i have a problem i'm sure many other bloggers face.
i am perfectly comfortable sharing intimate details about
my emotions with complete strangers i meet online
but shy away from expressing my true feelings to
anyone i know in real life
a woman in maine

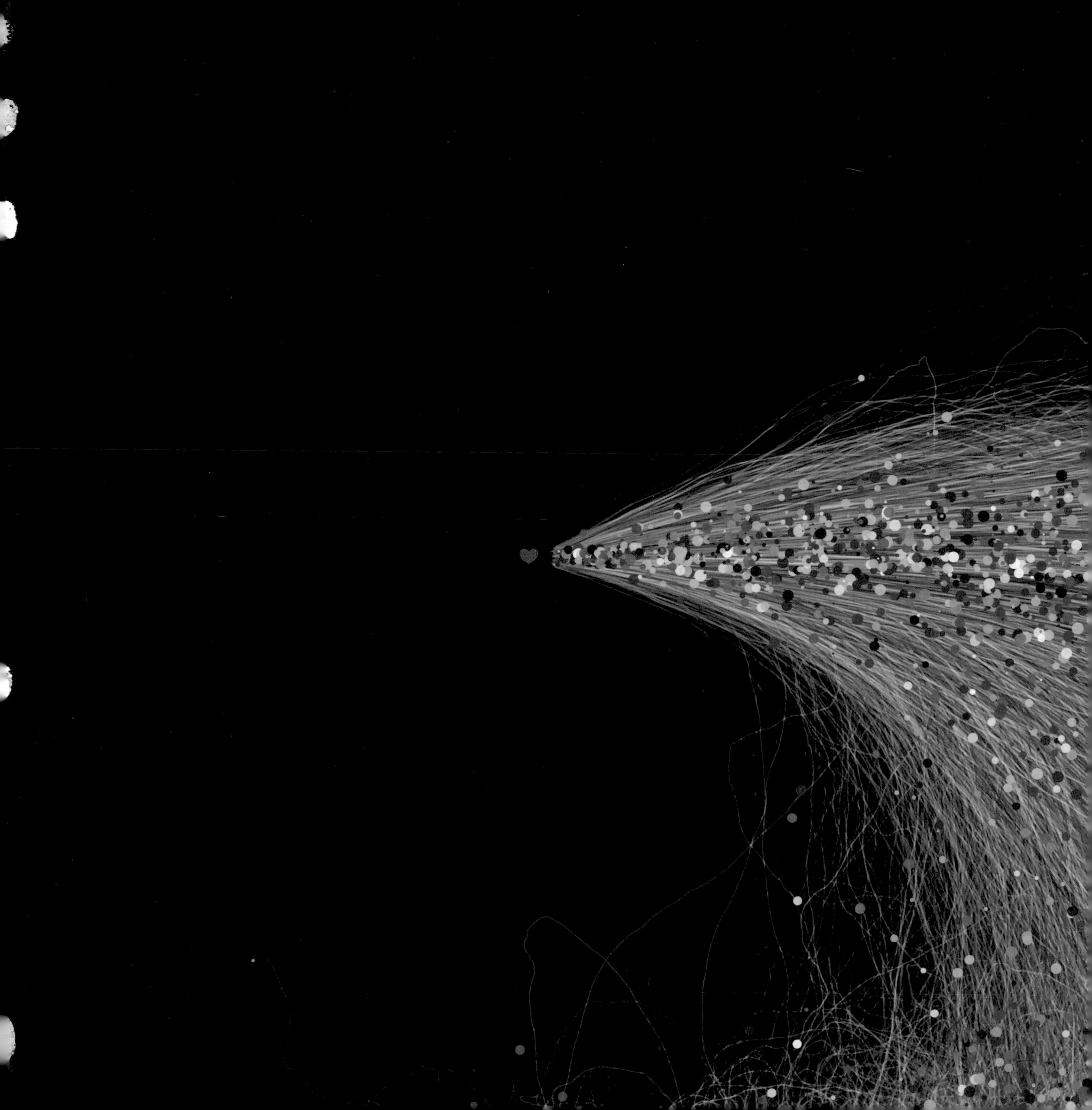

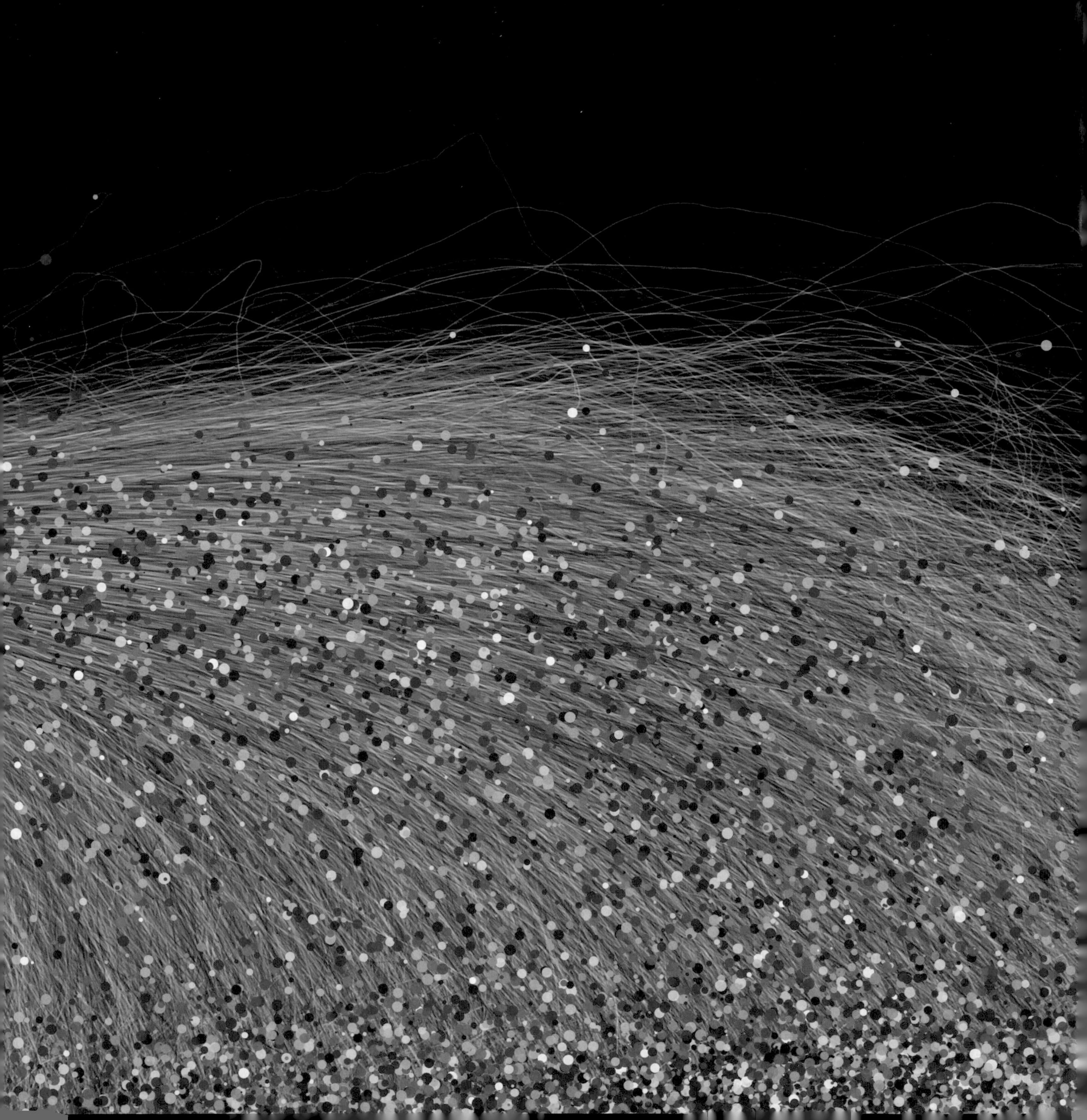

Drawing from a database of more than 12 million human feelings collected over 3 years from personal blogs on the Internet, **We Feel Fine** presents a comprehensive contemporary portrait of the world's emotional landscape, exploring the ups and downs of everyday life in all its color, chaos, and candor.

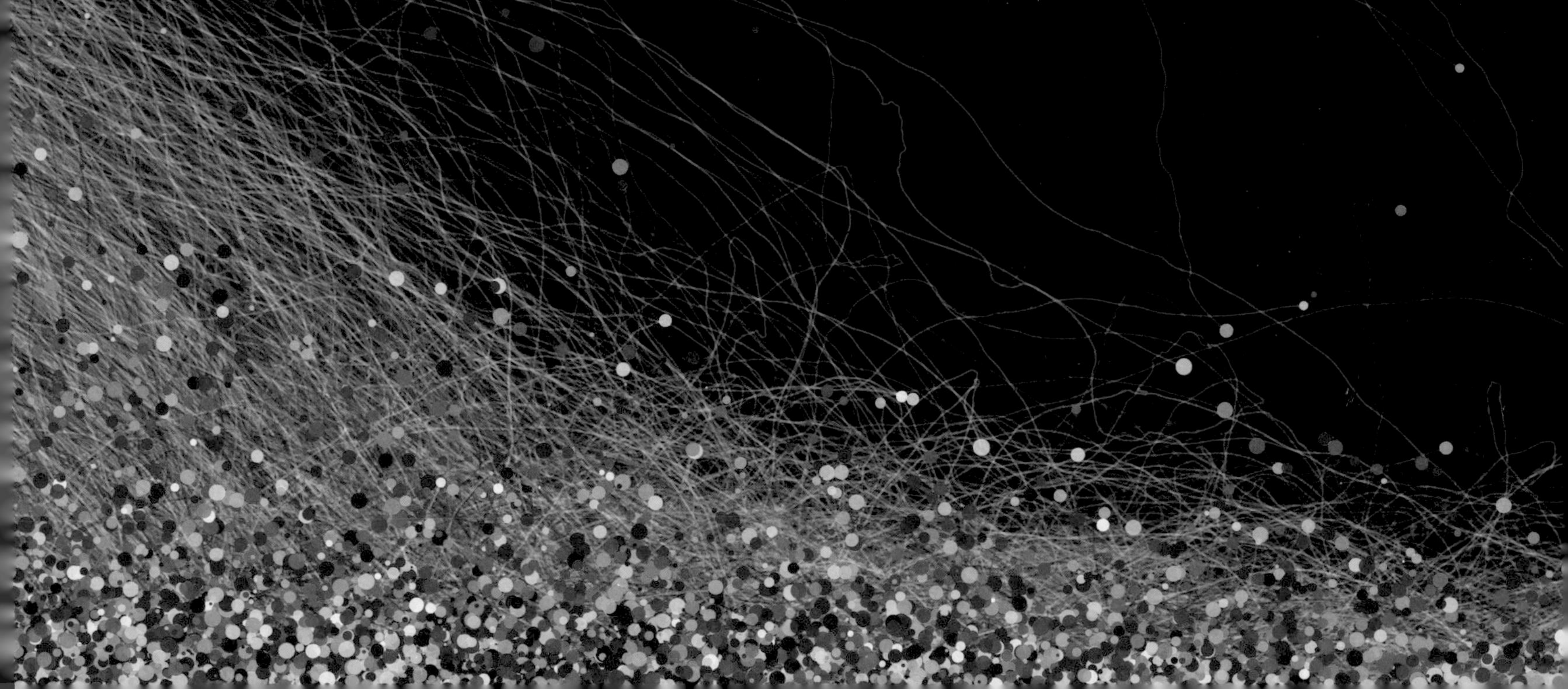

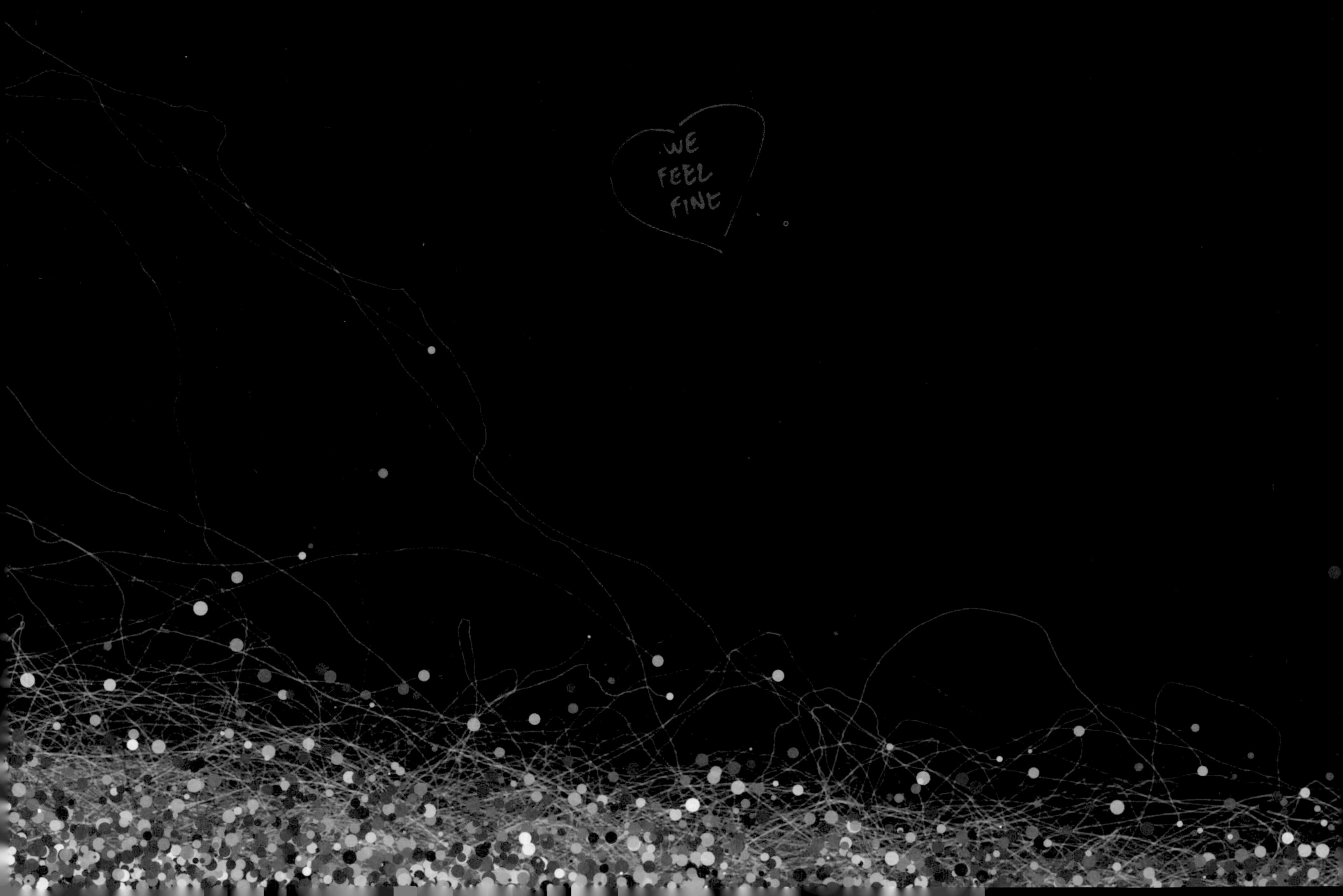
WE
FEEL
FINE

WE FEEL FINE

AN ALMANAC *of* HUMAN EMOTION

SEP KAMVAR AND JONATHAN HARRIS

SCRIBNER

NEW YORK · LONDON · TORONTO · SYDNEY

SCRIBNER
A Division of Simon & Schuster, Inc.
1230 Avenue of the Americas
New York, NY 10020

We Feel Fine: An Almanac of Human Emotion

Based on the website wefeelfine.org, where a live interactive version of *We Feel Fine* is available.

Knibb High Football Rules!

First Scribner hardcover edition December 2009

Designed by Jonathan Harris and Raul Gomez Valverde
Printed in the United States of America

1 3 5 7 9 10 8 6 4 2

ISBN 978-1-4391-1683-8

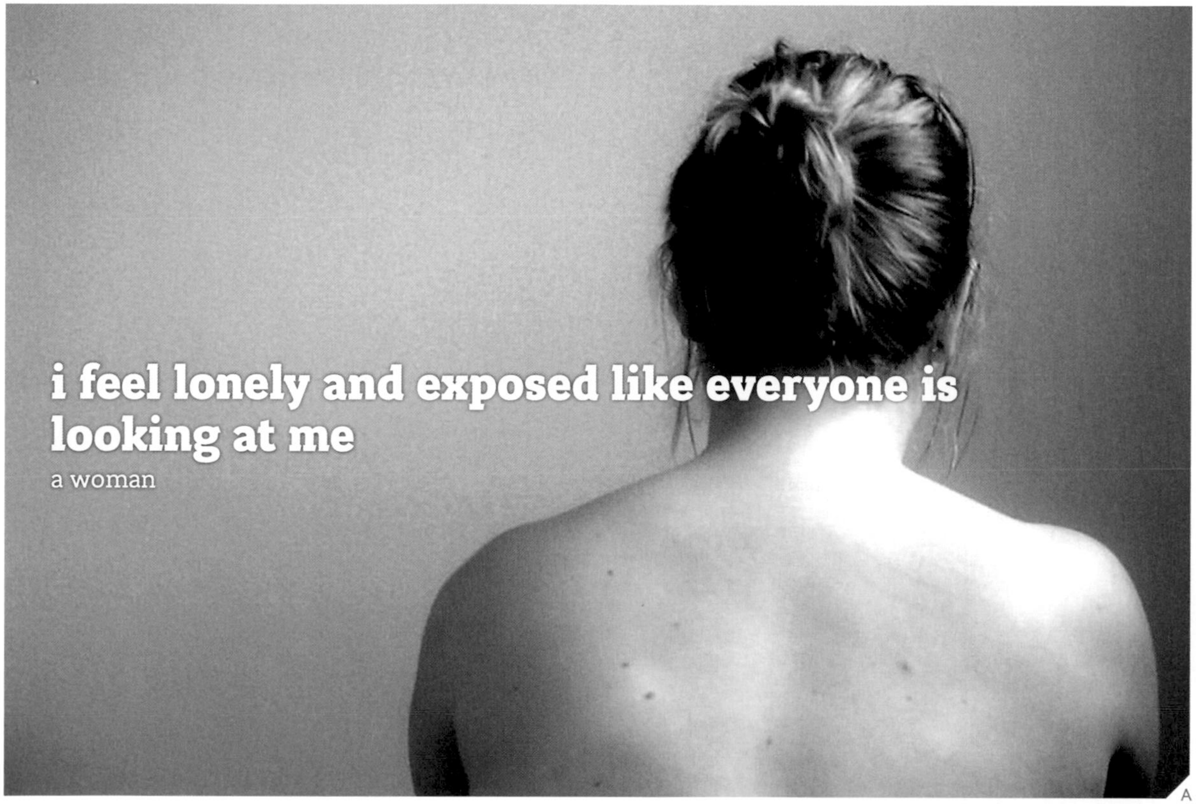

i feel lonely and exposed like everyone is looking at me
a woman

A

it feels so good to be alive
someone

B

Montáges, created automatically by *We Feel Fine* using photos and sentences found in the same blog post

i tell you how i feel but you don't care
someone

C

i feel beautiful again
a woman
A

i feel like a pimp
someone
B

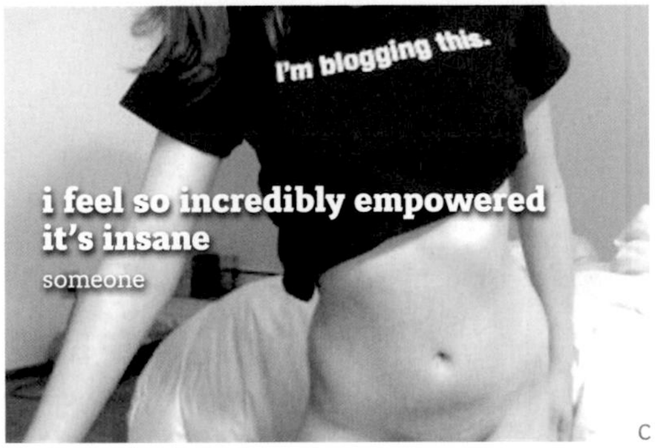
I'm blogging this.
i feel so incredibly empowered
it's insane
someone
C

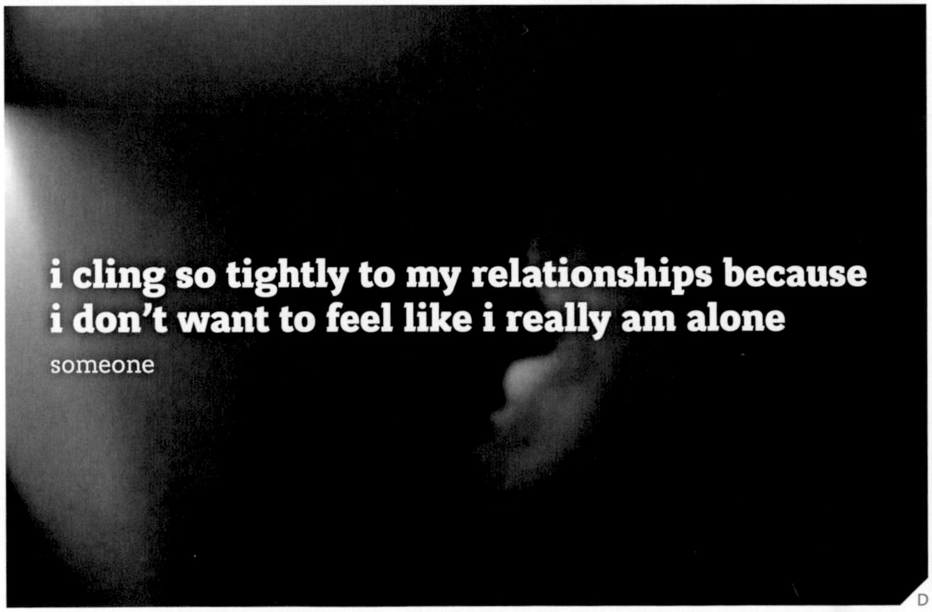
i cling so tightly to my relationships because
i don't want to feel like i really am alone
someone
D

i am feeling like flickr is
another home for me
a woman
E

i feel like i'm about to explode
a 23-year-old woman
A

i feel like a kid today
a man
B

i feel like the luckiest girl in the world
someone
C

i feel diagonally parked in a parallel universe
a woman
D

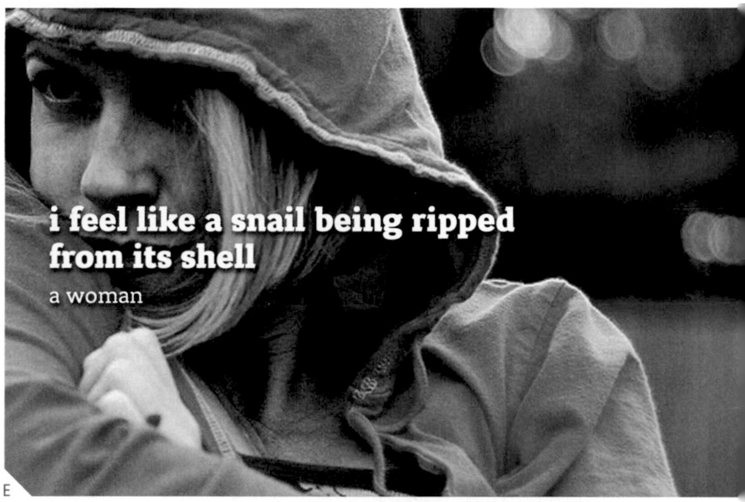
i feel like a snail being ripped from its shell
a woman
E

i feel like this
a woman
F

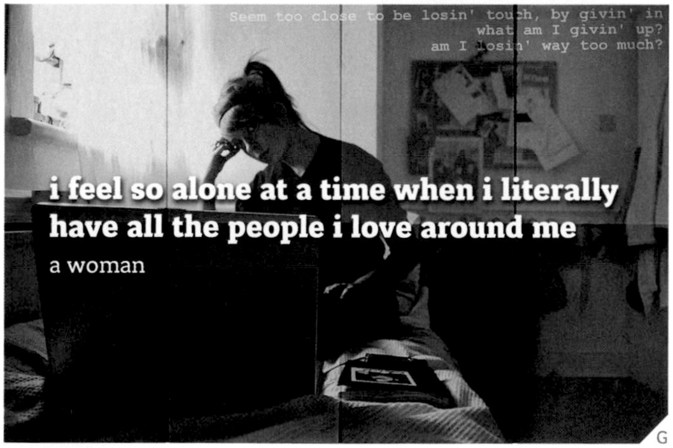
Seem too close to be losin' touch, by givin' in
what am I givin' up?
am I losin' way too much?
i feel so alone at a time when i literally have all the people i love around me
a woman
G

H

i feel like that tree
someone

i feel very warm to the touch
someone
I

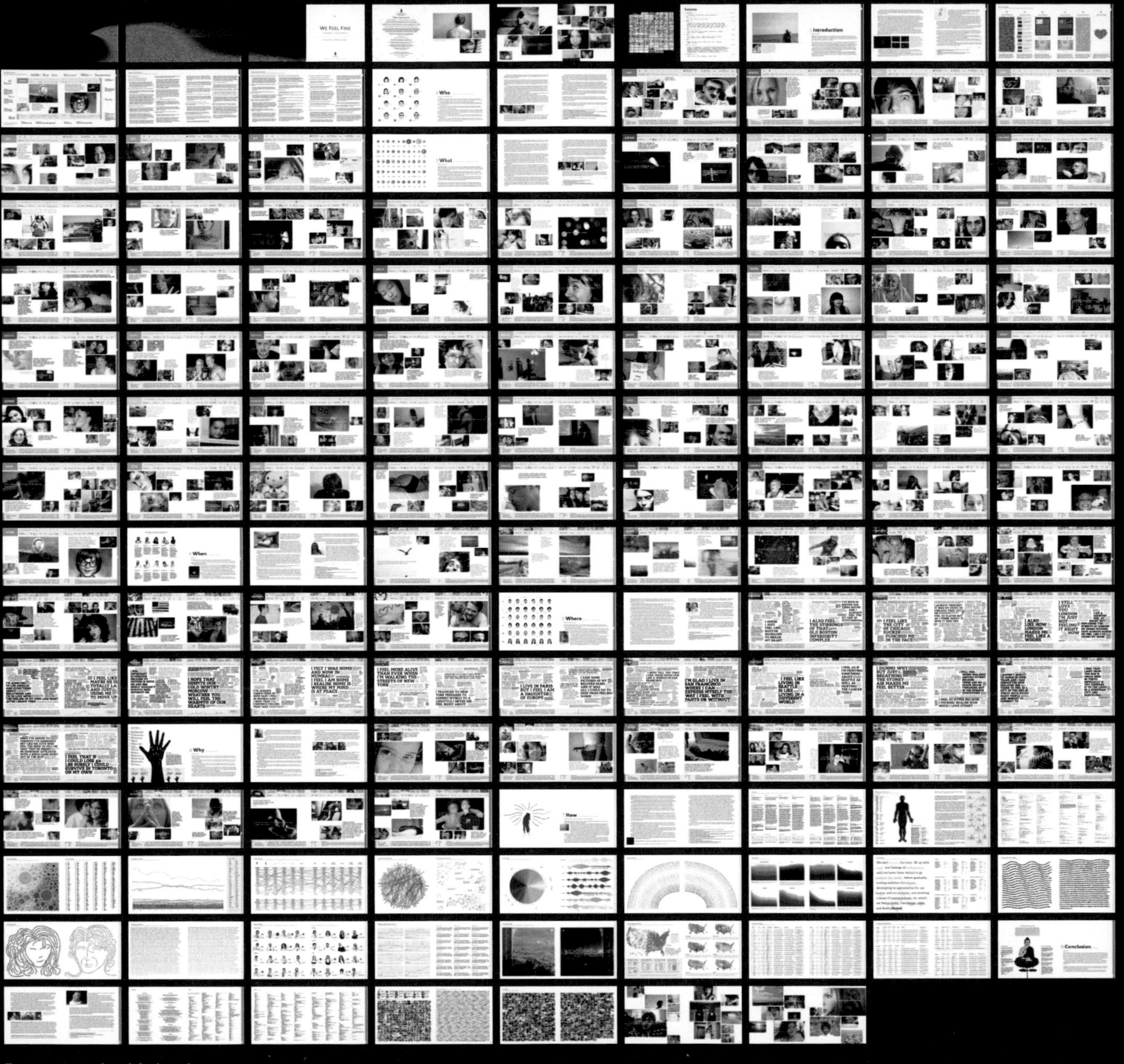

Every page in this book

Contents

i feel so much of my dad alive in me that there isn't even room for me
Oct 16, 2005 / from someone in wheaton, illinois, usa
WE FEEL FINE
A

Collected way back in October 2005, the above montage was one of the very first ones ever created by *We Feel Fine*, but it remains one of our favorites, and has become an unofficial mascot for the project in the years since. While putting together this book, we finally got in touch with the little girl in the picture, Meghan Orr, who is now 30 years old and living in Illinois with a husband and two little kids of her own.

1 Introduction

Tags: freedom, connection, blogging, we feel fine

Meghan Orr started blogging on September 14th, 2005. Her first post was about her cat, Billy. "It's kind of funny to me," she writes, "that I am writing my first blog ever about my cat Billy. Billy is a pretty cool cat." Billy, she wrote, loves to live free and do what he wants. He lets himself out and alternates between cuddling next to her and running away. Billy is ambivalent about technology—the day before Meghan's first blog post, Billy peed on her cell phone.[1]

About a decade before Meghan's first blog post, Justin Hall, then a freshman at Swarthmore College, started one of the first personal online diaries, *Justin's Links from the Underground*, where he posted his thoughts on topics from art to tai chi to college life to his relationship with his alcoholic father who had committed suicide. His first sentence, in January 1994, was: "Howdy, this is twenty-first century computing... (Is it worth our patience?) I'm publishing this, and I guess you're readin' this, in part to figure that out, huh?"[2]

By 1997, the public hadn't decided whether these online diaries were in fact worth their patience. There were only several dozen journals like Justin's, and they were not widely read outside of the technology community. But in 1999, the first major online publishing platforms were launched, the number of online journals jumped from a few dozen to thousands, and the term "blogging" was coined to describe this new phenomenon. The self-publishing revolution had begun.

The technology shift behind this revolution has been the subject of much discussion; easy mass-communication technologies have deeply influenced areas as diverse as journalism, entrepreneurship, and corporate responsibility. But equally interesting is the cultural shift that has accompanied this technological advance, where millions of people are suddenly happy to publish intimate details about their private lives for all to see.

This cultural shift has had a conspicuous effect on the web, which prior to the advent of blogs had been a great resource for information and commerce, but not a very emotional space. Blogs—and the microblogs and social networks that followed—changed that. The web of machines has become a web of people, rich with emotion, relationships, love, and flaws, just as nuanced and complex as the people who make it up.

We Feel Fine was born in the summer of 2005, a few weeks before Meghan Orr wrote her first blog post. The two of us were taking a road trip in Northern California, and the conversation turned to the emotional web, which by that point consisted not only of millions of blogs but also of rapidly growing social networks like MySpace and Facebook. We wanted to make something that could distill the beauty, humanity, and complexity that we saw in the web. We came up with the idea of writing a computer program that would continuously crawl all blogs on the web and extract any sentence containing the words "I feel" or "I am feeling."

Over the next several months, we wrote the code for *We Feel Fine*. We wrote backend infrastructure that would scan the blogosphere every minute and populate a live database of emotions, and a series of frontend visualizations that would allow people to see and interact with these emotions. Since many blog authors include biographical information on their blog profile pages, we could identify which feelings came from men or women, from 18-year-olds or 60-year-olds, from people in New York City or people in Tokyo. If a blog post contained both a feeling sentence and an image, we decided to overlay the sentence on top of the image to form what we call a "montage" composition. We have included many of our favorite montages in this book.

In May 2006 we launched the project at wefeelfine.org. We never expected the site to be as popular as it ended up being. Millions of people from all over the world have visited it. Newspapers, magazines, TV shows, and blogs have covered it, and museums from Athens to Houston to Melbourne have exhibited it. As for us, we could not stop looking at the blogs of the thousands of strangers whose feelings appeared on the site each day. We were consumed by a sense of empathy for people who we had never met, and at times we felt like we were looking in the mirror.

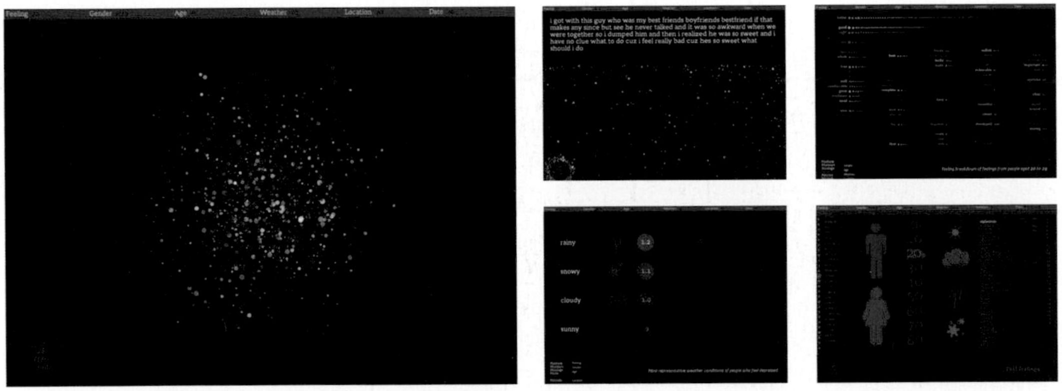

Screenshots from the interactive website, www.wefeelfine.org. Clockwise from far left: the Madness movement, showing the most recent 2,000 feelings represented as rainbow-colored dots; viewing a single sentence, or Murmur; the Mobs movement, showing the most common feelings overall; the search panel, allowing viewers to browse feelings from specific demographic groups; the Metrics movement, showing the current weather breakdown of the most recent 2,000 feelings.

"I actually see a lot of myself in Billy," writes Meghan in her first blog post. "Maybe that's why I'm so intrigued by him... Sometimes I really open up with people and show them how much I love them and how much they mean to me. Other times I feel so closed off from everyone and everything, like I am in my own world, and I am just running away."

"I feel like in some way or another we are all struggling for freedom... And what does that mean? To be free from worry? To be free from self doubt? To be free from sin? To be free from what the world says we should be? To be free to love? To be free to hate? To be free from the constraints of our culture and society?"[3]

The initial sketch for the *We Feel Fine* heart symbol, from 2005

These feelings are not unique to Meghan. The anthropologist Michael Wesch contends that people inherently crave both connection and freedom.[4] This dichotomy creates a tension that people often express by alternately opening up and closing off. We are frequently torn between building relationships and maintaining freedom from the constraints that those relationships impose.

According to Wesch, technologies like blogs and videocasting offer the promise of connecting without the constraints of commitment, which is why so many people take part. In the process, bloggers enter a quasi-anonymous world, writing about themselves to an audience they don't know and don't see. In this world everything is remembered, and anybody, including the blogger herself, can revisit any post at any time. The combination of physical distance and anonymity inspires intense self-reflection and remarkable depth on the part of the bloggers. "It's funny," writes Michelle Fry in her September 21st, 2005, blog post, "but I don't talk much in person. Yet, I can write and write." Blogging, she says, "is a good way of exploring ideas at length without the anxiety of having a one on one conversation. You can take your time with writing and take one thought at a time."[5]

Concurrently, this same distance and anonymity allow blog readers, in the words of Wesch, "to experience humanity without fear or anxiety." As readers, we can take our time, stare at people, and see them for who they are. Sometimes we can foster connections with bloggers that are more intimate than many real-life connections, because in real life it is impolite to stare.

By 2008, *We Feel Fine* had existed for two years and there were more than 10 million feelings in its database. However, there was still some work that we wanted to do. We wanted to curate and present some of our favorite feelings from the more than 10 million in our database, and we wanted to dive more deeply into the statistics of emotion. How do men feel differently from women? How do our emotions change as we grow older? What are the biggest drivers of jealousy? What causes sorrow?

We chose to present this emotional deep dive as a book rather than as another website because we felt the content would resonate more if people were given the chance to unplug and slow down. As technologists, we love how the web enables freedom and connectivity, but we also understand that too much technology can have the opposite effect.

Meghan, in writing about Billy the Cat's views on technology, wrote: "I think that if I were Billy I would also want to pee on my cell phone. I continue to struggle with all these electronic gadgets that are supposed to be bringing us all this increased freedom, when really it seems to me as if we are becoming their slaves."[6]

This is not, fundamentally, a book about technology (although we couldn't have written the book without it). This is a book about the human condition. As we said when we first launched *We Feel Fine* in 2006, we hope it makes the world seem a bit smaller, and that it helps people see the beauty of the everyday ups and downs of life. ♥

1. Meghan Orr. http://lifethroughmeghanseyes.blogspot.com/2005/09/billy-cat-its-kind-of-funny-to-me-that.html
2. Justin Hall. http://www.links.net/vita/web/start/original.html
3. Meghan Orr. See 1.
4. Wesch, Michael. "An Anthropological Introduction to YouTube." http://www.youtube.com/watch?v=TPAaO-lZ4_hU
5. Michelle Fry. http://verbalblog.blogspot.com/2005/09/midnight-in-garden-of-good-and-evil.html
6. Meghan Orr. See 1.

Harvesting Feelings

An overview of *We Feel Fine*'s system for automatically collecting feelings from the Internet

1 The Act of Self-Expression

Tens of millions of people chronicle the intimate details of their private lives on public blogs, producing hundreds of thousands of online diary entries per day, many of them incredibly personal.

2 Finding Emotional Entries

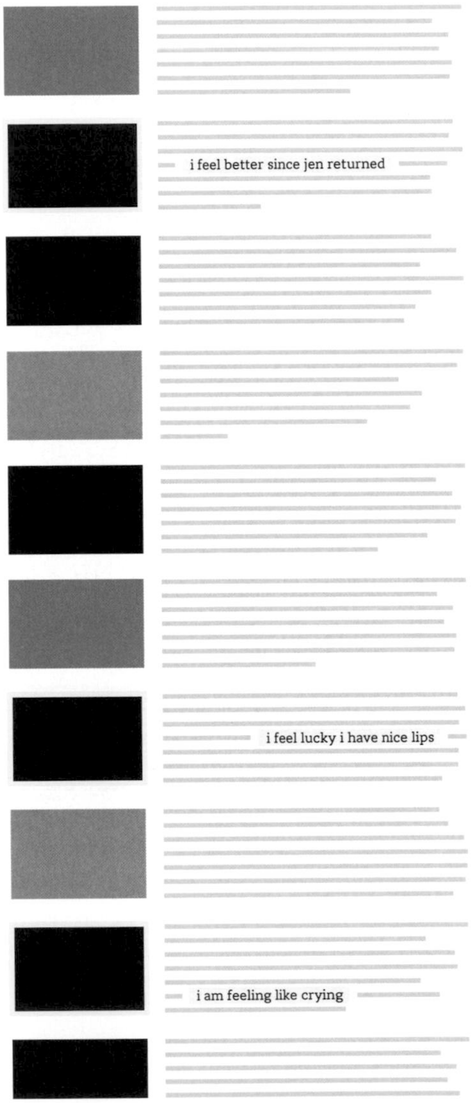
i feel better since jen returned
i feel lucky i have nice lips
i am feeling like crying

We Feel Fine examines these newly posted blog entries and isolates any that contain the phrase "i feel" or "i am feeling," usually finding around 10,000 such entries per day, mostly from English-speaking countries.

3 Emotional Extraction

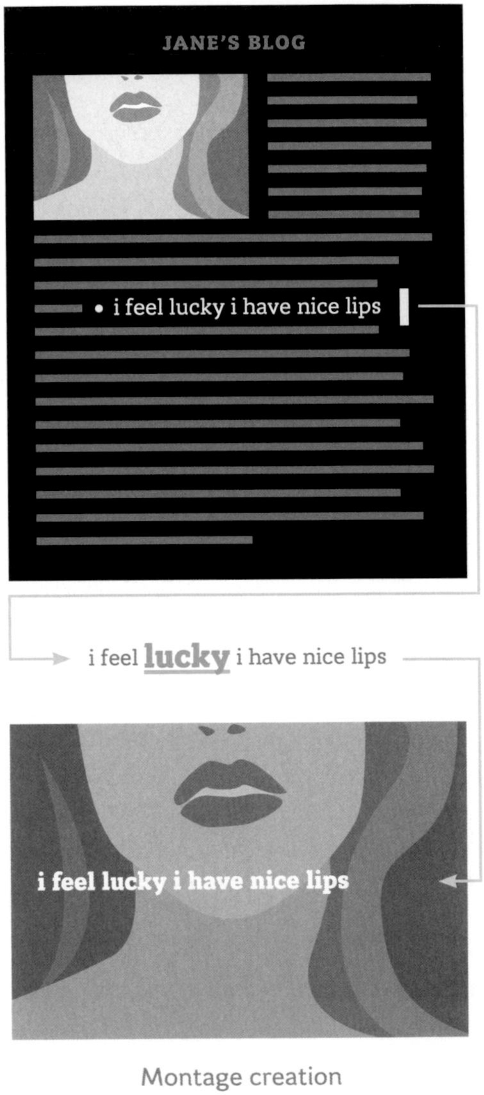
JANE'S BLOG
• i feel lucky i have nice lips
i feel lucky i have nice lips
i feel lucky i have nice lips
Montage creation

From these entries, *We Feel Fine* extracts any "i feel" sentence and identifies the "feeling" therein. If an image is included, it is merged with the sentence to form a montage composition, like those found in this book.

4

Demographic Discovery

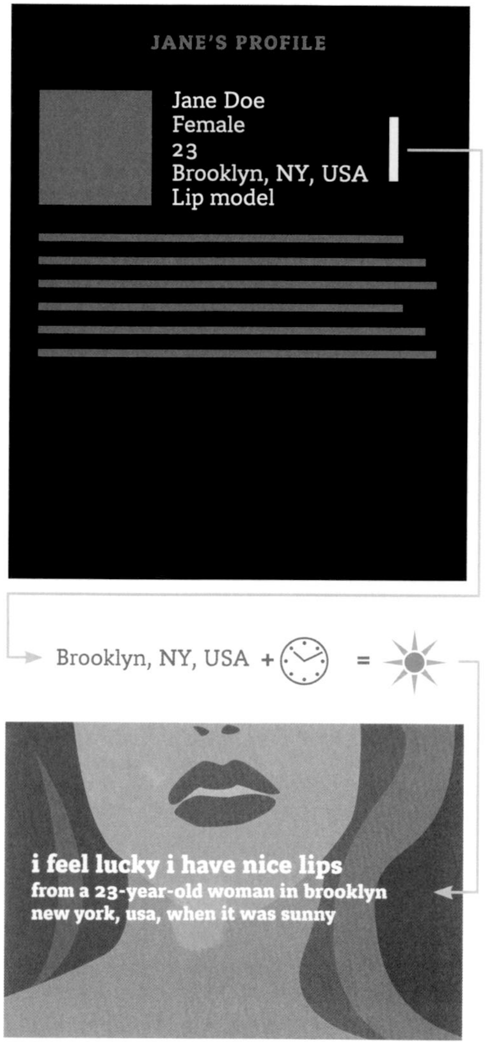

Byline creation

For each entry, *We Feel Fine* attempts to find the author's profile page, which it uses to identify the author's age, gender, and geographic location. It also tries to find the local weather conditions at the time of the post.

5

Databases Have Feelings Too

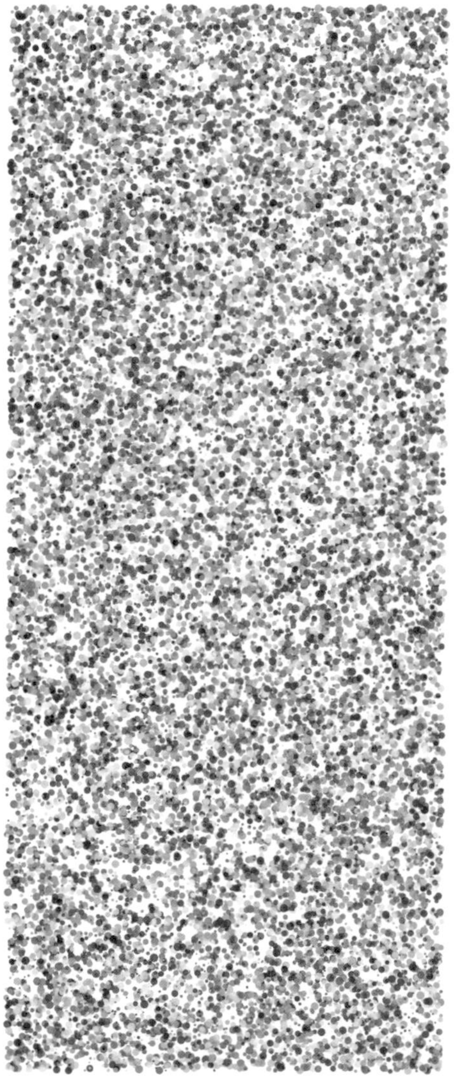

All this information is saved in a database that currently contains more than 12 million individual "feeling" sentences, and that can be queried along multiple demographic slices, many explored in this book.

6

Emotional Immortality

The feelings harvested by *We Feel Fine* attain a certain immortality, plucked from their original context and copied to a living archive of human emotion, which becomes a website (wefeelfine.org), a book, and more.

How This Book Works

An overview of the graphical system at work in this book, focusing on the "What" chapter, but applicable to all chapters

Rank and percentage
Rank / percentage of current feeling among all feelings

Gender
Gender breakdowns of current chapter

Age
Age breakdowns of current chapter

Header
Statistics

Title
Title of current chapter, colored accordingly

Montages
Automatically generated compositions created from photographs and sentences found in blog posts from real people, related to the current chapter

Stage
Curated content

Handwriting
Handwritten annotations provide the real-life backstories behind some of the most compelling montages in the book

Murmurs*
Handpicked sentences from real people talking about the current feeling

Footer
Definitions, usage examples, and other statistical insights

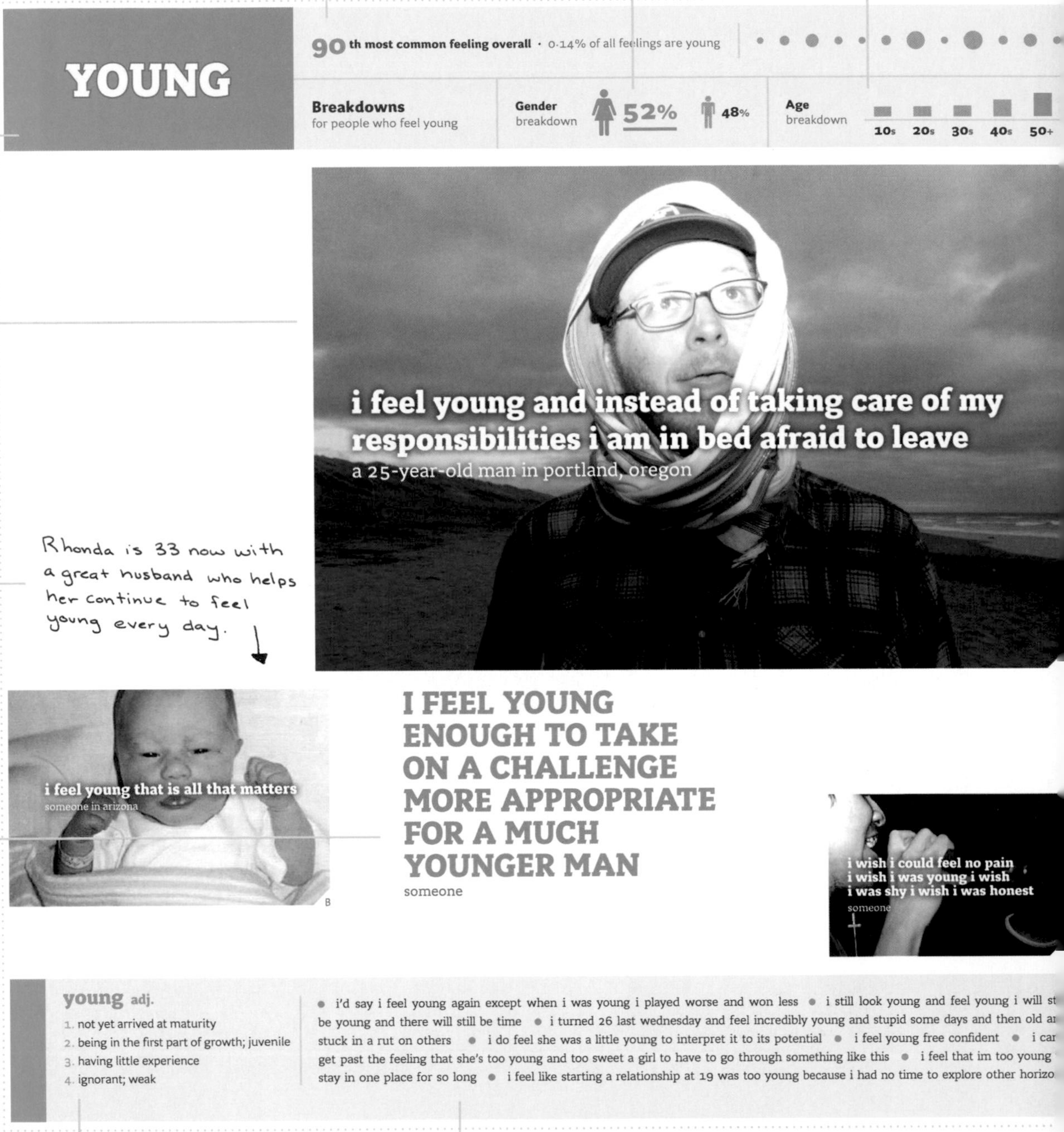

YOUNG
90 th most common feeling overall · 0.14% of all feelings are young
Breakdowns
for people who feel young
Gender
breakdown
52%
48%
Age
breakdown
10s 20s 30s 40s 50+
i feel young and instead of taking care of my responsibilities i am in bed afraid to leave
a 25-year-old man in portland, oregon
Rhonda is 33 now with a great husband who helps her continue to feel young every day.
i feel young that is all that matters
someone in arizona
I FEEL YOUNG ENOUGH TO TAKE ON A CHALLENGE MORE APPROPRIATE FOR A MUCH YOUNGER MAN
someone
i wish i could feel no pain
i wish i was young i wish
i was shy i wish i was honest
someone
young adj.
1. not yet arrived at maturity
2. being in the first part of growth; juvenile
3. having little experience
4. ignorant; weak
i'd say i feel young again except when i was young i played worse and won less • i still look young and feel young i will st
be young and there will still be time • i turned 26 last wednesday and feel incredibly young and stupid some days and then old a
stuck in a rut on others • i do feel she was a little young to interpret it to its potential • i feel young free confident • i ca
get past the feeling that she's too young and too sweet a girl to have to go through something like this • i feel that im too young
stay in one place for so long • i feel like starting a relationship at 19 was too young because i had no time to explore other horizo

Definitions
Dictionary definitions and other trivia about the current chapter

Usage examples
Sentences from real people describing feelings related to the current chapter, with color-coded dots dividing sentences

* The murmurs (big capitalized quotes) on the page come from different blogs than the photos and do not relate to the people in the photos.

Seasons
Seasonal breakdowns of current chapter by spring, summer, fall, and winter.

Related feelings
Feelings that frequently co-occur with the current feeling

Dots
Representing all feelings featured in the book, arranged alphabetically and sized by frequency

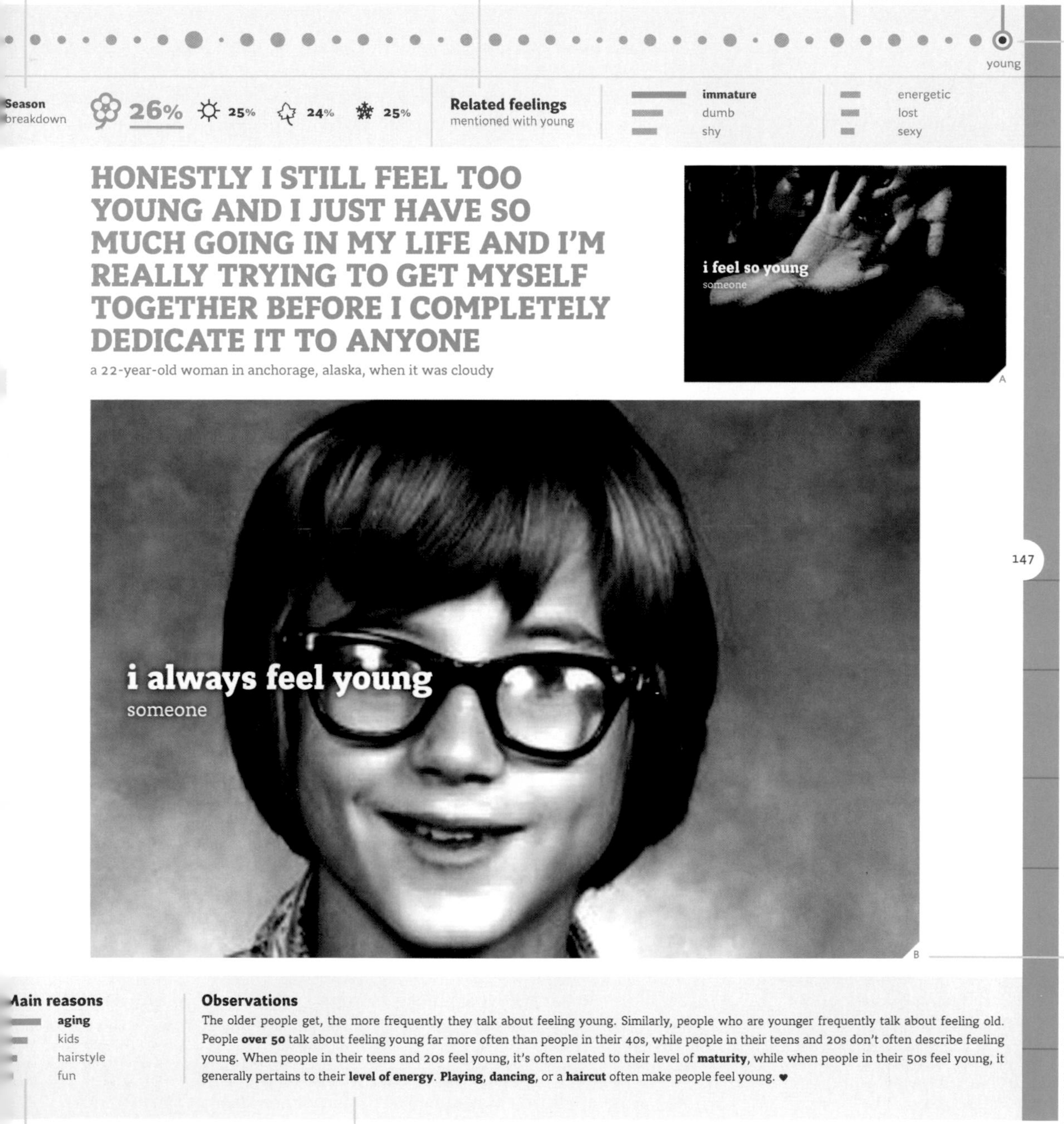
young
Season breakdown
26%
25%
24%
25%
Related feelings
mentioned with young
immature
dumb
shy
energetic
lost
sexy
HONESTLY I STILL FEEL TOO YOUNG AND I JUST HAVE SO MUCH GOING IN MY LIFE AND I'M REALLY TRYING TO GET MYSELF TOGETHER BEFORE I COMPLETELY DEDICATE IT TO ANYONE
a 22-year-old woman in anchorage, alaska, when it was cloudy
i feel so young
someone
A
i always feel young
someone
B
147
Main reasons
aging
kids
hairstyle
fun
Observations
The older people get, the more frequently they talk about feeling young. Similarly, people who are younger frequently talk about feeling old. People over 50 talk about feeling young far more often than people in their 40s, while people in their teens and 20s don't often describe feeling young. When people in their teens and 20s feel young, it's often related to their level of maturity, while when people in their 50s feel young, it generally pertains to their level of energy. Playing, dancing, or a haircut often make people feel young.

Current feeling
Current feeling highlighted in the appropriate color

Sidebar
Denotes current chapter color, current page number, and the page count proportions of all chapters in the book

Folio
Current page number, positioned accordingly

Web code
Provides online access to each montage. A given montage's web code is:
PAGE NUMBER + LETTER
For example, **147B** in this case.
Visit wefeelfine.org/book to enter montage codes and see the images in this book in their original context.

Main reasons
The main reasons why people feel a given way

Observations
Scientific insights into the current chapter topic, focusing on the most interesting observed trends

Frequently Asked Questions

Just about everything you'd ever want to know about *We Feel Fine* and more

Is this a book about blogs?

This is a book about people. Blogs are just the medium.

What about the non-English-speaking world?

Since *We Feel Fine* only scans blog posts containing the phrases "I feel" and "I am feeling," it is inherently limited to English-language blogs, which means the data in this book comes primarily from English-speaking countries (with some exceptions). In the future, it would be fun to do versions of *We Feel Fine* in other languages, but predicting the future is best left to soothsayers (and too often left to economists)!

Do the emotions of bloggers reflect the emotions of all people?

No. There is no group whose emotions reflect the emotions of all people. In particular, bloggers tend to be younger, more tech savvy, and more affluent than the general population.

At the same time, there is more universality to these results than one may imagine. To calibrate our findings, we looked at ten academic publications from the emotions research literature, where the studies involved the general population rather than the blogger population (pages 230–231). In almost all of these cases, we were able to replicate the results of these papers using *We Feel Fine* data, suggesting that when it comes to emotions, bloggers are a reasonable representation of the popluation at large. This is not to downplay the need for traditional experimental methodology, nor is it to suggest that studies using *We Feel Fine* will be able to replicate all the findings in the scientific literature. It is simply to say that the emotions of bloggers and non-bloggers are more similar than they are dissimilar.

Are the findings in the book scientific?

Yes and no. This was not intended to be a science book. So, for the purposes of the book, we skipped a number of steps that one would perform in a scientific study of emotion. For instance, we didn't do any manipulation experiments, we didn't use different methods to generate and to validate our hypotheses, and we didn't have this book peer-reviewed.

However, the statistical methods that we used are sound and our data analysis was rigorous. For many of our findings, we have found corroborating studies in the traditional psychology literature. For many others, we are in the process of corroborating our results with traditional experimental methods. And for yet other findings, we hope that academics and scientists will dig more deeply and explore further.

Science is a conversation and a body of continuous work-in-progress rather than a set of final results. We view the findings in this book as a piece of exploratory data analysis that is the beginning of a scientific conversation. We hope this conversation will not end with the publication of this book.

Are there any benefits to studying emotions through blogs rather than by traditional methods in emotions research?

There are some. Scale is one benefit. The ability to run an experiment with, say, 2 million people is not practical with traditional methods. Most of our experiments involve at least 2 million people. Time and cost are other benefits—once we built the infrastructure, the marginal cost of getting 20,000 more feelings is small—it only takes one day and a small amount of server space. The marginal cost of running a new experiment is also small. Our experiments take on the order of minutes to hours, rather than traditional experiments that take on the order of days to weeks. The final benefit is the ability to see how people feel in their day-to-day lives, rather than by interviewing people in the lab.

There are also drawbacks to this kind of study. There is a population bias that needs to be considered. More significantly, with these methods we cannot study causation, only correlation. Even in the "Main Reasons" sections, and the "Why We Feel What We Feel" spread (page 242), our findings are correlative. We cannot make statements about causality until we run more traditional experiments. For these reasons, we recommend these types of methods for hypothesis generation and exploratory data analysis, to be used in conjunction with, rather than as a replacement for, traditional methods.

What is the difference between feelings and emotions?

Many people use these terms interchangeably: *Webster*'s lists among its definitions for feeling: *an emotional state*, and for emotion: *a state of feeling*. Go figure. Where experts do make distinctions, they vary, which is not surprising as there is some debate among them on what exactly an emotion is in the first place.

We chose to study feelings in the broad sense of the term; we will use the word to describe sensation ("I feel hot"), perception ("I feel fat"), and sometimes even opinions ("I feel that people these days are addicted to the internet"), as well as emotion.

How does the relatively young age of bloggers affect the findings in this book?

Generally, where age would make an impact, we account for it by using a study population that samples equally from all age groups.

There are a couple of notable exceptions: seasons and reasons. In the "What" chapter, you may notice a pattern where many of the negative feelings are felt most strongly during the summer. This is due to an interesting phenomenon: younger people tend to have more strongly negative emotions, and in the summertime, when school is on break, there are a greater number of younger people blogging.

A second set of studies where we didn't normalize for age is the "Main Reasons" sections of the "What" chapter. This generally had little effect, but occasionally you will see "school" as a main reason for a given feeling, which would not have been the case if we had taken an equal sample from every age group.

Another area where age affects our findings is for people over 60. Since there are very few bloggers over 60, we have generally omitted the over-60 population from this book. This is a shame, but there were so few bloggers over 60 that our results for that age group were not statistically significant.

Are older people happier than younger people?

One of the strongest and most consistent patterns we found in studying this data is that people get happier as they get older. Because of the relative scarcity of bloggers over 60, we weren't able to come to conclusions for people over 60. But right up to age 60, people just keep getting happier. And more grateful.

Are people happier in New York or in San Francisco?

One thing we've found is that location doesn't have as strong an effect on emotion as, say, age. Culture does have a mediating effect on emotion, but for two cities in the same country, there are not large emotional differences. So, given our data, we can't tell you if people in San Francisco are happier than people in New York.

However, we can tell you that Sep is happier than Jonathan.

I read a study that Denmark is the happiest country on earth—can you corroborate that?

Unfortunately, our study is currently limited to English-language blogs, so we can't corroborate that. But we can tell you that, looking at our data, the United States looks a good bit happier than the UK (which was also a finding of that same Denmark study: *A Global Projection of Subjective Well-Being: A Challenge*, Adrian White, The University of Leicester, 2007).

I noticed that many of the feelings in the "What" chapter are felt more often by women than by men—is this because you have more women than men in your study?

We do have more women than men in our study, because women use "I feel" in blogs more than men do. But for the gender statistics in the "What" chapter, we sampled equal populations of men and women, so this doesn't explain your observation.

The truth is, when we picked the 50 feelings to feature with in-depth analysis (the "What" chapter), we picked them based on two criteria: that they be relatively common feelings, and that they be (in our opinion) interesting feelings. It just turned out that many of the feelings we picked happened to be felt more often by women. Some common feelings felt more strongly by men, such as "obligated", "compelled", and "justified", were not as interesting, while some of the interesting feelings felt strongly by men, like "hollow" and "inspired", were not as common.

Are women more emotive than men?

Certainly on blogs this is the case. In our data set, we find that on average women verbalize their emotions far more frequently than men do, and when men do verbalize their emotions, they often express them in a more attenuated manner. This may come as no surprise to our married readers.

In the observations sections, you say "People feel..."—wouldn't it be more accurate to say: "on blogs, people express feeling..."?

Yes. But we had space constraints so we shortened it. Every time we say "People feel..." you may substitute "On blogs, people express feeling..."

How did you compute the "Main Reasons" for a given feeling?

We wrote a program to determine which words occur in the same sentence as a given feeling with a frequency greater than the frequency those words occur in sentences without that feeling. We then manually examined each of these words and the corresponding sentences to see which ones represented legitimate reasons, and we took the top four to be the "Main Reasons".

I noticed that you sometimes say "Top Feelings" and other times you say "Distinctive Feelings"—what's the difference?

When we say "Top Feelings", we mean the most frequently expressed feelings in a given population. Generally, these are some variant of: better, bad, good, guilty, sick, sorry, well, alone, happy, and comfortable. When we say "Distinctive Feelings", we mean those feelings that may not be common in a given population, but that are expressed more frequently in that population than in the general population. For example, women feel "beautiful" much more commonly than men do. And older people feel "blessed" much more commonly than younger people do.

For those more mathematically inclined, Top Feelings for a given population are those whose probability **p(feeling|population)** is high, and Distinctive Feelings for a given population are those whose probability **p(population|feeling)** is high.

Frequently Asked Questions

Just about everything you'd ever want to know about *We Feel Fine* and more (continued)

How did you choose which photos went with which sentences?

When a blog post includes a sentence containing the phrase "I feel" or "I am feeling," and also includes an image, our program automatically overlays the sentence on the image and stores the resulting composition (which we call a "montage") in our database. So every image in this book comes from the same blog post as the sentence that overlays it. This was all determined by our computer program, without human intervention.

Are the sentences in the montages always about the people in the photo?

Not always. Our program automatically takes the sentences from the same blog post as the photo, and most of the time the sentence relates to the photo, but sometimes, the sentence is not by or about the people in the photos.

I see a letter at the bottom corner of each montage in the book—what's that?

Each montage in the book has a shorthand code, which is its page number and letter. These codes are used in the index, credits, and on the web, so you can see montages in their original context. For example, you can see the montage marked "A" on page 89 at www.wefeelfine.org/book/89A.

How do you know the age, gender, and location of the bloggers, and how do you know the weather?

Many blogs and social networks have public profiles, where people give their age, gender, and location. For such blogs, our program parses the profile along with the feeling sentence. For those blogs where the blogger specifies their location, since we know the date and time of the blog post and the location of the blogger, we can use publicly available weather databases to find what the weather was that day.

I noticed that some bylines say "a 57-year-old man in holmdel, new jersey, when it was sunny," and others just say "someone"—why is this?

Our program attempts to identity as much information as it can about a given blogger's demographics, which it then puts in the associated byline for a given montage. Some public profiles have less information than others, and some blogs have no profiles at all. The bylines in this book always include as much information as our program could find out.

We did get permission for all the photos in the book, and in doing so we got to know more about the authors than they put in their public profiles. But we decided to put in the montage bylines only what the program could find out.

Do you just get your sentences and photos from blogs?

We include feelings from micro-blogging platforms (like Twitter), photo sharing sites (like Flickr), and social networks (like MySpace). Since Facebook is a closed social network, we can't include feelings posted there. For simplicity's sake, we generally use the term "blogs" as an umbrella term for all of these types of sites, and the term "bloggers" to refer to their members.

Can I submit my feelings directly to We Feel Fine*?*

No. *We Feel Fine* finds feelings on blogs, in context, and doesn't let anybody submit feelings. We think that observing people in context and "in the wild" makes for more honest and unique statements of emotion than if we were to solicit people's feelings directly.

What about privacy?

We only crawl public blogs, which are viewable by many more people than the number of people who will buy this book.

Did you get permission from the bloggers whose photos you used in the book?

Yes. Communicating with these bloggers was one of the most enjoyable parts of writing this book.

Can you explain in more detail how your process for harvesting emotions works?

Sure. Take a look at pages 18–19. We have an in-depth description there. Or, for a more technical view, take a look at page 233.

I noticed that you have assigned each feeling a color—how did you choose the colors for each feeling?

For the most common 150 feelings (which include all the feelings in this book) we chose the colors manually, and we tried to choose colors that reflected the feeling—for example, the angry feelings we chose to be shades of red, the calm feelings shades of blue, and the happy feelings shades of yellow. For the rest of the feelings, we assigned colors randomly.

Did you write the handwritten sentences in the book?

We held a handwriting competition in the San Francisco Bay Area for high school students, and the winners of the handwriting competition were: Emily Ebbers, Jacqueline McGraw, Mandakini Mohindra, Lynn Nguyen, and Jessica Tran. They wrote all the handwritten sentences in the book (our friend, Hannah Knafo, helped out too).

How did you pick the feelings to showcase in the book?

We picked 50 that were both common and interesting to us.

How many bloggers did you contact while writing this book?

We got in touch with 12,765 bloggers, 2,411 responded, and 1,629 agreed to let us include their photos in the book.

Whoa! Did you e-mail them all yourself?

No, we had a small staff of two full-time research assistants (Matt and Hannah), without whom we could not have made this book.

How long did it take you to create this book?

It took us about nine months (working part-time around our day jobs) to write the data collection and visualization software in 2005 and early 2006. We then waited for a couple of years before starting to reach out to bloggers for inclusion in the book in late 2007. In early 2008, we pitched the book idea to several publishers, got a book deal, and started working on the spreads for the "Who," "What," "Where," "When," and "Why" chapters. We worked on the book full-time and in earnest for eleven months in late 2008 and 2009, and handed in our manuscript in August of 2009. Our publishers then produced the book and presold for the rest of 2009, in time for its release in December.

How did the two of you split up the work for this book?

Sep: *I am the creative genius and Jonathan is the pretty face.*
Jonathan: *Don't believe his pack of lies! I do all the work. Sep gets me coffee.*

Does Sep's mom really think he's handsome?

No.

Why did you write a book? Don't you already have a website?

This is a great question, and we thought about this a lot. There were certain things that lent themselves to this project being just a website. The website (wefeelfine.org) is real-time, showing feelings that have been posted to the web in the last few minutes, which is obviously impossible with a book. Since the material is coming from the web, it is fitting for the showcase to be on the web also. We are huge believers in the web as a medium, and we especially love its openness, accessibility, interactivity, equality, and reach.

But we decided to do a book because there were certain things that we could do with a book that don't work as well on the web. For instance, we wanted to curate some of our favorite photos, we wanted to have a narrative of substantial length, and we wanted to do some deep statistical data mining over the entire data set (which we can't do within the real-time constraints of the web browser). We also wanted to share our findings in a timeless, beautiful medium that anyone (including our parents!) can understand, and books are great for that.

Most importantly, many of us spend eight hours a day at work, staring at a computer. We wanted to be able to come home, lie down on the couch or sit outside in the sun, and read this book either alone or with a loved one, to share in a real-world experience of exploring emotions.

This book feels a bit disjointed. I'm used to books being more linear—what's going on?

At the beginning of Chapter 5 in Kurt Vonnegut's *Slaughterhouse-Five*, Billy Pilgrim finds himself in jail on the planet of Tralfamadore. Billy's captors give him some Tralfamadorian books to pass the time, and while Billy can't read Tralfamadorian, he does notice that the books are laid out in brief clumps of text, separated by stars. "Each clump of symbols is a brief, urgent message—describing a situation, a scene," explained one of his captors. "We Tralfamadorians read them all at once, not one after the other. There isn't any particular relationship between all the messages, except that the author has chosen them carefully, so that, when seen all at once, they produce an image of life that is beautiful and surprising and deep. There is no beginning, no middle, no end, no suspense, no moral, no causes, no effects. What we love in our books are the depths of many marvelous moments seen all at one time."

We aimed to write this book in the telegraphic, schizophrenic manner of tales from Tralfamadore, because that's where the flying saucers are.

You seem to represent feelings, both in your book and on your website, as brightly colored dots—why dots?

To the Tralfamadorians, the Universe does not look like a lot of bright little dots. Instead they see where each star has been and where it is going, so that the heavens are filled with rarefied, luminous spaghetti (kind of like our cover). But we're only earthlings, so we used dots.

Why did you bother making We Feel Fine*?*

In the sage words of Larry Walters, an American truck driver who, in 1982, attached 45 helium balloons to a standard lawn chair and then floated from his home in San Pedro, California, to an altitude of 16,000 feet, before eventually shooting a few of the balloons with a pellet gun and drifting into the controlled federal air space of Long Beach airport, where he crashed into a power line that caused a 20-minute blackout in a Long Beach neighborhood, "Well, a man can't just sit around."

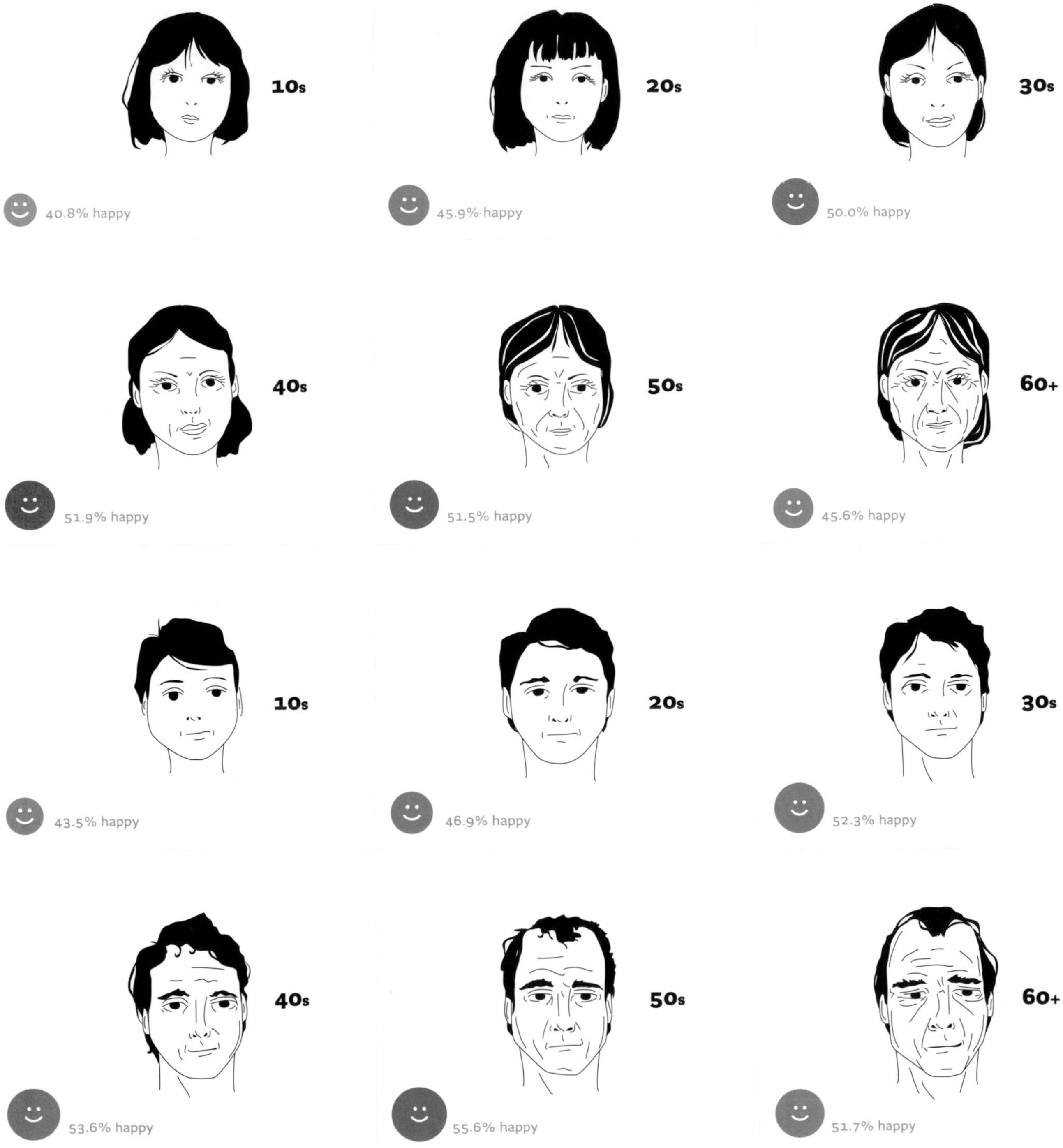

10s
40.8% happy
20s
45.9% happy
30s
50.0% happy
40s
51.9% happy
50s
51.5% happy
60+
45.6% happy
10s
43.5% happy
20s
46.9% happy
30s
52.3% happy
40s
53.6% happy
50s
55.6% happy
60+
51.7% happy

2 Who

On the effects of age and gender on emotions

Tags: social psychology, personality psychology

TJ Cardella turned 49 on May 23rd, 2007. "Well," she posted to her blog that day, "I'm another year older, but I feel about a million years wiser." TJ's past year had been a difficult one. After 19 years of marriage, her husband left her for one of her friends, and she had spent a lot of time reflecting on her life. "What have I learned?" she writes in her birthday blog post.[1]

1. *I have the most amazing family and friends in the world.* TJ's family and friends called her every day, brought her Kleenex and chocolate, took her out, and made her realize that "life hadn't ground to a halt because the love of my life had been seduced by a girl who claimed to be my friend."

2. *I am stronger than I ever realized.* TJ mentions that she grew up thinking that she was fragile, not capable of taking care of herself, weak and vulnerable. But the events of this past year, she writes, taught her that she is none of those things. "I'm making a home for myself, and I have love in my life in abundance."

3. *There are some people you just can't trust with your heart.* TJ realized that friendship is more than words. "Just because someone claims they're your friend doesn't mean they are," she writes. "I am not saying this from a space of bitterness. I have come to realize that I have undervalued myself to the point of not knowing how to protect myself. Now I know that I am worth protecting, and those people that I have in my life are those who deserve my friendship."

4. *I have learned that it is really hard to forgive, but it is necessary for your sanity to do so.* TJ notes that forgiveness doesn't mean excusing a person's actions, but showing mercy and generosity to the wrongdoer. "I try to do this every day," she writes, "and I think I'm getting better at it."

5. *Nobody knows what is coming next.* "Life is about surprises, and challenges and losses," she writes. "It's also about joy and understanding and love. Live for today, don't try to guess what might happen in the future, treasure what you have this moment. Hope springs eternal and true happiness is about being able to spot the moments."

TJ's birthday was both reflective and emotional, and her blog post was not only a contemplation of her marital situation, but also a reflection on age, emotion, and identity. "Every day that I've lived," she wrote, "and everything that I've done has brought me, as I am, to this place in my life, this who that I am."

In 1971, the psychologist Carroll Izard published his Differential Emotions Theory, which states that our abilities to feel and express many primary emotions (like fear, joy, disgust, sadness, anger, surprise, guilt, and contempt) develop during infancy.[2] But Izard also outlines emotional areas in which we do change as we age. The connections between our emotions and our thoughts and behavior become denser with age, allowing us to experience more complex emotions, to better regulate them, and to better read the emotions of others.

An analysis of the *We Feel Fine* database shows this increased sophistication and ability to regulate one's emotions with age. It also shows an interesting consequence: as we get older, we tend to have a greater sense of well-being (at least until our mid-sixties). While angst and high-arousal emotions are prevalent among bloggers in their teens and early twenties, by the time they reach their 50s and 60s, they tend to express more serenity and gratitude. TJ's sadness mixed with forgiveness, hope, and gratitude, as well as her ability to find peace and optimism in a difficult time, are hallmarks of a mature emotional outlook. Had TJ experienced a similarly distressing situation earlier in her life, she may have reacted much differently.

Our analysis shows an additional interesting finding of emotions and age—not only do people increase their well-being, but they also increase their sense of connectedness. As we grow older, we feel closer to the people around us.

In 1993, Stanford psychologist Laura Carstensen published her Theory of Socioemotional Selectivity. The theory states that when people view time as plentiful, as young people generally do, they focus on preparing for the future. To that end they spend their energy seeking new information and broadening their horizons. On the other hand when people see their time as limited, as people do when they get older, they focus on making their lives more emotionally meaningful. To that end they tend to strengthen their closest relationships and discard those friendships that are less emotionally meaningful.[3] TJ's sentiment that "those people I have in my life are those who deserve my friendship" is more common for people in their 50s than for people in their 20s, as is the sense of empathy that comes with feeling connected to the people around you.

From left: TJ Cardella; TJ's watercolor painting entitled "Strega"; TJ's watercolor entitled "La Huesera." More of TJ's art can be seen on her website, www.faeriechilde.com.

On November 10th, 2006, TJ posted to her blog the results of a quiz she took called "What Kind of Psychic Are You?"[4] The results told her that she had a finely tuned empathic sense, an ability to literally feel for someone else. "It gives you," said the quiz results, "the psychic ability to 'read' a person's aura, and interpret the information back to him or her. It can bring you amazingly close to others; you can sense their true emotional needs with unerring accuracy, and people may be drawn to you like magnets. But avoid absorbing other people's problems, as it's easy to get burned out."[5]

This finely tuned sense of empathy is likely due in part to her emotional maturity, but it is also a common trait among women in general—dozens of studies have shown that women have, on average, both a stronger ability to read the emotions of others and a greater tendency to "catch" the emotions of others than men do.[6] Other studies have also shown that women are more aware and expressive of their own emotions than men are.[7] Indeed, the *We Feel Fine* database shows that female bloggers use sentences containing the phrase "I feel" much more often than men do, and also that the average female blogger expresses a wider range of emotions than the average male blogger does.

These emotional contrasts can be explained by the fact that men and women often approach the world from different perspectives. The linguist Deborah Tannen suggests that men are more likely to engage with the world as individuals in a hierarchical social order, while women are more likely to engage with the world as interdependent people in a network of connections.[8] As such, men often learn to suppress their emotions, especially those that suggest vulnerability, while women often learn to tap into and express their emotions, especially those that involve intimacy. In line with this, the *We Feel Fine* database shows that feelings of pride, confidence, and detachment are more often expressed by male bloggers, whereas feelings of affection and empathy are more often expressed by female bloggers (see page 231).

This chapter explores the effects of age and gender on emotions. However it is important to note that age and gender are only two aspects of the "who" that TJ says she is. We are made up of thousands of intangibles that define each of us as individuals, and while we explore broad trends, it is important not to overapply these findings. Like our fingerprints, the emotional constitutions we possess share many similarities, but are also unquestionably unique.

"As I take my first steps into my 50th year (yup, when you turn 49, you are entering your 50th year...)," concludes TJ in her birthday post, "I hope to continue to be brave, to grow, and to be a representative of kindness here on this earth, and maybe, just maybe, show the way for other people who meet with trials they didn't expect—to help them see that even when you think your life is over, it might be just the beginning."[9]

PostScript: On August 6th, 2009, TJ sent us a note asking if we could add some text to this chapter, saying that she's mended fences with the girl. "I'm glad to have moved past it," she wrote, "and don't want her to feel like I'm still holding any sort of grudge. I know it's late to ask for this, but I would feel much better about it." ♥

1. TJ Cardella. http://blogs.myspace.com/index.cfm?fuseaction=blog.view&friendID=80981373&blogID=267769218
2. Izard, Carroll E. *The face of emotion*. (New York: Appleton-Century-Crofts, 1971).
3. Carstensen, Laura L. "Motivation for social contact across the life span: A theory of socioemotional selectivity." In J.E. Jacobs (Ed.) *Nebraska symposium on motivation: 1992, Developmental Perspectives on Motivation*. (Lincoln: University of Nebraska Press, 1993).
4. "What Kind of Psychic Are You?" http://www.okcupid.com/tests/take?testid=6709340901971304803
5. TJ Cardella Psychic Test. http://blogs.myspace.com/index.cfm?fuseaction=blog.view&friendId=80981373&blogId=191640202
6. Doherty, R. William. (1997). "The Emotional Contagion Scale: A Measure of Individual Differences." *Journal of Nonverbal Behavior*, 21, 131–154.
7. Brody, Leslie R. and Judith A. Hall (2008), "Gender and Emotion in Context." *Handbook of Emotions*, (New York: Guildford Press, 2008). Edited by Michael Lewis and Jeannette M. Haviland-Jones.
8. Tannen, Deborah. *You Just Don't Understand: Women and Men in Conversation*, (New York: HarperCollins, 1990).
9. TJ Cardella. See 1.

MEN

Top feelings among men

Above average / Men / Average

better | **good** | bad | **sorry** | alone | **down**

I FEEL LIKE MEAT SAUCE

a man

i feel disconnected from all of you wonderful people

a man

A

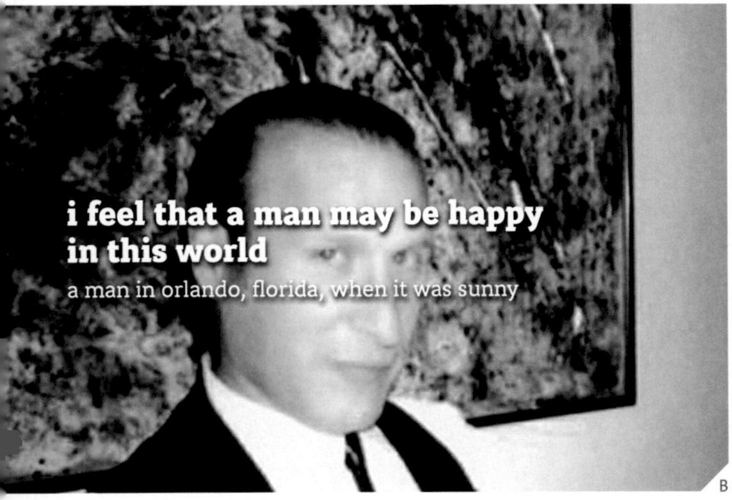
i feel that a man may be happy in this world

a man in orlando, florida, when it was sunny

B

i feel loved

a man

C

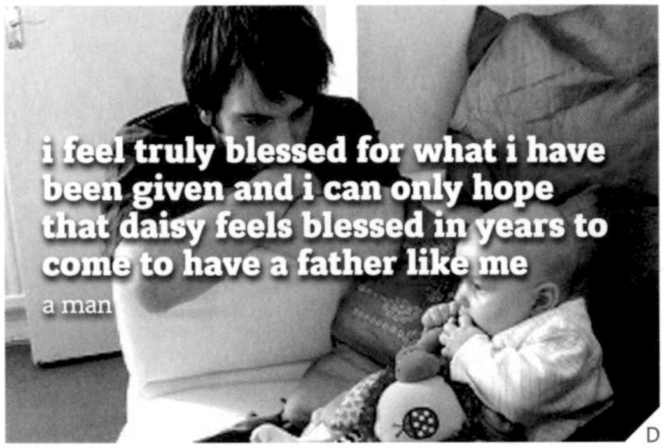
i feel truly blessed for what i have been given and i can only hope that daisy feels blessed in years to come to have a father like me

a man

D

i feel pretty

a man

E

i just feel a bit pissed

a man

F

i look and feel like i lost a fight but damn i feel good right now

a man

G

I LOVE YOU BUT YOU MAKE ME FEEL BAD AND DIRTY AFTER I DROP SO MUCH MONEY ON YOU

a man

men

1. adult male humans
2. 3,284,446,550 men globally (50.3%)
3. 41% of people in *We Feel Fine* are men
4. older bloggers are more often male

• i have been working too much to even feel like myself • i feel like a cat other times like a mouse • i feel like i'm watching many different things just happen in front of my face and i cant fix them • i want to tell everyone how i feel but i can't • i should hold the rod and strike when i feel the nibbles on the other end • i feel i am free in a world with many possibilities • i often feel like i need to start over again but time is running out • i feel like every man in america should be able to change out the hardware in their toilet • i feel and i feel plenty • i feel like because i volunteered to join the military no one held a gun to my head however i feel like i held it myself

Emotiveness Index Based on % of all sentences that contain feelings **3·0** / 10

Happiness Index Based on % of all feelings that are happy feelings **6·6** / 10

Sadness Index Based on % of all feelings that are sad feelings **2·8** / 10

great lost guilty **well** comfortable happy old sick sad ill **new** lonely

This blogger thought his life was over when his wife, high school sweetheart, and mother of his 2 daughters was sent to jail as a result of her drug addiction. For 4 years he would struggle to separate himself from his wife and make a new home for his children. Today, he is raising his two daughters, whom he has been awarded full custody. They all live in a house he recently bought with his new fiancée.

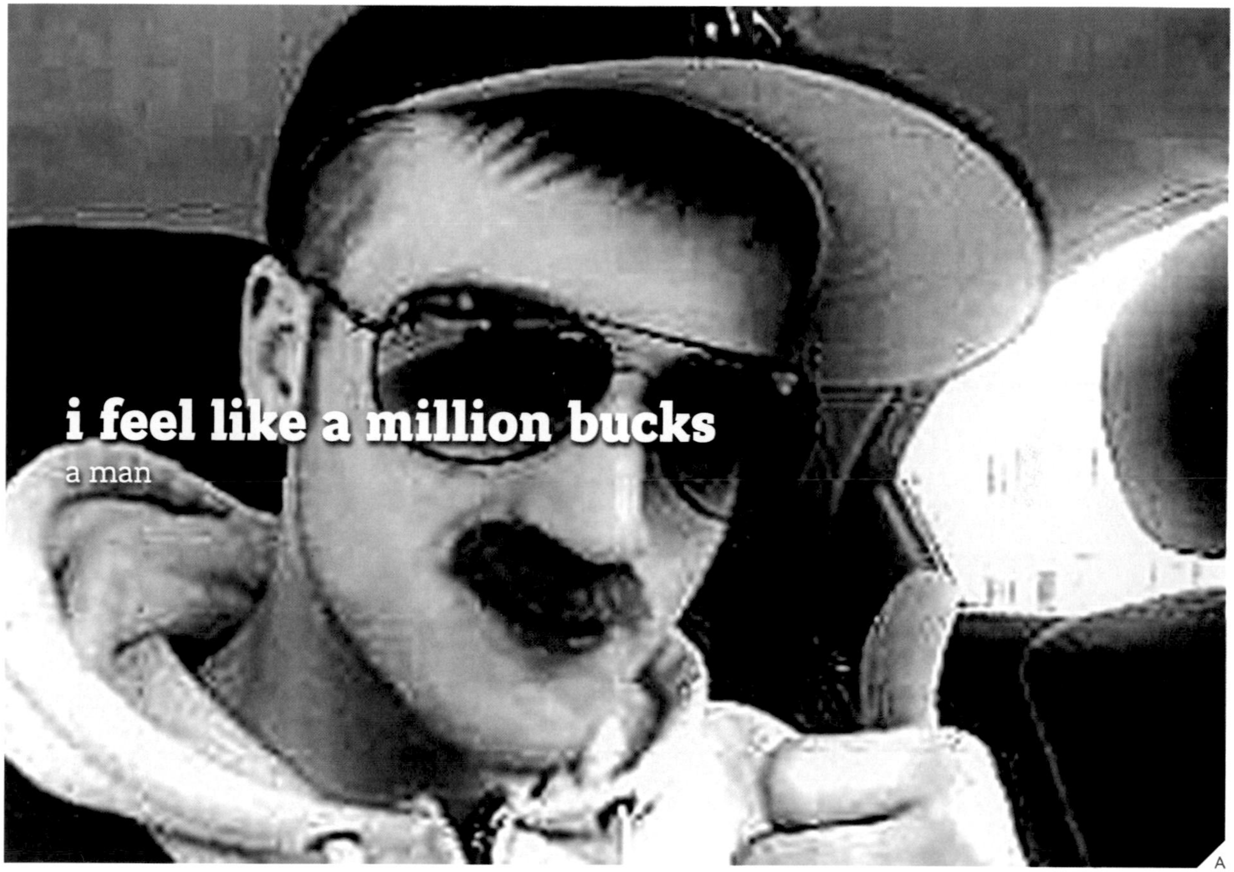

i feel like a million bucks

A

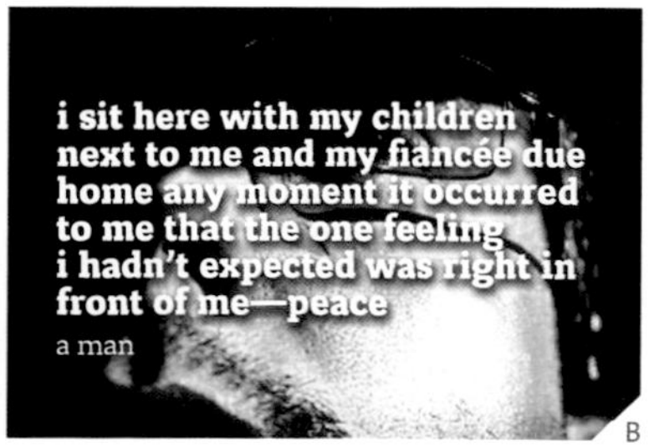

i sit here with my children next to me and my fiancée due home any moment it occurred to me that the one feeling i hadn't expected was right in front of me—peace
a man

B

i feel like i've done this 90 times before
a man

C

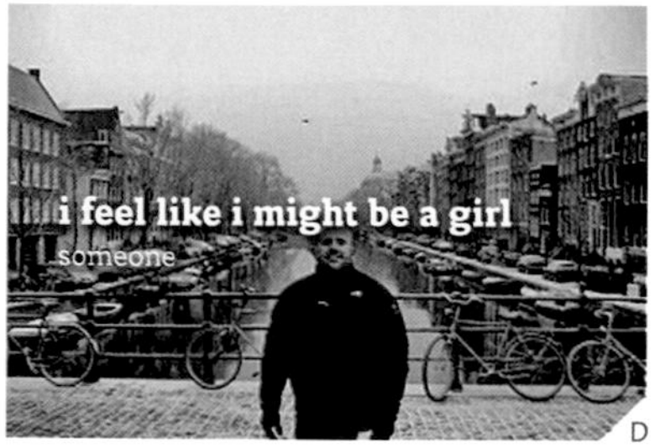

D

Observations

Men tend to express their emotions far less frequently on blogs than women do. They also tend to express a much smaller range of emotions than are expressed by woman. Men commonly express more **confidence** and **pride** than woman do, but also tend to express more **loneliness** than woman have been found to. Men tend to express emotions that communicate a greater sense of **individualism** and **detachment** than women, as well as a greater sensitivity to **power** and **success**. Men express the feelings **motivated** and **inspired** more often than women, but they also more often feel **uncomfortable** and **uneasy**. Men also express feeling **drunk** more often than women. ♥

WOMEN

10s | 20s | 30s | 40s | 50+

Top feelings among women — Above average / Women / Average

better · **bad** · good · sorry · **alone** · **guilty**

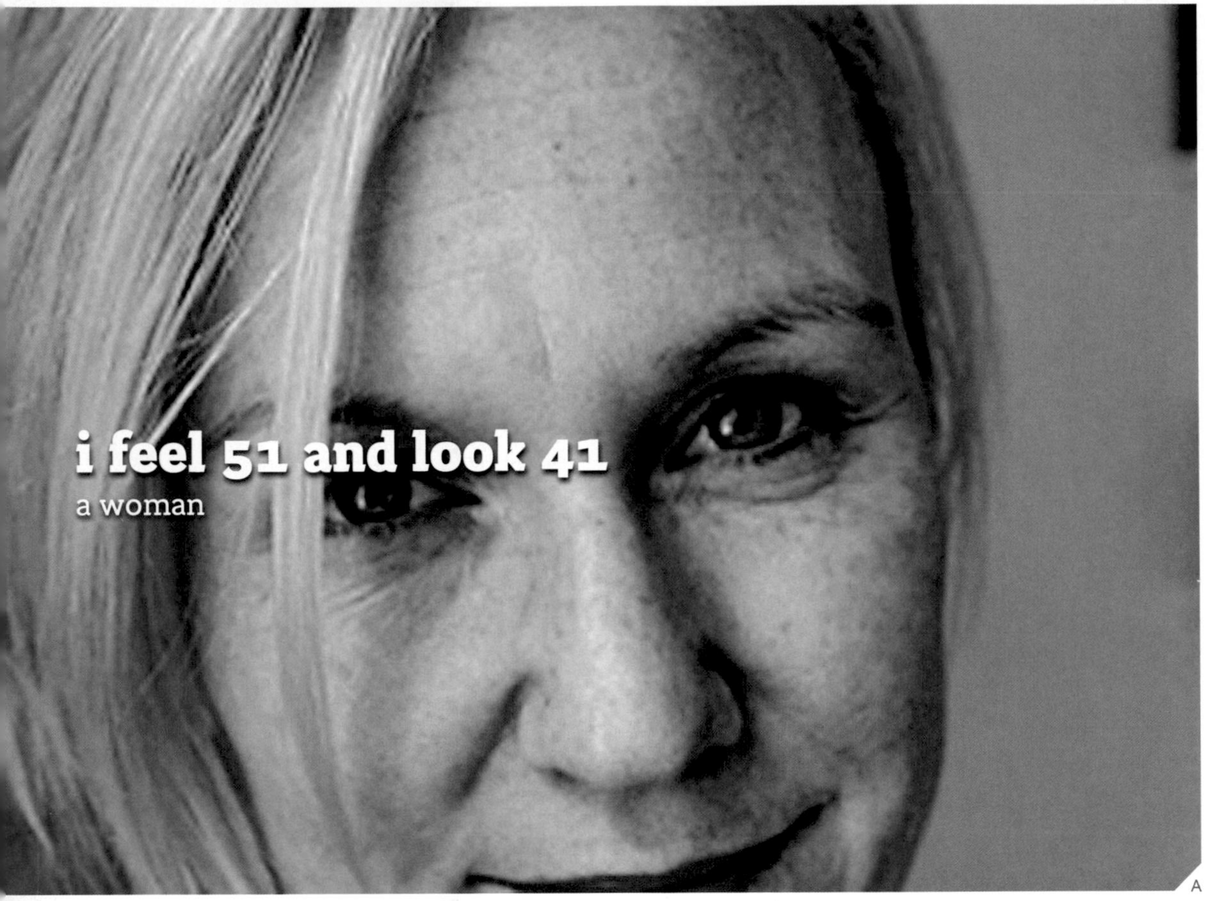

A

I FEEL SORRY FOR EVERYONE WHO NEVER RAN THROUGH SPRINKLERS AT NIGHT WITH CRAZY FRIENDS OR WHO NEVER DROVE TIL 2AM IN THE COUNTRY JUST FOR THE HELL OF IT

a woman

I FEEL PRETTY INVINCIBLE IN THESE PANTS

a woman

Emma is talking about recording artist Ben Lee. ↗

i feel quite positive that i'm going to marry him
a woman

B

C

women

1. adult female humans
2. 3,240,723,714 women globally (49.7%)
3. 59% of people in *We Feel Fine* are women
4. women blog more commonly than men

• i'm no feminist but i feel that women have a lot of pressure of society about what beauty is and they end up doing ridiculous things to try match the images they see in magazines especially young girls when the reality is they will never look that way because it's all computer generated • i believed that all my feelings of insecurity when he was around other women was simply my own poisonous jealousy and had no basis in reality • i miss being surrounded by women and feeling part of something so special and secret • i feel like there used to be more women in the public eye who stood for something worthwhile therein becoming role models • i feel like my face looks huge

Emotiveness Index Based on % of all sentences that contain feelings **7·0** / 10

Happiness Index Based on % of all feelings that are happy feelings **5·9** / 10

Sadness Index Based on % of all feelings that are sad feelings **3·5** / 10

down | **lost** | **sick** | happy | **sad** | great | **old** | well | comfortable | **stupid** | **safe** | **hurt** | **lonely**

A

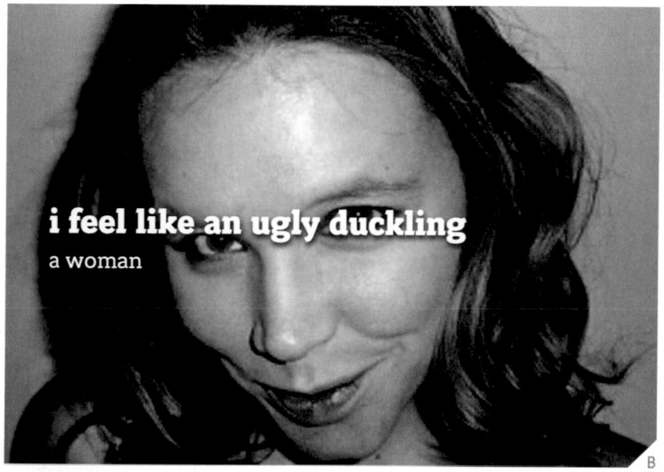

i feel like an ugly duckling

B

i feel good enough

C

i feel like i'm erring towards the slightly uh mental side
a woman

D

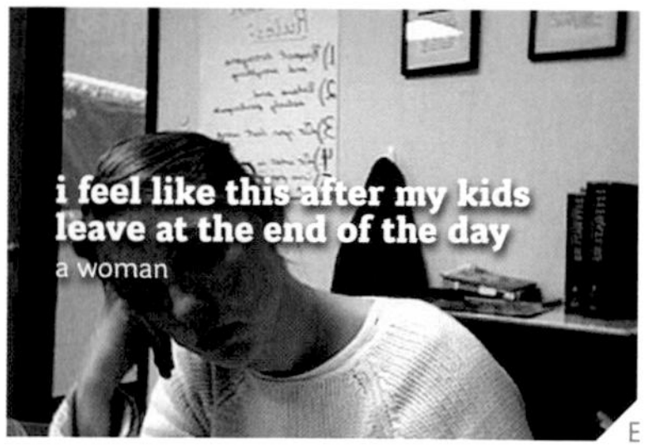

i feel like this after my kids leave at the end of the day
a woman

E

Karen is a teacher.

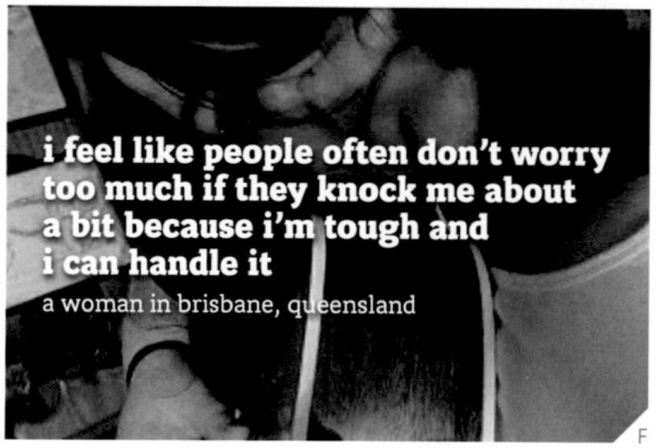

i feel like people often don't worry too much if they knock me about a bit because i'm tough and i can handle it
a woman in brisbane, queensland

F

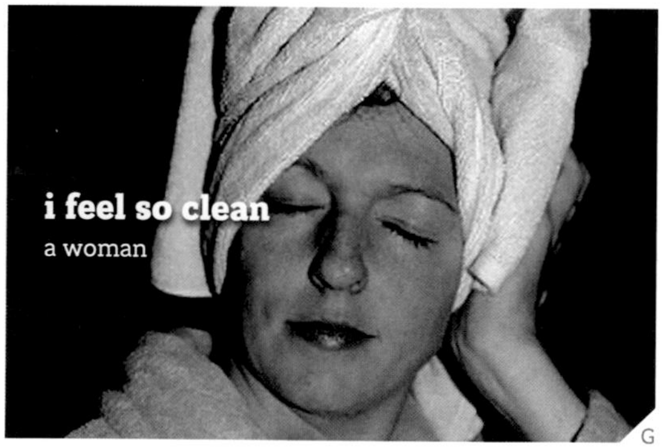

i feel so clean

G

Observations

Women tend to be far more expressive of their emotions on blogs than men. They tend to be exceedingly more personal in what they post, as well as more aware and affected by their relationships with the people close to them. They express feeling both **loved** and **unloved** more than men, and both **understood** and **misunderstood** more than men. While men are more in tune with power and success, women are more in tune with **security**, and express feeling **safe**, **secure**, **vulnerable**, and **threatened** with far more frequency than men. Women are more sensitive to **body image**—they feel both beautiful and ugly, and fat and fit more often than men. Women express **affection**, **gratitude**, and **sadness** more often than men do. ♥

Top feelings among teens

Above average / Teens / Average

better · **bad** · good · sick · guilty · alone

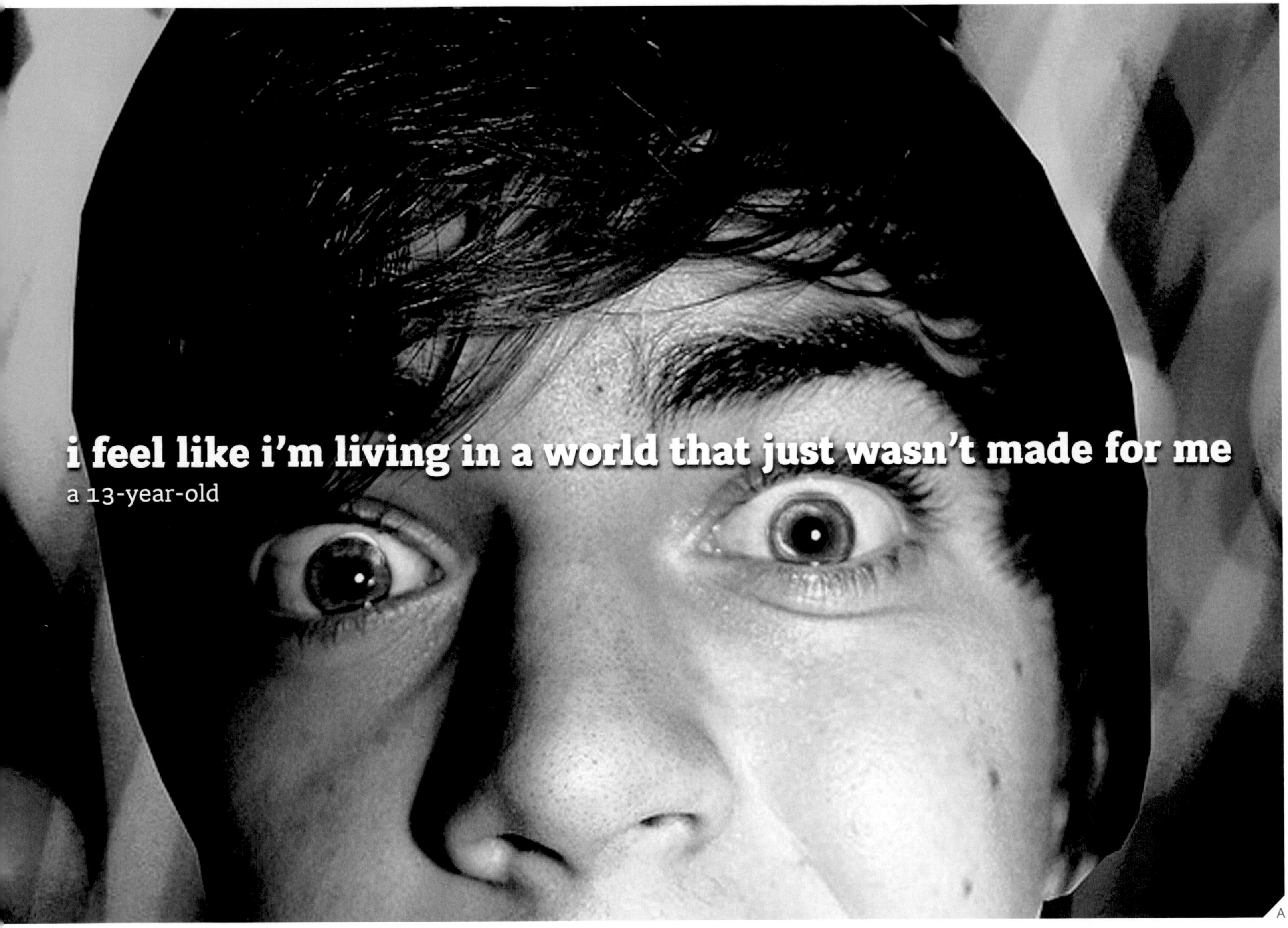

i feel like i'm living in a world that just wasn't made for me

a 13-year-old

A

10s

1. age group from 13 to 19
2. much development occurs
3. often referred to as adolescence
4. commonly known to be rebellious

● i think of how real life hasn't yet started i feel so tiny and insignificant and excited ● i'm feeling emo ● i think that subconciously i'm searching for my own meaning in life and making things feel more like the movies gives me this sense that sometime the plot will unfold and i'll figure out the direction to go ● i'm only friendly like sometimes when i feel like ● i love my dad and always will but his actions don't exactly reciprocate the same feelings ● i love high school i feel secure there the real world scares me a little ● i feel like it was my fault my family is broken now ● i'm just seeing the whole world in a different perspective at the moment and it makes me feel good

Emotiveness Index Based on % of all sentences that contain feelings **4·0** / 10

Happiness Index Based on % of all feelings that are happy feelings **4·6** / 10

Sadness Index Based on % of all feelings that are sad feelings **4·0** / 10

down sorry **happy** **lost** well **stupid** sad **ill** great comfortable **weird** **lonely**

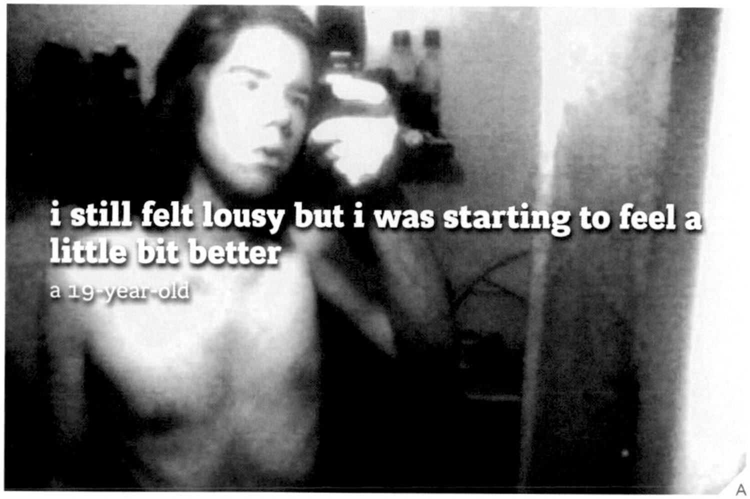

i still felt lousy but i was starting to feel a little bit better
a 19-year-old

A

i feel like I have nothing significant to say anymore
a 15-year-old

B

After having a strained relationship with his mother for years Brian found that his blog would eventually allow the two to communicate once again. His mother started reading his blog posts and responding in the comments and a new dialogue began. For the first time in a while they were able to tell each other they loved one another and discuss their problems.

I FEEL SO TRAPPED IN THIS IMAGINARY WAR BETWEEN YOU AND DAD AND IT'S SICKENING

a 19-year-old

i feel like my life isn't a pointless puddle of mud
a 18-year-old in singapore

C

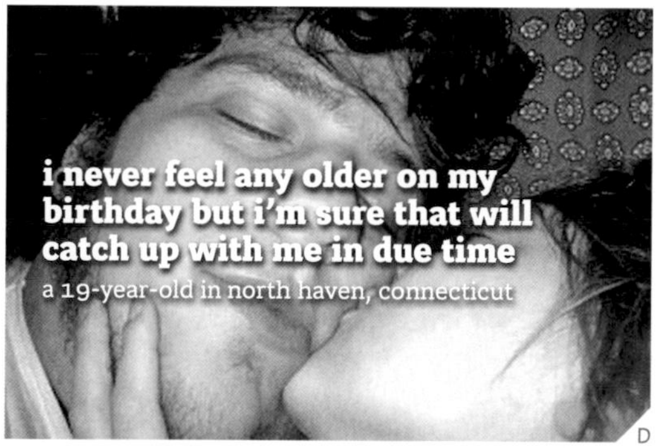

i never feel any older on my birthday but i'm sure that will catch up with me in due time
a 19-year-old in north haven, connecticut

D

I FEEL LIKE MY PARENTS SHOULDN'T HAVE HAD US BECAUSE THEY WEREN'T READY

a 19-year-old

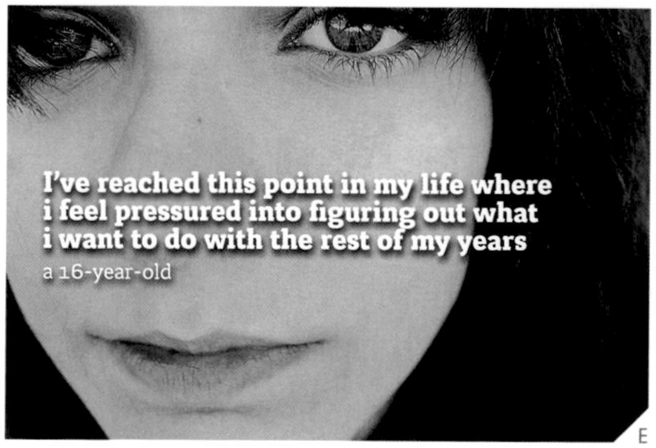

I've reached this point in my life where i feel pressured into figuring out what i want to do with the rest of my years
a 16-year-old

E

Observations

Of all the age groups in *We Feel Fine*, teens experience the most **angst**. They express feeling **awkward** and **weird**, as well as **restless** and **moody**, more than other age groups. They often express a sensitivity or awareness of their own levels of **maturity** and the maturity of others—teens express feeling both mature and immature more than other age groups. Teens express a higher level of **self-consciousness** and **self-doubt**, particularly with regard to how they fit in society or are viewed by others. They express feeling **stupid**, **retarded**, and **dumb**, as well as **worthless** and **unimportant**, more often than others. Teenagers also describe their emotions more colloquially than other age groups: they feel **pissed**, **fucked**, **shitty**, **bitchy**, and **screwed** more often. ♥

20s

10s | 20s | 30s | 40s | 50+

Top feelings among 20s — Above average / 20s / Average

better | bad | **good** | **guilty** | sorry | sick

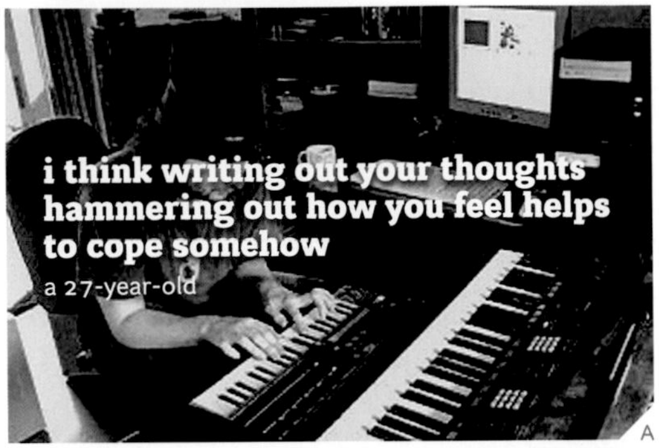

i think writing out your thoughts hammering out how you feel helps to cope somehow
a 27-year-old

A

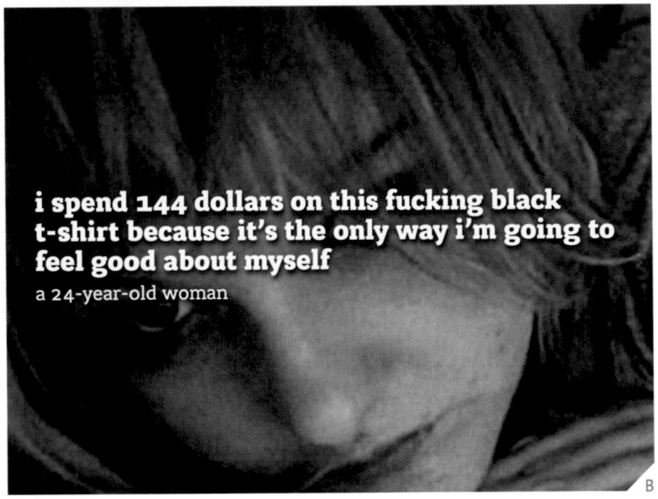

i spend 144 dollars on this fucking black t-shirt because it's the only way i'm going to feel good about myself
a 24-year-old woman

B

I FEEL SO LOST IN SO MANY ASPECTS OF MY LIFE AND IT WOULD JUST BE NICE TO HAVE THAT ONE PERSON BY MY SIDE NO MATTER WHAT

a 25-year-old

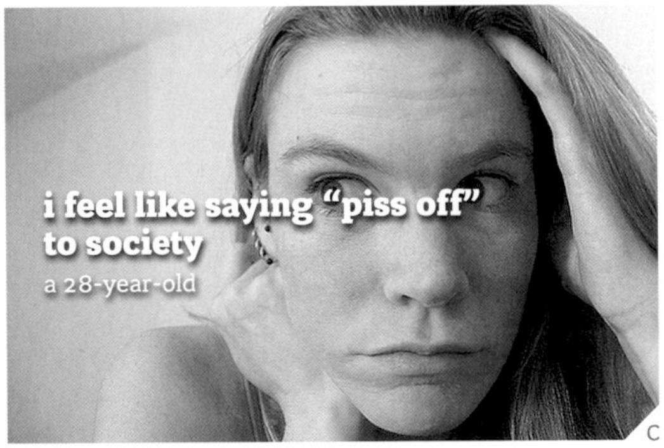

i feel like saying "piss off" to society
a 28-year-old

C

Terri's life is on track, but she feels like society expects her to have babies, a husband, and to own a home.

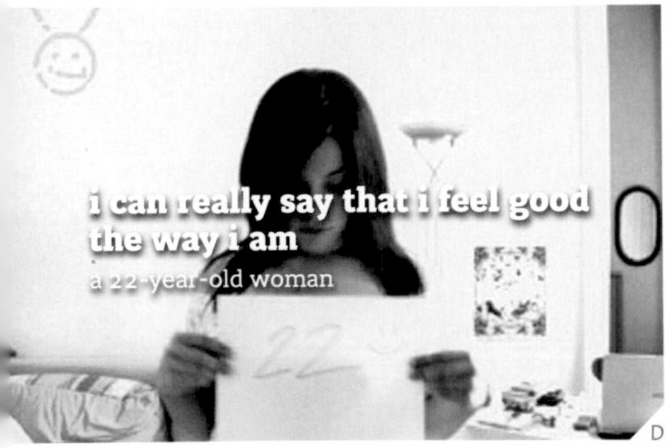

i can really say that i feel good the way i am
a 22-year-old woman

D

i can hardly wait to hold you feel my arms around you
a 22-year-old in moscow, russia

E

20s

1. age group from 20 to 29 years old
2. often referred to as early adulthood
3. full-time jobs, self-reliance are prevalent
4. marriage and families often begin

• i love kathryn so much and want to be with her not you but i still occasionally wake up from a dream about you and feel crap for the first couple of hours because we got on in it but now i'm awake and you're gone • i kinda feel bad for leaving my apartment kinda dirty and without doing dishes for my friend subletting • i feel depressed because i finished a book • i'm feeling ambitious on the weekends • i feel like i'm constantly waiting that my life is on hold • i feel like i'm walking on thin ice like my world is going to crumble at any moment • i'm currently experiencing another wave of sudden motivation which may have to do with the feeling of getting better at things

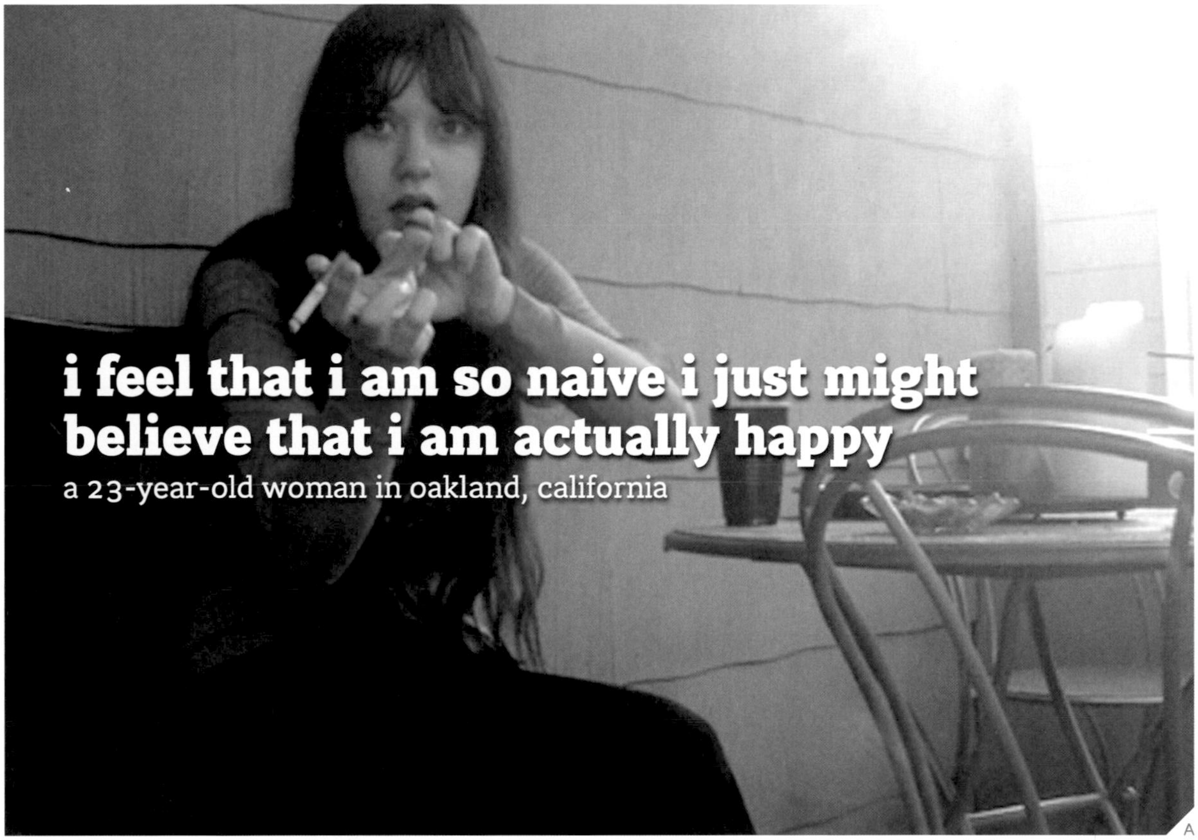

i feel that i am so naive i just might believe that i am actually happy
a 23-year-old woman in oakland, california

A

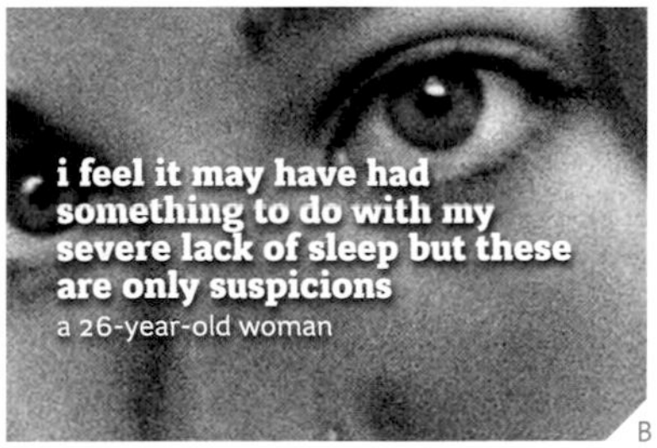

i feel it may have had something to do with my severe lack of sleep but these are only suspicions
a 26-year-old woman

B

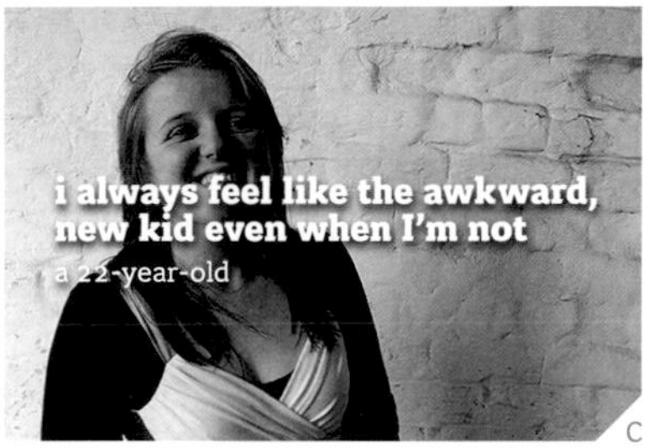

i always feel like the awkward, new kid even when I'm not
a 22-year-old

C

I JUST DON'T FEEL VERY CAPABLE AT ALL

a 23-year-old in russia

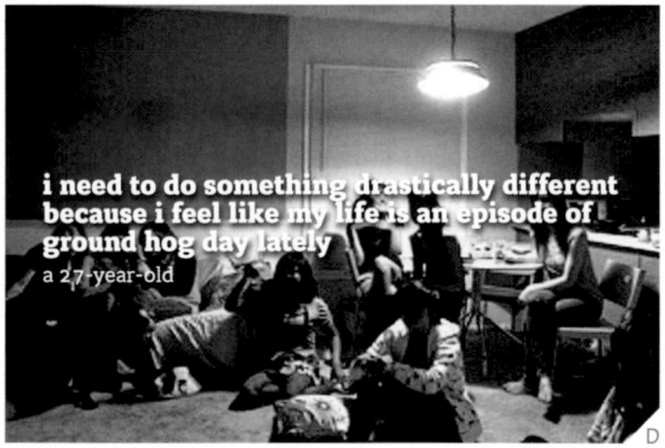

i need to do something drastically different because i feel like my life is an episode of ground hog day lately
a 27-year-old

D

Observations

Those in their 20s are a group whose emotions are marked by going out into the world and "making it." People in their 20s express a sense of drive far more than seen in other age groups. They express feeling **adventurous**, **accomplished**, **productive**, and **motivated** more often than people do at any other time in their lives. However, this drive is responsible for bringing about a flip side of **anxiety** and **stress**. In the early 20s, the years we identify as "college age," we witness emotions that suggest some sense of **confinement**. As people grow older and enter their late 20s we see a higher frequency of emotions that suggests a greater feeling and desire for **balance**, a desire often associated with **marriage** or **starting a family**. ♥

Top feelings among 30s

Above average
30s
Average

better · good · bad · guilty · sorry · well

I'M SO NERVOUS I GUESS IT'S TRUE WHAT THEY SAY ABOUT NOT FEELING GROWN UP UNTIL YOU'RE PAYING A MORTGAGE

a 35-year-old woman, when it was cloudy

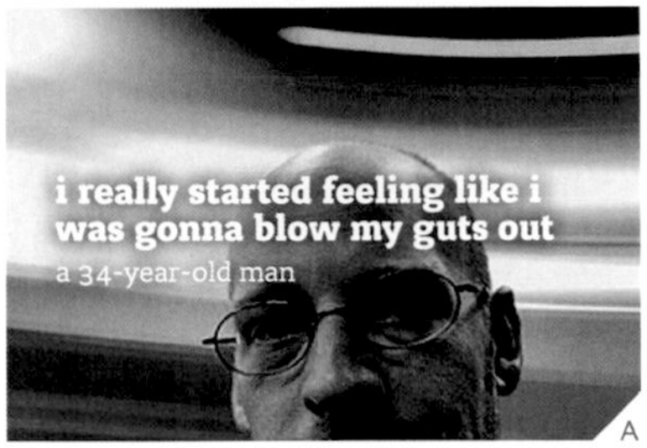

i really started feeling like i was gonna blow my guts out
a 34-year-old man

A

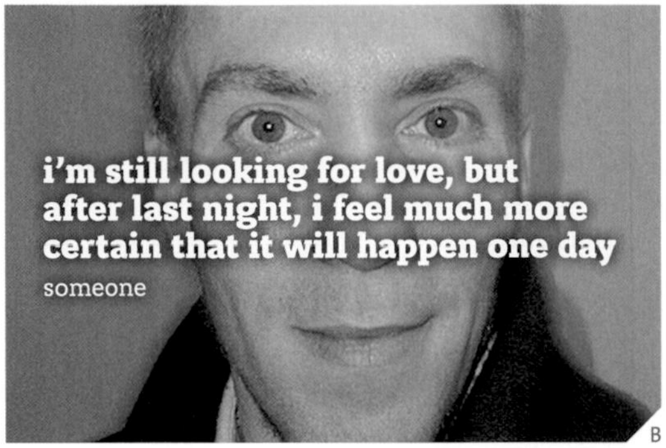

i'm still looking for love, but after last night, i feel much more certain that it will happen one day
someone

B

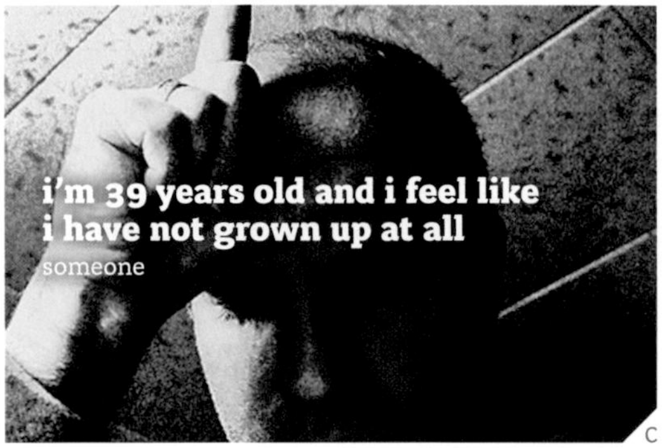

i'm 39 years old and i feel like i have not grown up at all
someone

C

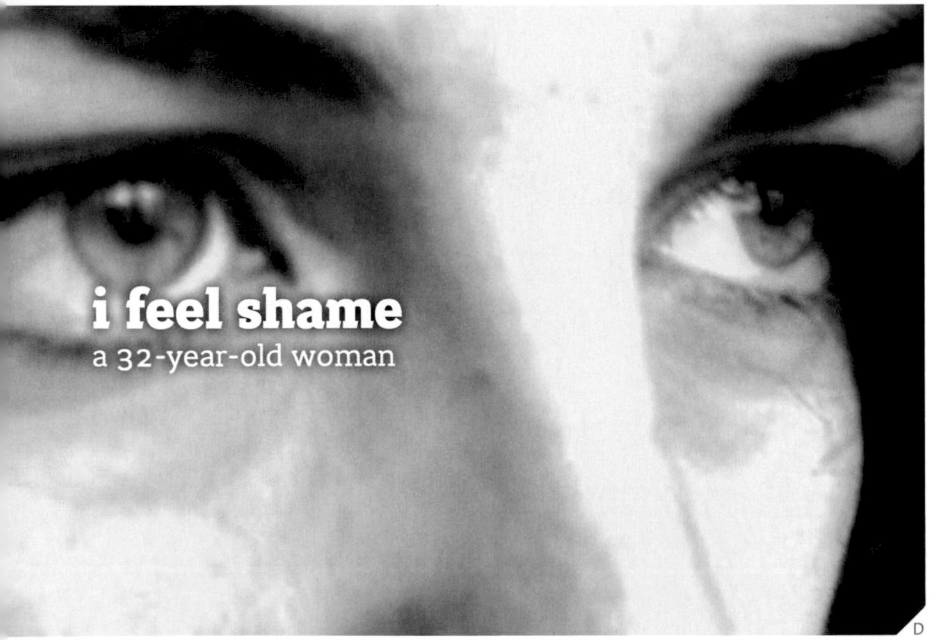

D

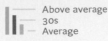

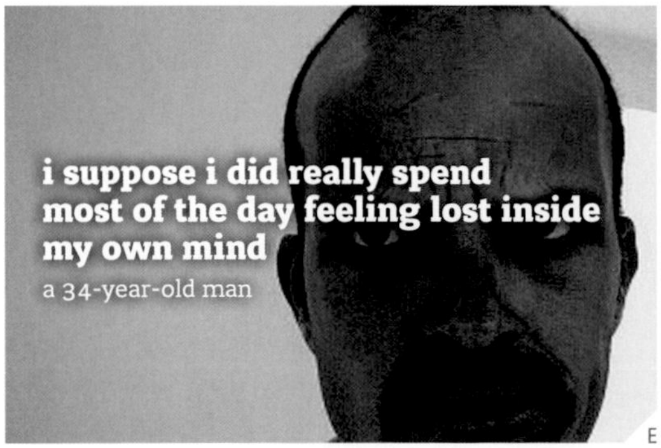

i suppose i did really spend most of the day feeling lost inside my own mind
a 34-year-old man

E

30s

1. age range from 30 to 39 years old
2. families usually started by this point
3. U.S. citizens can run for president at 35
4. family leadership role increases

• i'm looking toward the future with a sense of hope and promise i hope it's a feeling that remains for a long time • i feel like i need to focus on my career and finances and making myself happy and i'm not sure if i'm there yet but i'm getting to the point where i really don't give a shit • i feel emotional sickness when i think about the places from my childhood closing or worse getting torn down • i still love and miss her terribly to this day i feel that i would have been much better off for never have met her at all • i get to my parents house and it s a relief but there s a distinctly weird feeling driving my own car up the street i grew up on • i feel like i'm starting to gush like some love struck teenager

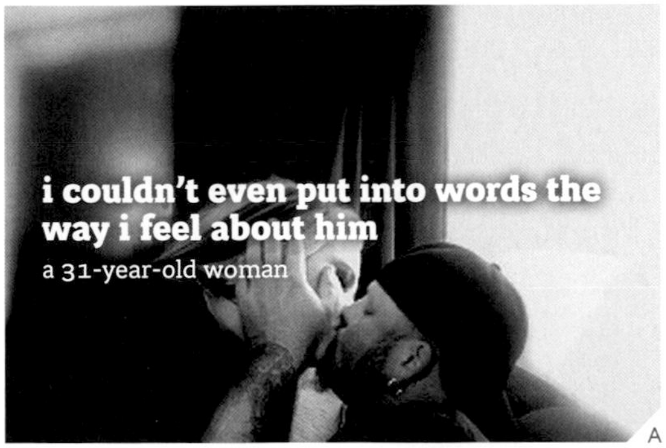

i couldn't even put into words the way i feel about him
a 31-year-old woman

A

i am a bum and i feel pretty good
a 39-year-old woman

B

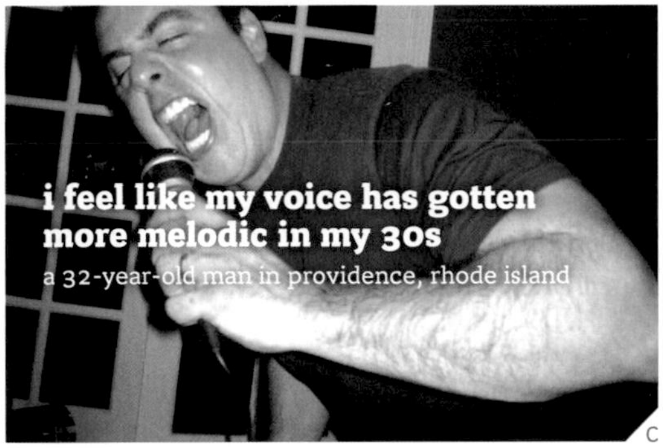

i feel like my voice has gotten more melodic in my 30s
a 32-year-old man in providence, rhode island

C

Ginger met her husband Gary on flickr.com where she came across his photographs. After emailing and chatting online they fell in love and were eventually married

i'm feeling like i should be carded for buying wine
a 38-year-old woman

D

i was feeling good so i jumped over a pile of horse poo
a 30-year-old man in brooklyn, new york

E

I FEEL OBLIGATED TO STOP PLAYING GAMES GET MARRIED AND BREED

a 36-year-old in cambridge, massachusetts

Observations

In their 30s, bloggers often express emotions associated with settling in and settling down. People are far more aware of their bodies and the subtle changes in their fluctuating **energy levels** and they express more often when they are feeling rested or energetic. People in their 30s commonly have new, young families and their emotions are extremely affected by this. People in their 30s often express a greater feeling of **gratitude** and **connectedness** with their surroundings than they did when they were younger. Individuals in their 30s also commonly express a feeling of possessing a stronger sense of **community** and **sense of spirituality** than they did when they were younger. ♥

40s

10s | 20s | 30s | 40s | 50+

Top feelings among 40s

Above average
40s
Average

better **good** bad **sorry** **guilty** **well**

sometimes i feel as if i should be doing more in my life
a 42-year-old

A

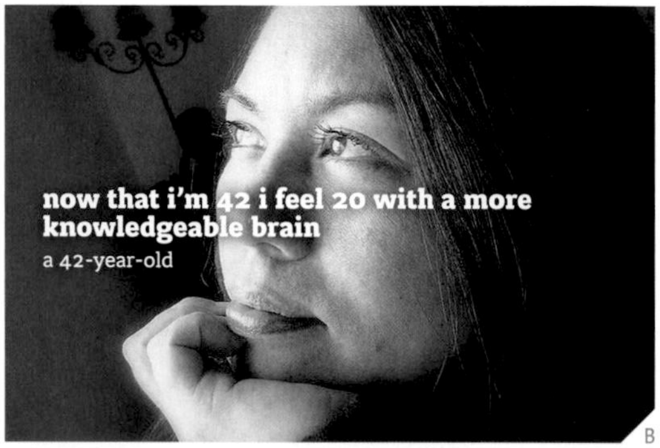

now that i'm 42 i feel 20 with a more knowledgeable brain
a 42-year-old

B

i find it interesting that now i'm 41 and feeling quite old...
i seldom wear makeup how much of that is my change in appearance and how much is that i feel better in my own skin
a 41-year-old

C

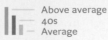

D

I FEEL GUILTY BECAUSE I AM LEAVING MY MOM IN THE NURSING HOME AND WALKING AWAY

a 48-year-old woman in hobbs, new mexico

40s

1. age group from 40 to 49 years old
2. often considered middle age
3. career usually firmly established
4. children sometimes entering their teens

• i want my wife and my children to feel loved every day because i show them and tell them • i understand times are difficult with two kids in college my family feels it too • i still feel like a kid waiting on my dad to play baseball with me to teach me the things that i need to know to survive in this world of ours • i didn't know i was capable of feeling so much before i was a mom • i wrestle so much with the fact that i really should love my wife even more then my kids but i just can't make myself feel that way toward her • i feel obligated to work with my dad • i feel that my body is at the end of it's rope • i always feel more energetic and excited as the moon waxes

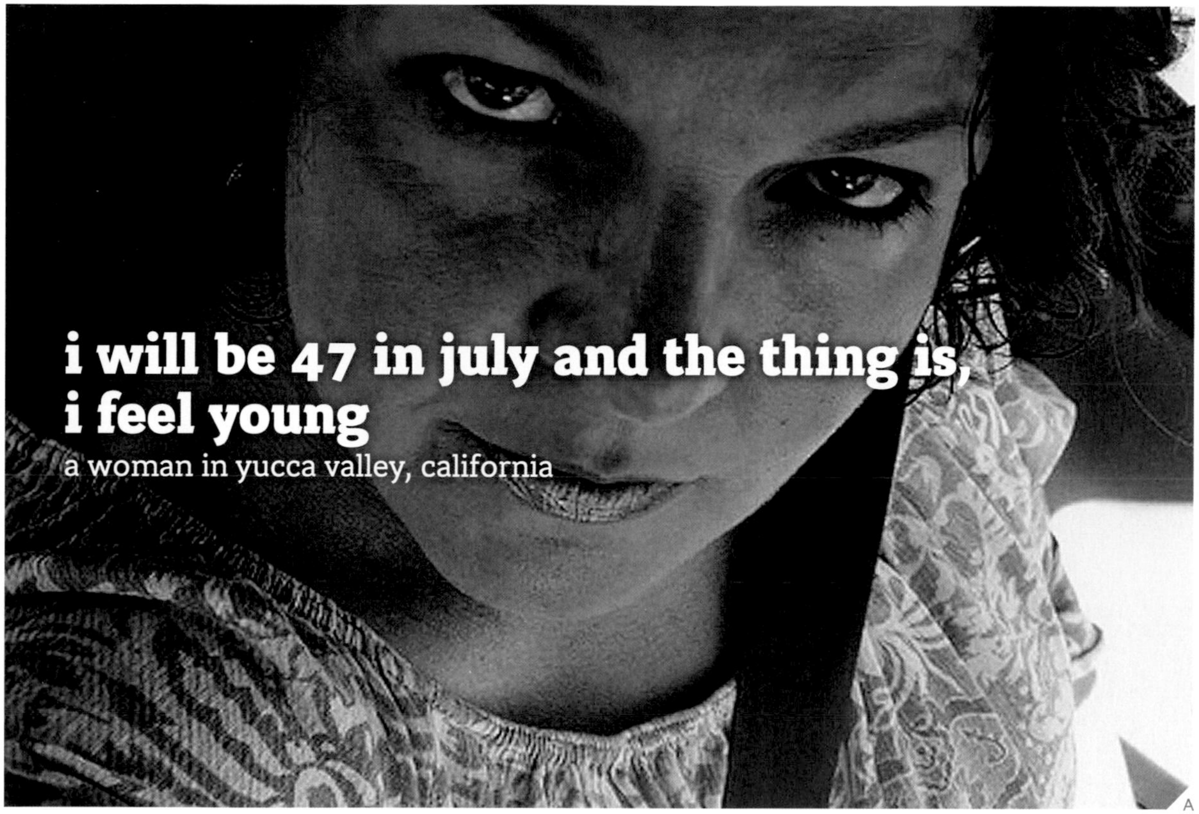

i will be 47 in july and the thing is, i feel young
a woman in yucca valley, california

A

B

I HAVE SEVERAL 40-YEAR-OLD FRIENDS THAT WILL CONTINUE TO FEEL LIKE A COMPLETE FAILURE UNTIL THEY GET MARRIED

a 42-year-old in saint joseph, michigan

i feel we are perched on the edge of fall
a 43-year-old man

C

Observations

In their 40s, just like in their 30s, bloggers continue to express a feeling of **gratitude** and **connectedness**. They also show an increase in **calm happiness.** Feelings such as **relaxed**, **secure**, and **calm** are expressed more frequently by bloggers in their 40s than by any other age group. Additionally, bloggers in their 40s also express a greater sense of responsibility. They feel a responsibility for both their children as well as their **aging parents**. It is also common for them to feel the greater **financial responsibility** of having a bigger home and an awareness of **retirement**. The feelings **responsible**, **frustrated**, **overwhelmed**, and **needed** are expressed more often by people in their 40s than by people at any other age. ♥

Top feelings among 50+

Above average 50+ / Average

better | **good** | bad | **well** | **guilty** | **great**

I FEEL I'M TOO OLD TO DATE FOR CRYING OUT LOUD I HAVE ADULT KIDS

a 55-year-old in hereford, england

i'm feeling better
a 51-year-old woman

A

i remember these trees being planted in 1956 and it makes me feel a bit dated
a 57-year-old man

B

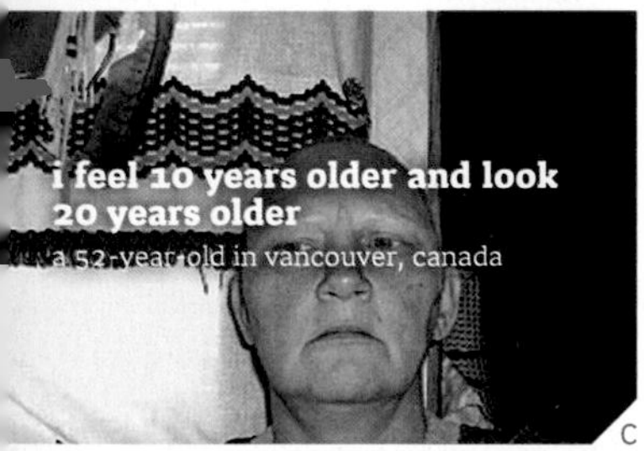

i feel 10 years older and look 20 years older
a 52-year-old in vancouver, canada

C

i climbed it alone feeling pretty proud of my 58 year old body
a 58-year-old man

D

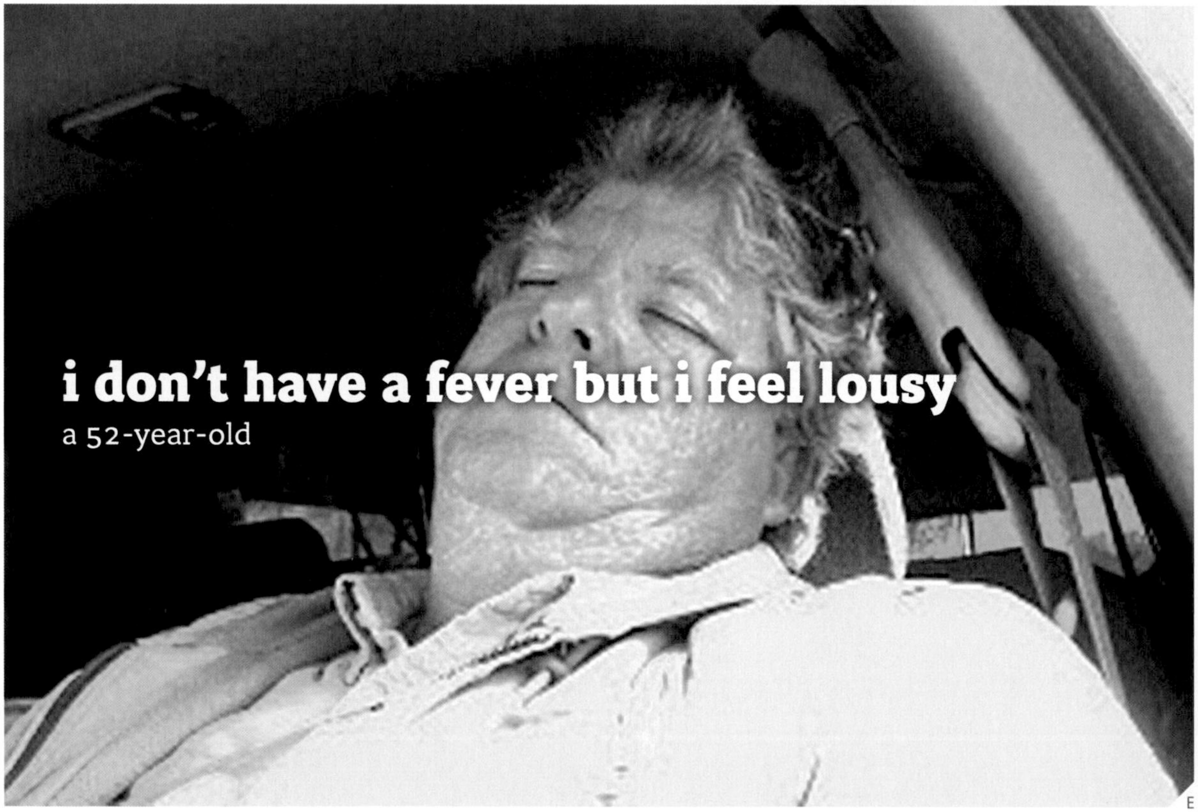

i don't have a fever but i feel lousy
a 52-year-old

E

50+

1. age group over 50 years old
2. children often enter late teens and 20s
3. families established, grandchildren
4. careers sometimes concluding

● i feel quite ok about things as i get older i don't want to die now obviously but i think that it is natural to become more accustomed to the idea as you get into real old age ● i should feel flattered but i'm mostly just sick to my stomach because i am never the girl that the guy falls in love with ● i feel really bad about myself and worry that i am gay ● i feel like i'm aging at a thousand miles an hour ● i feel that sense of failure of not being good enough ● i know part of my reluctance comes from the remainders of all my self doubts and self criticisms that overwhelmed my self esteem and kept me feeling small all my life

Emotiveness Index Based on % of all sentences that contain feelings **9·0** / 10

Happiness Index Based on % of all feelings that are happy feelings **9·0** / 10

Sadness Index Based on % of all feelings that are sad feelings **1·0** / 10

sad **comfortable** down alone **old** **safe** lost sick **blessed** **tired** **done** **new**

i feel so honored to call you my wife
a 57-year-old

A

2008 marked Susan and her husband's 40th anniversary. They eloped and were wed in Mexico when they were 17. They are still happily married.

I FEEL I HAVE A CHILD'S MIND IN AN ADULT'S BODY

a 57-year-old

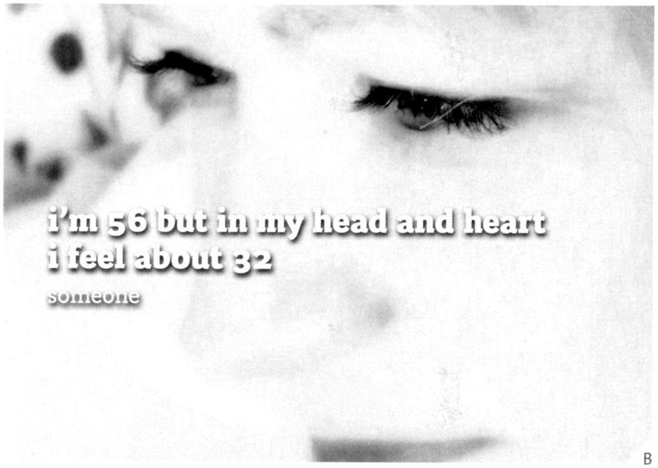

i'm 56 but in my head and heart i feel about 32
someone

B

I FEEL MORE LIKE I LOST A SON INSTEAD OF GAINING A DAUGHTER-IN-LAW

a 57-year-old woman in nashville, tennessee, when it was cloudy

i'm feeling better but i'm not 100% well yet
a 50-year-old woman

C

Observations

The number of bloggers in the *We Feel Fine* database decreases a huge amount as age increases. There are fewer bloggers ages 50 and older than there are in all the other age groups. The most distinct emotion expressed by bloggers in this age group is a feeling of being blessed and it is expressed largely in connection with their **children**. The feelings **blessed**, **grateful**, **fortunate**, and **honored** are expressed by people ages 50 and older far more often than they are expressed by people younger than 50. Overall, this is an age group that expresses a huge amount of positivity: the feelings **optimistic**, **wonderful**, **young**, and **positive** are expressed far more frequently after the age of 50 than ever expressed before. ♥

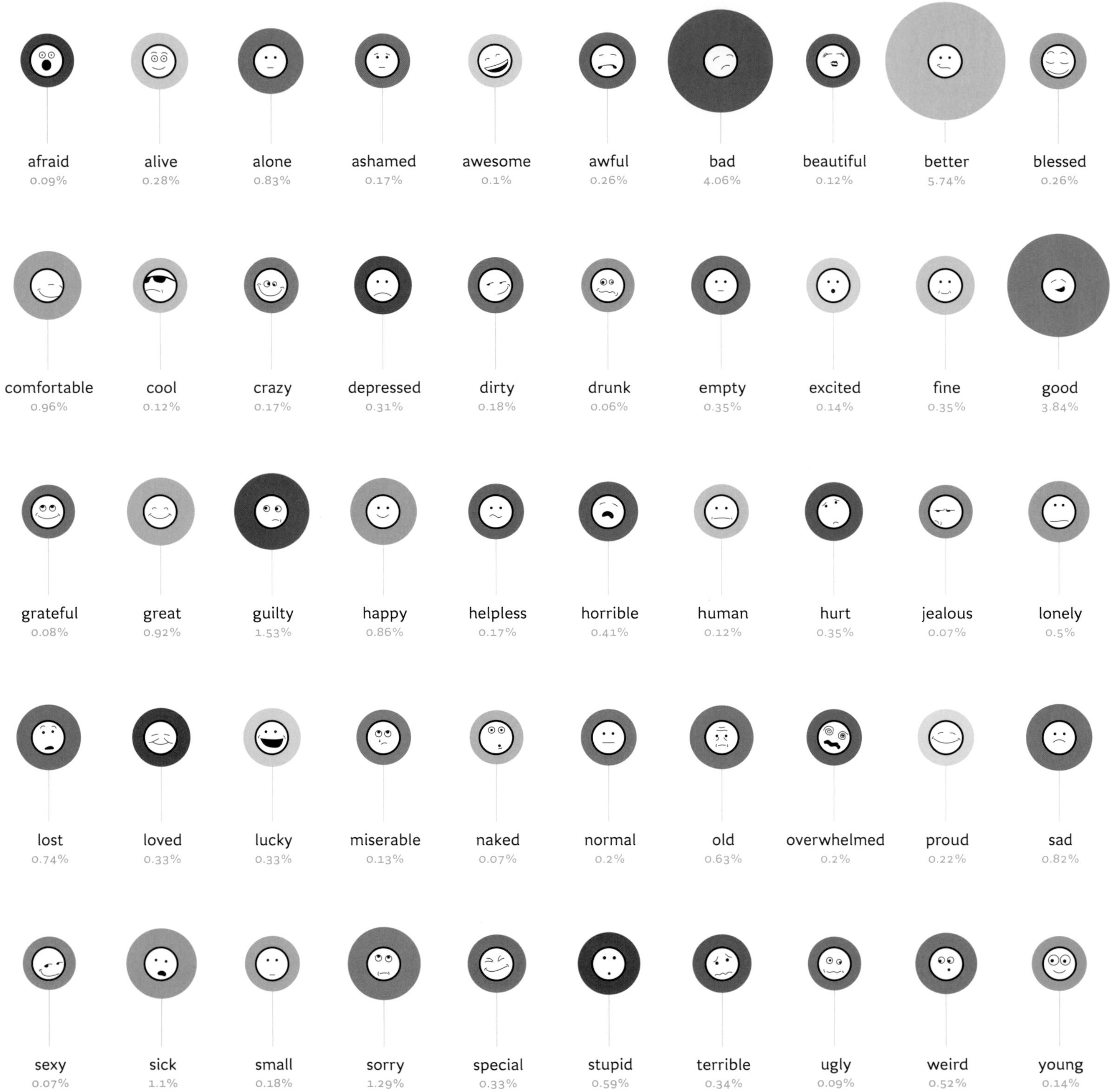
afraid 0.09%
alive 0.28%
alone 0.83%
ashamed 0.17%
awesome 0.1%
awful 0.26%
bad 4.06%
beautiful 0.12%
better 5.74%
blessed 0.26%
comfortable 0.96%
cool 0.12%
crazy 0.17%
depressed 0.31%
dirty 0.18%
drunk 0.06%
empty 0.35%
excited 0.14%
fine 0.35%
good 3.84%
grateful 0.08%
great 0.92%
guilty 1.53%
happy 0.86%
helpless 0.17%
horrible 0.41%
human 0.12%
hurt 0.35%
jealous 0.07%
lonely 0.5%
lost 0.74%
loved 0.33%
lucky 0.33%
miserable 0.13%
naked 0.07%
normal 0.2%
old 0.63%
overwhelmed 0.2%
proud 0.22%
sad 0.82%
sexy 0.07%
sick 1.1%
small 0.18%
sorry 1.29%
special 0.33%
stupid 0.59%
terrible 0.34%
ugly 0.09%
weird 0.52%
young 0.14%

3 What On the nature of emotions and their role in our lives

Tags: philosophy, neuroscience

Carolyn Scotchmer was living in Calgary at the end of 2006 when she decided at the age of 33 to shake things up a little bit. "I haven't gotten it all worked out yet," she writes in her December 2nd, 2006, blog post, "but the front running plan is to go to Egypt for a few weeks, then to Portugal and Spain to work on an organic farm for 4–6 weeks, and then back to Egypt, provided I still feel like that's where I'd like to be."[1]

Carolyn left her job two weeks later. A few weeks after that, she booked a plane ticket to London, where she had landed an interview with an adventure travel company for a job either in Egypt or Vietnam. The next day, the company changed their mind. They wouldn't be needing anybody until May. "I've spent today thinking about my next steps," she writes in her blog on January 11th, "and I realize that my biggest problem really is that there are too many options."

"Where I struggle is that for once in my life, I'm trying to follow my heart and not my overly logical head, and I'm a little out of practice. It's working so far, and it feels great, but sometimes I have a little trouble deciphering its messages. I overthink things and analyze them and second guess. But I know what the right choice is here, deep inside I know what I need to do. I'm leaving on February 5th. I know where I need to go. I just have to trust myself enough to do it."[2]

Since Socrates, philosophers have been debating the interplay between the heart and the head, between emotion and reason. Plato, his student, divided the soul into two parts, an irrational part and a rational part, and suggested that emotions arise from the lower, irrational part of the mind and pervert reason. Until recently Western philosophers have largely agreed with that mentality: that emotions are more basic, less intelligent, and more dangerous than reason. René Descartes distinguished emotions from "clear cognition," noting that they "agitate and disturb" the soul and render judgment "confused and obscure". But they can be controlled through rationality, he suggested: "To excite courage in oneself and remove fear, it is not sufficient to have the will to do so, but we must also apply ourselves to consider the reasons."[3]

Using reason to temper the emotions is not just an exercise for philosophers. Many of the bloggers in the *We Feel Fine* database use their blogs to introduce rationality to their emotions. "I feel good about my state of mind," writes one anonymous blogger in her April 19th, 2009, post. She had recently had an upsetting encounter with a girl who was trying to break up her relationship, but, she said, "I am close to being over that crazy girl and all that shit she caused. I have been very direct and calm rather than let anger and rage get the best of me. When I feel upset I just take a minute to decide if it's rational and reasonable as opposed to irrational and of psycho bitch status." And Justin Guber, on his June 9th, 2009, post, writes: "Last night I could feel those strange, weird, irrational feelings surface, and I started typing away and things felt a bit better after that."[4]

On September 13th, 1848, Phineas Gage, a 25-year-old railroad foreman, was impaled in the head with an iron rod in a construction accident outside Cavendish, Vermont. The 13-foot, 3.5-pound rod entered the side of his face, passed behind the left eye, and exited out the top of his head, landing about 80 feet away. Astonishingly, Gage was walking and talking within a few minutes, and sat upright in the ox cart that he rode in to see the town doctors, John Harlow and Edward Williams.

Williams wrote about the encounter: "Mr. Gage, during the time I was examining this wound, was relating the manner in which he was injured to the bystanders; he talked so rationally and was so willing to answer questions, that I directed my inquiries to him in preference to the men who were with him at the time of the accident... Mr. G. then related to me some of the circumstances, as he has since done; and I can safely say that neither at that time nor on any subsequent occasion, save once, did I consider him to be other than perfectly rational."[5]

Physically, Gage recovered tremendously well. He lost vision in his left eye, but he maintained all other physical abilities; he could walk, talk, and do complex physical tasks with ease. Further, he was still clearly intelligent. But there was a strange effect on his personality after the physical recovery: he seemed to have become a man-child. His doctor, John Harlow, mentioned that he became "fitful, irreverent, indulging at times in the grossest profanity which was not previously his custom, manifesting but little deference for his fellows, impatient of restraint or advice when it conflicts with his desires, at times pertinaciously obstinate, yet capricious and vacillating, devising many plans of future operation, which are no sooner arranged than they are abandoned."[6] His friends noted that "Gage was no longer Gage." His bosses, who before the accident had called him "the most efficient and capable" man in the railroad gang, refused to give him back his old job. He spent the rest of his life wandering between various jobs on horse farms, in the circus, and as a stagecoach driver in South America, seeming to have lost his ability to make reasonable decisions, his forethought, and his respect for social convention.

Almost a century and a half later, the neurologist Antonio Damasio encountered a patient whom he called "a modern Phineas Gage." The patient, whom he referred to as Elliot, was in his 30s and had undergone a radical personality change after an operation to remove a brain tumor on the surface of his frontal lobes. Elliot's intelligence, his ability to move, and his ability to use language were not harmed by the operation. But, like Phineas Gage, Elliot seemed to have lost the ability to make decisions and plan for the future. Since the operation, the formerly stable Elliot had started several ill-conceived business ventures, gotten himself bankrupt, and had two divorces. "The tragedy of this otherwise healthy and intelligent man was that he was neither stupid nor ignorant, and yet he acted often as if he were," said Damasio. "The machinery for his decision making was so flawed that he could no longer be an effective social being."[7]

Damasio struggled to figure out why Elliot had lost the ability to plan and make decisions. After all, his reason stayed entirely intact. Elliot scored above average on a battery of tests to determine the state of his rational mind—for long-term memory, short-term memory, perceptual ability, new learning, language, the ability to do arithmetic, the ability to make estimates based on incomplete knowledge, and logical competence. "After all these tests," wrote Damasio, "Elliot emerged as a man with a normal intellect who was unable to decide properly, especially when the decision involved personal and social matters. Could it be that reasoning and decision making in the personal and social domain were different from reasoning and thinking in domains concerning objects, space, numbers, and words?"[8]

It was at this point that Damasio gave Elliot a test that showed one additional post-operation change. Elliot had lost the ability to feel emotion. The case of Elliot led Damasio to the conclusion that the age-old dichotomy between emotions and reason is false. Emotions are crucial to reason, especially reasoning about social and personal issues. And while too much emotion can obstruct reason, according to Damasio, reduction in emotion can be an equally important source of irrational behavior. "The cold-bloodedness of Elliot's reasoning," writes Damasio, "prevented him from assigning different values to different options, and made his decision-making landscape hopelessly flat."[9] In a complex world with so many factors affecting our decisions, the heart needs to play a prominent role.

This chapter explores 50 common emotions through the lens of the *We Feel Fine* database. It explores the nature, the demographics, and the statistics around each of these emotions. In an interconnected world where emotions are so essential, this chapter provides one way to get to know our feelings more deeply.

From left: Carolyn Scotchmer at home; Carolyn in her suitcase; Carolyn waking up in Egypt's Sahara—"I wish we could bottle moments like this and save them for later, to be taken out and enjoyed at those times when we forget ourselves."

Carolyn Scotchmer did follow her heart and take that flight on February 5th, 2007, and moved to Egypt as was her original plan. After living in Cairo for a couple of months without a job, she ended up with the tour leader job she had wanted. In her May 24th, 2007, blog post, she wrote: "I can't believe this is actually happening! I know it won't be perfect, but I am so very excited to try this."[10] Her July 25th, 2007, blog post was entitled Ana Mapsutta, Arabic for "I'm happy."[11] ♥

1. Carolyn Scotchmer. http://ca.blog.360.yahoo.com/blog-6.JcFdoyerSpM9r2ysE3oO3yDBeMWAg4
2. Carolyn Scotchmer. http://www.flickr.com/photos/cscotchmer/353999270/
3. Descartes, René. *The Passions of the Soul*. 1649.
4. Justin Guber. http://guber.terapad.com/?fa=contentNews.newsDetails&from=list&newsID=100226

5–9. Damasio, Antonio. *Descartes' Error: Emotion, Reason, and the Human Brain*, (New York: Penguin, 1994).

10, 11. Carolyn Scotchmer. See 1.

AFRAID

142 nd most common feeling overall · 0.09% of all feelings are afraid

afraid

Breakdowns
for people who feel afraid

Gender breakdown 53% 47%

Age breakdown 10s 20s 30s 40s 50+

I FEEL SO AFRAID OF SCREWING THIS UP AND SCREWING UP THE SEMI FRIENDSHIPS I HAVE

a 22-year-old in burkina faso

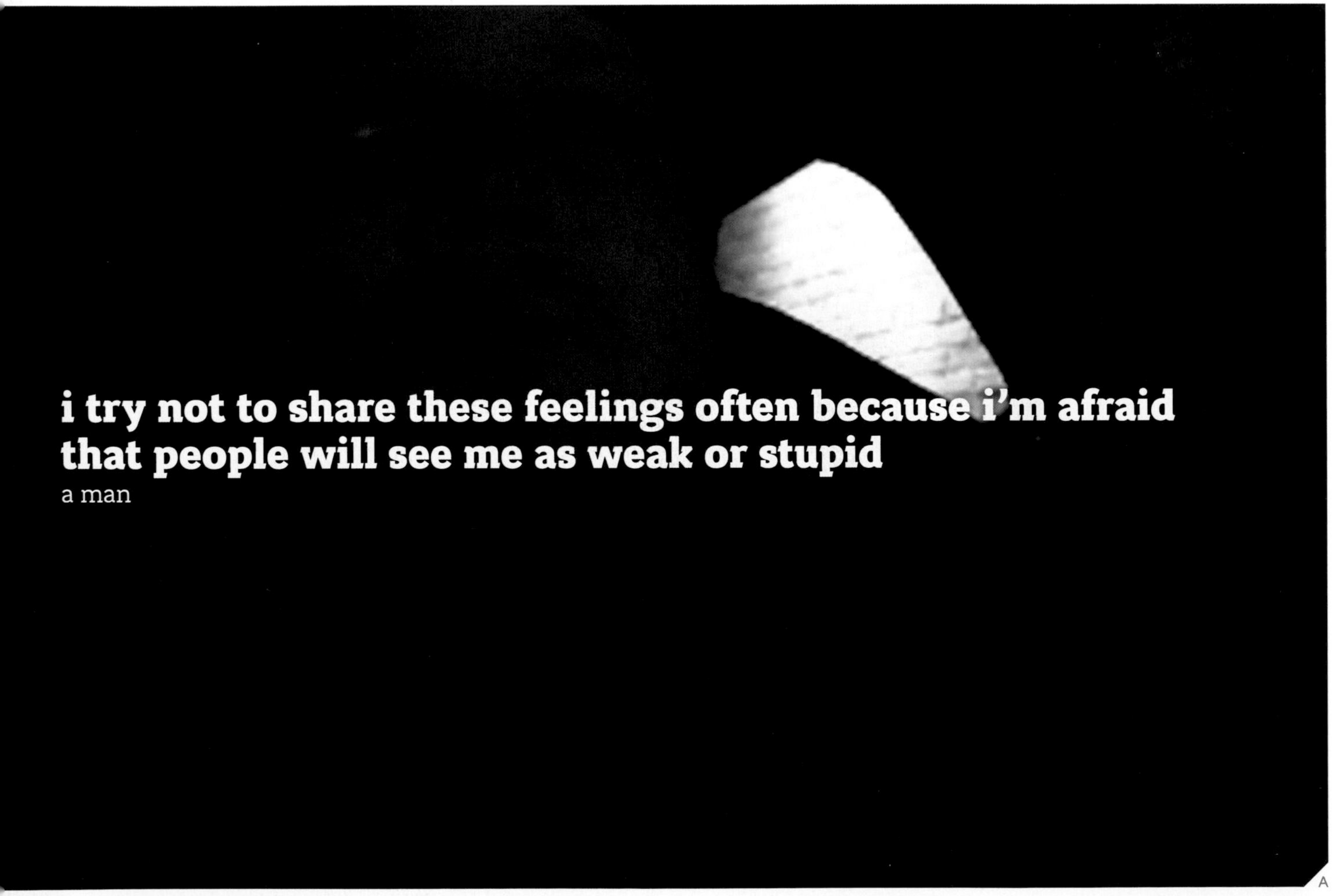

i try not to share these feelings often because i'm afraid that people will see me as weak or stupid
a man

A

afraid adj.

1. feeling fear
2. feeling regret or unhappiness
3. feeling reluctance or unwillingness
4. apprehensive

● i just kept touching him trying to warm him with my hands and talking to him so he would not feel any more afraid than he already must ● i don't know how he feels i'm afraid he'd stop talking to me cause he would think i've lost my sanity ● i want to love you too and not feel afraid while doing it ● i think you put on paper what many people feel but are afraid to say ● i almost never write how i feel cuz i'm afraid of what people will say ● i feel the need to maintain friends i've rarely had and to please my parents but i think it's because i'm afraid that once i commit to a path of opposition i'll never come back to the real world ● i feel like my mom is so afraid that she can no longer see reason

Season breakdown — **26%** | 23% | 26% | 25%

Related feelings mentioned with afraid

- **scared**
- hurt
- ashamed
- mad
- upset

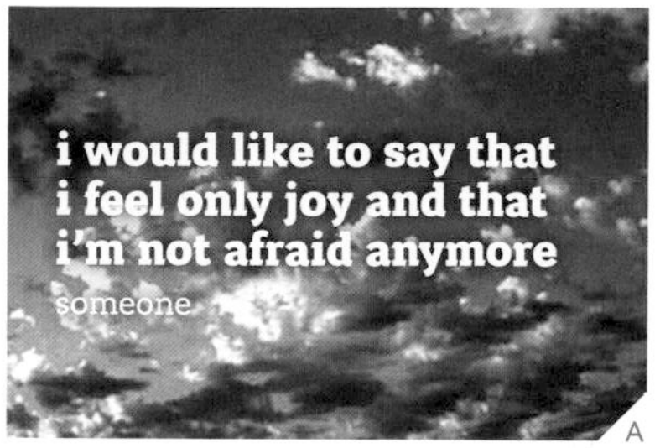

i would like to say that i feel only joy and that i'm not afraid anymore
someone

A

B

i feel afraid for this poor girl
a man in portsmouth, ohio, when it was raining

C

I FEEL LIKE I'M AFRAID TO LET MYSELF FALL IN LOVE AGAIN

a 21-year-old in altamonte springs, florida

Sarah has wanted to be a writer for a long time, but she had been afraid of failure. Recently, she has started to overcome her fear and is now a writer and a blogger.

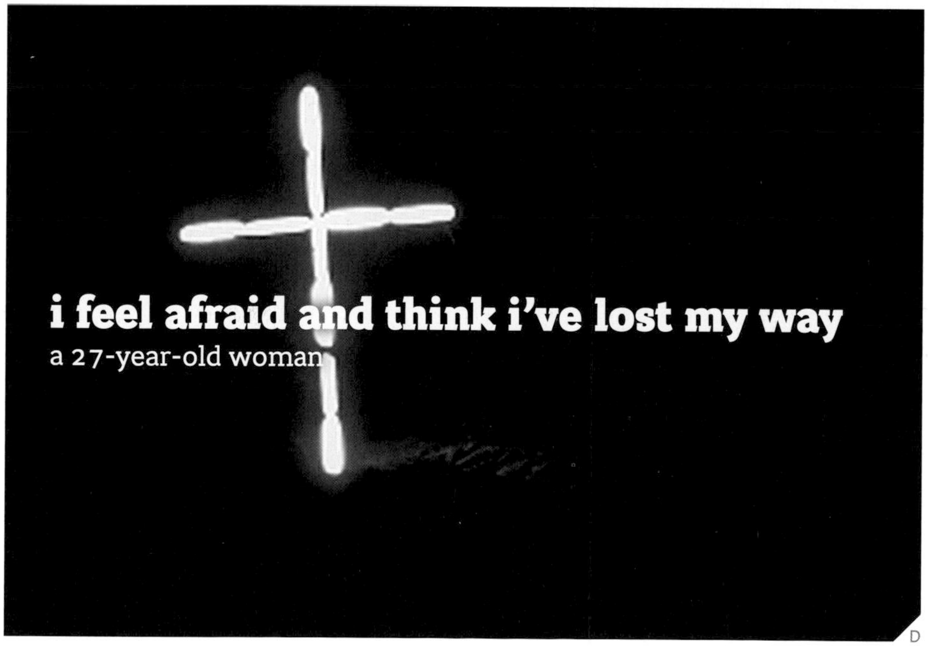

i feel afraid and think i've lost my way
a 27-year-old woman

D

Main reasons

- **love**
- being hurt
- loss
- rejection

Observations

People most commonly attribute the feeling of being afraid to a fear of **being in love** or of **losing love**. This trend parallels other commonly expressed fears: of **rejection**, of **being hurt**, and of **loss**. The fear of rejection grows less prevalent as people get older, as do any fears people have of **commitment**. **Women** express feeling afraid more than men, and interestingly enough more people in **Las Vegas** express feeling afraid than in any other American city. ♥

ALIVE

43 rd most common feeling overall · 0.28% of all feelings are alive

alive

Breakdowns
for people who feel alive

Gender breakdown 45% 55%

Age breakdown 10s 20s 30s 40s 50+

I NEED SOMEONE WHO MAKES ME FEEL ALIVE AND YOU JUST MAKE ME FEEL DEAD INSIDE

someone in indiana

i have experienced so much of life with him that it feels like i was never truly alive before i met him
a 32-year-old in brisbane, australia

A

i feel sooo alive
a woman

B

i feel so alive yet feel so alone
a 30-year-old

C

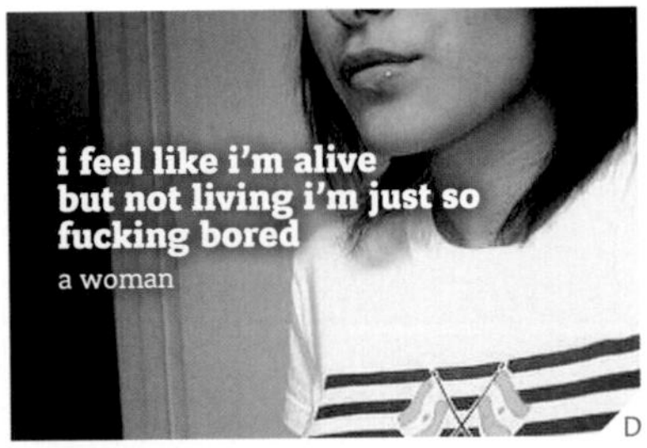

i feel like i'm alive but not living i'm just so fucking bored
a woman

D

alive adj.

1. having life; living
2. state of action; unexpired; existent
3. sprightly; lively; brisk
4. having lively feelings

● i feel more alive when i am me and i want to feel that way again ● i feel like i can do anything now i feel alive i see now why all that had to happen and it was because i didn't know who i was and grew further from god ● i crash down and burn out at least i'm gonna know what its like to feel alive oh i feel alive ● i know that when women start getting kooky that something about me feels alive inside ● i honestly can say i haven't done something crazy like that in a long time and even though it was just a dream i kind of feel more alive now ● i dyed my hair and now i feel brighter more alive ● i think i'll forgive myself and eat another bowl of ice cream to feel alive and celebrate such a book

Season breakdown 27% 22% 25% 26%

Related feelings mentioned with alive

dead
awake
strong
cool
beautiful
hot

i feel most alive when the things around me are dying
someone

A

I JUST OVERCAME CANCER AND WANTED TO FEEL ALIVE

someone

B

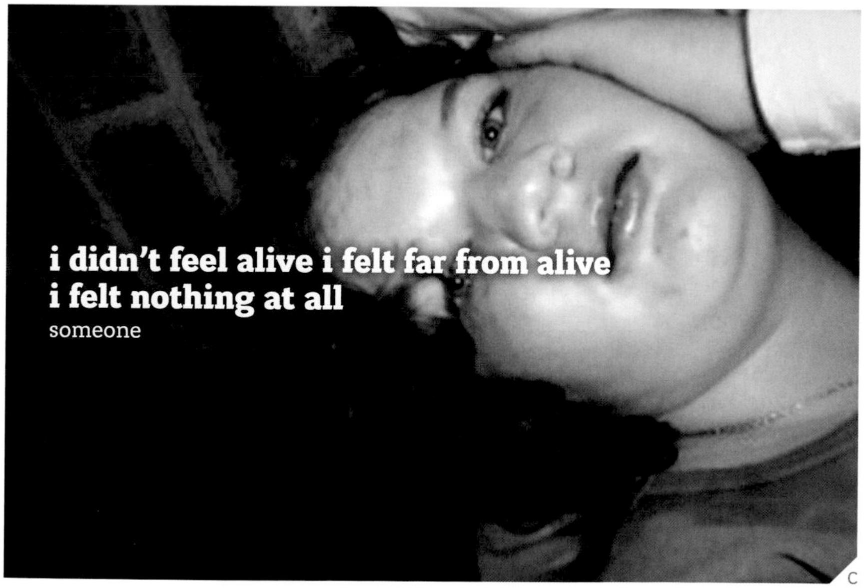

i didn't feel alive i felt far from alive
i felt nothing at all
someone

C

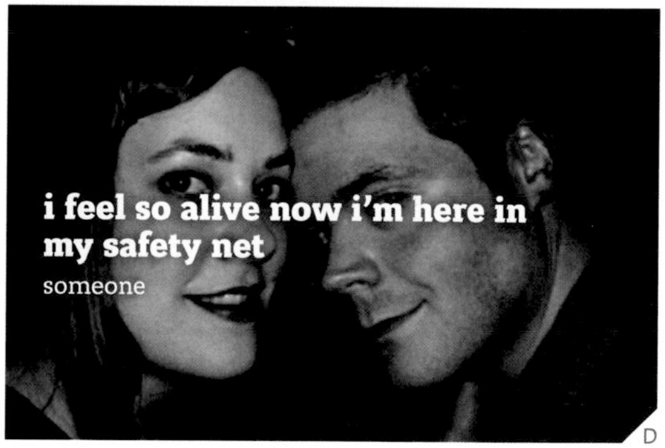

i feel so alive now i'm here in my safety net
someone

D

Main reasons

happiness
feeling pain
music
crying

Observations

People feel alive for many reasons, but often it is **adrenaline** associated with physical **pain**, **passion**, or sudden **happiness**. Playing music, singing, and **dancing** make people feel alive. People feel alive in the presence of **nature**, during **cold weather** or a hard **rain**, and people from the Rocky Mountain states feel most alive. People often feel alive and **energized** at the same time, and after periods of not feeling alive they correlate the feeling with the ability to **smile** again. People who are depressed often wistfully **remember** what it was like to feel alive. ♥

ALONE

13th most common feeling overall · 0.83% of all feelings are alone

Breakdowns
for people who feel alone

Gender breakdown: 53% women · 47% men

Age breakdown: 10s · 20s · 30s · 40s · 50+

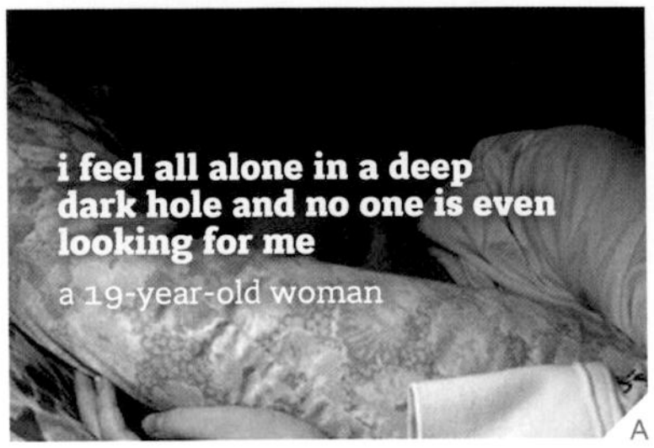

i feel all alone in a deep dark hole and no one is even looking for me
a 19-year-old woman

A

i'm feeling pretty alone here
a 52-year-old man

B

C

I HOPE YOU FEEL AS ALONE AND COLD AND MISERABLE AS I HAVE EVERY DAY SINCE YOU LEFT ME
a 31-year-old in connecticut

alone adj.

1. by one's self; exclusive of others
2. single, solitary
3. of or by itself
4. sole; only; exclusive

● i passed out with wet eyes and feeling more alone than i think i have ever felt ● i have a horrible feeling i'm going to be alone forever: i'd rather be dead then live like this till i die naturally i swear ● i feel even more alone not being able to touch you ● i feel really alone sometimes and its hard for me to make friends ● i feel so alone i cried myself to sleep last night ● i was having lots of fun sex and then didn't feel like being alone in my bed all night so i stayed at holden's and went back to 1212 at 8 o'clock this morning after waking up at 7 ● i feel so alone that i wonder if anyone would show up at my funeral ● i feel alone in a sea of people

Season breakdown — spring 24% · summer 24% · **fall 28%** · winter 24%

Related feelings
mentioned with alone

- **unloved**
- unwanted
- isolated
- abandoned
- misunderstood
- scared

I FEEL ALL ALONE I SIT ALL ALONE IN MY ROOM THINKING OF ENDING MY LIFE SOON

a 17-year-old woman in texas

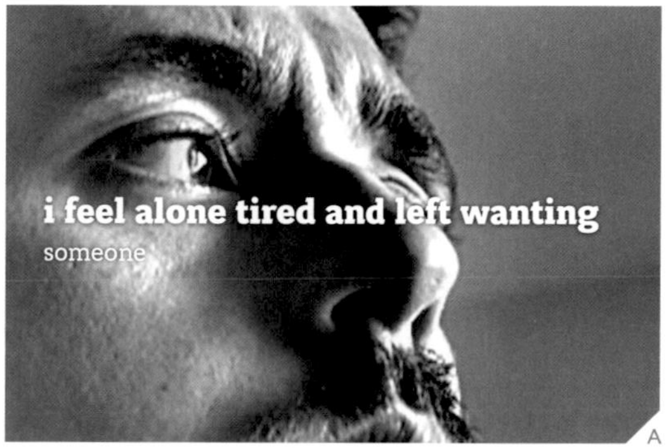

i feel alone tired and left wanting
someone

A

The blogger writes: So until I figure out what I want with this life, I stand here alone, watching the world pass me by, with envy, jealousy, regret, and fear, wondering what can be and what I already missed. But most of all I stand here with hope, that something will change and things will be better, someday.

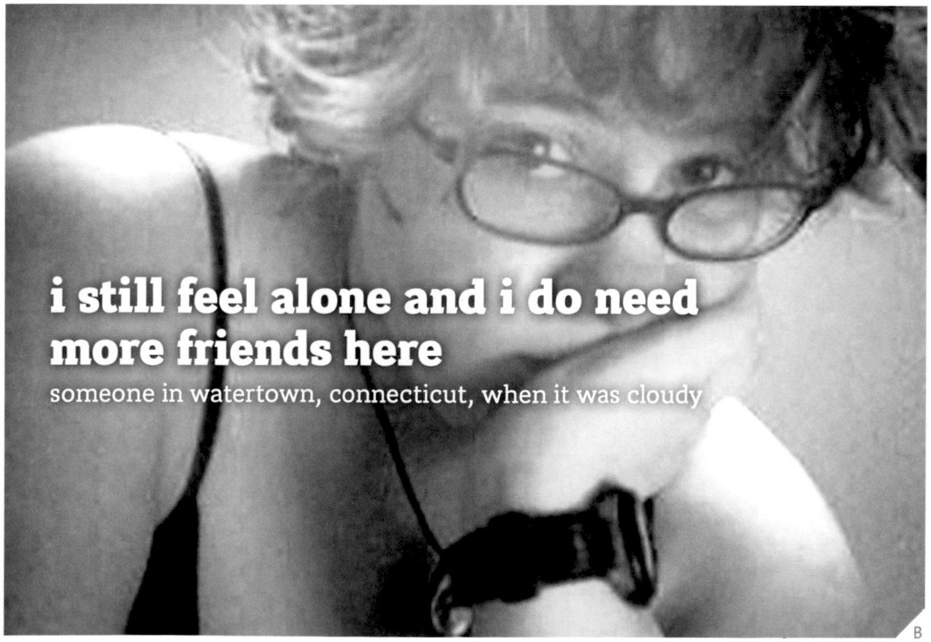

i still feel alone and i do need more friends here
someone in watertown, connecticut, when it was cloudy

B

Main reasons

- **lovelessness**
- friendlessness
- empty house
- crowds

Observations

People will often describe feeling alone in a **crowd** or in a crowded place, or when they are completley **surrounded** by people. People will also feel particularly alone when they feel that there is nobody in the world who cares about them. People who say they feel alone also tend to feel **lost**, **scared**, **abandoned**, **isolated**, **helpless**, or **vulnerable**. It is very rare for people to only feel mildly alone; they are more likely to describe feeling **utterly** alone or **completely** alone. It is very common for people to feel alone at **night**. ♥

ASHAMED

Breakdowns
for people who feel ashamed

Gender
breakdown 45% **55%**

Age
breakdown 10s 20s 30s 40s 50+

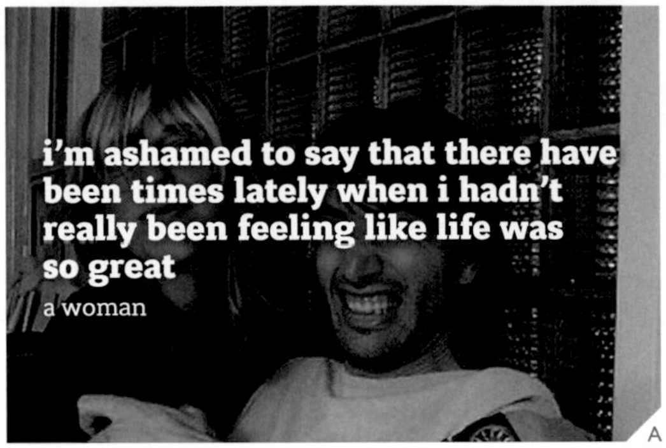

i'm ashamed to say that there have been times lately when i hadn't really been feeling like life was so great
a woman

A

i feel ashamed with myself
a man

B

Brandon is ashamed of his inability to jump over this fence.

i'm trying to get over feeling ashamed about what happened because i know now that it wasn't my fault
a woman in michigan

C

I FEEL SO ASHAMED I FEEL AS THOUGH I TOOK ADVANTAGE OF YOU AND THE SITUATION
a 28-year-old woman in stokesdale, north carolina

ashamed adj.

1. affected by shame
2. abashed or confused by guilt
3. conscious of impropriety
4. timid due to the anticipation of shame

• i feel ashamed and i feel like i stole from you • i feel very ashamed to be called a nigerian • i feel ashamed when they make me happy • i'd like to think that you would feel so ashamed if you saw what a wreck i was after what you did to me • i feel ashamed for falling into that trap of believing whatever is was that people told me about her • i want to bury my head in my pillow and feel ashamed for letting this happen all over again but it's of no use • i feel ashamed for treating a girl that disrespectfully and now it's on my conscience • i haven't been able to walk properly since june every single step has hurted which is why i've gained weight which for one makes me feel ashamed and disgusted

Season breakdown — 27% · 22% · 25% · 26%

Related feelings mentioned with ashamed

- **disgusted**
- embarrassed
- afraid
- scared
- proud
- angry

i did not feel ashamed to stare at a woman
a 23-year-old man in brighton, colorado

A

i feel sick to the stomach and ashamed
a man in leiden, the netherlands

B

I FEEL ASHAMED FOR HAVING BEEN MY STEPFATHER'S SEXUAL TOY AND PUNCHING BAG

a woman

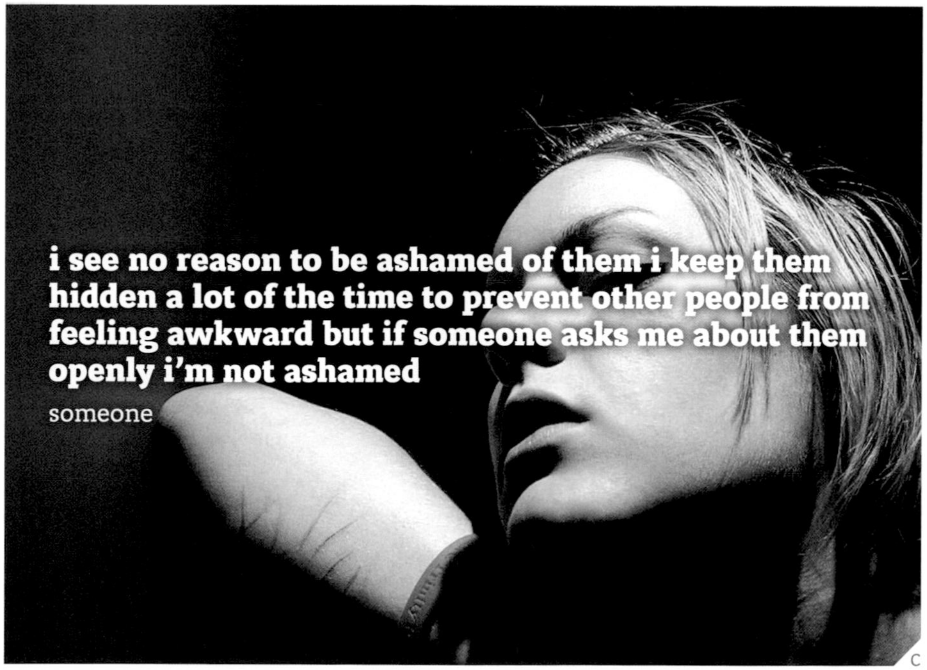

i see no reason to be ashamed of them i keep them hidden a lot of the time to prevent other people from feeling awkward but if someone asks me about them openly i'm not ashamed
someone

C

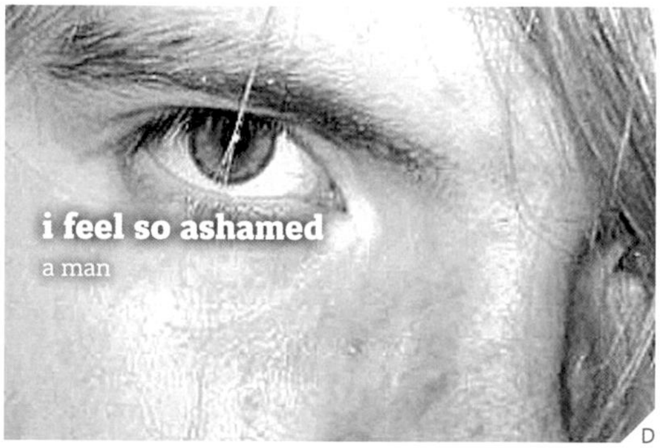

i feel so ashamed
a man

D

Main reasons

- **behavior**
- actions
- country
- past

Observations

People feel ashamed for all sorts of reasons. Sometimes they feel ashamed of their **country** (interestingly, a person's home country evokes feelings of both shame and pride). Sometimes they feel ashamed of their **past**. They feel ashamed to **admit** a view that they hold. But mostly, people express feeling ashamed for something that they did recently and now regret, whether it be an incident they caused or a way they behaved. Shame is often mentioned in conjunction with **disgust**, **fear**, or **anger**. People over 50 tend to feel less shame than people under 50. ♥

AWESOME

134 th most common feeling overall · 0.01% of all feelings are awesome

awesome

Breakdowns for people who feel awesome

Gender breakdown 52% 48%

Age breakdown 10s 20s 30s 40s 50+

i just feel really awesome
someone in indiana

A

I LOOK AT HIM AND I GET THIS FEELING IN MY STOMACH THAT IS SO AWESOME THAT THERE ISN'T EVEN WORDS TO DESCRIBE IT

a 25-year-old woman in new castle, pennsylvania

i feel completely awesome in this picture
a 24-year-old man

B

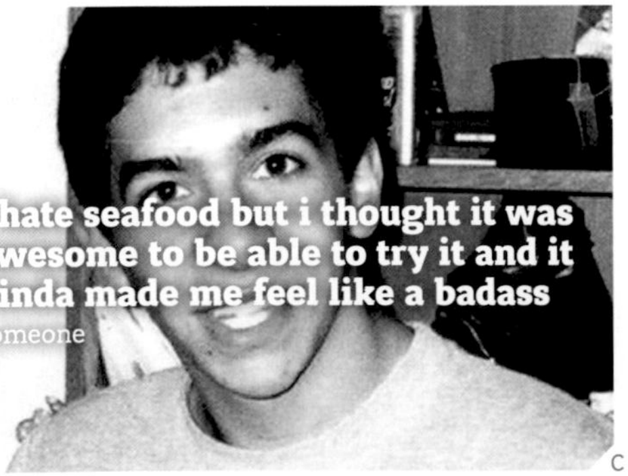

i hate seafood but i thought it was awesome to be able to try it and it kinda made me feel like a badass
someone

C

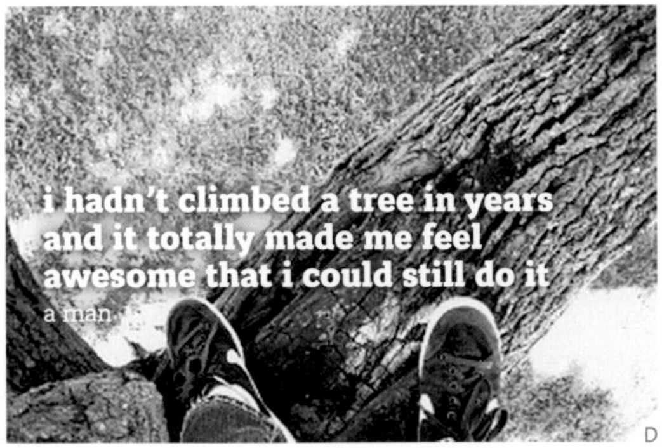

i hadn't climbed a tree in years and it totally made me feel awesome that i could still do it
a man

D

i was feeling pretty awesome
a 32-year-old man in chicago, illinois

E

awesome adj.

1. causing awe
2. appalling; awful
3. expressive of awe or terror
4. extraordinary

• i feel awesome and sometimes like i have everyone tricked into thinking i'm an adult • i feel awesome because i feel like i'm always tired even when i know i'm not • i feel like i'm an awesome lady but my back hurts and the chest pain is now a constant thing again • i have an eight-year-old son oliver who's becoming a little man and the feeling that he needs his awesome man around is becoming too strong for me to ignore • i feel like an awesome broken down palace once loved and taken care of but now am rarely visited and starting to fall apart • i just feel awesome next to all those young girls but i think i'm keeping up pretty good • i'm tired of feeling so awesome and used up

Season breakdown
24% | 27% | 24% | 25%

Related feelings
mentioned with awesome

cool
excited
incredible
amazing
great
super

A

B

i was doing my hair today and my roommate fruity asked me so how does it feel to be so awesome
someone in chicago, illinois, when it was cloudy

C

I MAY NOT BE THE COOLEST GUY BUT I FEEL PRETTY AWESOME RIGHT NOW

a 22-year-old in jonesboro, georgia

Main reasons

Being in love
Healthy diet
Friendship
Good news

Observations

Awesomeness is a feeling that is most commonly felt and expressed by young people. There are very few people older than 50 who claim that they feel awesome. People who feel awesome very often qualify the feeling by saying that they feel **freaking** awesome or **totally** awesome. When they feel awesome, they also commonly feel **cool**, and say that they **rock**. People often describe having an awesome **summer** or an awesome **weekend**, or will say they saw or will see an awesome **band**. Women tend to express feeling awesome slightly more than men do. ♥

AWFUL

46th most common feeling overall · 0.26% of all feelings are awful

awful

Breakdowns
for people who feel awful

Gender breakdown 62% 38%

Age breakdown 10s 20s 30s 40s 50+

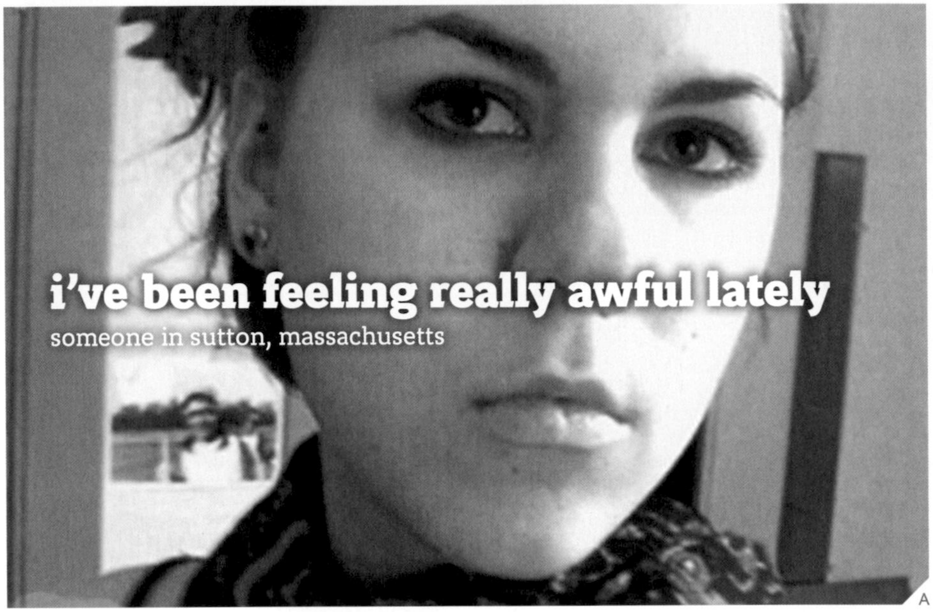

i've been feeling really awful lately
someone in sutton, massachusetts

A

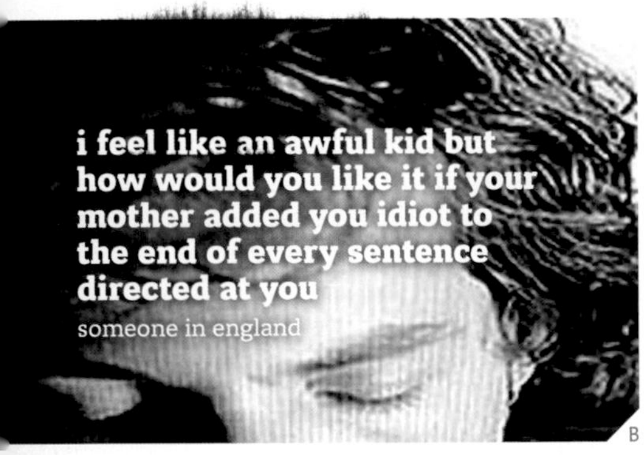

i feel like an awful kid but how would you like it if your mother added you idiot to the end of every sentence directed at you
someone in england

B

I FEEL AWFUL HAVING DATED A MARRIED WOMAN FOR 6 MONTHS

a 33-year-old woman in phoenix, arizona

C

awful adj.

1. oppressing with fear or horror; appalling
2. inspiring awe, fear, or reverence
3. profoundly impressive
4. struck or filled with awe; terror-stricken

• i want to be excited about school but honestly i just feel so awful • i kicked him in the head and i feel awful • i feel awful for sitting here alone next to my mom who's keeping me company because i seem lonely but i would also hate myself just as much if i was sitting there not saying anything with some people who don't know me at all • i am so sick of putting myself in situations that i think will be good and end up feeling awful about myself • he ran right to me and was shaking and i feel really awful • i lied there and i held you in my arms held you tight until you stopped feeling so awful and drifted off to sleep • i'm watching american idol and i feel awful for laughing at it sometimes

Season breakdown — 20% — **28%** — 27% — 25%

Related feelings mentioned with awful

- **upset**
- pissed
- sick
- disgusted
- selfish
- horrible

i'm feeling awful and not able to communicate well
someone

A

I FEEL AWFUL FOR MAKING YOU FEEL WORTHLESS

a 16-year-old woman in california

i feel slightly awful so it's fitting
a woman

B

Main reasons

- **fever**
- flu
- sleeplessness
- overeating

Observations

When people talk about feeling awful, it is most common for them to talk about feeling physically awful. It is usually mentioned when they are feeling **sick**, or when they have the **flu**, a **fever**, a **headache**, or an **infection**. It is also very common for people who feel awful to say that they **wake up** feeling awful. People also frequently say that they feel awful for **breaking up** with somebody who loves them. And people also feel awful for forgetting the **birthday** of someone who is close to them. ♥

BAD

2 **nd most common feeling overall** · 4.06% of all feelings are bad

bad

Breakdowns
for people who feel bad

Gender breakdown **54%** 46%

Age breakdown **10s** **20s** **30s** **40s** **50+**

I REALLY FEEL BAD NOW AS THOUGH I'M LEADING HIM ON

someone

i just feel like a bad mommy right now
someone

A

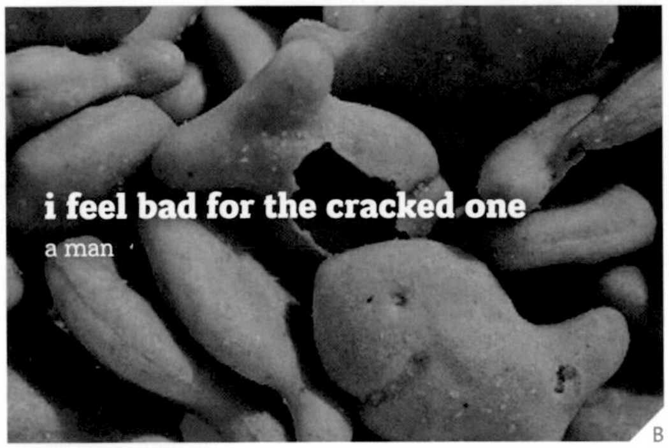

i feel bad for the cracked one
a man

B

C

bad adj.

1. injurious; hurtful; painful
2. inconvenient; unfavorable
3. morally defective; offensive
4. evil; vicious; wicked

● i don't normally do that i feel bad and lazy ● i feel bad because i had to postpone my math test again ● i hope he knows that he can't help how he feels and even though what happened 'that night' wasn't really bad it definately shouldn't have taken place given the fact that i do have a boyfriend ● i was also thinking about how since june started i have been taking alot of days off from work due to school things and i feel bad about it ● i do feel bad that i made someone cry though ● i've been bitching a lot lately to a few people and i do feel bad about that ● i don't think i ever really showed it but i still feel bad having thought it

Season breakdown — 23% · **27%** · 26% · 24%

Related feelings mentioned with bad

- **bitchy**
- rude
- mad
- nasty
- mean
- upset

i feel bad about it because i still love you
a 14-year-old

A

i feel bad 4 them
a woman

B

i feel like i'm just sitting here waiting for bad news
someone

C

i don't feel bad or anxious
someone

D

I FEEL SO BAD FOR NOT FINISHING MY STUFF ON TIME PLEASE KILL ME

someone in malaysia

i feel bad for them
someone

E

Main reasons

- **the poor guy**
- celebrities
- money
- leaving

Observations

People commonly feel bad, especially teens. People use the word when they feel guilty, sorry, sad, or down. People tend to feel bad for similar reasons that may make them feel guilty: being **neglectful**, **yelling**, **stealing**, forgetting a **birthday**, being **rude**, and having something bad happen that is their **fault**. During the 2008 election, Americans felt bad for John McCain and Sarah Palin (in that order). People tend to feel **kind of** or **sort of** bad. People feel bad when somebody **dies**, and since the economic crisis started in 2008, adults increasingly felt bad about **money**. ♥

BEAUTIFUL

102 nd most common feeling overall · 0.12% of all feelings are beautiful

beautiful

Breakdowns
for people who feel beautiful

Gender breakdown 64% 36%

Age breakdown 10s 20s 30s 40s 50+

i feel beautiful without you
someone

A

I FEEL THE MOST BEAUTIFUL WHEN I SURRENDER TO HIM

a 22-year-old in illinois

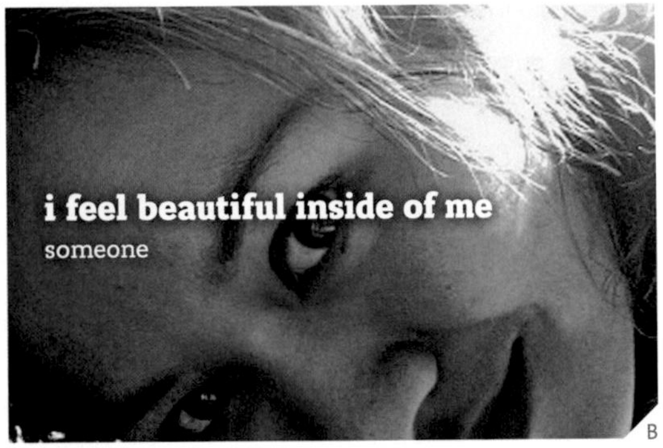

B

Richele had just broken up with her boyfriend of two years.

I FEEL BEAUTIFUL WHEN DEPRESSED OR STARVING AND I FEEL DEPRESSED WHEN I'M BEAUTIFUL

a 20-year-old in buffalo, new york, when it was cloudy

i don't feel beautiful anymore
a woman

C

beautiful adj.

1. possessing beauty
2. having qualities that constitute beauty
3. pleasing to the sight or mind
4. excellent; brilliant

● i want to tell every person that will listen how much i am in love with him and how fantastic this man is and how he makes me feel like the most beautiful person in the world ● i miss nights with someone on my shoulder reflecting on life and feeling beautiful ● i just wished he stayed alive a little longer to see feel and enjoy that beautiful sunny day ● i know i have so many people to call and everything but you know the feeling of just being held and told youre beautiful and shit like that i miss it soooo bad ● i feel beautiful when i am with him i like the fact that he tells me that he likes me so often ● i am no rookie to life and i do know how important it is for us women to look and feel beautiful

Season breakdown 27% 23% 26% 24%

Related feelings mentioned with beautiful

sexy	touched
smart	wonderful
ugly	cute

vicki is married and has a son. →

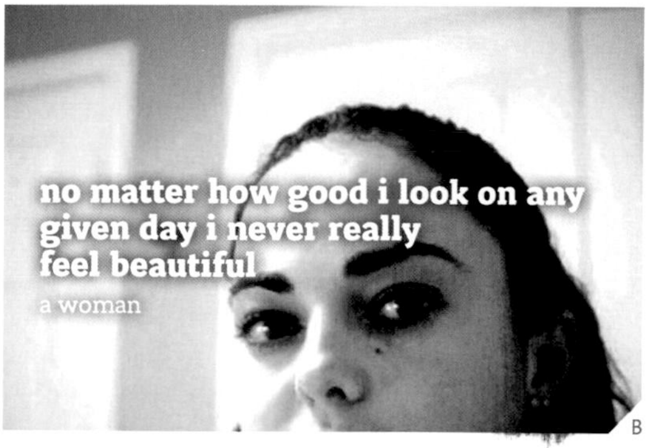

no matter how good i look on any given day i never really feel beautiful
a woman
B

I FEEL THAT WHEN I'M OLD I'LL LOOK AT YOU AND KNOW THE WORLD WAS BEAUTIFUL

a man

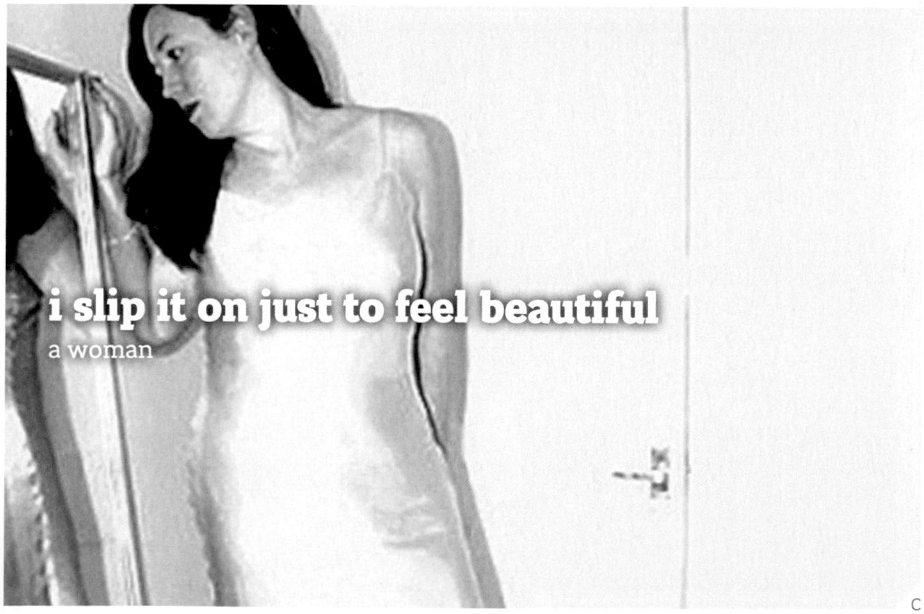

i slip it on just to feel beautiful
a woman
C

I WANT TO FEEL BEAUTIFUL NAKED AGAIN

a 21-year-old woman in pullman, washington

Main reasons

- **good hair**
- body image
- confidence
- compliments

Observations

Women feel beautiful and think about beauty in themselves far more than men, who mostly talk about beauty in women, **nature**, or **music**. Women feel beautiful when **loved**, and when they are in love, but also when they wear **makeup** and flattering **clothing**, or when they are **dancing**. People who feel beautiful also feel **happy**, **wonderful**, **amazing**, **sexy**, and close to **God**. Confidence is important, as is physical appearance; **eyes**, **heart**, **hair**, **body**, **smile**, and **soul** are most often mentioned. People **wish** they could feel beautiful, and **hope** that others feel beautiful. ♥

BETTER

1 st most common feeling overall · 5·74% of all feelings are better

better

Breakdowns
for people who feel better

Gender breakdown 53% 47%

Age breakdown 10s 20s 30s 40s 50+

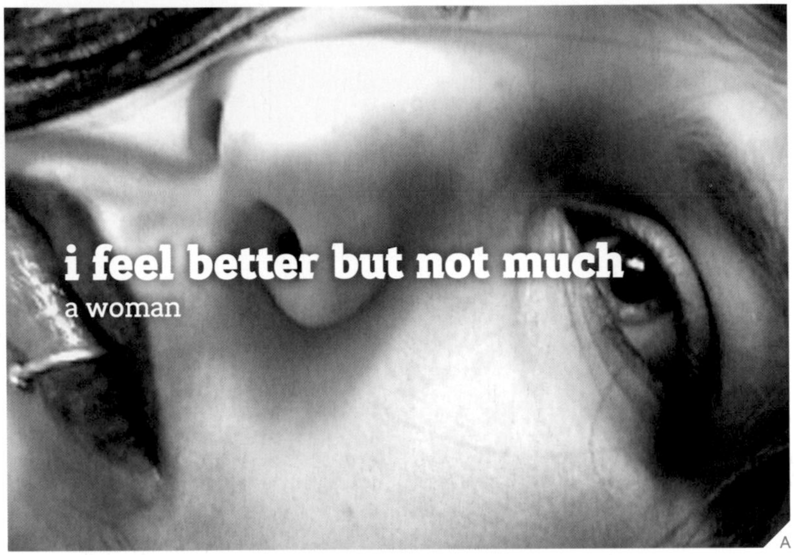

A

I LOVE YOU DEARLY AND I THINK HANGING OUT WOULD MAKE BOTH OF US FEEL MUCH BETTER
a 19-year-old in santa clarita, california, when it was sunny

i strive to lose weight because i do think i'll look better i'll look healthier i'll be able to dress myself better and i'll feel better about myself
someone

B

C

better adj.

1. having more good qualities than others
2. preferable in rank, value, or other respect
3. greater in amount; larger; more advanced
4. improved health; less affected by disease

• i just wish he was here so i could hug him and feel better about everything • i feel like that she may deserve someone way better than me • i feel like i need to make better choices with how i spend my nights • i was anxious to keep her near because she made me feel better • i feel every christmas gets better because you have more memories to cherish • i know just how you feel and though it may seem that things will never change it's better to try and fail than to leave an unfinished life • i always feel better when i'm well dressed • i can't wait to get the right dosage of this medicine so i'll start feeling better • i feel better about my years in the league because i was one of the clean guys

Season breakdown 22% 26% 27% 25%

Related feelings mentioned with better

healthier
stuffy
recovered
congested
glad

I'M ADDICTED TO MAKING MYSELF FEEL BETTER

an 18-year-old man in charlotte, north carolina, when it was cloudy

i feel better now after ranting
someone

A

Main reasons

feeling loved
talking
sleeping
happiness

Observations

People often **try** hard to make themselves or others feel better when they are down, but it's a difficult thing to do. One of the most effective ways to feel better seems to be to talk to somebody and get things off your **chest**. **Losing weight** often makes people feel better, as does exercise like **running** and **walking**. When people feel a bit **sick**, **sleeping** or **resting** and drinking **water** will often make them feel a bit better. People generally report feeling better when they have more **energy**, are **happier**, or have a greater sense of **control** over things. ♥

BLESSED

48 th most common feeling overall · 0.26% of all feelings are blessed

blessed

Breakdowns
for people who feel blessed

Gender breakdown — 65% female, 35% male

Age breakdown — 10s, 20s, 30s, 40s, 50+

i couldn't even fathom a baby that small and i feel very blessed that he weighed as much as he did
someone

A

B

I FEEL SO BLESSED TO BE ALIVE, TO BE BREATHING AND FREE FROM A HOSPITAL BED OR JAIL CELL

someone

i feel so blessed by what god has given me
someone

C

D

blessed adj.

1. hallowed; worthy of adoration
2. enjoying happiness or bliss; favored
3. imparting happiness or bliss; joyful
4. pertaining to spiritual happiness

● i feel so blessed to be married to her ● i feel truly blessed to share all this life love happiness stuff with somebody like jessica ● i feel so very blessed to have those in my life who have been here since the beginning those who came at my worst time and stayed and those who are just coming into it now ● i truly feel blessed to have been a part of such a unique group of people ● i feel blessed to have such an amazing group of friends and family ● i feel blessed to have been born and raised in such a beautiful place ● i feel blessed to have friends like you ● i feel blessed to not have to spend half of my waking hours in a job i hate making money for something to which i cannot relate

Season breakdown — 31% · 18% · 24% · 27%

Related feelings mentioned with blessed

- **thankful**
- humbled
- grateful
- honored
- privileged

i feel truly blessed to be a part of this wonderful community
someone

A

I LOOK AT MY CHILDREN EACH NIGHT AND FEEL TRULY BLESSED FOR WHAT GOD HAS GRANTED ME WITH

a 30-year-old woman in bismark, north dakota

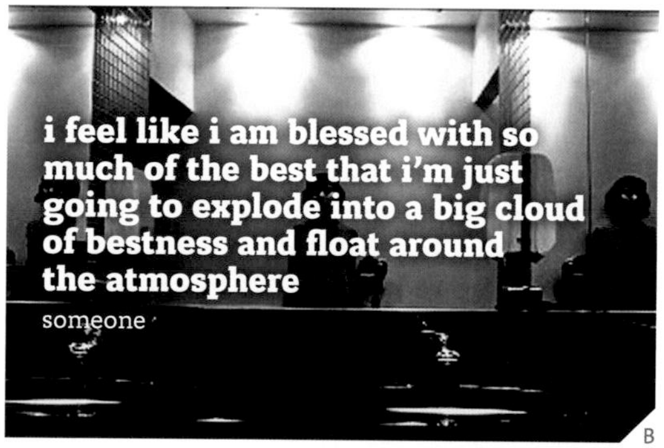

i feel like i am blessed with so much of the best that i'm just going to explode into a big cloud of bestness and float around the atmosphere
someone

B

i feel blessed and grateful to have a place to share my words
a woman in brooklyn, new york, when it was sunny

C

D

Main reasons

- **love**
- friendship
- family
- community

Observations

Blessed is a strong feeling with strong demographic tendencies. **Women** feel blessed more often than men, as do people in **Bible Belt** states, and there is a strong trend toward feeling blessed as people get **older**. This is particularly the case as people reach the age where they have **children**. Men and people in their 20s often feel blessed because of specific **opportunities**. Women of child-rearing age feel blessed because of their **kids**. People feel blessed for having **love** in their lives, and for having **family** and **friends**. People who feel blessed also feel **lucky** and **thankful**. ♥

COMFORTABLE

10 th most common feeling overall · 0.96% of all feelings are comfortable

comfortable

Breakdowns
for people who feel comfortable

Gender breakdown 48% 52%

Age breakdown 10s 20s 30s 40s 50+

i feel more comfortable here than i do anywhere else
a woman

A

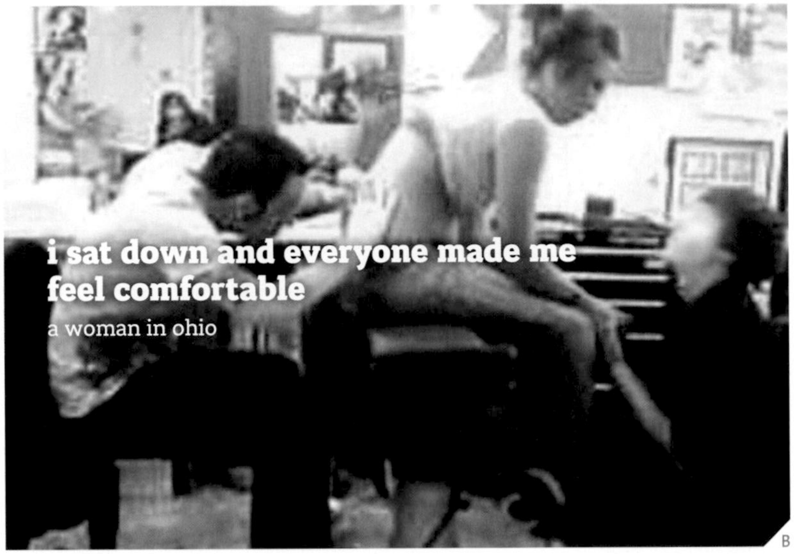

i sat down and everyone made me feel comfortable
a woman in ohio

B

I FEEL SO COMFORTABLE AROUND HIM WHICH IS WEIRD BECAUSE I AM NOT COMFORTABLE AROUND ANYONE

someone

i feel most comfortable with the term gender variant
someone in seattle, washington, when it was cloudy

C

comfortable adj.

1. providing comfort or consolation
2. able to comfort
3. in a condition of comfort
4. comparatively free of pain or distress

● i was feeling comfortable enough to start really just relaxing ● i feel comfortable in my own skin and that's what matters ● i should probably go with whatever makes me feel the least comfortable ● i feel more comfortable in my rumpled travelworn clothes unkempt hair and dusty shoes ● i'm at a place where i can trully feel comfortable with myself and that is sooo important ● i used to go spend a month or two with my grandparents in miami every summer from when i was five until i was ten when i decided i didn't really feel comfortable with them anymore ● i probably wouldn't feel totally comfortable with her reading it

Season breakdown 26% 25% 22% 27%

Related feelings mentioned with comfortable

familiar
shy
relaxed
nervous
social
friendly

I NEVER FEEL MORE COMFORTABLE SECURE OR PRETTY THAN WHEN I'M PLAYING DRESS UP IN PINUP STYLE CLOTHES

someone

i feel quite comfortable in my 178 centimeters
a woman

A

i feel like i'm 19 going on 30 and it shows because i am more comfortable around older people
a man

B

Main reasons

- **being at home**
- job familiarity
- friends
- jeans

Observations

People are frequently inclined to talk about feelings of comfort when discussing their **sexuality**, their **appearance**, their **relationships**, certain **places**, and their **solitude**. They will regularly express feeling comfortable with people when they **trust** them, and frequently feel comfortable in situations where they also feel **confident**. People also express feeling a high level of comfort when they become familiar with their **job**. ♥

COOL

103 rd most common feeling overall · 0.12% of all feelings are cool

cool

Breakdowns
for people who feel cool

Gender breakdown 46% 54%

Age breakdown 10s 20s 30s 40s 50+

i feel so cool
a 17-year-old in missouri

A

i feel cool on this mountain
a woman in shelburne, vermont

B

i'm sure he was just trying to make me feel like the barbies were cool
a woman

C

i feel so cool when i dance
someone

D

I MUST SAY I FEEL PRETTY COOL THAT I'M HANGING OUT WITH REAL FRENCH PEOPLE

a woman in san dimas, california, when it was sunny

cool adj.

1. moderately cold; between warm and cold
2. not ardent, warm, fond, or passionate
3. very good; excellent; fashionable; hip
4. manifesting coldness or dislike

• i always feel like such a loser when i'm with all these cool private school kids • i will never feel as cool as dave • i have decided that it would feel really cool to shave my head • i remember relaxing by a brook one night feeling the cool water cascade over my legs • i've just got to say that i have realized how incredibly grateful i am for not being the type of person that has to have a bunch of stuff to feel cool • i've never had an expensive bag and this one isn't either but it looks like it could be and that feeling is really really cool • i got the jurasic park feeling from all the booms that hit the windows that was cool • i feel that it is quite cool to have my own blog

Season breakdown — spring 24% · summer 29% · fall 24% · winter 23%

Related feelings mentioned with cool

- **refreshed**
- calm
- hip
- naked
- awesome

i feel so uncool when i look at it
someone in long beach, california

A

I KEEP SEEING FRESHMEN WANDERING AROUND LOST ASKING FOR DIRECTIONS AND IT MAKES ME FEEL PRETTY COOL

someone in appleton, wisconsin, when it was sunny

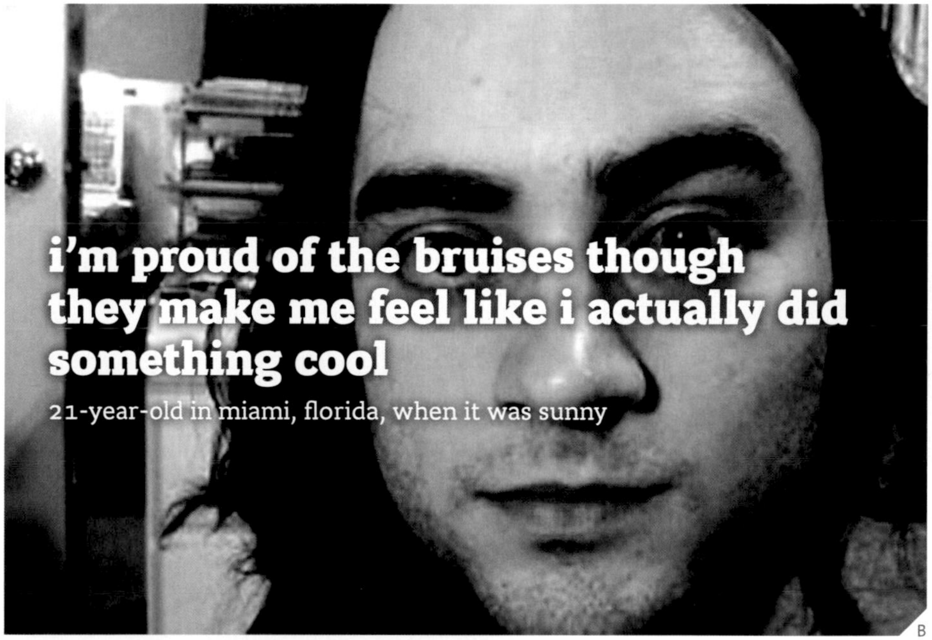

i'm proud of the bruises though they make me feel like i actually did something cool
21-year-old in miami, florida, when it was sunny

B

C

D

Main reasons

- **air temperature**
- breeze
- popularity
- status in school

Observations

In high school and in college, there is a fair amount of energy and thought devoted to being cool, especially when it comes to **popularity** and **social status**. Once people hit their 30s, they tend not to think about popularity and social status as much, so when they talk about feeling cool they are generally talking about the **temperature**. **Men** express feeling cool more than women, and in the **summer**, when people have a heightened awareness of the heat, they also tend to talk more about feeling cool. ♥

CRAZY

Breakdowns
for people who feel crazy

Gender breakdown 👩 **62%** 👨 **38%**

Age breakdown
10s 20s 30s 40s 50+

I AM IN LOVE WITH ISAAC NO MATTER HOW CRAZY I FEEL OR HOW CRAZY YOU THINK I AM

someone

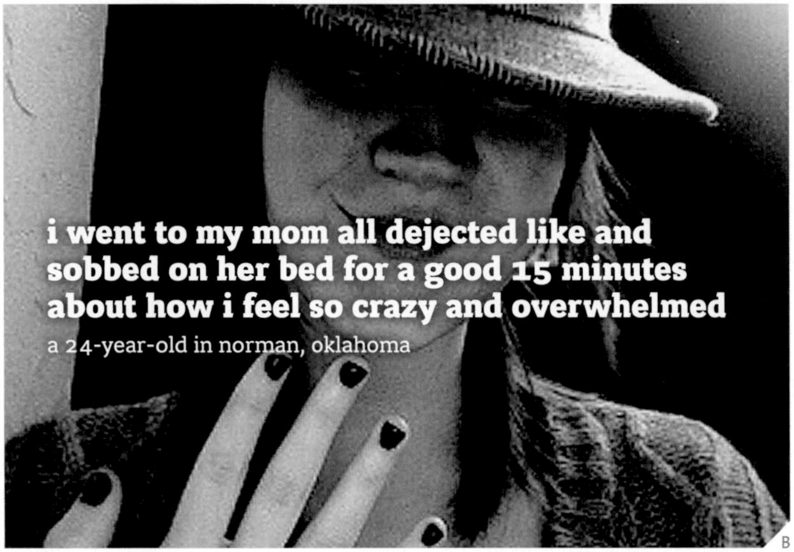

i went to my mom all dejected like and sobbed on her bed for a good 15 minutes about how i feel so crazy and overwhelmed

a 24-year-old in norman, oklahoma

B

i just try to put all this in a context that makes me feel a little crazy

someone

A

i had this stillness and it made me feel a little crazy

a woman

C

all i want to do is find a way to exist and not feel like i am going crazy

an 24-year-old in toccoa, georgia

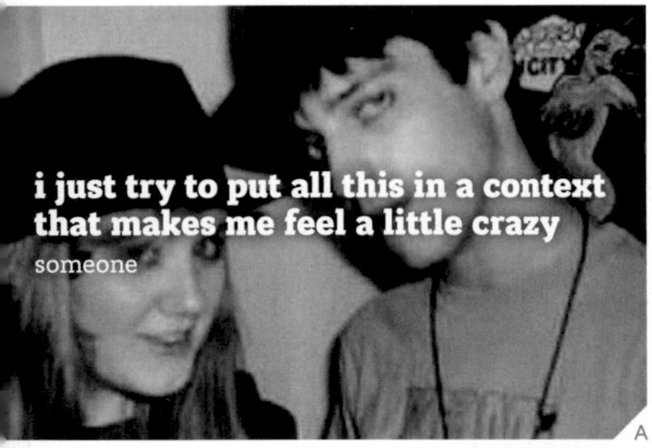

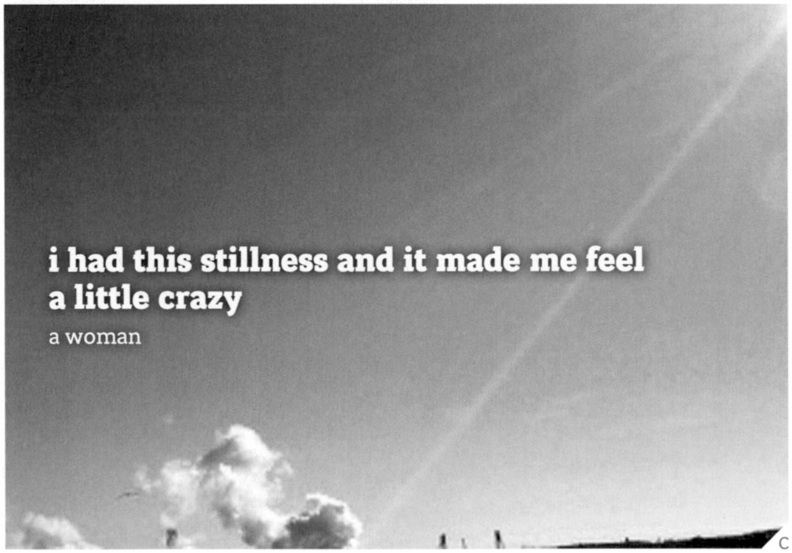

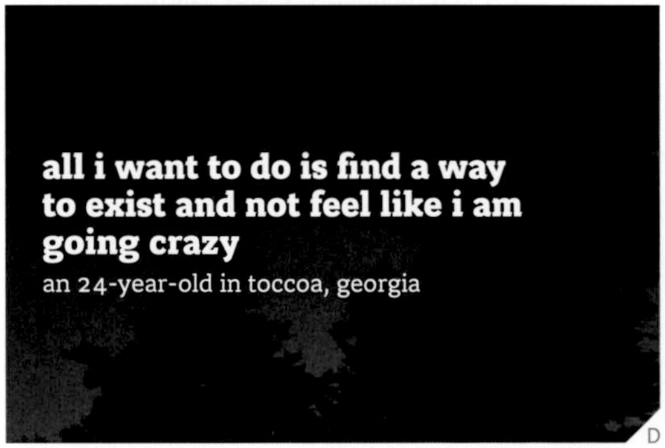

D

crazy adj.

1. demented or deranged in intellect
2. characterized by weakness or feebleness
3. broken; weakened
4. inordinately desirous; foolishly eager

- i always try try to play it off when im talking to you but its true and everything seems so deffernt since the day that i first layed eye's on you baby i never met a girl who can stop me on my track and it feels kind of crazy ● i feel crazy and like i'm bugging out
- i feel like god is the one putting this crazy thing on my heart ● i feel crazy oh so crazy i wouldn't mind if you planted a daisy
- i only had about half a doctor pepper and i feel like i'm going crazy ● i feel like a zombie work eat sleep and try to survive this crazy life
- i thought i was the only one who was starting to feel crazy because everyone else seemed so perfectly happy being rather insane

Season breakdown 23% 25% 27% 25%

Related feelings mentioned with crazy

wild
insane
helpless
mad
busy
nervous

A

I FEEL I'M GOING CRAZY I NEED A BREAK NOT A ONE-NIGHT STAND

a 21-year-old in sacramento, california, when it was cloudy

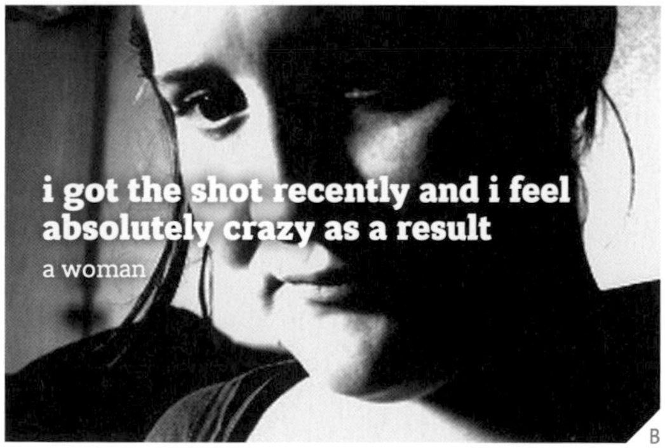

i got the shot recently and i feel absolutely crazy as a result
a woman

B

Main reasons

- **sleeplessness**
- loss of control
- the opposite sex
- emotions

Observations

Craziness is an emotion that is expressed for a very broad range of reasons. People most often express feeling crazy when they haven't had any **sleep**. But they also express feeling crazy when they feel like they are **out of control**, when they are experiencing a large range of strong **emotions**, or when they are exceedingly **nervous** or **stressed** out. It is far more common for a woman to express feeling crazy than it is for a man. People in their 20s and 10s say that they feel crazy far more often than older people do. ♥

DEPRESSED

40th most common feeling overall · 0.31% of all feelings are depressed

Breakdowns for people who feel depressed

Gender breakdown: 51% (female) · 49% (male)

Age breakdown: 10s · 20s · 30s · 40s · 50+

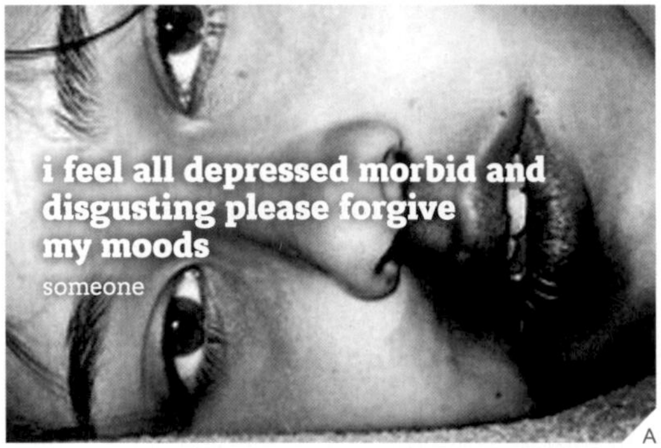

i feel all depressed morbid and disgusting please forgive my moods
someone

A

i just feel like theres no point in being depressed over matt anymore
someone

B

i started feeling kind of depressed as well as incredibly happy
someone in hirakata, japan

C

I AM STARTING TO FEEL VERY FRUSTRATED AND DEPRESSED AT THE IDEA THAT MY BABY COULD BE IN MORE DANGER BEING IN THERE THAN HE WOULD BEING OUT

someone

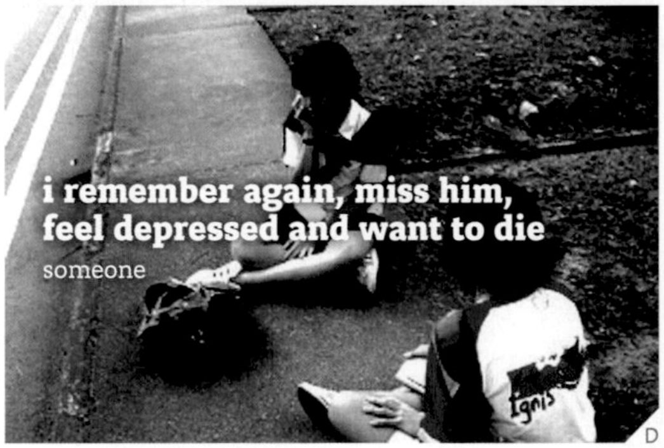

i remember again, miss him, feel depressed and want to die
someone

D

depressed adj.

1. dejected; dispirited
2. sad; humbled
3. pressed or forced down
4. lowered; sunk

● i feel i got no friends which makes me even more depressed ● i feel like shit and depressed and just fuck everything ● i feel so depressed right now the boy i like is avoiding me or something ● i have been here for almost 4 months and i have changed dramatically i feel depressed and every time my parents brother or like aunts uncles cousins try to talk to me i snap and i like turn into a cornered wild animal and i know i'm not like that ● i'm still managing to feel depressed enough to cry and give up ● i dunno why but i feel one of my depressed and alone moods coming on ● i've been feeling really depressed and sluggish and just worrying about my weight lately

Season breakdown 21% **29%** 27% 23%

Related feelings mentioned with depressed

suicidal
hopeless
angry
anxious
stressed
worried

I'VE BEEN FEELING SO DEPRESSED LATELY MAINLY DUE TO MY DETERIORATING MARRIAGE AND WORK STRESSING ME OUT

a 23-year-old man

i am tired of feeling shitty and depressed all the time
someone

A

Main reasons

no apparent reason
clinical depression
winter
anxiety

Observations

Men and women feel depression differently. Men feel **angry** or **mad**, while women feel **lonely**, **isolated**, or **anxious**. Women are more likely to **cry**, and men are more likely to feel **suicidal**. People feel less depressed as they get older, in frequency and intensity. While teens often feel **utterly** or **horribly** depressed, people in their 30s only feel it **mildly**. When depressed, people also often feel **hopeless** or **worthless** and often feel depressed for **no apparent reason**, especially in their teens. Later in life they will often recognize the feelings as a symptom of **clinical depression**. ♥

DIRTY

173 rd most common feeling overall · 0.07% of all feelings are dirty

Breakdowns
for people who feel dirty

Gender breakdown 37% 63%

Age breakdown 10s 20s 30s 40s 50+

I FEEL A LITTLE DIRTY BEING THIS CLOSE TO YOUR HEART

a 33-year-old man

i love his energy on stage outside of the musicals and the way he moves makes me feel very dirty
someone

A

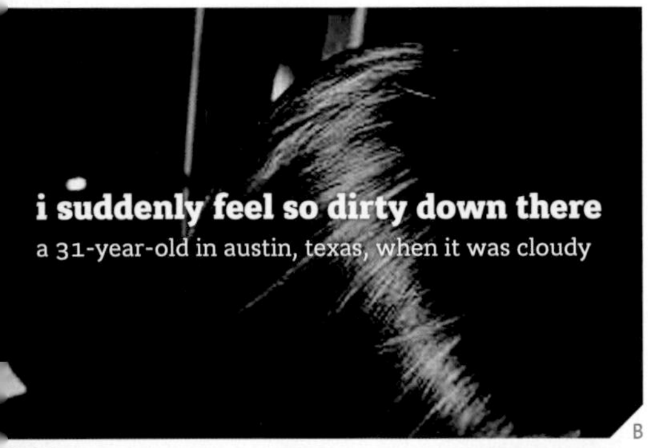

i suddenly feel so dirty down there
a 31-year-old in austin, texas, when it was cloudy

B

i feel so dirty dancing
a 25-year-old woman in brooklyn, new york

C

I KNOW THERE'S NO AVOIDING IT BUT IT MAKES ME FEEL A LITTLE DIRTY HAVING THIS MUCH INTEREST IN MY FATHER'S BOWEL MOVEMENTS

someone in madison, wisconsin

dirty adj.

1. defiled with dirt; foul; nasty; filthy
2. sullied; clouded
3. sordid; base; groveling
4. sleety; gusty; stormy

• i'm so bad with physical contact: it makes me feel dirty and enclosed • i feel so dirty even admitting bisexuality • i always try to make myself as clean and presentable as possible and having issues with my teeth is making me feel dirty or defective somehow • i feel like a dirty man • i feel dirty drinking this delicious soda • i don't know if i want a real friendship because i have a genuine affection for the person or if i just feel dirty for having shallow friendships and want to absolve myself of guilt • i feel so dirty even thinking about other girls so i just wait for her to show me a little attention • i just remember waking up feeling so dirty and wanting to cry

Season breakdown 27% 23% 23% 27%

Related feelings mentioned with dirty

gross
disgusted
clean
cheap
ashamed

I FEEL DIRTY BUT CHRIST HAS WASHED ME CLEAN

someone in virginia

I'VE HAD SEX WITH MORE THAN 30 PEOPLE AND THIS MAKES ME FEEL DIRTY

someone

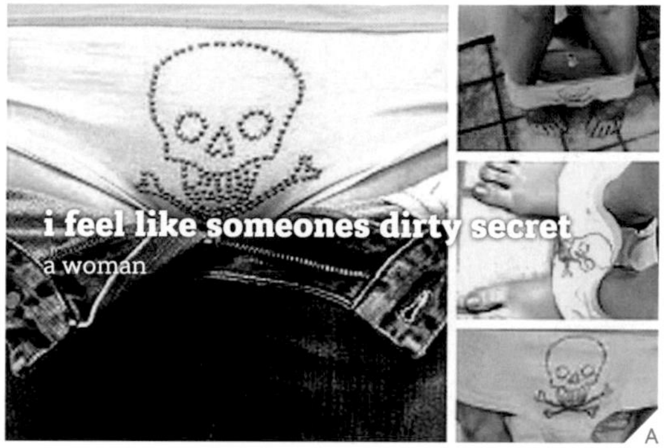

i feel like someones dirty secret

A

i feel dirty just looking at this photo
a man

B

← In July of 2007 We Feel Fine received permission to publish this photograph in this book. It was the first of many to come. (Thank you!)

Main reasons

not showering
voyeurism
sex
unclean clothes

Observations

People feel dirty for three primary reasons: when they have **sex** or sexual feelings, especially with somebody they don't love, when they are physically dirty and need to **shower**, and when they **do** or **admit** to something that they feel society doesn't accept. People feel dirty with many types of voyeurism, including **reading** or **watching** things that are private and that they shouldn't be seeing. People also often feel **cheap**, **ashamed**, **wrong**, **gross**, or **disgusting** when they feel dirty, and this feeling will often make them want to take a shower or **bath** immediately. ♥

DRUNK

180th most common feeling overall · 0.06% of all feelings are drunk

Breakdowns
for people who feel drunk

Gender breakdown: 46% · **54%**

Age breakdown: 10s · 20s · 30s · 40s · 50+

i feel drunk
someone

A

i managed to end the night not feeling too drunk
a 38-year-old man in london, england

B

I FEEL DRUNK AND I NEVER WANT IT TO STOP

a 22-year-old in belchertown, massachusetts

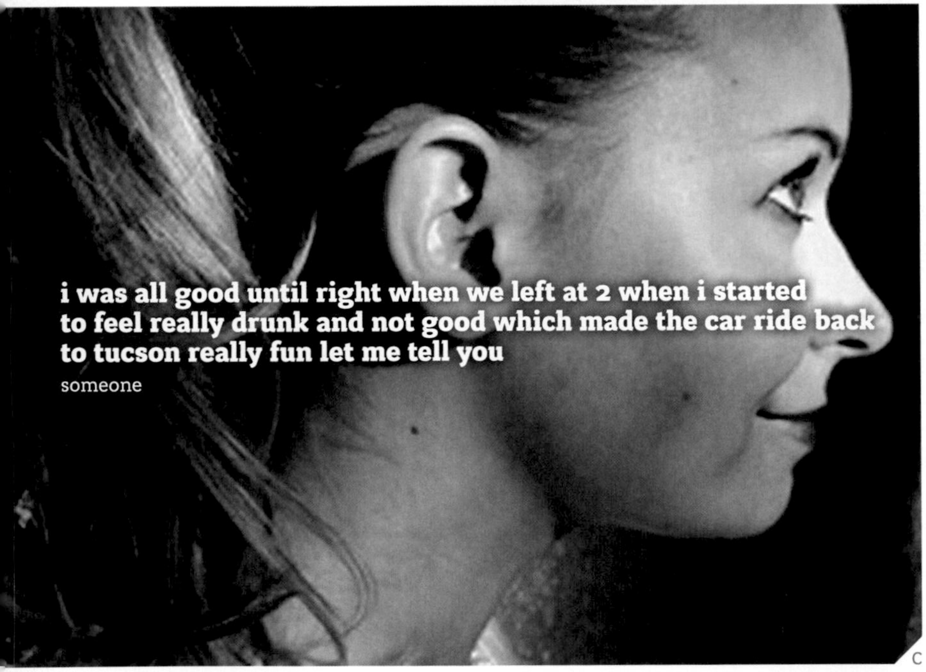

i was all good until right when we left at 2 when i started to feel really drunk and not good which made the car ride back to tucson really fun let me tell you
someone

C

I AM MASSIVELY DEVASTATED AND FEEL WIPED OUT DRUNK AND LOST BUT I'M SOBER AS A CHURCH MOUSE

someone

drunk adj.

1. intoxicated with, or as with, strong drink
2. inebriated
3. dominated by intense feeling
4. a chronic drinker

• i feel pretty drunk right now but what else can be expected of an irish lass set free on the world • i don't find her attractive in the slightest and i feel like a bit of a cock because i was drunk as a skunk and basically ended up gettin' off with her a few times • i feel like a drunk cinderella keep my eyes on the clock and worry that my carriage will turn into a pumpkin at the strike of noon • i could taste the whiskey i knew if i set foot out my front door and into a bar i would drink the night away and would feel like a tanker drunk of rotten asshole tomorrow • i believe in relationships and hopeless romanticism and all that good stuff i'm not a typical guy and i feel like one now because i'm drunk

Season breakdown 21% 26% 29% 24%

Related feelings
mentioned with drunk

- **sober**
- giddy
- insane
- dizzy
- sleepy
- stupid

i'm so tired i almost feel drunk
a 42-year-old woman

A

i went to work still feeling drunk and running on three hours of sleep but i think it was totally worth it
someone

B

I FEEL LIKE GETTING DRUNK AND FUCKING THE NEXT GUY I SEE JUST BECAUSE I CAN
a woman

Main reasons

- **beer**
- punch
- wine
- shots

Observations

College-age kids describe feeling drunk far more than anyone else at any other age. People tend to describe feeling drunk less and less as they get older. **Men** describe feeling drunk much more than women do, and when people feel drunk they commonly also describe feeling **giddy** and **dizzy**. The most common cause of feeling drunk is, unsurprisingly, **alcohol**. Although some people also describe feeling drunk as a product of serious **sleep deprivation**. ♥

EMPTY

31 st most common feeling overall · 0.35% of all feelings are empty

Breakdowns
for people who feel empty

Gender breakdown **51%** **49%**

Age breakdown **10s** **20s** **30s** **40s** **50+**

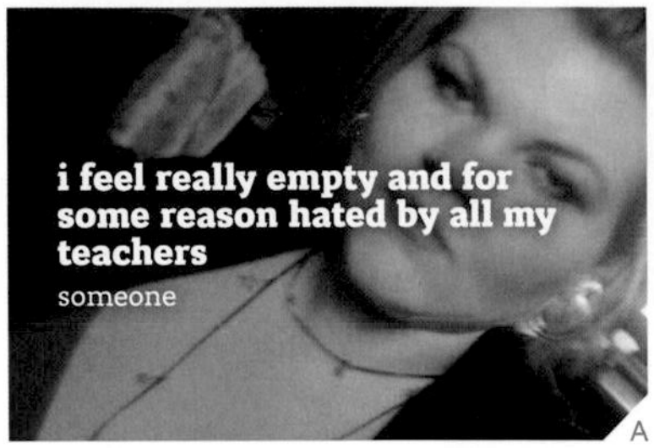

i feel really empty and for some reason hated by all my teachers
someone

A

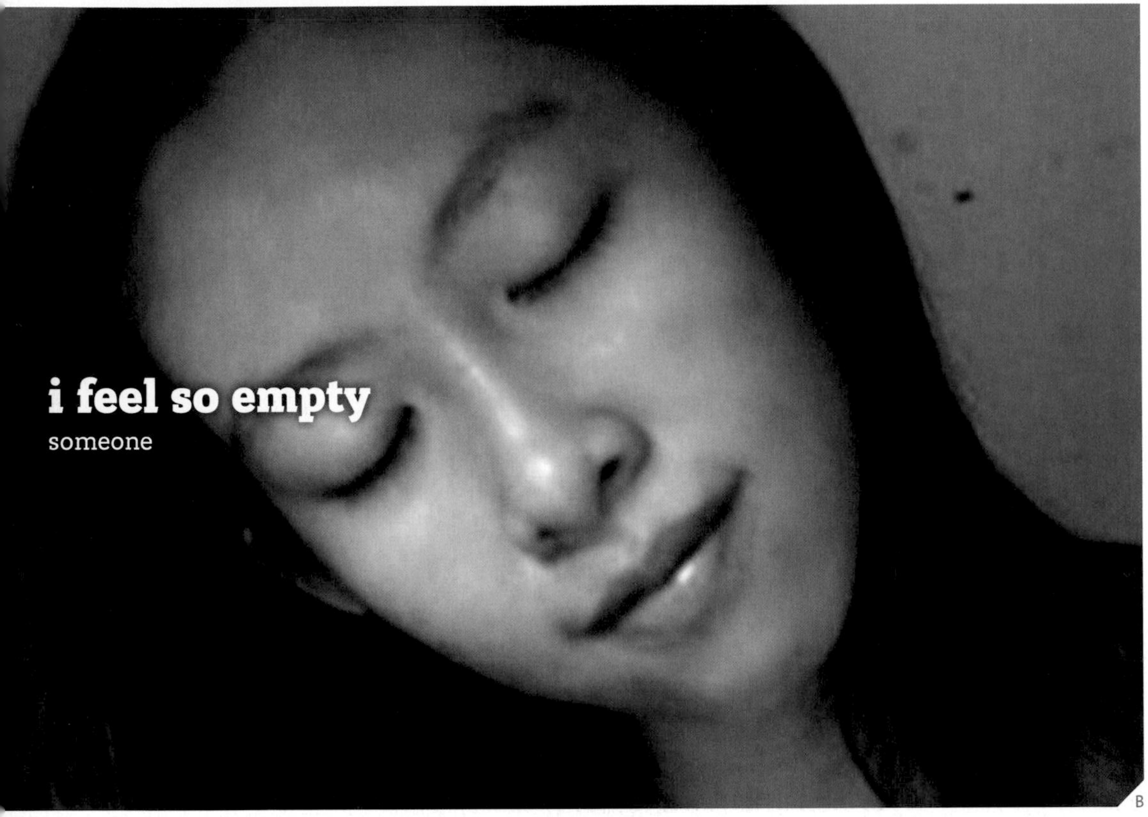

B

i am sad that you feel empty and unhappy
someone

C

I HAVE THIS GOD SIZED HOLE IN MY HEART AND I FEEL EMPTY

someone

empty adj.

1. containing nothing; not filled
2. having nothing to carry; unburdened
3. unable to satisfy; unsatisfactory; hollow
4. destitute of reality or real existence

● i feel intensely empty because i lack a cause or a reason for existence ● i feel so empty and numb right now you have no idea ● i feel so empty without someone in my life ● i'm thinking about how nice it would be to be up north right now and how coming back to the city has left me feeling empty and feeling down ● i love my boyfriend but it just feels empty to me right now ● i keep looking back to all the good times that we had and it makes me smile and glow inside but then i feel extremely empty inside because i dont have that special someone anymore ● i'm just sort of listless today and feel empty inside without my cellphone right next to me

Season breakdown: 24% · 24% · **28%** · 24%

Related feelings mentioned with empty

- **hollow**
- meaningless
- incomplete
- unfulfilled
- shallow
- numb

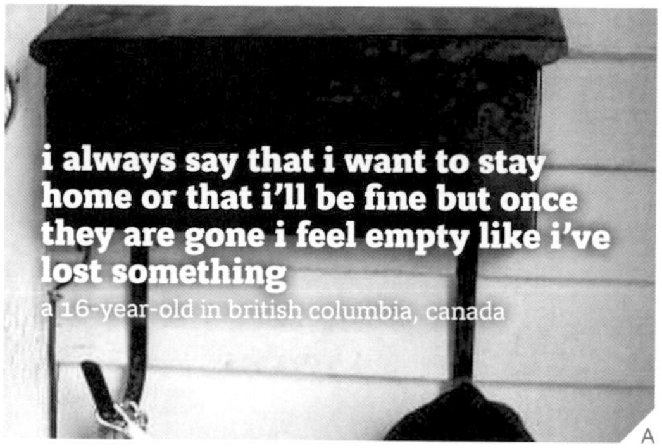

i always say that i want to stay home or that i'll be fine but once they are gone i feel empty like i've lost something
a 16-year-old in british columbia, canada

A

i can't see i can't hear and i can't taste anything i feel empty without feelings
a man

B

I FEEL EMPTY AND ALONE BECAUSE I KNOW YOU'RE GONE

a 24-year-old man in andalusia, alabama

i feel numb and empty and sad but can't cry
a 23-year-old in hamburg, new york

C

Main reasons

- **lovelessness**
- loss
- loneliness
- sadness

Observations

Like many painful feelings, emptiness is the result of a **lack of love** in one's life, and often comes from the **loss** of a loved one. The strongest feelings of emptiness come after the **death** of a loved one or after a **breakup**, and with many people, especially teenagers, when they have no **friends**. It is a physical feeling; people often report feeling it in their **heart** and their **body**. Many people feel empty when they come **home**, and at **night**, and feel it particularly when in **bed** alone. Teenagers feel most empty, and people feel less empty as they grow older. ♥

EXCITED

93rd most common feeling overall • 0.14% of all feelings are excited

Breakdowns
for people who feel excited

Gender breakdown 51% 49%

Age breakdown 10s 20s 30s 40s 50+

i'm feeling really excited about 2007
someone

A

I FEEL I'M EXCITED BUT I'M ABOUT TO MESS MY DRAWERS AT THE SAME TIME

a 22-year-old man in columbus, ohio, when it was cloudy

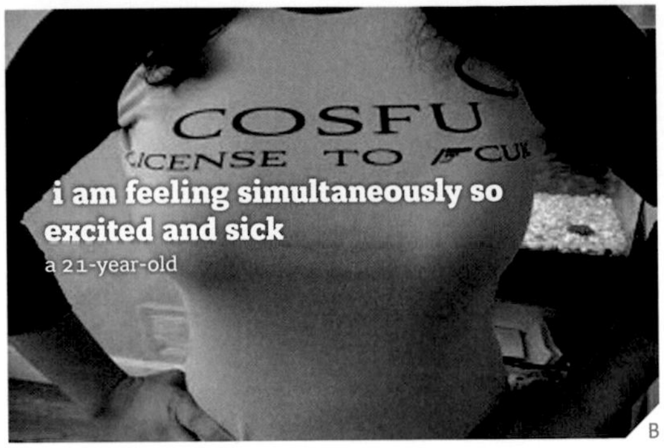

i am feeling simultaneously so excited and sick
a 21-year-old

B

i feel like such a geek being this excited about a scanner printer copier
a 30-year-old in long beach, california, when it was cloudy

C

i feel excited or scared or someother stupid emotion
someone in alameda, california

D

i checked out their menu online yesterday and feel very excited on the inside
someone

E

excited adj.

1. aroused or stimulated emotionally
2. called to increased activity
3. agitated
4. excessively affected by emotion

• i'm feeling really excited about a new work environment • i almost feel as though i shouldn't praise them but my overwhelming tendency is to be excited every damn time • i feel more excited about tomorrow than i did waiting to open presents on christmas eve • i just had this whole realization that there is no need to feel excited when boys call or text or are just nice • i arrived at school feeling excited and left feeling very depressed • i'm nervous but i feel excited and unstoppable to • i feel so excited about the future and sometimes i feel absolutely terrified because i don't know if i'm making the right steps to achieve my desired end • i feel freakin excited for prom tomorrow

Season breakdown 25% 25% 24% 26%

Related feelings mentioned with excited

nervous
apprehensive
scared
terrified
anxious
hopeful

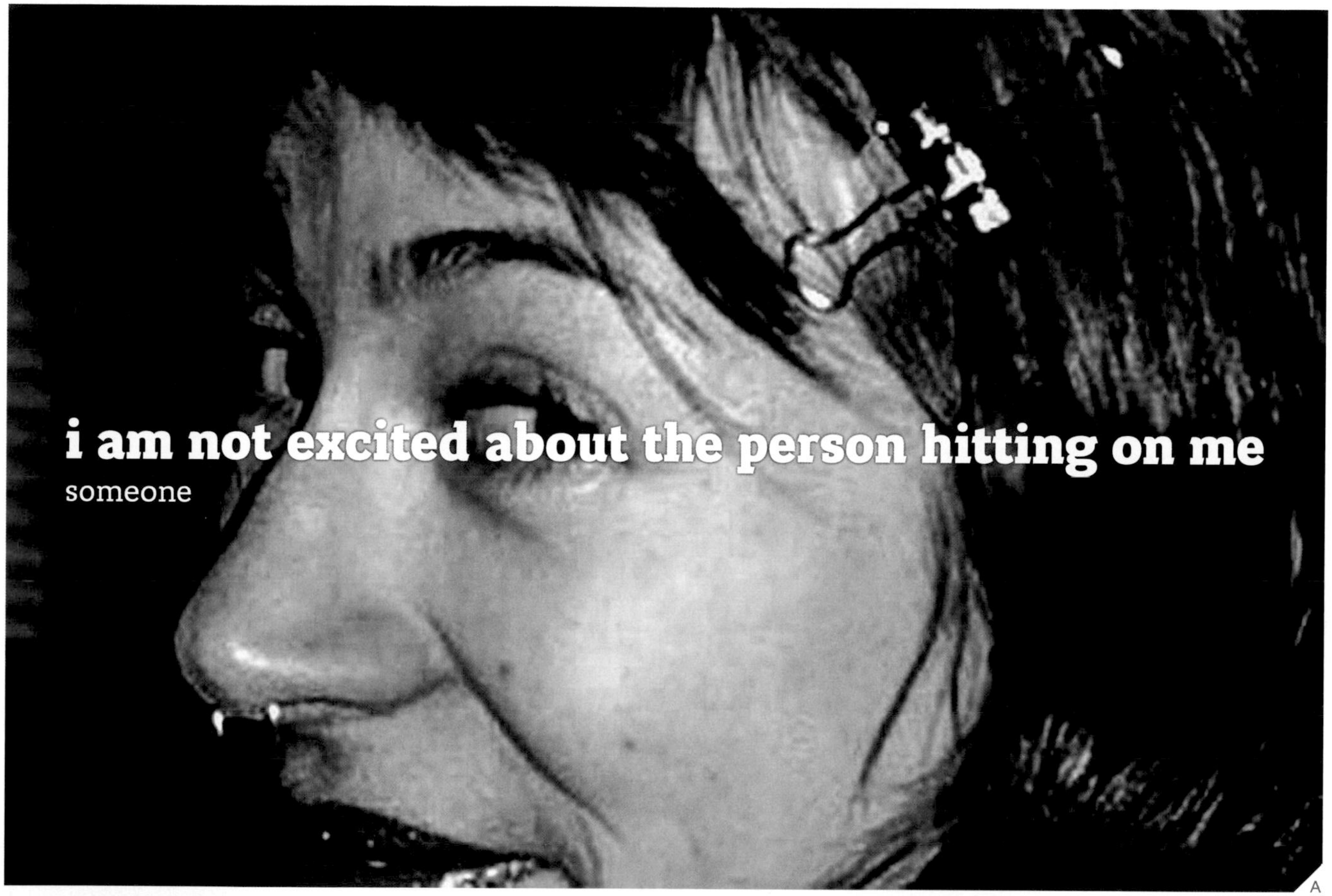

i am not excited about the person hitting on me
someone

A

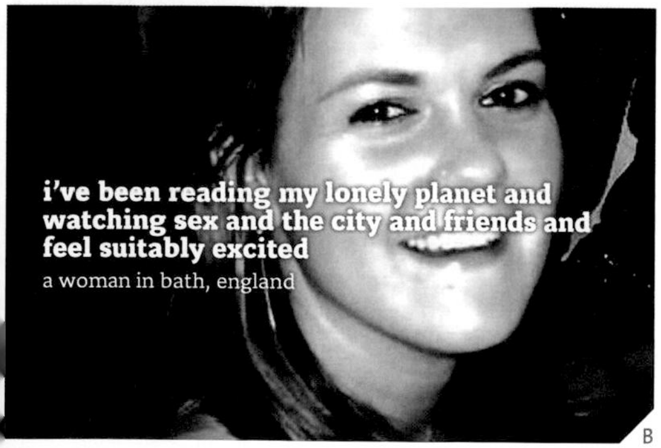

i've been reading my lonely planet and watching sex and the city and friends and feel suitably excited
a woman in bath, england

B

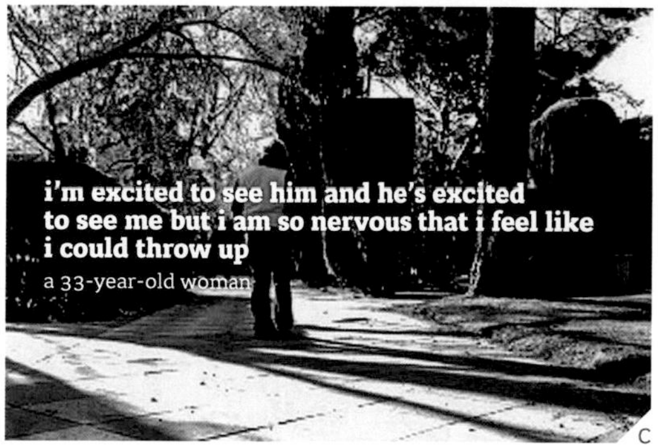

i'm excited to see him and he's excited to see me but i am so nervous that i feel like i could throw up
a 33-year-old woman

C

I FEEL LIKE A SCHOOL GIRL I AM SOOOOOO EXCITED AND I DO MISS HIM TERRIBLY
a 26-year-old woman in newbern, tennessee

Main reasons

school
seeing friends
new job
vacation

Observations

People who feel excited generally feel a mix of emotions. Mostly, people feel a **happy** excitement, but **nervous** and **scared** excitement is also very common. Since excitement often accompanies a **change** in one's life, like **moving** to a new place, getting **married**, or taking a **job**, it often comes with a tinge of **sadness** for leaving the old. People who are in school are often excited about the start of **school** and the start of **summer**, and many people across all age groups get excited about **Christmas**. And, as with many feelings, **new love** is a powerful force for excitement. ♥

FINE

29 th most common feeling overall · 0.35% of all feelings are fine

Breakdowns
for people who feel fine

Gender breakdown 40% 60%

Age breakdown 10s 20s 30s 40s 50+

i feel fine enough i guess considering everything's a mess
a woman

A

i feel fine now and the dr isn't really sure what was wrong
a woman

B

I SEEMED TO HAVE AVOIDED THE CONSEQUENCES OF MY ACTIONS THOUGH AS I WOKE UP FEELING FINE

a 22-year-old in melbourne, australia

fine adj.

1. finished; brought to perfection; refined
2. aiming at show or effect
3. nice; delicate; subtle; exquisite; artful
4. not coarse, gross, or heavy

• i feel fine now but a trip to the store yesterday almost made me pass out so i feel fine and i feel relaxed and more optimistic • i feel perfectly fine except that i feel like i have to pee every moment of every day • i'm well and almost contented there's just one tiny part of me which doesn't feel completely fine • i've had some drinks i feel fine now • i feel surprisingly fine and i've lost 2 kg since thursday • i can count the number of people who i trust and feel fine around on one fucking hand • i woke up with a blocked nose this morning but i feel fine and i'm sure the fresh air of chang mai will clear it up • i have no doubt that sex with you is gonna feel real fine

fine

Season breakdown 24% 25% 25% 26%

Related feelings mentioned with fine

okay
awake
alright
regular
sore

I HAVE BEEN GETTING BETTER SINCE I GOT THE PROZAC AND WHENEVER WE GO UP TO SANTA CRUZ I FEEL PERFECTLY FINE

a 19-year-old in california

A

Jessica was in a car accident.

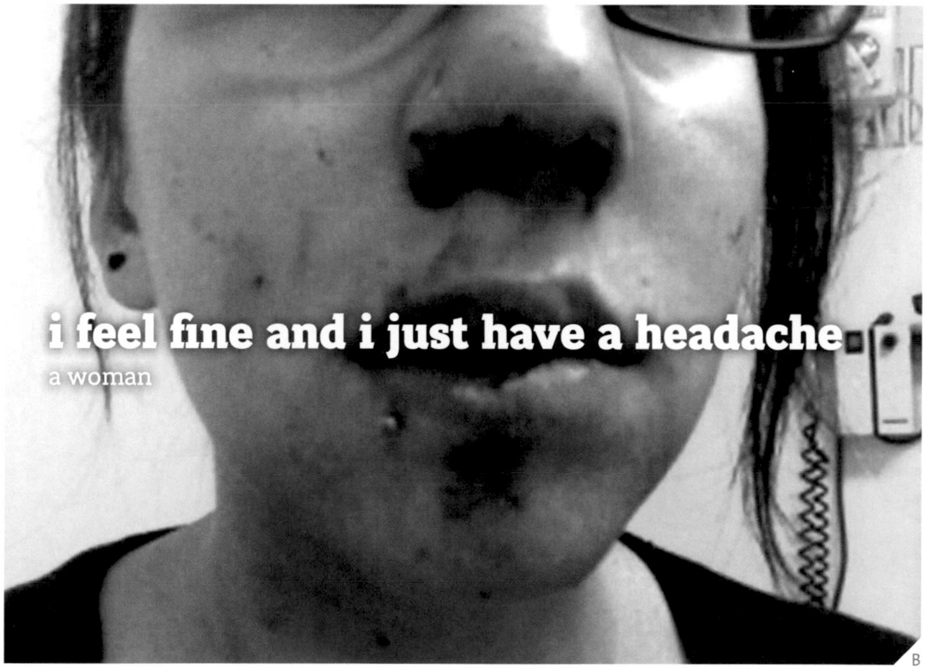

i feel fine and i just have a headache
i feel fine i just hurt
a woman

B

i feel fine but i'm tired of these freaking bandages
someone

C

i feel fine all dressed up

D

I FEEL FINE EXCEPT FOR THE PAIN

someone

Main reasons

- **waking up**
- enough sleep
- normality
- recovery

Observations

Feeling fine is often a way of people saying that their current physical or mental state is **manageable** or, simply put, **normal**. People often feel fine when they no longer feel **pain** or are no longer **sick**. They feel fine when they don't feel great, but don't feel terrible either. People also often feel fine when they **wake up**, before strong emotional stimuli enters into their day. Many people express feeling fine **except for** or in spite of some emotional or physical discomfort. As with many of the more nondescript emotions, men feel fine at a much higher rate than women do. ♥

GOOD

3 rd most common feeling overall · 3.84% of all feelings are good

Breakdowns
for people who feel good

Gender breakdown 47% 53%

Age breakdown 10s 20s 30s 40s 50+

I JUST MAY LIE TO MAKE YOU FEEL GOOD

a 21-year-old man in schererville, indiana, when it was sunny

A

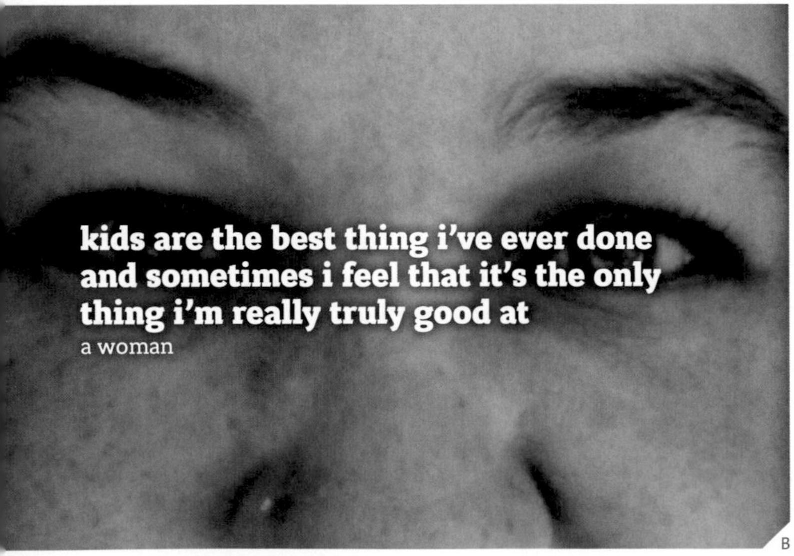

kids are the best thing i've ever done and sometimes i feel that it's the only thing i'm really truly good at
a woman

B

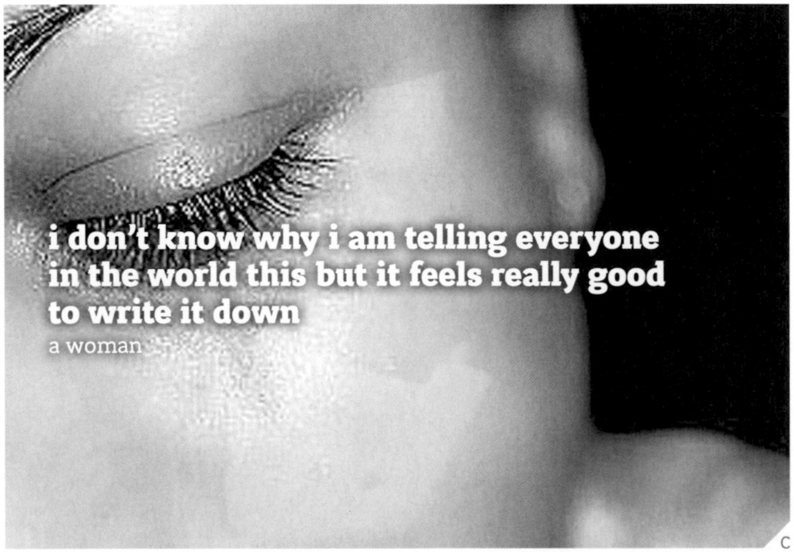

i don't know why i am telling everyone in the world this but it feels really good to write it down
a woman

C

good adj.

1. possessing desirable qualities
2. possessing moral excellence or virtue
3. kind; benevolent; gracious; polite
4. adequate; sufficient; competent

● i just gave blood and i feel so good about it ● i want to feel good about myself ● i feel like nothing i can every do for him will ever be good enough ● i had even started to lose weight and feel good about myself until yesterday when the self sabotage monster decided to make its loathsome appearance ● i'm feeling pretty good today considering it's the last day of my middle school years ● i live my life not by what the world society thinks is right but by what feels good to me ● i wonder when things will feel good again ● i really feel like i'm not good enough ● i feel pretty good about what i've accomplished in the past and i believe it will eventually lead me to where i want to be

good

Season breakdown 24% 25% 25% 26%

Related feelings mentioned with good

healthy
fresh
happy
wonderful
pleasant

i feel good la la la la la la la
a woman

A

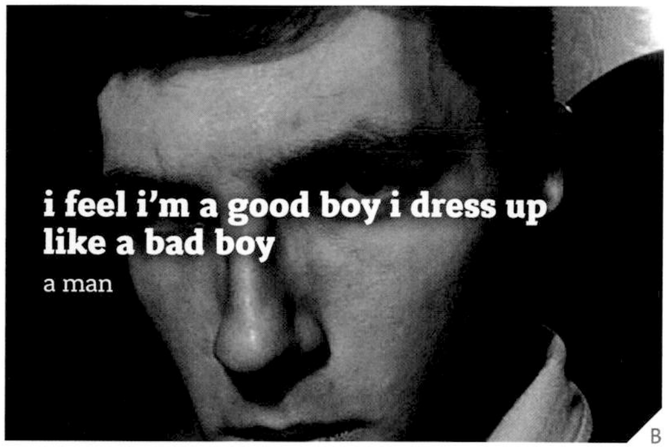

i feel i'm a good boy i dress up like a bad boy
a man

B

I GOT MARRIED SATURDAY TO MY BEST FRIEND AND THE LOVE OF MY LIFE AND TO BE HONEST I NEVER EXPECTED IT TO FEEL THIS GOOD

a 20-year-old woman
in timmonsville, south carolina

i feel so good after singing it out
someone

C

Main reasons

losing weight
sleep
exercise
eating healthy

Observations

Men and women of all age groups frequently express that living a healthy lifestyle makes them feel good. They commonly feel good after they have **exercised** in any way, but particularly after they have gone for a **run** or a **walk**. People regularly express feeling good about **money**. They feel good both about earning money and charitably giving it away to others who need it. People also often express feeling good about **themselves**. Men express feeling good more than women do, but women express feeling good about themselves far more frequently than men do. ♥

GRATEFUL

161 st most common feeling overall · 0.08% of all feelings are grateful

Breakdowns
for people who feel grateful

Gender breakdown 62% 38%

Age breakdown

A

i feel so grateful that our god is an awesome god
a 39-year-old man

B

I FEEL VERY GRATEFUL THAT I WAS ABLE TO CONCEIVE SO EASILY AND AT MY AGE

someone

C

grateful adj.

1. having a due sense of benefits received
2. pleasing to the senses; gratifying
3. willing to give thanks for benefits
4. kindly disposed toward a benefactor

● i feel so grateful to have such wonderful people in my life ● i do not feel grateful peaceful or otherwise good natured towards my fellow human beings ● i really do feel grateful and glad for every moment that is good or even decent ● i almost killed myself and so i feel grateful to allah for saving my life ● i feel grateful that it wasn't me who got hit ● i should be feeling grateful for their support and should learn to be tougher ● i feel so very grateful for chocolate ● i feel grateful for everything i have learned despite how hard it was to learn it ● i realized i didn't have to feel grateful for being adopted but that i am grateful for meeting other adoptees on all of our many walks of life grateful

Season breakdown 30% 21% 23% 26%

Related feelings
mentioned with grateful

- **humbled**
- thankful
- wonderful
- blessed
- amazing
- honored

I FEEL VERY GRATEFUL TO HAVE SOMEONE STAND IN FOR MY OWN MOM WHO PASSED AWAY WHEN I WAS 20 YEARS OLD

a 49-year-old woman in fresno, california, when it was cloudy

i feel grateful that my children have the privilege of getting to know her too
someone

A

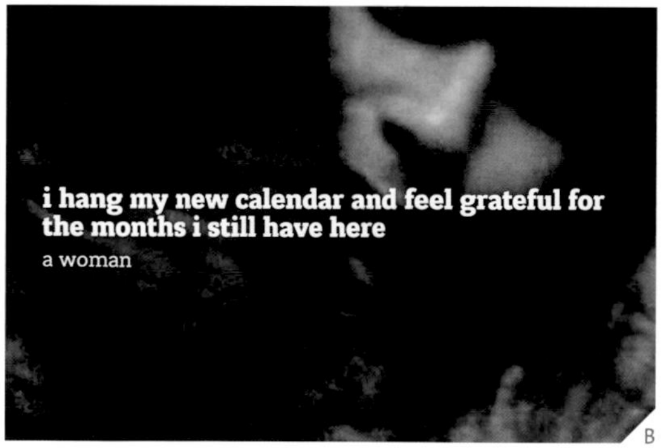

i hang my new calendar and feel grateful for the months i still have here
a woman

B

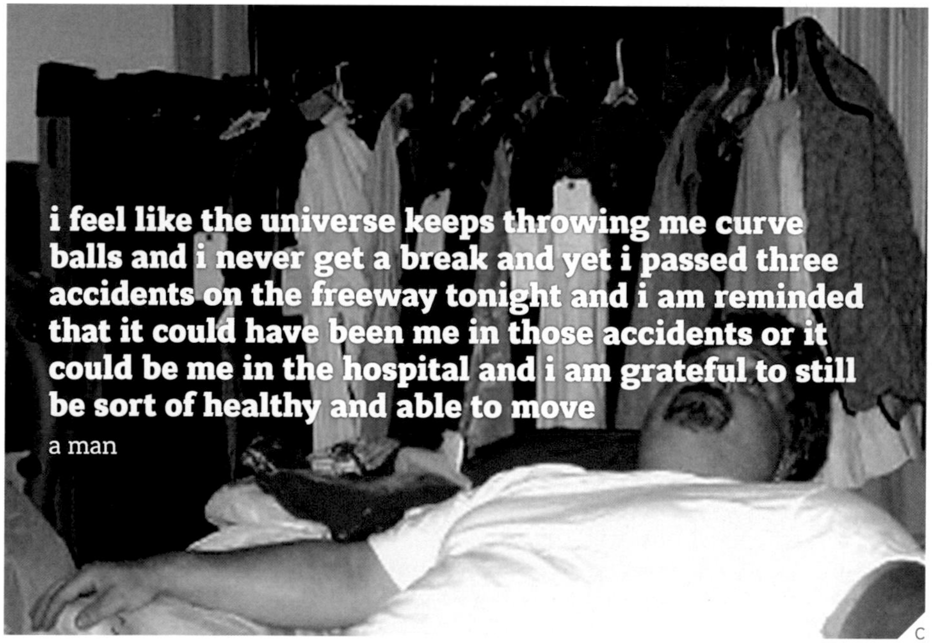

i feel like the universe keeps throwing me curve balls and i never get a break and yet i passed three accidents on the freeway tonight and i am reminded that it could have been me in those accidents or it could be me in the hospital and i am grateful to still be sort of healthy and able to move
a man

C

Main reasons

- **love**
- friendship
- family
- opportunity

Observations

Gratitude is a feeling expressed more often and more strongly as people get older, and far more by women than by men. People are often grateful for the **love** of their lives and their **friends** and **family**. They also feel grateful for good **opportunities** (such as trips to foreign countries, jobs, and chance meetings with influential people) and **experiences**. Often, when people express gratitude, they express it in strongly positive terms, feeling **incredibly** or **extremely** grateful for things that they describe as **wonderful**. People are most often grateful to God for their good fortune. ♥

GREAT

11th most common feeling overall · 0.92% of all feelings are great

Breakdowns
for people who feel great

Gender breakdown 44% 56%

Age breakdown 10s 20s 30s 40s 50+

i haven't done much of anything all day and it feels great
someone

A

I STILL FEEL GREAT ABOUT MY BODY AND LOVE THE WAY I LOOK IN THE MIRROR

someone

i may be worn out for a bit afterward but i feel great
a woman

B

i suck it up and pretend i feel great
a woman

C

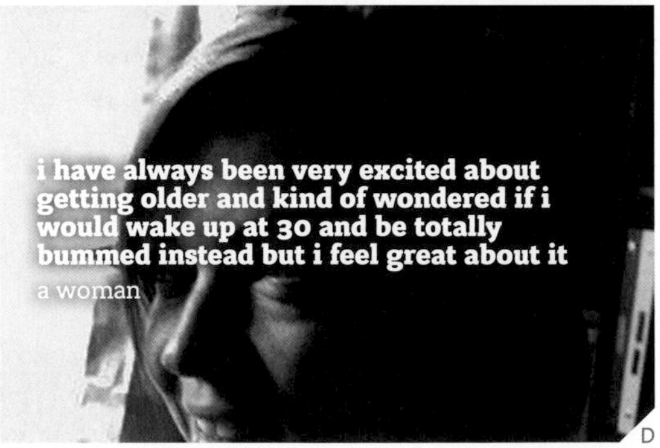

i have always been very excited about getting older and kind of wondered if i would wake up at 30 and be totally bummed instead but i feel great about it
a woman

D

This post was written on Kiona's 30th birthday. She is married and has a son.

great adj.

1. large in space; of much size; big; immense
2. large in number; numerous
3. endowed with extraordinary powers
4. more than ordinary in degree

• i feel great around her and i feel loved • i just dont love you like you love me i dont get that heart melting feeling when i see you you're a great friend and i'd hate to spoil that but i think i already have • i feel great about it: life is crazy life is hard but i've always known that some how love will find a way • i don't believe in standardized tests so i have a feeling its not going to be a great experience • i always feel great after a good workout • i lost four pounds this week i feel great • i'm a little over 57 hours into my fast so i'm feeling great about that • i started my yoga and stretching and with every stretch i felt energized and today on friday i feel absolutely great • i have a passion to look and feel great

great

Season breakdown 27% 23% 25% 25%

Related feelings mentioned with great

sore	excited
amazing	lost
wonderful	happy

I LOVE GETTING THE FEELING OF BUTTERFLIES IN MY STOMACH ITS JUST SUCH A GREAT HIGH YOU FEEL SO GOOD AND YOU KNOW YOU'RE IMPORTANT TO SOMEONE

someone in seattle, washington, when it was cloudy

i feel great
a man

A

it's such a great feeling to be underwater
a man

B

i may look like shit but i feel great
a woman

C

Main reasons

- **exercising**
- losing weight
- enough sleep
- accomplishments

Observations

The strongest reason why people say that they feel great is vigorous **exercise**. They most commonly feel great after going for a **run**, going to the **gym**, doing **yoga**, or going for a **swim**. While people commonly say that walks make them feel better, they do not frequently say that walks make them feel great. The other predominant reason people say they feel great is when they lose weight. People also feel great when they have gotten a good night's sleep, and when they lead healthy lifestyles in general. The British express feeling great less often than average. ♥

GUILTY

4th most common feeling overall · 1.53% of all feelings are guilty

Breakdowns
for people who feel guilty

Gender breakdown 57% 43%

Age breakdown 10s 20s 30s 40s 50+

I DON'T WANT TO LOSE HIS FRIENDSHIP BUT I REFUSE TO FEEL GUILTY FOR FINDING A NEW GUY THAT I REALLY REALLY REALLY LIKE

someone

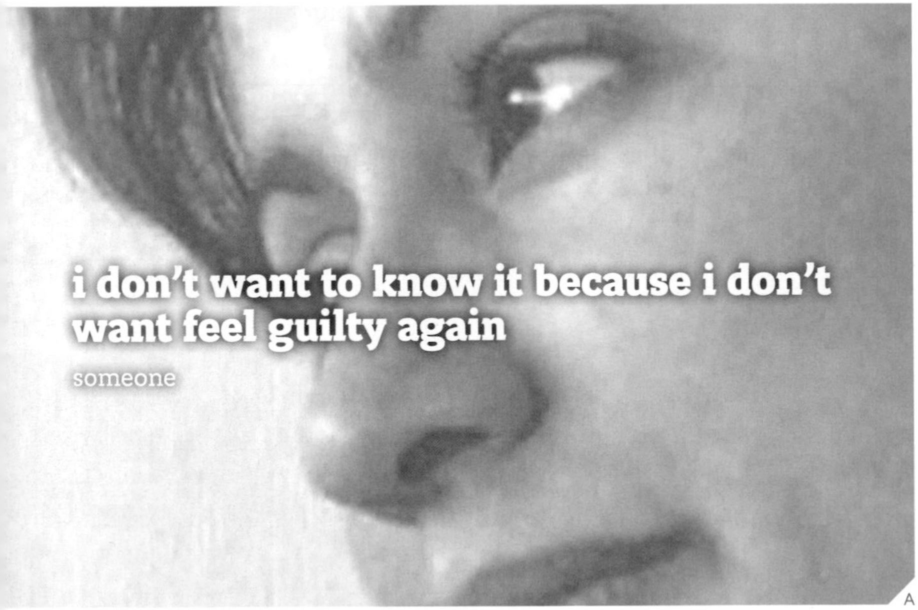

i don't want to know it because i don't want feel guilty again
someone

A

WHEN I THINK ABOUT ALL THE PAIN HE ENDURED WHILE HE WAS ALIVE I FEEL GUILTY FOR BEING ANGRY

someone in bridgeport, texas

↑ carolina feels guilty because a good friend of hers confessed his love and she does not share his feelings.

i feel so guilty every single time
i pay $5 for a starbucks
a woman
COFFEE

B

guilty adj.

1. having incurred guilt; delinquent
2. chargeable with something censurable
3. evincing or indicating guilt
4. conscious; cognizant of guilt

● i feel guilty for being satisfied ● i'm actually enjoying the cold weather i can indulge in my game addiction without feeling guilty because i should be outside working on something lol ● i can't help but feel guilty for the way i acted and feel sorry for myself in other respects ● i just feel so guilty i just end up throwing it up and crying my eyes out ● i feel guilty sometimes for things that i can't control ● i feel a little guilty starting my 5 year old down this path after my own 43 years of pain ● i turn him down because i feel guilty that someone has to help me i'm just use to doing things for myself ● i feel guilty because i don't really think this is the ideal christian response to this situation

Season breakdown 23% **26%** 25% 26%

Related feelings mentioned with guilty

- **selfish**
- mad
- angry
- ashamed
- upset

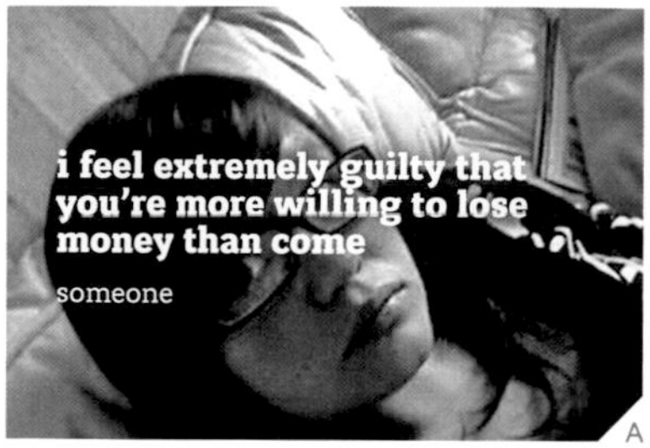

i feel extremely guilty that you're more willing to lose money than come
someone

A

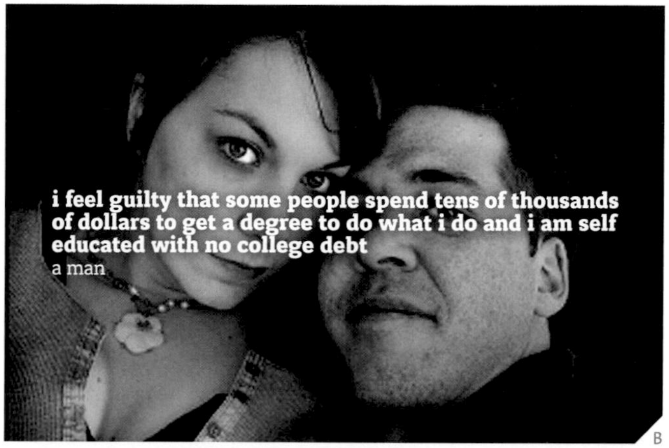

i feel guilty that some people spend tens of thousands of dollars to get a degree to do what i do and i am self educated with no college debt
a man

B

I HAVE PUT IN SO MANY YEARS OF GRUNT WORK, ASSHOLE BOSSES, SEXUAL HARASSMENT, BAD PAY AND SO MUCH MORE IN THIS BUSINESS THAT I REFUSE TO FEEL GUILTY FOR DOING WELL

a 21-year-old woman in las vegas, nevada

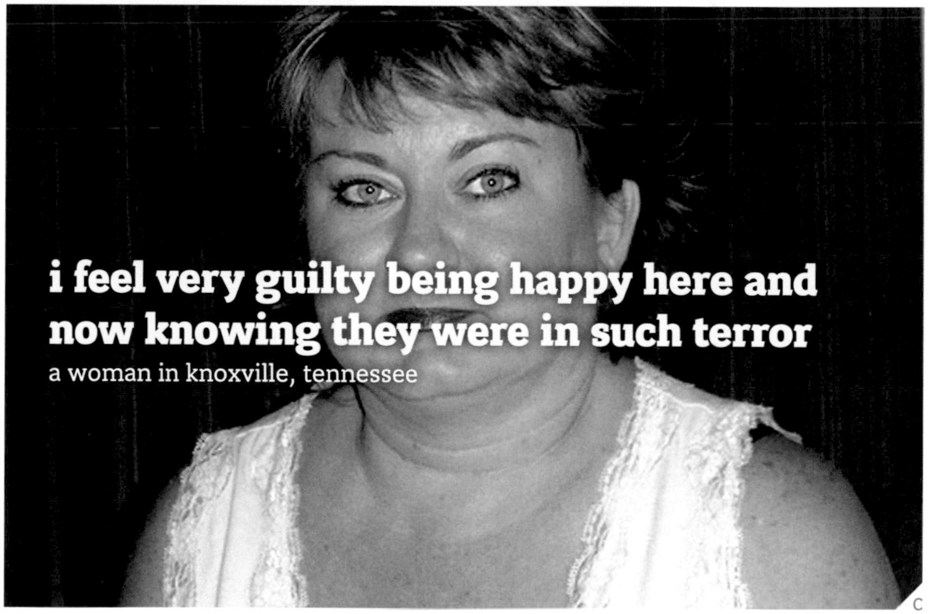

i feel very guilty being happy here and now knowing they were in such terror
a woman in knoxville, tennessee

C

Main reasons

- **money**
- overeating
- leaving
- sex

Observations

As people age they feel more guilty, but after middle age, the feeling lessens. **Women** feel guilty more than men. People often discuss feeling **horribly** or **terribly** guilty, but sometimes just **slightly** or **vaguely** guilty. Guilt is a feeling that people rebel against, saying that they **refuse** to feel guilty or that they **shouldn't** feel guilty. **Spending money** and **eating** are two reasons people feel guilty; also after **buying**, **neglecting**, **indulging**, **slacking**, **stealing**, **betraying**, and **yelling**. People in their teens and early 20s feel more guilt about having **sex**. **Catholics** frequently feel guilty. ♥

HAPPY

12 th most common feeling overall · 0.86% of all feelings are happy

Breakdowns
for people who feel happy

Gender breakdown 53% 47%

Age breakdown

i feel like my life just started over i am so happy and grateful
a woman

A

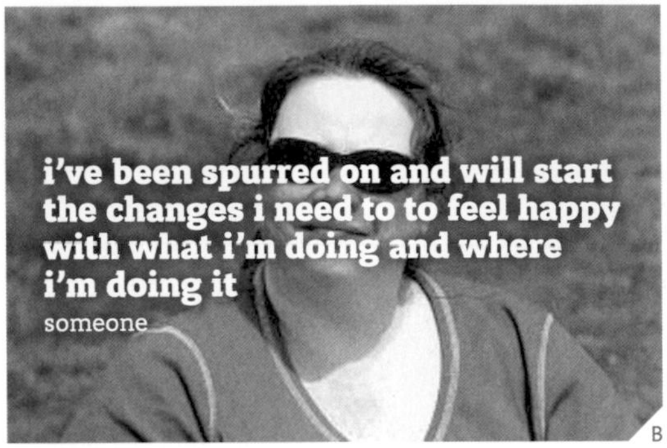

i've been spurred on and will start the changes i need to to feel happy with what i'm doing and where i'm doing it
someone

B

I WANT MY DAD TO FEEL HAPPY I WANT HIM TO RECOVER WHY CANT I HELP ANYTHING

someone

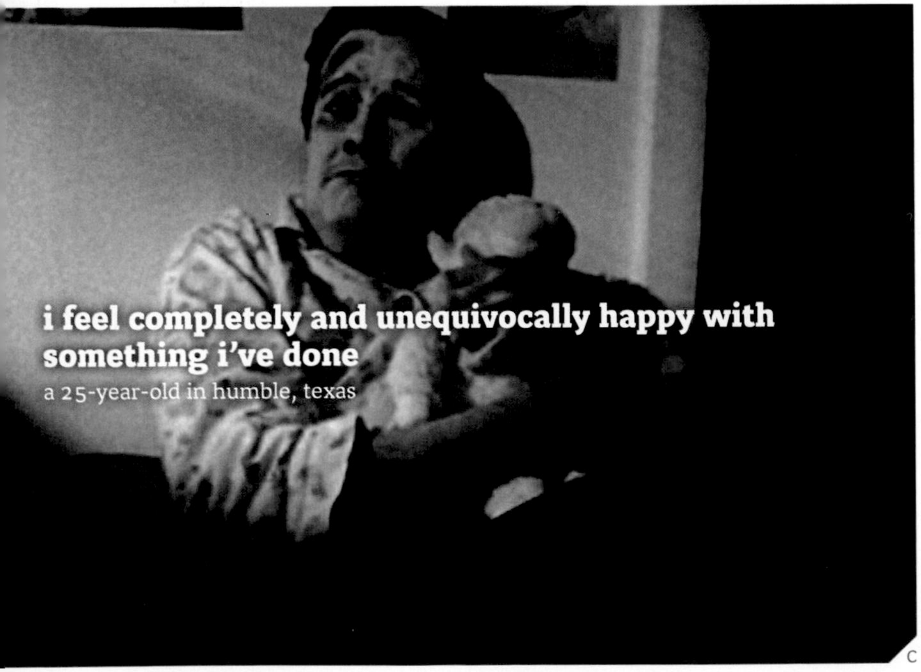

i feel completely and unequivocally happy with something i've done
a 25-year-old in humble, texas

C

I ALWAYS FEEL CHEATED BY A HAPPY ENDING BECAUSE I NEVER GET ONE MYSELF

someone in london, england

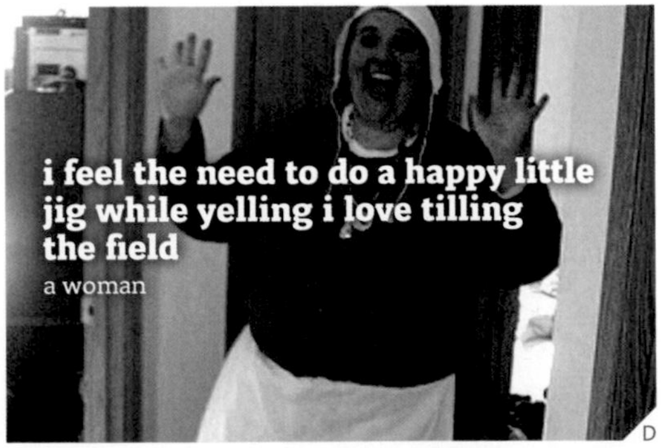

i feel the need to do a happy little jig while yelling i love tilling the field
a woman

D

happy adj.

1. the feeling arising from well-being
2. lucky; fortunate; successful
3. enjoying good of any kind
4. dexterous; ready; apt; felicitous

• i'm free free of all this hate this angst this fear this shaking sensation the heavy hearted feeling when i see other happy couples • i just got goosebumps all over because think of how everyone would feel happy all the time like spongebob that's how • i'm satisfied with my body and feel happy with myself i will continue to obsess and it doesn't make me a stupid person • i don't know what it is about poppies but i feel happy and smile when i see them • i feel so happy that all i want to do is make her happy • i'm sitting here in my cozy pajamas feeling really happy and sentimental • i moved my bed so that it was under my pretty pictures and now i feel so happy sleeping under them

Season breakdown 23% 28% 27% 22%

Related feelings mentioned with happy

content
joyful
sad
satisfied
upbeat
fulfilled

I SHOULDN'T NEED ANYONE ELSE TO MAKE ME FEEL HAPPY

someone in boston, massachusetts, when it was cloudy

i'm feeling happy and unstressed today
a 29-year-old man

A

i feel like even if she doesn't quite remember it the happy will stay with her
someone

B

Blu and her mother took her grandmother to her first male stripshow. Her grandmother, pictured, put money in that man's thong just seconds after this picture was taken. She didn't remember a few minutes later, but continued to smile.

Main reasons

love
friendship
going to school
family

Observations

Happiness is a great feeling. People **love** feeling happy and feel happy when they are in love. People are happy when with **friends** and **family**, and are **hopeful** that they are happy too. People are often happy to be **home** after being away and in the **morning**. People often feel happy and sad at the same time. As people grow older they express feeling happy less, but, in fact, people grow happier with age. This is because they find other words to express happiness. At a younger age people feel an **excited** happiness. As they grow older, they feel a **contented** happiness. ♥

HELPLESS

75th most common feeling overall · 0·17% of all feelings are helpless

Breakdowns
for people who feel helpless

Gender breakdown 57% 43%

Age breakdown 10s 20s 30s 40s 50+

i feel helpless please pray for my son he needs your love
a man
A

i feel so helpless watching you wither away
a woman
C

I JUST CAN'T GET ANY LOWER I FEEL TOTALLY HELPLESS AND GUILTY EVERYTIME I EAT

i feel pretty much helpless
someone

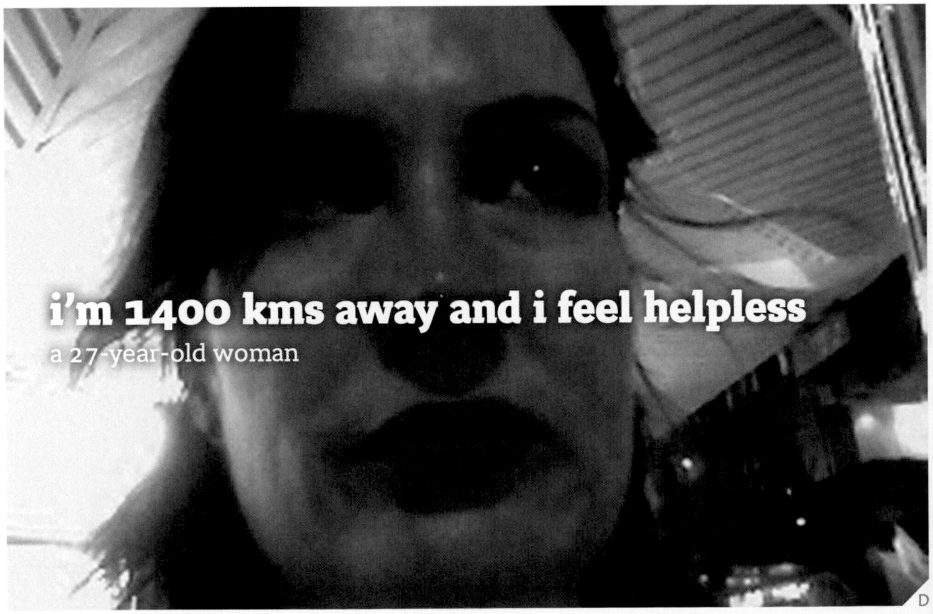

helpless adj.

1. destitute of help or strength
2. beyond help; irremediable
3. bringing no help; unaiding
4. unsupplied; destitute

• i have to step outside the box and educate myself on the health care system and politics to not feel so helpless • i was stuck arguing in a restaurant with my girlfriend feeling helpless as i watched my relationship slip through my fingers • i feel so helpless and anguished by the ineffective systems and my own limitations of time money and abilities • i feel so helpless and hopeless right now in the situation of the world today i frankly don't see that these ideas have very much possible influence over a situation involving millions of people and trillions of dollars • i feel so helpless but you can't just go out and buy a friend

Season breakdown 25% 24% **27%** 24%

Related feelings mentioned with helpless

hopeless
suicidal
useless
powerless
vulnerable
frustrated

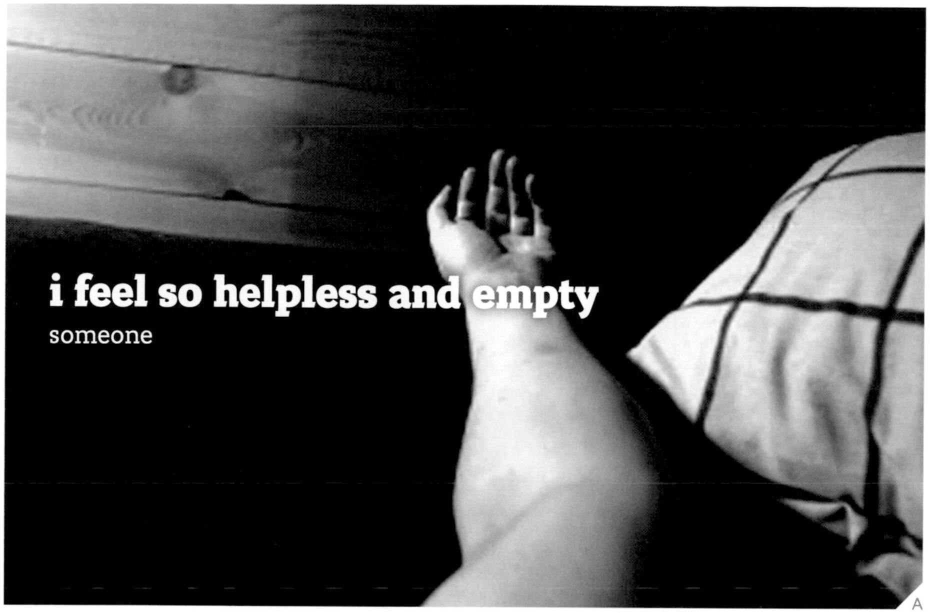
i feel so helpless and empty
someone
A

I FEEL HELPLESS AND I DON'T WANT TO LET YOU GO

a 23-year-old woman in melbourne, australia

i feel so helpless
a woman
B

i am feeling weaker and weaker
more helpless by the day
someone
C

I FELT MYSELF DRIFTING INTO MY QUIET LITTLE WORLD THE PLACE I TEND TO GO WHEN I FEEL AS THOUGH I AM HELPLESS OR DROWNING

someone

Main reasons

- **loss of control**
- pain
- illness
- suffering

Observations

People most commonly express feeling helpless when they feel they don't have **control** over a specific situation, such as when loved ones are **sick** or **in pain**. People also frequently feel helpless when they are confronted with things that are much larger than themselves, like most world events, which they feel completely powerless to **change**. When they feel helpless, people often also express feeling **hopeless**, **useless**, and **lost**, and say they want to **cry**. ♥

HORRIBLE

26th most common feeling overall · 0.41% of all feelings are horrible

Breakdowns for people who feel horrible

Gender breakdown: 61% (women) · 39% (men)

Age breakdown: 10s · 20s · 30s · 40s · 50+

I CHEATED ON YOU THE SECOND WEEK, AND I CHEATED ON YOU ON FRIDAY AND I FEEL HORRIBLE WHEN YOU HOLD MY HAND AND KISS ME, BUT FUCK I CAN'T HURT YOU AND TELL YOU AGAIN

a woman

i feel horrible
someone in virginia

A

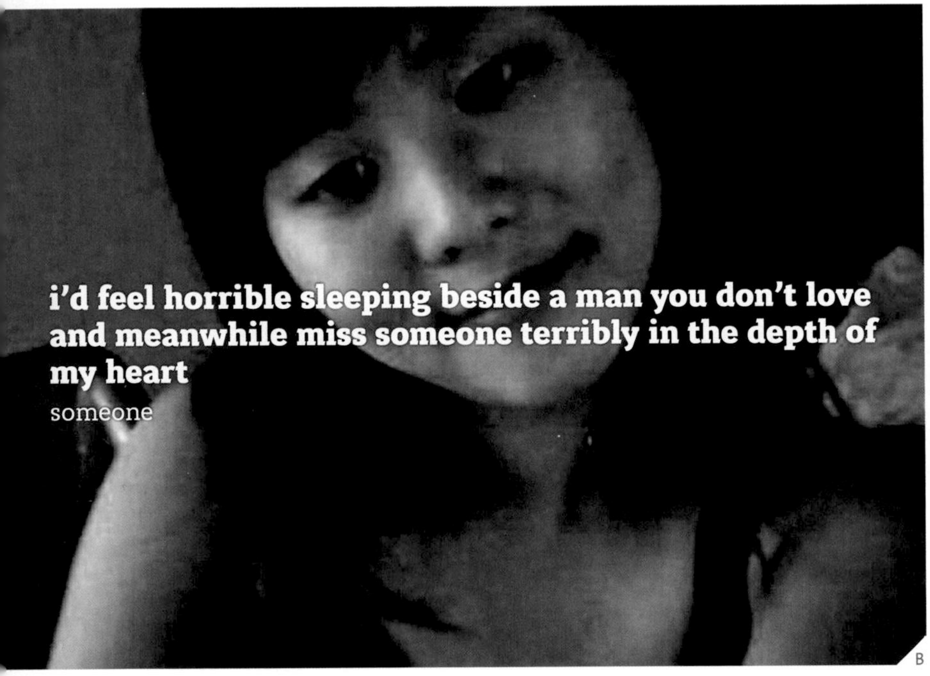

i'd feel horrible sleeping beside a man you don't love and meanwhile miss someone terribly in the depth of my heart
someone

B

i feel like the most horrible person in the world
a woman

C

Ling is a student in Shanghai, China, who blogs in English, her favorite academic subject. In this post, she is sad about a lost love interest and wondered if she would settle down and marry a local boy

I FEEL HORRIBLE SO HORRIBLE I WISH I WOULD'VE CALLED 911 WHEN I SAW THE SMOKE BUT I DIDN'T

someone

horrible adj.

1. tending to incite horror or fear
2. dreadful; terrible
3. shocking; hideous
4. atrocious; provoking horror

● i feel horrible for laughing during his rant speech even if it was almost all republican lies propaganda ● i would feel horrible subjecting kingsley to a life stuck in a teensy apartment with no backyard to stretch his legs ● i'm not thinking about her much b/c i feel horrible and miss her so much so i'm trying to think of other things and keep busy ● i feel horrible because dustin truly is a good kid and does not deserve this ● i feel like a horrible pet parent right now ● i feel so horrible to see you in pain to the point of tears ● i am also worried that even if it isn't i may feel so horrible as to not being able to have children that i will want to die ● i feel horrible when people fail to see the bigger picture

Season breakdown 21% **28%** 27% 24%

Related feelings mentioned with horrible

mad
ugly
selfish
upset
disgusting

i feel horrible because kathy's only son is moving far away to be with some girl he met on the internet
someone

A

Amber was 12 and growing up in Canada when she first met Matthew, her future husband, over the internet. He was 14 and in high school in Australia. It would be two years until they confessed their love for one another, 6 years until they met face to face, and 7 years until he would move to Canada and marry her. Amber is so happy, but feels guilty for taking Matthew away from his mom, Kathy.

I FEEL HORRIBLE THAT MY BABY IS GONE

a 22-year-old woman in tignall, georgia

Main reasons

- **illness**
- hurting others
- money
- cheating

Observations

People feel horrible when they **hurt** someone that they love. Parents, especially **mothers**, feel like horrible **parents**. People feel horrible if they feel **ugly**, **fat**, or **guilty** and they tend to feel it in their **stomach**. People feel horrible after they **eat**, especially if they have body issues, and feel horrible about **money**—spending money, taking money, or seeing others with money problems. Americans feel more horrible during the week of the **anniversary of 9/11**. The northeastern tip of the U.S. feels horrible more than most of the rest of the country and so do men and teenagers. ♥

HUMAN

112 th most common feeling overall · 0.12% of all feelings are human

Breakdowns for people who feel human

Gender breakdown 44% 56%

Age breakdown 10s 20s 30s 40s 50+

i didn't even feel human
a 34-year-old man

A

I ALSO FEEL SORT OF HUMAN IN MY LONELINESS

someone

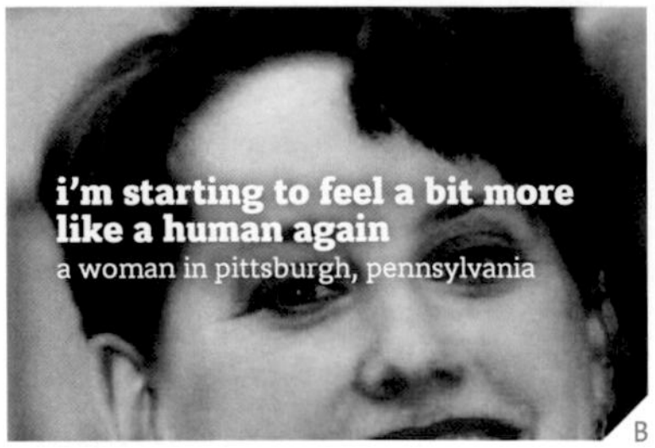

i'm starting to feel a bit more like a human again
a woman in pittsburgh, pennsylvania

B

i think by tomorrow i'll hopefully start feeling like a human again
someone

C

human adj.

1. belonging to man or mankind
2. having the qualities of mankind
3. of or pertaining to the race of mankind
4. characteristic of humanity

• i just made up the memory of butterflies to make myself feel human • i also feel sort of human in my loneliness • i have been using large quantities of nitrous in the am and pm of the last few weeks and i feel human again for the first time since 2001 • i am with jamie now he makes me feel like a human being again instead of just on object • i ran into a girl that was part of the bitches who made me feel like less of a human based on my social status • i feel the need to feel human and lose site of my disease • i think the medication is defintiely helping this time 'coz i actually feel human right now • i think i'm starting to turn the corner and feel human again

Season breakdown 25% 24% 25% 26%

Related feelings mentioned with human

real
awake
normal
capable
alive

i finished weeping & put some makeup on to feel human again
a 26-year-old in brunswick, maine
A

After struggling with Aspergers and Depression in his real life Torley found true happiness in his Second Life. He even found love.

I HAD A 2-HOUR SOAK IN THE TUB WITH A COUPLE OF SCOTCHES FROM THE MINI BAR AND I FEEL HUMAN AGAIN

a 58-year-old in london, ontario, when it was raining

i want to feel that i'm a real human
someone
B

Main reasons

enough sleep
showering
bath
exercise

Observations

When people talk about feeling human, they most commonly do so in the context of **starting** to feel human **again**, after experiencing a period of depression or sickness or numbness. People will frequently describe feeling only **halfway** or **remotely** human, and it is only very rarely that people describe feeling strongly human. People often say that they feel human again after getting a good night's **sleep** or taking a **shower**. Less frequently, a strong cup of **coffee** or a good **cry** will cause someone to feel human once again. ♥

HURT

32nd **most common feeling overall** · 0.35% of all feelings are hurt

Breakdowns
for people who feel hurt

Gender breakdown — 54% (women) · 46% (men)

Age breakdown — 10s · 20s · 30s · 40s · 50+

I HAD TO PRETEND THAT I REALLY ENJOYED MYSELF SO HIS FEELINGS WOULDN'T GET HURT

someone

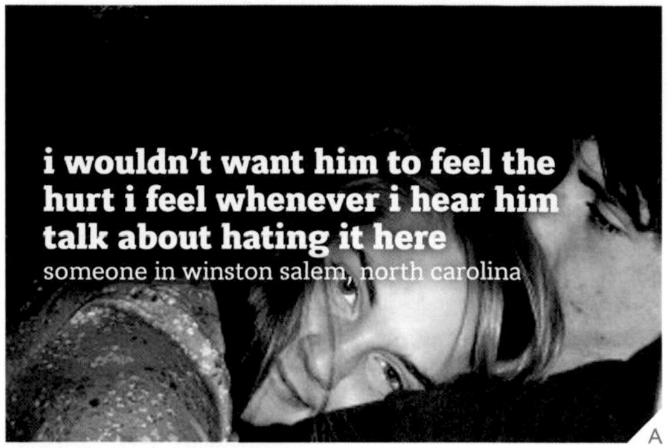

i wouldn't want him to feel the hurt i feel whenever i hear him talk about hating it here
someone in winston salem, north carolina

A

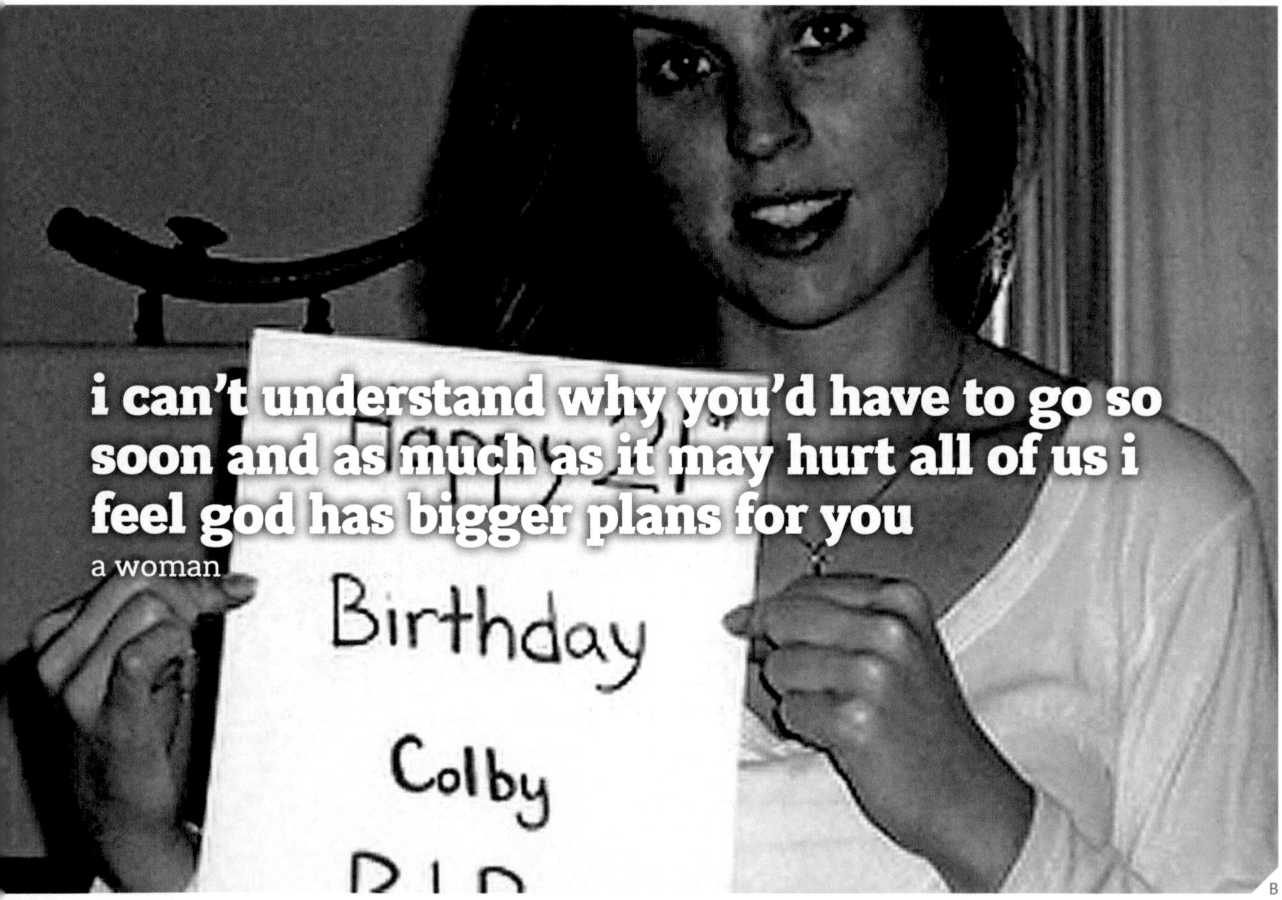

i can't understand why you'd have to go so soon and as much as it may hurt all of us i feel god has bigger plans for you
a woman

B

hurt adj.

1. to inflict physical pain or bodily harm
2. to impair the value or usefulness of
3. to wound the feelings of
4. offend in honor or self-respect

● i feel nothing but sadness and hurt ● i remember after talking to her that all i could feel was hurt i felt pain because i knew she was in pain ● i hurt someone with my words who is just a victim of an adult game yet i was feeling all this betrayal and hurt and it came out ● i really had my feelings hurt because it seemed like nobody appreciated anything that i did ● i was sick of her being mean instead of admitting when she was hurt or talking about it when she was angry ● i'm too scared to say how i feel because i don't want to get hurt ● i feel you're just pretending to be my friend so that you wont hurt my feelings hurt

Season breakdown		
spring 25%	summer 24%	**fall 27%**	winter 24%

Related feelings
mentioned with hurt

- **angry**
- abused
- rejected
- offended
- confused
- insulted

I'M SO USED TO BEING HURT IT FEELS LIKE IF I'M NOT HURT SOMEHOW SOMEWAY I DON'T FEEL ANYTHING

a woman in dorset, ohio

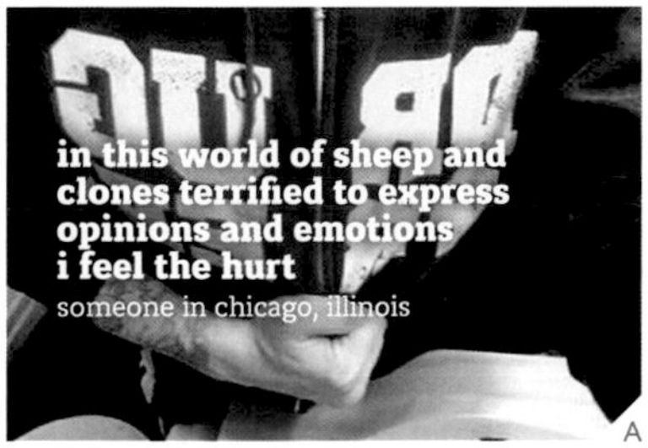

in this world of sheep and clones terrified to express opinions and emotions i feel the hurt
someone in chicago, illinois
A

Amanda is going through a terrible breakup with the re same guy for the third time.

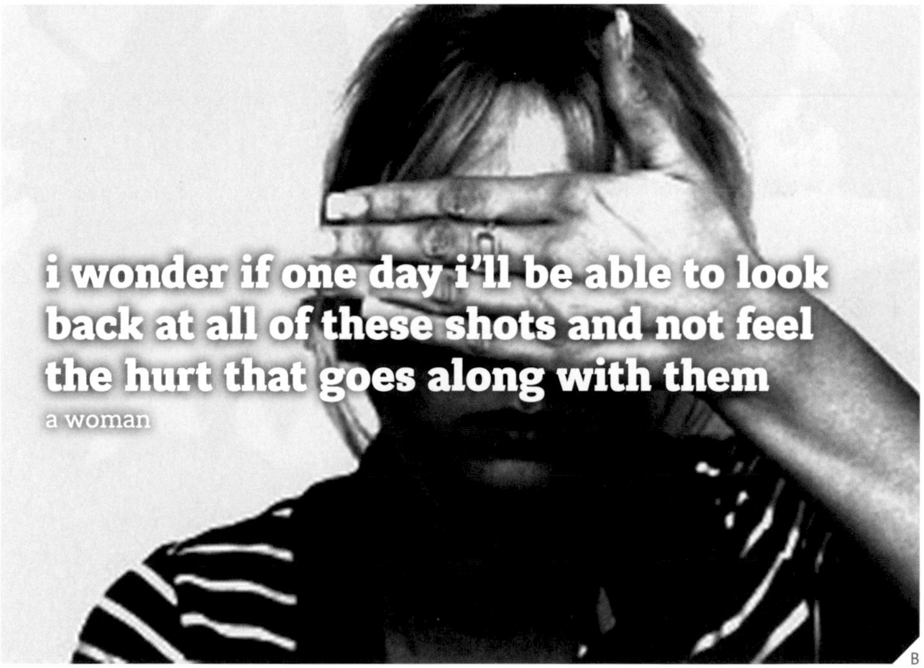

i wonder if one day i'll be able to look back at all of these shots and not feel the hurt that goes along with them
a woman
B

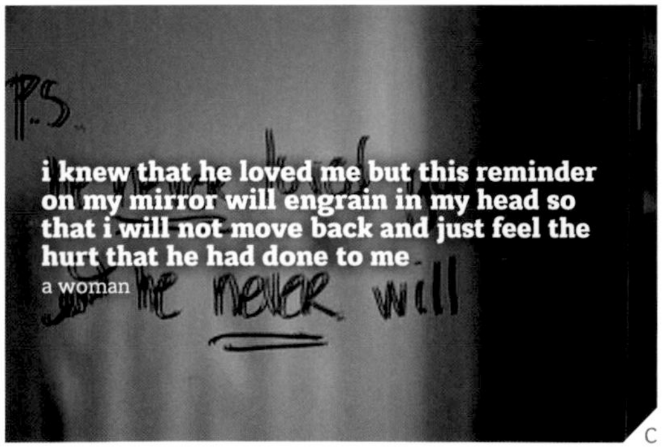

P.S.
he never will

i knew that he loved me but this reminder on my mirror will engrain in my head so that i will not move back and just feel the hurt that he had done to me
a woman
C

I FEEL LIKE I NEED TO HURT MYSELF

a 22-year-old in norman, oklahoma

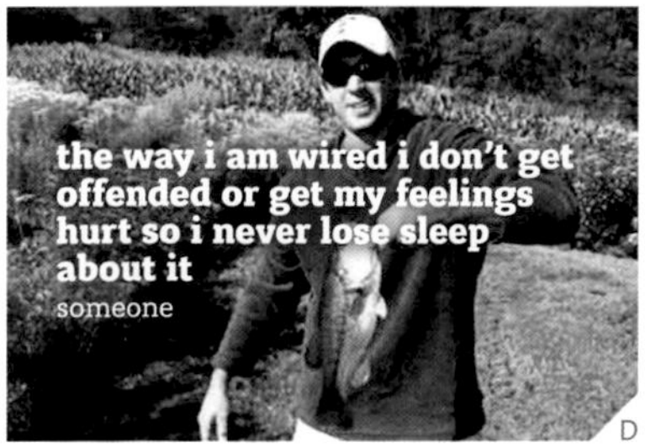

the way i am wired i don't get offended or get my feelings hurt so i never lose sleep about it
someone
D

I FEEL LIKE HE IS OUT ON A MISSION TO HURT ME

someone

Main reasons

- **pain**
- love
- betrayal
- harsh words

Observations

People use the word hurt to describe both a **physical** and an **emotional** feeling. When people feel hurt emotionally, it is often because they feel **betrayed**, and also due to feeling **rejected**, **offended**, or **insulted**. People who feel emotionally hurt also tend to experience feelings of **anger** and **confusion**. **Women** describe being hurt more than men do, but men describe feeling hurt physically more than women. As people get older, they feel less hurt. When people describe feeling hurt, they often describe wanting to **cry**, and less often, they describe wanting **to die**. ♥

JEALOUS

174 th most common feeling overall · 0.07% of all feelings are jealous

Breakdowns
for people who feel jealous

Gender breakdown: 55% | 45%

Age breakdown: 10s | 20s | 30s | 40s | 50+

they're all making me feel very jealous with their interesting mutterings about their talented lives
someone

A

B

I FEEL SO JEALOUS WHEN YOU NORMAL PEOPLE JUST OPEN YOUR MOUTH AND SPIT OUT WORDS SMOOTHLY

a 19-year-old in brisbane, australia

jealous adj.

1. morbid fear of rivalry in love
2. suspicious of faithfulness of partner
3. disposed to suspect rivalry; distrustful
4. apprehensive regarding others' motives

• i always feel a bit jealous when i see couples being all swoony with each other on vd although on the surface i know it is a ridiculous excuse for hallmark to make a profit • i'm a little hesitant because i have a feeling he's going to explain this to his friends as i was being a jealous dramatic freak • i read other's celebrating their 21st i cant help but feel abit jealous and also envious • i especially hate feeling jealous when there's honestly no good reason for it • i feel that i can't do anything else because of my constraints i am jealous with other people that have very great capability why not me • i also feel jealous your life is so action packed

Season breakdown 24% 27% 22% 27%

Related feelings
mentioned with jealous

- **envious**
- insecure
- angry
- annoyed
- mad
- ugly

i am feeling jealous and i am feeling not warm enough
a 25-year-old woman

A

I FEEL A LITTLE BIT JEALOUS WITH MY OWN SON BECAUSE MY WIFE NOW GIVES MORE ATTENTION TO HIM

someone

i am so feeling jealous of that because some of us are privileged enough to be there as guests of the almighty
someone
SAMSUNG
mobile

B

Main reasons

- **couples**
- ex
- romantic intrigue
- friends' opportunities

Observations

By far the main causes of jealousy are romantic issues. People are often jealous of others who are in **relationships**, talking to their significant others, or are close with somebody to whom they are attracted. In mild forms of jealousy, people talk about being **happy** for somebody, but also jealous at the same time. In stronger forms, people talk about being jealous and **angry**, and to a lesser degree **hurt**. Jealousy is a young person's emotion, and young women feel it most strongly. Women are usually jealous of other women, and men are usually jealous of other men. ♥

LONELY

22 **nd most common feeling overall** · 0.50% of all feelings are lonely

Breakdowns
for people who feel lonely

Gender breakdown — 52% (women) · 48% (men)

Age breakdown — 10s · 20s · 30s · 40s · 50+

I FEEL SO LONELY HERE LATELY I FEEL AS IF MY VERY BEST FRIEND IS NOT WHAT I THOUGHT HE WAS

a 33-year-old woman in phoenix, arizona

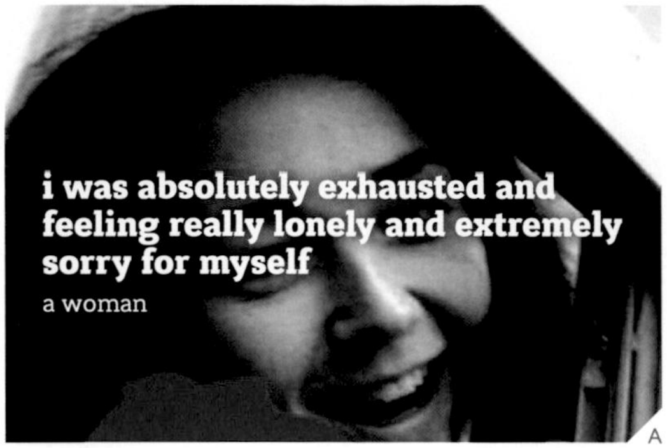

i was absolutely exhausted and feeling really lonely and extremely sorry for myself
a woman

A

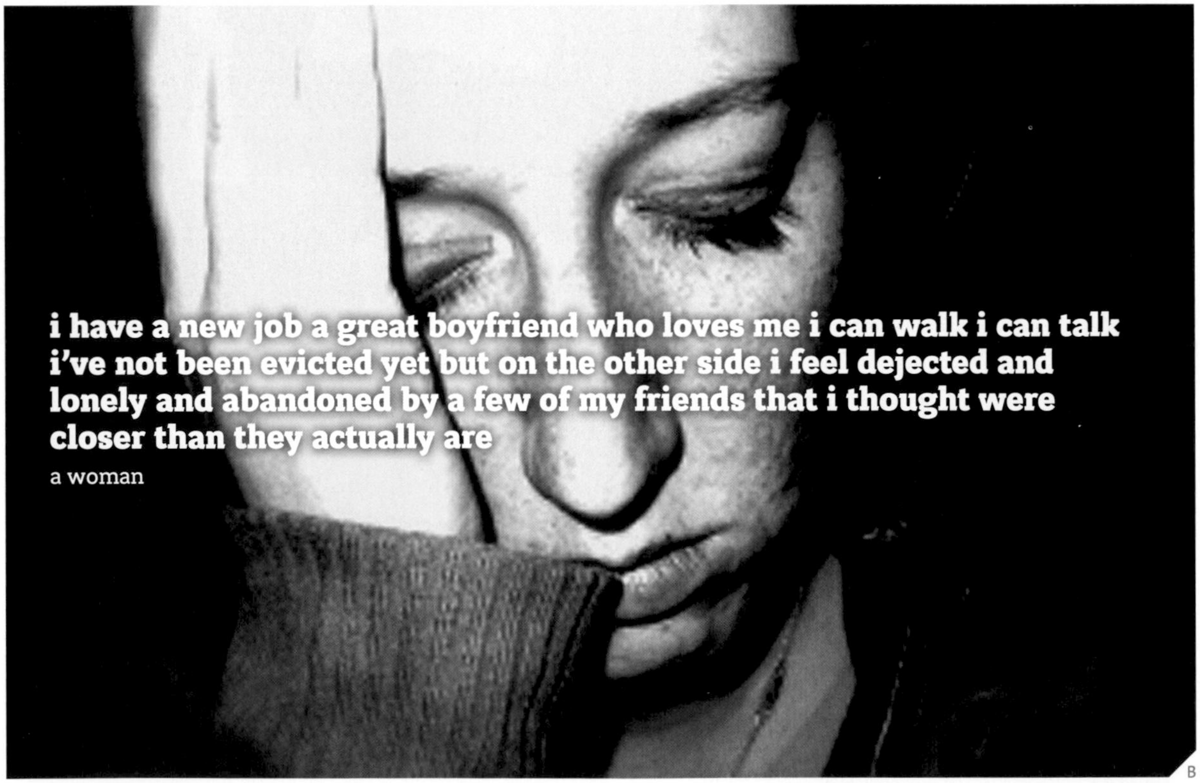

i have a new job a great boyfriend who loves me i can walk i can talk i've not been evicted yet but on the other side i feel dejected and lonely and abandoned by a few of my friends that i thought were closer than they actually are
a woman

B

i feel for you why is this world so lonely
a woman

C

lonely adj.

1. sequestered from company or neighbors
2. alone, or in want of company; forsaken
3. not frequented by human beings
4. lonesome

● i think she is thinking about the week he will be away with me and that she'll miss him and will feel lonely and thinking herself into being down i know how that feels ● i am not enjoying anything like the social life i was used to in geneva and was starting to feel desperately lonely and like i'd made a huge mistake coming home ● i feel like no one's there and when i'm lonely in my darkest hour you give me the power to sit and pretend ● i feel lonely again but i know that i'll see you again real soon ● i have my friends and family so never lonely in that way but yeah sometimes when your not with someone you feel lonely at times esp if everyone else around is all loved up

Season breakdown: 22% · 28% · 27% · 23%

Related feelings mentioned with lonely

- **unloved**
- isolated
- homesick
- unwanted
- misunderstood
- bored

i feel a bit lonely and the fact that no one else has felt about me the same way i feel about myself kinda makes me wonder
a woman

A

i feel so lonely and bad in riyadh
a man

B

I FEEL LONELY RIGHT BEFORE I GO TO SLEEP

a 16-year-old woman in california

i feel lonely scared more alone than ever
a woman

C

Main reasons

- **friendlessness**
- lovelessness
- separated from family
- depression

Observations

The predominant cause of loneliness, across all age groups and gender, is not having **friends**. This is followed by not having **love** in one's life and being away from **family**. The feeling is usually particularly strong when someone is surrounded by people who do have love in their lives. Interestingly, many people also describe feeling lonely in spite of being surrounded by friends, loved ones, or family. When people feel lonely, they also often feel **sad**, **depressed**, **empty**, and less often, **bored**. When lonely, people yearn to **talk** to somebody. People feel most lonely at **night**. ♥

LOST

15th most common feeling overall · 0.74% of all feelings are lost

Breakdowns
for people who feel lost

Gender breakdown: 54% (women) · 46% (men)

Age breakdown: 10s · 20s · 30s · 40s · 50+

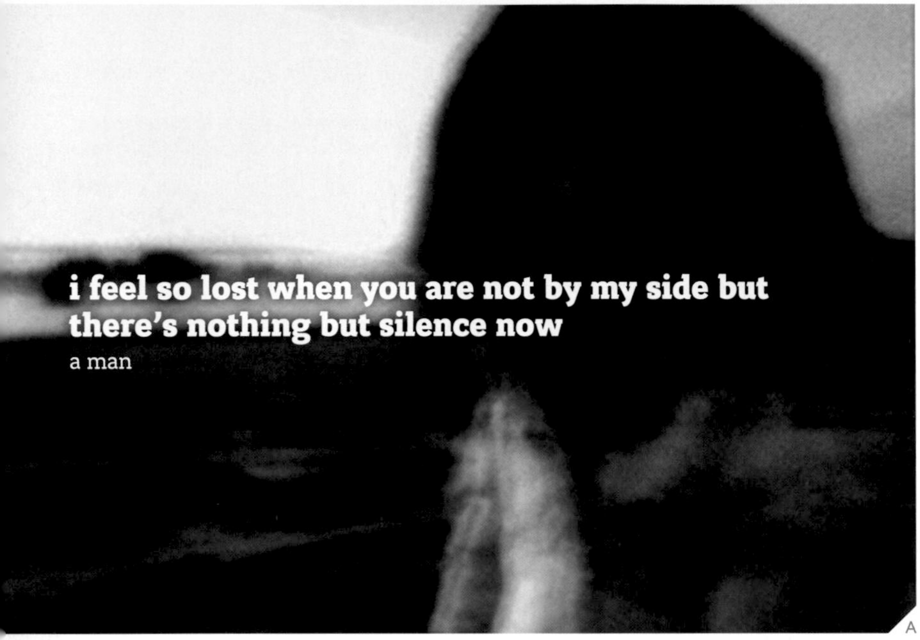

i feel so lost when you are not by my side but there's nothing but silence now
a man

A

I FEEL LIKE I'VE LOST EVERYONE CLOSE TO ME I'M MORE LONELY THAN I EVER HAVE BEEN BEFORE

a 20-year-old in louisiana

i have waited for years to begin work on my own projects but i must confess i feel a little lost
a man

B

i feel lost and wonder where i belong
a 26-year-old woman

C

i will never forget those weeks after this fire feeling totally lost

D

lost adj.

1. parted with unwillingly or unintentionally
2. no longer held or possessed
3. having wandered from or unable to find
4. hardened beyond sensibility or recovery

● i feel as though i'm going to be pretty lost without her next year ● i feel so lost so empty ● i feel completely lost in my world ● i'm feeling lost but there's got to be some place for me because if there isn't where will i go ● i feel strangly lost like i should be drinking more red bull and getting all the work done ● i feel lost in my empty state of mind at times traped by my own paranoia ● i feel lost and empty almost like the world is revolving around me in a dream ● i am feeling lost and alone even though i have family and friends who love me ● i totally feel lost not even your philosophy can help me ● i never had the feeling of being lost in my soul until now when i feel as though the world is against me lost

Season breakdown: 25% · 24% · **27%** · 24%

Related feelings mentioned with lost

- **confused**
- clueless
- unsure
- abandoned
- hopeless
- uncertain

i feel i'm getting lost
a woman

A

i feel i've lost my motivation to do great things
a 42-year-old man

B

I FEEL LIKE I WAITED TO GET TO THIS POINT FOR SO LONG AND NOW ITS HERE I'M IN COLLEGE AND I'M SO LOST
someone

Main reasons

- **loss of friendship**
- missing love
- confusion
- heartbreak

Observations

When people feel lost, they tend to express it in very strong ways. People who feel lost frequently express feeling **completely** lost or **totally** lost. People commonly express feeling lost when they are **alone**, after some type of **heartbreak**, or when they feel as though they do not know what they are doing and have **no direction** in life. When people feel lost, they also very often say they feel **confused**, and sometimes they say they feel **abandoned**. As people get older, they tend to feel less lost than they did when they were younger. ♥

LOVED

35 th most common feeling overall • 0.33% of all feelings are loved

Breakdowns
for people who feel loved

Gender breakdown 60% (women) 40% (men)

Age breakdown 10s 20s 30s 40s 50+

A

B

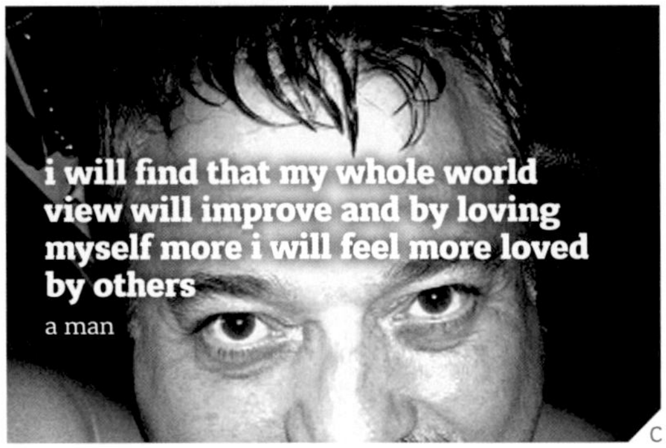

i will find that my whole world view will improve and by loving myself more i will feel more loved by others
a man

C

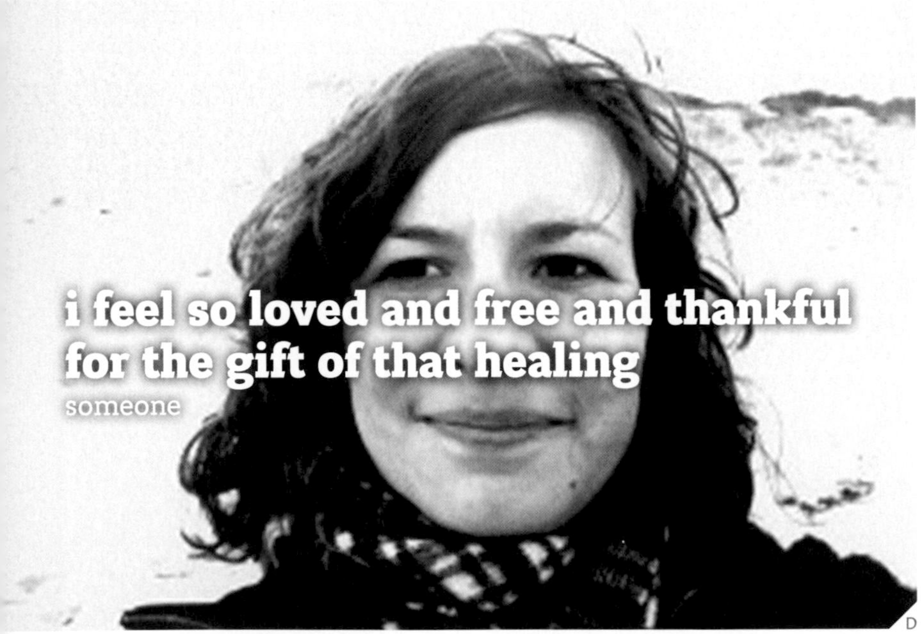

i feel so loved and free and thankful for the gift of that healing
someone

D

I ONLY FEEL LOVED WHEN I'M HAVING SEX WITH SOMEONE

someone

loved adj.

1. feeling of strong attachment
2. pre-eminent kindness or devotion
3. attachment to one of the opposite sex
4. affection; kind feeling; fondness

• i really just want someone to know that in order to make me feel loved you have to hold me • i stil feel loved and wanted and knowing that nikki is all mine makes me a thousand feet tall and ready to tackle the world • i feel loved when you celebrate my birthday with meaningful words written or spoken • i know what my weaknesses are: being lonely and wanting to feel loved • i can go from feeling totally in love totally loved and totally enraptured in one person one day and then feel totally in hate and kicking streetlights and cursing their day the next • i miss feeling loved and being hugged by people that mean it when they say i love you

Season breakdown 24% 24% **27%** 25%

Related feelings
mentioned with loved

- **appreciated**
- respected
- supported
- protected
- valued
- trusted

A

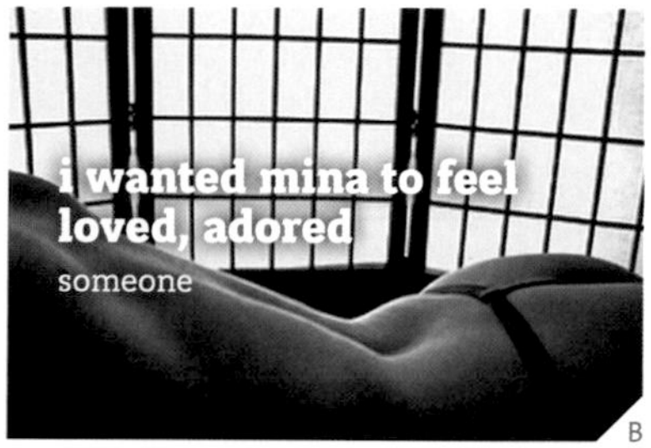

B

i feel so much irritation when being loved too much
someone

C

D

I FEEL LOVED BECAUSE GOD HAS FORGIVEN ME FOR CUTTING MYSELF OFF FROM HIM

someone

Main reasons

- **relationships**
- friendship
- family
- god

Observations

Women express feeling loved far more often than men do. Men and women across the board feel loved when they feel they are **cared for**, **valued**, **appreciated**, **accepted**, **supported**, and **protected**. People feel loved because their **significant others**, **friends**, or **family** have made them feel that way. **God** and **sex** also frequently make people feel loved. Feeling loved is often discussed in the context of **relationships**. ♥

LUCKY

34th most common feeling overall · 0.32% of all feelings are lucky

Breakdowns for people who feel lucky

Gender breakdown: 55% (women) · 45% (men)

Age breakdown: 10s · 20s · 30s · 40s · 50+

i've grown out of being invincible but i feel lucky
a man

A

I SHOULD FEEL LUCKY THAT MY INDULGENCE CONSISTS OF PIXELS RATHER THAN SOME MORE DAMAGING SUBSTANCE

a 25-year-old in lafayette, indiana

B

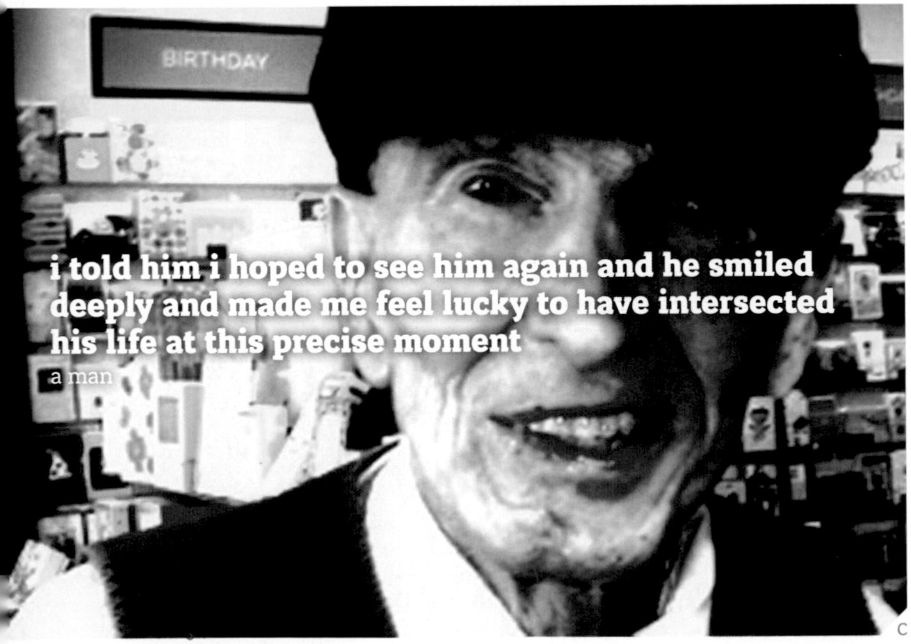

BIRTHDAY
i told him i hoped to see him again and he smiled deeply and made me feel lucky to have intersected his life at this precise moment
a man

C

I FEEL LUCKY TO HAVE A DAD WHO'S NEVER EVER AFRAID TO SAY HE LOVES US OR TO GIVE US A HUG

someone in indiana

lucky adj.

1. favored by luck
2. meeting with good success or fortune
3. producing good by chance
4. favorable; auspicious; fortunate

• i feel lucky when i get to hold his hand • i feel so lucky to have her as my little sister • i look at these family's and i feel like my parents and i are lucky • i love her so much and i feel so lucky to have her not only as a mom but as best friend • i feel very lucky to have people who want to see me happy and don't just mouth the words • i just lost a boyfriend and i feel lucky that i even had the time to spend those moments with him • i love what i do and feel so lucky to be able to do what i love for a living • i feel very lucky to have someone like julien in my life and i sometimes wonder if i am going to wake up and cry when i realise i was dreaming

Season breakdown

28% | 22% | 24% | 26%

Related feelings mentioned with lucky

wonderful
thankful
grateful
blessed
awesome
privileged

Melissa's grandmother was given this flag in honor of her son who recently passed away. He fought in the Vietnam war where he was exposed to agent orange, an herbicide used in combat. He died as a result. Melissa was honored to have seen the passing of the flag.

i feel lucky to have experienced it
a woman
A

I DO APPRECIATE CERTAIN ASPECTS OF HAVING MY FATHER ALIVE AND I FEEL VERY LUCKY

someone

i hope that you can appreciate every single day you see her get on that bus and feel as happy and lucky as you feel today
someone
B

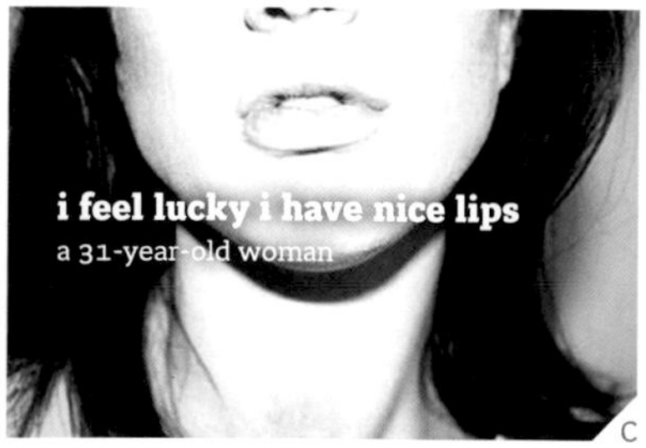

i feel lucky i have nice lips
a 31-year-old woman
C

i feel so lucky to live in sonoma
someone
D

Main reasons

significant other
friends
family
experiences

Observations

People who feel lucky are often the same people who feel grateful and blessed. **Older people** and women feel more lucky. Young women feel lucky for their **boyfriend**, while young men are less likely to say that about their **girlfriend**. However, married men are more likely to say they feel lucky to be with their **wives**. Everyone feels lucky for **opportunities** and **experiences**, and in their 20s they feel lucky to have a **job**. People often feel lucky around **Christmas**, and less strongly, **Thanksgiving**, because they see **friends** and **family**, have time to reflect, and in some cases, get gifts. ♥

MISERABLE

98 th most common feeling overall · 0.13% of all feelings are miserable

Breakdowns
for people who feel miserable

Gender breakdown — 52% · 48%

Age breakdown — 10s · 20s · 30s · 40s · 50+

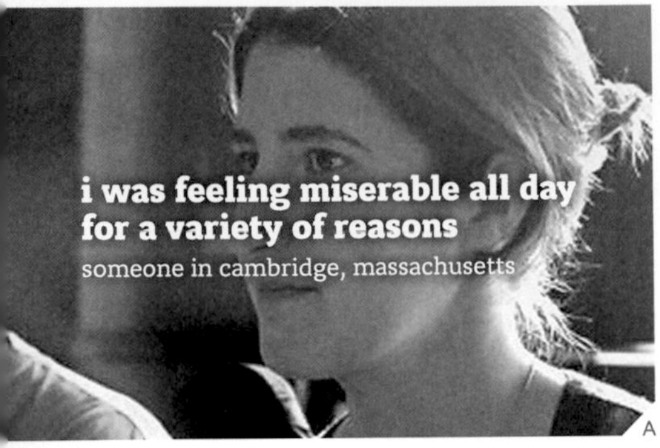

i was feeling miserable all day for a variety of reasons
someone in cambridge, massachusetts

A

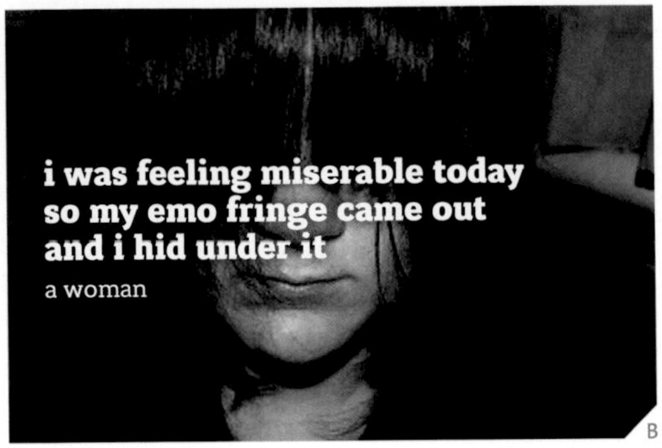

i was feeling miserable today so my emo fringe came out and i hid under it
a woman

B

I FEEL MISERABLE, I CAN'T REMEMBER THE LAST PERSON I ACTUALLY SPOKE TO, I FEEL ISOLATED, I FEEL LIKE A PRISONER AND AM FED UP WITH MY LIVING SITUATION AND MY HEALTH ISSUES

a 25-year-old in london, england

C

D

miserable adj.

1. very unhappy; wretched
2. causing unhappiness or misery
3. worthless; mean; despicable
4. abject; deplorable

● i don't think i could feel anymore miserable then i do right now ● i feel miserable because i felt helpless at my new job ● i feel absolutely miserable today mostly just physically miserable but that doesn't seem to bother my thinking at all ● i really can't handle hangovers at the moment they make me feel so miserable ● i feel miserable to miss him so much and send him whiny text messages that he doesn't even respond to ● i could see my sister dancing and having fun from afar and that made me feel somewhat miserable ● i'm feeling pretty miserable over some things that didn't happen this year ● i have been feeling so miserable for the past 7 weeks

Season breakdown 21% 26% 27% 26%

Related feelings mentioned with miserable

- **unhappy**
- depressed
- hopeless
- cold
- sore
- sick

i woke up feeling miserable yesterday and not wanting to go
someone

A

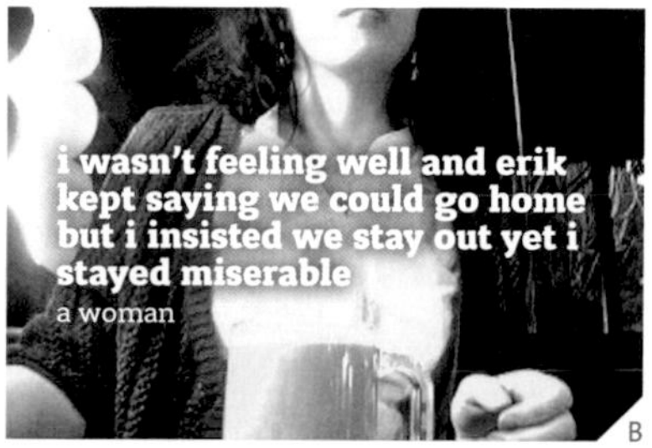

i wasn't feeling well and erik kept saying we could go home but i insisted we stay out yet i stayed miserable
a woman

B

i end up feeling even more miserable
someone

C

I JUST WANT TO BE ABLE TO BLAME SOMEONE FOR THIS AND BE ABLE TO SWEAR AT THEM FOR MAKING ME FEEL SO MISERABLE

someone

Main reasons

- **illness**
- sleeplessness
- school
- job

Observations

Miserable is an incredibly strong emotion. People commonly express feeling either **absolutely** miserable or **completely** miserable. Most often, they feel that way when they are **sick**, **tired**, or **sleepless**. People very often deal with their feelings of misery by going to **bed**. Women are frequently made to feel miserable when they are involved in a **bad relationship** or when **love has left** their lives. Men, on the other hand, are very different and are more likely to express **hope** that people who have hurt them in the past will end up feeling miserable. ♥

NAKED

171 st most common feeling overall · 0.07% of all feelings are naked

Breakdowns
for people who feel naked

Gender breakdown 54% 46%

Age breakdown 10s 20s 30s 40s 50+

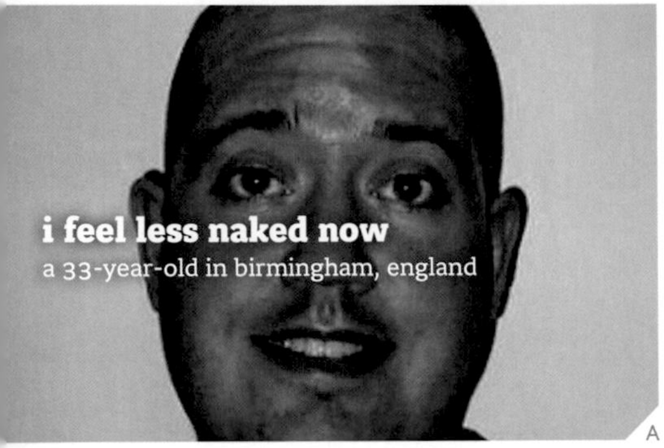

i feel less naked now
a 33-year-old in birmingham, england

A

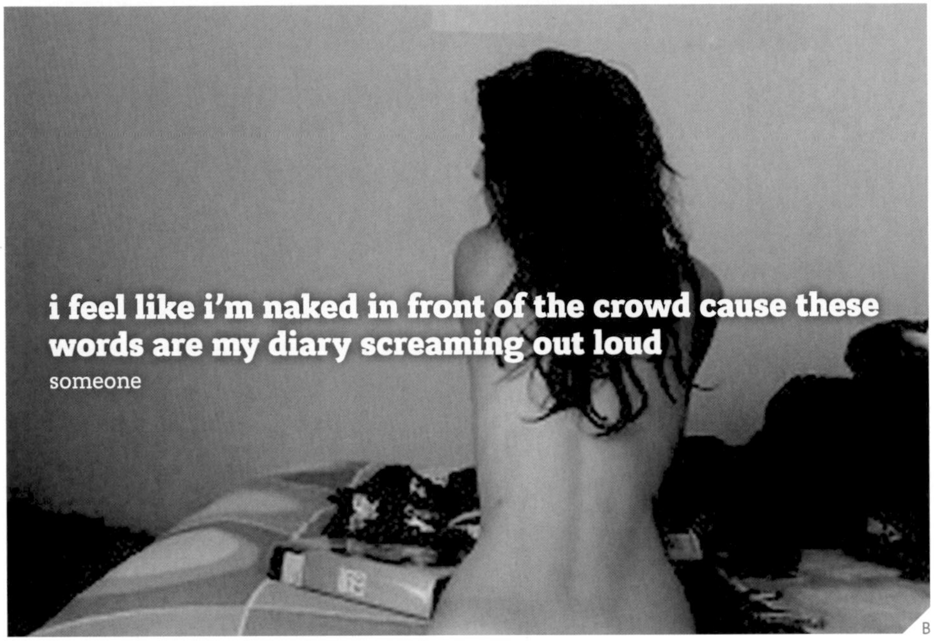

i feel like i'm naked in front of the crowd cause these words are my diary screaming out loud
someone

B

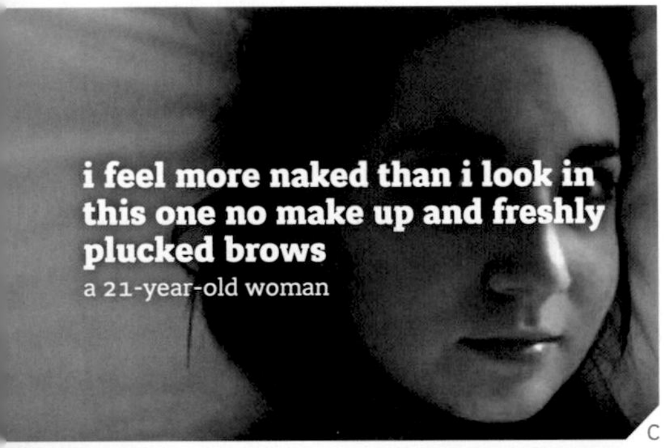

i feel more naked than i look in this one no make up and freshly plucked brows
a 21-year-old woman

C

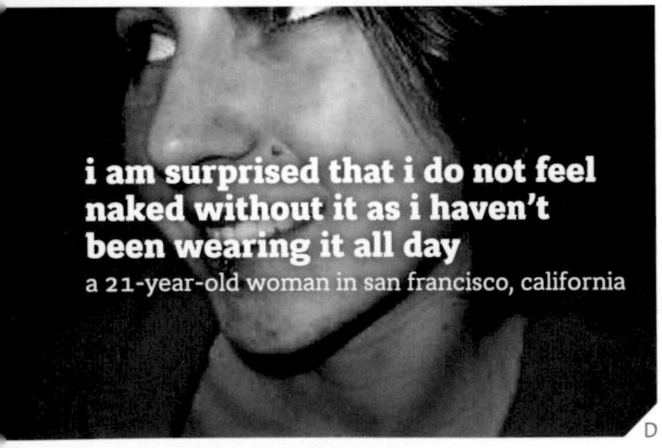

i am surprised that i do not feel naked without it as i haven't been wearing it all day
a 21-year-old woman in san francisco, california

D

I FEEL LIKE STRIPPING MYSELF NAKED BEFORE YOU AND TEARING OUT MY HEART AND SHOWING YOU HOW DARK IT REALLY IS AND THEN ASKING YOU TO STILL LOVE ME

someone in london, england

naked adj.

1. having no clothes on; uncovered; nude
2. having no means of protection
3. lacking desirable means of sustenance
4. mere; simple; plain

● i feel naked because i chose to wear a sparing low percentage of black today ● i feel so naked without my avatar ● i'll feel extremely naked without a car ● i feel weirdly naked under my clothes today ● i imagine this is what it feels like to sit naked in the rain and not care about anything at all ● i want to feel your touch on my naked flesh ● i feel naked without painted nails ● i feel naked without my lip piercings: and at the same time kinda annoyed that the retainers are still visible ● i cant believe how amazing it feels i look at my body naked in the mirror and i feel beautiful i feel like a woman not a child not a shinny and polished play thing for some porn magazine

Season breakdown 26% 25% 24% 25%

Related feelings mentioned with naked

bare
exposed
pure
vulnerable
cold
awake

I FEEL NAKED UNDER HIS GAZE AS IF HE CAN STRIP AWAY ALL AND SEE ME AS I TRULY AM

someone in latham, new york

i feel naked and scared and this world can be so cold
someone

A

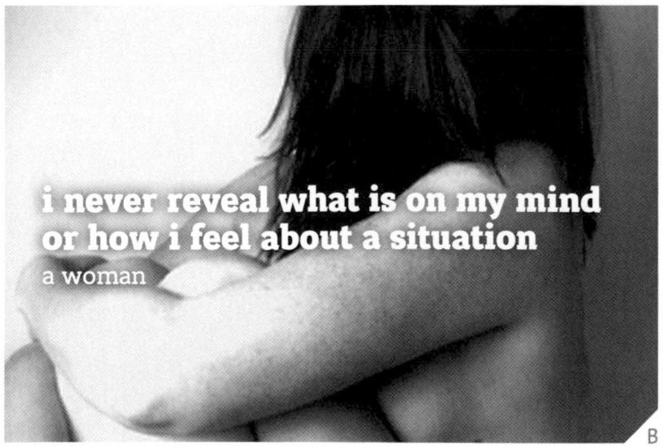

i never reveal what is on my mind or how i feel about a situation
a woman

B

C

I FEEL SO NAKED AND UGLY THESE DAYS

someone

Main reasons

not wearing clothes
missing an accessory
not wearing makeup
vulnerability

Observations

People most frequently express feeling naked when they are not wearing an accessory that they usually wear; examples include their **cell phone**, **watch**, **ring**, **earrings**, or their **glasses** (in that order). Women often feel naked after they have gotten a **haircut** or when they are not wearing any **makeup**. Men most commonly feel naked after they have shaved their **facial hair**. *We Feel Fine* noticed a strong trend of women reporting that they feel naked when they are also feeling **vulnerable** or **exposed**, while men almost never discuss feeling naked in that sense. ♥

Breakdowns
for people who feel normal

Gender breakdown 👩 **52%** 👨 **48%**

Age breakdown
10s 20s 30s 40s 50+

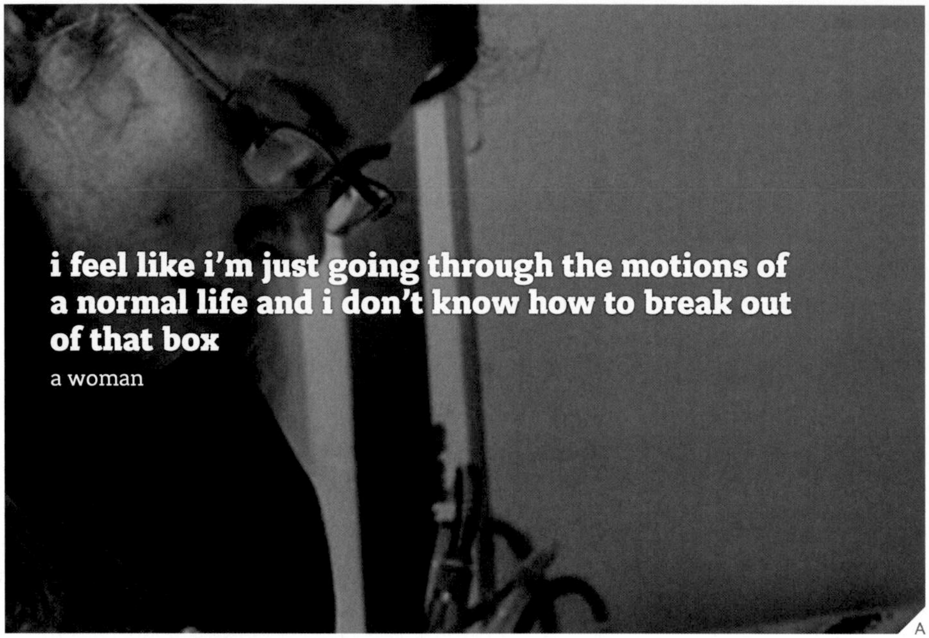

i feel like i'm just going through the motions of a normal life and i don't know how to break out of that box
a woman

A

he makes me believe i can feel normal again so i won't be afraid of life anymore
a woman

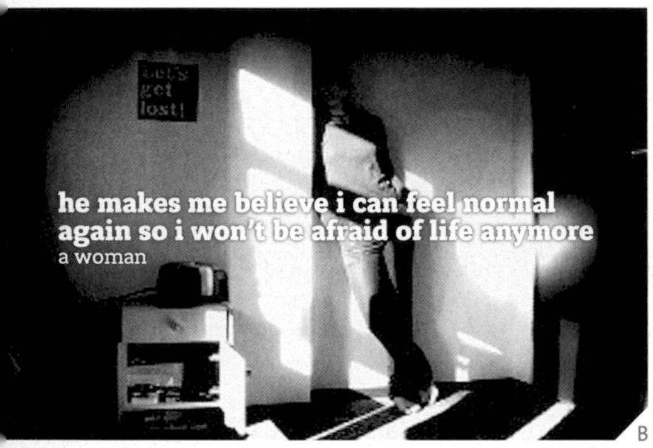

B

I DO PLAN ON TAKING HOWEVER LONG IT TAKES TO FEEL NORMAL AGAIN AND THIS MAY MEAN THAT YOU DON'T HEAR MUCH HAPPY STUFF FROM ME
someone

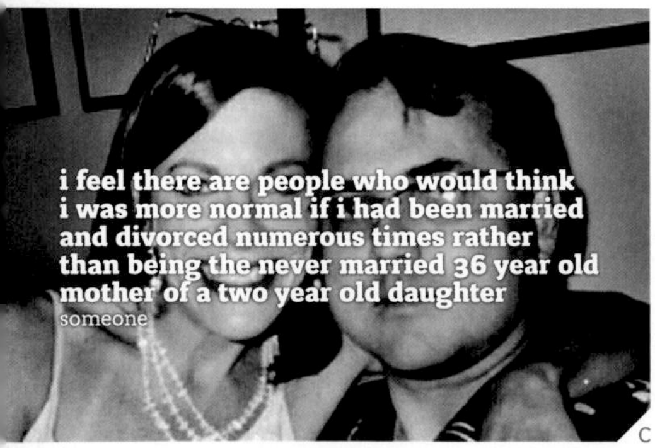

i feel there are people who would think i was more normal if i had been married and divorced numerous times rather than being the never married 36 year old mother of a two year old daughter
someone

C

i feel alternately normal and then sickly
a woman

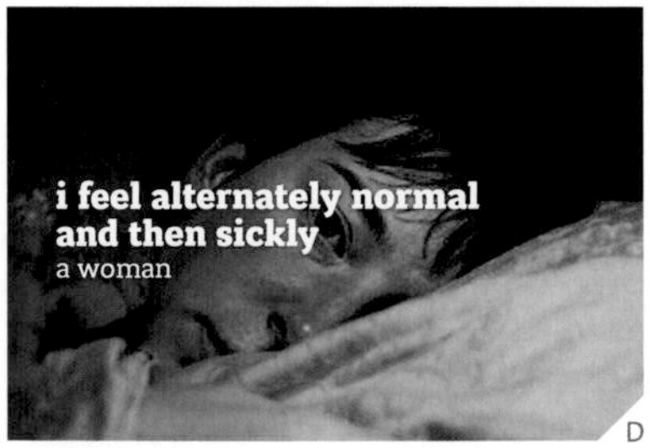

D

normal adj.

1. according to an established norm or rule
2. conformed to a type or standard
3. performing the proper functions
4. regular; natural; analogical

● i know that during the surgery nerves were severed and this will take some time before the skin will feel normal ● i feel completely normal even though i have the suspicion that i'm driving 100mph headlong into a brick wall ● i haven't had to take any pain meds today and one side of my jaw feels perfectly normal ● i feel like i have everything normal and everything abnormal in a father daughter relationship ● i suppose things feel more normal as of now but that would be under the presumption that i know what normal is these days ● i now feel a lot more like my normal self with a lot more energy too ● i just want to start feeling normal again so i can go to the gym

Season breakdown 24% 24% 25% 27%

Related feelings mentioned with normal

human
numb
average
healthy
accepted
crazy

I GET TWINGES OF JEALOUSY WHEN I SEE THEM FLIRTING I THINK ANYONE IN MY POSITION WOULD FEEL THAT WAY I THINK ITS NORMAL

someone

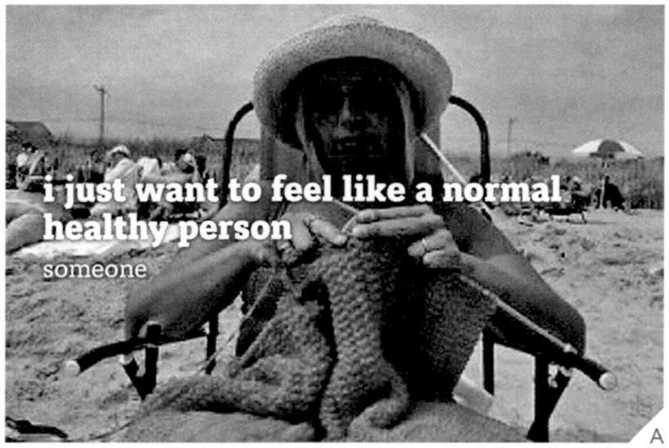
i just want to feel like a normal healthy person
someone

A

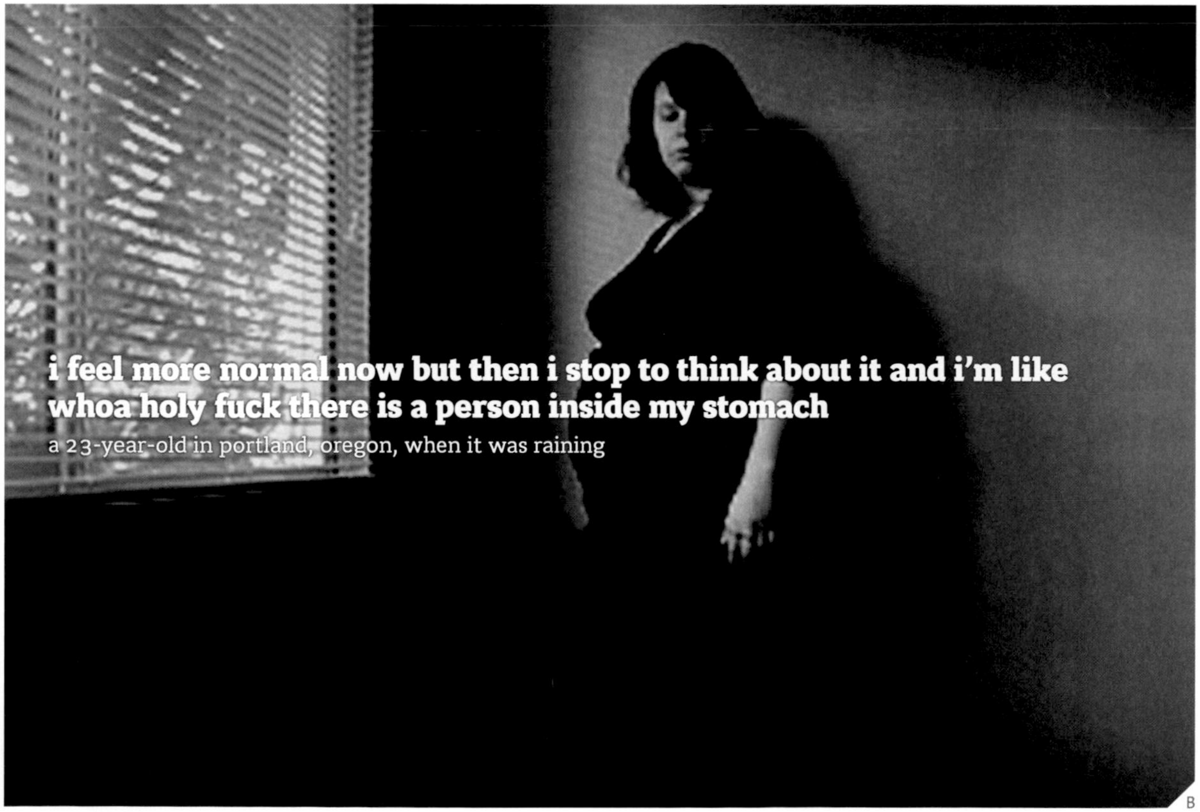
i feel more normal now but then i stop to think about it and i'm like whoa holy fuck there is a person inside my stomach
a 23-year-old in portland, oregon, when it was raining

B

I FINALLY FEEL SOMEWHAT NORMAL BUT I'VE LAPSED ON MY ANTI-DEPRESSANTS

someone

Main reasons

meds
sleep
coffee
recovery

Observations

People generally talk about feeling normal in contrast to recent abnormal feelings, and people say they feel **relatively** normal or **halfway** normal (although a large number of people do feel **perfectly** normal). One of the strongest reasons for feeling normal is **going on meds**, and less commonly, going **off meds**. People will often feel normal after coming out of a period of **depression** or prolonged **pain**. Women are more aware of how hormonal changes affect their feeling normal, especially during **pregnancy**. **Sleep** helps people feel normal. ♥

OLD

17th most common feeling overall · 0.63% of all feelings are old

Breakdowns
for people who feel old

Gender breakdown: 52% (women) · 48% (men)

Age breakdown: 10s · 20s · 30s · 40s · 50+

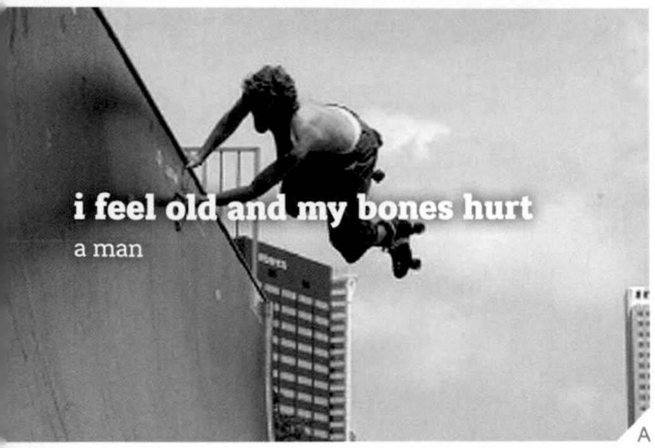

i feel old and my bones hurt
a man

A

I FEEL SO OLD YET IMMATURE USELESS AND UNACCOMPLISHED FOR MY AGE ALTHOUGH I KNOW I SHOULDN'T
a 22-year-old woman in arlington, texas

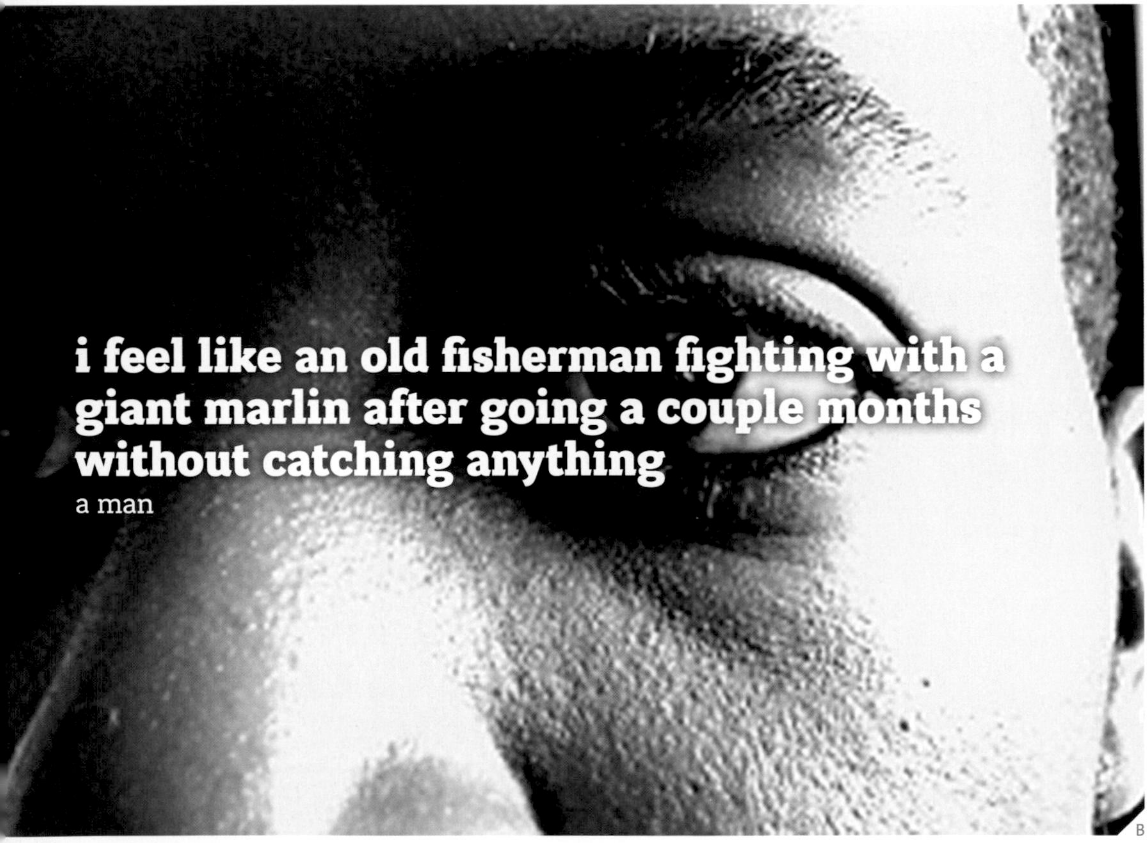

i feel like an old fisherman fighting with a giant marlin after going a couple months without catching anything
a man

B

i feel like i'm 75 years old
someone

C

old adj.

1. not young; advanced far in years or life
2. not new or fresh; not recently made
3. continued in life
2. worn out; weakened or exhausted by use

● i feel old and sometimes i feel like i have everyone tricked into thinking i'm an adult ● i feel old because i feel like i'm always tired even when i know i'm not ● i feel like i'm an old lady my back hurts legs hurt and the chest pain is now a constant thing once again ● i have an eight-year-old son oliver who is becoming a little man and the feeling that he needs his old man around is becoming too strong for me to ignore ● i feel like an old broken down palace once loved and taken care of but now am rarely visited and starting to fall apart ● i just feel old next to all those young girls but i think i'm keeping up pretty good ● i'm tired of feeling so old and used up

Season breakdown — 25% · 25% · 25% · 25%

Related feelings mentioned with old

- **aged**
- worn
- ancient
- mature
- wise

i agree that it is way to soon for you to be feeling old
a man

A

i feel like an old man at 21
a man

B

Dana is the eldest daughter of John, the blogger. (He has 8 children!) This photograph was taken before her senior prom

I'M GOING TO FEEL LIKE SUCH AN OLD WOMAN FOR SAYING THIS BUT: KIDS THESE DAYS SUCK

an 18-year-old in london, england, when it was rainy

i feel old saying this but i can remember when she was born
a woman

D

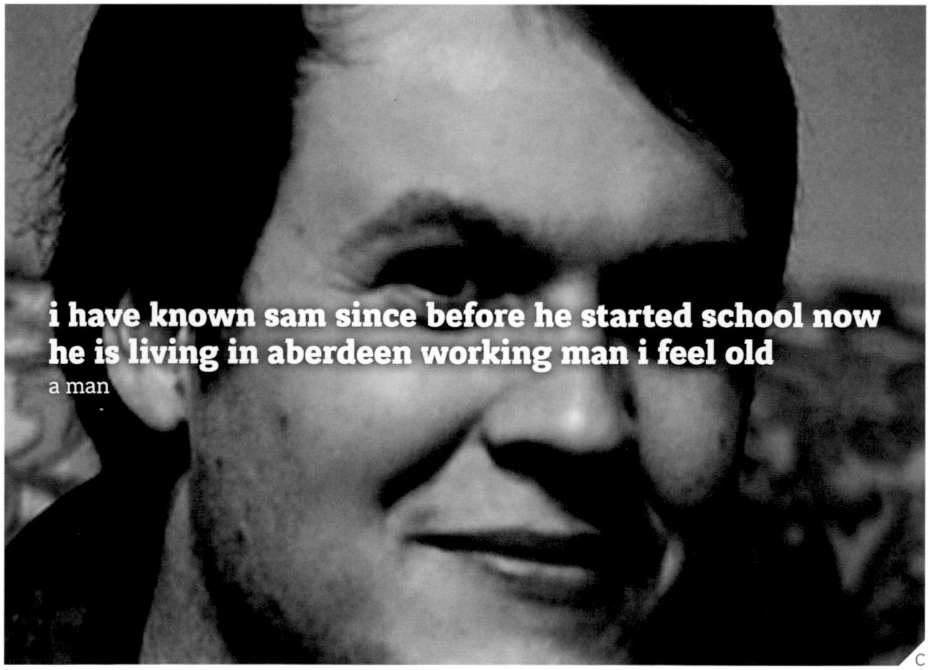

i have known sam since before he started school now he is living in aberdeen working man i feel old
a man

C

Main reasons

- **age**
- pain
- kids
- fatigue

Observations

As people get older, they feel older, but once they pass their 40s, old age and feeling old are no longer correlated. Most people who say they feel old express **anxiety over aging**, and many of them are quite young. There is a spike in feeling old in the **late 20s** and **mid 30s**. There is a lot of introspection around one's age in the **early 20s**, especially upon **graduating** college. Often, people will feel old on their **birthday**, when they are **tired** and feel they shouldn't be, or when they're **married**. **Nostalgia** makes people feel old, and younger people equate being old to being **boring**. ♥

OVERWHELMED

67th most common feeling overall · 0.20% of all feelings are overwhelmed

Breakdowns
for people who feel overwhelmed

Gender breakdown: 63% (women) · 37% (men)

Age breakdown: 10s · 20s · 30s · 40s · 50+

i feel overwhelmed just knowing its friday
a man

A

i feel completely overwhelmed when i'm with her
a 19-year-old in wales, united kingdom

B

I FEEL SO OVERWHELMED I JUST WANT TO SIT DOWN AND CRY
someone

This photograph was taken of a graveyard in Nunavut, the largest of the Northwest territories of Canada. Here, the youth suicide rate of its largely Inuit population is the highest in Canada. Maureen, who was in Nunavut for 18 months witnessed a small community of 1500 people lose 4 youths to suicide. ↓

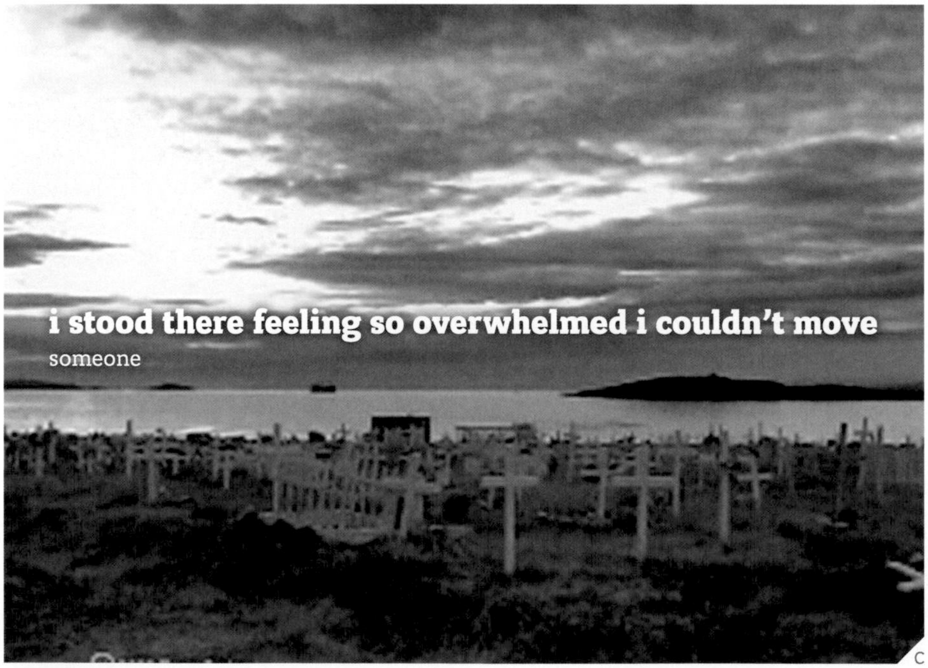

i stood there feeling so overwhelmed i couldn't move
someone

C

i feel overwhelmed by sadness
a woman

D

overwhelmed adj.

1. to cover over completely; bury; engulf
2. projected or impended over threateningly
3. completely surround or overpower
4. mentally or physically overpowering

● i feel so overwhelmed with life ● i don't choose to be this way but at times i just feel so overwhelmed ● i just say i feel so overwhelmed with joy right now cause im actually in school for science doing something productive ● i smile whenever i feel overwhelmed by guilt or shame ● i'm not the only one feeling a bit overwhelmed sometimes : cheers ● i feel overwhelmed by bureaucratic lunacy and unchecked child proofing ● i feel very overwhelmed right now with all the stuff i have to do to the point that it's causing me to just shut down ● i feel like i've been sort of overwhelmed lately and my thoughts and dreams keep getting the better of me

Season breakdown 23% **27%** 25% 25%

Related feelings mentioned with overwhelmed

- **pressured**
- stressed
- frustrated
- confused
- exhausted
- unsure

i was just feeling overwhelmed and a bit panicky and so i cried for a while
a 43-year-old woman
A

i'm feeling completely overwhelmed but in a good way
someone in portland, oregon, when it was raining
B

i feel overwhelmed by my heartbeats and i want be left alone
a woman
C

I FEEL HIS LOVE AND GOODNESS AND I FEEL OVERWHELMED

a woman

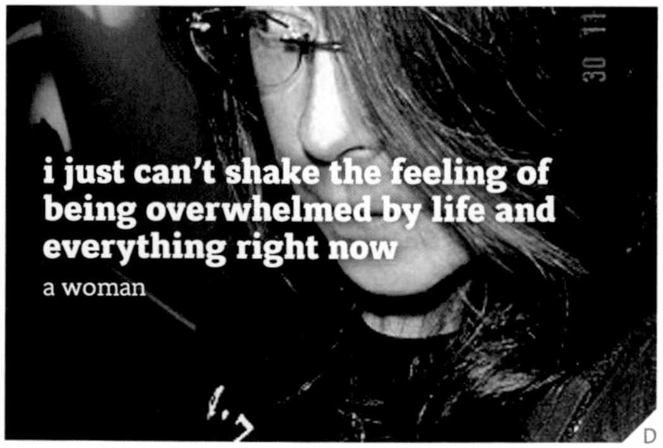

i just can't shake the feeling of being overwhelmed by life and everything right now
a woman
D

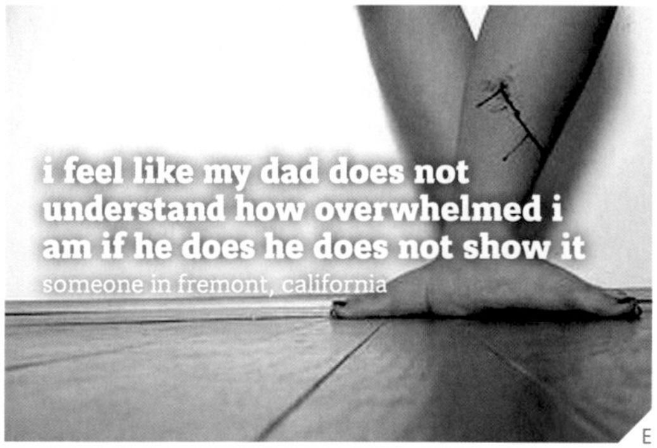

i feel like my dad does not understand how overwhelmed i am if he does he does not show it
someone in fremont, california
E

i got this overwhelming feeling today of loving her
someone
F

Main reasons

- **love**
- school
- business
- emotions

Observations

People feel overwhelmed when they are **starting** to feel overwhelmed, are **trying not** to feel overwhelmed, and are **completely** and **totally** overwhelmed. The biggest cause of being overwhelmed is too much **work**, whether it be a **job** or **school**; this causes a feeling of **stress** or **fatigue**. People are also overwhelmed by **emotions**, especially **love**, and when they feel overwhelmed they often turn to **God**. Women feel overwhelmed more than men. As people gain more responsibilities, they feel more overwhelmed, mainly in their **30s** and **40s**. ♥

PROUD

56 th most common feeling overall · 0.22% of all feelings are proud

Breakdowns
for people who feel proud

Gender breakdown 48% 52%

Age breakdown 10s 20s 30s 40s 50+

i feel proud and at the same time uncomfortable
someone

A

i feel somewhat proud though
a 20-year-old in istanbul, turkey

B

I WAS THINKING ABOUT HOW THESE HAVE BEEN SOME OF THE HARDEST MONTHS AND HARDEST TIMES OF MY LIFE AND HOW I SHOULD FEEL PROUD THAT I'VE HELD SHIT TOGETHER

someone

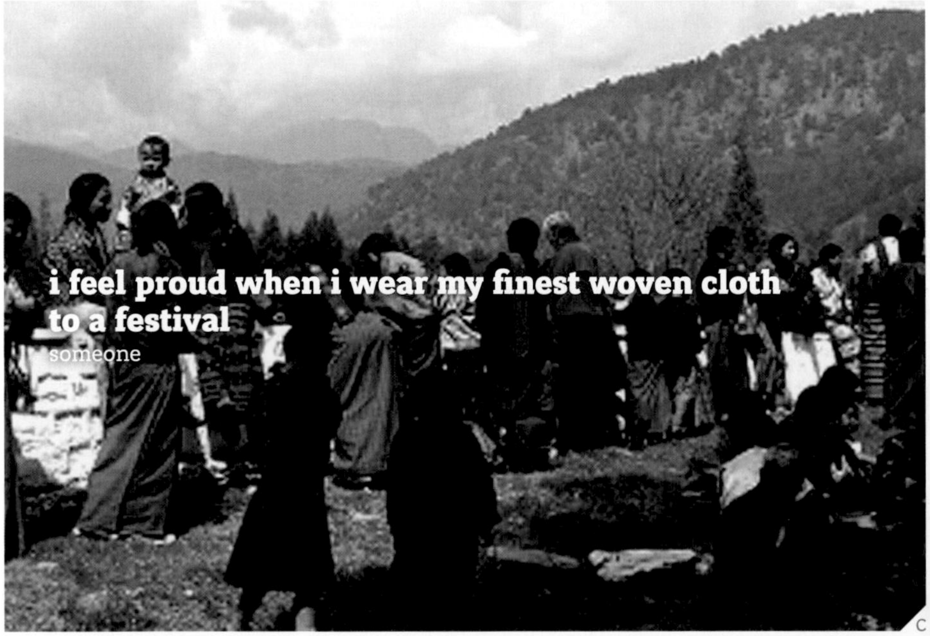

i feel proud when i wear my finest woven cloth to a festival
someone

C

proud adj.

1. feeling or manifesting pride
2. giving reason or occasion for pride
3. worthy of admiration; admirable
4. feeling self-respect

• i feel that you are proud of all the care that i put in • i would feel proud as a woman i would feel proud as an american • i'm not sure what but i hope you feel proud that you made the world that much of a better place by spreading the happy and the kind because i will not forget it • i feel like a proud mommy • i climbed it alone feeling pretty proud of my 58 year old body • i can speak from experience that seeing a child feel proud about something they have created is one of the most rewarding sights to behold • i honestly feel like i have nothing to say for myself like there's nothing for him to be proud of me for • i feel proud my relationship is now validated

Season breakdown 26% · 24% · 24% · 26%

Related feelings mentioned with proud

- **ashamed**
- smart
- brave
- successful
- privileged
- capable

i was feeling rather proud of myself
someone

A

i feel so proud to be holding the kansas flag
someone

B

I FEEL VERY PROUD TO DISCUSS MY MILITARY SERVICE WITH KIDS WHO ASK ME ABOUT IT

someone in iraq

i'll feel like such a proud parent when i let go of that bike seat and watch her ride off into the sunset
someone

C

↑ Pam was voted Miss Deaf Kansas on January 11, 2006. Her reign lasted 2 years.

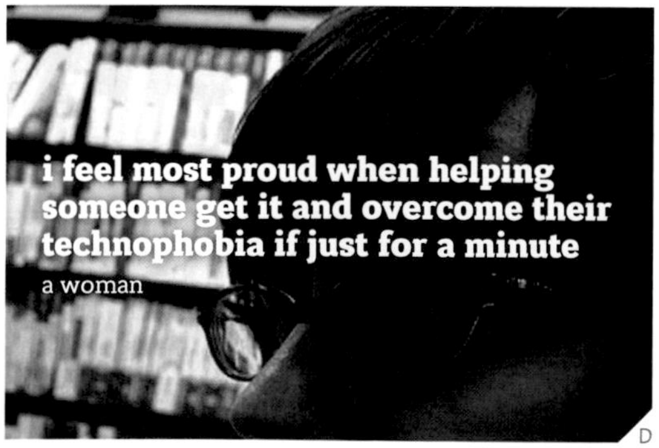

i feel most proud when helping someone get it and overcome their technophobia if just for a minute
a woman

D

Main reasons

- **myself**
- country
- achievements
- heritage

Observations

People most commonly express feeling proud of **themselves** and proud of their **country**. In the United States, there was a particularly strong feeling of national pride expressed on **Election Day 2008**, and the days immediately following. Many people state that they are proud of their **achievements**, their **heritage**, and their **children**, and when they or people close to them are **brave**, **smart**, or **successful**. *We Feel Fine* found that there is a particularly strong feeling of pride in **India**, and **men** tend to express feeling proud more often than women. ♥

SAD

14th most common feeling overall · 0.82% of all feelings are sad

Breakdowns
for people who feel sad

Gender breakdown 58% 42%

Age breakdown 10s 20s 30s 40s 50+

I FEEL SAD I WASN'T THE DAUGHTER YOU WANTED

someone

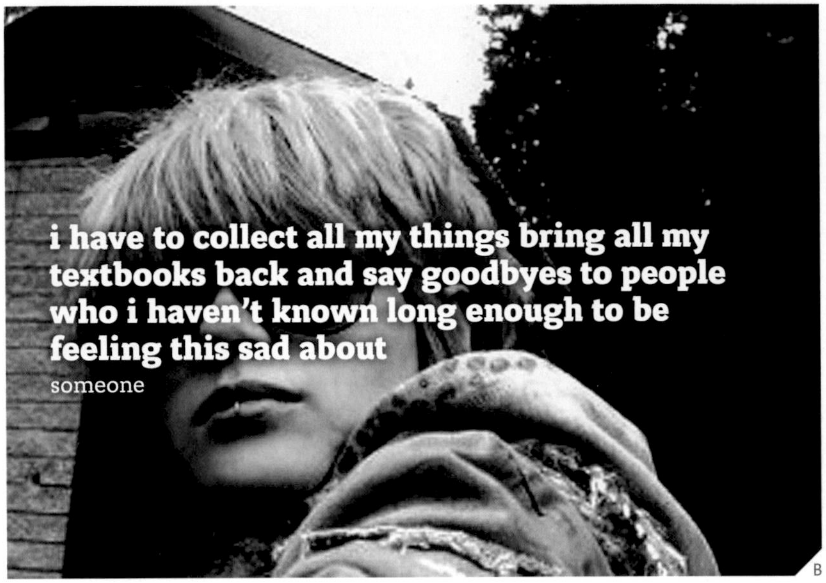
i have to collect all my things bring all my textbooks back and say goodbyes to people who i haven't known long enough to be feeling this sad about
someone
B

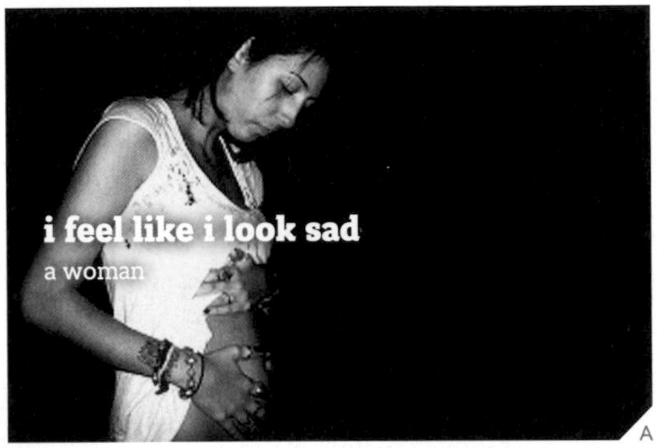
i feel like i look sad
a woman
A

i may feel sad when i see couples in love
a woman
C

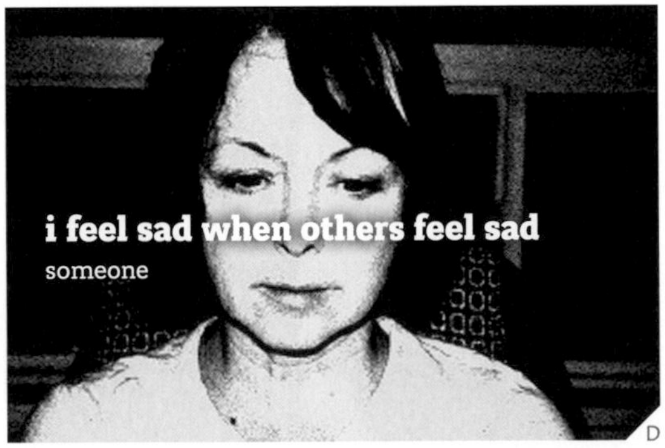
i feel sad when others feel sad
someone
D

sad adj.

1. depressing; of little worth
2. dull; grave; dark; somber
3. serious; grave; sober
4. affected with grief or unhappiness

● i don't understand why i feel sad every time i see you out with someone new ● i feel soo sad that my baby is growing out of his babyness right in front of my eyes ● i realized that i've been denying something for quite sometime to avoid feeling sad about it ● i start feeling sad because i miss you i remind myself how lucky i am to have someone so special to miss ● i don't have a girlfriend and i only have one friend but i feel sad ● i feel so sad for those people who lost friends in the shooting ● i've been feeling sad about getting my life stolen away from me so suddenly ● i feel sad because sarah and britney are complete bitches ● i still feel very sad 26 years after losing a baby full term

Season breakdown 25% **26%** 25% 23%

Related feelings mentioned with sad

angry
depressed
disappointed
lonely
confused
hopeless

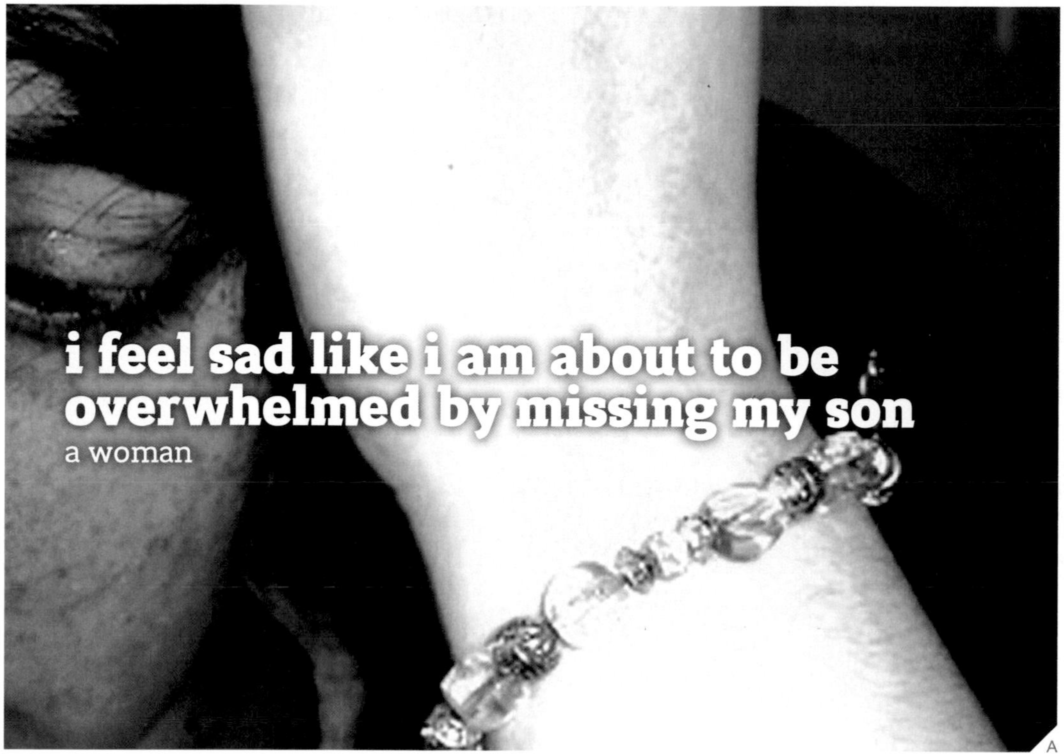

i feel sad like i am about to be overwhelmed by missing my son
a woman

A

This photograph was taken shortly after Heather lost her son Aodin R Hurd. Just 19 weeks after conception Aodin was stillborn. Two years after this tragedy she gave birth to Evi, a beautiful healthy little girl.

I FEEL SAD REMOVING HIS NUMBER FROM MY CELL TODAY

someone

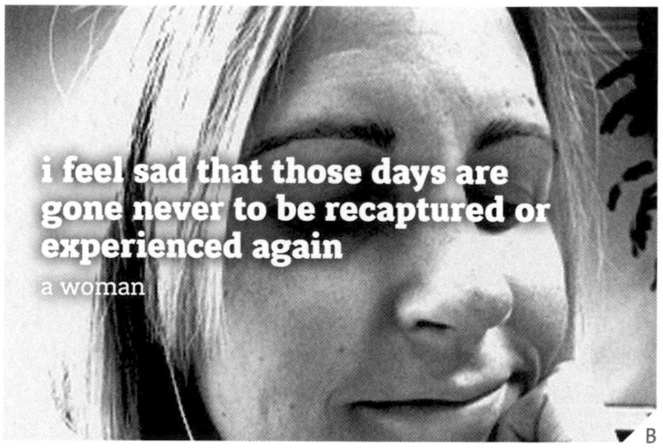

i feel sad that those days are gone never to be recaptured or experienced again
a woman

B

Main reasons

- **love**
- loneliness
- depression
- heartbreak

Observations

Being **lonely** is the single most commonly expressed reason for sadness. Unsurprisingly, people often feel sad and **depressed** at the same time. Curiously, people also feel sad and **angry** at the same time. People also frequently express feeling sad and **confused** at the same time, and this happens particularly when they are younger. The **death** of a family member, a friend, or a pet makes people feel sadness, and so does **heartbreak**. People regularly say that they will **wake up** feeling sad, and women express feeling sad far more than men do. ♥

SEXY

173 rd most common feeling overall · 0.07% of all feelings are sexy

Breakdowns
for people who feel sexy

Gender breakdown 64% 36%

Age breakdown 10s 20s 30s 40s 50+

i feel so damn sexy when i'm in my melrose street dress
a woman

A

I GOT TO GIVE LUKE A MAKESHIFT LAP DANCE ON SUNDAY WHICH WAS FUN AND MADE ME FEEL SEXY EVEN WITH MY FAT WHICH I KNOW HE DOESN'T MIND

i was feeling sexy so i took a self portrait
someone

B

sexy adj.

1. erotic or stimulating in a sexual way
2. pleasing, appealing, or beautiful
3. attractive
4. emitting sexuality

• i didn't feel sexy enough to pull those clothes off and it's been a sign of my lack of self esteem • i put on this black dress shirt that i bought a while ago and i have this sudden feeling of sexy • i feel sexy after my workout • i'm just feeling sexy damn it • i feel she's sexy because of the entire package • i am a 19 year old women who is looking for someone who can make me feel sexy • i am not feeling very sexy because i haven't gotten a brazilian wax in a long time • i am going to find a new corset since i gained a mess of weight it should help out plus it makes me feel sexy and i need that • i love feeling sexy and powerful and fucking proud of myself for once

Season breakdown 27% 25% 23% 25%

Related feelings mentioned with sexy

gorgeous
attractive
naughty
feminine
cute
sexual

A

I FEEL SEXY JUST BY CHANGING THE COLOR OF MY BRA

someone

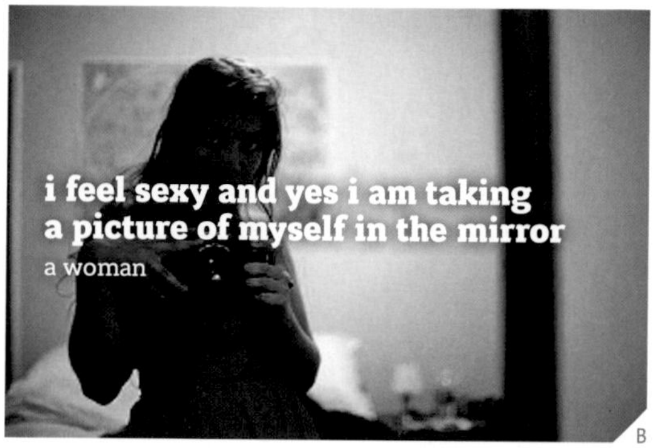

i feel sexy and yes i am taking a picture of myself in the mirror
a woman

B

C

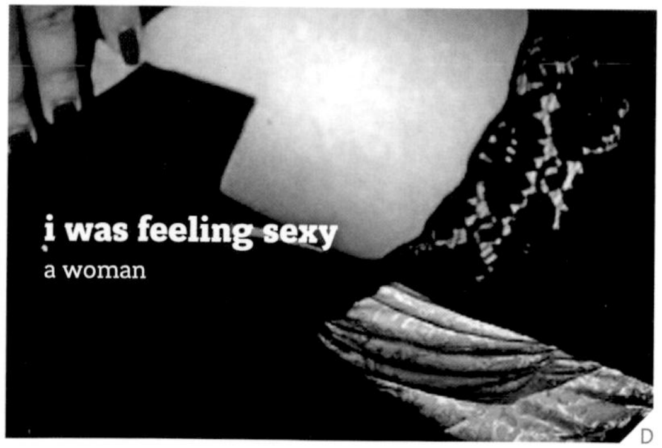

D

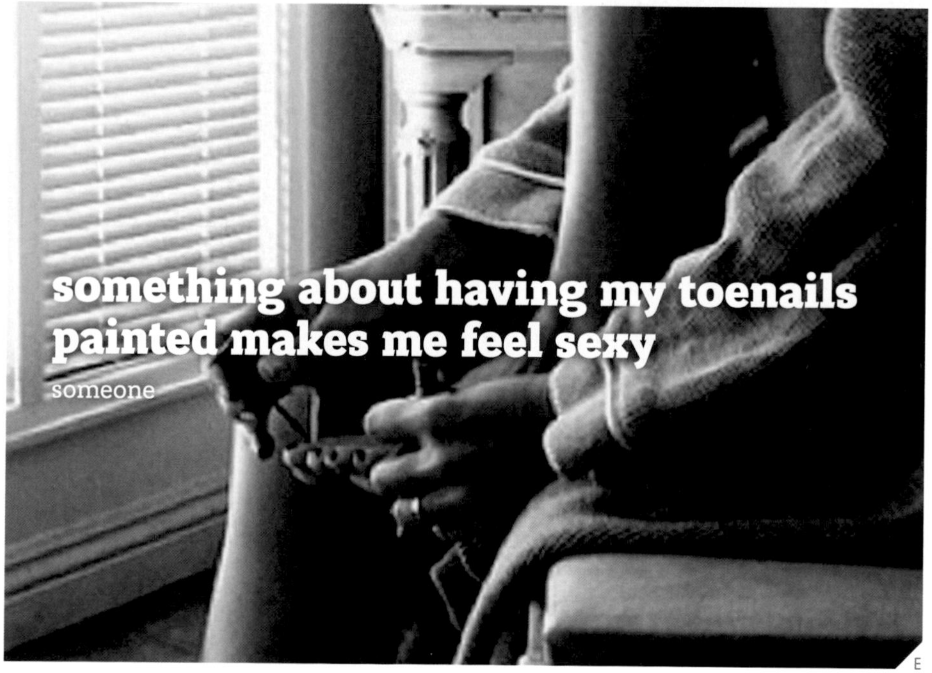

something about having my toenails painted makes me feel sexy
someone

E

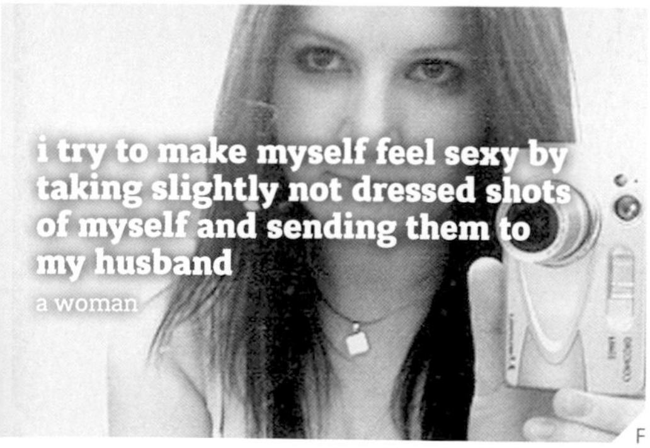

i try to make myself feel sexy by taking slightly not dressed shots of myself and sending them to my husband
a woman

F

Main reasons

- **being loved**
- clothing
- black lingerie
- high heels

Observations

Sexy is a feeling that is primarily felt and expressed by women. In comparison, men rarely say that they feel sexy. Women often feel sexy when wearing **lingerie**, particularly **black lingerie**, and when they wear **high heels** or **boots**. More generally, dressing in a certain article of **clothing** will often make a woman feel sexy, as will having **good hair**. Women in their **30s** feel more sexy than women at any other age. **Teenagers** and people over **50** express feeling sexy much less often than people in any other age group. ♥

SICK

7th most common feeling overall · 0.10% of all feelings are sick

Breakdowns
for people who feel sick

Gender breakdown 55% 45%

Age breakdown 10s 20s 30s 40s 50+

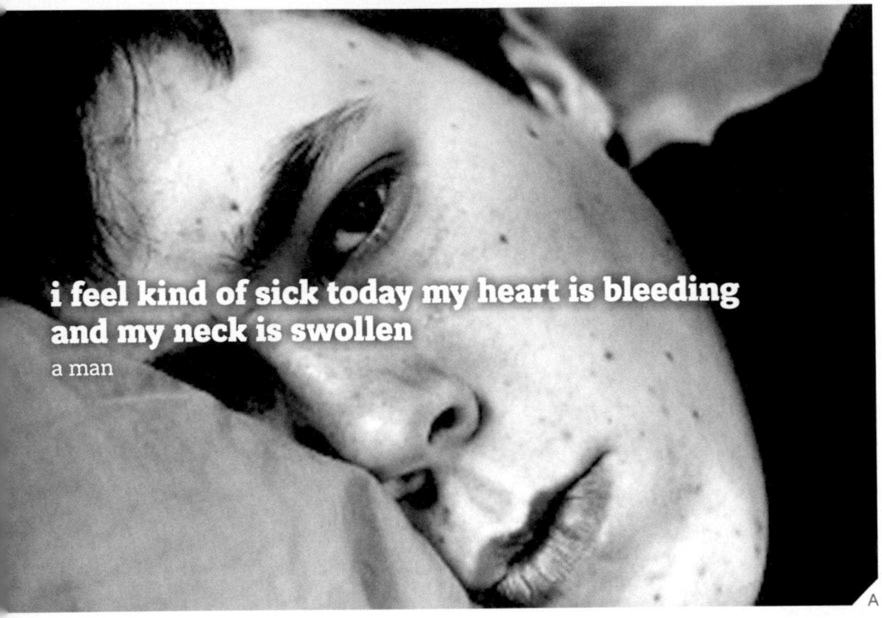

i feel kind of sick today my heart is bleeding and my neck is swollen
a man

A

I'M CRYING AND MY FACE LOOKS LIKE A BUS HIT IT AND I FEEL SICK AND I HATE EVERYTHING

a 17-year-old woman in melbourne, australia

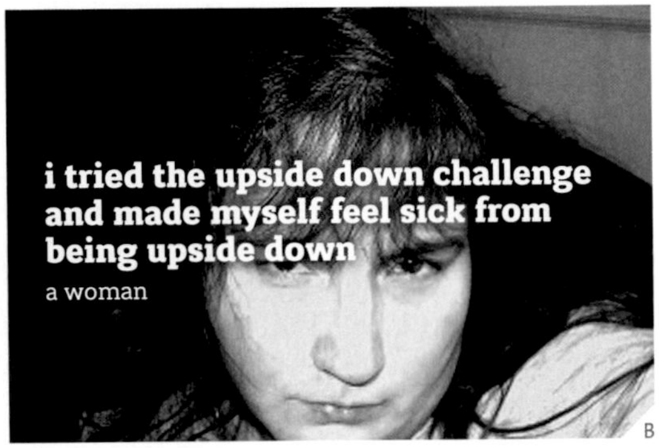

i tried the upside down challenge and made myself feel sick from being upside down
a woman

B

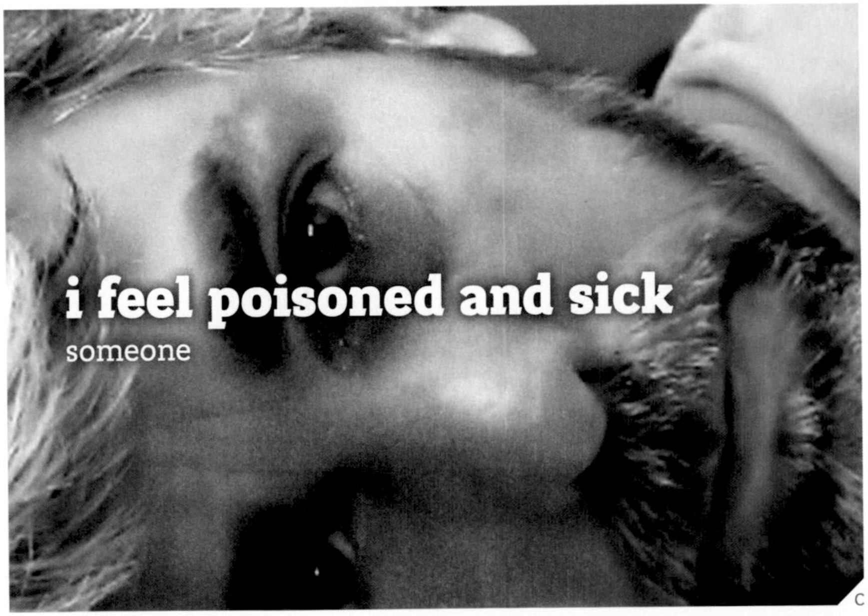

i feel poisoned and sick
someone

C

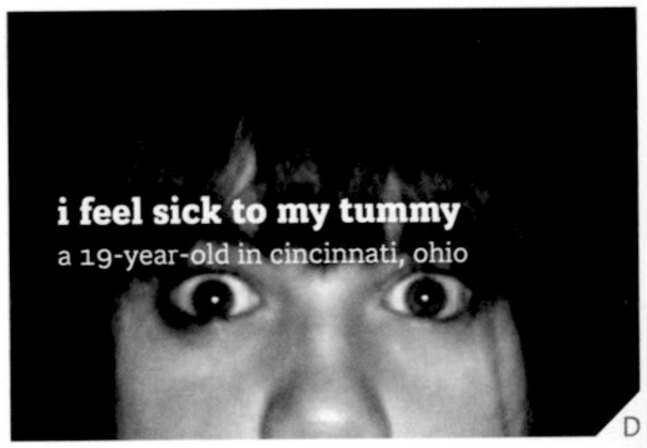

i feel sick to my tummy
a 19-year-old in cincinnati, ohio

D

sick adj.

1. affected with disease of any kind; ill
2. affected with, or attended by, nausea
3. having a strong dislike; disgusted
4. corrupted; imperfect; impaired

● i cant stop crying and i feel sick in the stomach and i wish that i would hear from dylan who is supposed to be my boyfriend but who has dissappeared and won't answer my calls or msgs and just ignores me ● i know the most beautiful girl on the planet and i just saw a new picture of her and i feel so sick ● i now feel sick and unclean and can't knock the feelin' that the old smelly fellas germs are in me system i think i need to bleach me insides or sumthin' ● i no longer feel that sick insecure feeling ● i now feel a sort of sick joy out of tainting those around me ● i'm sick of hating myself sick of waking up with these putrid feelings and sick of going to bed with them ● i feel so sick from the margarine

Season breakdown 20% **29%** 27% 24%

Related feelings
mentioned with sick

dizzy	sore
tired	weak
nauseous	exhausted

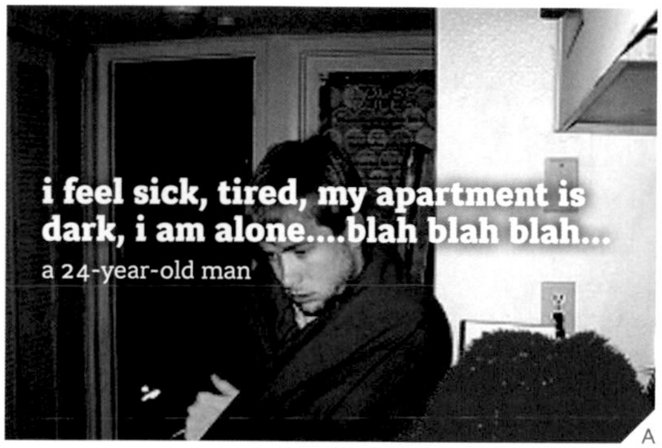
i feel sick, tired, my apartment is dark, i am alone....blah blah blah...
a 24-year-old man

A

i feel sick inside
someone

B

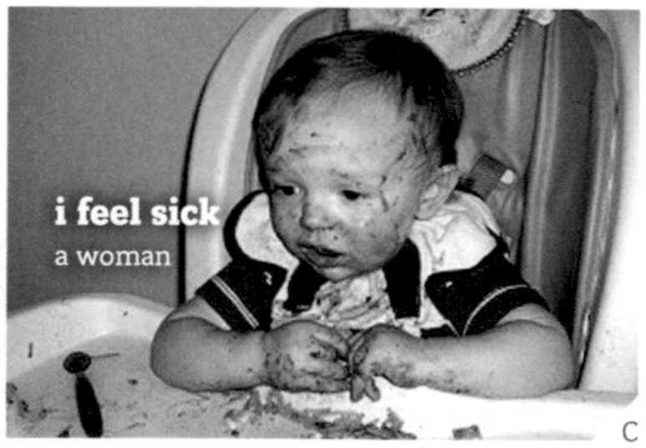
i feel sick
a woman

C

I WOKE UP FEELING SICK FEELING SPIRITUALLY EMPTY FEELING LIKE THERE WAS NO POINT IN LIVING
someone

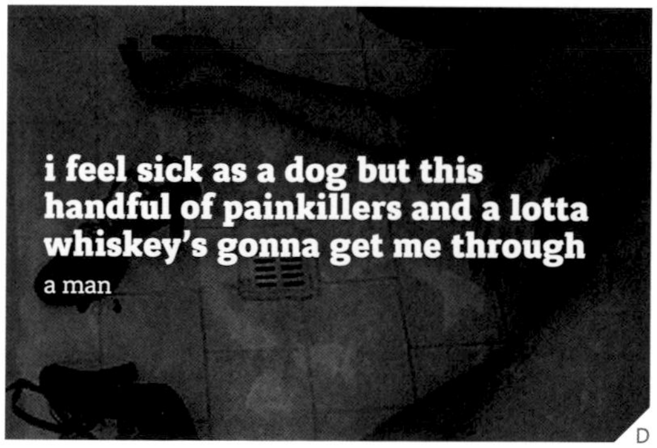
i feel sick as a dog but this handful of painkillers and a lotta whiskey's gonna get me through
a man

D

i think i feel myself getting sick
a 25-year-old man

E

Main reasons
- **eating**
- headache
- common cold
- nausea

Observations
When people say they feel sick, they generally feel **physically** sick. People feel sick after **eating** something bad or eating too much (especially **chocolate** or **junk food**). Many describe feeling sick from the common **cold**, **flu**, **drinking too much**, **pregnancy**, or just being generally ill. People most commonly feel sick to their **stomach**, followed by the **head** and then the **throat**. People who feel sick often take **medicine**, but also self-medicate with **water** or **soup**. If they have a stomachache, they will often just eat **toast**. ♥

SMALL

73 rd most common feeling overall · 0.17% of all feelings are small

Breakdowns
for people who feel small

Gender breakdown 52% 48%

Age breakdown 10s 20s 30s 40s 50+

i feel so small
a woman

A

I FEEL SO SMALL SO HELPLESS

someone in bristol, england

i feel so small
from a woman

B

i feel very small
someone

C

I WANTED TO BE SKINNY TO FEEL SMALL AND DISAPPEAR

someone

small adj.

1. having little size, comparatively
2. being of slight consequence
3. not prolonged in duration; short
4. weak; slender; fine; gentle; soft

• i feel like i'm a very small gear in a very big machine • i feel small but my thoughts are big • i feel that most of the time i only get to show a small piece of who i am • i feel very small in my life right now • i'm feeling very small and not so loved right now • i'm shrinking but i'm staying the same size so i get this dual feeling of being infinitely small and infinitely huge at the same time • i feel like a turtle because i'm making steps so small and slow that it almost doesn't feel like i'm moving at all • i made her feel small and defenseless and it was a shitty move on my part • i love to feel small • i wish i could do so much more to change the world but i feel so small

Season breakdown 28% 23% 23% 26%

Related feelings mentioned with small

insignificant
unimportant
powerless
worthless
vulnerable
useless

i feel small
a woman

A

I SEE MEN WITH MUSCLES AND FEEL SMALL AND YOUNG
a 28-year-old in minneapolis

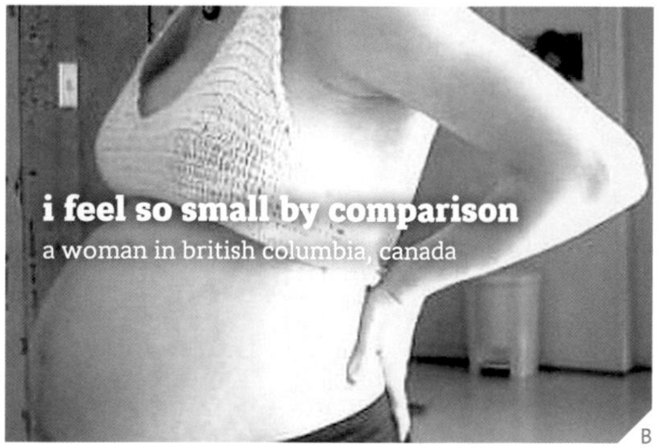
i feel so small by comparison
a woman in british columbia, canada

B

i feel small again
a woman

C

Main reasons

insignificance
god
the universe
silence

Observations

People express feeling small and feeling insignificant in comparison to things they consider big, in particular **God** and **the universe**. **Women** express feeling small, especially in the presence of God, more frequently than men do. When people express feeling small, they also express feeling **insignificant**, **unimportant**, **powerless**, **worthless**, **vulnerable**, and **useless**. Teenagers seldom describe feeling small. ♥

SORRY

6 th most common feeling overall · 1.29% of all feelings are sorry

Breakdowns
for people who feel sorry

Gender breakdown — 51% · 49%

Age breakdown — 10s · 20s · 30s · 40s · 50+

I FEEL SORRY FOR THAT GUY WHO'S FINGER YOU LOPPED OFF
someone

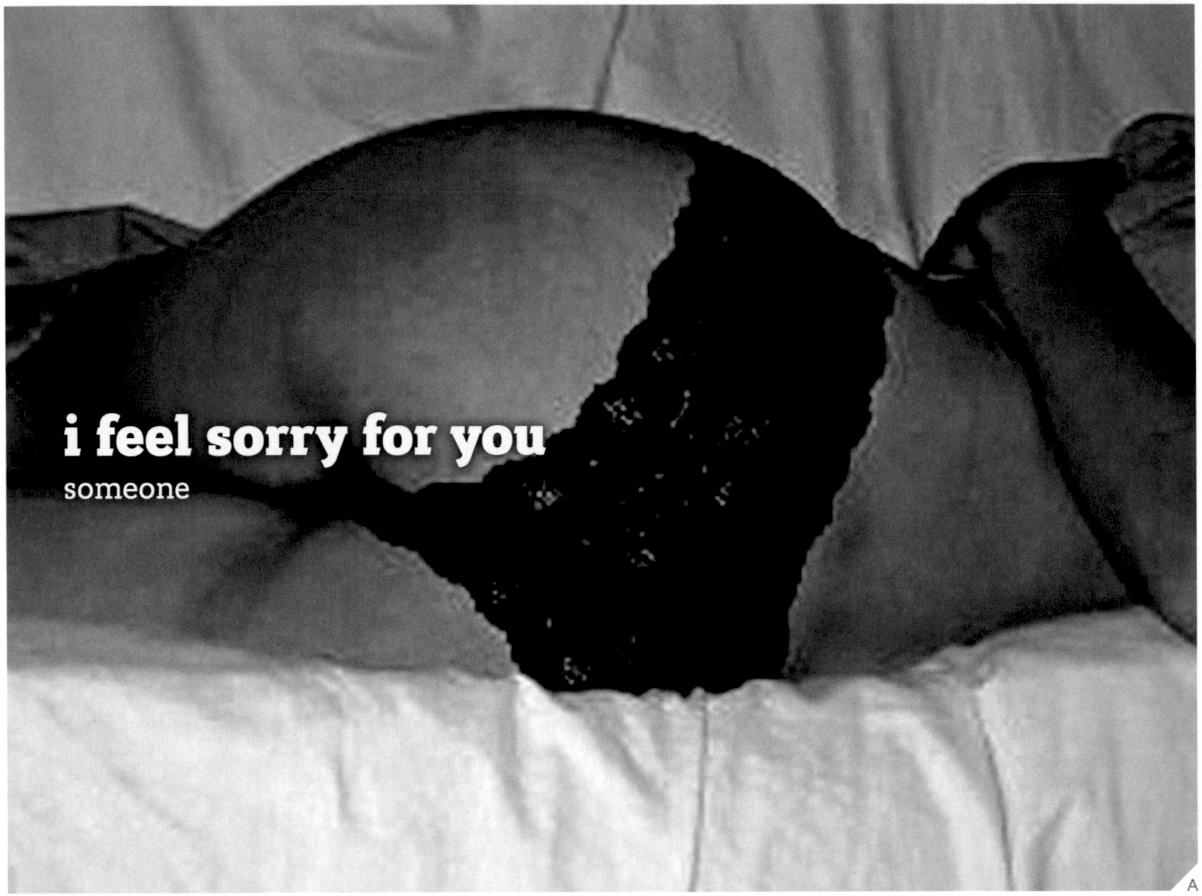

A

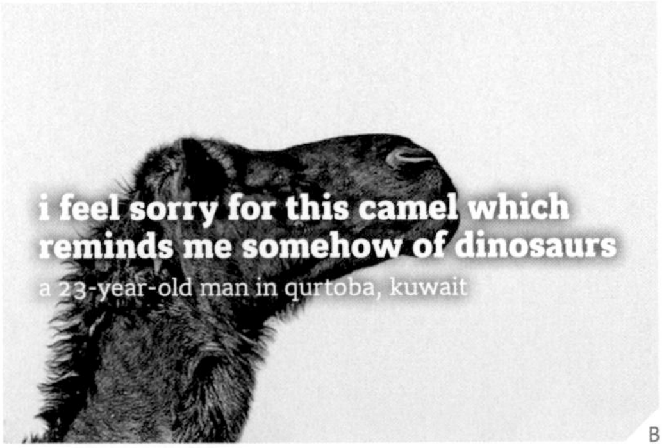

i feel sorry for this camel which reminds me somehow of dinosaurs
a 23-year-old man in qurtoba, kuwait

B

C

sorry adj.

1. inspiring sorrow, pity, scorn, or ridicule
2. feeling regret
3. melancholy; dismal; gloomy; mournful
4. pained for some evil

● i feel sorry for the girl ● i feel sorry for anyone who thinks they must eat a little lettuce boiled chicken and no carbs for lunch to be acceptable to the world ● i feel sorry for the greedy little gopher ● i feel sorry for all the people who ve never experienced life through a doll ● i can't help but to feel really sorry for mother earth ● i feel sorry for myself every time i close my eyes ● i feel sorry for those who spend real money for virtual money ● i cannot help but feel sorry for sarmiento ● i'm just feeling sorry for myself but i just hate not being able to just be with anyone ● i wont feel sorry for you because of something that happened to your ancestors ● i feel sorry for myself but it's better than hating

Season breakdown: 27% | 23% | 25% | 25%

Related feelings mentioned with sorry

- **poor**
- pathetic
- homeless
- abused
- ignorant
- cruel

I CAN ONLY FEEL SORRY FOR THE NEXT GIRL THAT FALLS FOR YOUR CHARMING AND MANIPULATIVE WORDS

someone

i was just generally feeling sorry for myself that day
a woman

B

i feel so sorry that i could not find a proper bicycle for her so far
someone

A

I NEEDED TO FEEL SORRY TO FEEL COMPLETE

a 24-year-old woman

i feel sorry for number four
a 42-year-old man

C

i feel sorry for him
a man

D

Main reasons

- **myself**
- somebody else
- their family
- kids

Observations

Many people feel sorry for **themselves**, and most people who do so also **hate** it. People tend to feel sorry for people they know who are going through something difficult, and for their **family**. People feel especially sorry for **kids**. They also often feel sorry for **public figures** who are going through difficult times. During the 2008 presidential election, people felt more sorry for the candidates than for anybody else: **John McCain**, **Sarah Palin**, and **Barack Obama** in that order. Very few people felt sorry for **Joe Biden**. ♥

SPECIAL

33 rd most common feeling overall · 0.33% of all feelings are special

Breakdowns for people who feel special

Gender breakdown 54% 46%

Age breakdown 10s 20s 30s 40s 50+

I HAVE TO SAY IT DOESN'T MAKE ME FEEL SPECIAL WHEN YOU TELL ME THAT YOU GET THE SAME FEELING FROM PLAYING XBOX WITH ME AS YOU DO HAVING SEX WITH ME

a woman

i feel so special with you

a 30-year-old man in boston, massachusetts

A

special adj.

1. particular; peculiar; different
2. extraordinary; uncommon
3. designed for a particular purpose
4. confined to a definite field of action

● i only sing it to the people who mean a lot to me so you should feel very special if you've ever heard it ● i truely love him with all my heart and the days that he does take time to make me feel special are well worth it ● i regret every word i said to make him feel special ● i love to make her smile and feel special ● i can tell him almost everything and he makes me feel special ● i remember feeling really special when i got a burger king crown ● i make her feel special and im glad i do b/c she does the same to me ● i won't dwell on the sorrow we all still feel here but instead will give you a glimpse of why he was so special and touched a nerve in everyone he ever met

Season breakdown 23% 24% 28% 25%

Related feelings mentioned with special

unique
appreciated
valued
loved
smart
popular

I HELP MAKE YOU FEEL SPECIAL INSIDE

someone

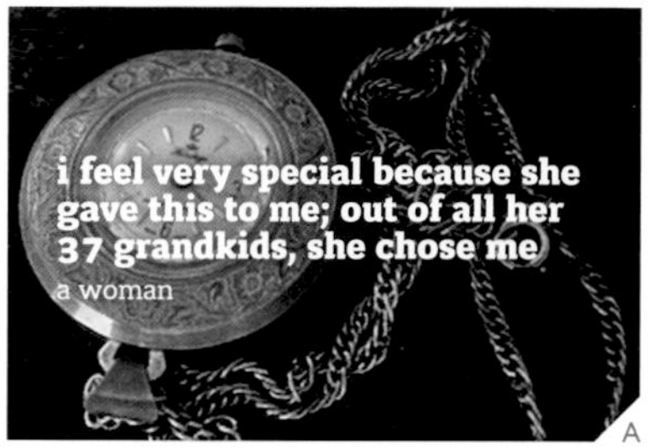

i feel very special because she gave this to me; out of all her 37 grandkids, she chose me
a woman

A

B

I TRULY FEEL SOMETHING SPECIAL FOR SOMEONE AND FIND IT EVEN SCARIER THEN BEING ALONE

someone in ontario, canada

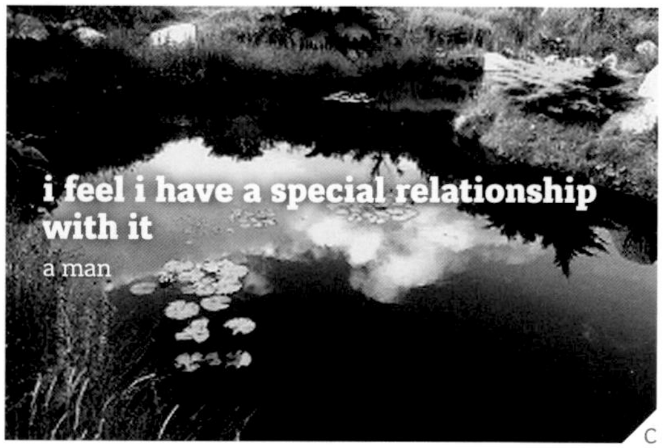

i feel i have a special relationship with it

C

Main reasons

being loved
being cared for
birthdays
gifts

Observations

People feel the most special when they are **loved**, **cared for**, and **appreciated**, and they feel special when they get tokens of that love, care, and appreciation. The tokens people discuss include **flowers**, **compliments**, **gifts**, and **hugs**. People tend to feel the most special on **Valentine's Day** and on their **birthdays** (although as people get older they begin to feel less special on their birthday). **Women** and **Australians** tend to feel particularly special, more so than any other group. When women feel special, they often also express feeling **beautiful**. ♥

STUPID

19th most common feeling overall · 0.59% of all feelings are stupid

Breakdowns
for people who feel stupid

Gender breakdown 58% 42%

Age breakdown 10s 20s 30s 40s 50+

I FEEL LIKE SUCH A STUPID RIDICULOUS WHINY LITTLE GIRL

someone in dartmouth, canada

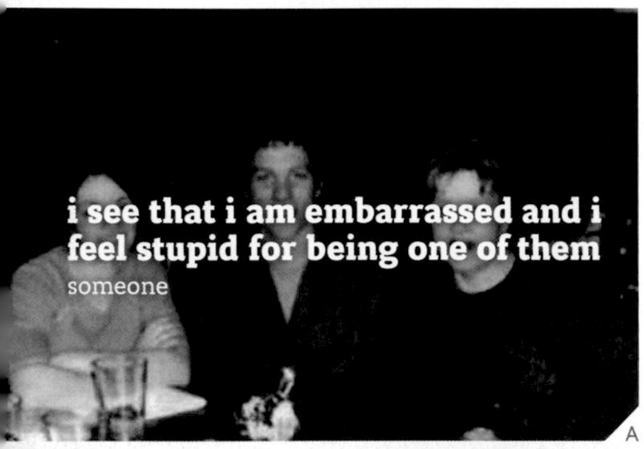

i see that i am embarrassed and i feel stupid for being one of them
someone

A

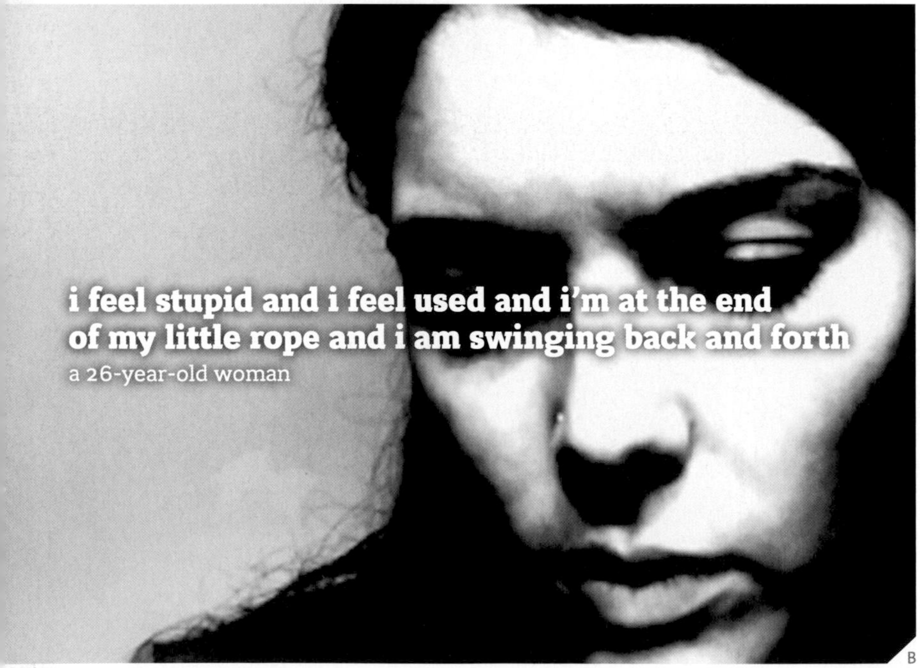

i feel stupid and i feel used and i'm at the end of my little rope and i am swinging back and forth
a 26-year-old woman

B

I USED TO BE ABLE TO PICK UP ON THE FEELINGS OF PEOPLE AROUND ME BUT NOW I'M TOO ABSORBED IN MY OWN STUPID PROBLEMS TO NOTICE

someone

stupid adj.

1. very dull
2. insensible; wanting in understanding
3. resulting from, or evincing, stupidity
4. formed without skill or genius; heavy

● i've been on such bumpy roads it's no wonder i feel ridiculously stupid for all the bad choices i made ● i feel stupid cuz jay's still here and i don't want to hurt him anymore than i already have ● i feel so stupid for even thinking some of the thoughts that i have ● i do not need to be made to feel stupid for feeling sad ● i never feel stupid for being with him so i guess that's a good sign ● i feel so stupid cause i actually believed her and she has been lying to me for months ● i want him to feel stupid and idiotic for having messed around on me like that sigh ● i feel stupid for saying i love you even though i never completely understood what i was saying ● i feel really stupid for crying in class

Season breakdown 22% 26% **27%** 25%

Related feelings mentioned with stupid

worthless
mad
pissed
dumb
embarrassed
useless

I AM TIRED OF NOT BEING NOTICED USED KICKED TO THE CURB AND TAKEN FOR GRANTED TAKEN AS NAIVE AND MADE TO FEEL STUPID

a 20-year-old woman in dayton, texas, when it was cloudy

2 2006

i feel so stupid for some reason
a woman

A

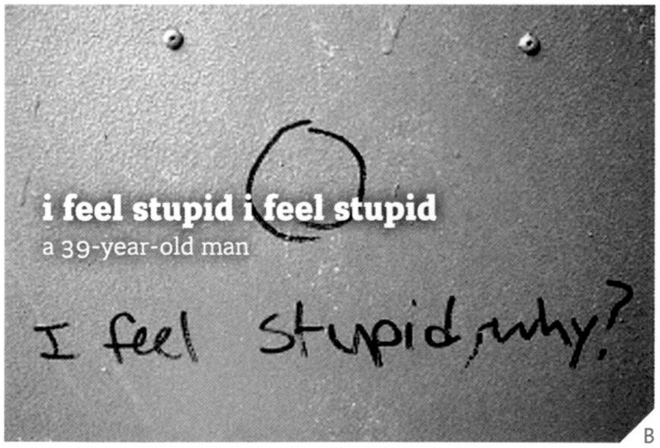
I feel stupid, why?

i feel stupid i feel stupid
a 39-year-old man

B

I WANT TO BE ABLE TO CRY WITHOUT FEELING STUPID

a 21-year-old

Main reasons

unrequited love
sharing feelings
speaking
embarrassment

Observations

People primarily feel stupid for social reasons. They often feel stupid for **loving** somebody who doesn't love them back, for **expressing feelings** or doing something that is **embarrassing**, or for **saying** something that they shouldn't have said. **Teenagers** feel stupid at a far greater rate than people of any other age group, and as people grow older, they feel progressively less and less stupid. While teenagers often feel stupid about something that happened at **school**, older people feel stupid when it comes to being irresponsible with **money**. ♥

TERRIBLE

33rd most common feeling overall · 0.34% of all feelings are terrible

Breakdowns for people who feel terrible

Gender breakdown: 54% (women) · 46% (men)

Age breakdown: 10s · 20s · 30s · 40s · 50+

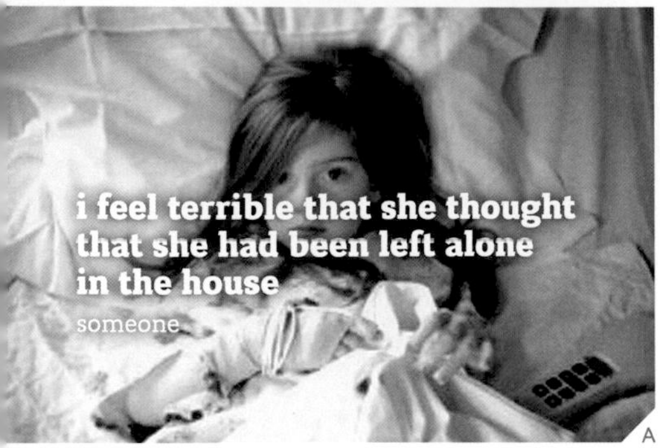

i feel terrible that she thought that she had been left alone in the house
someone

A

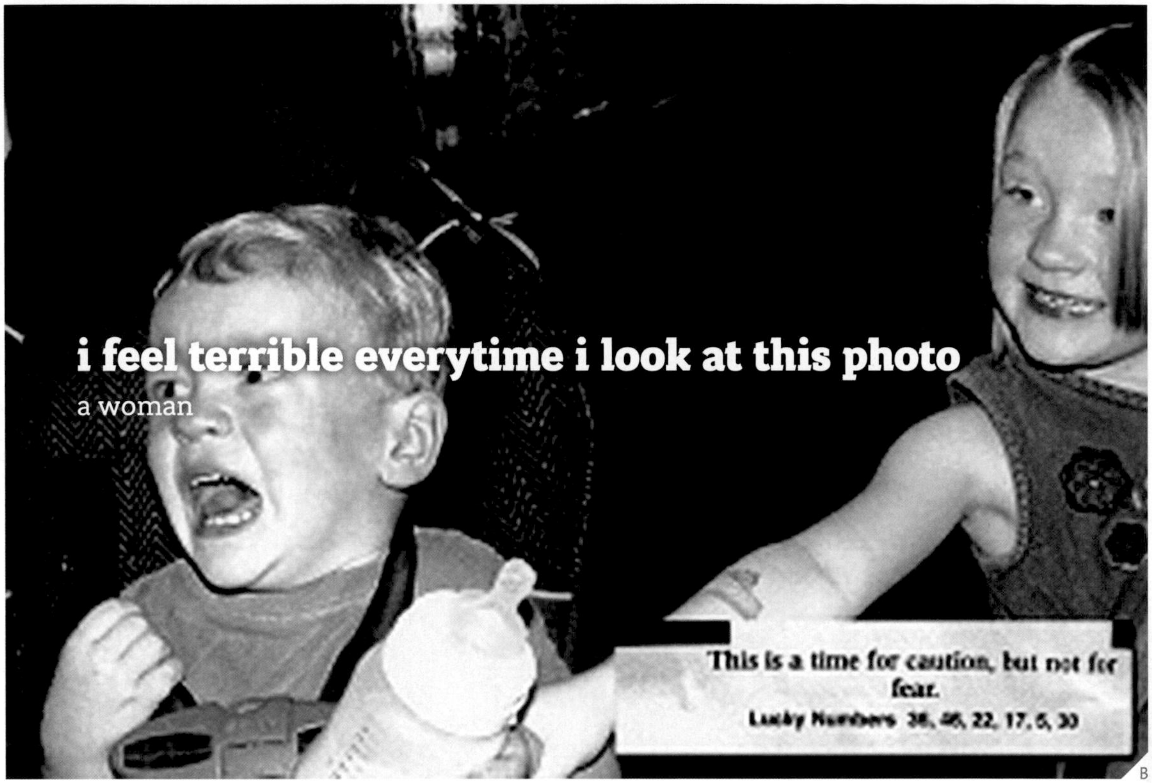

This is a time for caution, but not for fear.

i feel terrible everytime i look at this photo
a woman

B

This child, the blogger's son, is experiencing his first ever ride through a carwash.

i feel terrible tired and stuff
a woman

C

I WAS ALSO FEELING VERY TERRIBLE BECAUSE I LOOKED AT MYSELF IN THE MIRROR AND SAW REFLECTIONS OF SOMEONE WHO LOOKED NERDY UNFRIENDLY AND UGLY

someone in singapore

terrible adj.

1. likely to excite terror, awe, or dread
2. dreadful; formidable
3. excessive; extreme; severe
4. awful; causing fear or dread

• i'll never be able to explain that to you and that makes me feel terrible • i see so many people happy and in love and i just get nervous and i feel terrible • i understand a little i feel terrible despair when i see people bombed • i feel so terrible for her she will need to grow up in this world • i keep falling asleep now when i'm on the phone i never used to do that and i feel terrible • i mean i am 23-years-old and i have accomplished nothing but feeling terrible and shitty all of the time • i know i'd feel terrible afterwards because i hate confrontation and sharing my feelings and having to explain my actions to people • i feel terrible that someone had to clean it up terrible

Season breakdown 23% **26%** 25% 25%

Related feelings mentioned with terrible

upset
poor
fucked
mad
hurt
drunk

i feel terrible that i couldn't save him
a man

A

i would just feel terrible if i had to cancel
someone

B

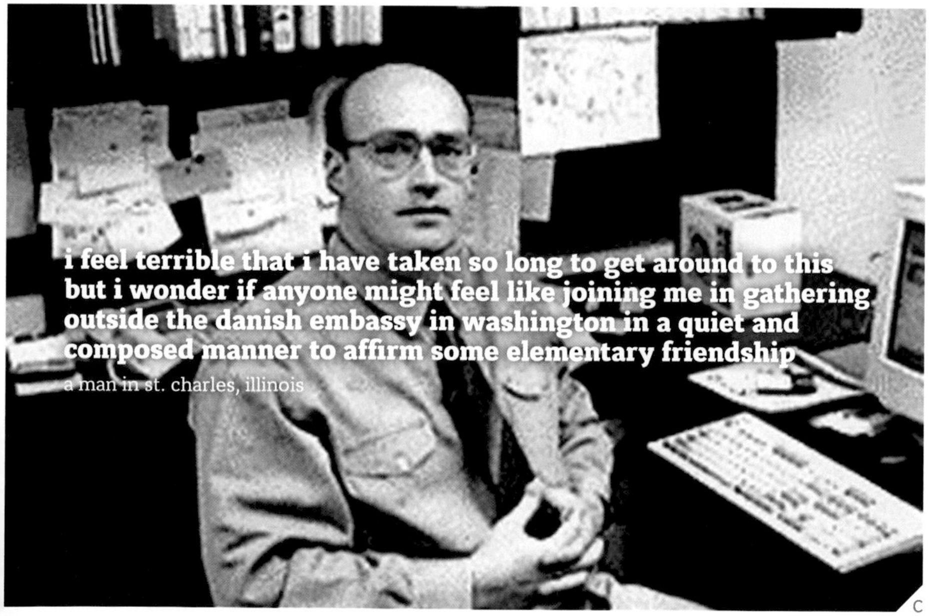

i feel terrible that i have taken so long to get around to this but i wonder if anyone might feel like joining me in gathering outside the danish embassy in washington in a quiet and composed manner to affirm some elementary friendship
a man in st. charles, illinois

C

I FEEL TERRIBLE I'M SCARED

an 18-year-old in mickleton, new jersey

Main reasons

lost love
hurting friends
pain
sickness

Observations

People often feel terrible when they forget somebody's **birthday**, are in **pain**, cause pain for someone else, or are **helpless** to stop the pain of a loved one. People with children often say they feel like they are terrible **parents**, particularly young parents and **mothers**. People feel terrible about **neglecting** something or somebody important to them. People feel terrible when they end a relationship, or when they are bad partners in a relationship. People also feel terrible when they are sick. Often when people are sick they **wake up** feeling terrible. ♥

UGLY

Breakdowns
for people who feel ugly

Gender breakdown **63%** **37%**

Age breakdown
10s 20s 30s 40s 50+

I STILL FEEL LIKE I'M AN UGLY PIECE OF SHIT

an 18-year-old in newark, delaware, when it was cloudy

i feel so ugly
a woman

i don't want to lose you but i just don't know to shake this ugly feeling
someone

B

i feel ugly right now
someone in troy, new york

C

i feel so ugly
a woman

D

i tried to take a picture that summed up how ugly i feel but i couldn't
a man

E

A

ugly adj.

1. offensive to the sight; unsightly
2. ill-natured; hideous; quarrelsome
3. unpleasant; disagreeable
4. surly; inclined to anger

● i can't even focus or work today i can't eat i seriously feel like it was an ugly break up and i am hoping against hopes that it was not that and you are not done with me ● i always feel ugly when i look at pictures of myself ● i feel so ugly and so much like a plain jane when i am around some of them ● i hate looking in the mirror because i feel ugly and fat ● i've feel that i am ugly fat disgusting stupid and slow as i am never any better than any of my sisters ● i feel that this life and this world is too ugly for their beautiful spirits ● i feel really ugly and look it and i cant fix it ● i feel i want to be ugly so that people would stop calling me superficial ● i feel so ugly and unloveable

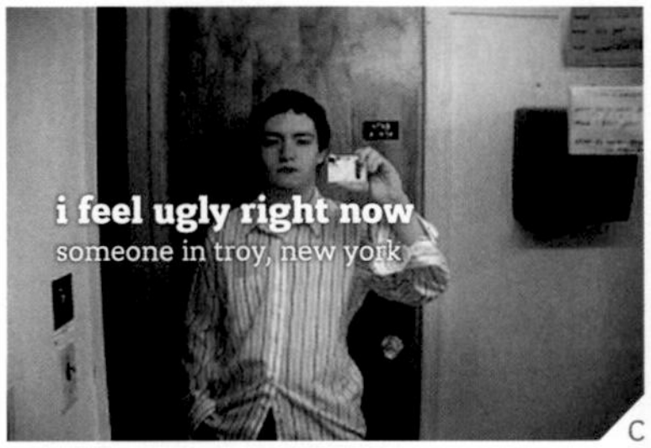

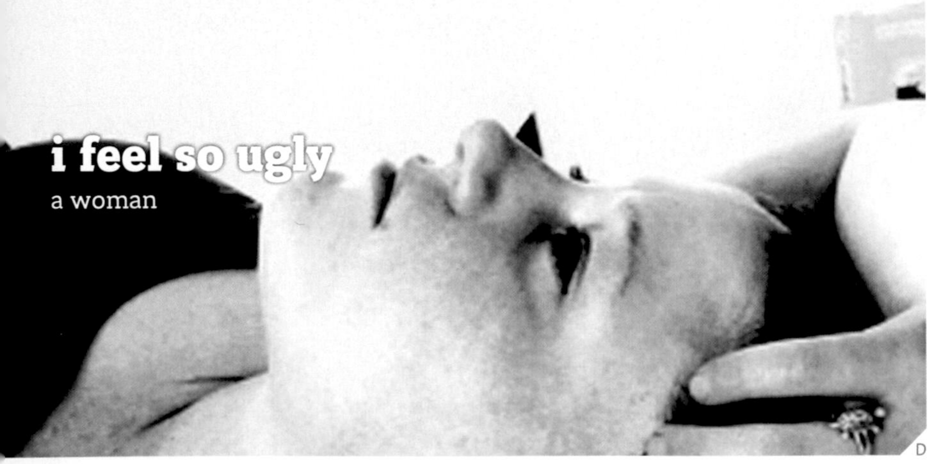

Season breakdown — 22% · 27% · **27%** · 24%

Related feelings mentioned with ugly

- **unwanted**
- fat
- unloved
- worthless
- disgusting
- gross

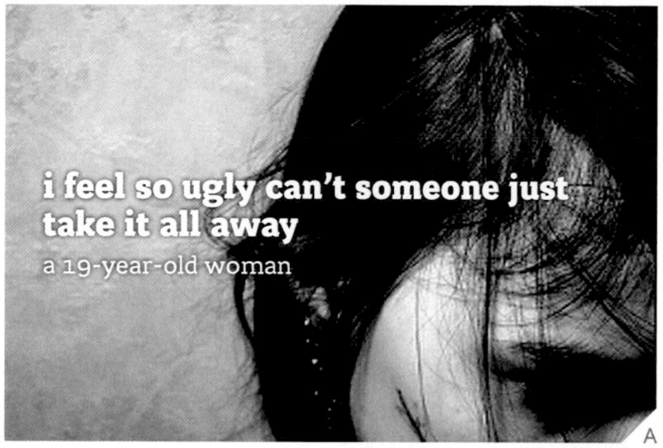

i feel so ugly can't someone just take it all away
a 19-year-old woman

A

I FEEL UGLY INSIDE

someone

when i feel ugly he makes me remember how beautiful life can be
someone

B

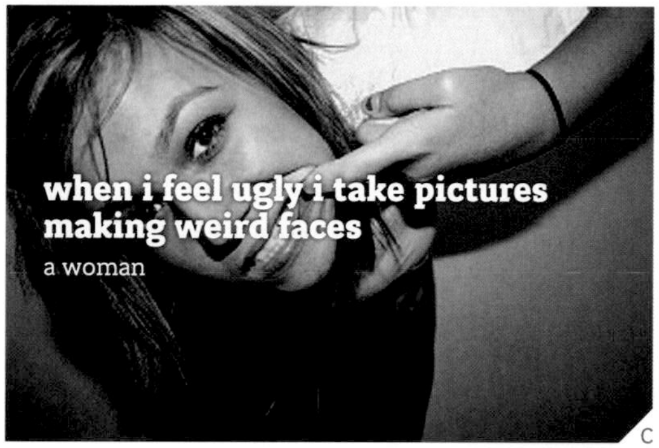

when i feel ugly i take pictures making weird faces
a woman

C

I MAY FEEL UGLY OR UNSEXY OR FAT BUT AT THE END OF THE DAY I NEED TO REALIZE HOW GOOD I HAVE IT AND HOW LUCKY I AM

someone

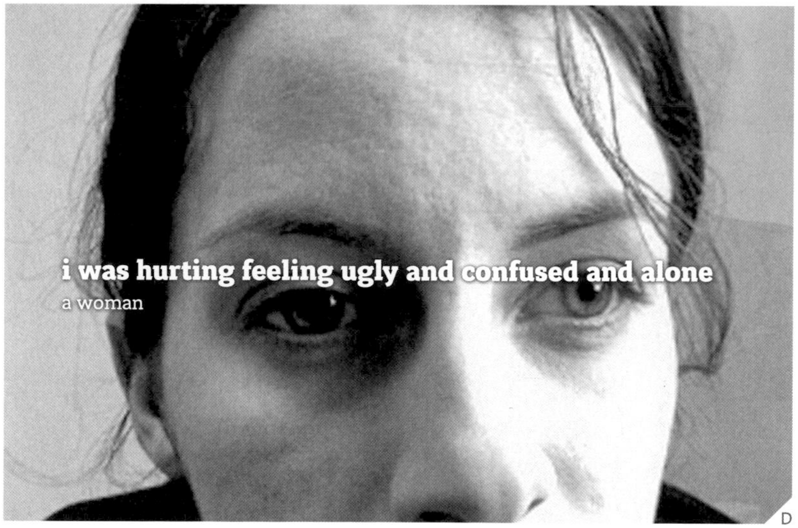

i was hurting feeling ugly and confused and alone
a woman

D

Main reasons

- **being overweight**
- bad hair day
- fatigue
- no makeup

Observations

There are remarkably strong demographic characteristics to this feeling. **Women** tend to feel ugly far more regularly than it seems men do, and **teenagers** express feeling ugly way more than people in any other age group do. It is most common for people to express feeling ugly when they are also feeling **fat**. People will say they feel ugly when they are having a **bad hair day**, when they are not wearing makeup, and when they are feeling **sick** or **tired**. When people feel ugly, they will also often express feeling **worthless**, **stupid**, and **unwanted**. ♥

WEIRD

21 st most common feeling overall · 0.52% of all feelings are weird

Breakdowns
for people who feel weird

Gender breakdown — 52% (women) · 48% (men)

Age breakdown — 10s · 20s · 30s · 40s · 50+

i'm trying to be brave but they still feel a little weird
a 26-year-old woman

A

i'm feeling weird like in a good mood
a 16-year-old in canada

B

i've been listening to some manics and feeling weird
a 22-year-old in london, england

C

I FEEL WEIRD LOOKING FOR THINGS THAT REMIND ME OF HOME SINCE I TRIED SO HARD TO ESCAPE
someone in the united states

i feel weird
someone in denver, colorado

D

weird adj.

1. strikingly odd or unusual
2. of or pertaining to fate
3. suggesting magical influence
4. supernatural; unearthly; wild

● i feel weird that i've never met him and i don't know what he looks like ● i get to fall asleep on stage for most of act 5 scene 1 which feels kind of weird since i m up there on stage well ok in the grassy spot where the stage is but pretty much unaware of what s going on around me ● i've been feeling weird all day like sitting around a lot and like crying a little kinda nauseous too ● i guess i'm so used to having it by my side wherever i go that it really feels weird to be separated from it ● i'm feeling kind of weird i guess because i haven't seen another human being today ● i've been feeling this weird longing to be back in my old catholic school atmosphere

Season breakdown 21% **30%** 25% 24%

Related feelings mentioned with weird

awkward
strange
confused
normal
random
naked

i feel weird seeing myself smiling

A

I FEEL WEIRD HAVING PHONE SEX

a 23-year-old man

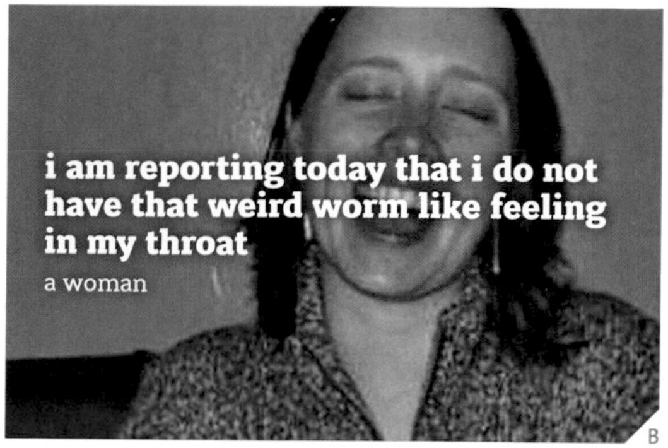

i am reporting today that i do not have that weird worm like feeling in my throat
a woman

B

i was having fun then my friend started telling me this stuff about how he felt about me i tried to not act like he made me feel weird but he made me feel so weird i could hardly stand it
someone

C

Main reasons

expressing things
new emotions
social situations
clothes

Observations

The older people get, the less weird they feel. This is largely because people feel weird in **new experiences**: **relationships**, **social situations**, **bodily changes**, **love**, and **new emotions**. They feel weird **saying** something that might be taken the wrong way. People often say they feel weird when they feel emotions they have trouble describing. They will use the words **kinda**, **stuff**, **dunno**, and **whatever** in these cases. People say that they feel weird **lately**, more than they feel weird about something specific. People refer to the **head** and **stomach** when they describe feeling weird. ♥

YOUNG

90th most common feeling overall · 0.14% of all feelings are young

Breakdowns
for people who feel young

Gender breakdown 52% 48%

Age breakdown 10s 20s 30s 40s 50+

i feel young and instead of taking care of my responsibilities i am in bed afraid to leave
a 25-year-old man in portland, oregon

A

Rhonda is 33 now with a great husband who helps her continue to feel young every day.

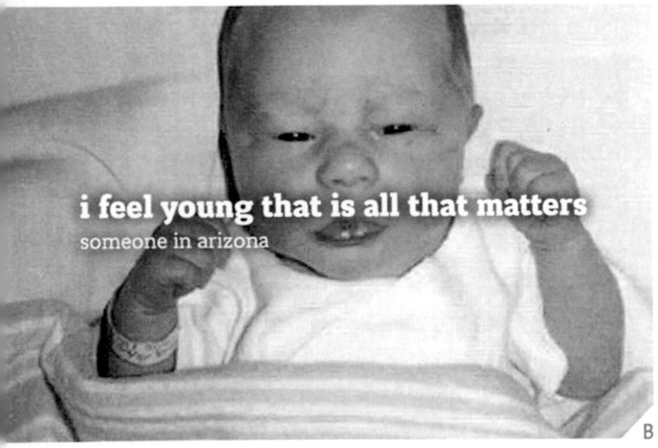

i feel young that is all that matters
someone in arizona

B

I FEEL YOUNG ENOUGH TO TAKE ON A CHALLENGE MORE APPROPRIATE FOR A MUCH YOUNGER MAN

someone

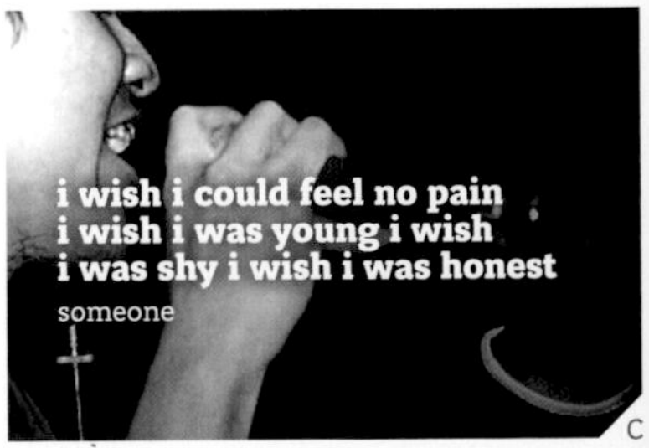

i wish i could feel no pain i wish i was young i wish i was shy i wish i was honest
someone

C

young adj.

1. not yet arrived at maturity
2. being in the first part of growth; juvenile
3. having little experience
4. ignorant; weak

● i'd say i feel young again except when i was young i played worse and won less ● i still look young and feel young i will still be young and there will still be time ● i turned 26 last wednesday and feel incredibly young and stupid some days and then old and stuck in a rut on others ● i do feel she was a little young to interpret it to its potential ● i feel young free confident ● i can't get past the feeling that she's too young and too sweet a girl to have to go through something like this ● i feel that im too young to stay in one place for so long ● i feel like starting a relationship at 19 was too young because i had no time to explore other horizons

Season breakdown 26% 25% 24% 25%

Related feelings mentioned with young

immature
dumb
shy
energetic
lost
sexy

HONESTLY I STILL FEEL TOO YOUNG AND I JUST HAVE SO MUCH GOING IN MY LIFE AND I'M REALLY TRYING TO GET MYSELF TOGETHER BEFORE I COMPLETELY DEDICATE IT TO ANYONE

a 22-year-old woman in anchorage, alaska, when it was cloudy

i feel so young
someone

A

i always feel young
someone

B

Main reasons

aging
kids
hairstyle
fun

Observations

The older people get, the more frequently they talk about feeling young. Similarly, people who are younger frequently talk about feeling old. People **over 50** talk about feeling young far more often than people in their 40s, while people in their teens and 20s don't often describe feeling young. When people in their teens and 20s feel young, it's often related to their level of **maturity**, and when people in their 50s feel young, it generally pertains to their **level of energy**. **Playing**, **dancing**, or a **haircut** often make people feel young. ♥

A Brief History of Western Emotional Philosophy

or, "Old White Men and What They Thought About Feelings"

Aristotle

384 BC – 322 BC

Aristotle saw the human soul as being composed of two parts, one rational and one irrational, both of which are necessary and complementary, and that emotions involve both halves of the soul. He argued that virtue is in large part an issue of feeling the right thing, and conversely that people's emotions are influenced by their moral beliefs.

The Stoics

3rd Cen. BC – 5th Cen. AD

The Stoics, founded in Athens by Zeno of Citium, taught strength of mind in the face of worldly events outside of our control, and a worldview where one can overcome destructive emotions such as anger, fear, and jealousy by maintaining a "Stoic calm."

René Descartes

1596 – 1650

Descartes, unlike Aristotle, saw the mental and physical aspects of human nature to be largely independent of one another, and suggested that the two come together in the pineal gland in the brain, where he suggested emotions originate.

David Hume

1711 – 1776

Hume saw emotions, rather than reason, as key in guiding our morality. Also, he divided emotions into two primary categories—direct emotions (which arise immediately from pain or pleasure) and indirect emotions (which are related to pain or pleasure in conjunction with the idea of somebody else).

Charles Darwin

1809 – 1882

Darwin argued that emotions in humans and animals are similar and suggested a large biological and evolutionary component to emotion. He argued that many emotions exist because they are useful in addressing the event that caused the emotion to arise (for example the adrenaline involved with fear facilitates fight or flight).

William James

1842 – 1910

James argued, controversially, that emotions are the recognition of bodily responses to some arousing event. In his words: "we feel sorry because we cry, angry because we strike, and afraid because we tremble."

Sigmund Freud

1856 – 1939

Freud's theories centered around the existence of an unconscious mind and the repression of painful thoughts and memories. In his writings on emotion he argues that at least part of an emotion (its underlying instincts and ideas) can be unconscious, which could lead to things like feeling guilt or anxiety without knowing why.

Martin Heidegger

1889 – 1976

Heidegger saw emotions, or moods, as centrally important and fundamental to being and awareness. He saw moods as the primary means, before reason, of disclosing what he called *Dasein*, or being-in-the-world.

Jean Paul Sartre

1905 – 1980

Sartre's main philosophical thesis is that humans are "condemned to be free," and that freedom extends to their emotions. So rather than seeing emotions as instinctual, like William James, he emphasized that humans are free to eliminate destructive emotions such as debilitating fear or envy.

Paul Ekman

1934 – present

Ekman shows the universality of facial expressions of emotion (particularly anger, disgust, fear, joy, sadness, and surprise) and, like Darwin, suggests that emotional responses are largely biological in origin.

4 When A brief history of emotion

Tags: history, news

Sam Zients was sitting in his apartment during his junior year at NYU when Barack Obama was elected president.

"I'm not sure if it has really hit me yet," he writes on his blog on election night. "When I mute the TV I can hear people on the street chanting and taxis honking in celebration. I see people on the screen gathered in crowds around the country absolutely beside themselves with happiness and exhilaration."[1]

On election night, November 4th, 2008, there was an outpouring of emotion onto the blogosphere. The feelings "proud" and "patriotic" spiked to levels we had not seen since we started tracking emotions in 2005. But perhaps most interestingly, there was an uptick in feelings of hope. "I feel like this is the dawn of a new optimism for America," writes Sam, "and I am absolutely elated to be a young person in this country right now." He ends his post by quoting Michelle Obama: "it feels like hope is finally making a comeback."[2]

Sam Zients climbing a ladder

Sam was not alone. Thousands of bloggers on election night talked of their hope for the future—Rob Brooks-Bilson, an engineer in Phoenix, wrote, "for the first time in 8 years I feel like there's a real chance in turning things around in this country and for that I feel like jumping around."[3] And Jun Loayza, a startup founder in Southern California, wrote, "unlike the other feelings I will always remember, like 9/11 or Princess Diana, this one is a feeling of hope and joy."[4]

It is not surprising that hope was so heavily expressed on election night—after all, Obama had made it the centerpiece of his campaign. What is surprising, however, is that this newfound hope didn't

An excited Rob Brooks-Bilson in his hotel room on Obama's election night

go away. Feelings like "elated" and "proud" spiked and then after a few days returned to their normal levels. But while hope declined after its spike on election night, it remained higher than it had been before the election. The United States had entered a period of greater hope.

On October 31st, 1517, Martin Luther famously nailed his Ninety-Five Theses to the door of the All Saints' Church, beginning the century and a half that came to be known as the Protestant Reformation. The period, according to historian Peter Stearns, was marked emotionally by a pervasive unhappiness, an appropriate Christian emotion at the time.[5] "The world is evil," wrote Martin Luther, "and this life is full of misery."[6] The mass quest for spiritual perfection espoused by Reformation leaders, as well as their deep-rooted consciousness of sin, led to a culture of sorrow. Stearns notes that paintings and diary entries of the time characteristically portrayed dolefulness and grief, and the sociologist Max Weber describes the period as one of "deep melancholy and moroseness."[7]

All of this began to change in the eighteenth century. The melancholy that had characterized the century before began to shift toward an insistence on happiness. Enlightenment philosophers such as John Locke and poets such as Voltaire were among the many who explored and advocated for happiness. "No previous age, in fact, wrote so much on the subject or so often," writes historian Darrin McMahon. "In France, Britain, and the Low Countries, in Germany, Italy, and the United States, disquisitions on happiness poured from the presses: reflections on happiness, treatises on happiness, systems of happiness, discourses, essays, sketches, and epistles."[8] The emotional philosophy of the time was illustrated even in the United States Declaration of Independence, which listed the pursuit of happiness as one of three inalienable rights. The Enlightenment's emphasis on reason created a culture where dogma was less pervasive and the fear of sin less encompassing, leaving people more free to focus on joy. As melancholy characterized the Reformation, happiness characterized the Enlightenment.

While basic human nature did not change dramatically during these periods, it is clear that the historical context did have an effect on the emotions people felt. What we feel, after all, is largely a product of what goes on around us.

The We Feel Fine database shows this most clearly when explored on a microhistorical level. The Virginia Tech Massacre in 2007, for example, prompted a spike in horror and sorrow, mostly among U.S. college students. "I can't even begin to explain how much sorrow I feel for those at Virginia Tech," wrote Taylor Rae, a freshman at FSU, the day after the shooting. "It's so hard to believe that a student did such a horrible thing. Being on a college campus, it's weird to think that it could've been here."[9] And Lissette Matos wrote, "I'm truly saddened by the events that took place yesterday at Virginia Tech. Though I may not be a student there, the pain they are suffering I feel here as well. As a college student myself, I can not even in my wildest imaginations ever think that something like this would happen while I'm in class."[10]

On June 25th, 2009, when Michael Jackson died, there was a spike in the feelings "shocked," "numb," "confused," and "sad." The pop megastar's passing caused the biggest one-day dip in happiness that we have seen in *We Feel Fine* since we started collecting feelings in 2005. Megan Smith, an editor in New York City, wrote, "I feel like a big part of my childhood has been shut away forever with Michael Jackson's death."[11] And Lance Foxx, a 30-year-old Navy reservist, wrote, "I grew up as a child of the 80s and I remember just about everything Michael Jackson did. He was one of the kindest and most giving celebrities the world will ever know. It is a true shame to see him go."[12]

While tragedies tend to evoke the most dramatic mass emotional swings on the blogosphere, the historical effects found in *We Feel Fine* are not limited to tragedies. Valentine's Day each year sees a dichotomous spike in love and loneliness, New Year's sees a spike in reflection and hope, and Christmas sees a spike in feelings of festiveness and generosity. Our emotions change based on the day, and big days provoke emotional changes. This chapter explores the "when" of emotion, looking at how people feel about selected events, holidays, and even weather conditions.

Laura Thieme and her daughter, Melina

A study of the *We Feel Fine* database shows that, at the time that Sam Zients wrote his election night blog post, hopefulness was not the only feeling that had changed its topography in the blogosphere's emotional landscape—over the previous sixteen months, anxiety about the economy had been steadily rising. In the second half of 2008, bloggers wrote about their feelings about the economy more than five times as often as they did in the first half of 2007. Laura Thieme, a small business owner, blogger, and mother-to-be, summarized the pervasive sentiment around the economy in her blog post on October 30th, 2008, just a few days before the election: "I'm scared about the unknown, scared about the economy, life's changes as a woman trying to solve problems for both clients, employees, students, and vendors, as well as herself and her new child."[13]

However, it is a testament to the optimism of human nature that on that same night, as on every night since *We Feel Fine* started collecting data from blogs, hope was expressed more often than anxiety. "I've made it this far," wrote Laura near the end of her post, "now it's time to make it a little further—and come home with my little child. I can then look forward to the Christmas holidays and ending this year with a family. It won't just be about me. It'll be including her in everything. I have chosen her to inspire me."[14] ♥

1, 2. Sam Zients. http://www.lolsam.com/?p=811
3. RobBrooks-Bilson. http://www.flickr.com/photos/brooks-bilson/3004797688/
4. Jun Loayza. http://www.junloayza.com/just-for-fun/i-am-so-proud-of-my-country/
5. Stearns, Peter N. "History of Emotions: Issues of Change and Impact" *Handbook of Emotions* (New York: Guildford Press, 2008). Edited by Michael Lewis and Jeannette M. Haviland-Jones.
6. Luther, Martin. *Large Catechism*. 1530
7. Weber, Max. *The Protestant Ethic and the Spirit of Capitalism*, translated by Peter Baher and Gordon C. Wells. (New York: Penguin Books, 2002).
8. McMahon, D. *Happiness: A History*, (Atlantic Monthly Press, 2006).
9. Taylor Rae. http://grimxreaper.livejournal.com/119006.html
10. Lisette Matos. http://craftygirly.com/2007/04/17/truly-saddened/
11. Megan Smith. http://www.megansminute.com/2009/06/michael-jackson-dead-at-age-50-rip-michael.html
12. Lance Foxx. http://lance-foxx.livejournal.com/181341.html
13, 14. Laura Thieme. http://www.laurathieme.com/a-fertility-journey/election-time-babies-to-deliver-economic-environmental-changes-oh-my.php

SUNNY

Distinctive themes
mentioned when sunny

sun	clouds	warmth
shine	moon	dawn
rays	melting	rainy

I DON'T REALLY FEEL LIKE PRAYING OR REFLECTING TODAY I JUST FEEL LIKE RELAXING LAUGHING AND WILING AWAY THIS SLEEPY SUNNY AFTERNOON

a 31-year-old in washington, d.c.

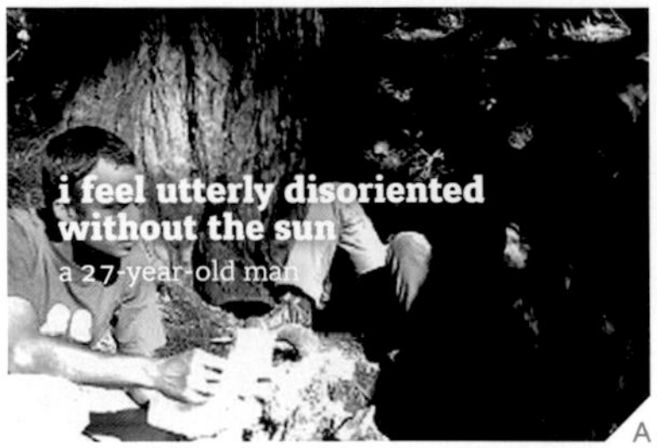

i feel utterly disoriented without the sun
a 27-year-old man

A

i feel the full breeze in my hair and see the sun shining strong on the leaves i will not ask for more
someone

B

sunny
1. of or pertaining to the sun
2. shining; bright; brilliant; radiant
3. exposed to the rays of the sun
4. cheerful; genial

● i could see the sun but i couldn't feel it ● i took fosse on a long walk and listened to music it was just one of those feel good about nature and the world walks where the weather gives you positive energy ● i feel so much more alive with the sun shining brightly above me ● i feel good because although i wasted perfect weather to catch up on sleep i slept ● i could feel the sun kissing me and my skin eagerly eating up all its radiation ● i feeling better but it felt like the weather was finally beginning to change into something more habitable ● i always feel sick after i've been in the sun for a while ● i don't know if it's the weather or what but i've been feeling sad ● i feel like i'm having sun stroke

Distinctive feelings

○ Sunny · Average

| ● **bright** | ● cheerful | ● warm | ● lovely | ● optimistic | ● special | ● happy |

I WISH THE SUN
WOULDN'T GO DOWN
SO EARLY BECAUSE
I FEEL LIKE THE
NIGHT COMES TOO
FAST AND THEN ALL
I EVER WANT TO DO
IS RUN AWAY

someone in los angeles, california

i always feel like looking at
something sunny and nice
a 36-year-old in sheffield, england

A

i feel the sun
someone

C

153

i feel sun in the sky it's a new day it's a new life for
me and i'm feeling good
someone

B

I LOOK OUT OF
THE WINDOW AND
IT'S SUNNY AND
I FEEL GUILTY FOR
EVEN CONSIDERING
TURNING THE
COMPUTER ON
someone

Observations

A sunny day often inspires **happiness** in people. When it is sunny outside people express feeling **joyful** and **cheerful**. They also express a feeling of lightheartedness while enjoying a clear sunny day. The sun also tends to inspire a great feeling of **optimism**. People are often struck by how beautiful the sun is and frequently recognize and acknowledge its **warmth** or **loveliness**. People will most often talk about the sun when it's shining brightly, when it emerges out of the clouds or after a hard rain, and also at **dawn** when it first appears. ❤

CLOUDY

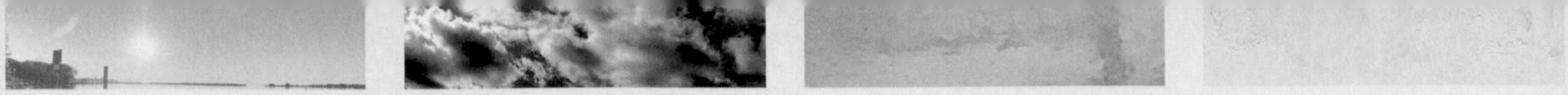

Distinctive themes
mentioned when cloudy

- **sunny**
- rainy
- skies
- storm
- silver lining
- sunlight
- rainy
- gray

i feel deep gratitude when i sit at the open window see moving clouds
a 24-year-old woman

A

I AM A WINTER GIRL AT HEART CLOUDY AND GREY SKIES MAKE ME FEEL AT PEACE

someone

i feel a storm a comin'
someone

B

I USUALLY FEEL HAPPY WHEN THE SUN'S SHINING DON'T EVEN TALK TO ME ON CLOUDY DAYS

someone

cloudy

1. overcast or obscured with clouds
2. consisting of a cloud or clouds
3. indicating gloom, anxiety, sullenness
4. confused; indistinct; obscure; dark

• i feel embarrassed because its a bit disconcerting wearing shades when its cloudy and dark out • i feel much happier when it's sunny outside and feel down when it's cloudy • i love cloudy weather it cools the house and me right down and i feel like i get so much more done • i kind of feel like i haven't left seattle it's been rainy cloudy since we got here • i had been feeling a bit down in the dumps for a while because it was so cloudy and rainy • whenever i wake to a dark cloudy morning i can't help but feel refreshed on the inside • i feel trapped in a cage as soon as the cold and cloudy weather moves in • i tend to hate cloudy weather because it makes me feel lethargic all day long

Distinctive feelings
○ Cloudy • Average

gloomy · dreary · cold · cool · depressed · afraid · lonely

i feel like a little child again when i look at clouds as beautiful as this
a woman

A

i feel emotion when i see the sky filled with clouds in red
a 38-year-old man

B

Observations

Cloudiness most commonly gives people a sense of **dreariness**. People often express feeling more **depressed** when it's cloudy outside than when the sky is clear. People also express feeling **fear** and **loneliness** more often when it is cloudy out than when the sun is shining. People frequently express feeling a strong physical effect when it's cloudy; that is, they feel cold or cool. People will often talk about the clouds in one of the following ways: in contrast to the sun or rain, when they predict a **storm**, and when it's **gray out**. ♥

RAINY

Distinctive themes
mentioned when rainy

pouring
drops
gloomy
storm
shelter
soaking
sunlight
sky
wet

i couldn't believe i had forgotten how wonderful it was to feel fresh rain
a woman

A

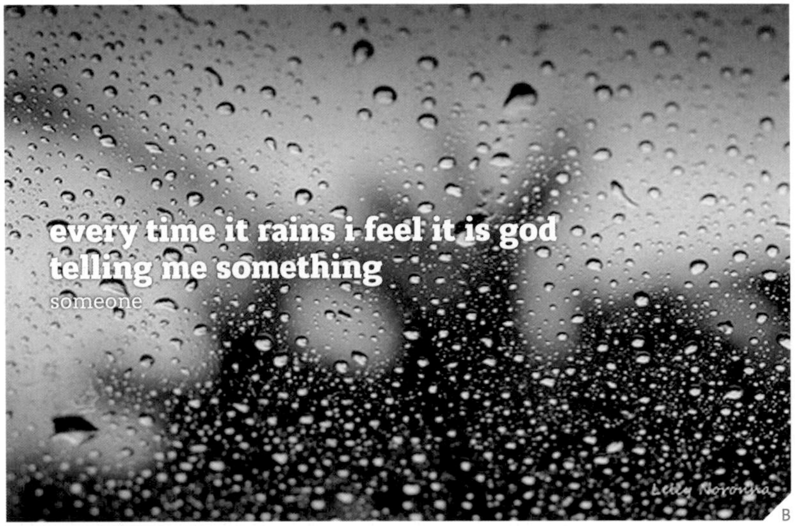

every time it rains i feel it is god telling me something
someone

B

i feel nice to be in a taxi
someone

C

I WANT TO NOT BE LONELY ON RAINY NIGHTS I WANT YOU TO NOT BE STUBBORN I WANT TO NOT FEEL SO DEFEATED EVERY TIME I THINK I CAN'T COMPLETE A SIMPLE TASK

someone

rainy

1. the weather condition when it rains
2. abounding with rain; wet; showery
3. to pour or shower down from above
4. the descent of water from the clouds

● i can feel it when i smell rain when the trees seem to be beckoning me down another path or when the only sound i hear is my heart racing with the wind ● i can still hear the rain pattering on the ground and i'm about to dismiss the noise before i realise that i can't feel said rain ● i feel bad for her because we have had lots of rain here and in an attempt to keep her from getting more moisture in her hair she has had to be kept in a stall ● i don't even feel like going out in the rain ● i feel i can climb into the seasons here get lost in the leaves and the rain that dumps on you for months and months ● i want to feel the rain against my cheeks ● i love the feeling i get when i walk in the rain

I FEEL ISOLATED AND IT'S RAINING AND I FUCKING HATE OVERCAST RAINY WEATHER

someone

when the rain falls i feel happy
someone

A

i can't describe how elevated gloomy weather makes me feel
someone

B

i wish i could say that i feel like dancing in the rain but the truth is i feel like crawling into bed
someone

C

Observations

People will very often express a deep sense of **melancholy** when it's raining outside. They express feeling **gloomy**, sometimes **sleepy**, sometimes **miserable**, and very often feeling **wet**. However, there is also a very large number of people for whom the rain has the opposite effect. They say that the rain inspires in them a feeling of **happiness** or **vitality**. The emotions expressed in rainy weather share many similarities to the emotions expressed when it is cloudy, including making people feel cold. People often talk about the rain when it's pouring or during a storm. ♥

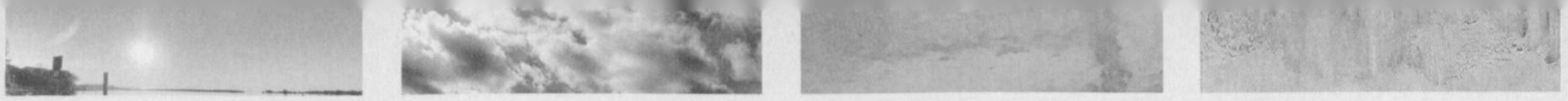

Distinctive themes
mentioned when snowy

- **christmas**
- mountains
- icy
- roads
- boots
- santa
- winter
- storm
- melting

i feel like a child again

A

i love the feeling of being inside on a snowy day feeling safe and warm
someone in montreal, canada

B

I NEED TO FEEL SAFE BECAUSE MY STUBBORN ASS OF A HUSBAND SEEMS TO THINK SNOW WILL NEVER GET IN HIS WAY OF GETTING SOMEWHERE

someone in bothell, washington

snowy

1. marked by the presence of snow
2. white like snow
3. abounding with snow
4. reminiscent of snow

• i can't stand winter except for how good it feels to enter a warm building after being outside for a long period of time • i am hoping this tired feeling is just tiredness and not the onset of winter depression • i can feel myself succumbing to the darkness of winter already • i am a winter girl but even i can't help but feel sad when i leave for work before the sun comes up and get out of class after it sets • i know people have different feelings about snow i love it • i still feel that childlike excitement about new fallen snow all crisp and glittery especially if i get a few hours off work • i feel robbed we got about 2 inches of snow last night but the areas just east of us got 8-10 inches

Distinctive feelings
○ Snowy • Average

freezing · cold · wet · peaceful · excited · alive · glad

i feel blessed to being able to enjoy all the wonderful things our 4 seasons offer
someone

A

I AM HOPING THIS TIRED FEELING IS JUST TIREDNESS AND NOT THE ONSET OF WINTER DEPRESSION

a 27-year-old in rochester, new york

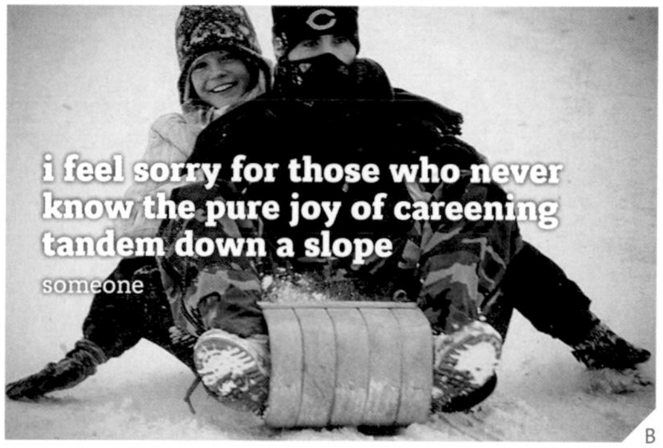

i feel sorry for those who never know the pure joy of careening tandem down a slope
someone

B

snow makes me feel kinda funny

C

i feel as if i had reached some point of balance and sanity
a 38-year-old man

D

i feel so calm and peaceful

E

i feel joy in my heart and snowflakes on my cheeks
a woman

F

Observations

Snow is most commonly associated with positive feelings. While people primarily talk about the temperature and feeling **cold** in the snow, for many snow brings about a feeling of **peacefulness**. However, for many others, the snow has the opposite effect and makes them feel **excited** or **alive**. Children and teenagers, in particular, tend to get excited when it snows. People tend to associate snow with Christmas, the mountains, and winter. ♥

CHRISTMAS

Distinctive themes
mentioned at Christmas

- **santa**
- holiday
- gifts
- spirit
- tree
- cheer
- shopping
- lights
- celebrate

A

I WANT MY CHRISTMAS TO FEEL LIKE IT USED TO

someone

This photograph was taken on the 2nd + last Christmas that Deborah was married to her husband. That christmas he was to return from D.C. where he relocated for work. When he never returned Deborah was crushed, but not surprised. Shortly after, she discovered that he had stolen her brother's identity and had become engaged to another woman whom he abandoned after running up 32K worth of credit card debt in her name. Deborah divorced her husband and is moving on.

I DON'T LIKE CHRISTMAS IN HOW I'M FORCED TO TRY AND FEEL LESS THAN CONTENT WITH WHAT I HAVE ALREADY

someone

i feel like i can be open about my love for them now because it's christmas time and socially acceptable to be wearing monkeys with santa hats
someone

B

christmas

1. annual Christian holiday on Dec. 25th
2. commemorates Christ's birth
3. often celebrated with a church service
4. gifts are usually exchanged

● i'm addicted to christmas and everything associated with it even if it makes me feel nostalgic for snow ● i feel that i have an excuse to go and while i have most of my christmas shopping done i have bought a lot for myself too ● i have the sinking feeling my novel will never be done by christmas for my parents and i will cry bucketloads ● i spent 10 at an antique store for something i wasn't that thrilled about all the while feeling like i just wished i had a christmas book from my childhood ● i felt a little bad for agreeing because it was obvious that he still didn't feel well but we recently decided that we won't be able to come home for christmas so i'm thankful for the quality time together

Distinctive feelings
○ Christmas • Average

festive · cozy · joyful · magical · cheerful · spoiled · generous

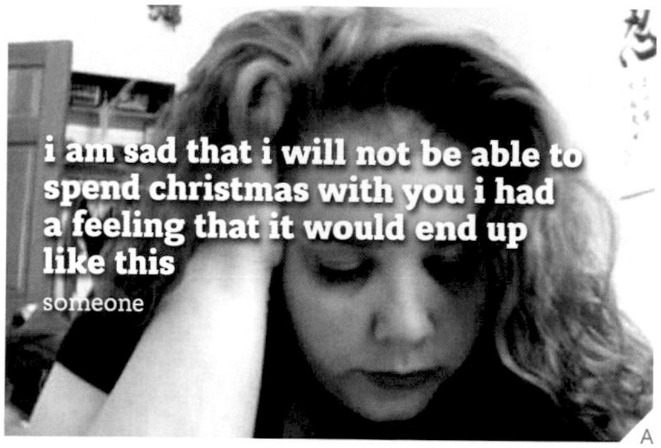

i am sad that i will not be able to spend christmas with you i had a feeling that it would end up like this
someone

A

B

i know its early but i am feeling the christmas spirit
someone

C

i always feel a little sad after christmas has gone
someone

D

i don't even feel christmasy at all
a woman in selangor, malaysia

E

DECEMBER

6	7	8	9	10	11	12
13	14	15	16	17	18	19
20	21	22	23	24	**25**	26
27	28	28	30	31		

Observations

On Christmas, people express feeling a great deal of **joy** and **cheer**. This is due mostly to the gathering of family and friends. People also express feeling cozy, especially when surrounded by loved ones. The traditions, especially the Christmas trees and Christmas lights, make people feel **magical** and **festive**. The giving and receiving of **gifts** play an interesting role in people's feelings about the day. People express **gratitude** for getting gifts, but more often they express a feeling of **generosity** during Christmas time, and people often express feeling **spoiled** on Christmas. ♥

Distinctive themes
mentioned on Election Day

vote
returns
november
patriotic
volunteer
democrats
senate
campaign
obama

I FEEL LIKE I KNOW WHAT AN HISTORIC MOMENT REALLY MEANS NOW

a 23-year-old

On November 4th, 2008 Barack Obama was elected president of the United States.

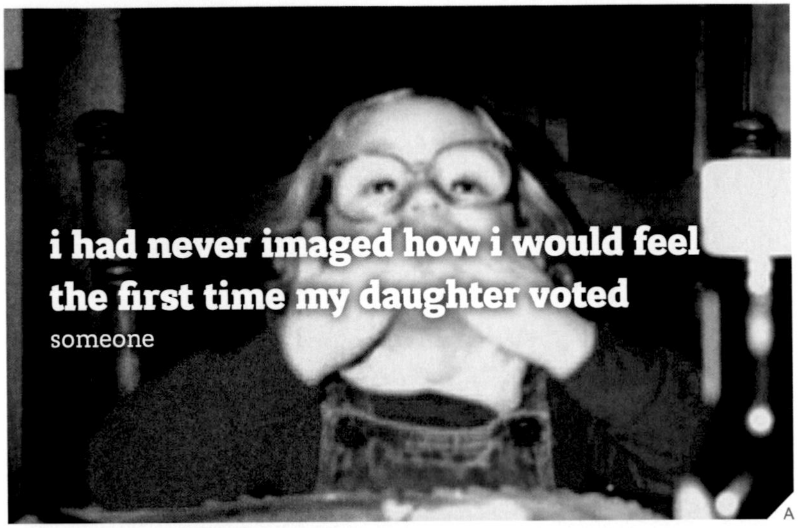

i had never imaged how i would feel the first time my daughter voted
someone

A

In this election voter turnout was the highest it had been for 40 years.

i imagine i feel the way that other generations felt when they voted for jfk
a man

B

He won the election with 52.9% of the vote and 365 electoral votes.

i feel like they blew up the death star
a man

C

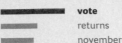

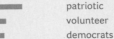

i feel like he really could win this
someone
CHANGE

D

election day 2008

1. day to vote for elected officials
2. 1st Tuesday after 1st Monday in Nov.
3. Barack Obama elected president of U.S.
4. first African American president

● i watched indiana turn bright blue and senator obama become president elect obama and i cried and i feel like i can breathe again because we actually did it ● i feel differently i am inspired moved and more hopeful than i have ever been ● i feel safe enough to predict that astrology is going to become a part of the mainstream of consciousness pretty soon ● i feel better but i wonder if it's because mccain palin lost rather and obama biden winning ● i have studied the local issues a bit i still didn't feel that i had spent enough time to really understand all the candidates ● i feel nothing but pride that barack obama has been elected for once i can t wait to see what a president might do for the country

Distinctive feelings
○ Election Day • Average

patriotic | confident | proud | depressed | beautiful | excited

i feel pretty good right now

A

I DON'T CARE HOW YOU FEEL ABOUT HIM POLITICALLY YOU HAVE TO SAY THIS IS AMERICA AT ITS GRANDEST

someone

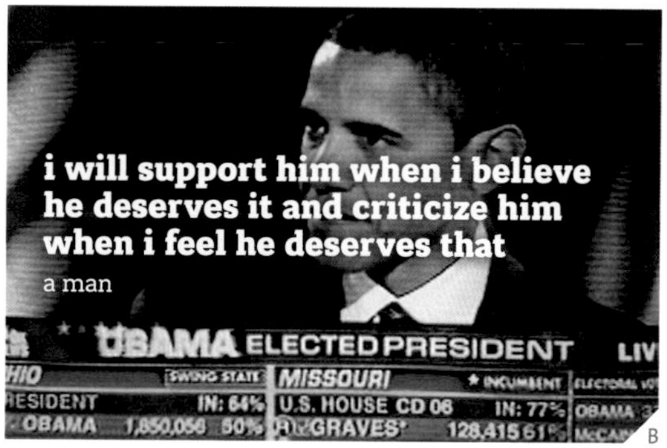

i will support him when i believe he deserves it and criticize him when i feel he deserves that

B

The feeling "proud" spiked on blogs to 4 times the normal level, and it remains the proudest day since we started collecting feelings in 2005.

C

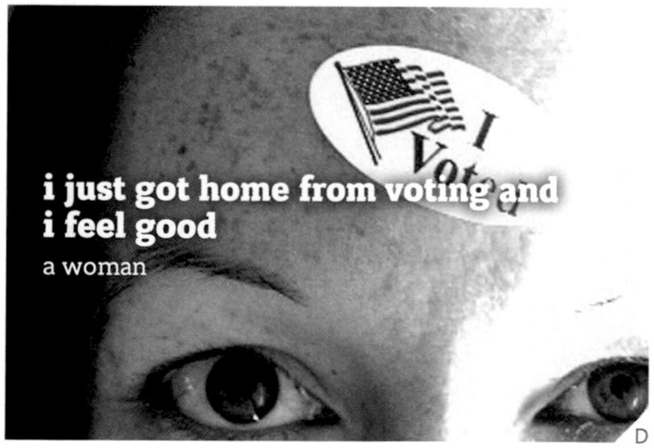

i just got home from voting and i feel good
i feel like i can take a breath for a minute
a woman
I Voted

D

I FEEL LIKE A LONG NIGHTMARE IS OVER TONIGHT

someone

NOVEMBER 2008

2	3	**4**	5	6	7	8
9	10	11	12	13	14	15
16	17	18	19	20	21	22
23	24	25	26	27	28	29

Observations

Election Day 2008 saw a flood of emotions on the web. Overwhelmingly, people felt **patriotic** because they **voted** in an historical presidential election. Many Obama supporters expressed their **confidence** and felt that Barack Obama was sure to win. As the blogosphere is somewhat left-leaning, when Obama won, people expressed feeling **proud**, **excited**, and very **hopeful** for the future. John McCain also had a large number of supporters in the blogosphere, and, at his loss, they expressed feeling very **depressed**. ♥

HALLOWEEN

Distinctive themes
mentioned on Halloween

- **costume**
- candy
- parties
- dressing up
- trick or treating
- pumpkins
- october
- scary movies
- fun

i can't feel my hands
a 23-year-old in bridgeton, missouri

A

i'm not really into the whole halloween thingy as i feel it is more of an american tradition
a man

B

I FEEL THAT SO MANY AMERICAN KIDS ARE SO SPOILED ANYMORE THAT THERE'S NO SPIRIT OR LIFE NO JOY IN THE TYPICAL TRADITIONS AND FESTIVITIES OBVIOUSLY HALLOWEEN IN PARTICULAR

someone in new york city

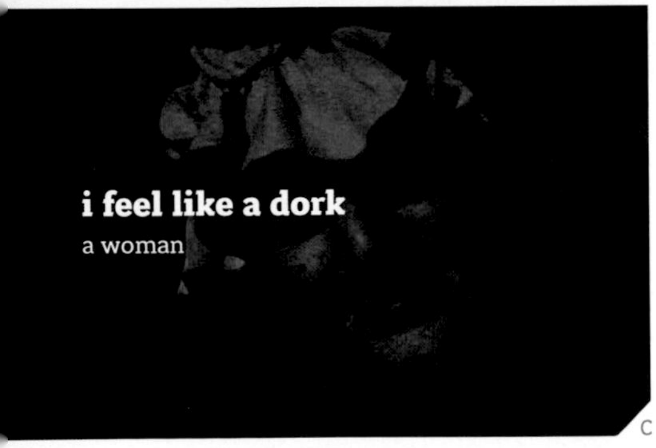

i feel like a dork
a woman

C

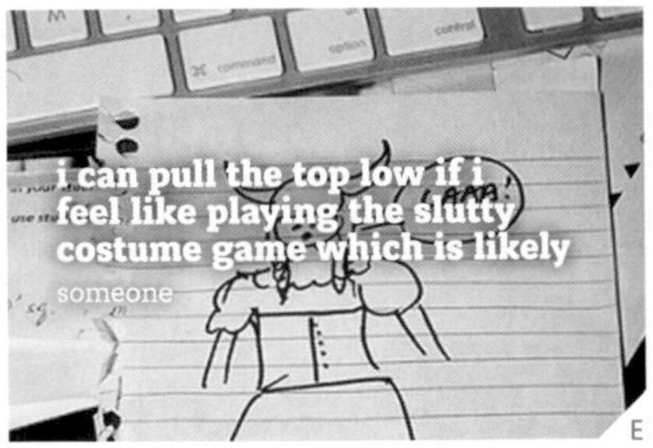

i can pull the top low if i feel like playing the slutty costume game which is likely
someone

E

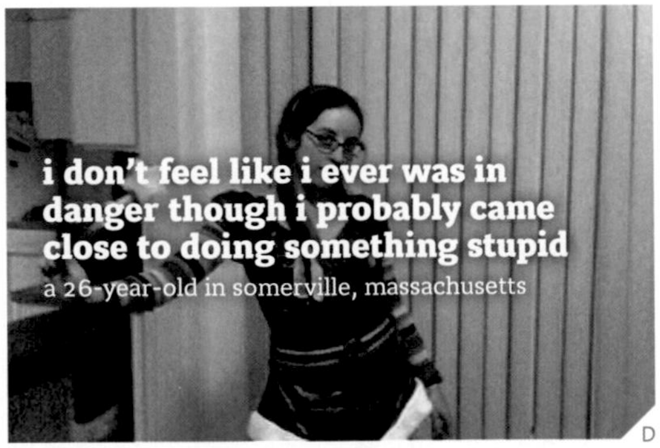

i don't feel like i ever was in danger though i probably came close to doing something stupid
a 26-year-old in somerville, massachusetts

D

halloween

1. the evening preceding All Saints' Day
2. in the U.S., celebrated on October 31st
3. traditionally celebrated with costumes
4. has roots in Celtic festival of Samhain

● i realized it was halloween and that i woke up without that magical omg it's halloween feeling ● i feel kinda like a killjoy for not doing it but i've never really been into halloween at least not to the point of actually thinking about a costume until yesterday and by then it was just too late ● i know that when we start cutting pumpkins and getting costumes ready and digging through the candy it will feel like halloween ● i smiled to myself feeling i had decieved them into thinking i was normal that i was just dressed up for halloween and not just some crazy girl in a weird costume ● i feel alone in my appreciation for halloween ● i don't know what the halloween equivalent to scrooge is but i feel it

Distinctive feelings
○ Halloween • Average

excited · lame · awesome · shitty · silly · blah · sexy · creative

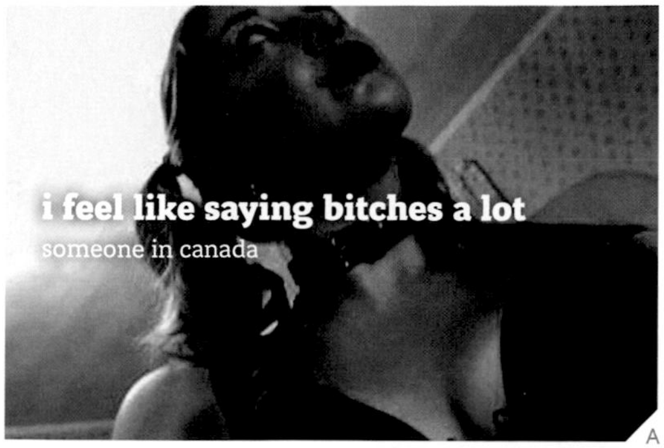

i feel like saying bitches a lot
someone in canada
A

i feel i don't know her
someone
B

i feel my belly growing
someone
C

i feel a storm a brewin'
someone
D

OCTOBER

6	7	8	9	10	11	12
13	14	15	16	17	18	19
20	21	22	23	24	25	26
27	28	28	30	**31**		

Observations

Halloween is a holiday that evokes the emotions of youth, as we primarily associate the holiday with **fun** and **excitement**. However, we see a dichotomy in how people feel about the holiday; while many people express feeling that Halloween is **awesome**, others express the feeling that it is **lame**. Of all the elements that make up Halloween, people talk most frequently about their **costumes**. Costumes give people the opportunity to feel **creative** and many people take the opportunity to wear costumes that make them feel **sexy**. ♥

JULY 4TH

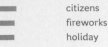

Distinctive themes
mentioned on July 4th

	patriotic		citizens		american
	parade		fireworks		beer
	celebration		holiday		americans

you know how i feel about all things american
someone

B

i feel like mel's face is truly representative of the direction our country's leaders are taking us
- a man

A

i feel the winds of change blowing and the pendulum swinging back
a man

C

i woke up not exactly feeling proud to be an american on this independence day
a 30-year-old in seattle, washington

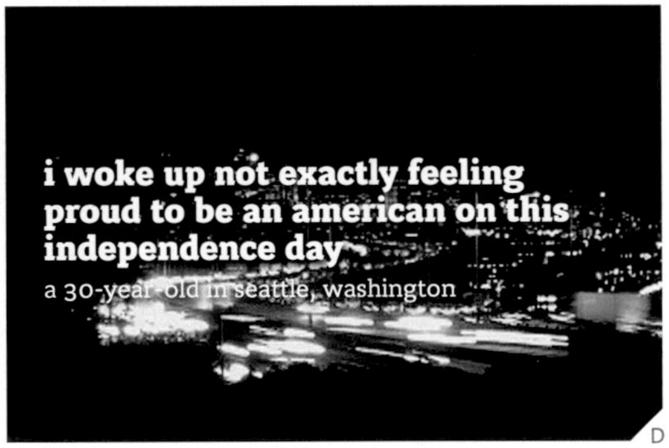

D

I AM AN UNABASHED PATRIOT AND FEEL BLESSED TO HAVE BEEN BORN IN AMERICA
someone

july 4th

1. date commemorating U.S. independence
2. commonly celebrated with fireworks
3. legal holiday in the U.S.
4. Declaration of Independence was 1776

● i feel like i'll have much more freedom there than anywhere else ● i feel like the fourth of july is just another tool for judging patriotism and another weapon in the republican arsenal for turning liberals into the bad guys ● i know i must be odd but to me it doesn't really feel like the fourth of july until i watch the boston pops orchestra ● i can't really feel like an honest to good american if i don't see fireworks on the fourth i guess i will have to embrace that canadian heritage i have oh canada ● i like the fourth of july the fireworks the bbq's that could happen but this year i just don't feel the same as i used to ● i am an unabashed patriot and feel blessed to have been born in america

Distinctive feelings
○ July 4th • Average

patriotic · american · political · proud · excited · free

I HIGHLY DOUBT I WILL EVER UNDERSTAND WHY AMERICANS FEEL THE NEED TO CELEBRATE AND SHOW THEIR PATRIOTISM WITH EXPLOSIVES

someone in auburn, washington

i feel hope for our beautiful nation
someone

A

i love my country but today i don't feel much like celebrating
someone

B

Kevin posted this photo on July 4th, 2008. He expressed that patriotism included "the responsibility to carry out public discourse on political matters and demand change when we see fit." In his post, he expressed concern for environmental policy, the Iraq war, and Guantanamo.
On July 4th, 2009, he sent us an e-mail saying that he felt like America is back on the right track and he once again feels like celebrating.
↵

JULY

		1	2	3	**4**	5
6	7	8	9	10	11	12
13	14	15	16	17	18	19
20	21	22	23	24	25	26

Observations

The 4th of July, unsurprisingly, evokes strong feelings of **patriotism** throughout the **United States**. On Independence Day, people express feeling **patriotic**, **American**, and **proud**. The day also evokes political sentiments, as the holiday rightly inspires people to take the time to **reflect** on the state of American **politics**. These sentiments are often more mixed on the blogosphere, and were especially mixed in 2006 through 2008. But overall, the general sentiment is one of **fun**, **excitement**, **pride**, **patriotism**, **fireworks**, **parades**, and **beer**. ♥

NEW YEAR'S

Distinctive themes
mentioned at New Year's

- **eve**
- resolution
- christmas
- celebration
- holidays
- midnight
- calendar
- parties
- goals

i can either keep feeling the way i do or do something about it
someone

A

i feel like this is the first new year that i've met face to face
someone in new york

B

I HAD NO NEW YEAR'S KISS AND FELT LIKE AN IDIOT, BUT THAT WASN'T GOING TO STOP ME HAVING FUN

a 26-year-old

i feel a new chapter beginning
a woman

C

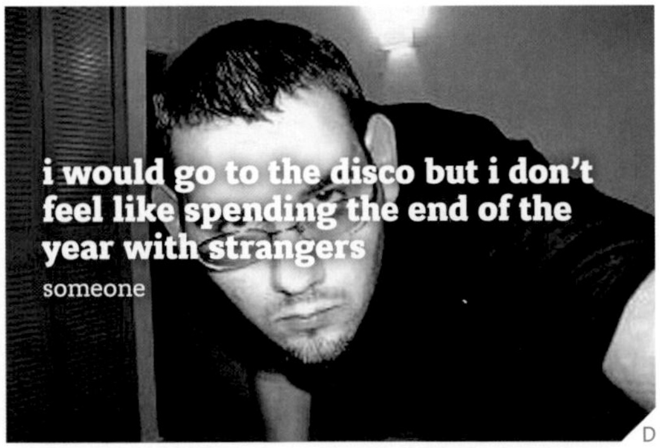

i would go to the disco but i don't feel like spending the end of the year with strangers
someone

D

new year's

1. in the West, January 1st
2. marks beginning of calendar year
3. celebrated with midnight countdown
4. often celebrated with fireworks

• i'm working tonight so wont be out partying but i must admit i'm not a fan of the whole new year thing anyway i'm not sure why but it always makes me feel sad • i feel lonely while living with someone • feel like new year resolutions are just an excuse to talk up plans and not act on them • i dont feel like its a new year • i feel as if life has changed alot this past year for me • i was fragile and very insecure when i got here and i'm feeling stronger and better now • i make the same two resolutions every year with one physical one thrown in just so i can feel like a failure when i don't do it • i feel so much stronger as a person over last year • i feel myself once more

Distinctive feelings
○ New Year's • Average

hopeful | drunk | happy | optimistic | excited | ready

i feel like i got my ass kicked too
a woman

A

Sarah's resolution for 2007 was to keep her mind open. She thought she might move from Arizona to Portland, or meet someone and elope to Vegas. In 2007, she moved to LA, hated it, moved back to Arizona, and decided she likely won't get married until she is 35. Her only resolution for 2009 was to be happy. ↓

I DON'T BELIEVE IN MAKING RESOLUTIONS BECAUSE IF YOU FEEL YOU NEED TO CHANGE SOMETHING ABOUT YOURSELF WHY WAIT TILL JANUARY 1ST

a 27-year-old man in mayville, wisconsin

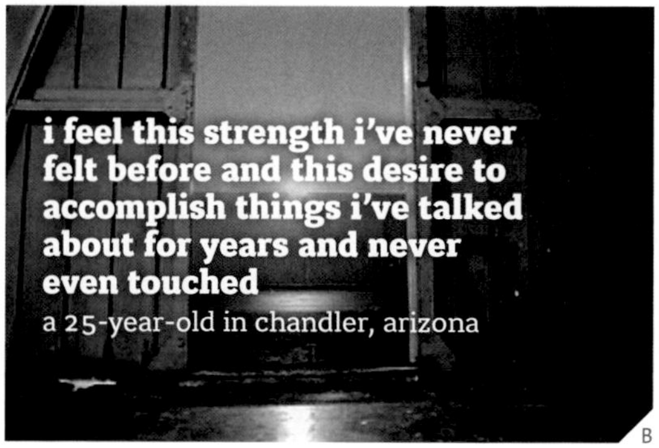

i feel this strength i've never felt before and this desire to accomplish things i've talked about for years and never even touched
a 25-year-old in chandler, arizona

B

JANUARY

		1	2	3	4	5
6	7	8	9	10	11	12
13	14	15	16	17	18	19
20	21	22	23	24	25	26

Observations

New Year's is a time of **reflection** and **partying**. On both New Year's Day and New Year's Eve, people often express feeling **hopeful**, **optimistic**, **excited**, and ready for the new year to begin, but are also **contemplative** of the previous year. The **excitement** and **happiness** of the upcoming new year is very strong, although it is commingled with a seasonal **post-holiday depression** that begins a couple of days after Christmas and continues until a few days after the new year. On New Year's Eve, people most commonly express feeling **drunk**. ♥

Distinctive themes
mentioned on Valentine's Day

roses
candy
couples
gifts
cards
flowers
chocolate
love
single

i feel sick and colorless and extra extra cranky
a 26-year-old woman

A

i feel blessed by having a wonderful partner in crime great family and creative friends
a 32-year-old man

B

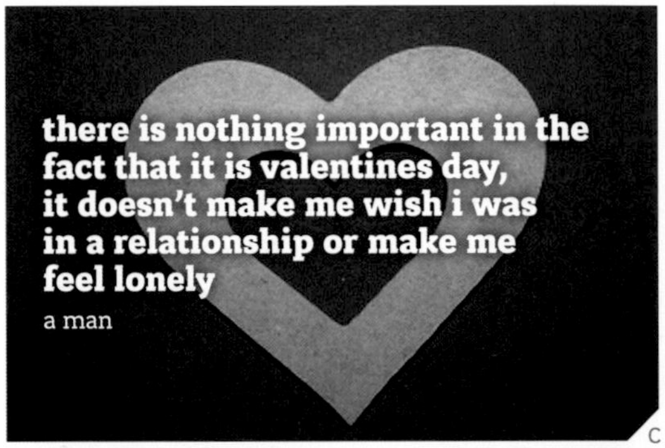

there is nothing important in the fact that it is valentines day, it doesn't make me wish i was in a relationship or make me feel lonely
a man

C

This photograph was taken four years after the couple started dating, six months after they were engaged, one month after they broke the engagement, and one month before Jennifer, the blogger, was diagnosed with Bipolar Disorder. They are still happily together.

i feel like a loser for being single
a man

D

E

I'M BLESSED TO HAVE SOMEONE THAT MAKES ME FEEL LIKE ITS VALENTINE'S DAY EVERYDAY

someone in makati city, philippines

valentine's day

1. February 14th of each year
2. often involves the exchange of flowers
3. a day to celebrate loved ones
4. Cupid is the traditional mascot

• i'm single but i really don't care that i am because i'm sharing valentines day with my closest friends and family and that makes this day feel special • i know i have wonderful friends they make me feel important on valentines day • i don't feel lonely today i'm actually happy being single on valentines day • i dont feel i need valentines day to express it because i will say and do things everyday to show it • i wonder if i will go to bed on valentines day feeling like i outsmarted them all • i would then use information contained in the book to justify to my girlfriend at the time why i did not participate valentines day and therefore did not feel need to purchase dinner cards candy etc

Distinctive feelings
o Valen. Day • Average

romantic · cheesy · lonely · special · cute · forced · depressed · evil

I ASSUMED THAT ONCE I HAD A BOYFRIEND SOMEONE TO SHARE IT WITH I WOULDN'T FEEL THIS WAY

someone

i feel so loved
a 38-year-old man

A

i hope that someone you care about helped you feel as special as i did today
someone

B

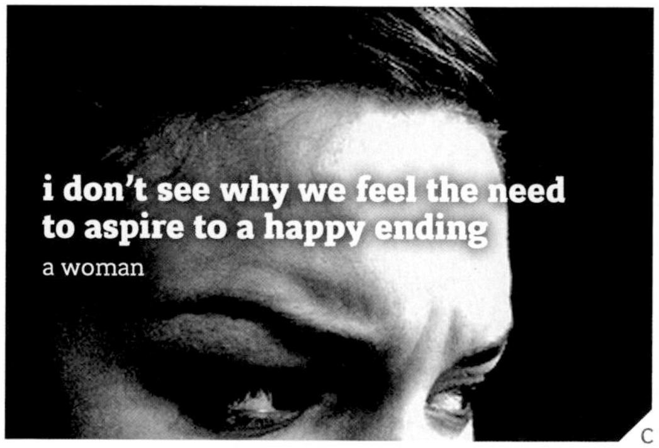

i don't see why we feel the need to aspire to a happy ending
a woman

C

FEBRUARY						
6	7	8	9	10	11	12
13	**14**	15	16	17	18	19
20	21	22	23	24	25	26
27	28	28				

Observations

Valentine's Day is an emotionally dichotomous day. Many people feel **loved** and **special** on Valentine's Day, while many others feel **lonely** and **depressed**. This dichotomy is also reflected in how people feel about the day itself: many feel that it's a **romantic** holiday, while many others feel that it is **cheesy**. Interestingly, while feelings like "loved" and "special" spike right on Valentine's Day, the feeling of "loneliness" starts climbing a few days before Valentine's Day. The most talked about gift on Valentine's Day are **roses**, followed by **candy**, **cards**, **flowers**, and **chocolate**. ♥

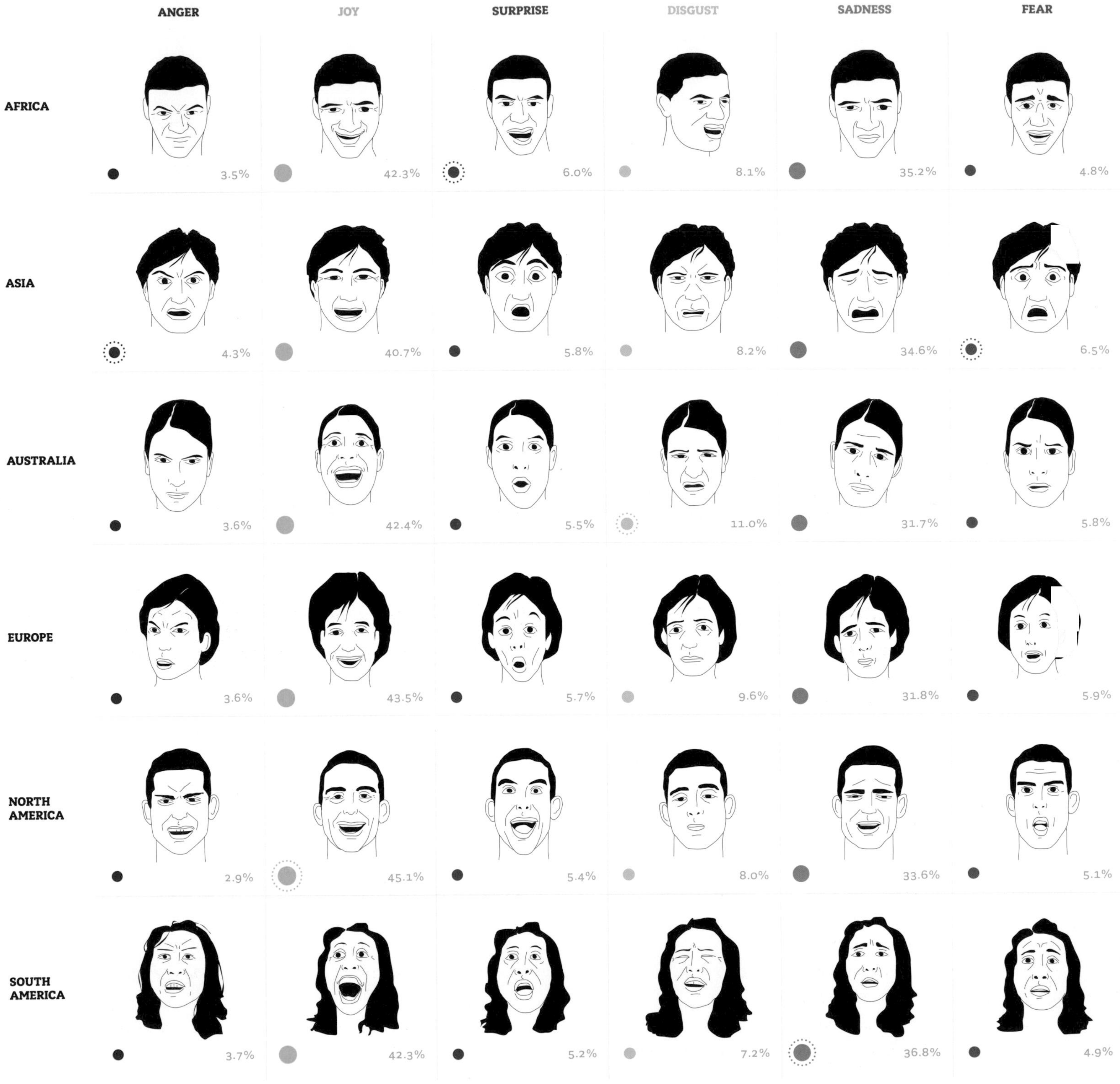
ANGER
JOY
SURPRISE
DISGUST
SADNESS
FEAR
AFRICA
3.5%
42.3%
6.0%
8.1%
35.2%
4.8%
ASIA
4.3%
40.7%
5.8%
8.2%
34.6%
6.5%
AUSTRALIA
3.6%
42.4%
5.5%
11.0%
31.7%
5.8%
EUROPE
3.6%
43.5%
5.7%
9.6%
31.8%
5.9%
NORTH AMERICA
2.9%
45.1%
5.4%
8.0%
33.6%
5.1%
SOUTH AMERICA
3.7%
42.3%
5.2%
7.2%
36.8%
4.9%

5 Where On the effects of culture on emotion

Tags: cultural anthropology, geography

On March 23rd, 2009, John Deal came home from Japan. What began as a one-year trip when he was 33 had reached its terminus some four and a half years later, and he found himself "rocketed (back) to New York City to make my way amid immigrants, miracles, rabbis, and one lovely wife."[1]

John didn't think that he would miss Japan. Even after four and a half years there, he felt like an outsider. It wasn't so much that he wanted to be an insider, but it hurt his pride that he never felt like he had the option. In his March 11th, 2009, blog post, John quotes the author Will Ferguson, writing: "Like a hostess in a snackbar, Japan flirts its way into our hearts, it pours our drinks, it strokes our ego, it smiles and sighs and listens to our stories, and then, in a moment of silence, it asks: 'How did you ever get so fat?' It is not that I want inside and can't that bothers me. I do not want to be Japanese. What rankles my Western heart is that it doesn't matter what I do or do not want."[2]

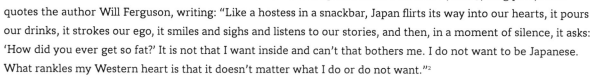

John Deal in Japan

A few days later, John was walking home from a cheap dinner along the cracked blacktop and stained concrete when his wife stopped and pointed out a slender, shaking tree, clad in faint pink. It was a plum tree. "Cherry trees get all the press," he wrote in his blog post that evening, "and they are extraordinary, but the sight of a grove of white plum trees has comforted me during the rainy walks to the train station every February and March since 2005. Plum trees aren't flashy, but they exude a quiet, reassuring loveliness. And like the *sakura*, they are everywhere, which means that all those unremarkable tangles of black branches you hurried by eleven months of the year will suddenly surprise you with a fan-dance of color and scent one morning in late winter... Japan is like that: a country of moments, fleeting glimpses that shock you with unpredicted beauty."[3]

In 1954, the psychologist Paul Ekman began his lifelong research on facial expressions by trying to refute Charles Darwin. Darwin had suggested that emotions were universal, biological in origin, and that many nonhuman mammals shared the same primary emotions as humans. Ekman, on the other hand, hypothesized that emotions were largely cultural in origin. In other words, that where people are from influences how they feel.

However, as he spent time researching the topic, Ekman reversed his views, and has since produced a large body of research supporting that basic emotions, like joy, sorrow, fear, anger, suprise, and disgust, are pan-cultural.

Ekman's turning point came in his study of the isolated Fore tribe in Papua New Guinea in the late 1960s. He showed the tribespeople photos of various facial expressions, from cultures to whom the Fore had not yet been exposed. The Fore were able to reliably recognize the facial expressions of fear, disgust, anger, and surprise. Furthermore, when the Fore were told a story designed to elicit one of those emotions, they would respond with the same facial expressions as would a typical Westerner when told the same story. Whether we are American or Japanese or Fore, Ekman concluded, we are wired for the same basic emotions.[4]

A decade later, the anthropologist Catherine Lutz spent nine months living on the tiny island of Ifaluk, Micronesia, with a population of only 430 people. Lutz's time on Ifaluk led her to a conclusion that was somewhat different than Ekman's.

Ifaluk, an atoll on the Caroline Islands, has a total land area of about half a square mile, much smaller than New York's Central Park. At its highest point, Ifaluk rises only eight meters above sea level. The closest island to the Ifaluk is the 800-person island of Woleai, which is 40 kilometers away, and the nearest big city is Port Moresby in Papua New Guinea, about 2,000 kilometers away. The seas around the island are hazardous, and the traditional songs of the Ifaluk contain many laments to loved ones lost at sea.

The small size, isolation, and natural dangers make for an incredibly strong sense of community in Ifaluk, as Lutz quickly learned. During her first few weeks there, she saddened a group of women who came to visit her hut by asking, "Do you want to get some drinking water with me?" It was not until later that she realized that by addressing the women as "you," she implied a separation between her and them. A more correct way to ask this would have been to say, "We'll go and get water now, OK?" indicating the interdependence and collective decision making that were valued in the Ifaluk society.

Lutz found the emotions expressed by the Ifaluk to be quite different than those expressed in the United States, so much so that many of the words that the Ifaluk used to describe emotional states had no direct translation into English. The Ifaluk word *ker*, for example, loosely translates to "excited happiness." *Ker* was seen by the Ifaluk to be an emotion that can separate people from one another, and was rarely expressed on the island. Rather, the predominant form of happiness was *maluwelu*, or "gentle/calm/quiet." And while hotheaded anger was almost nonexistent on Ifaluk—in the nine months that Lutz lived on Ifaluk, the most serious aggressive act was one man touching the shoulder of another—an emotion that was expressed more commonly was *song*, or "justifiable anger," which generally occurred if someone publicly violated social customs. Unlike the Western concept of anger that arises when we feel that our rights have been violated, *song* arises among the Ifaluk out of social duty when they feel that social harmony might have been disturbed. The general response to *song* is *metagu*, an "anxiety/fear/shame" that prompts the offender to apologize and make reparation, thereby restoring the peace. The most important emotion on the island, Lutz found, was *fago*, or "compassion/love/sadness," especially for loved ones in need. In such an interdependent society, empathetic love reigns and disruptive emotions are suppressed.[5]

While the Ifaluk provide a particularly salient example of a strongly collectivist society and the emotions of its members, it is by no means unique. Japan, for example, places a stronger emphasis on societal interdependence than the heavily individualistic United States, and the dominant emotions in both countries reflect this cultural difference. Anger is far less commonly expressed between Japanese friends than between American friends, and the Japanese emotion *amae* (loosely translated as "the dependence on the kindness of loved ones") is so much less common in the United States that there is no direct English translation.[6, 7] Even Japanese and English emoticons differ—two of the most commonly used Japanese emoticons are those for "apologizing" (*m(_ _)m*) and "shy" (*(^^;)*), for which there are no English equivalents.[8]

John and his wife, Kat, happily back in the U.S.A., here at New York's Coney Island

As among the Ifaluk, disruptive, high-arousal emotions are less commonly expressed among Japanese than among Americans. "My experience," wrote John Deal in his May 20th, 2008, blog post, "is that most Japanese teens and adults who spend any amount of time in the United States find it hedonically overwhelming—not unlike the way Pinocchio and friends regarded Pleasure Island, but without the ears and braying. In general they find Americans likeable if a bit scary—kind of like big, overenthusiastic Irish wolfhounds."

Conversely, given his American upbringing, John feels a bit emotionally stifled in Japan: "I think the main thing Japanese people love about America is that we don't really have the whole *honne/tatemae* thing. *Tatamae* is your "face": how you must behave to fulfill your role, which is often a pretty illusory—but powerful—function of your sense of what everyone else wants from you. It blocks the expression of true feelings much of the time; only in a few rare contexts can you let your *honne*, or inner emotional life, show." John concludes: "Whatever flaws America possesses, we are by and large a highly emotionally *accessible* culture, albeit sometimes to the point of maudlin overshare."[9] While where we live, as Ekman discovered, doesn't affect our potential for expressing emotions, it can, as Lutz found, affect our practice.

The We Feel Fine database does not lend itself well to the statistical study of the geographic effects on emotion, since it collects only English-language blogs. We have some sense, for example, that people in England express happiness less frequently than people in the United States, but a comparative study of the United States and Japan is difficult because those blogging in the English language in Japan are unlikely to be representative of the Japanese population at large. We can, however, get a qualitative view of how people feel about the places in which they live. We can do this by exploring the singular moments—the fleeting glimpses of unpredictable beauty—which is what we will do in the pages that follow. ♥

1. John Deal. Blog URL withheld by request.
2. Will Ferguson. *Hitching Rides with Buddha*. (Edinburgh: Canongate Books, 2006).
3. John Deal. See 1.
4. Ekman, P.; Sorenson, E.R.; and Friesen, W.V. (April 1969) "Pan-Cultural Elements in Facial Displays of Emotion." *Science*, 164(3875):86-88.
5. Lutz, C. *Unnatural Emotions. Everyday Sentiments on a Micronesian Atoll and Their Challenge to Western Theory*. University of Chicago Press, 1988.
6. Oatley, Keith, Dacher Keltner, and Jennifer Jenkins. *Understanding Emotions*, (Oxford: Blackwell Publishing, 2006).
7. Doi, Takeo. *Anatomy of Dependence*. (Tokyo, Kodansha International, 2002).
8. Japanese Emoticons. http://whatjapanthinks.com/2006/08/14/japans-top-thirty-emoticons/
9. John Deal. See 1.

BOSTON

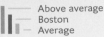

Top feelings in Boston

Above average / Boston Average

better | bad | **good** | **guilty** | **well** | sick

I LOVE BOSTON ON A LOT OF LEVELS AND THIS AREA WILL PROBABLY NEVER STOP FEELING LIKE HOME TO ME WITH ITS SQUEAKY TRAINS AND MASSHOLESPERSONALLY FEEL THE SPIRIT OF BOSTON HAS BEEN ABUSED BY SELFISH POWER HUNGRY PEOPLE HUGELY WELCOME IN BOSTON

I DO FEEL AT HOME IN BOSTON AND THAT'S NICE

I SPENT MOST OF MY ENTIRE DAY AT BOSTON BOWL PLAYING ITG2 AND TAKING MOST OF THE EASY AND MEDIUM SCORES AND RACK IT UP IN THE 99'S JUST TO MAKE THOSE KIDS FEEL BAD

I KNOW I SHOULD BE MORE OPTIMISTIC BECAUSE SPRING IS COMING BUT IN BOSTON YOU DON'T REALLY FEEL IT UNTIL MID APRIL

I HAVE REALLY ENJOYED MY TIME IN BOSTON BUT I THINK THE WEST COAST IS WHAT WILL ALWAYS FEEL LIKE HOME

I SORTA FEEL LIKE IM LOSING PATIENCE WITH EVERY PASSING DAY OR MAYBE BOSTON HAS JUST TURNED ME INTO A BITCH CUZ HERE IT'S KINDA EASY TO BE ONE

I'LL FEEL BETTER ONCE I GET BACK TO BOSTON AND AFTER HE HELPS MIKE AND WALKS INTO THE DOOR FINE THEN I'LL BE OKAY

I FEEL LIKE YOU ARE ONE OF THE REASONS I WAS DESTINED TO MOVE TO BOSTON

I DON'T REALLY FEEL READY TO LEAVE BOSTON

I JUST HAVE A LOT OF PRIDE IN BOSTON TEAMS SO I FEEL I CAN CALL THEM MY OWN

I REALLY DON'T WANT TO GO BACK TO BOSTON TONIGHT TO FACE CLASSES AND WORK ALL WEEK AND THE ONE THING THAT ALWAYS MAKES ME FEEL BETTER CURRENTLY HATES ME

I DON'T FEEL LIKE READING BOSTON BIASED NEWS

I GUESS I JUST FEEL LIKE BOSTON MANAGED TO BREAK MY HEART

I FEEL A CALM IN THIS STRANGE POCKET OF TIME I'M EXPERIENCING HERE IN BOSTON WITH SO FEW PEOPLE AROUND

I FEEL THAT I WANT TO STAY IN BOSTON I REALLY LIKE IT UP HERE AND MAYBE I CAN TOUGH OUT MY RESIDENCY PROGRAM

I FINALLY STARTED TO FEEL LIKE BOSTON WAS GROWING ON ME

I'M A BOSTON RED SOX FAN BECAUSE IT MAKES ME FEEL CLOSER TO MY FATHER

I'M NOT SURE THAT I BELIEVE THERE IS A SUCH THING AS HELL BUT IF THERE IS I AM QUITE SURE ABOUT HOW IT WILL FEEL JUST LIKE DOWNTOWN BOSTON DURING THE BIG DIG

Boston

Massachusetts, United States

Population	616,535
Population density	12,375 / mi²
GDP per capita	$47,000 USD

• i feel like the red sox just won the world series all over again • i'm working on feeling good on the inside and i honestly think i'm getting some great progress • i feel so embarrassed to tell anyone that i had to tuck my tail and come home due to how much of a loser it makes me feel like to live at home again • i feel more religious or spiritual than i did before • i find myself feeling like the universe has steered me into having exactly the skill set i need in order to be able to pull this off • i don't feel like digging out those 21 steps down to the front door • i feel like my eclectic and busy life style attracts girls but in time pushes them away because i am so self indulgent when it comes to these activites

I FEEL LIKE I JUST NEED A LITTLE TIME TO COLLECT MY THOUGHTS WITH AN OCEAN IN BETWEEN ME AND BOSTON

I WILL RETURN TO BOSTON NEXT YEAR BUT I WILL NO LONGER FEEL MY HEART JUMP IF I SEE SOMEONE ON THE STREET THAT LOOKS LIKE YOU

I'VE BEEN IN BOSTON FOR THREE HOURS AND I ALREADY FEEL THE ICY GRIP OF HYPOTHERMIA

I LEAVE THE HOUSE FEELING LIKE I OWN BOSTON

I FEEL TERRIBLE AND WORST PART ABOUT BEING SICK IS THAT I COULDN'T GO WITH MY BOYFRIEND TO GO SEE BON JOVI TONIGHT AT THE GARDEN IN BOSTON

I MISS BOSTON SO MUCH BUT I CAN ONLY DO THE SAME THING FOR SO LONG BEFORE I FEEL LIKE I'M RUNNING IN PLACE

I GUESS THE MAIN LESSON OF MOVING TO BOSTON HAS TO BE WORKING THROUGH THAT FEELING OF BEING OK WITH NOT ALWAYS HAVING PEOPLE I KNOW WELL TO HANG OUT WITH

I MOVED TO BOSTON, HAVING SOME OF HIS THINGS AROUND HELPED ME TO FEEL CLOSE TO HIM

I FEEL SO FUCKING HOPELESS AND I THINK THAT I NEED TO GET OUT OF BOSTON

I ALSO FEEL THE STIRRINGS OF THAT OLD BOSTON INFERIORITY COMPLEX

I FEEL SO READY TO MOVE ON FROM THIS SCHOOL AND FROM BOSTON

I THINK THE FINAL BULLET TO THE BLEEDING SOON TO BE DEAD ENTITY WAS THAT I REALLY DIDN'T FEEL ANY GUILT WHEN I SUBSEQUENTLY FOOLED AROUND WITH ANOTHER GIRL WHILE I WAS IN BOSTON

I DON'T REALLY WANT TO MOVE OUTSIDE OF BOSTON THOUGH I FEEL I'D BE WAY TOO LONELY SURROUNDED BY QUIET FAMILIES AND SUCH

I'M ALSO HIDING IN MY APARTMENT PRAYING THAT AUTHORITIES DON'T HAUL ME OUT OF BOSTON FOR HAVING ALLOWED MYSELF TO BE DRAGGED ON A DUCK TOUR

I FEEL LIKE CLUBS IN BOSTON NEED A LOGISTICS PERSON TO COME IN AND TELL THEM HOW TO DO THINGS

I DON'T FEEL TERRIBLY SAFE IN BOSTON

I WENT TO BOSTON WITH GRETA, BEN, AND LESLEY AND IT WAS REALLY FUN WE WENT TO FIRE AND ICE AGAIN AND THEN WALKED AROUND AND I STOLE A BUNCH OF STUFF AND NOW I FEEL GUILTY

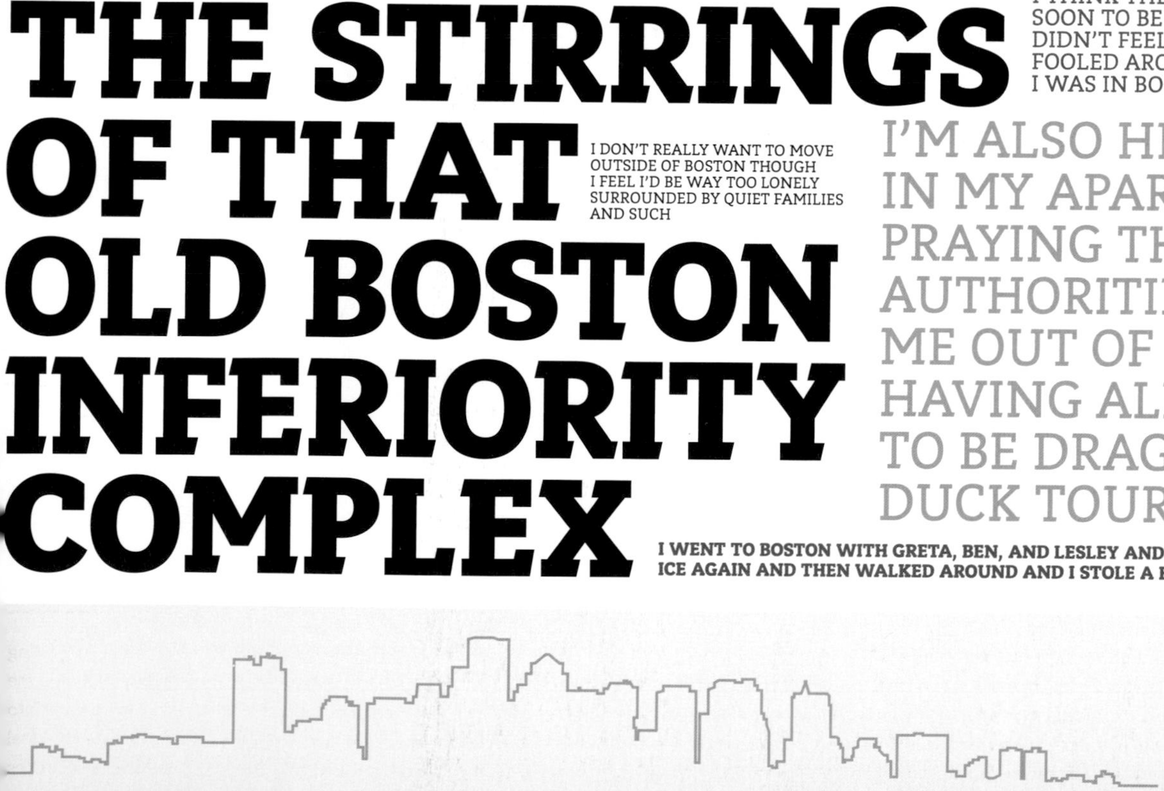

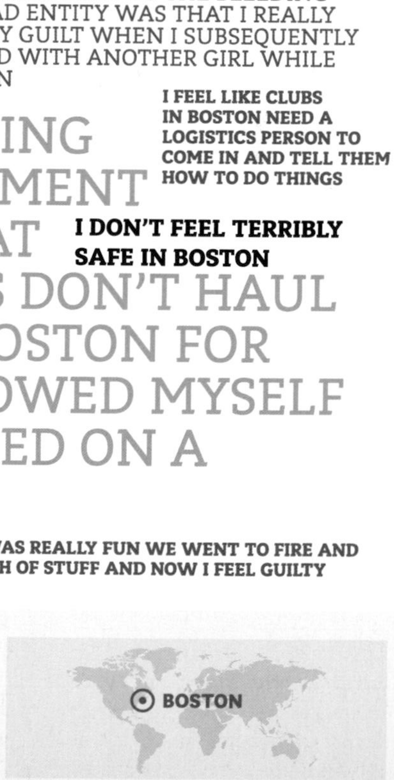

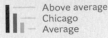

Top feelings in Chicago

Above average · Chicago · Average

better · **good** · bad · guilty · **down** · **well**

I LIKE CHICAGO MUCH BETTER THAN INDIANA GEOGRAPHICALLY AND JUST FEEL A NATURAL EXCITEMENT FOR THE DAAA BEARS

I FEEL REALLY JAZZED AND LUCKY AND PROUD THAT I CALL CHICAGO MY HOME

I FEEL THAT THE NEW CAR SMELL OF CHICAGO HAS EVAPORATED

I JUST FEEL SUN ON MY BARE SHOULDERS IN MY OWN BACK YARD IN CHICAGO

I GUESS WHAT I MEAN IS THAT I AM HOME IN MY HOMETOWN WHERE I FEEL SAFE AND RELAXED CHICAGO

I FEEL LIKE CHICAGO APPEALS TO MY CURIOSITY AND MY ADVENTUROUS SPONTANEOUS SIDE BUT NOT MY INTROVERTED HOME BODY OUTDOORSY TOM BOY SIDE

I FEEL I AM TOO CAUTIOUS FOR A 19 YEAR OLD WITH THE CITY OF CHICAGO TO HER DISPOSAL

I FEEL TOTALLY CUT OFF FROM NATURE LIVING IN CHICAGO AND IT MAKES ME SORT OF DEPRESSED SOMETIMES

I DON'T HAVE FAMILY HERE IN CHICAGO BUT NOW IT'LL FEEL LIKE I DO

I FEEL AS TRAPPED AS I DID IN CHICAGO SIX YEARS AGO AND I'M SAYING THE SAME THINGS NOW THAT I DID THEN

I MOVED TO CHICAGO FEELING REFRESHED AND READY TO START OVER AND CONFIDENT PRETTY SMART

I FEEL LIKE THE CITY OF CHICAGO SUCKER PUNCHED ME IN THE FACE

I HOPE TO CAPTURE THAT FEELING AND PUT IT IN A BOX AND BURY IT SOMEWHERE IN CHICAGO

I GET NERVOUS ABOUT THE MOVE TO CHICAGO IT MAKES ME FEEL SO MUCH BETTER WHEN I REMIND MYSELF THAT I'LL HAVE HER WITH ME

I FELL IN LOVE WITH MY NEW LIFE IN CHICAGO AND THERE IS SOMETHING INTOXICATING ABOUT STARTING OVER IN A NEW CITY ESPECIALLY WHEN YOU'RE FEELING SUFFOCATED BY RECENT EVENTS

I DO NOT FEEL AT HOME IN CHICAGO

I KNOW THAT'S HARSH BUT I FEEL IT TOO AND HONESTLY DON'T REALLY KNOW HOW TO DEAL WITH THE REALITY OF POVERTY WHICH I WITNESS RIGHT IN FRONT OF ME HERE ON THE STREETS OF CHICAGO

I GOT FUCKED OVER BY A LOT OF PEOPLE IN CHICAGO AFTER BEING FUCKED OVER BY A LOT OF PEOPLE IN COLLEGE BUT I REFUSED TO LET MYSELF FEEL THE ANGER AND AS SUCH I JUST LOCKED MYSELF AWAY FROM THE WORLD

Chicago

Illinois, United States

Population	2,836,658
Population density	12,649 / mi²
GDP per capita	$51,100 USD

• i dont really feel i'm at the point in my life where the city is right for me anymore • i dont feel like i have any friends here that really give two shits about me or that between us we have time to see each other • i just feel like what's the point of being here • i fee like i am waking up everyday and going to bed every night without accomplishing a damn thing and i have no idea how to get past this • i am not ready to have feelings for someone again • i feel like a hypochondriac • i didn't really feel that the white sox were wel represented so we'd get pretty excited every time we saw some • i feel like obama is the most in line with what i see as america at its bes

sorry | **comfortable** | sick | **great** | alone | **old** | lost | happy | ill | stupid | weird | sad | tired

I'VE BEEN TRYING TO FIGURE OUT WHAT GOD WANTS ME TO DO NEXT AND THIS WEEKEND I REALIZED HE WANTS ME TO MOVE TO A DIFFERENT PART OF THE COUNTRY I FEEL LIKE I'VE GROWN ALL I CAN HERE IN CHICAGO

I ALWAYS THOUGHT IT WAS MY MOVE TO CHICAGO THAT LET ME FEEL SO ELATED BUT AS I THINK ABOUT IT NOW IT WAS HER

I LIVED A WHOOOLE LOT OF LIFE IN CHICAGO AND LIKE OTHER ASPECTS OF MY LIFE FEEL THEY DESERVE THE TIME OF DAY YOUR TIME OF DAY

I FEEL THE NEED TO TELL YOU THAT CHICAGO HAS THE LARGEST POPULATION OF POLISH PEOPLE OUTSIDE OF WARSAW

I MISS THE SMALL BIG CITY FEEL OF SOMEPLACE LIKE CHICAGO

I FEEL LIKE I'M IN A CHICAGO SNOW GLOBE IT'S SO BEAUTIFUL

I FEEL LIKE I HAVEN'T MADE THE MOST OUT OF CHICAGO THOUGH AND THAT'S MY OWN FAULT

I JUST DON'T WANT TO FEEL STUCK IN CHICAGO FOR ANOTHER YEAR IF I DON'T CHOOSE THAT

I MISS CHICAGO BUT I FEEL IT'D BE NO DIFFERENT FROM THE WAY THINGS ARE HERE RIGHT NOW

I FEEL AS IF I AM LOSING SOMETHING BY LEAVING CHICAGO

I HAVE DECIDED THAT BECAUSE I HAVE NO FRIENDS HERE IN CHICAGO AND I AM BLOATED AND FEELING LIKE POO AND BECAUSE IT'S FINALLY THE WEEKEND

I FEEL LIKE I WAS MEANT TO LIVE IN CHICAGO

I GREW UP IN A CHICAGO TRIBUNE HOUSE SO I ALWAYS FEEL A BIT DIRTY READING THE OTHER CHICAGO PAPER

I'VE BEEN TRYING TO FIGURE OUT HOW TO EXPLAIN HOW I FEEL ABOUT PROVIDENCE AND CHICAGO RESPECTIVELY AND ALL I CAN COME UP WITH IS SOME CHEESY METAPHOR ABOUT FIRST LOVES AND SOUL MATES

I AM IN CHICAGO I FEEL ALIVE I KNOW THAT THIS SOUNDS CORNY BUT IF YOU LIVE SOMEWHERE THAT YOU LOVE YOU KNOW WHAT I MEAN

ONCE I GET HOME FROM WORK TODAY I AM NOT GOING TO LEAVE THE HOUSE EXCEPT FOR THE MAIL AND MAYBE A WALK UNTIL MONDAY MORNING

I HAVE MANAGED TO CONVINCE THE STUDIO THAT CHICAGO IN THE SUMMER HAS JUST THE ROMANTIC FEEL YOU'RE LOOKING FOR

I FEEL VERY SPECIAL GROWING UP IN CHICAGO

I FEEL LIKE I'M STARTING TO RECOGNIZE A LOT OF FACES IN CHICAGO'S SMALL BUT DIE HARD ELECTRONIC MUSIC SCENE

I DON'T KNOW ABOUT YOU BUT I FEEL A LOT SAFER KNOWING THE CHICAGO POLICE ARE ON THE PROWL FOR PROSTITUTES

I LONG FOR THAT IN CHICAGO I FEEL LIKE I GOT MARRIED AND SUDDENLY EVERYONE THOUGHT I WAS TOO BUSY OR JUST ASSUMED I WOULD NOT WANT TO COME

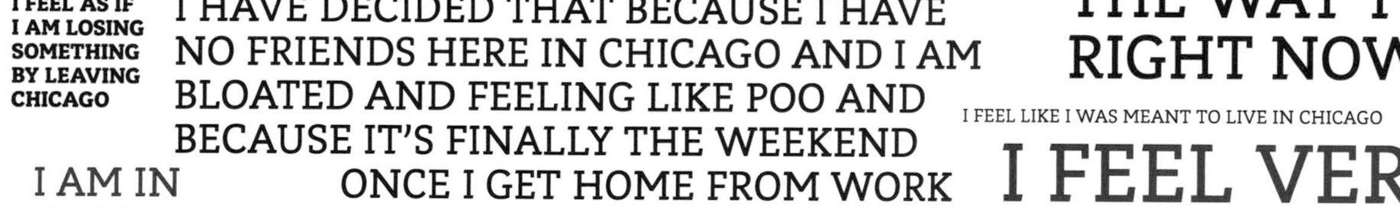

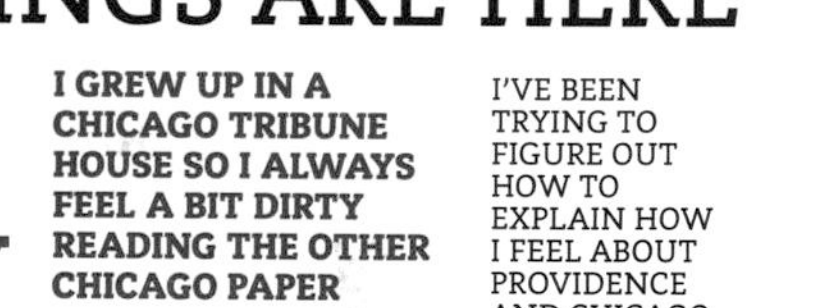

Top feelings in London

Above average London Average

better | bad | good | **guilty** | **sorry** | **sick**

I FEEL THAT I COULD MAKE LONDON MY HOME IF I ONLY HAD A CHANCE

I FEEL A BIT LIKE I AM DOOMED IN LONDON

I OFTEN FEEL HOMESICK FOR LONDON BUT LONDON IS NOT MY HOME NEW YORK IS

I'M BACK IN LONDON AND I REMEMBER HOW THIS CITY USED TO GLINT AND GLITTER FOR ME USED TO FEEL SO EXCITING AND VIBRANT

I DON'T FEEL LIKE I WANT TO STAY IN LONDON FOR MUCH LONGER WITH THE INCREASE OF YOUTH CRIME IT'S TOO MUCH AND I FEEL LIKE IT'S THE WRONG PLACE TO LIVE

I ALMOST FEEL SUFFOCATED BY THE WEALTH OF HISTORY CULTURE ACTIVITY PEOPLE DIVERSITY THAT LONDON HAS

I FEEL QUITE AT PEACE IN MY QUIET CORNER OF LONDON

I LOVED LIVING IN LONDON IT DID MAKE ME FEEL LIKE MY LUNGS WERE FULL OF HORSE SHIT AND BURNING TIRES

I WAS REALLY SHOCKED BY IT AND FELT PERSONALLY ATTACKED LONDON FEELS A BIG PART OF ME

I ALMOST CRIED PUTTING MY FEET IN THE SAND FOR THE FIRST TIME HAVING ALMOST FORGOTTEN WHAT IT FEELS LIKE TO FEEL SAND UNDER MY FEET AFTER SO LONG IN SMOGGY LONDON IT WAS WONDERFUL

I OFTEN FEEL I MISS OUT ON SOME GREAT TRAVEL OPPORTUNITIES THAT LIVING IN LONDON THROWS AT YOU

I FEEL BAD BECAUSE I'M LIKE IN LONDON AND I DON'T WANT TO WASTE TIME

I REALIZED I HAVE MADE SOME REALLY GOOD FRIENDS IN LONDON BUT BECAUSE I CONSTANTLY FEEL INFERIOR I DON'T MAKE ENOUGH EFFORT TO SEE THEM OUTSIDE THE CLUBS

I ALSO LIKE HOW LONDON MAKES ME FEEL LIKE A WHORE

I MISS LONDON I MISS DAVE I MISS ENGLAND I MISS MY FRIENDS IN ENGLAND

I AM HERE I FEEL UGLY I FEEL A FAILURE I SEE MYSELF DIFFERENTLY IN LONDON MIRRORS

I FEEL THAT EVERYONE SHOULD GET TO WITNESS AT LEAST ONE MURDER OR MANSLAUGHTER IN NORTH LONDON

I FEEL SAFE I LOVE TO SEE BIG BEN TO HEAR IT MAKES ME REALIZE HOW SPECIAL LONDON IS

I KIND OF FEEL THAT I'LL STAY IN LONDON LONGER THAN I HAD ACTUALLY PLANNED BECAUSE I HAVE A FUCKING GREAT TIME AT THE MOMENT

I NOW FEEL DIRTY CHEAP AND USED IN LONDON

London

England, United Kingdom

Population	7,355,400
Population density	12,331 / mi²
GDP per capita	$62,423 USD

• i didn't feel quite as safe as i would walking around southwest london or camden • i really feel that i have as many aussie friends in london as in australia so spending chrissy here does feel a lot like spending it at home • i was happily surprised by how i feel being back in london • i celebrate having been born and brought up in london i always feel part of it • i also studied the tube map today and looked at the places i might like to live in london so i feel a bit better now that i have some idea of exactly where wifey will be • i don't know why anyone living in london doesn t feel like an idiot living there • i feel very comfortable in london

down ill well happy tired comfortable sad great old lost weird alone

I STILL LOVE YOU LONDON I'M JUST NOT FEELING IT RIGHT NOW

I FEEL THAT I'VE DEVELOPED A RELATIONSHIP WITH LONDON ITSELF

I THINK IT WOULD IMPROVE THE AMENITY AND THE FEEL OF LONDON IF IT WAS FELT TO BE A CYCLING CITY

I FEEL STRONGLY THAT LONDON IS MY ONLY HOME TOWN

I LOVE MEETING PEOPLE RANDOMLY IN LONDON IT MAKES IT FEEL LIKE A VILLAGE MY VILLAGE

I HAVE NO REAL GOOD ANSWER JUST THIS FEELING THAT LONDON WILL BE HERE AND THAT I CAN GO DO MY THING FOR A WHILE AND COME BACK

I MUST LEAVE THE COUNTRY OR LEAVE LONDON OR THE HOUSE AT VERY LEAST TO FEEL BETTER AND RUN FROM ALL MY PROBLEMS

I AM HERE I FEEL UGLY I FEEL A FAILURE I SEE MYSELF DIFFERENTLY IN LONDON MIRRORS

I AM A COUNTRY GIRL AT HEART BUT EXPLORING THE STREETS OF LONDON ON WARM SUMMER DAYS ALWAYS MAKES ME FEEL LIKE I'VE FOUND MY HOME

I'VE HEARD SO MANY HORROR STORIES ABOUT LONDON THAT THERE'S NO COMMUNITY AND ABOUT PEOPLE ARRIVING HERE WITH NO FRIENDS FEELING LONELY GOING IN TO DEBT AND THEN RETURNING TO THEIR HOMETOWN CITY

I FEEL ROMANTIC IN LONDON

I JUST HAD THIS FEELING OF COMPLETENESS WALKING AROUND THE CITY OF LONDON

I LOVE WALKING ABOUT OLD SOUTH LONDON AND FEELING IT IN MY BLOOD

I FEEL LIKE I'VE LOST MYSELF SOMEWHERE OVER THE OCEAN COMING TO LONDON

I WAS ON THE PHONE TO MY HOMEOPATH DURING THE LUNCH HOUR NEARLY IN TEARS ON THE STREETS OF LONDON BECAUSE I COULD NOT FEEL THAT THINGS WERE GETTING BETTER AND I COULDN'T SEE MY FUTURE DOING THIS

I FEEL EXTREME SADNESS SEEING MY TWO PARENTS IN THE LAST DAYS OF THEIR LIVES AND BEING HERE IS LEES PAINFUL THAN BEING IN LONDON AT LEAST HERE I CAN HELP

I ALWAYS FEEL A STRANGE BLEND OF EXHILERATION AND UNEASE IN LONDON

Top feelings in Los Angeles

Above average · Los Angeles · Average

better · bad · good · **guilty** · sorry · down

I FEEL LIKE LOS ANGELES WITH ITS LAYOUT IS A LONELY PLACE

I FEEL CALLED TO LOS ANGELES AND IN-N-OUT BURGER AND PINKBERRY FROYO AND STAR TOURS AND WESTWOOD

I DON'T GET ALLERGIES IN LOS ANGELES I GET HEADACHES NASTY ONES THAT MAKE ME FEEL LIKE MY RIGHT EYEBALL IS ON FIRE TO BE PRECISE

I FEEL THERE IS MORE RACISM AND IGNORANCE HERE IN LOS ANGELES THAT I EVER FELT AT HOME IN RURAL GEORGIA

I'VE MOVED OUT TO LOS ANGELES I FEEL LIKE I LOST A PART OF MYSELF

I REALIZE THAT LOS ANGELES DIDN'T FULFILL MY DREAMS BUT DESTROYED THEM COMPLETELY CHEWED THEM UP SPIT THEM OUT AND MADE ME FEEL HOLLOW

I FEEL LIKE LOS ANGELES IS NOT ONLY THE CITY THAT SUITS ME BEST BUT IT'S WHERE I AM PROUD TO CALL HOME

WHEN I LEFT FOR LOS ANGELES MY FAMILY TOLD ME FEELINGS THEY HAD ABOUT ME THAT WERE HARD TO LISTEN TO

I FEEL LIKE I'M TREADING WATER IN LOS ANGELES

I FEEL AN IMMEDIATE CLOSENESS TO ANYONE WHO LOVES NEW YORK OR HATES LOS ANGELES

I FEEL LIKE THERE'S A RACE BEING RUN IN LOS ANGELES FOR SOME UNATTAINABLE GOAL TO BE THE BEST THE SKINNIEST THE MOST BEAUTIFUL

I GAVE HIM A PART OF ME THAT I WOULDN'T GIVE TO ANYONE I'M NOT LIKE OTHER GIRLS HERE IN LA OR ANYWHERE ELSE I WILL ONLY SLEEP WITH SOMEONE I DEEPLY LOVE AND I KINDA FEEL LIKE HE MAY HAVE MADE A MISTAKE OR SOMETHING MAYBE HE USED ME

I'M ADDICTED TO LOS ANGELES AND EVERYTHING ABOUT HOLLYWOOD AND I'M IN LOVE WITH THE FEELING OF MY OWN LEGS RIGHT AFTER I SHAVE THEM

I AM A MOTHER OF TWO LIVING IN LOS ANGELES WHO DOESN'T REALLY FEEL LIKE SHE BELONGS

I DON'T LIVE IN LOS ANGELES I LIVE CLOSE ENOUGH TO FEEL THE EFFECTS OF THE WHOLE SURREAL LALA LAND MENTALITY

I FEEL PRETTY LONELY LIVING HERE IN LA

I LIVE IN LOS ANGELES AND I CAN'T TELL YOU HOW MUCH SAFER I FEEL KNOWING THAT PARIS HILTON IS BEHIND BARS

I AM HERE IN LA SURROUNDED BY THE RIGHT PEOPLE AND I'M ON THE RIGHT PATH TO FINALLY CHASE AND CATCH MY DREAMS AND SOMETIMES I FEEL LIKE I SABOTAGE MYSELF A BIT

Los Angeles

California, United States

Population	3,849,378
Population density	8,205 / mi²
GDP per capita	$53,000 USD

• i feel like i know los angeles pretty damn well and well i couldn't tell you a damn store in brentwood • i live in los angeles and this is the first place that i feel like this is it • i keep having these feelings of contentedness that i don't think i have ever had while living in los angeles • i had quite the day in los angeles and feel the need to spread the word • i am realizing that since this accident i have been feeling extremely isolated living in los angeles • i feel as if i left los angeles and returned to another dimension of what was los angeles • i feel really comfortable in big cities like los angeles • i'm cute makes me feel like they only like me because i'm cute or just because i'm a movie star

sick comfortable great well alone sad lost old happy stupid weird ill

I DRIVE A BMW BECAUSE I FEEL LIKE IT AND I DON'T WANT TO GET CARJACKED IN LOS ANGELES

I MISS LOS ANGELES AND LENNY AND FEELING INSPIRED

I WANTED TO GO TO LA FOR SINGING BUT I DON'T NEED TO MAKE IT BIG TO FEEL WHOLE

I CUT OFF SOME PEOPLE WHEN I MOVED TO LA AND FEEL NO GUILT AT ALL OVER IT

I FEEL LIKE LIVING IN LA WE SUFFER A FATE SIMILAR TO OUR AIR

I'M BACK IN LOS ANGELES I FEEL LIKE I'M LOSING ALL THOSE IDEALS

I FEEL THAT MOVING FROM SOUTH CAROLINA TO LA HAS GIVEN ME A FUCKED UP PERCEPTION OF SPACE

I REMEMBER BEING SO IN LOVE WITH LOS ANGELES WHEN I WAS YOUNGER AND NOW I JUST FEEL OVERWHELMINGLY SICKENED BY IT

I REALLY FEEL AT HOME IN LOS ANGELES

I FEEL LIKE MAYBE HE IS TOTALLY LA AND JUST USING ME TO MOVE UP

I KNOW NEW YORK CITY IS FULL OF HUSTLERS TOO BUT THEY JUST FEEL SO DIFFERENT IN LOS ANGELES SOMEHOW

I FEEL SO BLESSED TO HAVE THE FRIENDS I DO ESPECIALLY IN A CITY LIKE LOS ANGELES

THE OLDER I GET AND THE LONGER I LIVE AWAY FROM THE HOUSE I GREW UP IN THE MORE STRONGLY COMING BACK TO LOS ANGELES FEELS LIKE HOME

I FEEL STRANGELY FOND OF LA SOMETIMES IT REDUCES ME TO TEARS OF IMPOTENT RAGE AND ANGUISH

I WANT THE LOVELY HIPPIE FEELING OF SF WITH THE BEAUTIFUL WEATHER OF LA

183

I FEEL SO BLESSED TO HAVE THE FRIENDS I DO ESPECIALLY IN A CITY LIKE LOS ANGELES

I FEEL LIKE I ATE A PORTION OF EVERYONE'S FOOD IN LOS ANGELES COUNTY

I FEEL THAT WAY BECAUSE WOMEN IN LOS ANGELES ARE REALLY SUPERFICIAL AT TIMES AND DON'T WANT TO DATE BUTCHES OR EVEN OVERLY TOMBOYISH FEMALES

I ALWAYS ASK MYSELF SELF WHY DO SO MANY PEOPLE SEEM TO LOVE THIS SHIT HOLE OF A CITY THEN I GET REAL SAD BECAUSE I'M IN LOS ANGELES AND I HATE IT HERE SO I GO GET ICE CREAM TO MAKE MYSELF FEEL BETTER

I DON'T CARE WHO YOU ARE HOW BEAUTIFUL YOU ARE HOW TALENTED YOU ARE HOW EDUCATED HOW RICH YOU ARE IN FAMILY BLESSINGS LOS ANGELES WILL MAKE YOU FEEL LIKE SHIT ABOUT YOURSELF IN TIME

Top feelings in Moscow

Above average
Moscow
Average

good better bad **sorry** **happy** **sad**

I HAVE A FEELING THAT WHEN WE DO GET TO THE AIRPORT HIS TICKET WILL SAY SYDNEY AND MINE WILL READ MOSCOW

I PERSONALLY FEEL SAFE IN MOSCOW AND OFTEN WALK THE STREETS AT NIGHT BY MYSELF THERE IS DEFINITELY AN ELEMENT OF DANGER HERE

I FEEL THE NEED TO TALK WITH MYSELF I GUESS ABOUT CROSS CULTURAL RELATIONS AND HOW MOSCOW TURNS EVERYTHING ON IT'S HEAD

I FEEL IMPORTANT IN MOSCOW BECAUSE MY MOTHER IS WITH ME AND SHE SIMPLY COULDN'T SURVIVE HERE WITHOUT ME

I THINK I FEEL TOWARDS MOSCOW THE SAME WAY I WOULD FEEL TOWARDS A PERSON

I LIVE IN MOSCOW AND I FEEL MUCH MORE COMFORTABLE HERE BECAUSE WE DON'T HAVE THE POLICE LAWLESSNESS THAT CONTINUES IN ST PETERSBURG

I'M FEELING A BIT DEFEATED BY THE MOSCOW APARTMENT SCENE

I WON'T FEEL SAFE IN MOSCOW EVEN THOUGH I THINK I'VE FIGURED A LOT OF IT OUT

I AM CALLING ON YOU PRESIDENT BUSH NOT TO AVERT YOUR EYES FROM THE MANY RUSSIAN CITIZENS IN GROZNY NASRAN BESLAN VOLGODONSK NIZHNY NOVGOROD MOSCOW MURMANSK AND SAINT PETERSBURG WHO FEEL NEGLECTED AND IGNORED IN BOTH THEIR PROTESTS AND SUFFERING

I WISHED I COULD BE IN MOSCOW RIGHT NOW AND FEEL THE FLAIR OF THAT CITY

I DIDN'T PARTICULARLY ENJOY MOSCOW BUT FEEL I NEED TO GO BACK IN ORDER TO GET A BETTER GRASP OF IT

I FEEL LIKE A SEAMSTRESS IN MOSCOW GOING OVER THE SAME PATTERNS OVER AND OVER AND NEVER BEING ALLOWED TO CHANGE A THING

I BOTH COMMENTED ABOUT HOW STRANGE IT SEEMS TO BE HERE IN MOSCOW AND HAVE IT FEEL FAMILIAR

Moscow

Central Federal District, Russia

Population	12,382,754
Population density	29,668 / mi²
GDP per capita	$16,800 USD

- i was going to go back to moscow tonight but i layed down for longer than expected and i don't really feel like driving back in the dark
- i'm out here to support my fellow moscow nude news industry workers and because i feel all of us deserve the benefits of executive level management
- how strange to be here in moscow and have it feel familiar
- i sat on a bench at the lubianka moscow underground feeling happy
- i feel guilty for coming to moscow and not seeing red square
- i didn't know how good it would feel to be back in moscow
- i blame the war but i feel i should be visiting moscow more

down | alone | guilty | empty | tired | comfortable | old | lonely | different | great | well

I FEEL MUCH BETTER AFTER SOME GOOD TIMES AND EXPLORING MORE OF MOSCOW IN HER INFINITE BEAUTY

I FEEL HAPPY THAT I HAVE ANOTHER "FIRST TIME" TO ADD TO MY GROWING LIST OF FIRST TIMES IN MOSCOW

I JUST GET THE FEELING THAT OF ALL THE PLACES I HAVE BEEN MOSCOW IS THE ONE MOST LIKELY TO HAVE A TERRORIST BOMBING IN A BIG PUBLIC PLACE WHERE I MIGHT BE

I DON'T KNOW WHY BUT TODAY WHEN I STROLL ALONE ABOUT THE MOSCOW'S STREETS

I HOPE THAT DESPITE OUR COLD WINTRY MOSCOW WEATHER YOU WILL FEEL THE WARMTH OF OUR HEARTS

I FEEL THAT OUR SOULS ARE VERY LOOK LIKE TO EACH OTHER

I FEEL LIKE SIGHING OH IF WE COULD ONLY GET TO MOSCOW

I FEEL DISGUSTINGLY DIRTY AND DIZZY AND READY TO BE IN MOSCOW

I FELT RISING UP IN ME A PROFOUND FEELING OF RESPECT FOR LENIN DESPITE MY RECENT CONVICTION THAT HE WAS RESPONSIBLE FOR THE ANNIHILATION OF THE ANARCHIST ORGANIZATION IN MOSCOW WHICH HAD BEEN THE SIGNAL FOR THE DESTRUCTION OF SIMILAR ORGANIZATIONS IN MANY OTHER CITIES

I'M BEGINNING TO FEEL WEIRD THAT THE HIGHLIGHT OF MY TRIP TO MOSCOW IS MY TRIP TO SAINT PETERSBURG

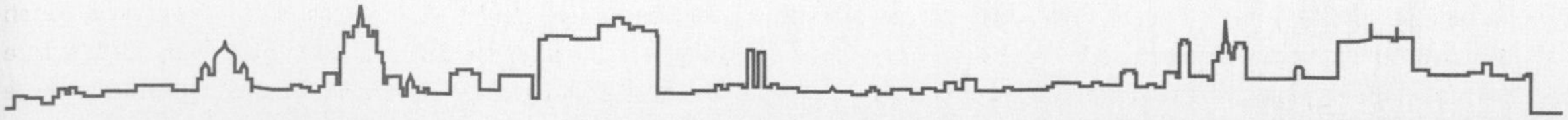

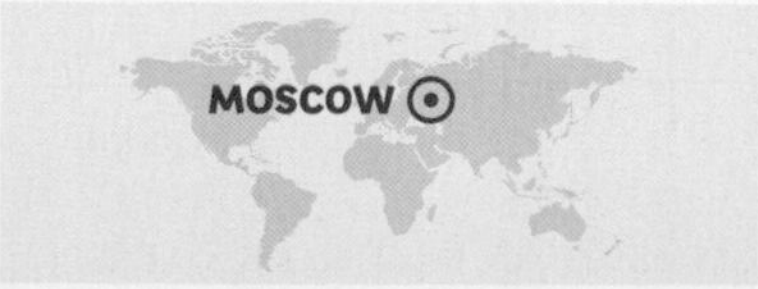

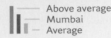

Top feelings in Mumbai — Above average / Mumbai / Average

good · better · bad · **happy** · guilty · **sad**

I FEEL LUCKY FOR HAVING GROWN UP IN BOMBAY

I DON'T WANT TO OFFEND ANYONE IN MUMBAI OR ANYTHING AND IT BEING MY BIRTHPLACE I KIND OF FEEL EMBARASSED BUT I MISS NYC

I FEEL FAR LESS DEFEATED FAR MORE OPTIMISTIC ABOUT THE FUTURE THAN I DID THE FIRST FEW DAYS AFTER MUMBAI WAS ATTACKED

I WAS LEAVING HOME TO COME HERE MY SEVEN YEAR OLD DAUGHTER SAID PLEASE TELL THE POLICEMEN OF MUMBAI THAT I FEEL SAFE AND SECURE IN MY HOME BECAUSE OF THEM

I FEEL HUGELY WELCOME IN MUMBAI

I FEEL DEEPLY PAINED AS DO MANY PEOPLE IN PAKISTAN OVER THE TRAGIC EVENTS THAT TOOK PLACE IN BOMBAY

I FEEL DISLOCATED AND VAGUELY SAD WHENEVER I'M BACK IN MUMBAI AND UNINTENTIONALLY SPEAK DELHI'S HINDI

I LIVE IN BOSTON AND MY PARENTS LIVE IN MUMBAI BUT THE VAST DISTANCE ISN'T INDICATIVE OF THE PRESSURE WHICH I FEEL

I FEEL MUMBAI IS A LITTLE UNSAFE FOR GIRLS

I FEEL LIKE MUMBAI SHOULD LOOK LIKE PARIS FUNCTION LIKE NEW YORK AND HAVE THE VALUES OF ZURICH

I HAVEN'T GRIEVED AT ALL THAT'S WHY I HAVE THIS SICK FEELING IN MY STOMACH AND NOW I WANT EVERYONE TO REALLY MOURN NOT ONLY FOR THE 190 ODD PEOPLE WHO HAVE DIED IN THE SERIAL BOMB BLASTS BUT ALSO FOR THE CITY OF MUMBAI

I DONT KNOW WHY BUT I ENJOYED THE BUS RIDES ALMOST EVERYTIME I TOOK IT AND THINK THAT IF ONE WANTS TO SEE AND FEEL BOMBAY IN REAL SENSE ONE MUST TRAVEL BY THESE RED ENGINES AT LEAST ONCE

I FEEL THAT HINDI CINEMA IS AN IMPORTANT REASON FOR THIS CHANGE BECAUSE IT'S SLOWLY MOVING AWAY FROM THE TRADITIONAL 'BOY FALLS IN LOVE WITH GIRL' STORIES TO ONES WHICH ADDRESS CERTAIN SOCIAL ISSUES

I'VE ALWAYS TAKEN PRIDE IN HOW SAFE I FEEL IN MUMBAI AND I HOPE THAT I'LL CONTINUE FEELING THAT WAY

MUMBAI AIRPORT IS THE ONLY AIRPORT WHICH GIVES ME THE SCHMANCY WANCY FEEL OF BEING IN AN AIRPORT

I FEEL IN MUMBAI NO ONE IS BOTHERED ABOUT WHAT OTHER ONE IS DOING

I SUPPOSE BOMBAY IS SO BIG SO CROWDED AND AT TIMES SO CHAOTIC THAT ANYWHERE ELSE FEELS EASIER TO DEAL WITH

I KNOW IT SOUNDS SILLY BUT ALL I HAVE TO DO IS LOOK AT A PICTURE OF KRISHNA OR THE CITY OF BOMBAY OR A BEAUTIFUL BOLLYWOOD WOMAN WITH A BINDI ON HER FOREHEAD AND I FEEL LIKE THIS WORLD IS A FASCINATING EVER CHANGING PLACE OF WONDER

I HAVE LIVED BOTH IN CALCUTTA AND BOMBAY AND I STRONGLY FEEL THAT THESE CITES NEED MORE THAN A CHANGED NAME

Mumbai

Maharashtra, India

Population	13,662,885
Population density	35,213 / mi²
GDP per capita	$7,000 USD

• i know that i should not be feeling scared considering that i do not live in south bombay • i too feel angry and sad about the mumbai terror attacks • i feel like the world's eyes are on mumbai now and while i know the city has tragic stories to share with us i'm glad we also get to see this story about the power of love in the face of everything else • i feel even more depressed to hear that the egregious spread of any number of types of yoga has extended back to india itself the home of yoga where fashionable girls in mumbai are taking it up for the first time because madonna does it

sorry down different lonely lost great sick tired well old comfortable

I FELT I WAS HOME AND NOW IN MUMBAI I FEEL I AM HOME I REALISE HOME IS WHERE MY MIND IS AT PEACE

I'M TRYING TO GET THE HELL OUT OF MUMBAI AS I FEEL I'VE GOTTEN ALL I COULD POSSIBLY WANT FROM THIS CITY

I FEEL A SHIVER OF EXCITEMENT RUN DOWN MY SPINE EACH TIME I FEEL THE COLD BOMBAY WIND BLOW OVER ME

I FEEL ENOUGH HAD BEEN ENOUGH LONG BEFORE THIS ATTACK ON MUMBAI

I DON'T KNOW HOW I'D FEEL ABOUT MUMBAI GIN AS OPPOSED TO BOMBAY GIN

I VISITED MUMBAI AND WITNESSED ALL THE STREET URCHINS RUNNING AROUND BUT I WAS DESENSITIZED BY MY FAMILY BECAUSE THE GENERAL FEELING IS THAT IT'S SAD BUT THAT YOU CAN'T DO ANYTHING ABOUT IT

I WAS IN MUMBAI AND FEELING LIKE A TRUE TOURIST I TOOK ADVANTAGE OF THE OPPORTUNITY THAT VACATION ALLOWS AND BOUGHT A COCONUT TO DRINK

I STILL IN A WAY FEEL LIKE THE WANNABE STARLET IN BOMBAY TRYING TO MAKE MORE OF MY DREAMS A REALITY GETTING THERE SLOWLY BUT SURELY

I PERSONALLY FEEL THE SPIRIT OF MUMBAI HAS BEEN ABUSED BY SELFISH POWER HUNGRY PEOPLE HUGELY WELCOME IN MUMBAI

I FEEL LOST WHEN I GO TO BOMBAY I GET OVERWHELMED BY THE ENORMITY OF THAT CITY

I CRAVE THE FEELING I GET WHEN I READ ABOUT LIFE IN THE SLUMS OF BOMBAY

I FEEL THE PAIN AND SUFFERING OF MUMBAI THIS WAS AN ATTACK ON OUR NATIONHOOD

I WANTED TO WRITE ABOUT THE MUMBAI MADNESS BUT I THOUGHT THAT HARSH HAS ALREADY EXPRESSED ALL THE FEELINGS OF ANGER DESPAIR FEAR FRUSTRATION AND EXTREME SORROW THAT WE ARE ALL FEELING AT THE MOMENT

I CAN'T GET PAST HOW IT EXPLOITS THE HORRORS OF THE MUMBAI SLUMS FOR PATHOS AND THEN WRAPS EVERYTHING UP WITH AN UPBEAT BOLLYWOOD NUMBER SO THAT ITS NOT TOO PAINFUL FOR THE AUDIENCE

I DON'T FEEL TOO GOOD TODAY GOT A TOUCH OF THE MUMBAI TUMBAI

Top feelings in New York

Above average
New York
Average

better | bad | good | **guilty** | well | **comfortable**

I FEEL MORE ALIVE THAN EVER WHEN I'M WALKING THE STREETS OF NEW YORK

I FEEL KINDA LUCKY THAT I LIVE IN NEW YORK RATHER THAN A SWING STATE

I FEEL AT HOME IN NEW YORK

I FEEL SAFE IN A CAGE IN NEW YORK CITY

I FEEL LIKE MY HEAD IS IN NEW YORK

I DO FEEL MORE THAN EVER THAT I NEED TO LEAVE NEW YORK NOW

I FEEL LIKE NEW YORK IS TOO MUCH

I SEE IT IN THE CONTEXT OF THE ALIENATION DISTANCE AND MYSTERY THAT I FEEL SO OFTEN IN NEW YORK

I FEEL EVEN MORE SORRY NOW FOR NEW YORKERS

I FEEL LIKE JAZZ IN NEW YORK IS NOT REALLY SPECIAL ANYMORE

I LEFT NEW YORK FEELING THAT I DID THE RIGHT THING

I HAVE MIXED FEELINGS ABOUT MAUREEN DOWD OF THE NEW YORK TIMES BUT THIS ARTICLE RULES

WHAT I LOVE ABOUT NEW YORK MORE THAN ANY OTHER CITY IN THE WORLD IS THAT PEOPLE JUST GO WITH WHAT THEY FEEL AND I BELIEVE THAT'S WHAT FASHION IS: FASHION IS EXPRESSING YOURSELF

I FEEL LIKE THAT IS ONLY OUR FIRST OF MANY ONLY IN NEW YORK MOMENTS

I JUST WANTED A FRESH START A DIFFERENT LOOK A DIFFERENT FEEL WHEN I WAS IN NEW YORK I WORE 11 FOR ISIAH THOMAS BECAUSE HE WAS SO INSTRUMENTAL IN BRINGING ME THERE

I REALLY FEEL LIKE MY VISIT TO NEW YORK THREW ME OFF TRACK

I FEEL SO WELCOME IN NEW YORK

I FEEL LIKE SO MUCH OF NEW YORK IS THIS SHELL OF WHAT IT USED TO BE

I WAS TALKING WITH MY FRIEND SARAH THE OTHER DAY AND SHE SAID EVERYBODY THAT COMES TO NEW YORK FEELS LIKE THEY HAVE TO PROVE SOMETHING

I FEEL LIKE CRYING IN NEW YORK

I FEEL ALIVE AND POWERFUL AND ALSO INVISIBLE IN NEW YORK

I FEEL LIKE IF I WENT TO NEW YORK I WOULD DO IT TO IMPRESS YOU

I HAVE THIS HORRIBLE HORRIBLE FEELING I'M RUNNING ON NEW YORK TIME AGAIN

I JUST FEEL THAT WAY BECAUSE I LIVE IN NEW YORK AND I'M A SNOB

New York City

New York, United States

Population	8,274,527
Population density	27,130 / mi²
GDP per capita	$61,000 USD

• i'm finally happy but i'm feeling like i'm missing out on things in new york i'm all out of the circle • i feel like heading to the whirlwind that is contemporary new york city • i feel all corny for being like what happens in new york stays in new york but after last night i gotta plead the 5th • i have no feel whatsoever for the beauty of new york • i cannot wait to get to new york you just cannot beat the big city feeling of so many people in one place all going around doing their own business • i'm from new york i love the pace getting lost in the crowd and all that so a place like prague shouldn't feel overwhelming • i feel like i need to see as much new york theatre as i can before i leave the states

sorry | down | great | sick | **ill** | **weird** | alone | sad | lost | happy | **different** | old

I FEEL YOUR PAIN NEW YORK

I FEEL SO QUINTESSENTIALLY NEW YORK RIGHT NOW EATING A SLICE WHILST TYPING TO YOU DEAR READER

WHEN I WAS IN NEW YORK NO MATTER HOW LATE IT WAS OR HOW DRUNK I WAS DID I EVER FEEL THE SLIGHTEST BIT UNSAFE EVEN WITH IPOD AND CAMERA IN HAND

I REALLY FEEL LIKE BEING DEPRESSED TONIGHT IN AN ARTISTIC DISMAL SMOKING A CIGARETTE SOMEWHERE IN A FILM NOIR PART OF NEW YORK WAY

I FEEL LIKE I'M IN NEW YORK

I FEEL LIKE I'VE RUN THE NEW YORK MARATHON

I'M RECRUITING GUINEA PIGS IN NEW YORK IF ANYBODY'S FEELING AT ALL DARING

WHENEVER I GO TO NEW YORK I WEAR A PROFESSIONAL VERSION OF FUCK ME BLACK AND I FEEL DRESSED RIGHT EVERY TIME

I SAID TO MY HUSBAND THESE ARE THE BEST OF NEW YORK CITY AND ON THIS ANNIVERSARY I CANNOT HELP BUT FEEL THAT WHAT WE WENT THROUGH ON 9/11 WAS BECAUSE OF RELIGIOUS FANATICS IN THE NAME OF RELIGION WANTING TO HARM AND KILL AMERICANS

I FEEL AT HOME IN THIS CITY LIKE A NEW YORK CITY PIGEON LOOKING AT WATER TANKS ALL DAY LONG

I REMEMBER FEELIN THAT SHORT SPAT OF HURT FOR THEM FIREMEN IN NEW YORK

I HOPE MEMORIES OF THEIR NEW YORK ESCAPADE DON'T MAKE ME FEEL TOO LEFT OUT BECAUSE I'M NOT A BIG FAN OF ISOLATION

I AM BEGINNING TO FEEL COMFORTABLE IN BROOKLYN LIKE I LIVE THERE AND IT MAY POSSIBLY ONE DAY BE CALLED HOME

I FEEL LIKE NEW YORK IS MINE

I FEEL GULITY SAYING THIS BUT I'M GLAD I DON'T LIVE IN NEW YORK

I'M FEELING LIKE THAT OLD SONG THE ONLY LIVING BOY IN NEW YORK

I NEVER FELT THAT THERE WAS A FEELING IN NEW YORK LIKE THERE HAD BEEN IN SAN FRANCISCO

I FEEL THE CITY OF NEW YORK SINKING DEEP INTO MY STOMACH

I HAVE NO FEEL AT ALL FOR THE BEAUTY OF NEW YORK

I TRAVELED TO NEW YORK PREPARED TO COMMIT MYSELF TO A LIFESTYLE I NEVER DID FEEL RIGHT ABOUT

I FEEL LIKE NEW YORK PIZZA

189

I FEEL SORRY FOR THE SLUTS OF CHICAGOLAND BECAUSE THEY POSSESS A CHARACTERISTIC NOT SEEN IN NEW YORK

I FEEL LIKE I COULD WALK RIGHT INTO NEW YORK CITY TOMORROW AND BOTH PROSECUTE CRIMES AND SOLVE THEM

I FEEL HE IS JUST TRYING TO BURN EVERY POSSIBLE BRIDGE LEFT FAMILY FRIENDS WORK BEFORE HE MOVES TO NEW YORK

I READ AN INFORMAL STUDY A WHILE BACK THAT FOUND THAT NEW YORK IS THE MOST POLITE OF 35 MAJOR CITIES TORONTO CAME IN THIRD BUT REALLY THERE'S A DIFFERENT FEEL TO MANY DAY TO DAY INTERACTIONS HERE

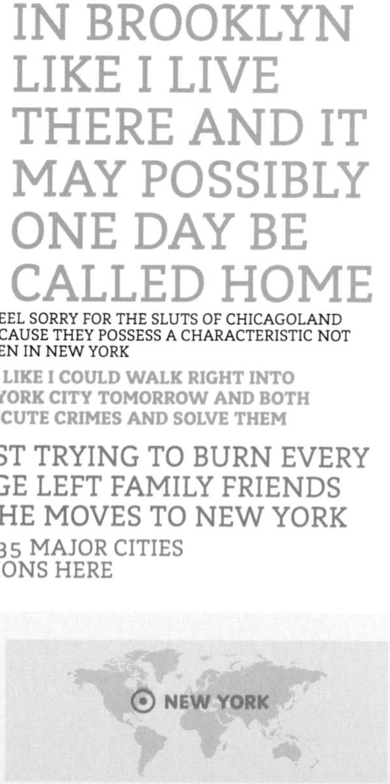

Top feelings in Paris

Above average Paris / Paris / Average

better · good · bad · **guilty** · **sorry** · down

I ALWAYS FEEL A REAL SENSE OF EXCITEMENT PULLING INTO PARIS

I KNOW IT I'M LEAVING PARIS AND I FEEL ON THE PLANE A SWIFT REVULSION AT THE IDEA OF RETURNING AS WELL AS A HOMESICKNESS FOR PARIS WHICH AFTER JUST A DAY HAD FELT LIKE HOME

I LOVE SHOWING OFF PARIS WHICH I FEEL REALLY POSSESSIVE ABOUT

I DID MOVE TO PARIS AND I AM HAPPY HERE BUT I FEEL LIKE I'M DRIFTING

I ALREADY FEEL MYSELF GAINING WEIGHT AS I TYPE THIS BUT I DIDN'T COME TO PARIS TO WATCH WHAT I EAT WELL YES I DID BUT IN A TOTALLY DIFFERENT WAY THAN I DO AT HOME

I FEEL FABULOUS I'M YOUNG HEALTHY AND I LIVE IN PARIS

I FEEL SO AT HOME HERE IT'S AS IF PARIS IS MY REAL HOME AND CANADA WAS A PLACE I WAS STUCK IN CANADA SUCKS SO MUCH ETC

I FEEL THAT PARIS IS A PLACE THAT STILL APPRECIATES ITS SHOWGIRLS

I AM WALKING THROUGH PARIS AND LOOK INTO ONE OF THOSE QUIET COURTYARDS WHERE NOTHING HAS CHANGED FOR DECADES I FEEL ALMOST PHYSICALLY THE CURRENT OF TIME SLOWING DOWN IN THE GRAVITATIONAL FIELD OF OBLIVION

I WAS SAD TO LEAVE IT'S WEIRD HOW OFTEN I'VE SIGHED AND SAID THAT I DIDN'T REALLY FEEL LIKE GOING BACK TO PARIS

I FIGURED OUT OVER THE NEXT FEW DAYS YOU CAN WALK AND WALK AND WALK IN PARIS AND STILL FEEL LIKE YOU HAVEN'T GOTTEN ANYWHERE

I LIVE IN PARIS BUT I FEEL I AM A DAUGHTER OF EUROPE

I FEEL THAT THE VIEW FROM THE TOP IS THE MOST BEAUTIFUL IN PARIS SINCE IT IS THE ONLY PLACE FROM WHICH YOU CANNOT SEE THE TOWER HAHA

I FEEL THAT PARIS IS A ROMANTIC PLACE TO GO AND BEST TO GO WITH LOVED ONE

I THINK THE ULTIMATE PARIS THING TO DO IS RELAX BY THE RIVER AT MIDNIGHT WATCHING THE EIFFEL TOWER SPARKLING YOU KNOW MILLIONS HAVE DONE IT BEFORE YOU AND IT S JUST AN INCREDIBLE FEELING

I FEEL A LITTLE BIT OUT OF CHARACTER FOR ME BUT PARIS HAS SEEMED TO BRING OUT SOME BURIED FEELINGS BOTH GOOD AND BAD AND I'M REALLY NOT SURE WHAT TO MAKE OF IT

I FEEL LIKE SUCH A JERK FOR WANTING TO LEAVE THIS PLACE AND IT'S NOT THAT I'M MISERABLE OR THAT I'M NOT EXPERIENCING PARIS BUT LIKE I DON'T KNOW I GET IT ALREADY

I'M BEGINNING TO FEEL WORRYINGLY AT HOME IN PARIS

I FEEL THE BEST LOOKING CARS IN HISTORY CAME FROM PARIS BASED COACHBUILDERS IN THE GOLDEN ERA OF 1936 TO 1939

I THINK I'VE FELT LIKE EVERY FEELING THAT I CAN FEEL TOWARDS PARIS IN A SPAN OF 7 WEEKS

Paris

Île-de-France, France

Population	2,167,994
Population density	40,150 / mi²
GDP per capita	$46,000 USD

• i always feel a real sense of excitement pulling into paris • i really feel comfortable in paris and it's going to be hard for me to leave if it's not possible for me to continue my studies here right away • i feel i'm throwing my arms around paris • i was thinking of going to the musee d'orsay but since it is really nasty out and i really don't feel like getting dressed i am just going to stay home and read and watch movies • i have to do that to not feel in danger when i want to go home after the last metro when i'm too far to walk • i don't see why i should feel sorry for someone just because they don't know how to do their job • i'd love to stop feeling guilty about every dime i spend

I FEEL SAFE IN PARIS

I LOVED PARIS AND THE ROMANTIC FEEL TO IT AND I LOVED ROME AND ALL THE HISTORY BUT NEITHER OF THEM HAS THE TRANQUILITY OR THE CHARM OF MADRID

I FIND IT STRANGE THAT PEOPLE I KNOW ARE PROMPT TO DESCRIBE PARIS AS BEING GAY WITHOUT BATTING AN EYELID LET'S SEE THEM USE IT WHEN THEY FEEL HAPPY

I COULDN'T HELP BUT FEEL A SERENE HAPPINESS MAYBE PARIS WAS FINALLY GETTING TO ME AND SEEPING INTO MY VEINS

I'M HAPPY IT'S RAINING IN PARIS SO THAT TONIGHT I WON'T FEEL SO BAD ABOUT SPENDING MY FREE TIME WORKING ON A ROMANCE NOVEL I'M TRYING TO FINISH ABOUT MY TIME HERE LAST FALL

I DON'T KNOW HOW I FEEL ABOUT PARIS BUT THE THINGS I'VE DONE HERE ARE THINGS I'LL NEVER FORGET I MEAN HOW MANY PEOPLE CAN SAY THEY RIDE PAST THE MOULIN ROUGE EVERY DAY TO WORK

I AM ALREADY BEGINNING TO DREAD FEELING LEFT OUT WHILE I'M IN PARIS

I TRULY FEEL PARIS BELONGS TO ME

I THINK PEOPLE LOVE PARIS BECAUSE THEY FEEL THAT PARIS LOVES THEM BACK

I SAW SOME PICTURES OF MY BELOVED PARIS AND IT WAS ALL I COULD DO TO KEEP FROM FEELING DOWN

I EVER BECOME A SUPER VILLAIN I MUST MAKE SURE TO START MY EVIL PLAN BY DESTROYING PARIS IT JUST WOULDN'T FEEL RIGHT OTHERWISE

I FEEL PARIS EVOKES THIS SPECIAL FEELING FOR ME BUT I CANNOT CAPTURE IT VISUALLY AT ALL

I DID NOT REALLY FEEL WELCOMED IN PARIS

I CLIMBED THE TOWER I SAW THE SHEER SIZE OF PARIS AND IT MADE ME FEEL SO SMALL AND INSIGNIFICANT

I ALWAYS FEEL SO SAD WHEN I COME BACK TO PARIS

I THINK ONCE MY HONEY IS FEELING BETTER WE'RE GONNA TAKE A FAIRY TO PARIS FOR A WEEKEND AND RELAX

AS DISCONNECTED AS I FEEL NOW FROM THE NAIVE PERSON I BELIEVE I WAS THEN; PARIS WAS MY COMING OF AGE AND A TRULY TRANSFORMATIVE TIME IN MY LIFE

I HAVE GUILT ISSUES AND FEEL LIKE IT S A HORRIBLE CRIME TO SPEND A DAY IN PARIS ONLY GOING TO CLASS OR WORKING

I READ SOMEWHERE THAT PARIS SMELLS OF COFFEE CIGARS AND CHEESE AND ALTHOUGH I HAVE HAD NOTHING EXCEPT PEANUTS AND COOKIES AND WATER I FEEL LIKE EXPLORING THIS ASPECT OF THE PARISIAN POP CULTURE

Top feelings in San Francisco

Above average / San Francisco Average

better · **good** · bad · **guilty** · sick · **well**

I LOVE SAN FRANCISCO AND FEEL IT IS THE MOST BEAUTIFUL AND EXCITING CITY IN THE WORLD

I THINK THE ABSOLUTE WORST PART OF SAN FRANCISCO IS HOW INCREDIBLY SMALL IT MAKES YOU FEEL I DON'T HAVE MANY IF ANY AT ALL CLOSE FRIENDS HERE

I FEEL LUCKY TO LIVE IN SAN FRANCISCO

I WANT SO MUCH TO BE ABLE TO RE ENTER MY LIFE WITH NEW EYES TO APPRECIATE FRESH THE BEAUTY OF SAN FRANCISCO TO FEEL MORE CONSCIOUS GRATITUDE FOR THE EXTENT OF THE LUXURY I CALL HOME

I COULD FEEL THIS JOY IN SAN FRANCISCO LIKE A DREAM WAS COMING ALIVE

I MUST TELL YOU THAT I FEEL MUCH MUCH LESS LIKE A WEIRDO IN SAN FRANCISCO

I LIVE ALONG WASHINGTON SQUARE PARK WHICH ALWAYS FEELS SO SAFE AND I ALWAYS THOUGHT OF HOW ODD IT WAS THAT I FELT SAFER IN NEW YORK THAN I FELT IN SAN FRANCISCO WHEN SF IS SUPPOSED TO BE LIKE PARTY LOVE LOVELY TOWN AND NY IS USUALLY THOUGHT OF AS GRITTY BIG SCARY LAND

I FEEL IT IS MY DUTY TO LET YOU KNOW SAN FRANCISCO IS YOUR SANCTUARY

I FEEL SORRY FOR THE CHILDREN BORN IN SAN FRANCISCO

I MOVED TO SAN FRANCISCO AND I REALLY FEEL LIKE I'M GOING TO MAKE A REALIZATION ABOUT WHAT I WANT MY FUTURE TO BE

I KNOW EVERYONE IS LOOKING FOR A JOB RIGHT NOW BUT SAN FRANCISCO ISN'T THE WORST JOB MARKET IN THE WORLD SO I'M STILL REFUSING TO GIVE UP

I DIDN'T REALIZE UNTIL I CAME HOME HOW BAD SAN FRANCISCO MAKES ME FEEL ABOUT MYSELF

I FEEL LIKE A SISSY COMPLAINING ABOUT COLD WEATHER WHEN I LIVE IN SAN FRANCISCO

I TRIED IT ON AT AGENT PROVOCATEUR IN DOWNTOWN SAN FRANCISCO TODAY AND IT MADE ME FEEL LIKE THE HOTTEST BITCH EVER

I HAD BEEN FEELING LESS ENTHUSIASTIC ALMOST RELUCTANT EVEN TO MOVE TO SAN FRANCISCO AND DO THE GRAD SCHOOL THING

I FEEL COMPLETE IN SAN FRANCISCO

WHEN I'M IN SAN FRANCISCO I FEEL LIKE I'M BEING HUGGED

I DON'T FEEL SEXY OR DON'T KNOW WHAT IS SEXY IN SAN FRANCISCO

I LIVE IN SAN FRANCISCO AND THERE ARE HUGE PARTS OF THIS CITY I WOULDN'T FEEL SAFE HOLDING MY GIRLFRIEND'S HAND

I FEEL I FEEL AS THOUGH I LEFT MYSELF IN SAN FRANCISCO AND AM COMING BACK TO THE TIMID PERSON I DON'T WANT TO BE

I MISS SAN FRANCISCO SO MUCH ITS ACTUALLY MAKING ME FEEL SICK

I MEET FAR TOO MANY GAY MEN IN SAN FRANCISCO WHO FEEL TERRIBLY ISOLATED

San Francisco

California, United States

Population	764,976
Population density	16,380 / mi²
GDP per capita	$58,000 USD

• i gingerly made my way down to the train from chinatown not sure what expression i was wearing since i couldn't feel half of my face • i arrived at mission bay and i started to feel good again • i feel like i've lived in sf for a long time but yet stupidly never really explored the grocery stores in the mission • i love my neighbors and seeing them makes me happy but all those accidental run ins on valencia make me feel bad inside: anxious and sour • i didn't feel like hanging in the mission waiting for muni and i figure he hangs at the dr so he can't be killler • i walked montgomery that night i noticed that they painted a certain building on the corner and north beach didn't feel the way it used to

down | **great** | sorry | alone | comfortable | **sad** | **weird** | **old** | happy | **tired** | ill | lost

I FEEL LIKE SAN FRANCISCO IS A SHIP THAT HAS ALREADY SAILED FOR ME

I FEEL LIKE A COMPLETELY DIFFERENT PERSON THAN THE ONE 5 YEARS AGO THAT MOVED TO SAN FRANCISCO

I WANT A WARM CITY WITH AN EAST COAST FEEL AND SAN FRANCISCO IS THE CLOSEST I'M GONNA GET I THINK

I DIDN'T REALIZE WHAT LIVING IN SAN FRANCISCO CAN DO TO A GUY OTHER THAN MAKE HIM FEEL CONFIDENT IN HIS HOMOSEXUALITY

I FEEL LIVING IN SAN FRANCISCO IS SURE OPENING MY EYES TO NEW EXPERIENCES

I'LL FEEL GUILTY AND NERVOUS FOR EVERY PENNY THAT I SPEND IN SAN FRANCISCO NOW

I'M GLAD I LIVE IN SAN FRANCISCO WHERE I CAN EXPRESS MYSELF THE WAY I FEEL WITH PANTS OR WITHOUT

I LIVE IN THE CASTRO IN SAN FRANCISCO ONE OF THE GAYEST NEIGHBORHOODS IN THE WORLD AND I LOVE LIVING HERE AND I FEEL LUCKY THERE IS STILL A VIBRANT SCENE HERE

I FEEL LIKE HOLLYWOOD IS TRYING TO TELL ME SOMETHING WHEN SKYNET CHOOSES TO PUT ITS HEADQUARTERS IN SAN FRANCISCO

I'VE BEEN IN SAN FRANCISCO FOR ABOUT A YEAR NOW AND WHILE I ABSOLUTELY LOVE IT HERE I AM ALSO STARTING TO FEEL RESTLESS

I FEEL THAT SAN FRANCISCO IS A LOT HILLIER THAN ONE MIGHT FIRST THINK WHEN WALKING OR TAKING BUSES

I'VE SOBERED UP I FEEL LIKE I OWE HALF THE POPULATION OF SAN FRANCISCO AN APOLOGY

I SIMPLY WANTED TO BRING YOU JOY AND A FEELING OF PHYSICAL CONNECTEDNESS IN THIS DARK CRUEL CITY WE CALL SAN FRANCISCO

I LOVE SAN FRANCISCO SO MUCH IT HURTS BUT I ALSO FEEL AS THOUGH I DON'T REALLY BELONG HERE SOMETIMES

I HAD MOVED TO SAN FRANCISCO JUST ABOUT YEAR AGO SO EXCITED TO MEET NEW PEOPLE BUT NOW I FEEL LIKE IT'S GETTING OLD FOR ME

I FEEL THAT I HAVE TAKEN EVERYTHING I NEED FROM SAN FRANCISCO AND THERE IS NOTHING LEFT FOR ME TO DISCOVER ABOUT THIS CITY OR MYSELF

I FEEL LIKE I'LL BE HAPPY TO JUST HANG OUT IN SAN FRANCISCO FOR THE NEXT YEAR AND PROCESS IT ALL WITHOUT TOO MANY STIRRINGS OF WANDERLUST

Top feelings in Seattle

Above average / Seattle / Average

better · good · bad · guilty · well · sorry

I FEEL SO UNWANTED IN SEATTLE

I FEEL LIKE I'M A CRAZY LEFTIST SOMETIMES BUT AS FAR AS SEATTLE GOES I'M SLIGHTLY CONSERVATIVE I THINK

I DO THINK ABOUT AND MISS A LOT OF PEOPLE WHO I DON'T GET MANY CHANCES TO TALK TO ANYMORE BUT I DON T GET HOMESICK BECAUSE I FINALLY FEEL THAT SEATTLE IS MY HOME COMPLETELY

I LIVED IN SEATTLE FOR ABOUT 20 YEARS BUT SOON AFTER MY SON WAS BORN I BEGAN TO FEEL THE URGE TO MOVE

I TRULY FELT AND FEEL LIKE THERE LACKED RESOURCES AND COMMUNITY FOR SEX WORKERS IN SEATTLE

I GREW UP IN KETCHUM IDAHO AND I FEEL LIKE WEST SEATTLE HAS THIS WONDERFUL ENERGY MUCH LIKE A LITTLE RESORT TOWN

I FEEL ABOUT SEATTLE BEING THE FIRST OF PROBABLY MORE TO COME OF OTHER CITIES BEING REDUCED TO ONE NEWSPAPER SOURCE

I FEEL LIKE LIVING IN SEATTLE IS LIKE LIVING IN A DIFFERENT WORLD

I FEEL LIKE I WENT THROUGH ONE OF THOSE LIFE CHANGING TIMES DURING THE MOVE TO SEATTLE

I WAS UNEMPLOYED IN SEATTLE FOR A TOTAL OF 5 DAYS FOR WHICH I FEEL VERY FORTUNATE

I FEEL LIKE I'M THE ONLY GIRL IN SEATTLE NOT WEARING A SKIRT BUT I'M IN DESPERATE NEED OF A LEG WAXING SO I'LL JUST HAVE TO BE HAPPY WITH JEANS AND FLIP FLOPS

I FEEL LIKE I'M JUST SORT OF EXISTING UNTIL I GET TO LEAVE FOR SEATTLE AND SEE MY FRIENDS

WHEN I EAT DUNGENESS CRAB I FEEL VERY SEATTLE

I FEEL AS IF NO ONE FROM SEATTLE OR THE GREATER SEATTLE AREA IS REALLY ORIGINAL

I HAVE A FEELING I'LL LOOK BACK AT SEATTLE AND FEEL AS IF I COULD OF SKIPPED THE ENTIRE THING BECAUSE REALLY I HAVE ACCOMPLISHED NOTHING BY LIVING HERE

I FEEL LIKE ALL OF MY STRESS WAS LEFT IN SEATTLE

I HAVE A FEELING THE LANDSCAPES I SAW IN THE INDUSTRIAL PART OF SEATTLE YESTERDAY ARE GOING TO BECOME VERY PERMANENT PARTS OF MY DREAMSCAPES FOR AWHILE

I'VE LONG HAD A FEAR OF LIVING IN A LARGE CITY AND BECOMING HOMELESS AND SEATTLE FEELS REALLY BIG TO ME

I HAD WANTED SOME NEW SWEATERS FOR THIS BITING SEATTLE COLD AND RAIN I PUT ON THE ONES I HAVE AND FEEL THEIR COZINESS WITH ADORATION INSTEAD OF WISHING THEY WERE NEW

I FEEL LIKE SEATTLE WILL BE A GREAT PLACE TO LIVE IF I EVER DECIDE TO SETTLE DOWN OR SOMETHING

I'M FEELING THE BURNING NEED TO GO TO BACK TO SEATTLE

Seattle

Washington, United States

Population	594,210
Population density	7,085 / mi²
GDP per capita	$56,000 USD

• i stood in a line for coffee that was longer than the beer lines drinking starbucks tastes like shopping at walmart feels: tainted but occasionally necessary • i would feel bad about saying this but i have yet to meet the mariners fan who defends or enjoys having silva on our team • i feel badly for richie but hugely relieved for the mariners • i do not need nor want any new guys in my life and have great friends to keep me feeling loved • i desire you because you make me feel good you look good or you give me what i want • i find myself laying in bed with another man and feeling the same exact feelings i've felt for my ex but rather stronger feelings of love

sick **comfortable** down **great** lost **sad** **tired** alone **weird** ill happy old

I FEEL BADLY FOR SEATTLE AS THEY ARE TALENTED BUT CLUELESS

I REALLY LOVE MY FAMILY AND I'M FINDING IT REALLY HARD TO UNDERSTAND MY LIFE RIGHT NOW BECAUSE I FEEL LIKE SO MUCH OF MYSELF BELONGS IN SEATTLE AND SO MUCH OF MYSELF BELONGS WITH MY FAMILY

I FEEL AS IF I'M FIGHTING SOMETHING ABOUT SEATTLE AS WELL AS FIGHTING THE CANCER ITSELF

I JUST FEEL GOOD THIS MORNING I THINK IT IS SOMETHING TO DO WITH THE SEATTLE SKYLINE OUT SIDE MY WINDOW REFRACTING BITS OF MORNING LIGHT

I FEEL LIKE I'M GOING TO COME OFF A BIT ON THE SNOBBY SIDE AFTER SPENDING THIS TIME IN SEATTLE

I FEEL CLOSER TO SEATTLE THAN I DO MY OWN FAMILY

I FEEL LIKE THE 8 YEARS OF OUR LOVE WOULDN'T FIT IN THE WHOLE OF SEATTLE LET ALONE A BOX OF CHOCOLATES

I FEEL LIKE ALL OF MY FRIENDS IN SEATTLE HAVE WAY COOL NAMES FOR THEIR CATS AND I'M JEALOUS

I DO HAVE FRIENDS BUT AS MUCH AS I HAVE TRIED TO MAKE CONNECTIONS WITH THE CATS IN SEATTLE SOMEHOW I FEEL AS IF I NEVER REALLY FIT

I FEEL MOVING TO SEATTLE THOUGHTS IN THE AIR

I PRETTY MUCH WANT EVERYONE TO KNOW HOW SHITTY I HAVE BEEN FEELING SINCE MOVING TO SEATTLE

I FIRST MOVED TO SEATTLE IN '94 I REMEMBER MY VERY FIRST NIGHT IN THE CITY AND THIS INCREDIBLE FEELING THAT WASHED OVER ME

I'VE MADE SUCH GREAT FRIENDS BOTH IN SEATTLE AND AROUND THE WORLD AND REALLY FEEL AS THOUGH I'VE FOUND A PLACE TO BELONG

I WANT TO WRITE ABOUT HOW I FEEL AS THOUGH I AM FALLING OUT OF LOVE WITH SEATTLE

I REALLY FEEL LIKE SEATTLE IS ONE OF THE MOST BEAUTIFUL PLACES IN THE COUNTRY TO LIVE

I FEEL LIKE SEATTLE MAY NOT WORK OUT VERY WELL CONSIDERING THAT MY FAMILY AND I ARE BOTH BROKE

I WAS HOPING THAT I WOULDN'T MOVE AGAIN ANY TIME SOON BUT SEATTLE JUST MAKES ME FEEL LIKE I'M INVISIBLE

I REMEMBERED BEING FAT AND MISERABLE IN SEATTLE FEELING HUNGRY NO STARVED RAVENOUS MY HUNGER LIGHTING UP EVERY MOMENT OF EVERY DAY LIKE A FLASHING NEON SIGN AND I FOUND I VASTLY PREFERRED THE ALTERNATIVE: EATING FREELY AND JOYFULLY IN A CITY I LOVED

Top feelings in Sydney

Above average / Sydney / Average

better | bad | good | **sick** | **guilty** | **sorry**

I DUNNO WHY BUT JUST BREATHING THE SYDNEY AIR MAKES ME FEEL BETTER

I FEEL OUT OF PLACE IN SYDNEY NOT SO MUCH BECAUSE I'M ALONE BUT BECAUSE I AM SO STRONGLY AWARE THAT THIS IS NOT WHERE I'M CALLED

I SEE SYDNEY HARBOR I FEEL THIS MIXTURE OF COMFORT SAFETY AND MAGIC

I FEEL LIKE I LIVE IN HOLLYWOOD I'VE OFTEN REFERRED TO SYDNEY AS THE HOLLYWOOD OF THE SOUTHERN HEMISPHERE ESPECIALLY IN THE LAST DECADE WHEN ALL THE BEAUTIFUL PEOPLE SEEM TO BE ABOUT TOWN ALL THE TIME

I AM ALONE AND PRETTY BORED HERE IN SYDNEY SO I GUESS I FEEL A BIT BLACK AND WHITE

I'M THIRTY I JUST MOVED TO MAITLAND FROM SYDNEY AND I'M TRYING TO SORT OUT MY LIFE AND MAKE MYSELF FEEL HAPPY AND FULFILLED

I LOVE RUNNING AT NIGHT I USED TO DO IT WHEN I LIVED IN SYDNEY BUT I DON'T FEEL SAFE DOING IT IN LONDON

I REGRET COMING TO SYDNEY I FEEL LIKE I SHOULD HAVE STAYED BACK IN HOUSTON WITH MY MOTHER

I FEEL OUT OF PLACE IN SYDNEY NOT SO MUCH BECAUSE I'M ALONE BUT BECAUSE I AM SO STRONGLY AWARE THAT THIS IS NOT WHERE I'M CALLED

I FEEL LIKE I'M RUNNING AWAY FROM SYDNEY AND NOT RUNNING TO ANYTHING PARTICULAR

I FEEL A DISCONNECTION WITH THE REAL WORLD LIVING IN THE MIDDLE OF SYDNEY

I FEEL LIKE WHEN I LEFT SYDNEY IT'S LIKE I JUMPED OFF A CLIFF

I FEEL LIKE I AM LIVING THREE LIVES: MY SINGAPORE LIFE MY SYDNEY LIFE AND MY IMAGINED LIFE

I WISH WE WERE BACK IN SYDNEY AND WE COULD GO TO THE BEACH FOR NYE AND DRINK CHAMPAGNE AND I COULD MAKE NEW FRIENDS AND HAVE A SOCIAL LIFE OF MY OWN SO I DON'T FEEL SO UNBEARABLY DEPENDENT

I FEEL I'M MEANT TO GO TO SYDNEY

I SOMETIMES FEEL CLAUSTROPHOBIC AND STRESSED WALKING AROUND SYDNEY

I AM LIVING IN SYDNEY DURING THE SEMESTERS I ALWAYS FEEL LIKE I AM MISSING OUT ON THOSE SPECIAL MARKERS WHICH INDICATE THE CHANGING SEASONS

I FEEL SO LONELY IN SYDNEY

I FEEL IF I LEFT SYDNEY LOSING CERTAIN THINGS WOULD LEAVE A HOLE TOO

Sydney

New South Wales, Australia

Population	4,284,379
Population density	913 / mi²
GDP per capita	$39,000 USD

• i spent the whole afternoon on the harbour kayaking it was surprisingly good: i loved being out on the water in the sun it's impossible to describe but feels amazing • i feel like my head is more screwed on now and i am much more sensible will sydney be the great undoing of all of this • i feel like i live in hollywood i've often referred to sydney as the hollywood of the southern hemisphere especially in the last decade when all the beautiful people seem to be about town all the time • i didn't feel like i really had a christmas last year in sydney i spent all of dec sweating and broiling at the beaches and having hot summer nights in the city with friends • i def feel like a little mini holiday in the blue mountains

down | happy | tired | sad | comfortable | well | ill | lost | great | old | stupid | alone

I GET THE FEELING THAT IF I TRAVEL AROUND SYDNEY ALL ALONE I WOULD START MUTTERING TO MYSELF TOO

I WOULD LOVE TO GET A JOB IN SYDNEY BUT I AM GETTING IMPATIENT AND NEVER SEEM TO FEEL HAPPY HERE SO HOME MAY BE ON THE HORIZON

I'M REALLY WISHING I CAN SLOW DOWN TIME CAUSE I DON'T FEEL LIKE LEAVING SYDNEY QUITE YET

I STILL FEEL WEIRD WALKING AROUND SYDNEY BECAUSE THERE ARE NO CRACK HEADS TWEAKING OUT IN THE STREETS DOWNTOWN

I HAVE DECIDED TO TAKE OFF AND PACK IT ALL IN AND SAY A HUGE FUCK YOU TO SYDNEY AND JOB HUNTING AND FEELING DEPRESSED

I KNOW IT'S ONLY BEEN SIX MONTHS OR SO BUT I FEEL CONTENT THAT I'VE ASSEMBLED PARTS OF SYDNEY I CAN CALL MY OWN AND IT'S CROSSED MY MIND TO MOVE TO ANOTHER CITY

I HAVE THIS HUGE SPIRITUAL FEELING ABOUT SYDNEY HARBOR

I DO FEEL SAD IN LEAVING SYDNEY A CITY I LOVE A NEIGHBOURHOOD I LOVE AND FRIENDS I LOVE

I REALLY FEEL AT HOME IN SYDNEY AND IT'S AMAZING HOW MUCH BETTER I'M ABLE TO HANDLE SITUATIONS IN THE CITY

I STILL FEEL QUITE UNSAFE IF I HAVE TO WALK ON THE STREET ALONE IN SYDNEY

I SAW THE OPERA HOUSE I COULD FEEL THE BREDTH OF MY DECISION TO MOVE HERE AND IT WAS THE BEST FEELING IN THE WORLD TO KNOW THAT I COULD FINALLY CROSS SEEING THE SYDNEY OPERA HOUSE OFF MY LIST OF THINGS TO DO IN THIS LIFE TIME

IT HAS A LOVELY WAY OF MAKING YOU FEEL LIKE A TOURIST EVEN IF YOU'VE LIVED IN SYDNEY FOR 20 YEARS

I FEEL TRAPPED HERE IN SYDNEY

I KINDA FEEL LIKE LEAVING SYDNEY BEHIND WAS A HUGE MILESTONE

I KNOW MANY OF US CAN BE WARY OF PIANO SALESPEOPLE AND YOU MAY FEEL THAT THEY ARE STEERING YOU IN A CERTAIN DIRECTION BUT PIANO SALES COMPANY THAT HAVE BEEN IN THE MARKET FOR A LONG TIME SUCH AS HUTCHINGS PIANOS IN SYDNEY ARE QUITE REPUTABLE

I THOUGHT THAT ABSOLUTELY NOTHING COULD FEEL WRONG ONCE I AM IN SYDNEY AND THAT HERE I SHALL BE ETERNALLY HAPPY

I FEEL SO HYPER BECAUSE I FUCKING REALISE HOW MUCH I LOVE SYDNEY

I FEEL SO SMALL BY WINDY SYDNEY

I OFTEN FEEL A LACK OF COMMUNITY IN SYDNEY

Top feelings in Tokyo

Above average Tokyo Average

better | **bad** | good | **sorry** | **lonely**

I AM COMING FROM FUZHOU BUT JUST THE LOOKING DOWN AT YOUR FEET WHEN WALKING ON THE STREETS YOU CAN FEEL HOW MUCH CLEANER TOKYO IS THAN THE AVERAGE CHINESE CITY

I STILL HATE HOW NO MATTER HOW GOOD I GET AT THIS LANGUAGE TOKYO CAN STILL MAKE ME FEEL LIKE A RANK BEGINNER

I FINALLY FEEL LIKE I'M RETURNING TO TOKYO MY HOME AND I BELONG HERE

I FEEL LIKE THESE PEOPLE WHO HAVE DEEP POCKETS DON'T REALLY GET TO EXPERIENCE THE TOKYO THAT I SEE

I FEEL LIKE EVERYWHERE IN ANYTIME IS CROWDED IN TOKYO

I FEEL THE WAY I CURRENTLY DO BUT WHAT COULD POSSIBLY COMPARE TO LIVING IN TOKYO

I HAVEN'T BEEN TO JAPAN IN SOME YEARS AND I HAD FORGOTTEN HOW ISOLATED ONE TENDS TO FEEL IN A CITY OF THE SIZE OF TOKYO WITH SOOOO MANY PEOPLE AND NOBODY TO CONNECT TO

I FEEL LIKE TOKYO IS AN ADULT WHILE BEIJING IS ONLY A SMALL CHILD

I WAS BORN IN TOKYO AND I THINK THAT I FEEL MORE AT HOME WHEN I'M THERE

I WENT TO TOKYO YESTERDAY AND I FEEL LIKE I'VE RUN A MARATHON

I HAVEN'T EVEN COME CLOSE TO EXPERIENCING A FRACTION OF WHAT TOKYO HAS TO OFFER I FEEL LIKE I'VE DONE WHAT I NEEDED TOO

I WAS FEELING PRETTY SHITTY AND I KNEW IT WOULD BE ONE OF MY LAST SHOWS IN TOKYO

I WOULD FEEL TOTALLY SAFE GOING OUT AT NIGHT IN EITHER KYOTO OR TOKYO

I AM ACTUALLY BEGINNING TO FEEL A LITTLE TIRED OF TOKYO THOUGH I SUPPOSE THAT IS JUST THE WALKING AND THE SHOPPING

I FEEL GUILTY THAT I'M IN TOKYO AND I SIT IN MY APARTMENT EVERY DAY AND READ

I DIDN'T HAPPEN TO GO TO GINZA THIS CHRISTMAS DAY BECAUSE I FEEL GINZA HAS THE MOST CHRISTMAS FEELING OF ANY PLACE IN TOKYO FOR SOME REASON

I NOW FEEL LIKE I CAN FACE THE COLD TOKYO CROWDS WITH A SMILE

I FEEL STRANGE THAT I CAN NEVER BE IN NEW YORK AND TOKYO SIMULTANEOUSLY

I COULD DO WITH MORE TOKYO TIME BUT I GET THE FEELING THE PLACE WILL EITHER DO MY HEAD IN OR I'LL LOVE IT

I FEEL SOMEWHAT NOSTALGIC FOR 1950'S TOKYO WHENEVER I SEE THE TOWER

I CAN FEEL A PART OF ME DYING IF I DON'T GO TO TOKYO SOON ENOUGH

I WANT TO BE ABLE TO WALK THROUGH TOKYO CONFIDENTLY AND NOT FEEL LIKE WHALE WADDLING DOWN THE STREET

Tokyo

Kanto, Japan

Population	12,790,000
Population density	9,412 / mi²
GDP per capita	$34,000 USD

• i arrived in tokyo more than a month ago and i feel like i'd better start journaling both to keep me sane and record my fun and sometimes horrible memories • i was missing tokyo sooooo badly and this helps to make me feel a tad better • i live in tokyo the more i think that this whole country is a paradox on its own foreigners always praise the harmony of traditions and technology but i have a feeling that the japanese are under pressure of designing new things because the basics for living are literally crumbling away • i had a wonderful time in okinawa but now i'm home in tokyo and i feel oh so lonely • i can't feel enough of myself to know if suicide is the answer

comfortable | sick | well | weird | guilty | down | happy | great | ill | sad | alone | stupid

I STILL HAVE SOMEWHAT MIXED FEELINGS BUT HERE IN TOKYO WHICH IS SORT OF MY ALONE CITY I'M COMFORTABLE WITH THE SEPARATION COMFORTABLE WITH THE NOTION THAT IT'S NOT AN IRREVOCABLE CHANGE BUT JUST SOMETHING I'M DOING FOR A WHILE

I AM WALKING THROUGH TOKYO FEELING ESPECIALLY TALL

I THINK IT IS INTERESTING TO NOTE THAT TOKYO HAS AS MUCH ITS OWN FLAIR AND STYLE AND HISTORY AS PARIS OR HONG KONG THE CITY NEVER FEELS LIKE IT S ABOUT TO RIP ITSELF APART THE WAY MORE DIVERSE CITIES LIKE LOS ANGELES DO

I DON'T FEEL LIKE DOING ANY ACTUAL RESEARCH TO PROVE IT BUT CONSIDER A FEW SOLID FACTS: LIKE A KAJILLION PEOPLE LIVE IN TOKYO

I FEEL LASER BEAMS OF DISBELIEF SHOOTING IN MY DIRECTION FROM TOKYO

I FEEL KIND OF BORED HERE NOW AS WE HAVE ALREADY GONE TO SO MANY PLACES IN TOKYO AND DON'T KNOW WHAT ELSE TO DO

I JUST GOT BACK FROM TOKYO AND MY EYES FEEL LIKE THEY ARE GOING TO FALL OFF MY FACE

I REALLY FEEL TOKYO MAY BE THE WAY TO GO

I STILL FEEL A SLIGHT GRAVITATIONAL PULL BETWEEN MY LIFE HERE IN TOKYO IN THE NOW WHERE I COME FROM AND WHERE I WOULD LIKE TO HEAD IN THE FUTURE

I EXPECTED TOKYO TO BE SOME HUGE CITY BUT IT DIDN'T FEEL LIKE IT

I FEEL LIKE I HAVE LIVED MY LIFE IN TOKYO TO THE FULLEST

I FEEL THAT LIGHT FROM THE SUN IS WEAK HERE IN TOKYO ESPECIALLY IF YOU COMPARE IT TO THE LIGHT IN A EUROPEAN CITY LIKE BARCELONA

I DUNNO I'M JUST NOT FEELING TOKYO LATELY ALTHOUGH MUCH OF THAT MUST BE DUE TO THE WEATHER AND MY SUBSEQUENT INABILITY TO WANDER AROUND AS FREELY AS I'D LIKE TO

I WAS WALKING AT NIGHT IN SMALL TOKYO ALLEYWAYS AND NOT ONCE DID I FEEL UNSAFE

I REALLY DON'T KNOW HOW I ENDED HERE IN TOKYO BUT AGAIN EVERYTHING JUST FEELS SO NATURAL ALTHOUGH CERTAIN PEOPLE MAY THINK THAT I'M THIS BRAVE ADVENTEROUS SOUL

I KNOW IN TIME THAT THINGS WILL CHANGE AND I'LL FEEL A LOT BETTER AND MORE CONFIDENT ABOUT LIVING IN TOKYO

I HAVE A STRANGE FEELING OF BELONGING IN TOKYO ALBEIT IT IS A VERY SLIGHT FEELING

I FEEL LIKE THE COUNT OF THE GREATER TOKYO METROPOLITAN AREA

I KNOW I HAVE ENDLESS AMOUNTS OF SUSHI AND OTHER GLORIOUS THINGS IN TOKYO BUT SOMETIMES A GIRL JUST WANTS A LITTLE BROCCOLI RABE TO MAKE THINGS FEEL ALL RIGHT

I WASN'T SURE IF I WAS GOING TO MAKE IT THROUGH BUT FORTUNATELY I DID THANKS TO A CERTAIN SOMEONE'S NEVERENDING SUPPORT AND MY AWESOME FRIENDS HERE IN TOKYO AND NOW THAT I'VE EMERGED FROM THE FIRE MOSTLY UNSCATHED I FEEL LIKE I'M READY TO CONQUER ANYTHING

I WENT AWAY TO TOKYO AND DID NOT HAVE MANY FRIENDS AT FIRST THERE WAS A TIME WHEN I DID FEEL AWFULLY LONELY AND I USED FOOD TO SUBSTITUTE THAT PAIN

I STILL FEEL BLESSED BEYOND BELIEF AND I CAN'T FREAKIN WAIT TO LAND IN TOKYO AND START ON MY FIRST ASSIGNMENT

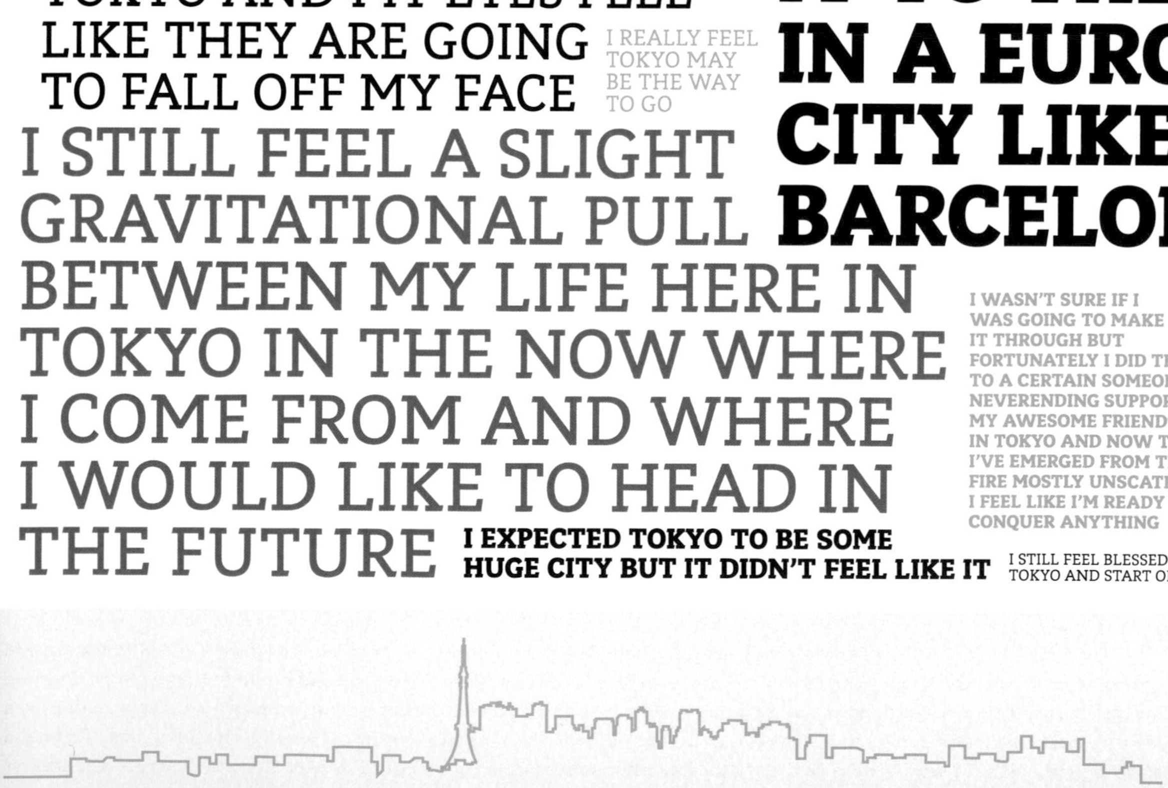

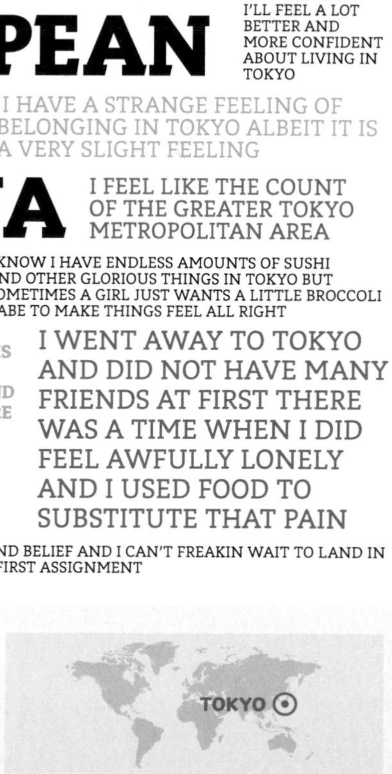

Top feelings in Toronto

Above average / Toronto / Average

better · bad · good · guilty · sick · sorry

I FEEL ALMOST COMPELLED TO GO BACK TO TORONTO SOON AND SPEND SOME TIME IN THE AREA WHERE I FIRST SAW HER

I DO NOT FEEL SAFE IN TORONTO

I'M IN TORONTO WHERE I CANNOT ESCAPE THE FEELING THAT I SHOULD BE DOING SOMETHING

I WAS KINDA DOWN ABOUT THINGS I REMEMBER FEELING REALLY ALONE ALL THE TIME I KNEW THERE WERE OTHER GAY PEOPLE IN TORONTO BUT THEY WERE MUCH OLDER THAN ME

I FELT LOST IN TORONTO AND I FEEL SO FOUND HERE

I KEPT THINKING GOD I PRAYED ABOUT THIS DECISION TO MOVE TO TORONTO AND I'M FEELING LIKE IT WAS THE WRONG ONE

SINCE I'VE MOVED TO TORONTO I'VE RANDOMLY MET LIKE SIX GUYS WHO FEEL THE NEED TO TELL ME THAT THEY'RE BIKERS OR SOMEHOW AFFILIATED WITH A BIKER GANG RIGHT OUT OF THE BLUE

I FEEL THAT THE ONLY THING THAT WOULD MAKE ME HAPPY AND MY LIFE WORTH LIVING AGAIN WOULD BE TORONTO

I FIND MYSELF BACK IN TORONTO UNDER MY PARENT'S WATCHFUL GAZE AND I CAN'T HELP BUT FEEL SUFFOCATED

I FEEL SO TORONTO IT HURTS

I'VE SAID BEFORE AND WILL DO AGAIN I FEEL LIKE TORONTO IS MY HOME BUT I AM NOT READY TO RETURN

I GUESS MAKING SOMEBODY IN TORONTO FEEL BAD IS IT'S OWN REWARD

I MOVED TO TORONTO I FEEL LIKE I HAVE A SOLID BASE NOW A FAMILY

I FEEL SO COMFORTABLE WITH THE IDEA OF BEING AWAY FROM TORONTO FOR A LOT LONGER THAN I INITIALLY ANTICIPATED

I REALLY REALLY FEEL LIKE I SHOULD LEAVE TORONTO BUT I DON'T KNOW IF I CAN GIVE UP THAT CRAZY MIX OF RANDOMNESS AND ANONYMITY THAT DEFINES URBAN LIFE

I FEEL LIKE I'M NOT GIVING TORONTO A FAIR REVIEW ACCORDING TO ME SO FAR THIS CITY HAS ARTSY HOT DOG VENDORS AND HUMPING ROOSTER ART

I GUESS I FEEL TORONTO IS IN A BUBBLE OF SORTS

I FEEL MYSELF BEING LIKE I JUST WANT TO STAY IN TORONTO AND WORK AND NOT HAVE TO THINK OR SHARE WASHROOMS OR MAKE FRIENDS AWKWARDLY

I WALK DOWN THE STREETS OF TORONTO ALL CLEAN AND FEELING LIKE I SMELL A BIT TOO MUCH LIKE A HIPPIE TO BE ENTIRELY MYSELF

I FEEL LIKE I'M SURROUNDED BY IDIOTS IN FACT THE TREADMILLBIKE PRETTYMUCH SUMS UP TORONTO TO ME

Toronto

Ontario, Canada

Population	2,503,281
Population density	10,287 / mi²
GDP per capita	$40,900 USD

• i tooled around the area earlier this week and found it a pleasant area that doesn't feel like being in toronto at all due to the lake • i'm kinda glad i came back to toronto but at the same time i feel kinda bad for partying soo hard every week like this • i have a feeling she really enjoyed toronto but i'm not sure if it's the city itself or just the fact that it's not home • i'm applying for a busker's licence here in toronto so i can feel free to go play my music on the streets for moneys • i look at house prices in toronto i want to scream because it feels like we'll never get the house we want in an area that we want • i feel like nothing happens in toronto

well | down | great | comfortable | happy | ill | sad | tired | old | lost | stupid | weird

I FINALLY FEEL LIKE FOR THE FIRST TIME IN TORONTO I AM IN THE RIGHT JOB RIGHT PLACE AND TIME

I FEEL SADDENED TO SAY I THINK THE GOOD NEEDS TO BE TEMPORARILY REMOVED FROM TORONTO UNTIL CITY COUNCILORS CAN GET THEIR ACTS TOGETHER AND THINK ABOUT THE PEOPLE

I FEEL AS THOUGH ESPECIALLY IN TORONTO I SURROUNDED MYSELF FOR A LONG TIME WITH A CROWD I PROBABLY WAS NEVER REALLY PART OF BUT STUCK WITH AS IT WAS ALL I KNEW HAD HERE

I HAVE A FEELING THOUGH MY MOM MAY KILL ME UPON MY ARRIVAL INTO TORONTO

I DON'T FEEL HAPPY IN TORONTO BUT IT'S JUST MORE QUIET AND SERENE HERE

I STILL FEEL LIKE I'M RUNNING A MARATHON IN A TOO SMALL CORSET AND I CAN'T FUCKING BREATHE THIS SAME TORONTO AIR ANY MORE

I LOVE TORONTO AND I LOVE WHO I AM I JUST NEED TO FEEL LIKE I AM GETTING SOMEWHERE

I FEEL LIKE THIS TORONTO LIFE IS A PRACTICE LIFE

I LOVE TORONTO BECAUSE YOU CAN GO TO LITTLE INDIA AND FEEL LIKE YOU ARE IN A TOTALLY DIFFERENT PLACE

I ALWAYS FEEL LIKE I'M WATCHING MY BACK IN TORONTO AND IT IS QUITE EXHAUSTING AFTER A WHILE

I FEEL PARTICULARLY FORTUNATE TO LIVE IN THE VIBRANT CULTURALLY DIVERSE AND TOLERANT CITY OF TORONTO

I HAD TO CANCEL OUR PLANS TO GO UP TO THE COTTAGE THIS WEEKEND AND HERE IT IS A BEAUTIFUL WEEKEND IN TORONTO AND I STILL FEEL LIKE A BAG O' SHIT

I FEEL THAT IF I COULD LOSE 50 LBS SURELY I COULD SURVIVE IN TORONTO ON MY OWN

I FEEL THAT TORONTO IS A WATERED DOWN AMERICA THERE ARE MANY THINGS IN TORONTO AND WITHIN CANADIAN CULTURE THAT ARE VERY AMERICAN

I FEEL ABOUT TORONTO I HAVE MET SOME AMAZING PEOPLE THERE AND IT'S WHERE MY LIFE IS NOW

I FEEL LIKE IN TORONTO I'M TRYING TO LOOK FOR A CIRCLE IN A STURDY FIXED SQUARE

I WAS BORN IN 1950 IN TORONTO AND HAVE LIVED IN 15 CITIES INCLUDING IN THE USA SO I'VE BEEN AROUND AND ABOUT AND AT TIMES I FEEL LIKE A WALKING TOXIC DUMPSITE

I FEEL PEER PRESSURE FROM TORONTO KIDS

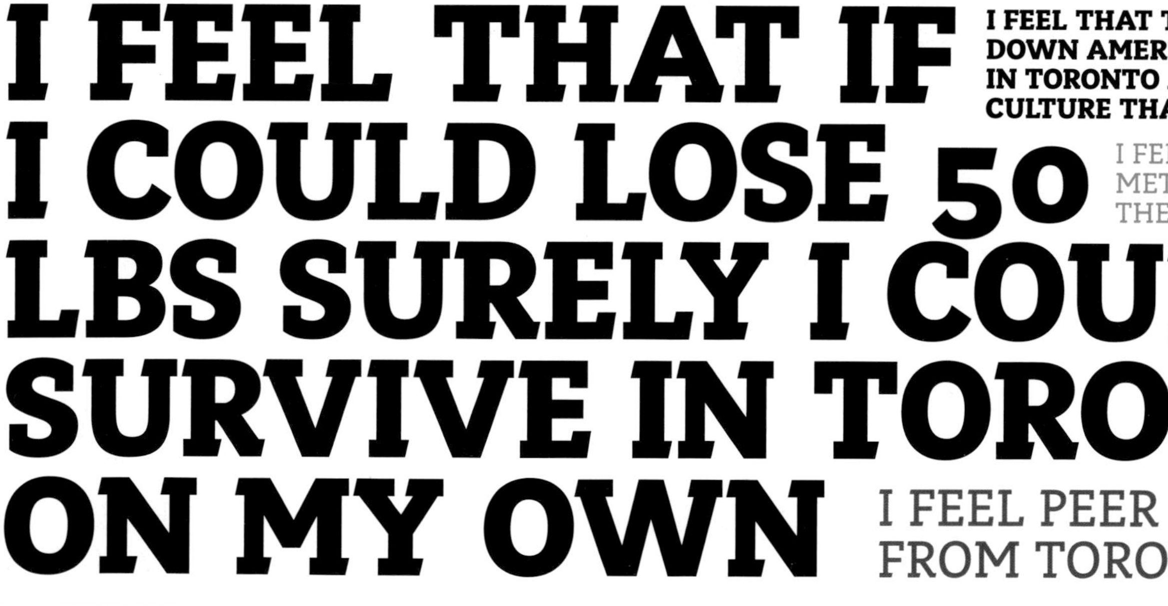

The Lines of the Hand

ranked by the percentage of feelings that specifically mention each topic

Life 2.79% of feelings
- vitality, physical health, general well-being
- length is *not* associated with length of life

Heart 1.06%
- emotional stability, romance, depression
- wavy = many lovers; straight = self-control

Head 1.01%
- intellectualism, thirst for knowledge
- curved = creative; straight = practical

Sex 0.47%
- sexual desire and drive
- capacity for romance

Money 0.41%
- skill and technique for acquiring cash
- does *not* determine material wealth

Luck 0.39%
- how lucky one is
- lottery, business, love

Health 0.28%
- overall health and sickness
- broken / wavy = problems

Spirit 0.21%
- depth of spirituality
- ability to achieve inner peace

Travel 0.12%
- influence of travel on one's life
- lines crossing travel line = danger on trips

Marriage 0.05%
- light line = romance; strong line = marriage
- closer to pinky finger = romance later in life

Fate 0.03%
- effect of external events on one's life
- deep line = strongly controlled by destiny

Fame 0.01%
- social rewards of success
- broken line = sporadic recognition

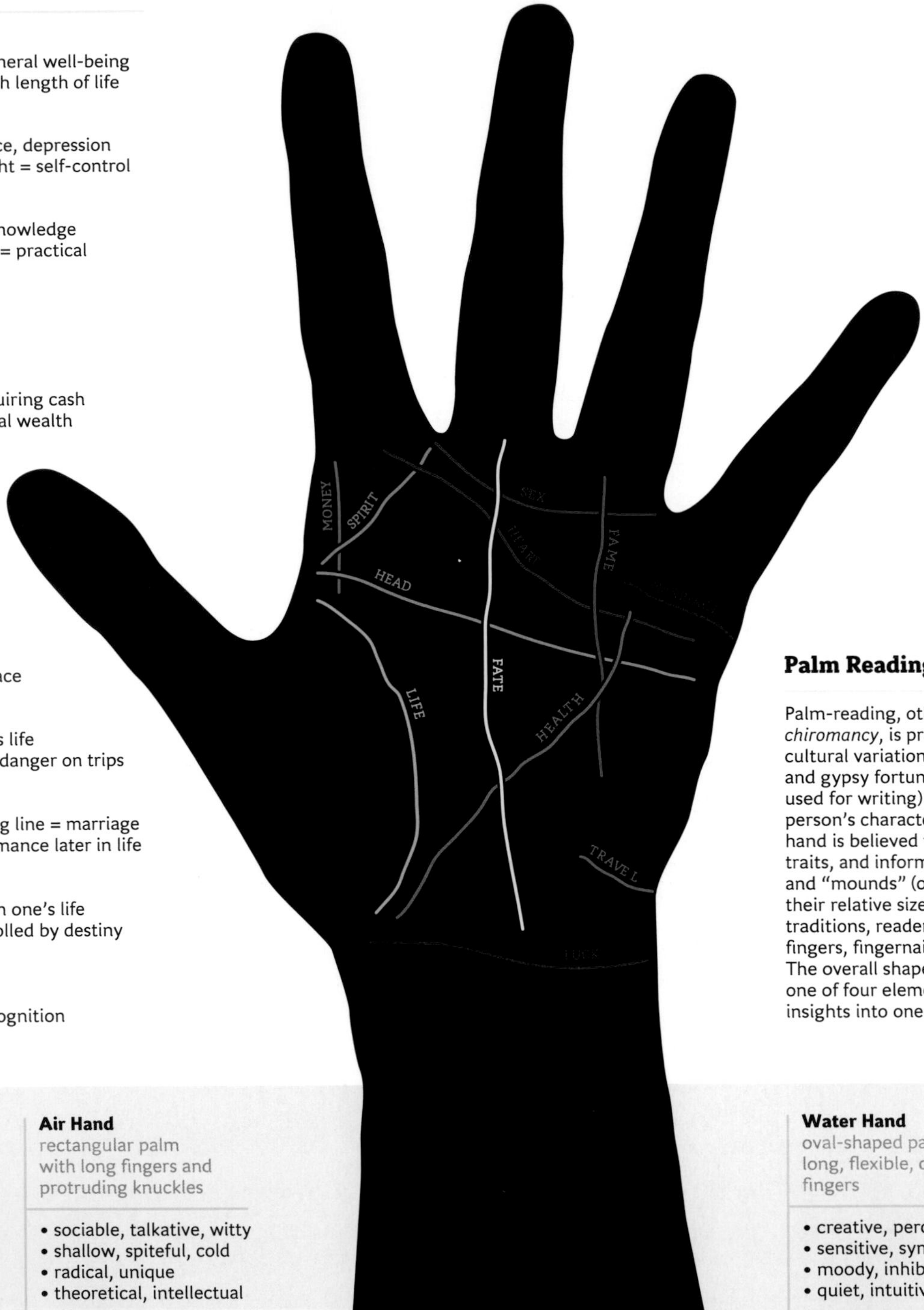

Palm Readings

Palm-reading, otherwise known as *palmistry* or *chiromancy*, is practiced all over the world with many cultural variations, finding its roots in Indian astrology and gypsy fortune-telling. The dominant hand (the one used for writing) is said to contain information about a person's character and fate, while the non-dominant hand is believed to encode hereditary conditions, family traits, and information from past lives. Various "lines" and "mounds" (or bumps) are interpreted by examining their relative sizes, qualities, and intersections. In some traditions, readers also inspect characteristics of the fingers, fingernails, fingerprints, and palmar skin patterns. The overall shape of the hand is typically classified into one of four elemental types, which are believed to provide insights into one's personality.

Earth Hand
broad, square palm and fingers; thick or coarse skin; ruddy color

- solid values, centered
- practical, responsible
- stubborn, materialistic
- dextrous, physical

Air Hand
rectangular palm with long fingers and protruding knuckles

- sociable, talkative, witty
- shallow, spiteful, cold
- radical, unique
- theoretical, intellectual

Water Hand
oval-shaped palm with long, flexible, conical fingers

- creative, perceptive
- sensitive, sympathetic
- moody, inhibited
- quiet, intuitive

Fire Hand
square or rectangular palm; flushed or pink skin; shorter fingers

- spontaneous
- enthusiastic, optimistic
- egoistic, insensitive
- bold, instinctive

6 Why
On the reasons why we feel

Tags: sociology, biology

On April 28th, 2007, Meg Moore bought a train ticket from Portland, Oregon, to Tacoma, Washington, to spend 5 days with her mom. She was excited to go out to dinner with her mom for her 19th birthday, to go shopping together, and most of all, to repair their relationship. "Sometimes," Meg posted on her blog that day, "it makes me wanna cry when I think about it (like right now). How much I hurt her, and all the shit I put her through. And how hard I was on her when I didn't get things the way I wanted... I was such a fucking brat, I still am, in all honesty."[1]

Meg was born with cystic fibrosis, a disease that causes chronic lung and digestion problems. She never knew her biological mother, who had been in and out of drug and alcohol rehab 18 times before the alcohol took her life on Valentine's Day 2004. Meg was off to visit her adoptive mother.

"She is the strongest person I know, in all fucking honesty," Meg writes in the post. "All the times she had to go to the ER with me, and sit there... whether it be because I couldn't breathe and needed oxygen, and she sat there worried about my health (knowingly going into situations like that having adopted me, and knowing all about CF being a nurse). Or having to sit with me because I tried to kill myself again, and wondering what she did wrong. She didn't do anything wrong."[2]

Meg, like her biological mother, has gone through her own bouts of addiction. Her February 24th, 2008, blog post starts, "Hi, I'm Meg. I'm an alcoholic and an addict." Meg had just gotten home from rehab: "There is still a tremendous amount of anger inside me, I think I found that out when I kicked a hole in the wall before I left. I need to find out where that is coming from, and give up my resentments."[3] Meg sometimes wishes her biological mother were alive so she could perhaps empathize with Meg's experiences with addiction.

Meg Moore

Meg blogs about a wide range of topics, from living with cystic fibrosis, to her battle with addiction, to her love for Ozzy Osbourne. But Meg's most poignant posts are those that talk about her relationships with the people in her life, like her biological grandmother whom she met a year after her biological mother died, her boyfriend, Marko, the community that reads her blog, many of whom, like herself, have cystic fibrosis, and of course, her mom.

"I wanna repair this relationship more than anything in my life, more than meeting Ozzy, more than not having CF," she writes. "I remember when I was a teenager, and we tried family counseling, it was so fucking hopeless. And up until about a month ago, I never really thought it was reparable, and everyone around me told me the same thing. But in the past month, I have realized what's most important to me, and one of those things is my mom. One of the only things probably."[4]

On May 17th, 2009, Tiffany Cheng, a 17-year-old high school student, posted to her blog, echoing a question that has been asked by philosophers and scientists throughout time. "Why do we have emotions?" she asks. "Can't you help but wonder that?"[5]

In 1872, 13 years after he published his groundbreaking *Origin of Species*, Charles Darwin proposed an answer to Tiffany's age-old question in his book *The Expression of Emotion in Man and Animals*. We have emotions, Darwin surmised, because they are useful in dealing with emotion-arousing situations.

In the century and a half since Darwin, a large body of scientific evidence has been put forth to support this theory. When we experience fear, for example, blood rushes to our large muscles, making it easier to run away (or to fight). Adrenaline is released, increasing our heart rate and constricting blood flow to the face and stomach (so that our face goes white and our stomach feels tied up in a knot), and so that blood flows to the arms and legs where it's needed most. Our pupils dilate to see better, our reflexes become hypersensitive, and our blood sugar rises. All of these responses would be useful if we were to be, say, attacked by a bear.

The facial expressions for fear are easy to identify—the eyes widen, the pupils dilate, the mouth opens, and the brows draw together. This signaling mechanism is useful if one person in a group, say, were to see a bear. When one person becomes afraid, others can quickly and easily read his fear, instinctively mimicking his physiological response, "catching" his emotion without needing to understand its cause.

A physiological response similar to fear occurs when we feel excited. If we were spear-hunting for dinner and were suddenly to see a buffalo, our body would release adrenaline, blood would rush to our big muscles, and our heart rate would rise, all increasing our chance of catching the buffalo.

In today's world, where we are rarely attacked by predators and where we prefer the supermarket to the hunt, does Darwin's theory still answer Tiffany Cheng's question, or are human emotions the vestiges of an evolutionary process that changes much more slowly than human society?

When we analyzed the *We Feel Fine* database for the top "whys" of emotion, we found a curious phenomenon. Among people not directly affected, large-scale but remote issues like the Iraq War had far less emotional impact than we had expected. The biggest drivers of emotion were immediate, direct, and above all, personal. This chapter explores the "why" of emotion—highlighting some of the most prominent emotional drivers, according to the *We Feel Fine* database.

A study of the *We Feel Fine* database shows that the most common drivers of emotion are the actions of people close to us. Our emotions help guide us through the complex social fabric in which we live. We get angry with those who slight us, we fear those who threaten us, and we love those who support us. We make our decisions about who to spend our time with (and how to spend that time) based on these emotions.

Interestingly, the experience of love causes the opposite physiological reaction to the experience of anger and fear. With love, heart rate and blood pressure decrease, the processes that facilitate growth and reproduction are triggered, and our salivary glands and stomach secretions activate to stimulate digestion. Overall, we feel a calm and contentment that is useful for cooperation.[6]

In the present day, the ability to hunt for food or escape from predators is less useful than it once was. What is more useful today is our ability to form nurturing relationships and avoid toxic ones, which is due in large part to the guiding force of our emotions. In the words of psychologist Richard Davidson: "All emotions are social. You can't separate the cause of an emotion from the world of relationships—our social interactions are what drive our emotions."[7]

From left: Meg Moore with her adoptive mother; Meg with her biological grandmother; Meg and her adoptive mother at the tattoo parlor, when Meg took her mom to get her first tattoo.

The view of emotions as being good for developing social relationships—and thus useful for survival—is a scientific view, but we may also come to the same conclusion that Tiffany Cheng ultimately reached: that emotions bring beauty to our lives.

The first comment on Meg Moore's blog post about repairing her relationship with her mom was by a young woman from Fort Pierce, Florida, named Stephanie Steele, who was also suffering from cystic fibrosis. "Meg this post made me cry," wrote Steph, "because I went through the same thing with my mother when I was 18. I moved out into friends' houses before my 18th b-day and now at 21 I moved home in order to live back with her for my final days... It's weird being home and I had that long talk with my mother. It was hard because I put my mother through hell. We are really close too, so when we didn't talk it was hard on the two of us, and when I moved out it really hurt her. She's so happy I'm home now."[8]

A couple of months later, on June 7th, 2007, Steph passed away. Her mother has picked up her blog where Steph left off, and continues to post there. In her post on December 26th, 2008, she wrote, "When I reach eternity I cannot wait to hold you and tell you how much I love you and how I was honored by God that you chose me to be your mom."[9] ♥

1, 2. Meg Moore. http://megmucus.livejournal.com/78612.html
3. Meg Moore. http://megmucus.livejournal.com/117405.html
4. Meg Moore. See 1.
5. Tiffany Cheng. http://whoisjincheng.blogspot.com/2009/05/relationships.html
6. Goleman, Daniel. *Emotional Intelligence*. (New York: Bantam Dell, 1995).
7. Goleman, Daniel. *Social Intelligence*. (New York: Bantam Dell, 2006).
8. Stephanie Steele comment. http://megmucus.livejournal.com/78612.html?thread=159252#t159252
9. Stephanie Steele. http://cfkitty.livejournal.com/202057.html

BLOGGING

Breakdowns
for feelings about blogging

Gender breakdown: 43% | 57%

Age breakdown: 10s | 20s | 30s | 40s | 50+

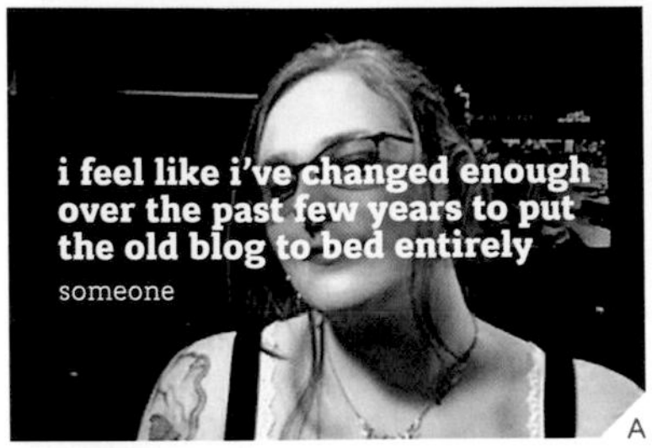

i feel like i've changed enough over the past few years to put the old blog to bed entirely
someone

A

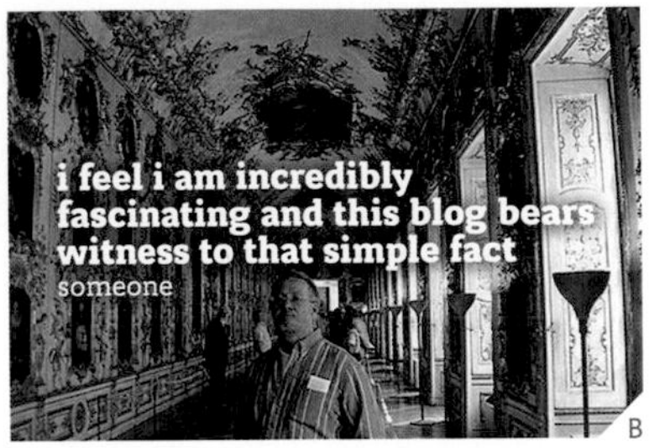

i feel i am incredibly fascinating and this blog bears witness to that simple fact
someone

B

I HAVE A TWITTER NOW I FEEL LIKE SUCH A FAILURE

a woman

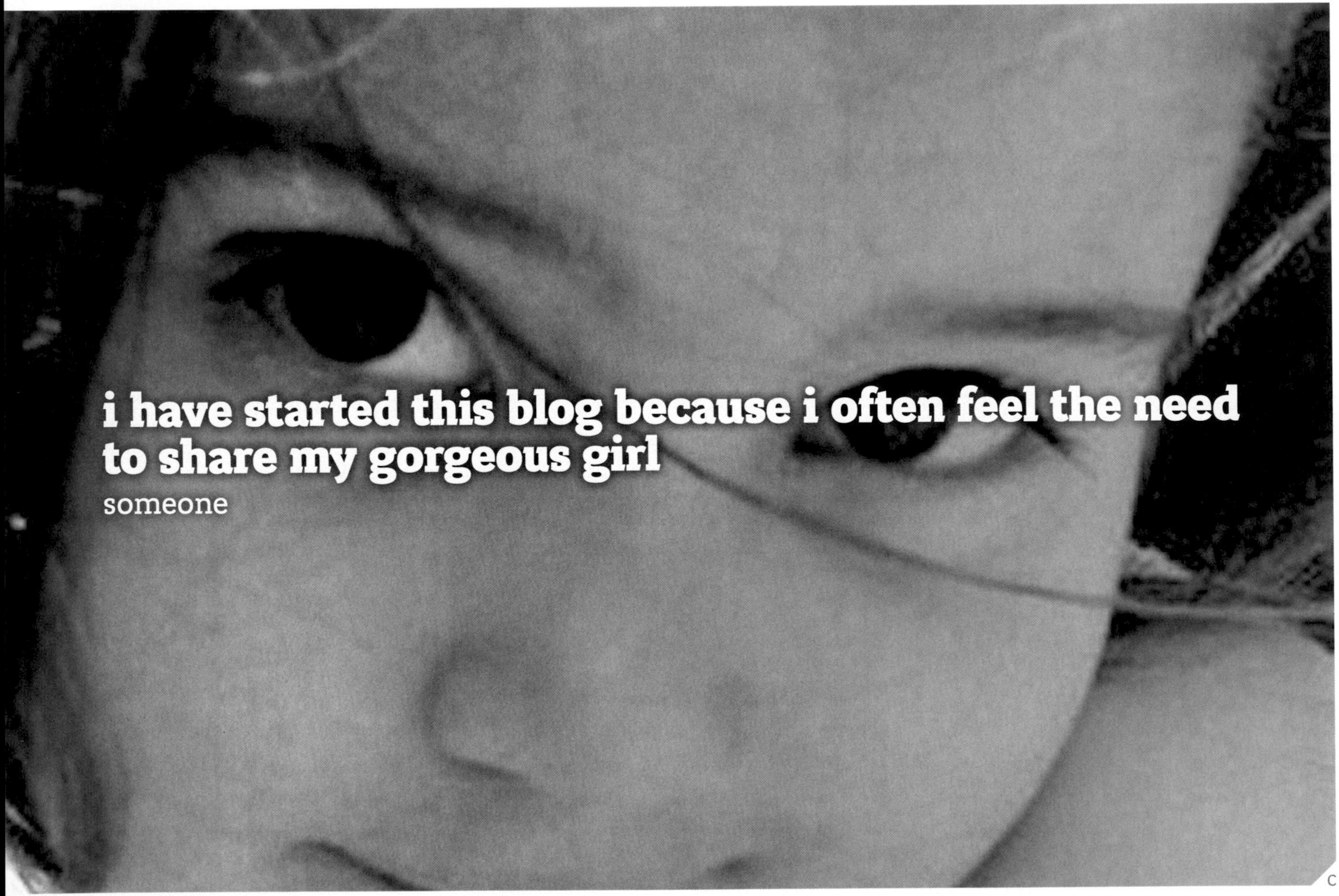

i have started this blog because i often feel the need to share my gorgeous girl
someone

C

blogging

1. keeping a website with regular entries
2. maintaining or adding content to a blog
3. keeping a personal online diary
4. providing social commentary, news

• i come away from blogging with a feeling of belonging to the greatest family in the world • i think that is why i love this blog it is a way of telling someone how i feel without being written off • i thought blogging about it would make me feel better but i was wrong i think i am better off drinking a cyanide cocktail • i absolutely feel blogging has challenged me in ways i never thought possible • i feel like a total zombie and i don't even know why i'm here blogging when i'm already half dead • i started blogging and dieting again and i think i've lost a little bit of weight and i certainly feel better • i enjoy most about blogging is being able to help others feel better

Distinctive feelings
o Blogging • Average

interesting | public | boring | personal | serious | random | inspired

I ALWAYS WANT TO RESPECT HER WISHES AND NEVER MAKE HER FEEL LIKE MY BLOG IS MORE IMPORTANT OR THERE TO HARM HER

someone

i feel naked inside and out on this blog
a 27-year-old man

A

i'm feeling really uninspired lately and hating my flickr stream
a woman

B

i feel guilt now if i'm not uploading photos
someone

C

I FEEL MUCH BETTER ABOUT SPENDING 825 BILLION IN TAXPAYER DOLLARS IF I KNOW SOMEONE'S GOING TO BE BLOGGING ABOUT IT

someone

sometimes i feel like the last person left alive all alone in my apartment with my cat my blog and my dvd collection
someone

D

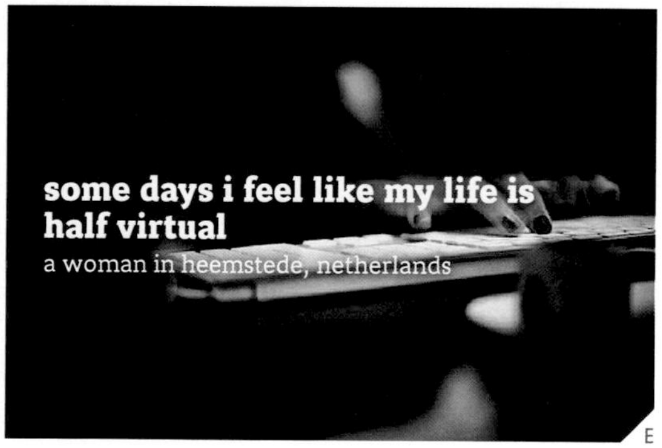

some days i feel like my life is half virtual
a woman in heemstede, netherlands

E

Related themes

- **rambling**
- readers
- post
- venting

Observations

When people talk about their blogs, there is often a sense of **self-consciousness** involved, specifically in the way that their audience may perceive them. **Interesting** and **boring** are two of the most common feelings when people talk about their blogs, and people often express that they feel like they are **rambling**. People also express a sensitivity toward the **public nature** of the medium and the **personal nature** of what they write about. While younger people blog more than older people, those over 50 are more self-conscious and blogging itself arouses emotions in them. ♥

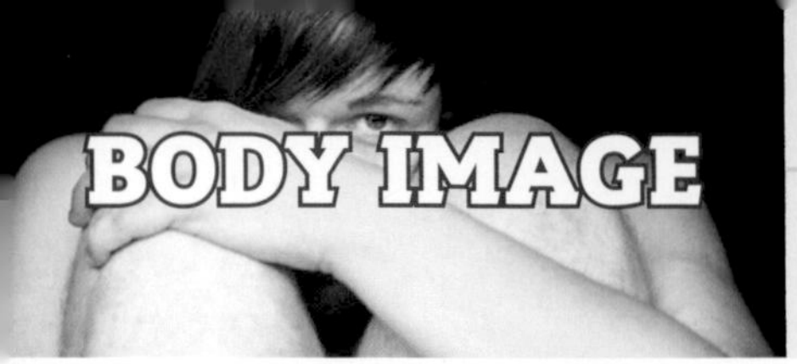

BODY IMAGE

Breakdowns
for feelings about body image

Gender breakdown — 52% (female) · 48% (male)

Age breakdown — 10s · 20s · 30s · 40s · 50+

i feel fat
someone

A

I FEEL GOOD ABOUT MYSELF KNOWING YOU ARE SKINNIER THAN I AM AND STILL HATE YOURSELF

a 24-year-old in littleton, colorado

i feel like crap today
a woman

B

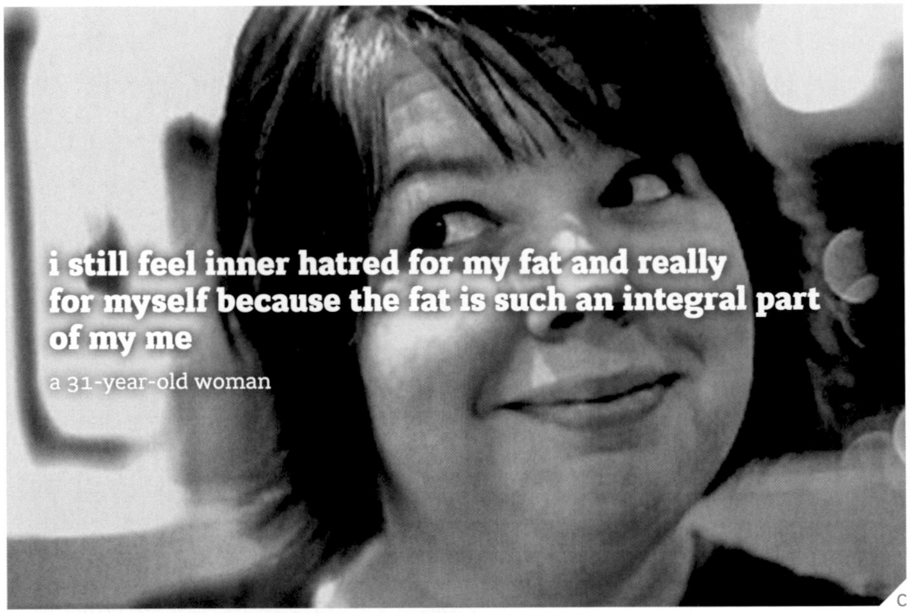

i still feel inner hatred for my fat and really for myself because the fat is such an integral part of my me
a 31-year-old woman

C

i've dropped 10 pounds and love how i look
someone in tuanton, massachusetts

D

i feel fat today
a 29-year-old woman

E

body image

1. perception of one's physical appearance
2. perception of appearance by others
3. internal sense of having a body
4. a person's sense of physical self

● i feel fatter than i ever have before and it makes me want to die ● i i'm just the ugly fat friend that people keep around to make themselves feel better ● i feel like i get picked on more about being skinny than a fat person would be picked on for being fat ● i hang out with fat girls so i look and feel skinny ● i have gained so much weight i feeel so disgusted i dont even want to have sex with him because i feel like it is wrong ● i hate that my boyfriend is skinnier than me it makes me feel so self conscious especially when he is so healthy and i sit there eating cookies ● i decided i think people who hate fat women actually just feel threatened at the idea that a fat woman can be happy

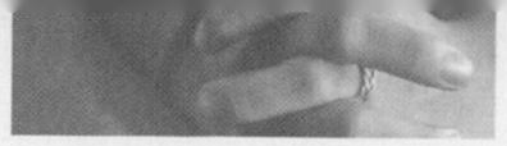

Distinctive feelings
○ Body image • Average

fat · beautiful · ugly · sexy · disgusting · bloated · crummy · unattractive

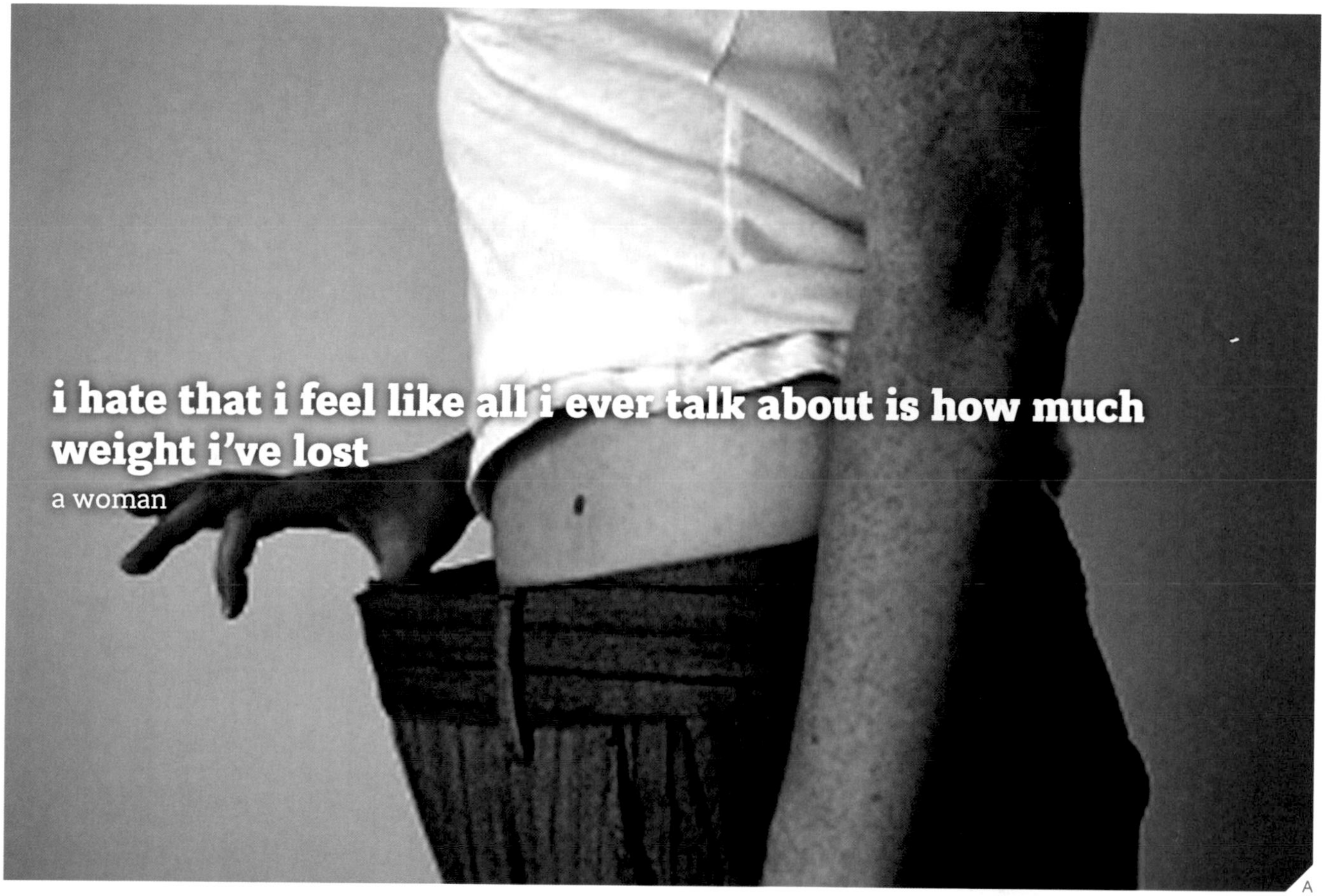

i hate that i feel like all i ever talk about is how much weight i've lost
a woman

A

I ALWAYS FEEL EMOTIONALLY FREE AFTER I SHAVE OR WAX OFF MY BODY HAIR AND PLUCK MY EYEBROWS

a man

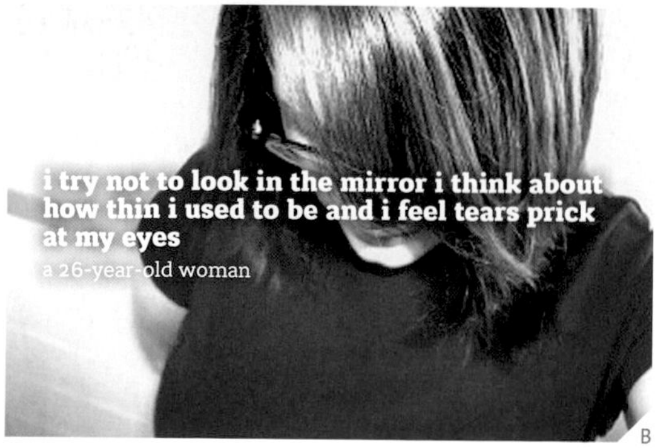

i try not to look in the mirror i think about how thin i used to be and i feel tears prick at my eyes
a 26-year-old woman

B

Related themes
- **mirror**
- makeup
- scale
- ass

Observations

Women are more likely to discuss their feelings about their bodies and do so far more frequently than men do, especially as their issues pertain to their **weight**. People in their late teens and early 20s are more expressive of the feelings pertaining to their **body image** and discuss it more frequently than any other age group, and as people get older, body image will often tend to evoke a bit less emotion. The emotions aroused by people's body image are more commonly **negative** than positive, and are often feelings of **insecurity**. ♥

DEATH

Breakdowns
for feelings about death

Gender breakdown 44% 56%

Age breakdown 10s 20s 30s 40s 50+

i feel i have lost one of my best friends, someone that touched everyone she met
a 31-year-old

A

I WANNA KNOW HOW IT FEELS LIKE TO DIE THOUGH I'M SCARED OF DEATH

someone in singapore

Matt is speaking of his mother who he lost to a brain tumor.

Susan, photographed with her grandmother, was often teased for being her gram's favorite. She writes: "she was the Gram who didn't ask questions when I showed up at her house when I was really supposed to be in school, or at work. I think it was because she really thought that I could do no wrong. She called me the daughter she never had. I loved it." Susan's grandmother passed away in 2005 and she is not done greiving for her.

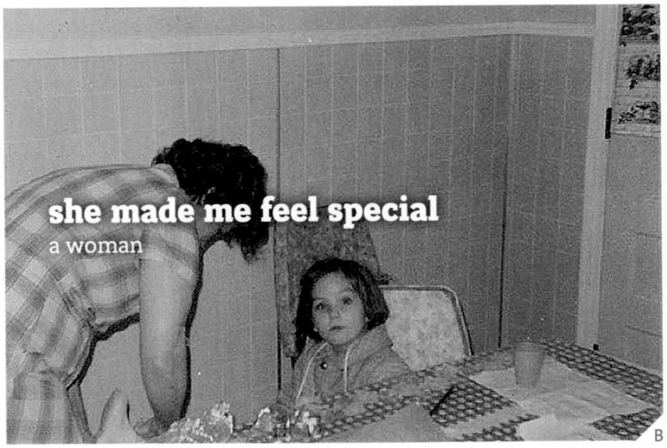

she made me feel special
a woman

B

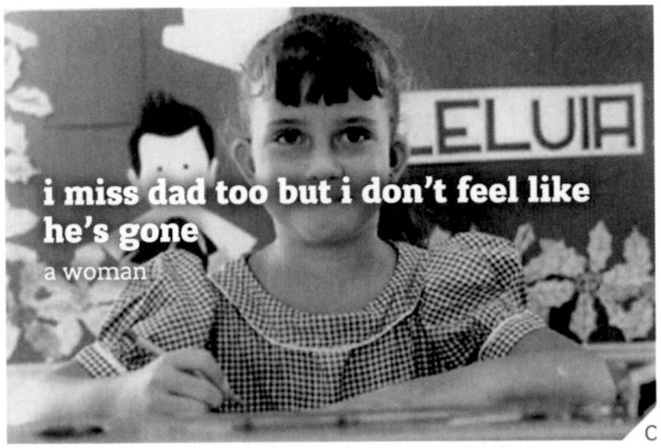

i miss dad too but i don't feel like he's gone
a woman

C

death

1. manner of dying
2. act or state of passing from life
3. cessation of one's biological functions
4. the absence of life; state of being dead

● i wish i was cold enough to tell him that if he died i would feel relief ● i feel like some days i'm waiting to die that i might live ● i don't want to die feeling like nobody really knew me ● i left school and dad died i feel like i don't know anything about anything ● i don't ever want someone i love or respect to die without knowing how i feel about them ● i haven't been able to shake the feeling of wanting to die ● i can't actually put into words how i feel about this and how much guilt and remorse that i have for the fact that i could not put my pride away for one day to go and visit a dying friend ● i don't care about me dying but i'll feel eternally sorry for those i leave behind

Distinctive feelings
○ Death • Average

numb | scared | frightened | troubled | crushed | haunted | afraid

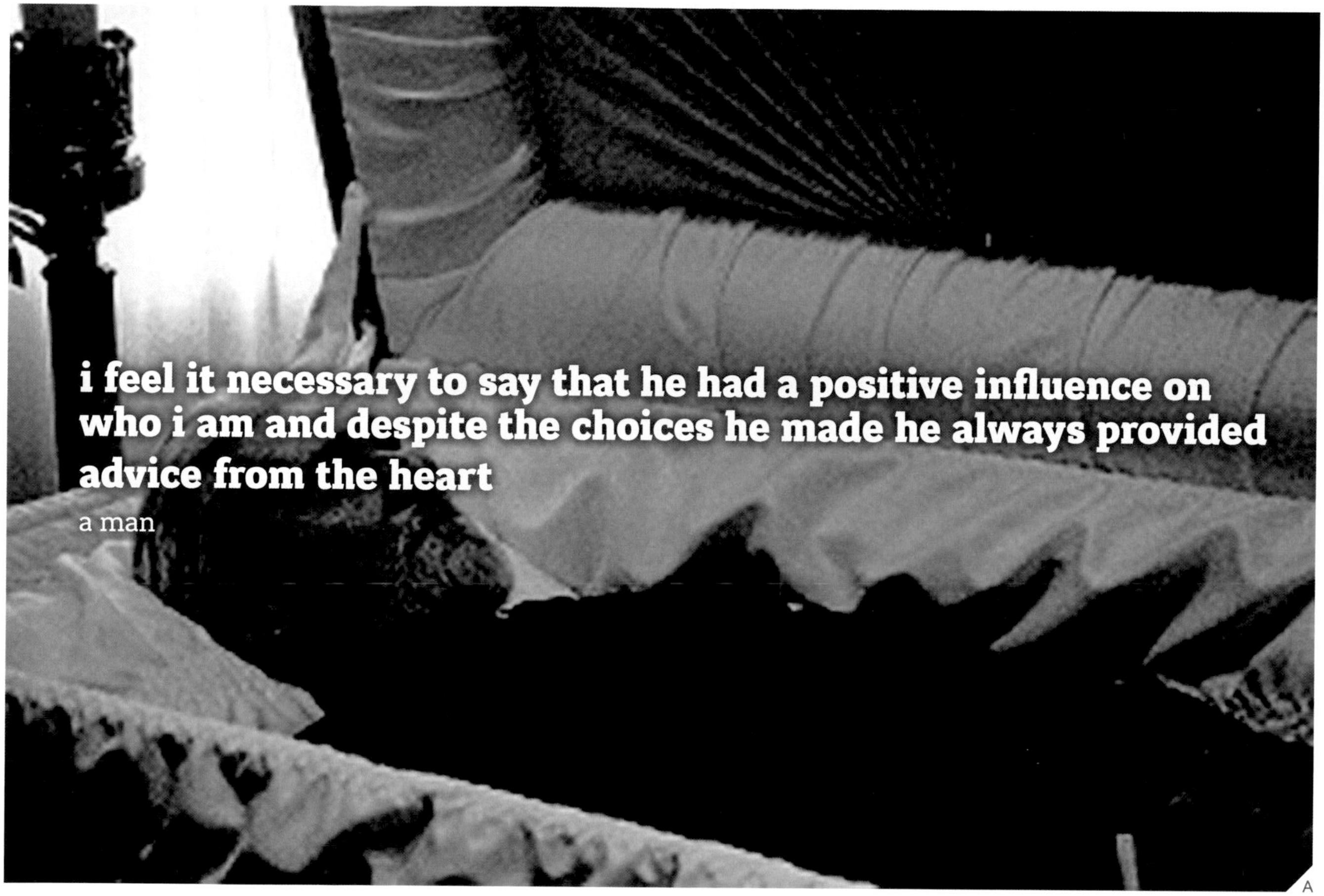

i feel it necessary to say that he had a positive influence on who i am and despite the choices he made he always provided advice from the heart
a man

A

I DIDN'T WANT HIM TO SUFFER AND I WANTED HIS MIND TO BE FREE FROM FEAR AND PAIN SO THAT WHEN HE DIED HE COULD FEEL MY LOVE AND BE COMFORTED BY IT

someone

Related themes
- **agony**
- suicide
- mourning
- grave

Observations

The most common emotion people express when contemplating death is **fear**, along with feeling **scared**, **frightened**, and **afraid**. People who have experienced the death of somebody close to them often express deep **sadness and pain**. People who express feeling **numb** to the world around them commonly say that they feel as if they are already dead, or feel they want to die. Overall and not surprisingly, the emotions about death are largely negative. Men discuss their emotions about death on blogs more frequently than women do. ♥

FRIENDSHIP

Breakdowns
for feelings about friendship

Gender breakdown — 51% (women) / 49% (men)

Age breakdown — 10s 20s 30s 40s 50+

i really just want to feel accepted by my guy friends too like how i accept them
someone

A

i feel inspired today by my wonderful group of friends
someone

B

i am in love with this place this feeling my friends and my family
someone

C

i feel like this with nick: new friend, but old friendship
someone

D

i feel like my friends know me better than my parents do
a woman in los angeles, california

E

I HAVE A FRIEND WHO LOVES IN THE MOST PERFECTLY PURE WAY AND WITH HIS UNCONDITIONAL LOVE MAKES ME FEEL PERFECT TOO

a woman

friendship

1. the state of being friends
2. friendly relation or attachment
3. aptness to unite; affinity
4. not inimical or hostile; not a foe

● i have found that close friends who are good at recognizing and expressing their own feelings are helpful in supporting me in learning more about my own feelings ● i still want to be with you but if the knowledge of my feelings for you is going to negatively effect our friendship and keep us from becoming better friends i am deeply sorry i ever told you ● i am with others friends i feel safe and loved enough by that the crisis feels less threatening and easier to control ● i know that despite the utter happiness i feel for my friends and my loved ones i continue to have this emptiness in my chest or in my uterus as it may be ● i love my friendships with all the boys but it means that i really can't feel like a girl

Distinctive feelings
o Friendship • Average

supported · close · supportive · abandoned · surrounded · comforted

I FEEL SO LUCKY TO NOT ONLY HAVE THE FRIENDS THAT I HAVE BUT EXTREMELY LUCKY THAT THEY ARE THE KIND OF PEOPLE WHO DON'T HAVE LAME WEDDINGS

someone

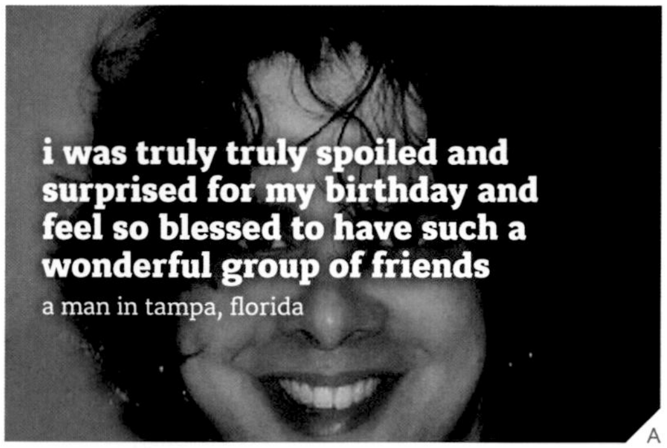

i was truly truly spoiled and surprised for my birthday and feel so blessed to have such a wonderful group of friends
a man in tampa, florida

A

Jason, photographed here with his dear friend Allison, the blogger, died from cancer at the age of 26. He was first diagnosed in 2004 and beat the cancer 3 times before his death in September of 2008.

i sometimes wonder how people become friends and why the bonds can feel so strong
someone

B

Related themes
- **family**
- coworkers
- enemies
- strangers

Observations
Friendship is one of the most common elicitors of emotions on blogs. Especially in the teens and early 20s, but continuing through all ages, friends play a very big social role in people's emotional lives. Largely, the emotions surrounding friendship are of **support** and **comfort**: **supported** and **supportive** are two of the most common feelings associated with friendship. Because the supportive role of friendship is so central, people often express strong negative emotions when friends don't play that role and particularly when they feel **abandoned** by their friends. ♥

KIDS

Breakdowns
for feelings about kids

Gender
breakdown 👩 55% 👨 45%

Age
breakdown

10s 20s 30s 40s 50+

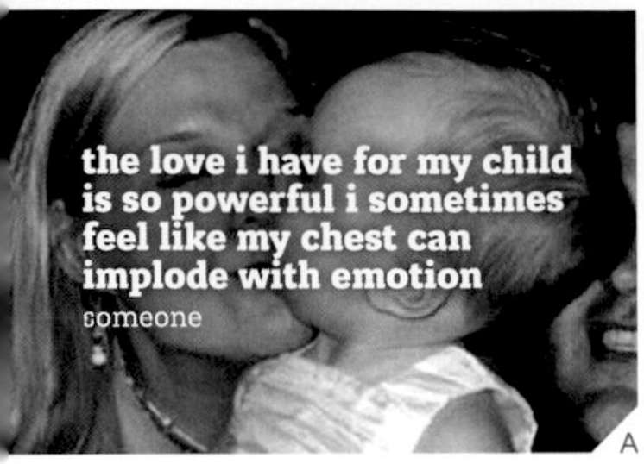

the love i have for my child is so powerful i sometimes feel like my chest can implode with emotion
someone

A

i have been in love a few times but nothing prepares you for the love you feel for your childs
a 33-year-old man in birmingham, alabama

B

i feel like my children teach me much more than i teach them
someone

C

I FEEL AS FULFILLED SHUTTLING KIDS AS I DID BRINGING HOME A PAYCHECK

someone

i hope that my children feel safe and loved and wanted and understood
someone

D

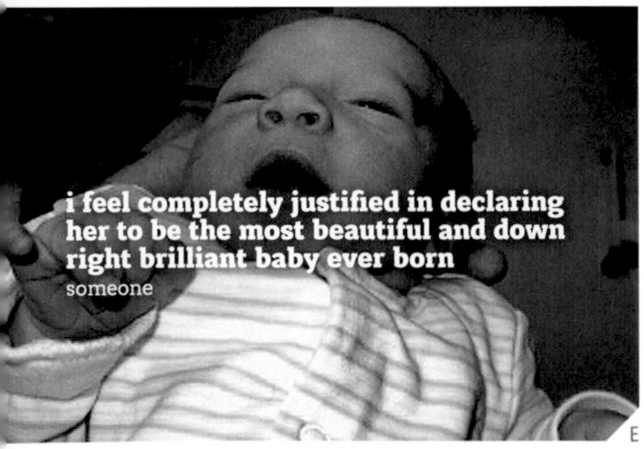

i feel completely justified in declaring her to be the most beautiful and down right brilliant baby ever born
someone

E

kids

1. sons or daughters
2. immediate progeny of human parents
3. young persons of either sex
4. those who exhibit childlike qualities

● i think kids can feel the truth which is a great gift to have knowing the essence of a situation without it ever being said forthright ● i feel bad that he doesn't have any toys so i go buy him more and he just murders them too ● i feel very loved when my children tell me high points of their days at school ● i would never wish this feeling or period of life upon anyone and sometimes i think that it would be best to not have kids so that they will never have to go through this ● i feel that i love my kids in as balanced and normal a way as i possibly could ● i think i will never feel completely self assured in this area of my life that the decisions i make for my kids are the right ones

Distinctive feelings
o Kids • Average

blessed · grateful · protective · caring · wonderful · responsible · supportive

I LOVE MY CHILDREN DEARLY BUT SERIOUSLY AM I SUPPOSED TO FEEL COMPLETE JUST BECAUSE I TAUGHT THEM THE ALPHABET OR HOW TO COUNT OR BASIC LIFE SKILLS

someone

i feel our baby days slipping away
someone

A

i just hope he feels about me the way i feel about my dad in 28 years
a man

B

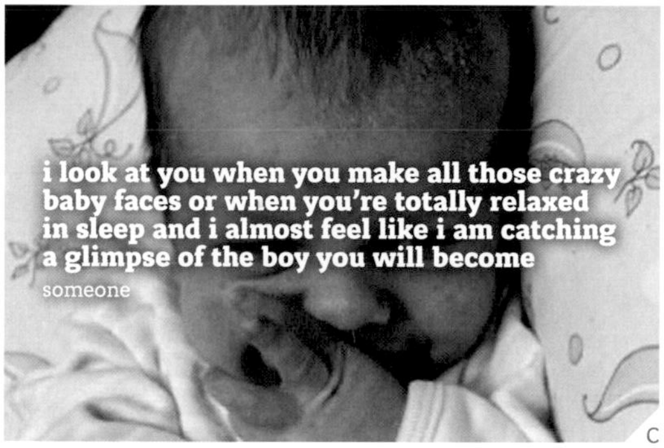

i look at you when you make all those crazy baby faces or when you're totally relaxed in sleep and i almost feel like i am catching a glimpse of the boy you will become
someone

C

Kristy married her high school sweetheart two weeks after she graduated from college. They now have 4 children together, including this little girl. Kristy just weaned their last child after more than nine years breastfeeding.

i feel honoured and privileged and tired
someone

D

215

Related themes
- **adults**
- marriage
- raising
- parents

Observations

Having children is a big turning point in one's emotional life, for both men and women but especially for women. The predominant emotion surrounding kids is **gratitude**: people frequently express feeling **blessed** and **grateful** for their children. People also express feeling a big sense of **responsibility** for their roles in their children's lives—**protective**, **caring**, **responsible**, and **supportive** are frequently expressed emotions. People in their 30s talk about their emotions about their children the most, as people in their 30s are those who most commonly have young children. ♥

MONEY

Breakdowns
for feelings about money

Gender breakdown 44% 56%

Age breakdown

i feel like every day here is all about making enough money to get by
someone

A

I AM A MAN SOMETIMES I CRY BECAUSE I FEEL SO ANGRY THAT I CAN'T MAKE ENOUGH MONEY TO BUY THE MEDICINES THAT MY WIFE NEEDS TO GET BETTER BUT WHAT CAN I DO

someone

i feel cheap
a woman

B

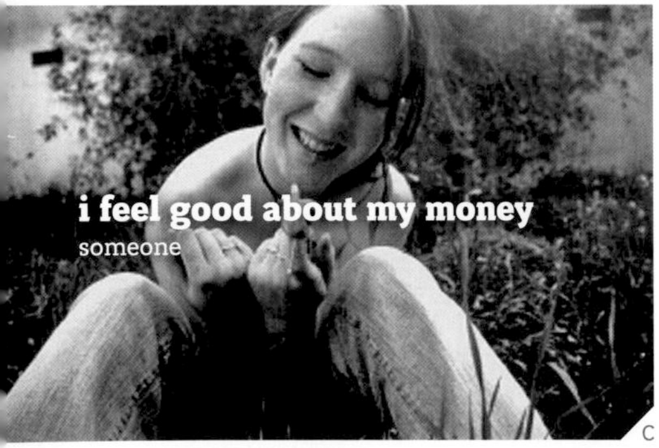

i feel good about my money
someone

C

money

1. a medium of exchange
2. usually government-issued tender
3. any currency used in buying and selling
4. wealth; property

● i never wanted to become sick rich just to have money and feel better than others ● i appreciate what my parents do for me but seriously sometimes it feels like they just provide me with money ● i don't feel like i want to talk with him because he sold my dog for his own pocket money ● i didn't start our vegetable garden to save money but when the economy started to slide we didn't feel the pinch like some of our friends did ● i feel i'm running out of money faster and trying to find ways to buy food for my family ● i am thinking about this economic stimulus plan and i really don't feel stimulated by it at all

Distinctive feelings
○ Money • Average

generous · rich · ambitious · ridiculous · broke · cheap · poor · guilty

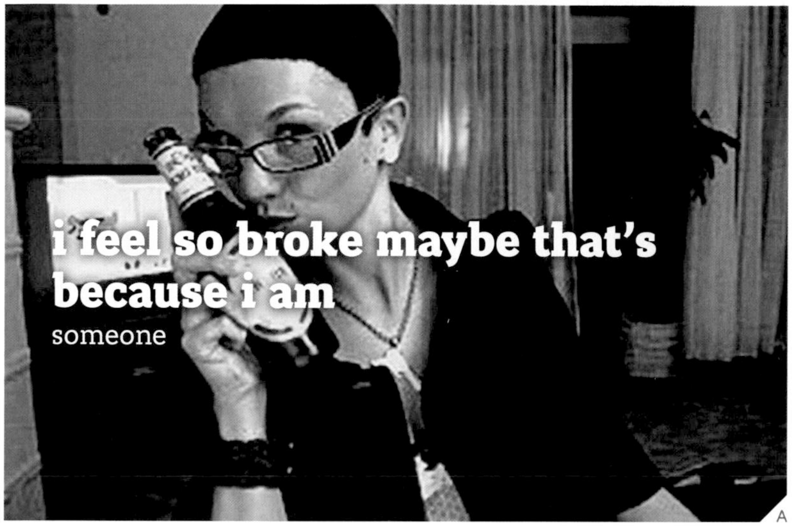

i feel so broke maybe that's because i am
someone

A

I FEEL STRONG WHEN I REMEMBER SITTING ON THE STEP IN FRONT OF A BANK IN SPAULDING LETTING IT SINK IN THAT I WAS HOMELESS AND WAS RUNNING OUT OF MONEY

a 22-year-old man in corydon, indiana

i still owe her money and i feel bad about it
a woman

B

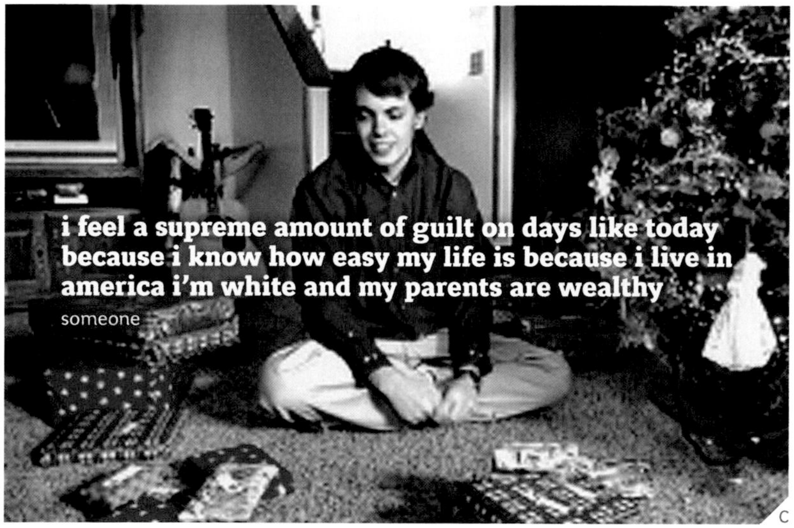

i feel a supreme amount of guilt on days like today because i know how easy my life is because i live in america i'm white and my parents are wealthy
someone

C

Related themes
- **earning**
- spending
- saving
- wasting

Observations

Money causes emotional expression in men more frequently than it does in women. Much of the emotion around money comes from the **anxiety** causing feelings that there is not **enough** or the desire to have more; **broke**, **cheap**, and **poor** are three of the most commonly expressed emotions on the topic. Money also often causes people to feel a great amount of **guilt**, for spending it unwisely, for having too much, or for **owing** somebody some. Additionally, people often get great **joy** from being generous with their money, and also enjoy those who are **generous** with theirs. ♥

RELATIONSHIPS

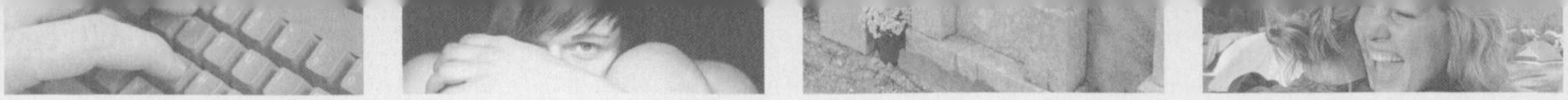

Breakdowns
for feelings about relationships

Gender breakdown: 53% | 47%

Age breakdown: 10s 20s 30s 40s 50+

I FEEL LIKE MY RELATIONSHIPS IS HOLDING ME BACK FROM DOING THE THINGS I TRULY WANT TO DO

someone

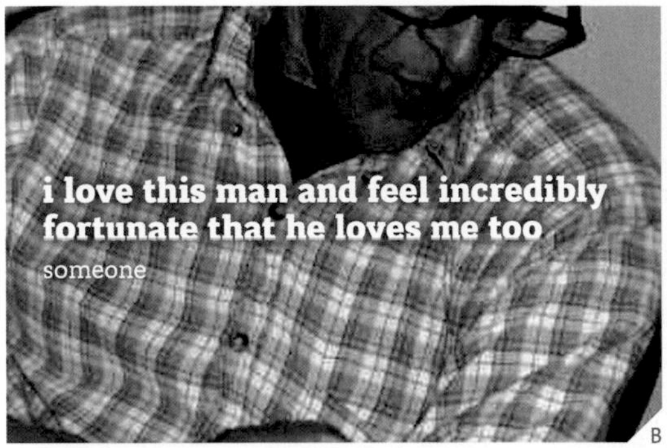

i love this man and feel incredibly fortunate that he loves me too
someone

B

i feel really confident about the relationship i'm in
a 20-year-old in mississauga, canada

A

Valerie and her husband hoped to have a child, but doctors told them they would be unable to conceive. In 2005 they decided to adopt and Valerie began blogging to document the process. On May 21, 2007 they brought home their beautiful adopted son Jensen from China. →

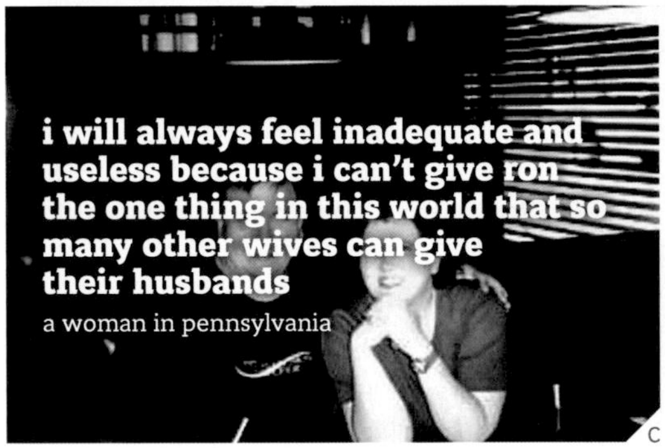

i will always feel inadequate and useless because i can't give ron the one thing in this world that so many other wives can give their husbands
a woman in pennsylvania

C

I WANT TO LOVE WITH EVERY INCH OF MY BODY AND WHEN I FINALLY DO SETTLE DOWN I WANT TO LOVE AND FEEL SO MUCH PASSION FOR THAT PERSON I CAN'T STAND IT

someone

my girlfriend makes me feel like I'm glowing
someone

D

relationships

1. state of connectedness between people
2. active physical or emotional intimacy
3. related by kindred or affinity
4. long-term associations between people

• i'm sick of relationships i'm sick of falling in love i'm sick of men and their crap i'm sick of worrying about someone else i'm sick of being made to feel like i'm not good enough even though it's not on purpose • i wish losing felt more like winning when it comes to relationships and i could feel happy leaving a relationship that just wasn't a good fit for me • i didn't want to be bogged down with a relationship but now i'm kind of missing that bogged down feeling the feeling of knowing someone will be there for you even if you fuck up • i cling so tightly to my relationships because i don t want to feel like i really am alone • i feel like our relationship is dying

Distinctive feelings
○ Relationships • Average

committed · romantic · intimate · sexual · complicated · loving · incredible

A

I REALIZED NOW MORE THAN EVER THIS RING FEELS MORE LIKE A DEAD WEIGHT THAN A PROMISE FOR THE FUTURE

someone

i feel guilty for letting relationships fall through the cracks
an 18-year-old in new jersey

B

Related themes

- **commitment**
- intimacy
- friendship
- lifestyle

Observations

The most commonly associated sentiment around relationships is one of **commitment**. The second is **intimacy**, especially an emotional intimacy. A large amount of emotional **energy** goes into relationships, both having them and also **searching** for them. Not surprisingly, women discuss their emotions about relationships more than men do. People often feel that they are in **complicated** relationships, especially when they are younger. But overall, emotions about relationships are positive, and people often describe themselves as having an **incredible** or a **loving relationship**. ♥

Breakdowns
for feelings about religion

Gender
breakdown
54% 46%

Age
breakdown

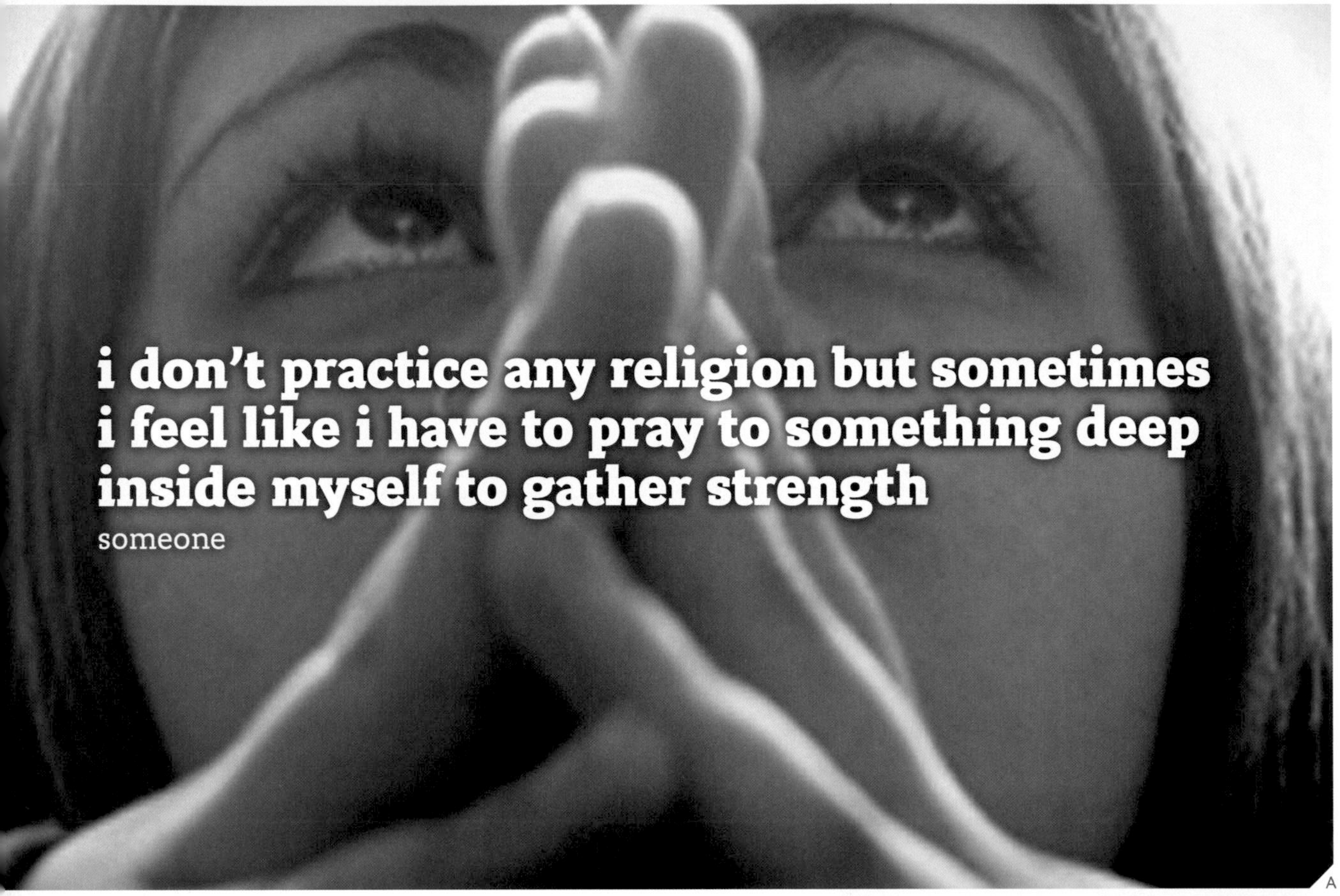

i don't practice any religion but sometimes i feel like i have to pray to something deep inside myself to gather strength
someone

A

I FEEL AN INTRINSIC DESIRE FOR THE SORT OF COMMUNAL CONNECTION THAT RELIGION PROVIDES

someone

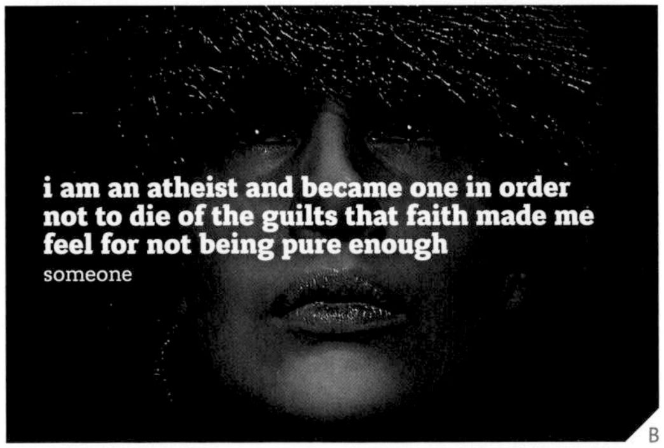

i am an atheist and became one in order not to die of the guilts that faith made me feel for not being pure enough
someone

B

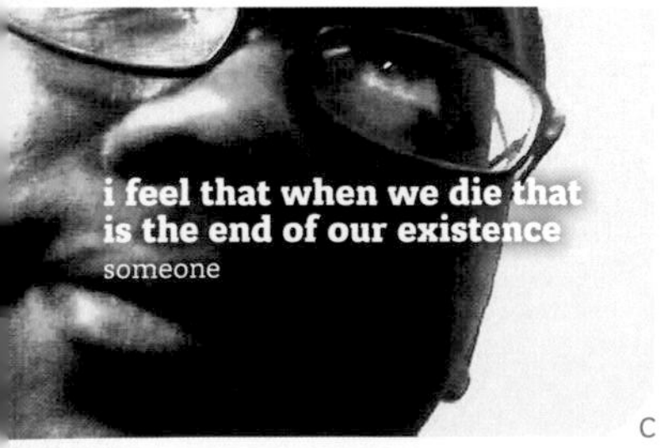

i feel that when we die that is the end of our existence
someone

C

religion

1. system of faith and worship
2. recognizing the existence of a god
3. feeling of love, awe of supreme power
4. a manifestation of piety

● i distinctly remember feeling shame as a child whenever i did something that violated the moral code that my parents and my church instilled in me ● i don't know how i feel about religion but i keep the idea of god present in my mind all the time ● i feel assured because he told me islam is not about abuse of power it's not about corruption it's about your soul your commitment to the integrity and dignity of the human being it's about your heart ● i feel increasingly certain that there are more fundamental forces at large than those promoted by organized religions no matter what the brand names christianity islam judaism hinduism they're all the same to me utter poppycock

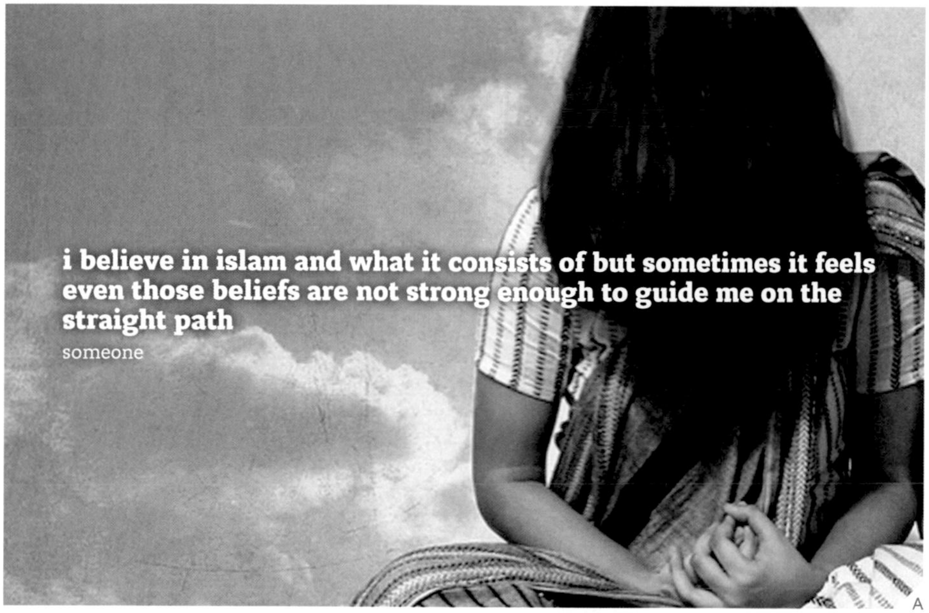

i believe in islam and what it consists of but sometimes it feels even those beliefs are not strong enough to guide me on the straight path
someone

A

I FEEL THE POINT OF CHRISTIANITY FOR ME IS LOVE NOT JUDGMENT AND CERTAINLY NOT HELL TALK

someone

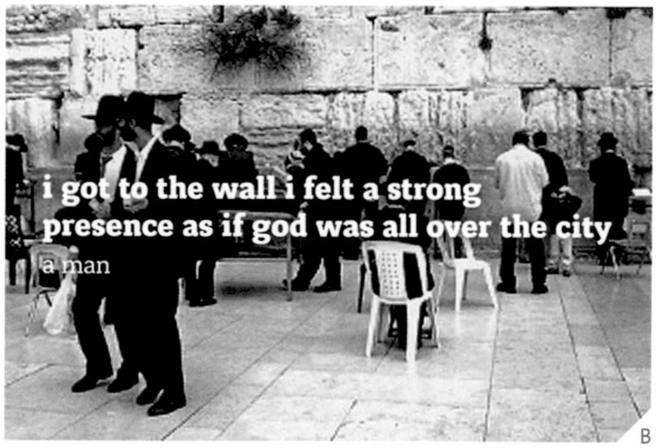

i got to the wall i felt a strong presence as if god was all over the city
a man

B

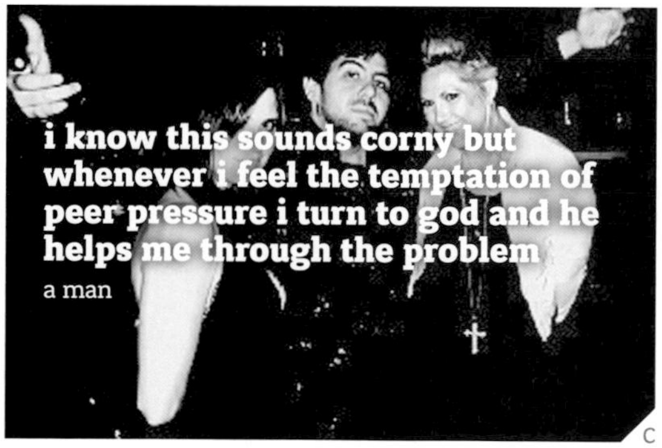

i know this sounds corny but whenever i feel the temptation of peer pressure i turn to god and he helps me through the problem
a man

C

I FEEL LIKE MY RELIGION STIFLES MY SEXUALITY

someone

every time i feel afraid i hold tighter to my faith
someone

D

Related themes

- **worship**
- prayer
- bible
- faith

Observations

Religion evokes emotions more as people get **older**. We find on the blogosphere that people get more **spiritual** as they get older, and their feelings reflect this. Women discuss their emotions about religion on blogs more often than men. Often, people express feeling the **power** of **God** and religion in the practice of religion, specifically in **prayer** and **worship**. Those who express **faith** on their blogs express it in a manner more emotional than **cerebral**. People often grapple with **organized religion** or their own level of adherence to religion. ♥

Breakdowns
for feelings about sex

Gender breakdown 46% 54%

Age breakdown 10s 20s 30s 40s 50+

I DON'T HAVE SEX TO MAKE MYSELF FEEL GOOD ABOUT WHO I AM

a woman

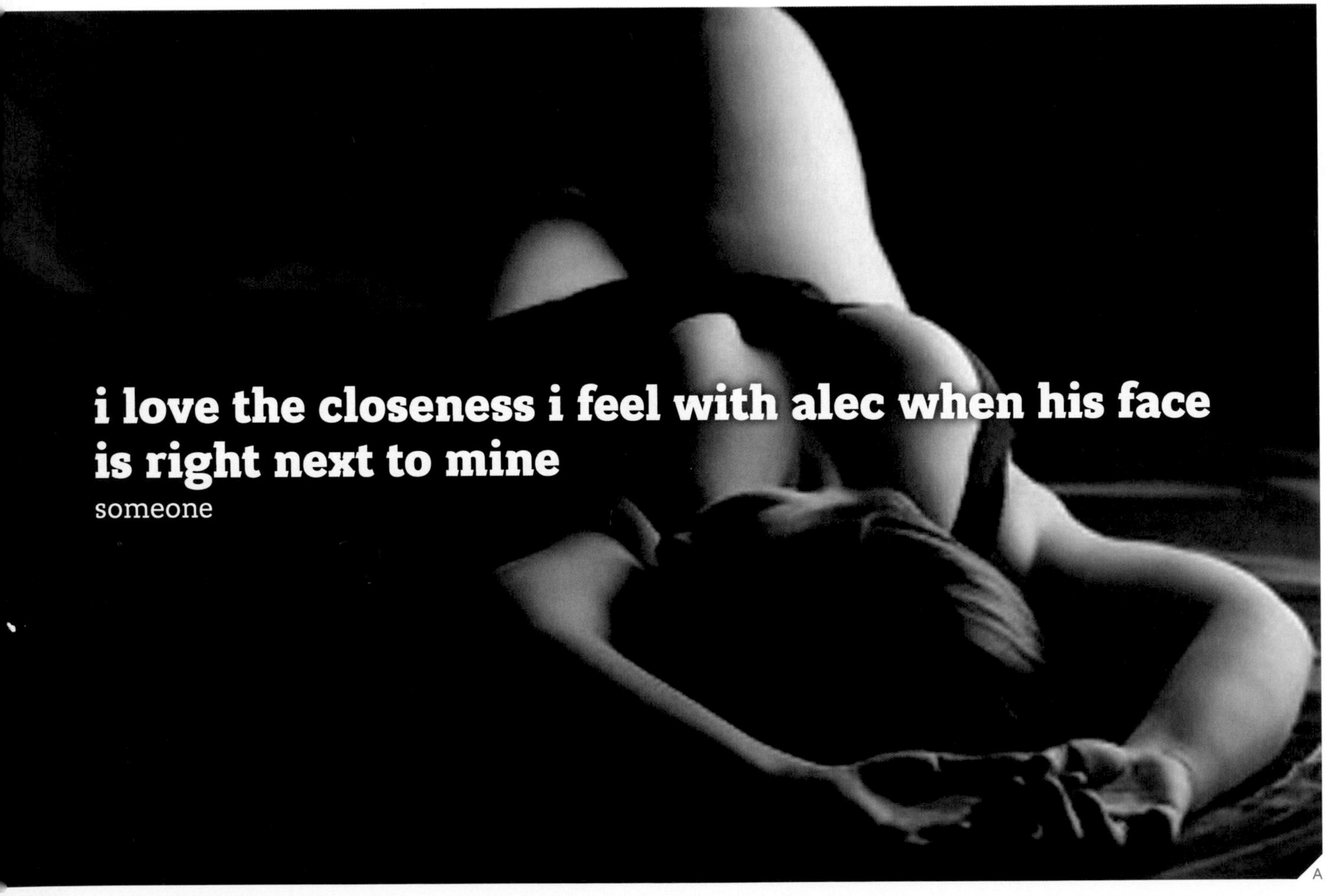

i love the closeness i feel with alec when his face is right next to mine
someone

A

sex

1. sexual activity; intercourse
2. one's gender or sexual characteristics
3. preference of sexual identity
4. traits by which gender is distinguished

● i can't have sex when i don't feel sexy ● i feel incredible guilt for having premarital sex ● i began to feel a bit like man meat like she was the one in it for the sex not me ● i don't feel any guilt when i think about the amount of sex i had ● i lost my virginity when i was 14 i didn't feel dirty i didn't feel gross ● i think i need more sex and less feelings ● i feel closer to someone after sex than after a year of casual conversation ● i was some sex toy he can feel up any time he wants ● i like having sex outside i love the way a breeze or rain feels like a shock against my hot sweaty body ● i feel the best choices anyone makes around sex aren't going to be based in fear

Distinctive feelings
○ Sex • Average

sexual · sexy · horny · naughty · wild · erotic · tender

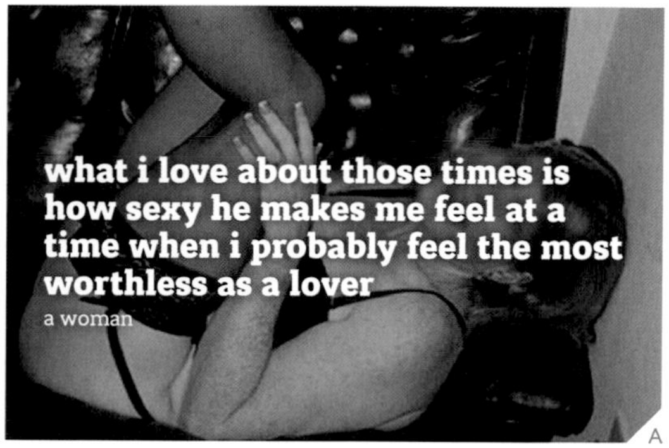

what i love about those times is how sexy he makes me feel at a time when i probably feel the most worthless as a lover
a woman

A

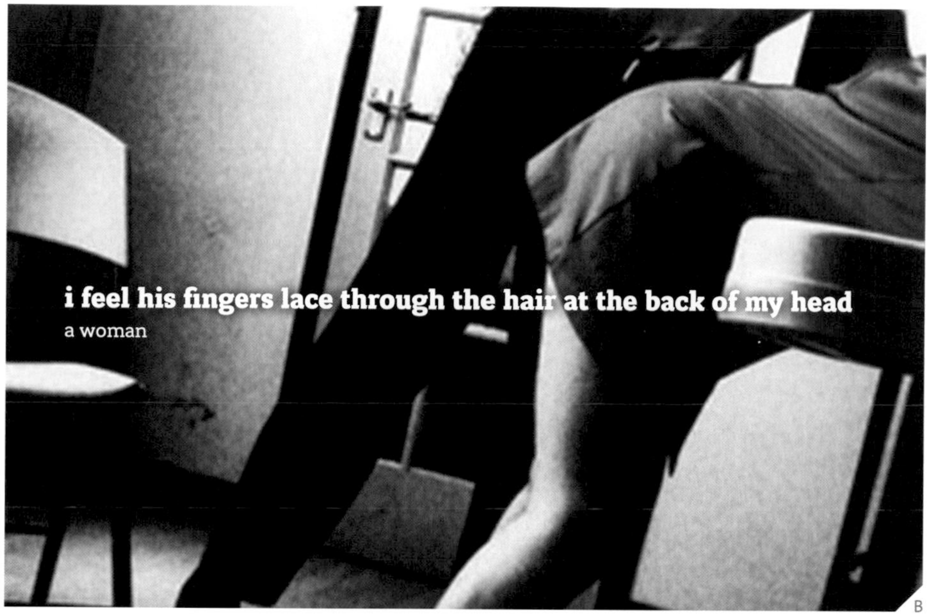

i feel his fingers lace through the hair at the back of my head
a woman

B

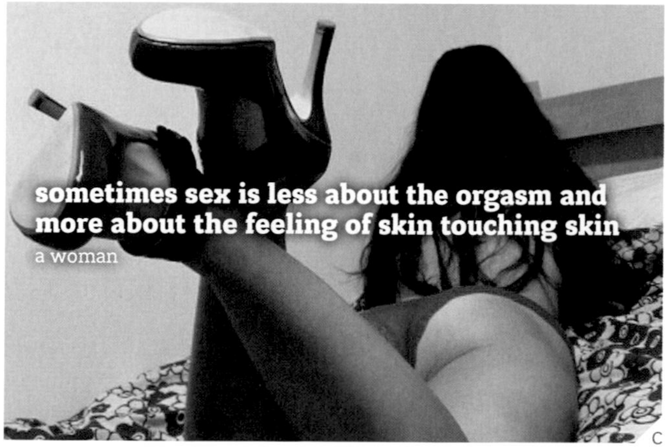

sometimes sex is less about the orgasm and more about the feeling of skin touching skin
a woman

C

I FEEL BAD FOR AMERICAN HIGH SCHOOL KIDS WHO HAVE TO SIT THROUGH ABSTINENCE CLASSES BECAUSE IT'S A WASTE OF THEIR TIME AND I'M SURE THEY HAVE BETTER THINGS TO DO LIKE HAVE SEX WITH ONE ANOTHER

someone

Related themes

- **partner**
- toy
- lover
- marriage

Observations

The feelings people express on the blogosphere about sex are incredibly complex. Most people enjoy sex and many of them **pursue** it with a great amount of **energy**. For other people, it often brings up feelings of **guilt** or feelings about their **self-esteem**. Men **talk** about sex a good deal more than women, and women are more likely than men to use the words **love** and sex in the same sentence. People in their **30s** talk about sex more often than people do at any other age. ♥

Breakdowns
for feelings about work

Gender breakdown 48% 52%

Age breakdown 10s 20s 30s 40s 50+

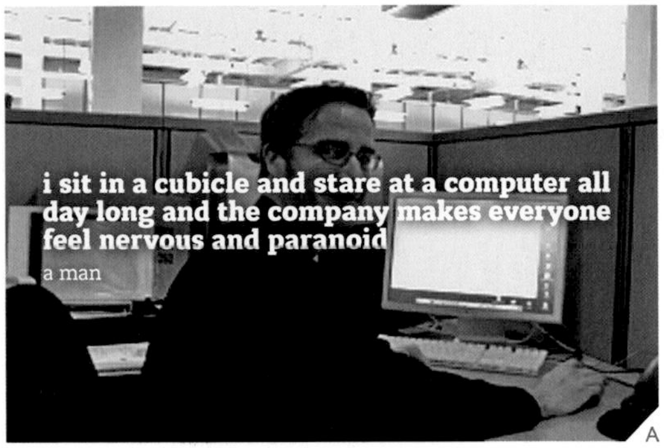

i sit in a cubicle and stare at a computer all day long and the company makes everyone feel nervous and paranoid
a man

A

i feel lucky to even have a job
someone

B

I KNOW MY JOB LEAVES A GREAT DEAL TO BE DESIRED BUT IT IS A JOB AND IN THESE ECONOMIC TIMES I'M FEELING PRETTY LUCKY TO EVEN HAVE ONE

someone

i have work for the first time in ten days but it is good, i feel refreshed i feel ready to go back
someone in australia

C

the financial grey cloud is over my head and as usual work is starting to feel like a chore
someone from singapore

D

work

1. exertion of strength or faculties
2. physical or intellectual effort
3. business; employment
4. engaging in the performance of a task

• i feel like my day job metaphorically jacked off on my thigh and told me to be grateful—then didn't even offer me a towel • i was focusing on the many reasons why i couldn't possibly quit the job i hated or how impossible it was to do the things that really mattered to me to go for the things that made me feel truly alive • i feel utterly worthless despite having a diploma and a degree • i feel overwhelmed because i work day by day with big problems and negative feelings • i feel guilty staying in this job but i feel irresponsible leaving it • i have been feeling clogged and restless in my job and in our culture

Distinctive feelings
○ Work ● Average

◉ **hectic** ◉ stressful ◉ busy ◉ competent ◉ valued ◉ rewarding ◉ cynical

i'm happy and i really feel like sometimes i am making a break through with my work

someone in teaneck, new jersey

A

i have been feeling surprisingly good to be at work
a 34-year-old woman

B

i feel proud of myself today because i have a job
a 23-year-old in manchesterford, england

C

I HATE MY JOB AND IT MAKES ME FEEL STUPID AND INSIGNIFICANT

a 22-year-old in texas

225

Related themes
quitting
salary
desk
boss

Observations

Work and jobs tends to elicit many different kinds of emotions. On the one hand, it is very common for people to express feeling **stressed** or **burned out** because of their jobs. But on the other hand, people also express that their jobs make them feel **valued** and that their work is **rewarding**. Men tend to discuss their **emotions** about work more often than women do, and like sex and children, it is talked about most frequently by people in their **30s**, but also very commonly by people in their **20s**. It is very common for people to express the fact that they feel like they want to **quit** their jobs. ♥

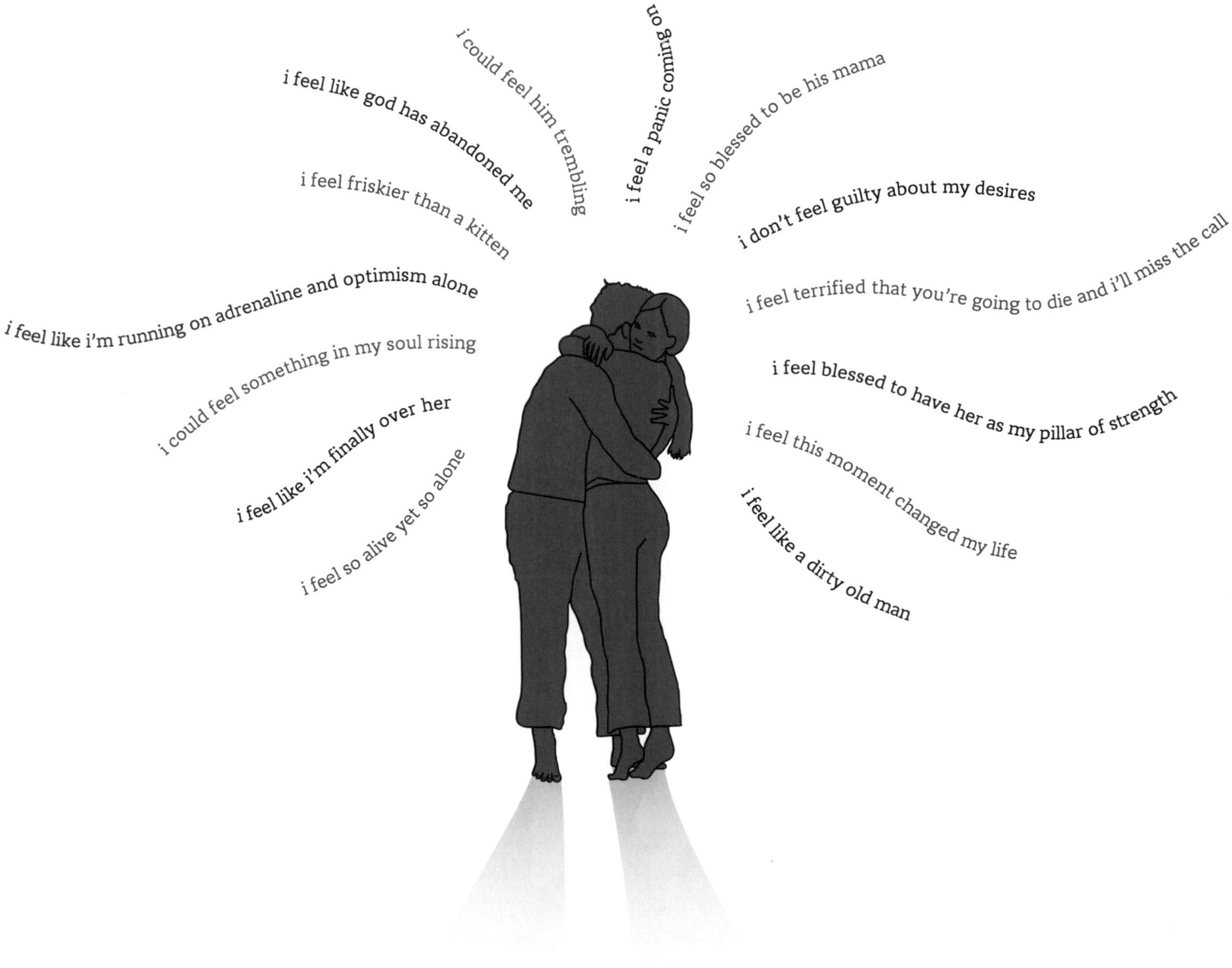
i could feel him trembling
i feel a panic coming on
i feel like god has abandoned me
i feel so blessed to be his mama
i feel friskier than a kitten
i don't feel guilty about my desires
i feel like i'm running on adrenaline and optimism alone
i feel terrified that you're going to die and i'll miss the call
i could feel something in my soul rising
i feel blessed to have her as my pillar of strength
i feel like i'm finally over her
i feel this moment changed my life
i feel so alive yet so alone
i feel like a dirty old man

7 How

On how emotional research is conducted

Tags: psychology, statistics, computer science, bioinformatics, information visualization

On March 21st, 2009, Shasta Gibson posted an intense emotional self-examination to her blog. "I was able to examine my feelings," she wrote at the end, "and put them into perspective."

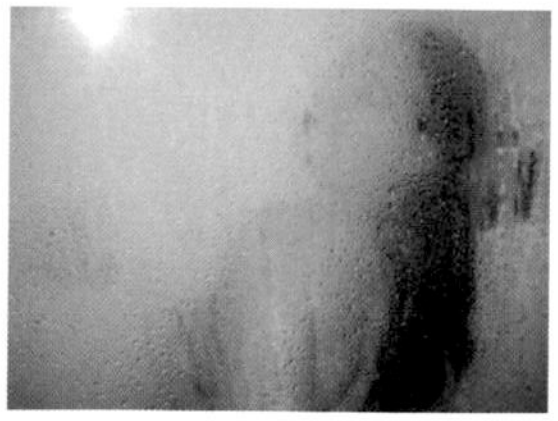

Shasta Gibson, cleansing

Shasta and her husband Jack are polyamorous, and the night before, Jack had had sex with a couple without her. Even though she and Jack had been polyamorous for 3 years, this was his first (in her words) "all-the-way" sexual encounter with another woman. Upon his return she felt a whole range of emotions; she was not worried that he loved her less, yet she felt incredibly disturbed and did not want to be near him. He tried to hold her hand, and she pulled away. "I wasn't angry with him, and I'm not angry at him now. I just didn't want him to touch me."

She cried softly all night, and could not stop picturing him with the other woman. "It's like having something really special to you," she wrote, "something precious, handled by someone else. Someone you don't know, who may not care much about your precious object." That feeling continued throughout the next morning, and as things started to lighten up the next afternoon, she sobbed, "great gasping sobs that make my whole body rattle with effort." Then Jack hugged her, and "murmured quietly into my ear while all the hurt and disgust drained out of me. It was almost certainly the sort of moment that one will remember for the rest of their days." "Really," she wrote, "today was almost perfect."[1]

Her exploration of her emotions prompted a similar introspective self-examination by many of her readers. One of her readers, Nia, commented on her post: "Our emotions defy our logic, our preparations, and even our other emotions at times. Sometimes there's a lot under them, sometimes there's nothing." And another reader, Adam, commented: "As you know, one of the wonderful things about being poly is that you have to examine yourself and the way you feel or it doesn't work. I can't help but feel it's good for people to do this. I think most people just work their way through life never really examining themselves."

For most of history, the scholarly investigation of emotion has fallen into the domain of philosophers, and the primary means of studying emotion has been through introspective self-examination. "Everyone has experience of the passions within himself," said the philosopher René Descartes, "and there is no necessity to borrow one's observations from elsewhere in order to discover their true nature."[2] Like Shasta, philosophers from Aristotle to Aquinas would examine their own feelings in order to learn their nature.

The earliest psychologists were philosophers themselves. During the Islamic Golden Age, the 9th-century Arab philosopher al-Kindi explored the relationship between the intellect and emotion and developed cognitive techniques to combat depression,[3] and the 10th-century Persian philosopher Ibn Sina linked emotions to physiology by observing the heart rate of a lovesick subject.[4]

In the West, modern psychology began to emerge as a field distinct from philosophy in the late 1800s. In the United States, Harvard philosophy professor William James established the first psychology lab in 1875, around the same time that Wilhelm Wundt, the chair of philosophy at the University of Leipzig in Germany, established his own psychology laboratory. Given its roots in philosophy, it's not surprising that experimental psychology was also based largely on self-examination. Wundt's laboratory work consisted primarily of controlled methods of observation and self-report, or as he called it: *Experimentelle Selbstbeobachtung* (experimental self-examination).[5] James, too, emphasized the importance of self-report: "Introspective observation," he wrote, "is what we have to rely on first and foremost and always."[6]

Introspective self-report has remained the prominent method of study in personality and social psychology, and particularly in the study of emotion.[7] A research study in the psychology of emotions will often consist of sending out self-report questionnaires that ask about personality traits, subjective feelings, or how one would feel in hypothetical scenarios. In many cases, the subjects are "primed" before they fill out the self-report—for example, a subject may do a word puzzle that involves money-related words in order to make them think about money before they fill out the questionnaire. Comparing the primed group with the control group (who would do a similar word puzzle, but with neutral words) will show whether there are emotional differences between people who are thinking about money versus those that aren't.

On August 6th, 1991, Tim Berners-Lee posted to the *alt.hypertext* newsgroup, introducing his invention, the World Wide Web: "The WorldWideWeb (WWW) project aims to allow links to be made to any information anywhere," he wrote. "The WWW project was started to allow high energy physicists to share data, news, and documentation. We are very interested in spreading the web to other areas, and having gateway servers for other data. Collaborators welcome!"[8]

That same year, Stephen Fodor, a young biochemist in Palo Alto, published with his colleagues a paper detailing one of the most impactful advances in biology in recent times: the microarray. The microarray is a piece of technology that allows scientists to measure the presence of a gene in a DNA sample much faster than was previously possible. In the past, gene expression needed to happen one gene at a time, but the microarray allowed for thousands of genes to be tested simultaneously.[9]

This had a significant effect on the amount of biological knowledge that was produced. An article in *Science* magazine a few years later declared, "The growing use of relatively inexpensive microarrays to monitor the expression of thousands of genes at once is creating a flood of data on everything from strawberry ripening to viral pathogenicity."[10] The sheer volume of data produced by microarray experiments increased the importance of statistics, computer science, and mathematics in biomedical research. Indeed, the microarray (along with the Human Genome Project that preceded it) is largely responsible for the rise of the fields of bioinformatics and computational genomics.

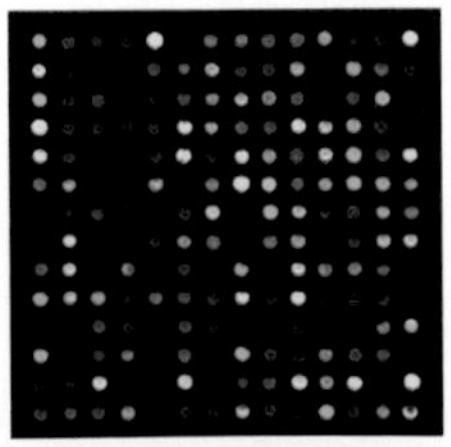

The microarray's effect on the biological sciences foretells the influence the blogosphere and overall social web could

Left: A DNA microarray is a glass slide containing thousands of discrete spots of DNA. Gene expression in an experimental sample is indicated by the color of the fluorescent label at each given spot.

have on emotions research, and on the social sciences in general. Blogs give us countless instances of introspective observation and self-report. With tools like *We Feel Fine* analyzing the social web, we can run self-report experiments on millions of people in seconds. Besides scale and speed, these self-reports have the benefit of being unsolicited and "in the wild" instead of in a lab setting.

Like microarray experiments, large-scale social science studies using the web are not perfect—there are limitations to the computational techniques and biases in the data set. But as with the microarray, techniques will evolve and tools will be built to handle these biases, and the flood of data will increase the importance of computer science, mathematics, and statistics in the social sciences. We expect that as these tools continue to be developed and adopted, fields like psychoinformatics, computational sociology, cultural informatics, and computational sociolinguistics will arise and serve as useful complements to the traditional social sciences.

In addition to the quantitative ability to do very-large-scale statistical analyses of emotions (or attitudes, language, etc.), the social web gives us the ability to look at people qualitatively in depth. The psychiatrist Carl Jung once said: "Anyone who wants to know the human psyche will learn next to nothing from experimental psychology. He would be better advised to abandon exact science, put away his scholar's gown, bid farewell to his study, and wander with human heart through the world. There in the horrors of prisons, lunatic asylums and hospitals, in drab suburban pubs, in brothels and gambling-halls, in the salons of the elegant, the Stock Exchanges, socialist meetings, churches, revivalist gatherings and ecstatic sects, through love and hate, through the experience of passion in every form in his own body, he would reap richer stores of knowledge than textbooks a foot thick could give him."[11]

Indeed, we have learned as much about emotions from reading people's blogs as we have from running our statistical tools. Through the eyes of bloggers, we have been able to wander throughout the world, exploring the drab suburban pubs and the salons of the elegant, meeting mothers in New Mexico and travel guides in Egypt, teenage Ozzy Osbourne fans and young polyamorists. They have given us rich stores of knowledge about emotions, and we hope to pass along what we've learned in this inch-thick book.

This chapter focuses on the "how" of *We Feel Fine*: how we built the software, how we wrote this book, and how people feel around the world. It shows how our feelings change, as we age and over the course of the day, and where our feelings come from, on the map and in the body.

"I use this blog," wrote Shasta Gibson in her March 14th, 2006, blog post, "as a place to reflect and examine my emotions."[12] This chapter looks into how we borrowed the observations of more than 2 million people like Shasta, and what we discovered about the nature of emotions in the process. ♥

1. Shasta Gibson. http://shastagibson.com/2009/04/05/the-heart-is-deceitful-above-all-things-and-desperately-wicked/
2. Descartes, René. *The Passions of the Soul*. 1649.
3. Haque, Amber. "Psychology from an Islamic Perspective: Contributions of Early Muslim Scholars and Challenges to Contemporary Muslim Psychologists." *Journal of Religion and Health*. (December 2004). 43(4):4, 357–77.
4. Syed, Ibrahim B. "Islamic Medicine, 1000 years ahead of its time." *Journal of the International Society for the History of Islamic Medicine*, 2. (2002).
5. Wundt, Wilhelm M. *Principles of Physiological Psychology*. Translated by Edward B. Titchener. (New York: MacMillan, 1904).
6. James, William. *Principles of Psychology*, (Dover Publications, 1950).
7. Baumeister, Roy F., Kathleen D. Vohs, and David C. Funder. "Psychology as the Science of Self-Reports and Finger Movements: Or, Whatever Happened to Actual Behavior?" *Perspectives on Psychological Science*. (December, 2007). 396–403.
8. Tim Berners-Lee. http://www.w3.org/People/Berners-Lee/1991/08/art-6484.txt
9. Fodor, Stephen P., J. L. Read, M.C. Pirrung, L. Stryer, A.T. Lu, and D. Solas. "Light-directed spatially addressable parallel chemical synthesis." *Science*. (February 15, 1991). 251(4995):767-773.
10. Marshall, E. "Do-It-Yourself Gene Watching." *Science*. 286(5439):444–47.
11. Jung, Carl G. *The Collected Works of CG Jung*, Volume 7. (Princeton, NJ: Princeton University Press, 1967).
12. Shasta Gibson. http://shastagibson.com/2006/03/14/emotional-angst-is-more-exciting-than-this/

Lit Review

A summary of some of the academic literature in emotions research, and *We Feel Fine*'s take on each study

The finding:

Negativity decreases with age, while positivity increases.

The Academy says:

Gross, J.J.; Carstensen, L.L.; Pasupathi, M.; Tsai, J.; Goetestam-Skorpen, C.G.; & Hsu, A.Y.C. (1997)
Emotion and aging: Experience, expression, and control. Psychology and Aging, 12. 590–599.

Age differences in emotional experience, expression, and control were investigated in 4 studies. A community sample of 127 African Americans and European Americans (ages 19–96) was used in Study 1; a community sample of 82 Chinese Americans and European Americans (ages 20–85) was used in Study 2; a community sample of 49 Norwegians drawn from 2 age groups (ages 20–35 and 70+) was used in Study 3; and a sample of 1,080 American nuns (ages 24–101) was used in Study 4. Across studies, a consistent pattern of age differences emerged. Compared with younger participants, older participants reported fewer negative emotional experiences and greater emotional control.

Also:

Consedine, N.S., & Magai, C. (2006)
Emotion development in adulthood: A developmental functionalist review and critique. In C. Hoare (ed.), The Oxford Handbook of Adult Development and Learning. New York: Oxford University Press. 123–148.

Magai, C. (2001)
Emotions over the lifespan. In J.E. Birren & K.W. Schaie (eds.), Handbook of the Psychology of Aging, 5th ed. San Diego, CA: Academic Press. 310–344.

We Feel Fine says:

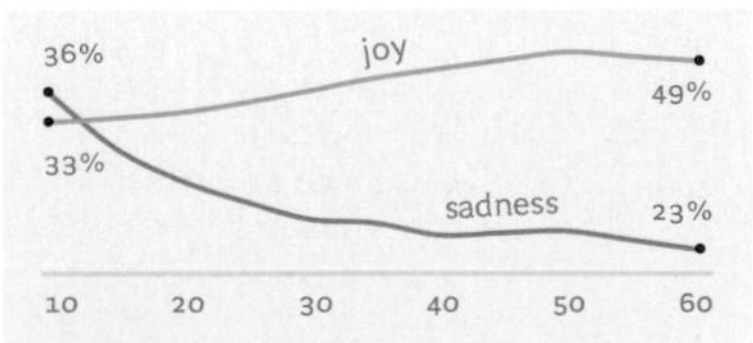

The *We Feel Fine* data shows a slight increase in joy, and a marked decrease in sorrow, as one ages.

The finding:

However, there is a slight decrease in positivity starting in the mid 60s.

The Academy says:

Mroczek, D.K., & Spiro, A. (2005)
Change in life satisfaction during adulthood: Findings from the Veterans Affairs Normative Aging Study. Journal of Personality and Social Psychology, 88. 189–202.

Change in life satisfaction was modeled over a 22-year period in 1,927 men. A curvilinear relationship emerged. Growth-curve models indicated that life satisfaction peaked at age 65 and then declined, but showed significant individual differences in rate of change. Extraversion predicted variability in change, with higher levels associated with a high and flat life satisfaction trajectory. Time-varying physical health and marital status were associated with higher life satisfaction. Proximity to death was associated with a decline in life satisfaction. On measurement occasions that were within one year before death, trajectories showed steeper decline, and this effect was not attributable to declines in self-rated physical health. The findings are at odds with prior (cross-sectional) research showing that subjective well-being improves with aging.

Also:

Charles, S.T.; Reynolds, C.A.; & Gatz, M. (2001)
Age-related differences and change in positive and negative affect over 23 years. Journal of Personality and Social Psychology, 80. 136–151.

We Feel Fine says:

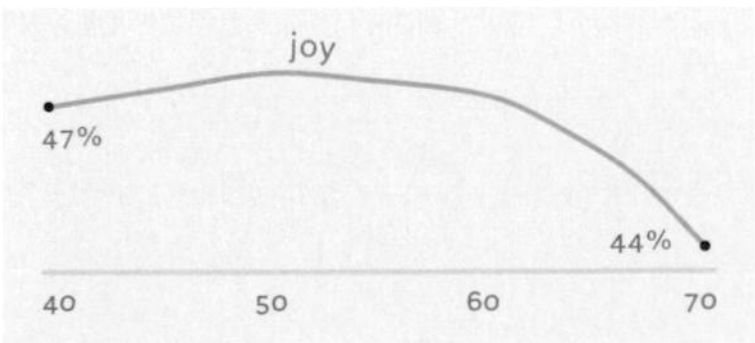

In the 60s, we start to see a dip in joy.

The finding:

Anxiety and shyness decrease with age.

The Academy says:

Lawton, M.P.; Kleban, M.H.; & Dean, J. (1993)
Affect and age: Cross-sectional comparisons of structure and prevalence. Psychology and Aging, 8. 165–175.

The self-reports of 207 young-adult (ages 18–30), 231 middle-aged (ages 31–59), and 828 older-adult (age 60 and over) subjects were used to study the structure of affect. Affects were represented by terms included in various circumplex arrays of emotions as presented by previous investigators. A set of 46 affects was subjected to exploratory analysis, and a final set of 38 affects was subjected to confirmatory factor analysis. The goodness of fit of each group's factor loadings to the hypothesized factors of positive affect, depression, anxiety-guilt, contentment, hostility, and shyness was not up to the desired .90 level, and some significant differences in factor structure were observed for each age-group comparison. There were few age differences in levels of positive affect. Depression was most frequent among younger subjects and least frequent among older subjects. Younger subjects were most often anxious and shy. Older subjects were most often content and least often hostile.

Also:

Consedine, N.S., & Magai, C. (2003)
Attachment and emotion experience in later life: The view from emotions theory. Attachment and Human Development, 5. 165–187.

We Feel Fine says:

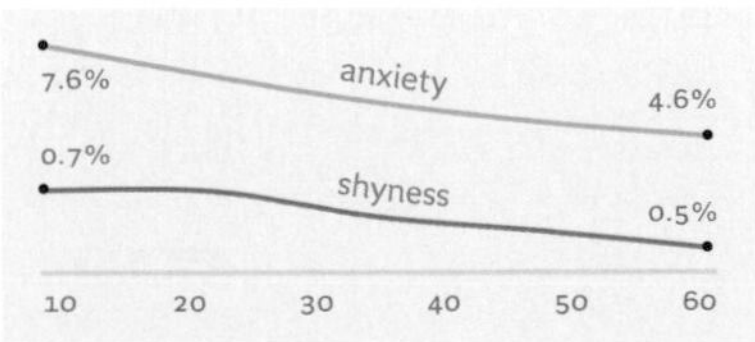

We see a decrease in both anxiety and shyness with age.

The finding:

Fear and anger decrease with age.

The Academy says:

Birditt, K., & Fingerman, K.L. (2003)
Age and gender differences in adults' descriptions of emotional reactions to interpersonal problems. Journal of Gerontology: Series B. Psychological Sciences, 58B. 237–245.

This study examines age and gender differences in descriptions of emotional reactions and reports of the intensity and duration of those emotional responses to interpersonal tensions. As part of a larger study, 185 (85 male and 100 female) participants aged 13 to 99 described the last time they were upset with members of their social networks. Participants then described how they felt and rated the intensity and duration of their distress. Participants' reported emotions were grouped by use of theoretically derived categories and empirically derived post hoc categories. Three emotion categories were examined: anger, sadness, and nonspecific negative emotions. Adolescents and young adults were more likely than older adults to describe anger. Adolescents and young adults also reported more intense aversive responses than older adults. Women rated their distress as more intense than men. With the exception of middle-aged and oldest-old adults, women reported that they experienced distress for a longer duration than men. Findings are interpreted in terms of theories regarding age and gender differences in emotion regulation and interpersonal tensions.

We Feel Fine says:

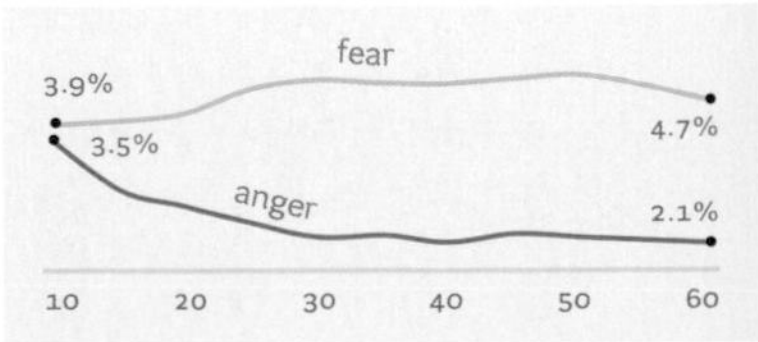

We see a marked decrease in anger with age, but fear holds relatively steady.

The finding:

Women express more negativity than men, while men express more positivity than women.

The Academy says:

Simon, R.W., & Nath, L.E. (2004)
Gender and emotion in the United States: Do men and women differ in self-reports of feelings and expressive behavior? American Journal of Sociology, 109. 1137–1176.

U.S. emotion culture contains beliefs that women are more emotional and emotionally expressive than men and that men and women differ in their experience and expression of specific emotions. Using data from the 1996 emotions module of the General Social Survey, the authors investigate whether men and women differ in self-reports of feelings and expressive behavior, evaluating whether the patterns observed for men and women are consistent with cultural beliefs as well as predictions from two sociological theories about emotion and two sociological theories about gender. Surprisingly, self-reports do not support cultural beliefs about gender differences in the frequency of everyday subjective feelings in general. Men and women do, however, differ in the frequency of certain positive and negative feelings, which is explained by their difference in social position. The implications of the findings for theory and research on both gender and emotion are discussed.

We Feel Fine says:

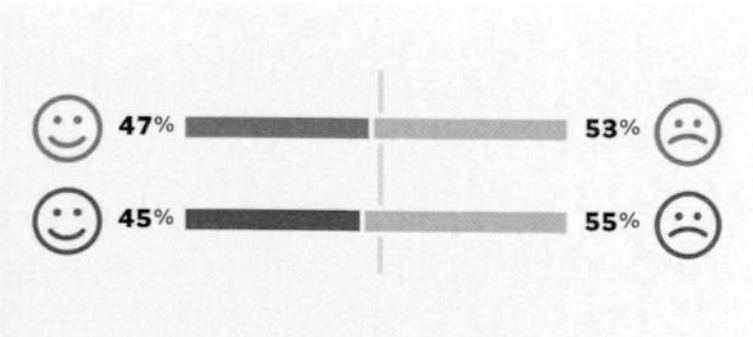

The *We Feel Fine* dataset shows that women express more negative emotions than men.

The finding:

Women express more love, affection, and warmth than men.

The Academy says:

Allen, J., & Haccoun, D. (1976)
Sex differences in emotionality: A multi-dimensional approach. Human Relations, 29, 711–720.

An Emotionality Survey was developed to assess sex differences in three dimensions of emotion: covert responding, interpersonal expression, and attitudes toward responses and expressions. Situational determinants of responses were also investigated. Within each of these areas, four types of emotion were distinguished: anger, fear, joy, and sadness. In general, females exceeded males in reported emotionality, but sex differences varied as a function of dimension and type of emotion. Differences were greatest for interpersonal expression, and for fear and sadness. Females also reported more of an interpersonal basis for their emotional responses. The findings suggest a sex difference in the functional significance of emotion, and support a multidimensional approach to the investigation of sex differences in emotionality.

Also:

Brody, L.R. (1993)
On understanding gender differences in the expression of emotion: Gender roles, socialization and language. In S. Ablon, D. Brown, E. Khantzian, & J. Mach (eds.), Human feelings, Exploration in affect development and meaning. Hillsdale, NJ: Analytic Press. 89–121.

Fisher, A.H., & Manstead, A.S.R. (2000)
The relation between gender and emotion in different cultures. In A.H. Fischer (ed.), Gender and emotion: Social psychological perspectives. New York: Cambridge University Press. 71–98.

We Feel Fine says:

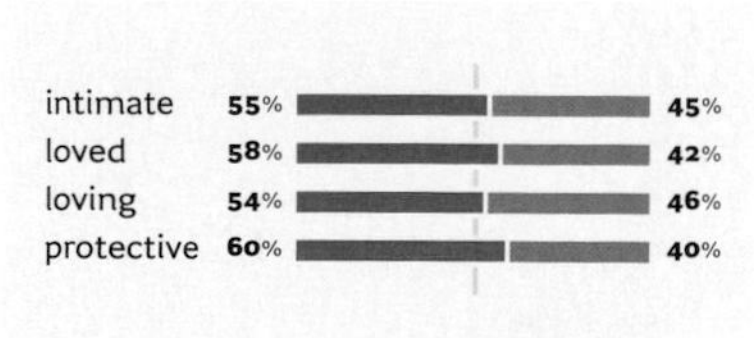

We see that women are more likely to express feelings related to affection and warmth. For instance, of the people who feel protective, 60% are women.

The finding:

Women express more sadness, fear, anxiety, hurt, and shame than men.

The Academy says:

Fischer, A.H.; Rodriguez Mosquera, P.M.; van Vianen, A.E.M.; & Manstead, A.S.R. (2004)
Gender and culture differences in emotion. Emotion, 4. 87–94.

In this article, the authors report a secondary analysis on a cross-cultural dataset on gender differences in six emotions collected in 37 countries. The aim was to test the universality of the gender-specific pattern found in studies with Western respondents, namely that men report more powerful emotions (e.g., anger), whereas women report more powerless emotions (e.g., sadness, fear). Overall, the gender-specific pattern of women reporting to experience and express more powerless emotions and men more powerful emotions was replicated, and only some interactions with measures of status and societal role in different cultures were found.

Also:

Hess, U.; Senecal, S.; Kirouac, G.; Herrera, P.; Philippot, P.; & Kleck, R.E. (2000)
Emotional expressivity in men and women: Stereotypes and self perceptions. Cognition and Emotion, 14. 609–642.

Simon, R.W., & Nath, L.E. (2004)
Gender and emotion in the United States: Do men and women differ in self-reports of feelings and expressive behavior? American Journal of Sociology, 109. 1137–1176.

Brody, L.R. (1999)
Gender, emotion, and the family. Cambridge, MA: Harvard University Press.

We Feel Fine says:

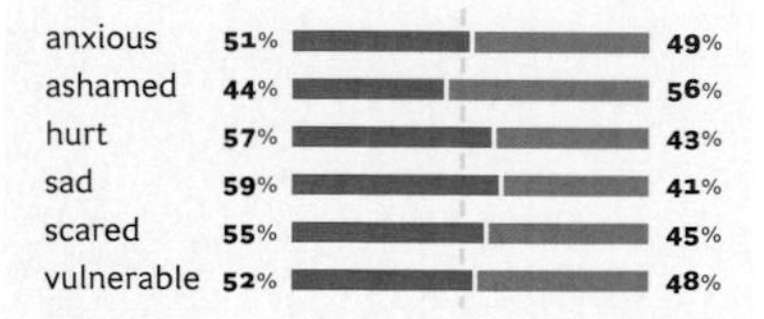

We see that women are more likely to express anxiety, hurt, sorrow, fear, and vulnerability than men. We are not able to replicate that women express more shame.

The finding:

Men express more loneliness, pride, confidence, guilt, and excitement than women.

The Academy says:

Brody, L.R. (1993)
On understanding gender differences in the expression of emotion: Gender roles, socialization and language. In S. Ablon, D. Brown, E. Khantzian, & J. Mach (eds.), Human feelings: Exploration in affect development and meaning. Hillsdale, NJ: Analytic Press. 89–121.

Forty-three male and 53 female college seniors maintained the Rochester Interaction Record for two weeks, providing information about every social interaction of ten minutes or more. Subjects then completed the revised UCLA (University of California, Los Angeles) Loneliness Scale and the Personal Attributes Questionnaire, measuring sex-role orientation. For both sexes, loneliness was negatively related to the amount of time spent with females and to the meaningfulness of interaction with males and females. However, meaningfulness with males was more important than meaningfulness with females.

Also:

Brody, L.R. (1999)
Gender, emotion, and the family. Cambridge, MA: Harvard University Press.

Simon, R.W., & Nath, L.E. (2004)
Gender and emotion in the United States: Do men and women differ in self-reports of feelings and expressive behavior? American Journal of Sociology, 109. 1137–1176.

Wheeler, L.; Reis, H.; Nezlek, J. (1983)
Loneliness, social interaction, and sex roles. Journal of Personality and Social Psychology, 45. 943–953.

We Feel Fine says:

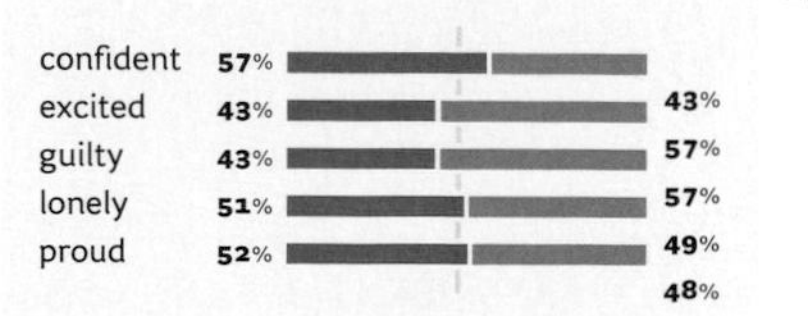

In the *We Feel Fine* dataset, men express more confidence, loneliness, and pride. However, we do not replicate men feeling more guilt and excitement.

The Anatomy of Emotion

Our most emotional body parts, and the feelings they feel

Body part / feeling	Times average
Heart	
broken	16 times average
aching	12.2
healed	7.0
crushed	6.2
gentle	5.8
tender	5.5
heavy	5.1
throbbing	4.5
longing	4.4
wounded	4.3
hollow	3.5
wild	3.4
burning	3.2
bruised	3.1
healing	3.1
loving	2.7
touched	2.7
precious	2.6
empty	2.4
numb	2.4
fragile	2.2
pure	2.1
Head	
spinning	15.0
throbbing	9.8
stuffy	5.0
cleared	4.6
aching	3.7
swollen	2.9
congested	2.9
heavy	2.8
dizzy	2.2
Stomach	
queasy	20.0
sick	15.1
bloated	14.4
nauseated	12.5
hollow	8.6
Chest	
tight	21.9
heavy	14.3
aching	14.0
smooth	5.7
hairy	5.3
Legs	
aching	20.9
throbbing	12.7
sore	12.5
itchy	9.7
Arms	
muscular	8.4
strong	2.7
Fingers	
tingling	21.1
tingly	14.9
Toes	
tingling	19.7
freezing	13.5

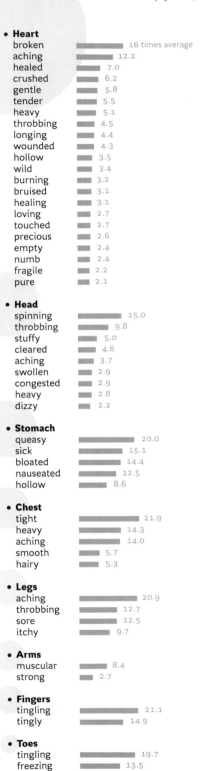

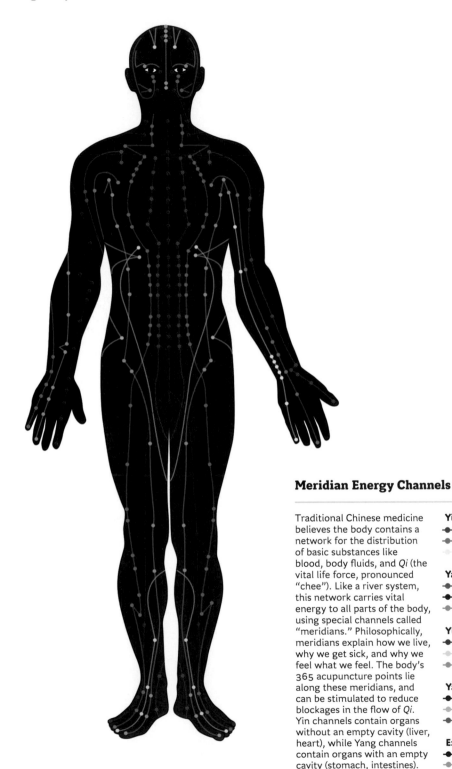

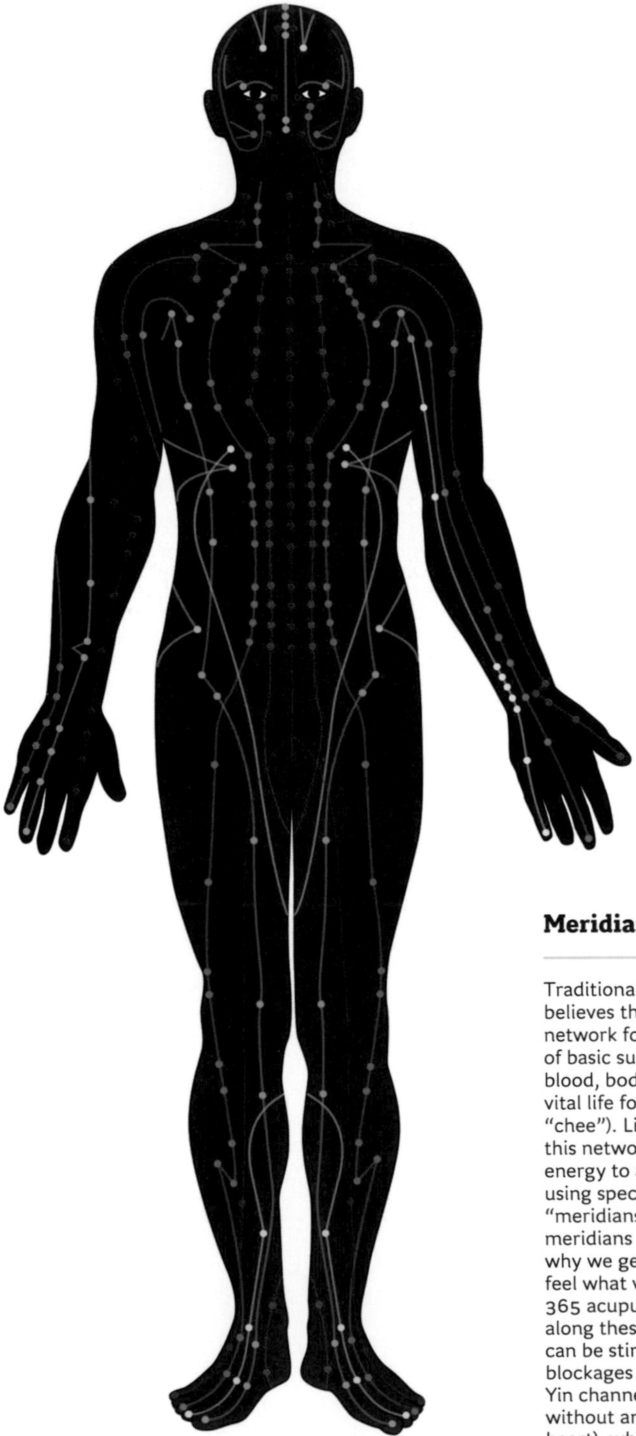

Meridian Energy Channels

Traditional Chinese medicine believes the body contains a network for the distribution of basic substances like blood, body fluids, and *Qi* (the vital life force, pronounced "chee"). Like a river system, this network carries vital energy to all parts of the body, using special channels called "meridians." Philosophically, meridians explain how we live, why we get sick, and why we feel what we feel. The body's 365 acupuncture points lie along these meridians, and can be stimulated to reduce blockages in the flow of *Qi*. Yin channels contain organs without an empty cavity (liver, heart), while Yang channels contain organs with an empty cavity (stomach, intestines).

Yin Arm Channels
- Lung / Taiyin
- Pericardium / Jueyin
- Heart / Shaoyin

Yang Arm Channels
- Small Intestine / Taiyang
- Large / Yangming
- Triple Heater / Shaoyang

Yin Leg Channels
- Kidney / Shaoyin
- Liver / Jueyin
- Spleen / Taiyin

Yang Leg Channels
- Urinary Bladder / Taiyang
- Gall Bladder / Shaoyang
- Stomach / Yangming

Extra Channels
- Conception Vessel / Ren
- Governing Vessel / Du

The Anatomy of a Large-Scale Emotional Search Engine

High-level architecture of the *We Feel Fine* system

The architecture of the *We Feel Fine* system is composed of fourteen main components, illustrated in the diagram at right and explained below. A **URLServer** (1) collects the URLs of blog posts to be crawled, and sends that list to the **Crawler** (2), which fetches the blog posts from the web. At the moment, the Crawler is a single dedicated machine, but has been designed so that we can easily add more crawling machines if desired.

The Crawler then sends the fetched pages to the **Feeling Indexer** (3), which determines whether there is a feeling sentence in the blog, and if so, parses out the feeling sentence or sentences, the time and date of the post, and any demographic information from the blogger's profile (such as gender, age, and location). The Feeling Indexer also sends the sentence to the **Emotional Lexicon** (4), which determines whether there is a feeling word in the sentence (like "happy," "sad," etc.), and if so, sends the feeling word back to the Feeling Indexer. If there are images in the post, the Feeling Indexer determines the biggest image in the post (determined by file size of the image file), and sends it to the **Image Repository** (7). For those posts where the location is specified, the Feeling Indexer sends the location, time, and date of the post to the **Weather Server** (5), which determines the weather of that location at that time and date using several public weather databases.

When the Feeling Indexer has finished this processing, the feeling sentence and metadata are sent to the **We Feel Fine Database** (6), a MySQL database that stores the emotional data, including sentence, feeling, date, time, post URL, weather, and author gender, age, and location. At the moment, the *We Feel Fine* Database is a single dedicated database server, but has been designed to be easily sharded by date range if desired. We chose to design for sharding by date range because most database queries are for the most recent feelings, and the API returns feelings in reverse chronological order. Sharding by date range will allow common queries to hit the fewest number of shards.

Several entities communicate with the *We Feel Fine* Database. The **Sentiment Mining Server** (9) is used to compute statistics over the entire database, like the ones seen in this book. The **API Server** (10) defines a RESTful API, translating specified URLs into SQL queries, and then returning the SQL results to the browser as XML-formatted text. This is an open API, documented at wefeelfine.org/api.html. To decrease query latencies, we continuously cache the most common queries to the API, and store the results in the **Query Cache** (8). The API Server first communicates with the Query Cache, and if the query is not in the cache, it hits the database.

The **We Feel Fine Frontend** (13), which is a Java applet written using Processing (processing.org) and viewable at wefeelfine.org, communicates with the API Server, translating user actions to API queries, and translating the XML-formatted results into interactive visualizations. When there are images involved, the Frontend also communicates with the **Montage Server** (11), which, given a feeling ID, overlays a sentence on the appropriate image and displays the resulting montage to the user through the Frontend. Users may also choose to save a montage to the **Montage Gallery** (14), in which case the Montage Server will save the montage to the database so that others may view it in the gallery from that point on. Viewers of the Montage Gallery may choose to view the montages in the gallery ranked by recency or popularity, and they may also use the gallery to e-mail montages to friends.

And finally, since the API is open for non-commercial use, there are dozens of **Third-Party Applications** (12) that communicate with the *We Feel Fine* API, visualizing the data in a number of ways that we never previously imagined.

We Feel Fine Component Diagram

The 14 main components composing the *We Feel Fine* system

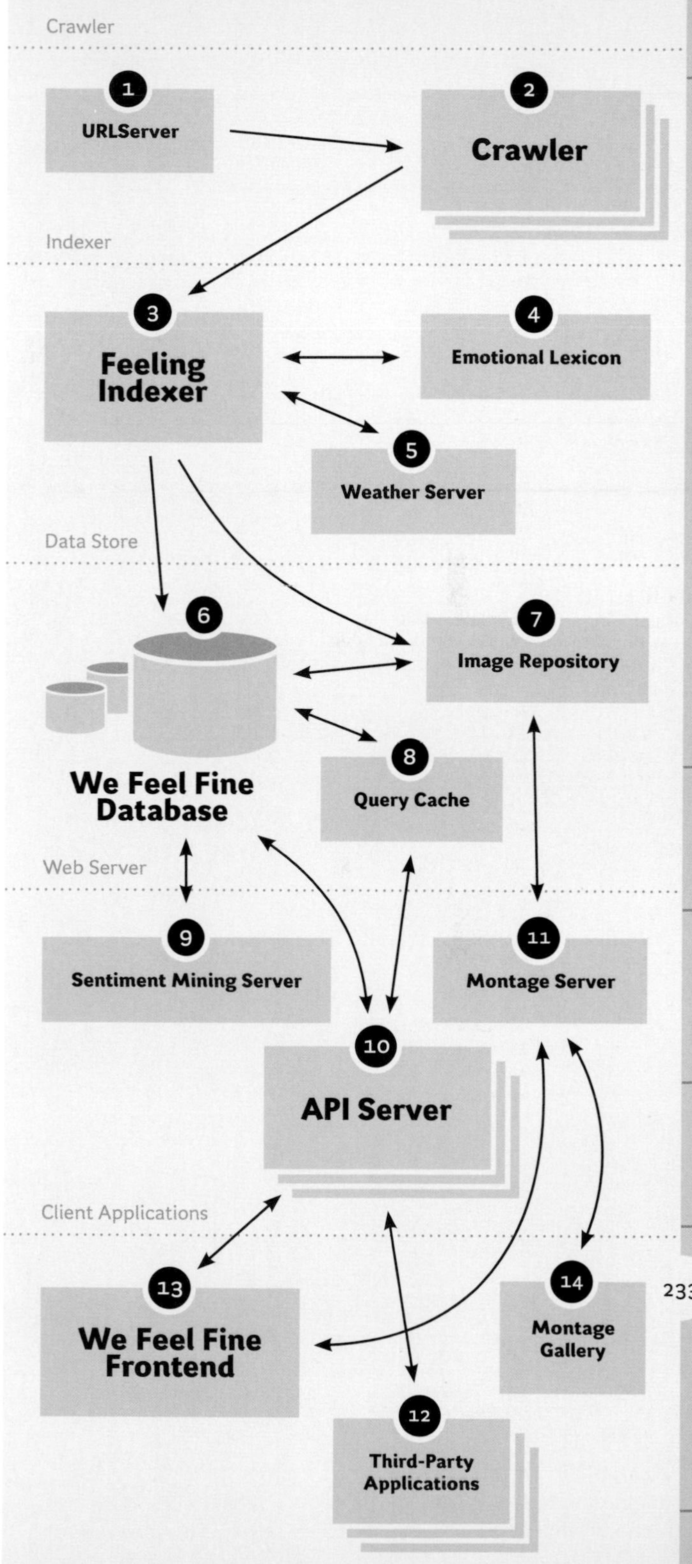

Source Code: Backend

A partial and simplified version of the code that *We Feel Fine* uses to extract feeling sentences from a set of blog posts (written in Perl)

```
#!/usr/bin/perl

use XML::Simple;
use SOAP::Lite;
use LWP::Simple;
use LWP::UserAgent;
use HTTP::Request;
use Digest::MD5;
use lib "/home/wefeelfine/perl/lib/perl5/site_perl/5.8.6/";
require WWW::RobotRules;
use LWP::Simple qw(get);

# Function to check if a URL can be downloaded,
# based on the corresponding robots.txt
sub off_limits {
  local ( $url ) = @_;
  local ( $server, $port, $path, $robotfile, $atype, $ret );
  my $robotsrules = new WWW::RobotRules 'WeFeelFine';

  # Gopher masquerading as http, assume okay
  if ( $url =~ m#^http://[^/]+:70[^0-9]#i ) return 0;

  # Parse URL
  ( $server, $port, $path ) =
       ( $url =~ m#^([a-z]+://[^/]+(:[0-9]+)?)(.*)#i );
  $server =~ tr/A-Z/a-z/;
  $robotUrl = $server . "/robots.txt";
  my $robots_txt = get $robotUrl;
  $robotsrules->parse( $robotUrl, $robots_txt );

  # Now we are able to check if a URL is valid for those servers that
  # we have obtained and parsed "robots.txt" files for
  if ( !$robotsrules->allowed( $url ) ) return ( 1 );

  return ( 0 );
}

# Given an array of blog URLs, extract feelings and usernames
sub extractFeelingsFromPosts {
  my ( @postlist ) = @_;
  my $feelingcount = 0;
  foreach my $posturl( @postlist ) {
    print "Extracting feelings from $posturl\n\n";
    sleep 1;
    # Get HTML of post as string
    if ( !off_limits( $posturl ) ) {
      my $post = geturl( $posturl );
      # Look for feelings in post
      my $count = findFeelings( $post, $posturl );
      $feelingcount += $count;
    }
  }
  return $feelingcount;
}

# Generic function to find the first adjective in a sentence
# assumes the sentence being passed is User::clean'd
sub findAdjective {
  my $sentence = @_[ 0 ]; # Sentence to search
  my $adjFound = 0;
  my $adjective = "";

  # Clean up the sentence further
  $sentence = lc( $sentence ); # Make lowercase
  $sentence =~ s/[':]//g;

  # Only start looking after the word "feel"
  $sentence = substr( $sentence, $feelLoc );

  # Find first adjective in string
  foreach my $word ( split( / /, $sentence ) ) {
    if ( !$adjFound ) { # If adj hasn't already been found for this entry
      if ( exists( $main::feelings{ $word } ) ) { # Adj found, print it
        # pretty and real are common adverbs
        if ( $word ne "pretty" && $word ne "real") $adjFound = 1;
        $adjective = $word;
      }
    }
  }
  return $adjective;
}
```

```
# Generic function to find the feeling sentence(s) in an HTML page
sub findFeelings {
  my $post = @_[ 0 ]; # Blog post
  my $posturl = @_[ 1 ]; # URL of blog post
  my $feelingcount = 0; # Number of feelings found
  my $sentence;
  my $reject = 0;

  # if somebody puts a nofeelings tag in their post, don't scrape it
  if ( $post =~ "nofeelings" ) $reject = 1;

  # If body tags exist, only keep content between body tags
  if ( $post =~ /<body(.*?)>(.+?)<\/body>/igs ) $post = $2;

  # Remove HTML comments from cntry
  $post = removeComments( $post );

  # Setup regular expressions for "I .... feel .... EOS"
  $regex_I = "(I[\\s\\'][^\\.\\?\\!>]*?)";
  $regex_Feel = "feel.+?";
  $regex_EOS = "(\\.|\\?|\\!|<\\/div>|<\\/td>|<\\/p>|<hr>)";
  $regex = $regex_I . $regex_Feel . $regex_EOS;

  # Check for occurrences of "feel" after the first sentence
  while ( $post =~ m/($regex)/isg ) {

    # Remove HTML tags from sentence
    $sentence = removeHTML( $1 );

    # Clean up sentence even more
    $sentence = clean( $sentence );

    # Make sure sentence is not too short (only "i feel")
    if ( $sentence =~ /feel\s*$/i ){
      print "Sentence is too short\n";
      return;
    }

    # Make sure sentence is not too long
    if ( length( $sentence ) > $sentenceLimit ) {
      print "Feeling found, but sentence is too long (longer
            than $sentenceLimit chars)\n";
      return;
    }

    my $feeling = findAdjective( $sentence );
    print "Feeling ($feeling) found in: $sentence\n\n";
    $feelingcount++;
  }
  return $feelingcount;
}

# Function to grab an HTML page
sub geturl {
  my ( $url, $options ) = @_;
  my $ua = new LWP::UserAgent;
  my $request = new HTTP::Request( 'GET', $url );
  my $timeout = 20;

  $ua->proxy( http => $constants->{ http_proxy } )
                if $constants->{ http_proxy };
  $ua->agent( "Mozilla/4.0" );
  $timeout = $options->{ timeout } if $options->{ timeout };
  $ua->timeout( $timeout );
  my $result = $ua->request( $request );
  if ( $result->is_success ) {
    return $result->content;
  } else {
    print "Url Fetch Failed: $url";
    print $result->status_line . "\n";
    return "";
  }
}

# Remove HTML comments
sub removeComments {
  local ( $page ) = @_[ 0 ] ;
  $page =~ s{ <! (.*?)(--.*?--\s*)+(.*?)>}{
                if ($1 || $3) { "<!$1 $3>"; } } gesx;
  return $page;
}
```

```
# Remove HTML tags
sub removeHTML {
  local ( $page ) = @_[ 0 ] ;

  # After noscript, kill the rest of the line -- hack for Flickr
  $page =~ s/<noscript>\n<div>.*//;

  # Replace <br> tags with a space
  $page =~ s/<br.*?>/ /igs;
  $page =~ s{ <(?: [^>'"] * | ".*?" | '.*?' )+> }{ } gsx;
  return $page;
}

# Helper function to strip whitespace and tags
sub clean {
  my $str = @_[ 0 ] ;  # The string to clean
  my $situation = @_[ 1 ] ;  # Any extra instructions

  # Remove tags
  $str =~ s/<.*?>//ig;
  $str =~ s/<\/.*?>//ig;

  # Remove ASCII encodings
  $str =~ s/&[a-z0-9]{4,5};/ /ig;
  $str =~ s/&#[a-z0-9]{4,5};/ /ig;

  if ( $situation ne "keeppunctuation" ) {
    # Remove all non alphanumeric chars (replace with space)
    $str =~ s/([^a-z0-9\s\'\:]+)/ /igs;

    # Remove any trailing colons
    $str =~ s/\:$//s;
  }

  # Remove spaces before and after main text chunk
  $str =~ s/^\s*(.*?)\s*$/$1/ig;

  # Remove newline characters
  $str =~ s/[\n\r]/ /igs;

  # Remove any multiple whitespaces
  $str =~ s/\s+/ /ig;

  # Remove any leading and trailing whitespaces
  $str =~ s/\s+$//g;
  $str =~ s/^\s+//g;

  return lc( $str );
}

# Sets up hash table of valid "feelings" (adjectives)
sub loadFeelings {
  my %feelings;

  # Define list of adjectives
  $adjectives = get "http://www.wefeelfine.org/data/validWords.txt";

  my @lines = split /\n/, $adjectives;
  foreach my $line ( @lines ) {
    # Remove newlines
    $line =~ s/\n//g;
    $line =~ s/\r//g;
    $feelings { $line } = 1;
  }
  return %feelings;
}

# MAIN ------------------------------------------------------------

# Maximum sentence length allowed
$sentenceLimit = 300;

# Load valid feelings
%feelings = loadFeelings();

# URLs to search
@posturls = ( "http://www.wefeelfine.org/sample-post.html" );

# Extract feelings from posts
extractFeelingsFromPosts( @posturls );
```

Source Code: Frontend

The code used to generate the dot explosion images at the front of this book (written in Processing / Java)

```
import processing.pdf.*;

// Number of dots to start with and number to add each frame
int NUM_INITIAL_DOTS = 2000;
int NUM_EXTRA_DOTS = 75;

// Render PDF - always set to false - click mouse to output PDF
Boolean bRenderPDF = false;

// Render on screen - set false to optimize performance
// N.B. set to false when rendering a PDF with many dots
Boolean bRender = true;

// Valid dot colors (will be used randomly)
color[] colors = {
  #FFA401, #07548A, #FFF700, #E97802, #004E6F, #2E9127,
  #017E94, #00553A, #00696F, #E6C637, #18213E, #595884,
  #FF7F00, #FFD801, #40B6B8, #043F69, #7EC31B, #014872,
  #027975, #273E67, #F70059, #08468F, #352C65, #263D67,
  #11581C, #E4010A, #0A3B8A, #EA3137, #FE992D, #F44387,
  #3688BA, #1B2958, #F30263, #73207C, #3A4AA1, #F30172,
  #243C96, #283152, #99D013, #99CF15
};

ArrayList dots;
PGraphics pdf;

void setup() {

  // Prepare canvas
  int w=1600, h=800;
  size( w, h );
  smooth();

  // Prepare PDF
  pdf = createGraphics( w, h, PDF, "explosion.pdf" );

  // Create initial dots
  dots = new ArrayList();
  for ( int i=0; i < NUM_INITIAL_DOTS; i++ ) {
    addDot();
  }
}

// Add a dot to the mix
void addDot() {
  float r = random( 1, 8 ); // Radius
  float a = random( .8, .9 ); // Alpha
  dots.add( new Dot( getRandomColor(), r, a ));
}

void draw() {

  // Add extra dots
  for ( int i=0; i < NUM_EXTRA_DOTS; i++ ) {
    addDot();
  }

  // Update dot positions
  for ( int i=0; i < dots.size(); i++ ) {
    ((Dot) dots.get( i )).update();
  }

  println( dots.size() + " dots - click to save PDF" );

  // Clear background
  if ( bRenderPDF ) {
    pdf.beginDraw();
    pdf.background( 0 );
    println( "Saving PDF with " + dots.size() + " dots" );
  } else background( 0 );

  // Draw dot motion trails
  for ( int i=0; i < dots.size(); i++ ) {
    if ( bRender || bRenderPDF ) ((Dot) dots.get( i )).renderTrail();
  }

  // Draw dot circles
  for ( int i=0; i < dots.size(); i++ ) {
    if ( bRender || bRenderPDF ) ((Dot) dots.get( i )).renderDot();
  }

  // If rendering PDF, clean it up and revert to normal
  if ( bRenderPDF ) {
    pdf.dispose();
    pdf.endDraw();
    bRenderPDF = false;
    bRender = false;
    println( "PDF saved" );
  }
}


class Dot {

  color c; // Dot color
  float r; // Dot radius
  float a; // Dot alpha

  // Physics
  float gravity, friction, bounce, pull, wander, quiver;
  float vxlimit, vylimit; // Max velocities
  PVector vel, pos; // Velocity and position
  ArrayList pts; // All points dot has passed

  Dot( color c, float r, float a ) { // color, radius, alpha

    // Save color and radius
    this.c = c;
    this.r = r;

    // Scale alpha from [0, 1] to [0, 255]
    this.a = rescale( a, 0, 1, 0, 255 );

    // Set physics variables
    gravity = random( .3, .8 );
    friction = random( .8, .95 );
    bounce = random( -.95, -.85 );
    pull = random( -.02, -.01 );
    wander = random( 1, 3 );
    quiver = random( .1, .2 );

    // Maximum velocities
    vxlimit = vylimit = 85;

    // Initial velocity and position
    vel = new PVector( random( 60, 100 ), random( -10, 2 ), 0 );
    pos = new PVector( 100, height/2 + random( -1, 1 ), 0 );

    // Positions
    pts = new ArrayList();

  }

  void update() {

    // Add wander
    vel.add( random( -wander, wander*1.15 ),
             random( -wander, wander ), 0 );

    // Add quiver
    vel.add( random( -quiver, quiver ),
             random( -quiver, quiver ), 0 );

    // Not too fast!
    if ( vel.x > vxlimit ) vel.x = vxlimit;
    else if ( vel.x < -vxlimit ) vel.x = -vxlimit;
    if ( vel.y > vylimit ) vel.y = vylimit;
    else if ( vel.y < -vylimit ) vel.y = -vylimit;

    // Add forces
    vel.x += pull;
    vel.y += gravity;
    vel.mult( friction );

    // Add velocity to position
    pos.add( vel );

    // Did we hit the floor?
    if ( pos.y > height ) {
      pos.y = height-r;
      vel.y *= bounce;
    }

    // Did we hit a side wall?
    if ( pos.x < 0 ) {
      pos.x = r;
      vel.x *= bounce;
    } else if ( pos.x > width ) {
      pos.x = width-r;
      vel.x *= bounce;
    }

    // Remember current position
    pts.add( new PVector( pos.x, pos.y, 0 ));

  }

  // Render trail
  void renderTrail() {

    if ( bRenderPDF ) {
      pdf.beginShape();
      pdf.stroke( c, a/3 );
      pdf.strokeWeight( 1 );
      pdf.noFill();
    } else {
      beginShape();
      stroke( c, a/3 );
      strokeWeight( 1 );
      noFill();
    }

    // Render all trails
    for( int i=0; i < pts.size(); i++ ) {

      PVector v = ( PVector ) pts.get( i );

      // Extra vertex for ends of curve
      if ( i == 0 || i == pts.size() - 1 ) {
        if ( bRenderPDF ) pdf.curveVertex( v.x, v.y );
        else curveVertex( v.x, v.y );
      }
      if ( bRenderPDF ) pdf.curveVertex( v.x, v.y );
      else curveVertex( v.x, v.y );
    }
    if ( bRenderPDF ) pdf.endShape();
    else endShape();
  }

  // Render dot
  void renderDot() {

    if ( bRenderPDF ) {
      pdf.fill( c, a );
      pdf.noStroke();
      pdf.ellipse( pos.x, pos.y, r, r );
    } else {
      fill( c, a );
      noStroke();
      ellipse( pos.x, pos.y, r, r );
    }
  }

}


// Return a random color
color getRandomColor() {
  return colors[ floor( random( 0, colors.length - 1 )) ];
}


// Rescale a number, specifying the old and new ranges
float rescale( float old, float olo, float ohi, float nlo, float nhi ) {
  return nhi - ((( ohi - old ) / ( ohi - olo )) * ( nhi - nlo ));
}


// Mouse clicked: render PDF
void mouseClicked() {
  if ( bRenderPDF == false ) bRenderPDF = true;
}
```

Top 2,500 Feelings

Each circle is a feeling, scaled to show how many times it was felt from 2006-2009

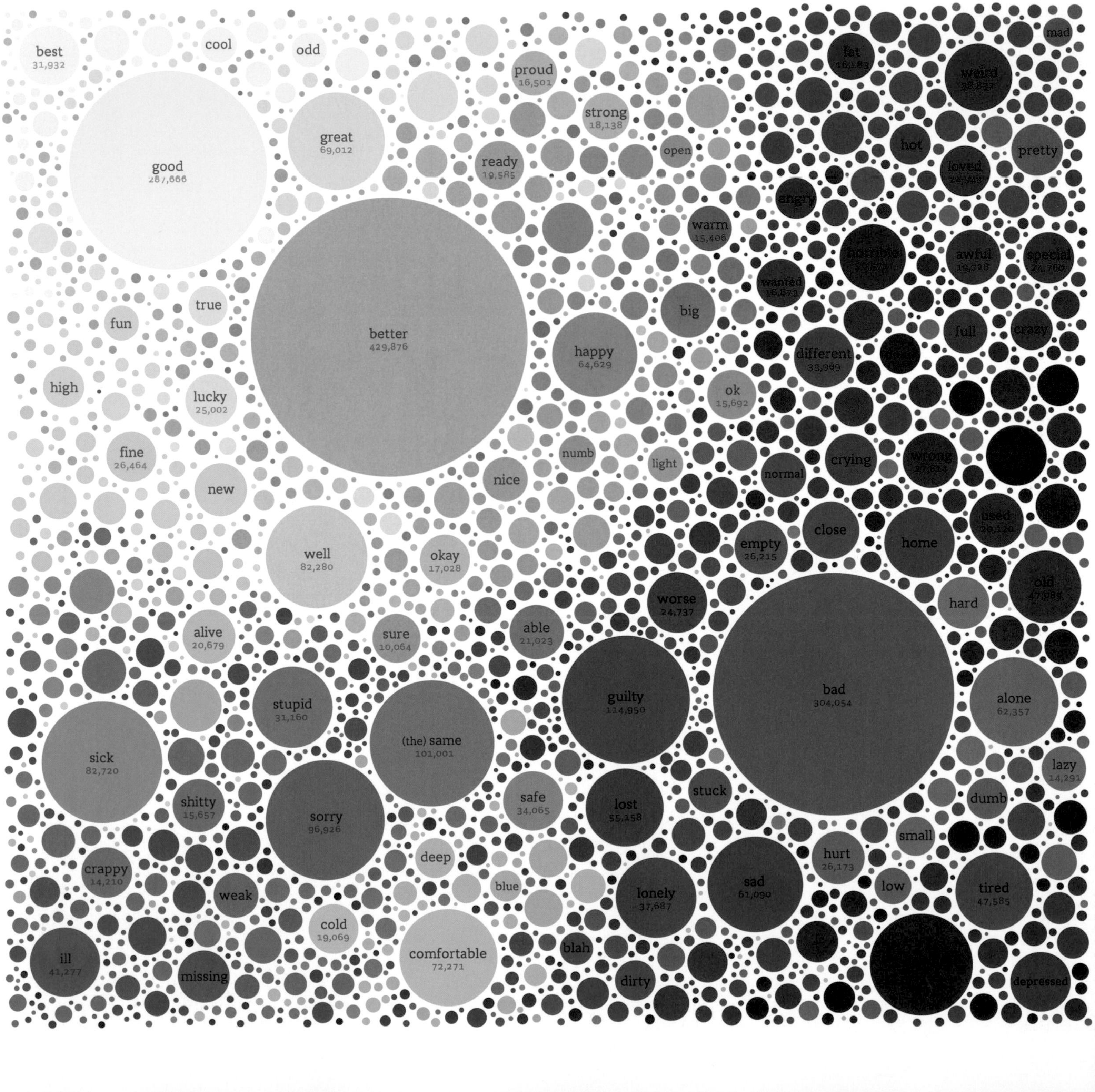

Top 500 Feelings

Showing the number of times each feeling was felt from 2006–2009

429,876	better
304,054	bad
287,666	good
114,950	guilty
101,001	(the) same
96,926	sorry
82,720	sick
82,280	well
78,912	down
72,271	comfortable
69,012	great
64,629	happy
62,357	alone
61,090	sad
55,158	lost
47,585	tired
47,089	old
46,951	(at) home
44,456	stupid
41,277	ill
38,832	weird
37,687	lonely
34,065	safe
33,969	different
31,932	best
30,571	horrible
29,646	confident
27,814	wrong
26,464	fine
26,359	important
26,215	empty
26,173	hurt
25,496	terrible
25,002	lucky
24,943	loved
24,760	special
24,737	worse
23,302	close
23,054	uncomfortable
22,862	depressed
21,023	able
20,717	compelled
20,679	alive
20,120	used
19,957	complete
19,728	awful
19,585	ready
19,560	blessed
19,069	cold
18,540	accomplished
18,367	sure
18,138	strong
17,028	okay
16,873	wanted
16,798	certain
16,501	proud
16,183	fat
15,892	full
15,748	awkward
15,692	ok
15,657	shitty
15,406	warm
15,192	taxing
15,023	normal
14,865	behind
14,834	nice
14,819	overwhelmed
14,601	strange
14,472	stuck
14,335	weak
14,291	lazy
14,210	crappy
13,847	small
13,416	dirty
12,932	helpless
12,710	crazy
12,467	high
12,435	ashamed
12,430	hot
12,219	angry
12,164	trapped
12,149	mean
11,948	stressed
11,422	pretty
11,384	dead
10,915	useless
10,895	nervous
10,878	obligated
10,865	silly
10,737	young
10,582	needed
10,229	dumb
10,204	excited
10,088	low
9,973	numb
9,953	scared
9,899	relaxed
9,781	miserable
9,655	light
9,579	hungry
9,558	executive
9,500	amazing
9,356	cool
9,232	upset
9,172	connected
9,067	whatever
9,027	beautiful
8,962	dizzy
8,942	bored
8,866	secure
8,832	drained
8,771	human
8,648	super
8,626	relieved
8,509	sleepy
8,501	confused
8,485	wonderful
8,472	open
8,402	inspired
8,325	exhausted
8,231	worthless
8,106	grown
8,087	content
8,078	odd
8,036	frustrated
7,990	gross
7,983	positive
7,975	anxious
7,967	funny
7,857	broken
7,806	wasted
7,629	happier
7,429	alright
7,244	awesome
7,239	selfish
7,188	fit
7,152	insecure
7,120	refreshed
7,094	blah
7,079	productive
6,979	older
6,856	afraid
6,854	fortunate
6,776	disappointed
6,762	blue
6,646	calm
6,636	embarrassed
6,634	responsible
6,551	ugly
6,510	satisfied
6,477	pathetic
6,126	nauseous
6,110	emotional
6,106	heavy
6,102	perfect
5,916	worst
5,861	beat
5,834	motivated
5,805	inadequate
5,790	creative
5,686	grateful
5,657	hopeless
5,563	uneasy
5,475	disconnected
5,458	mad
5,390	welcome
5,388	honored
5,330	fucked
5,296	spent
5,235	healthy
5,148	naked
5,100	isolated
5,067	sexy
5,053	jealous
5,037	icky
4,919	lame
4,909	vulnerable
4,846	awake
4,820	busy
4,787	drunk
4,778	restless
4,661	clean
4,630	obliged
4,522	boring
4,493	nostalgic
4,390	torn
4,366	disgusting
4,335	sore
4,305	prepared
4,298	threatened
4,267	honest
4,250	glad
4,238	distant
4,225	smart
4,212	justified
4,193	social
4,118	slow
4,099	optimistic
4,083	fair
4,077	soft
3,992	pissed
3,942	worried
3,936	fresh
3,910	fantastic
3,877	poor
3,847	pressured
3,812	rested
3,740	abandoned
3,732	annoyed
3,731	random
3,726	negative
3,589	bloated
3,583	lousy
3,541	broke
3,531	powerful
3,490	violated
3,467	inferior
3,462	fake
3,441	ridiculous
3,395	insane
3,389	younger
3,370	forgotten
3,323	foolish
3,322	neglected
3,274	pushed
3,257	sweet
3,253	bitter
3,214	appreciated
3,190	privileged
3,116	wet
3,078	rejected
3,044	rushed
3,005	giddy
2,995	unhappy
2,960	present
2,935	deprived
2,931	disgusted
2,923	shy
2,909	attached
2,860	ignored
2,837	invisible
2,827	incomplete
2,822	interested
2,807	passionate
2,805	worn
2,797	loving
2,794	burnt
2,782	lacking
2,777	desperate
2,757	defeated
2,749	evil
2,745	screwed
2,739	hopeful
2,729	retarded
2,703	gay
2,700	empowered
2,698	capable
2,697	peaceful
2,685	healthier
2,663	thankful
2,584	incredible
2,574	queasy
2,566	powerless
2,562	detached
2,561	homesick
2,553	successful
2,552	decent
2,512	unloved
2,455	unwanted
2,446	superior
2,446	energetic
2,416	tense
2,398	accepted
2,387	lethargic
2,385	hollow
2,369	fulfilled
2,368	liked
2,323	spiritual
2,300	liberated
2,285	cheap
2,256	annoying
2,238	pleased
2,225	cute
2,221	yucky
2,188	aware
2,174	touched
2,163	intimidated
2,150	exposed
2,133	spoiled
2,122	mature
2,085	rich
2,045	irritated
2,021	entitled
2,021	attractive
1,990	paranoid
1,982	surrounded
1,972	insulted
1,965	offended
1,955	nauseated
1,951	crushed
1,935	sluggish
1,931	unsure
1,911	significant
1,890	rotten
1,802	unprepared
1,759	unsafe
1,754	groggy
1,732	blind
1,721	thin
1,700	vindicated
1,697	stable
1,692	generous
1,682	melancholy
1,681	unwell
1,679	brave
1,670	independent
1,668	plain
1,652	nasty
1,636	understood
1,629	woozy
1,628	longing
1,626	alienated
1,595	genuine
1,593	honoured
1,579	insignificant
1,576	dull
1,566	unworthy
1,560	unique
1,529	lovely
1,523	sexual
1,520	alien
1,510	focused
1,476	protected
1,459	comforted
1,449	loud
1,446	wise
1,444	unappreciated
1,431	tall
1,414	bothered
1,401	fabulous
1,388	apathetic
1,387	cross
1,381	popular
1,376	horny
1,373	improved
1,361	indifferent
1,358	uninspired
1,356	claustrophobic
1,347	wide
1,338	professional
1,337	beaten
1,335	romantic
1,331	unmotivated
1,324	unsettled
1,298	fragile
1,297	ruined
1,275	rusty
1,269	sane
1,269	crummy
1,263	holy
1,260	cranky
1,257	creepy
1,246	wild
1,239	shaky
1,235	suicidal
1,232	sensitive
1,224	christian
1,213	renewed
1,205	welcomed
1,192	grumpy
1,190	stretched
1,179	validated
1,176	surprised
1,176	invincible
1,167	false
1,165	excellent
1,163	moody
1,159	bare
1,151	drowsy
1,149	encouraged
1,140	scary
1,132	naughty
1,124	punished
1,123	cramped
1,104	dangerous
1,102	organized
1,093	intelligent
1,077	centered
1,076	comfy
1,073	sentimental
1,070	gentle
1,066	feverish
1,060	affected
1,059	average
1,054	profound
1,050	needy
1,038	outcast
1,036	driven
1,030	tremendous
1,030	shallow
1,022	complicated
1,022	active
1,017	balanced
1,012	helpful
1,009	fuzzy
999	political
999	horrid
986	elated
982	valuable
973	enlightened
969	stiff
958	friendly
956	immature
944	girly
944	bitchy
942	hip
940	precious
931	resentful
926	apprehensive
920	itchy
912	protective
910	jaded
906	unproductive
890	relevant
890	misunderstood
889	hated
872	uncertain
862	saved
858	unsatisfied
853	unhealthy
852	mighty
850	committed
847	unattractive
840	incompetent
828	ignorant
828	ambitious
814	stagnant
811	nuts
811	childish
806	humbled
796	modern
779	incapable
773	grand
751	weary
750	review
748	larger
748	accurate
746	skinny
746	restricted
733	cheerful
732	effective
718	defensive
712	wretched
711	released
709	adventurous
703	buried
697	valued
691	wronged
685	cynical
679	enormous
676	terrified
667	mellow
666	unimportant
666	envious
659	heartbroken
655	chinese
650	tingling
642	available
636	surreal
607	feminine
606	temporary
601	wicked
599	famous
594	shocked
577	cruel
576	abused
575	fatter
572	winning
569	gloomy
568	traveling
565	vain
561	artistic
557	sticky
557	discovered
556	par
555	determined
553	sympathetic
551	supported
550	unnecessary
546	disturbed
545	developing
544	ambivalent
539	sold
539	received
537	witty
529	fancy
528	doomed
527	completed
523	pleasant
518	clever

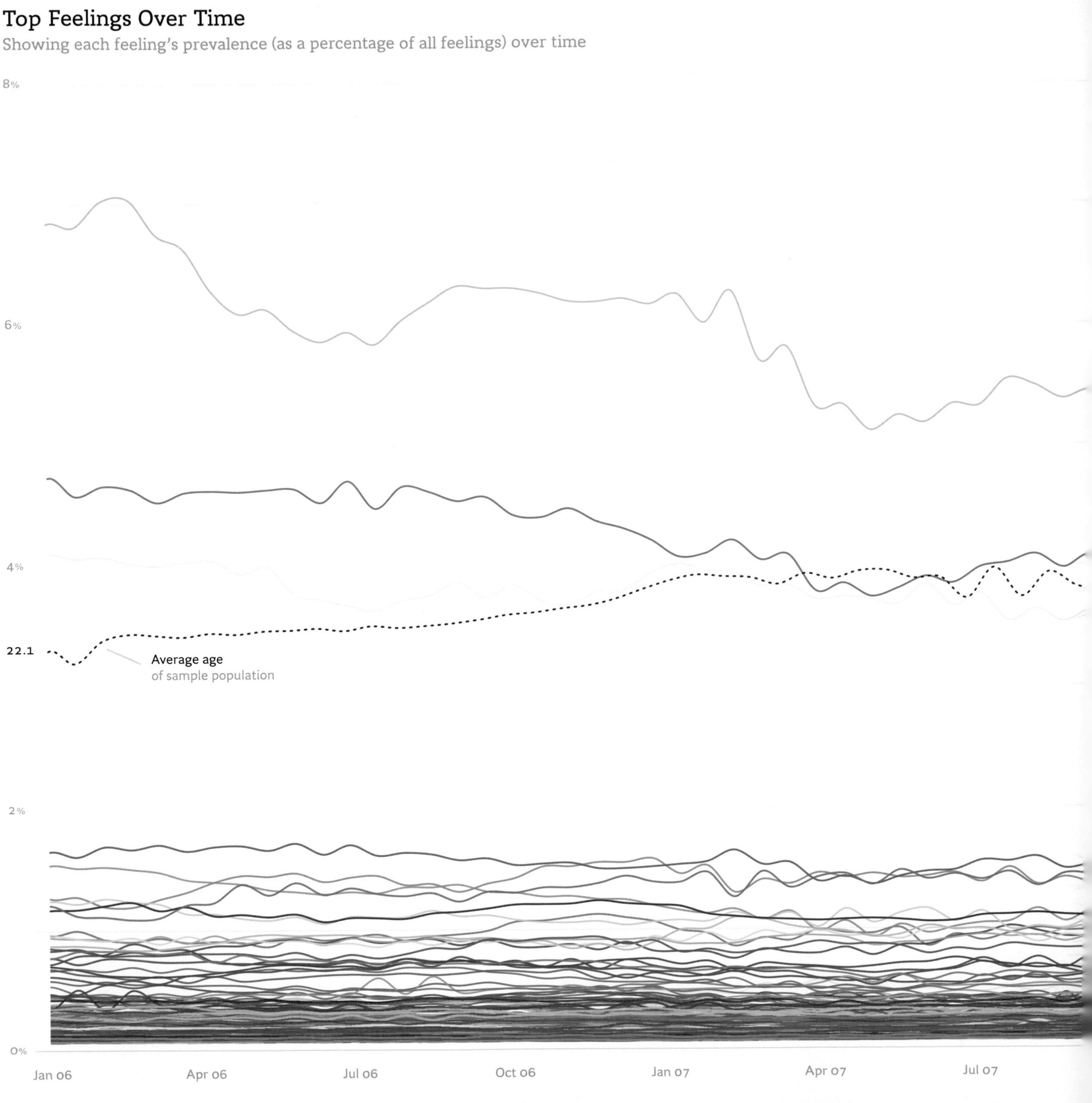
Top Feelings Over Time
Showing each feeling's prevalence (as a percentage of all feelings) over time
8%
6%
4%
22.1
Average age
of sample population
2%
0%
Jan 06
Apr 06
Jul 06
Oct 06
Jan 07
Apr 07
Jul 07

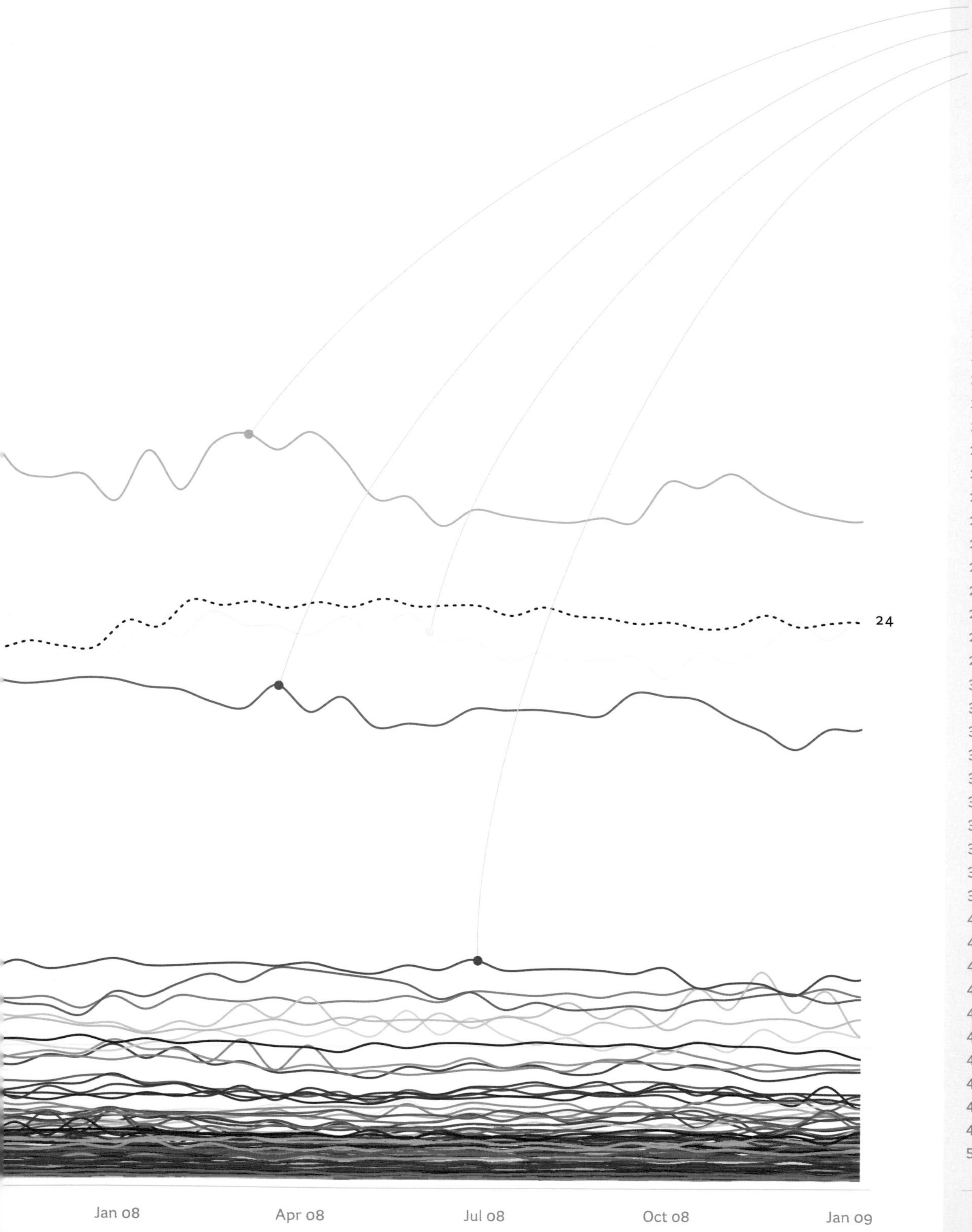

Top 100 feelings *

1 better
2 bad
3 good
4 guilty
5 (the) same
6 sorry
7 sick
8 well
9 down
10 comfortable
11 great
12 happy
13 alone
14 sad
15 lost
16 tired
17 old
18 (at) home
19 stupid
20 ill
21 weird
22 lonely
23 safe
24 different
25 best
26 horrible
27 confident
28 wrong
29 fine
30 important
31 empty
32 hurt
33 terrible
34 lucky
35 loved
36 special
37 worse
38 close
39 uncomfortable
40 depressed
41 able
42 compelled
43 alive
44 used
45 complete
46 awful
47 ready
48 blessed
49 cold
50 accomplished
51 sure
52 strong
53 okay
54 wanted
55 certain
56 proud
57 fat
58 full
59 awkward
60 ok
61 shitty
62 warm
63 taxing
64 normal
65 behind
66 nice
67 overwhelmed
68 strange
69 stuck
70 weak
71 lazy
72 crappy
73 small
74 dirty
75 helpless
76 crazy
77 high
78 ashamed
79 hot
80 angry
81 trapped
82 mean
83 stressed
84 pretty
85 dead
86 useless
87 nervous
88 obligated
89 silly
90 young
91 needed
92 dumb
93 excited
94 low
95 numb
96 scared
97 relaxed
98 miserable
99 light
100 hungry

* Data sampled at weekly intervals

Common Ground

The top 25 feelings and the top 10 emotional catalysts across various demographics. Emotionally, everyone is largely the same.

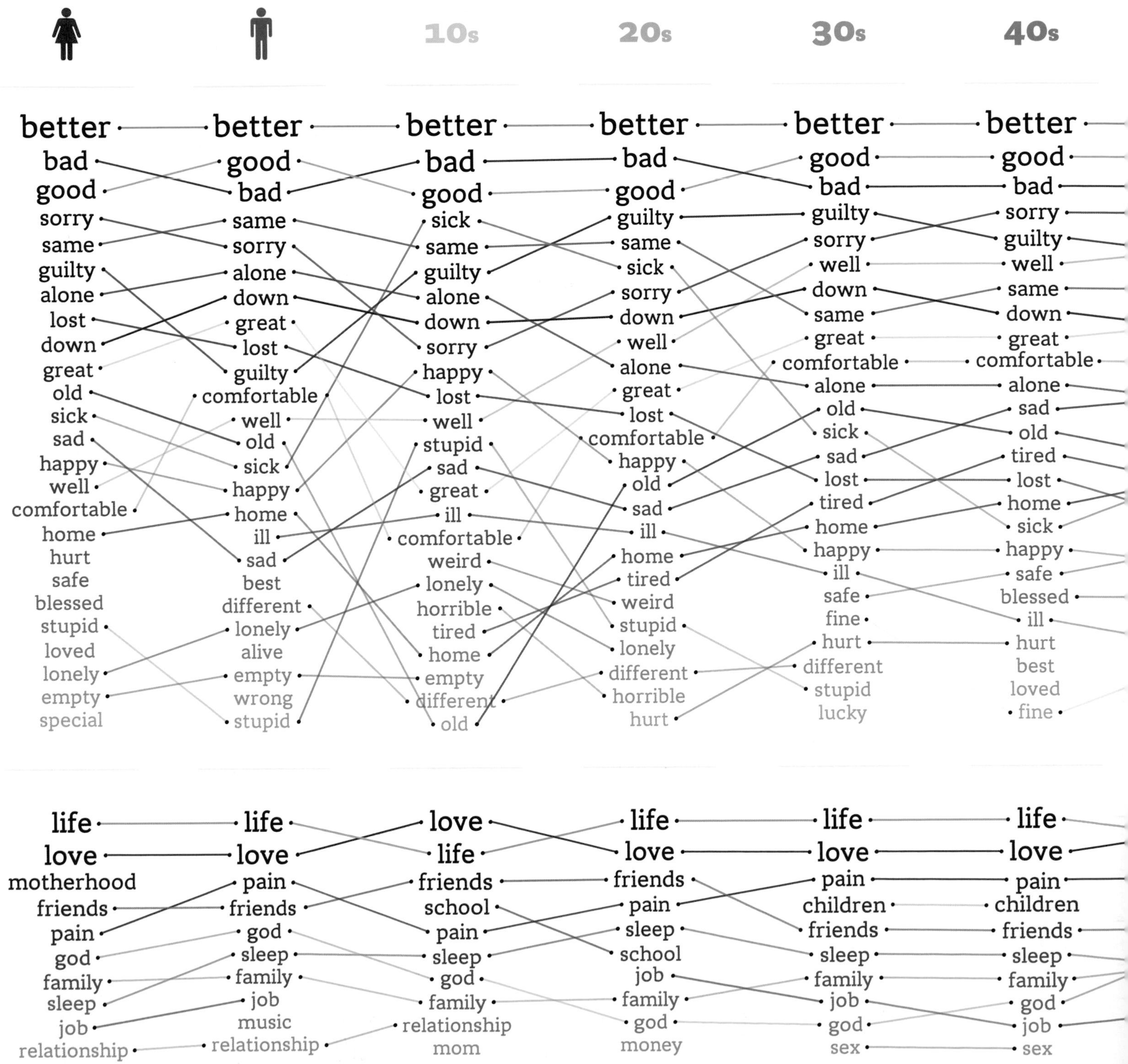

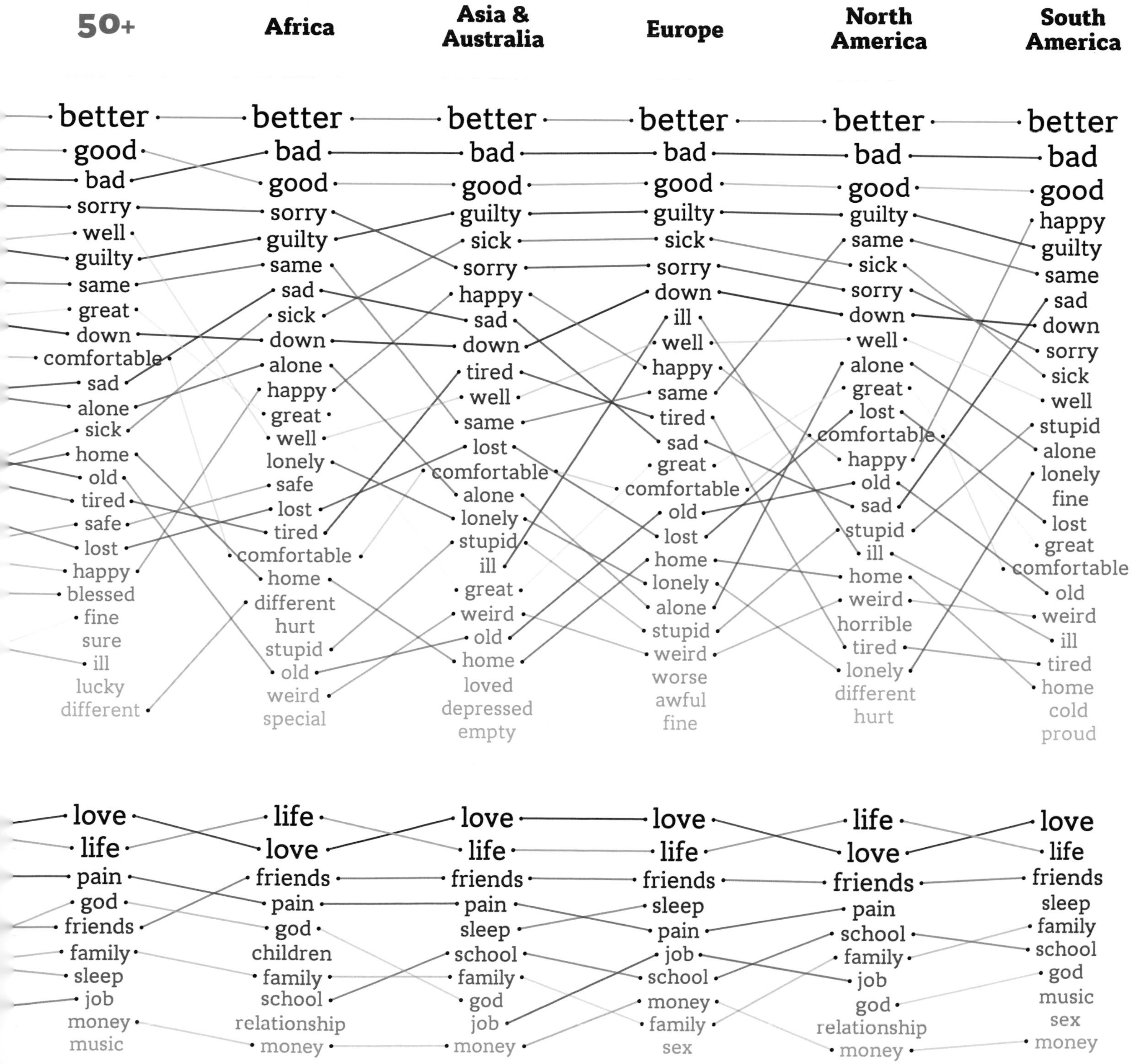

50+
Africa
Asia & Australia
Europe
North America
South America
better good bad sorry well guilty same great down comfortable sad alone sick home old tired safe lost happy blessed fine sure ill lucky different
better bad good sorry guilty same sad sick down alone happy great well lonely safe lost tired comfortable home different hurt stupid old weird special
better bad good guilty sick sorry happy sad down tired well same lost comfortable alone lonely stupid ill great weird old home loved depressed empty
better bad good guilty sick sorry down ill well happy same tired sad great comfortable old lost home lonely alone stupid weird worse awful fine
better bad good guilty same sick sorry down well alone great lost comfortable happy old sad stupid ill home weird horrible tired lonely different hurt
better bad good happy guilty same sad down sorry sick well stupid alone lonely fine lost great comfortable old weird ill tired home cold proud
love life pain god friends family sleep job money music
life love friends pain god children family school relationship money
love life friends pain sleep school family god job money
love life friends sleep pain job school money family sex
life love friends pain school family job god relationship money
love life friends sleep family school god music sex money

Why We Feel What We Feel

Feelings (in color) connected to their primary causes (in black) by colored lines

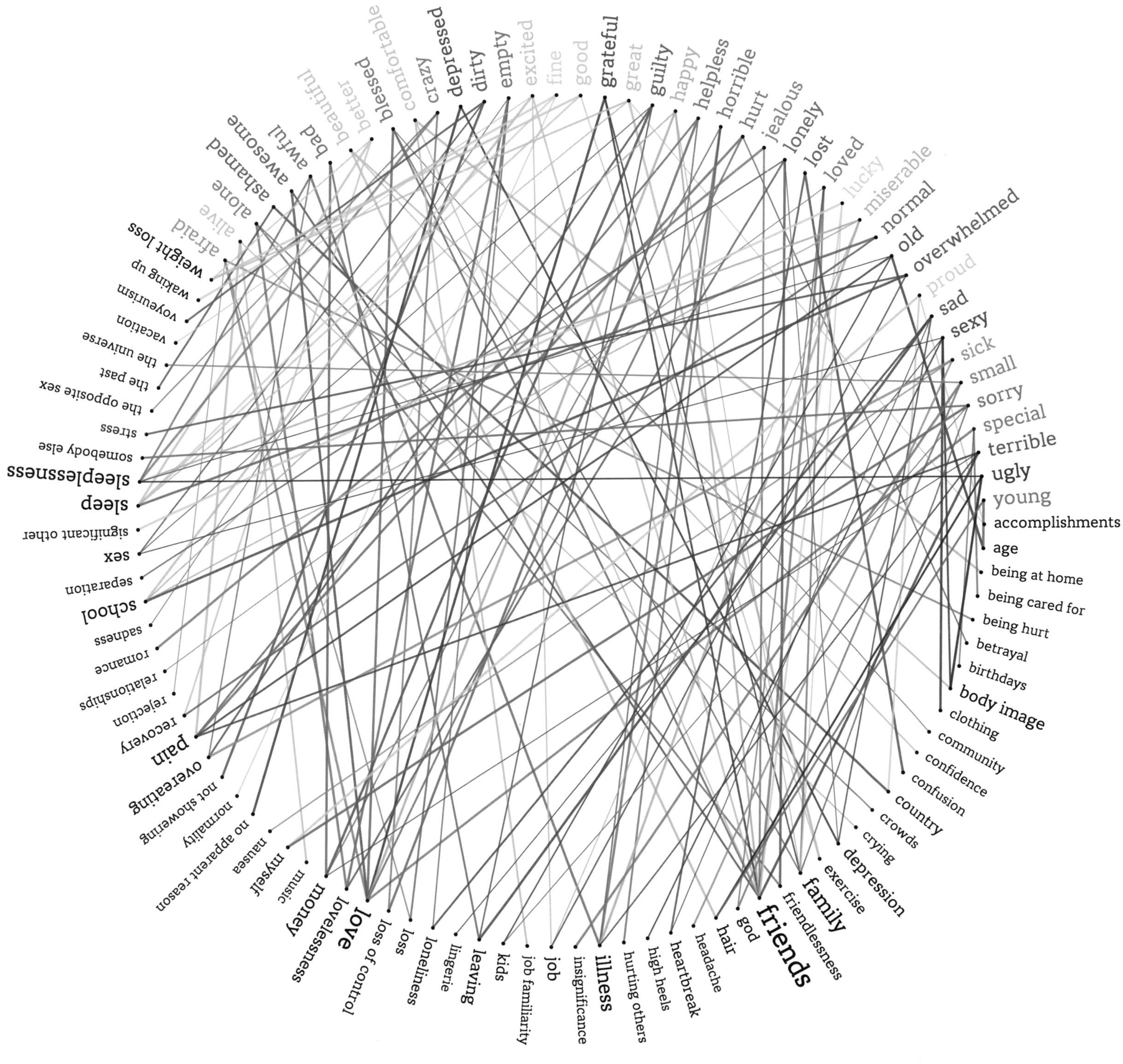

The Tangled Web of Emotions

Feelings that frequently co-occur in the same sentence are connected by lines

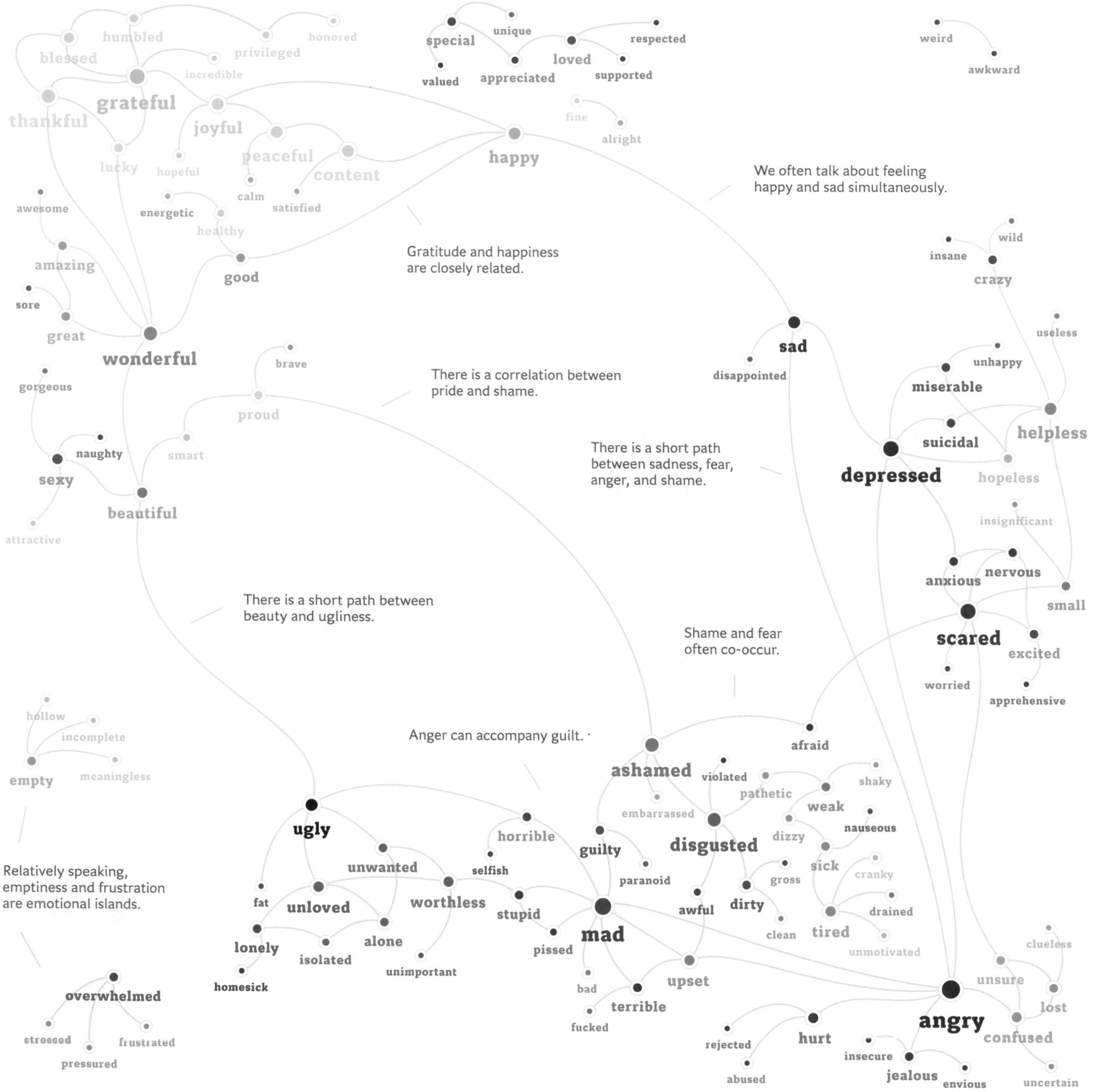

243

Mood Swings

The top 130 feelings from 2006–2009, organized into the eight basic emotions

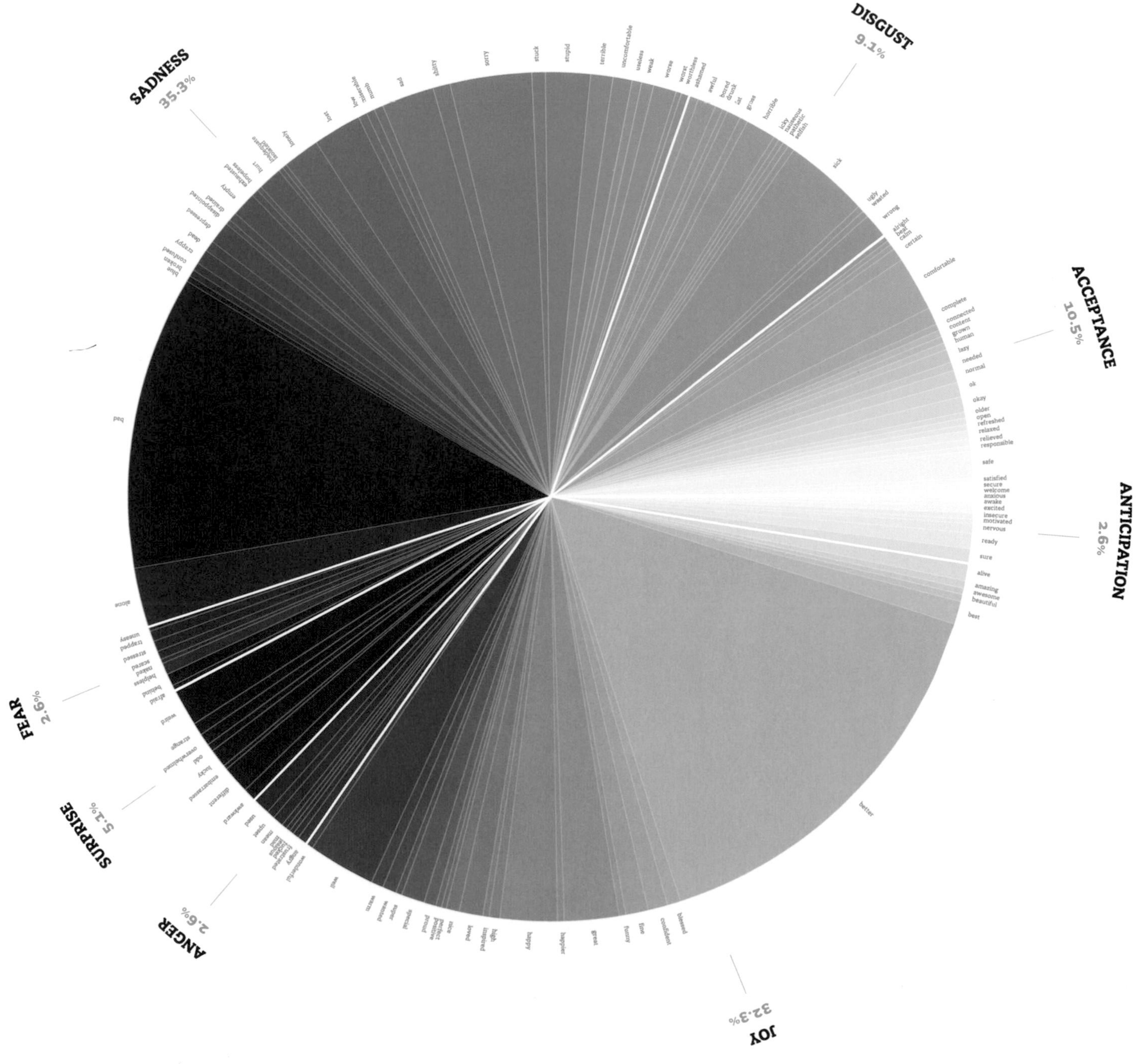

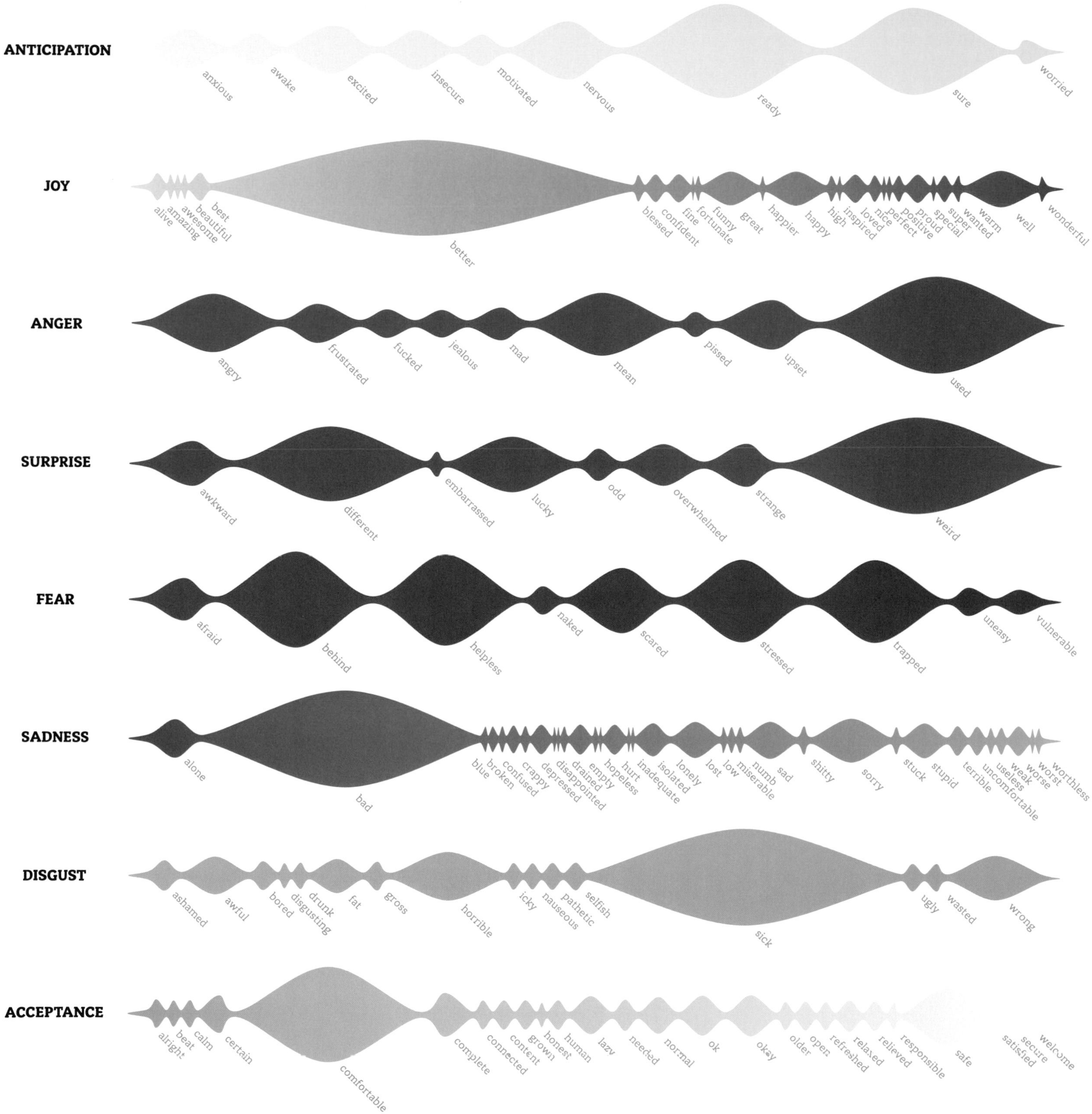
ANTICIPATION
anxious awake excited insecure motivated nervous ready sure worried
JOY
alive amazing awesome beautiful best better blessed confident fine fortunate funny great happier happy high inspired loved nice perfect positive proud special super wanted warm well wonderful
ANGER
angry frustrated fucked jealous mad mean pissed upset used
SURPRISE
awkward different embarrassed lucky odd overwhelmed strange weird
FEAR
afraid behind helpless naked scared stressed trapped uneasy vulnerable
SADNESS
alone bad blue broken confused crappy depressed disappointed drained empty hopeless hurt inadequate isolated lonely lost low miserable numb sad shitty sorry stuck stupid terrible uncomfortable useless weak worse worst worthless
DISGUST
ashamed awful bored disgusting drunk fat gross horrible icky nauseous pathetic selfish sick ugly wasted wrong
ACCEPTANCE
alright beat calm certain comfortable complete connected content grown honest human lazy needed normal ok okay older open refreshed relaxed relieved responsible safe satisfied secure welcome

Shades of Emotion

A rainbow of feelings, from thrilled to suicidal

• i like him that's why i feel sooo thrilled • i feel so freaking joyous and festive • i feel so jubilant right now just knowing that is how i'm living life • i feel so
• i wish to always feel the way i do now blissfully deliriously and unashamedly exultant • i feel like i have a totally excellent social life • i find few things
• i also see the vulnerability she has and i feel elated to care for her and protect her • i feel so delighted when you say you're really excited by me
• i feel merry just after a storm • i feel positively tickled at the idea of doing only what makes me happy and not worrying about another soul
• i'm glad for the experiences i've had good or bad because i feel i've changed a lot since my school days • i feel gratified that i've done
• i feel alright today • i'm feeling really pessimistic about school • i feel glum which sucks cause i have so many hopes this week
• i was feeling a bit down so i began to reread frankenstein • i was feeling downcast melancholy and bored so i made up a
• i was being a drama queen and feeling all blue and weepy • i'm already feeling distant from my boyfriend although
• i don't know why but i couldn't tell ben all the things that he was doing to make me feel so dissatisfied • i dont
• i feel lonely although i don't really miss very many people anymore • i feel sad that she died at a very very
• i always feel hollow sometimes i drown in feelings they overtake me and i sink through them unable
• i've been going through my days almost lifeless aside from the happy face i pull off i feel vacant
• i wanted to have sex so i could feel blank • i feel empty inside like someone took out my
• i look up at him and feel more melancholy than i have in a long time • i feel so very
• i guess it really sunk in this week that i have no job and i was feeling depressed
• i feel despondent and powerless • i feel so completely destroyed inside
• i feel sometimes as if i'm a robot or some inanimate lifeless science
• i feel like emotionally i'm already dead and that soon it won't

ecstatic about accomplishing my life-long goal of becoming a therapist • i feel wonderful when i wear my swan headpiece to the city • i feel psyched yeah

more invigorating than listening to books while working out at the end of the hour i feel awesome focused and super competent like a kung fu master

• i shouldn't be feeling postively gleeful about it but ha ha • i have been feeling peppy and very soon i am going to start my daily dance routine

• i feel pretty upbeat • i think i feel happy so why do i keep wanting things to stop • i feel good and i bought a cute pretty pink furry wallet

my life's work • i feel pleased in the end for what i have • i feel somewhat satisfied • i feel almost completely fine • i feel ok now

• i feel like i'm a decent enough human being and i deserve the chance to be happy yet whenever i try to be happy i get hurt

new game • i was feeling kind of bummed out about some work stuff today so my husband and i went to lunch together

he doesn't know it • i've been feeling moody ever since yesterday • i feel so discouraged and like my life is a failure

know why i just feel unhappy and depressed when i step into church • i have been feeling low since christmas

young age • i feel a sorrowful anger when i realize how long i'll really be alone until i find that one person

to feel anything but them • i seem to have lost focus in every direction and have been feeling low

• i have my moments when i'm feeling a bit morose and so go into hiding for a while to cope

skeleton took out the organs took out all the vital parts leaving behind the useless parts

miserable without you it's almost like having you here • i feel totally wrecked now

• i left the mommy group feeling pretty horrible about my parenting skills

• i feel like a truck demolished my body • i feel hopeless and helpless

project rather than a human being • i feel like the end is coming

just be emotionally • i was feeling suicidal and started cutting

A Moody Life

The rise and fall of our various moods as we age

ANTICIPATION

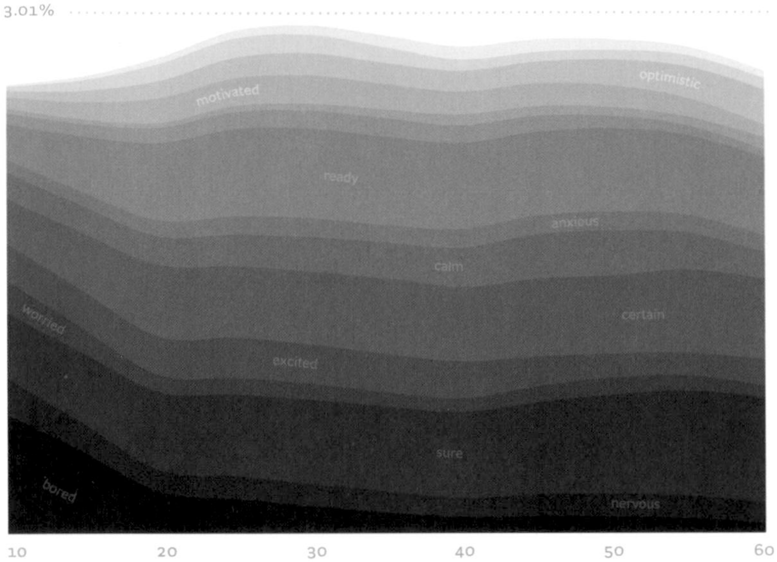

Anticipation contains: bored, nervous, sure, worried, excited, certain, calm, anxious, ready, inspired, hopeful, motivated, optimistic, prepared, threatened

JOY

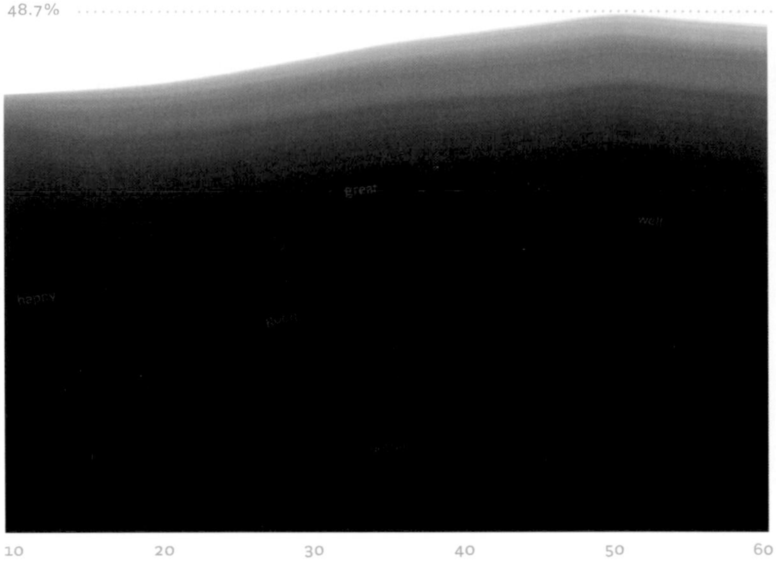

Joy contains: better, good, happy, well, special, loved, great, safe, proud, nice, fine, best, wanted, complete, warm, super, alive, high, confident, happier, perfect, excited, relieved, content, beautiful, secure, lucky, blessed, awesome, wonderful, relaxed, liked, inspired, energetic, amazing, loving, glad, giddy, hopeful, accepted, satisfied, refreshed, honored, fortunate, fantastic, optimistic, grateful, fulfilled, incredible, peaceful

ANGER

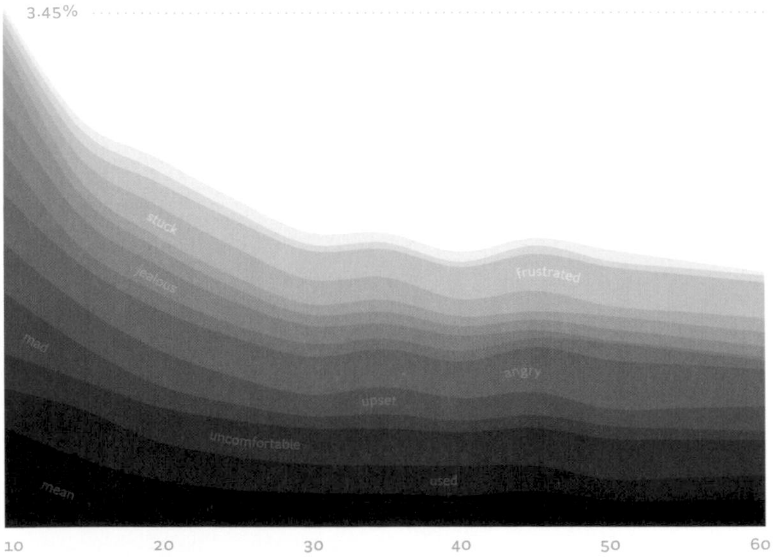

Anger contains: mean, used, uncomfortable, mad, upset, angry, jealous, fucked, pissed, annoyed, stuck, frustrated, screwed, bitter

SURPRISE

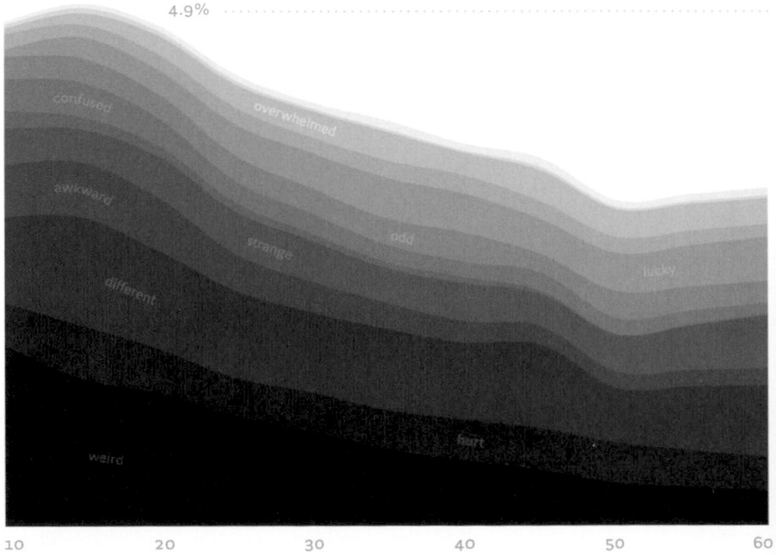

Surprise contains: weird, hurt, different, awkward, strange, fucked, confused, odd, lucky, disappointed, overwhelmed, screwed, embarrassed

FEAR

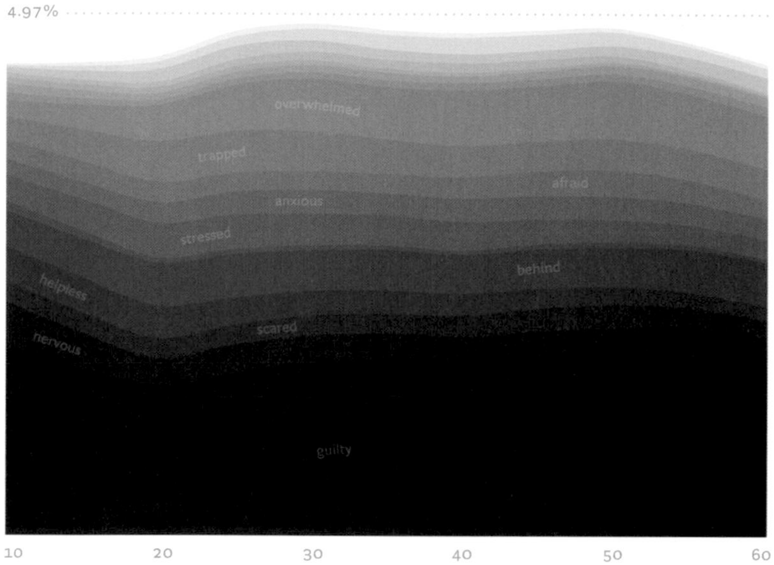

Fear contains: guilty, nervous, helpless, scared, behind, worried, stressed, anxious, afraid, trapped, overwhelmed, tense, desperate, unprepared, queasy, uneasy, threatened, unsure

SADNESS

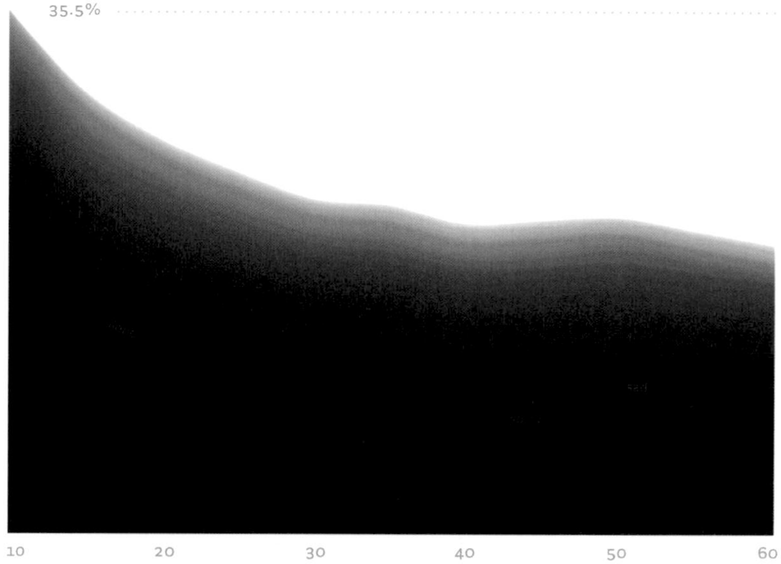

Sadness contains: bad, guilty, sorry, sad, horrible, alone, lonely, depressed, terrible, lost, worse, wrong, empty, awful, hurt, dead, crappy, used, uncomfortable, useless, miserable, helpless, broken, shitty, jealous, confused, ashamed, weak, unloved, numb, ignored, drained, worst, hopeless, worthless, stuck, low, disappointed, violated, rejected, crushed, melancholy, incomplete, frustrated, unhappy, lousy, homesick, embarrassed, deprived, blue, hollow, abandoned, lacking, isolated, inadequate, defeated

DISGUST

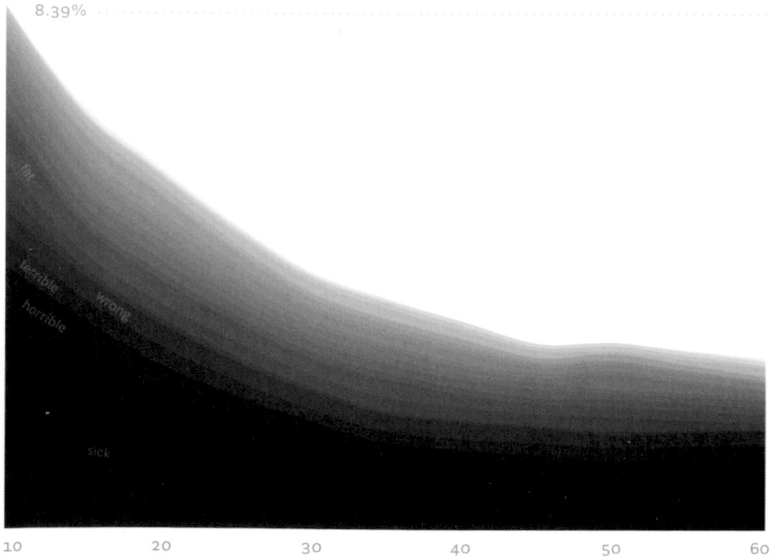

Disgust contains: sick, horrible, terrible, wrong, bored, awful, fat, miserable, selfish, ugly, ashamed, pathetic, icky, worthless, gross, evil, disgusting, nauseous, yucky, nauseated, disgusted

ACCEPTANCE

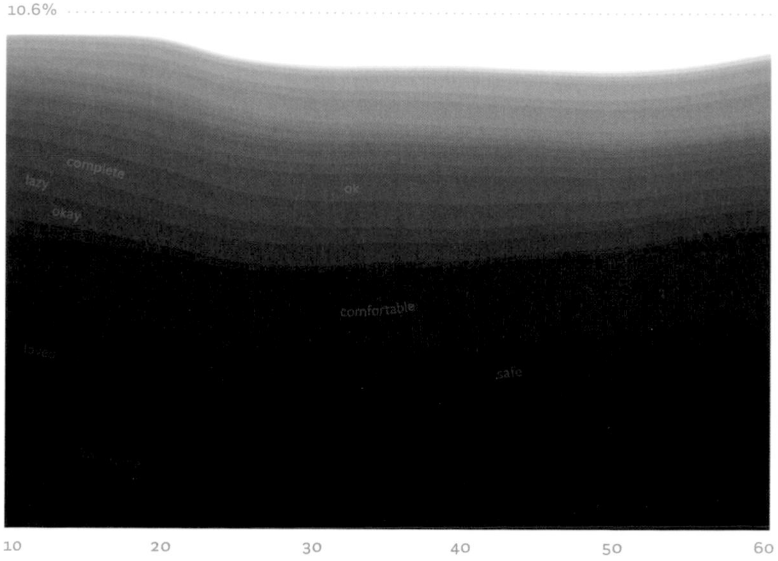

Acceptance contains: (the) same, loved, safe, comfortable, dead, okay, lazy, complete, ok, relieved, numb, drained, hopeless, alright, content, secure, normal, beat, relaxed, loving, satisfied, fulfilled, peaceful, defeated

A Life Sentence

The major emotional themes as we age, summarized in a single (annotated) sentence

We start **simple** 11–14, but soon fill up with **angst** 15–18 and feelings of **confinement** 19–22, until we leave those behind to go **conquer the world** 23–26, before gradually trading ambition for **balance** 27–30, developing an appreciation for our **bodies** 31–35 and our **children** 31–35, and evolving a sense of **connectedness** 36–40, for which we feel **grateful** 36–40, then **happy** 41–49, **calm** 41–49, and finally **blessed** 50+.

simple / 11–14

People in their early teens use a reasonably **narrow** range of words to describe their emotions compared to older age groups.

unique emotions per 1,000 feelings among 11-14-year-olds **337**

normal amount **443**

angst / 15–18

In the later teenage years, the high school social environment seems to cause feelings of angst and **isolation**. There is also a heightened awareness of changing **maturity** levels and a tendency to feel **dumb**.

isolation
- unappreciated
- unloved
- unwanted
- heartbroken

maturity
- matured
- immature
- childish

dumb
- retarded
- stupid
- dumb

confinement / 19–22

College-aged kids experience confinement and **disconnect** more than other age groups. Often they feel **unhealthy** in their college lifestyles, and continue to have an awareness or concern around **maturity**.

disconnect
- stranded
- dependent
- stifled
- confined

unhealthy
- unhealthy
- fatter

maturity
- naive
- innocent
- irresponsible
- childish

conquer the world / 23–26

People in their early professional years are out to conquer the real world and are more **driven** to be validated than other age groups, in their career and their life. This is accompanied by a sense of **unease** with inaction or lack of success.

driven
- capable
- justified
- adventurous
- successful
- professional
- validated
- entitled
- vindicated

unease
- stagnant
- anxious
- unsettled
- defeated

balance / 27–30

In the late 20s, while there are still overtones of **ambition** and desire for success and validation, these feelings trend downward and there is the emergence of a sense of **balance** and appreciation.

ambition
- vindicated
- entitled
- successful
- energetic
- ambitious

balance
- rested
- blessed
- pleased
- balanced
- fortunate
- grateful

bodies & children / 31–35

In their early 30s, people start becoming aware of their body and **energy levels**, and there is a continuation of the trend toward **gratitude**, which is strongly correlated to having children and building a **family**.

energy levels
- rested
- sluggish
- energetic

gratitude
- fortunate
- grateful
- blessed
- honored

family
- husband
- wife
- kids

grateful & connected / 36–40

In the late 30s, the trend toward **gratitude** and connectedness continues, and there is a new trend toward **happiness**. Along with continued emphasis on family and children, we see a stronger sense of spirituality and **community**.

gratitude
- fortunate
- blessed
- honored
- grateful

happiness
- positive
- wonderful
- glad

community
- community
- culture
- spiritual

happy & calm / 41–49

People in their 40s show an increased gratitude and **calm happiness**. Additionally, we see the a weight of **responsibility** on their shoulders.

happy & calm
- blessed
- human
- connected
- positive
- wonderful
- relaxed
- secure
- calm

responsibility
- responsible
- frustrated
- overwhelmed
- needed

blessed / 50+

Many people in their 50s talk about feeling **blessed**, largely in connection with their children.

blessed
- blessed
- lucky

The Ups and Downs of Aging

What we feel about our age, year by year from 1–60

• i never felt that my dad loved me; later when my parents divorced my mother said that after i was **1** my father never touched me
• i feel surrounded by ghosts of my own past since i've been coming here since i was **2** years old • i feel a little guilty for killing a bunch of bumblebees when i was **3** • i have been feeling this pain since i was **4** years old • i remember first feeling fat when i was **5** years old • i had been holding up all these emotions and feelings since i was **6** years old and finally i just snapped • i was **7** years old and already feeling the beginnings of an early puberty • i was **8** when i fell in love with him • i was **9** years old and still to this day i feel the ache of missing him • i feel like i'm in the middle of that piano competition when i was **10**, wearing glasses, hopelessly awkward and shy • i wish it were not true, but i have been having sexual feelings since i was **11** years old • i feel like i'm **12** again and i have been neglectful in writing in my diary • i was **13** years old and yes i was young and just wanted to have a so called boyfriend just to know what it feels like • i feel like a **14** year old girl, only less composed and not as proficient at text messaging • i'm **15**, terrified of life, of growing up, of my family problems, and of how i'm in love with someone i can never be with • i'm now **16** and very introverted and depressed because i feel like i can't do anything about it • i'm **17** and already feel like i'm grown up; i can't imagine how my imagination will run wild when i'm older • i'm **18** and within my legal rights to take a walk at night, but seeing the cops drive around makes me feel like a criminal • i feel **19**, rebellious, and alive
i feel ridiculous i'm nearly **20** years old and i'm writing an internet diary • i'm **21** years old wow i feel so old • i'm **22** and i feel fatter than ever • i was **23** years old and the thought of a little horrible creature growing in my tummy made me feel ill
• i'm **24** years old although sometimes i feel about 40 and other times i act about 17 • i feel so weird to almost be **25** and to still be single and never having had an actual boyfriend • i am only **26** years old right now and i feel like i have a very bright future • i'm **27** and my search for answers has taken me to india; now with sufism i feel i don't have to search, for i've found
• i'm now **28** and have been traveling all over the world performing but feel now it is time to settle back in edinburgh
• i wonder if my cousin feels guilt for being **29**, unmarried, and now never able to present her mother with grandchildren

• i want to head bravely into my **30s** feeling more secure and aware than i spent the end of my twenties • i feel pretty lucky to be able to say that at **31**, i am in by far the best shape of my life • i am **32**, weigh over 250 pounds, and still fighting to feel accepted by my dad • i'm **33** and i'm doing the voice of a chihuahua in beverley hills chihuahua and it feels completely right • i am **34** years old and i feel like i'm a total failure in my life • i am **35** and feel like i am going through puberty with my 13 year old son who is also fighting with acne • i'm feeling ancient in all of my **36** years • i have to admit that at **37** i feel completely out of touch with anyone between 13-17 • i'm **38**, but fuck if i feel like i'm the tiniest bit past my prime • i'm **39** and there's nothing in my professional life that comes close to the pride and contentment i feel at home • i look in the mirror and i see wrinkles and creases that make me feel every single one of those **40** years • i'm **41** and i feel like i just woke up from a 20 year bad dream • i was **42** and it was one of the few times in my life up to that point when i did not feel any hostility from white people • i'm **43** and i feel too old to be chasing around a busy toddler • i think it's safe to say that he lived more in his **44** years than a lot of people do in 94, but i feel so bad for his wife & kids • i feel as if i'm in the halftime of my career, being **45**, and that makes me think i've entered the locker room of life • i was taken back and made to feel old when i realized that stunning brunette from the breakfast club is already **46** • i'm **47** and i feel every damn year month day hour minute and second of it • i'm **48** and when i divorced my husband i wasn't sure i'd ever feel that kind of passionate intensity for a man again • i feel a bit like a spoiled child right now bemoaning this disability since i've had **49** years of amazing physical ability • i don't feel **50**, so most of the time i don't let it bother me, but when i think how long 50 years is, it's kind of depressing • i'm **51** and most times i feel i need to pee i have to do it right away, why is this? • i feel much younger than **52**, but i know i've been alive more than half a century and a lot can happen in that much time • i'm **53** and no longer want to work for money but for joy, and to answer the call to service i feel so clearly in my heart • i am **54** years old and am just starting to blog and i will blog my skating experiences • i'm **55**, my sister was just diagnosed with breast cancer, and to be honest i feel like i've been diagnosed with it too • i'm **56**, have a son who's 29 and makes me feel older than i am, and a daughter who's 8 and makes me feel younger • i have also been tired and while i'm just **57** i don't feel like moving very fast now • i'm **58** and i feel like the biggest cow ever • i'm **59** years old and i feel young again • i'm **60** years old and i feel much better now

He Said, She Said

What we feel about the opposite sex

i love the feeling of being naked and exposed like this while jane is still clothed as it adds to the feeling that she is in total control
i feel bad because yesterday i found out alexis didn't like me so i called her and was like oh my god
i'd just proposed the day before and i found the love that rebecca and i had when we first met
i really feel that this is a new start and caroline is feeling pensive i guess
spiritually i know god has a great destiny for beth and i and we both feel that we are at a tipping point in our lives
i feel happy for natalia
i feel myself growing farther and farther away from amanda
i called melissa earlier today and she made me feel like absolute shit just for calling her
i took jenna off of my top friends so i wouldn't be tempted to see her profile and feel the abandonment again
i feel sorry for sarah
i feel loved by ruth
i can't sleep i can barely work because i cant keep my head straight megan is avoiding and ignoring me since i asked her on a date she said yes but i think it was because she didn't want to hurt my feelings
i love angie it just feels awesome i know it was meant to happen i just know it
i thought i had coped with breaking up with lauren but even now i still sometimes feel bad that we aren't friends
i called michelle feeling too weak to face her
i talked to hannah that afternoon which made me feel a little better
i feel like a baby around anne
i feel that one of the problems i had while dating lauren was lying to myself about who i was
i have gone to such lengths as to text message sarah telling her that i hope she dies she's a pathetic excuse for a human i hope she can never conceive a child again i hope she burns in hell i hope she feels like putting a gun to her head every time she has an abortion
i miss jessica so much i kinda feel like dying
i dont think about nicole and the love i feel for her
i feel crazy for jen
i feel sad that my post made amanda cry more
i have low self esteem and unlike my ex jenny doesn't want me to feel bad about myself
i feel like michelle has abandoned me
i didn't know how to explain that to rachel without her feeling guilty
i feel like i lean too heavily on laura sometimes
i feel you jo
i feel your pain annie
i feel like i take it out on amanda
i feel like wendy is such a slut
i feel sad when i think about holly
i love you vanessa and i'm kind of in shock right now and i can't think straight and i feel really bad for you
i still feel like it exists and still do love mary jo with all my heart
i feel like my prayers have finally been answered by this woman kim
i feel ok around tia
i feel blessed as ever because katie and i are stepping out in faith toward our future together
i feel so mad at kate
i feel so alive with jen
i feel like quinn just sets me free
i have broken up with ashley and now i feel like crap
i told jane this morning that i feel like i just got my ass kicked in a fight
i saw to lisa and made sure that she got home to her own bed safely and i walked away from her house with mixed feelings
i feel like shit ok well kristin i just wanna say i love you and i know my past isnt the best but yours isnt either and i dont hold anything against you
i feel dead without liz
i never want charlotte to feel invisible or unimportant
i told anna how i feel i told her what i think and all she did was throw it back in my face for the most part
i can still feel elizabeth's kiss
i can feel the emptiness left by nora

i was with my soon to be ex-husband for 4 years and what i had for him is nothing compared to what i feel for **bill**

i came to the conclusion that **nathan** can feel whatever he feels

i can't describe what i feel towards **neil** it's almost like an emptiness but not if that makes any sense

i feel better now i can go talk to **ryan** without ripping his head off

i love **justin** with all my heart and just want to know that he feels the way he says he does because for some unknown reason he doesnt make me feel very good

i feel like i m starting to gush about **peter** so i'll stop here

i know **gabe** is just across the street but i would feel better if he was just across the hall

i guess i could try to sleep but have a feeling i won't be able to until **matt** gets home

i didn't even feel it with **zach**

i could feel myself care less and less about the relationship because of the way **jason** treated me

i love my **steve** even though i don't tell him enough and sometimes feel like he's doing so much for me

i wonder if **frank** feels anything at all

i'm in love with someone else, unhappy with **sam**, and i feel i can't leave him

i feel much closer to the lord through **conor**

i feel so sorry for **rob** i try to control myself but these damn hormones are getting the best of me

i feel like such a douche asking **kevin** for a kiss

i feel crazy for **miles**

i feel ok with **joe**

i feel my heart aching for **nick**

i want a reason to feel like shit i mean yeah **ben** has a daughter it shouldnt really effect me because i am over him but then i make myself believe that i am not over him

i have this feeling that lovings from **chuck** just aren't enough

i think what **jack** is looking for and what i'm looking for is how it feels to be loved

i feel like **james** is a loser

jeff makes me feel wanted

ben makes me feel beautiful even though i'm not

i just feel like **jimmy** doesn't listen

i feel so weak without **kyle**

i feel like i'm driving **pete** crazy

i feel bad about betraying **jim**

i broke up with **paul** because i have feelings for my neighbor

i feel optimistic about **max** and me

i'm still feel things for **mark**

i can't decide how i really feel about **dan**

i bet **nathan** must feel very sad

i feel terrible for **joe**

i feel ok, **matt**

i feel like **henry** lied to me

i feel safe with **alex**

i want to feel things for **bill** but i just don't

i feel sad for **joe**

i am so over my feelings for **robbie**

every time i see **joe** i get an icky feeling that i was so stupid to have ever touched hin

i feel it's time to have sex with **john**

i feel i remember **jonathan**'s life better than my own

i know just how you feel **peter**

i still have feelings for **raul** but i'm used to hiding my feelings away in a corner and putting on a fake happy smile

i really thought that i loved **jon** but after meeting you i know that whatever i felt with him couldn't possibly be love because it isn't nearly as strong as what i feel when i'm with you

i would just text **mike** and talk to him about how i feel but i'll just never ever do that will i?

i feel for **jasoı**

Feeling Like a (Wo)man

Distinctly male (blue) and female (pink) feelings, based on usage frequency among men and women

focused wise decent unique reborn invincible outcast energetic genuine popular vindicated social interested cross superior fine dirty evil welcome present lethargic justified obligated paranoid cold obliged dull privileged offended soft compelled uneasy alien thin slow embarrassed cool alienated stable melancholy aware awake wronged bitter bothered false creative fucked hollow alive beat drunk inspired wet fresh crushed disconnected spiritual odd random uncomfortable lacking detached strange motivated pissed disgusted distant alright responsible positive christian ill spent powerless humbled younger best confident fulfilled wide sore rich accepted dead optimistic burnt capable glad welcomed liked wasted human ashamed great jaded exposed insignificant nice attached poor incredible successful light warm cheap beaten same fake significant sentimental young holy comfortable honest worried fair certain productive satisfied good rested pushed sleepy different awkward foolish powerful wrong behind wanted awesome bored able drained used pathetic sure surrounded down open close full boring useless heavy retarded longing bloated emotional depressed refreshed funny tired proud complete negative deprived well needed ready whatever sweet tall forgotten weak fortunate healthy strong incomplete lazy gentle lonely empty shitty mature unworthy precious centered nostalgic disappointed fit nasty weird happier relaxed worse loud important worn high connected saved isolated terrible alone fantastic prepared inferior abandoned attractive ok low older unwanted anxious trapped queasy sorry ignored perfect home worst calm mean frustrated passionate nervous screwed neglected afraid angry accomplished dumb dizzy small tense touched normal special worthless inadequate content numb miserable rejected misunderstood lost renewed old happy broken vulnerable hopeless lovely wild clean amazing better desperate unsure stupid liberated rotten appreciated relieved bad sane blue rushed insane exhausted grown sick ridiculous unhappy lousy loving upset shy secure scared silly intimidated torn honored annoyed restless healthier threatened annoying stuck crappy naked hot insecure lame mad nauseous hurt helpless empowered confused brave lucky guilty smart okay excited loved understood jealous safe busy broke violated horrible sad ugly nuts pressured wonderful punished independent disgusting grateful entitled unsafe pretty thankful crazy stressed hopeful awful plain selfish defeated homesick unloved beautiful fat overwhelmed spoiled super giddy blessed blah nauseated sexy gross invisible peaceful hungry cute unappreciated icky protected

protected unappreciated hungry peaceful invisible gross sexy nauseated blah blessed giddy super spoiled overwhelmed fat beautiful unloved homesick defeated selfish plain awful hopeful stressed crazy thankful pretty unsafe entitled grateful disgusting independent punished wonderful pressured ugly nuts sad horrible violated broke busy safe jealous understood loved excited okay smart guilty lucky confused brave empowered helpless hurt nauseous mad lame insecure hot naked crappy stuck annoying threatened healthier restless annoyed honored torn intimidated silly scared secure shy upset loving lousy unhappy ridiculous sick grown exhausted insane rushed blue sane bad relieved appreciated rotten liberated stupid unsure desperate better amazing clean wild lovely hopeless vulnerable broken happy old renewed lost misunderstood rejected miserable numb content inadequate worthless special normal touched tense small dizzy dumb accomplished angry afraid neglected screwed nervous passionate frustrated mean calm worst home perfect ignored sorry queasy trapped anxious unwanted older low ok attractive abandoned inferior prepared fantastic alone terrible isolated saved connected high worn important loud worse relaxed happier weird nasty fit disappointed nostalgic unworthy precious centered mature shitty empty lonely gentle lazy incomplete strong healthy fortunate weak forgotten tall sweet whatever ready needed well deprived negative complete proud tired funny refreshed depressed emotional bloated longing retarded heavy useless boring full close open down surrounded sure pathetic used drained able bored awesome wanted behind wrong powerful foolish awkward different sleepy pushed rested good satisfied productive certain fair worried honest comfortable holy young sentimental significant fake same beaten cheap warm light successful incredible poor attached nice insignificant exposed jaded great ashamed human wasted liked welcomed glad capable burnt optimistic dead sore rich accepted wide fulfilled confident best younger humbled spent powerless ill christian positive responsible alright distant disgusted pissed motivated strange detached lacking uncomfortable random odd spiritual disconnected crushed fresh wet inspired drunk beat alive hollow fucked creative false bothered bitter wronged awake aware melancholy stable alienated cool embarrassed slow thin alien uneasy compelled soft offended privileged dull obliged cold paranoid obligated justified lethargic present welcome evil dirty fine superior cross interested social blind vindicated popular genuine energetic outcast invincible reborn unique decent wise gay

Approval Ratings

● Positive sentiment ● Negative sentiment ○ Circle size denotes volume of sentiment

How we feel about those most ogled and adored, mocked and maligned members of society—our sacred celebrities

* In January 2009, Barack Obama's approval rating was 76% and Michael Jackson's was 55%, which proves the age-old truths that people like politicians better before they take office, and rock stars better after they're dead.

Rockers

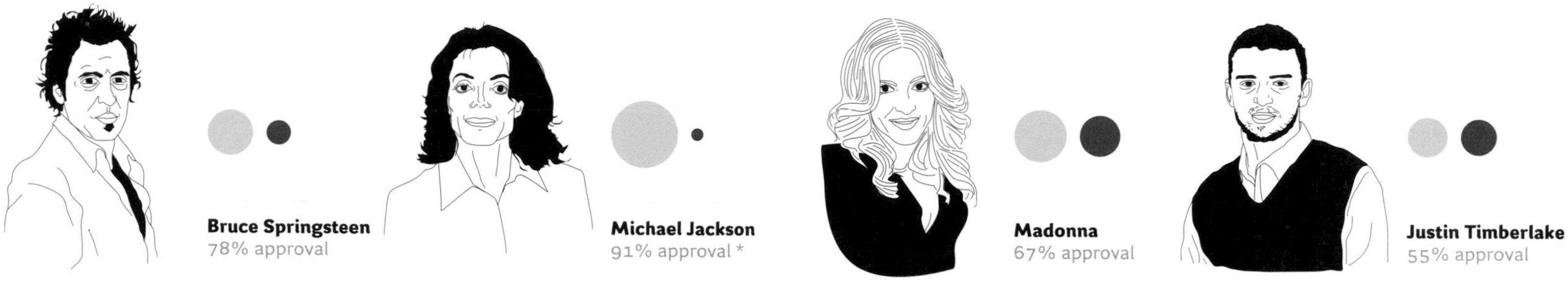

Rappers

Idols

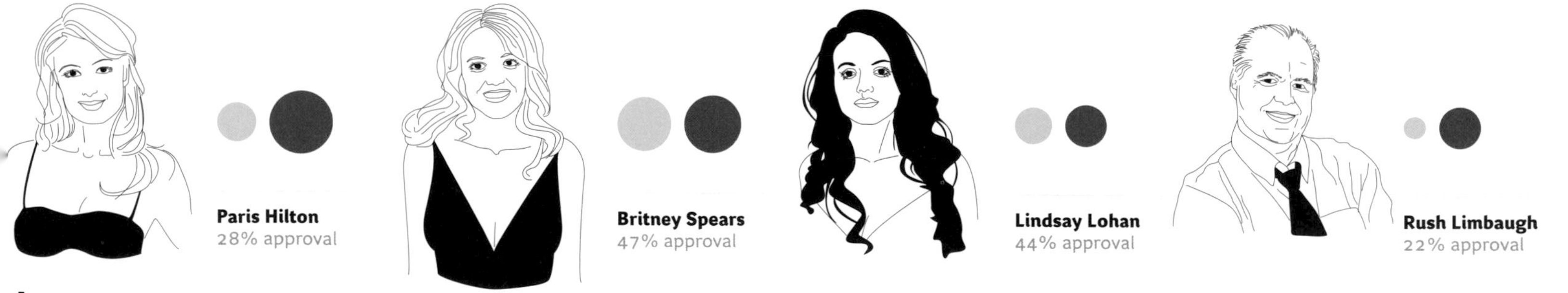

Icons

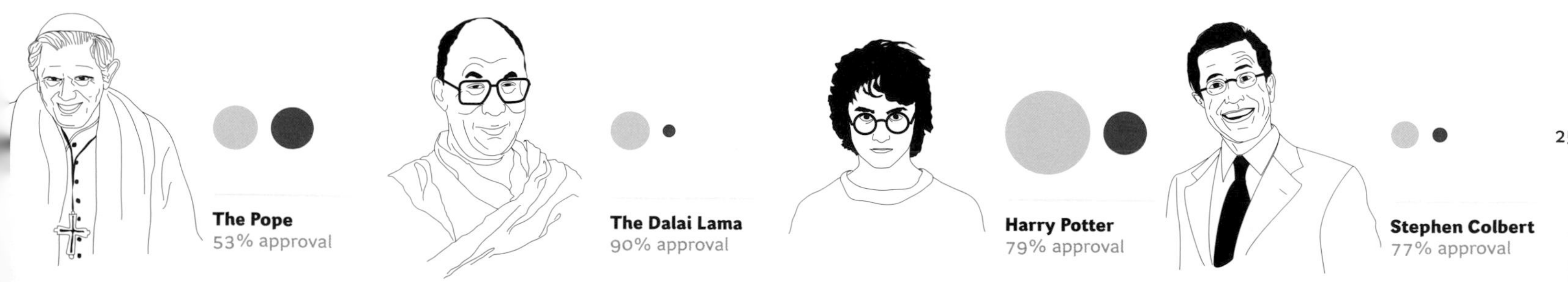

Feeling the Calendar and the Clock

A calendrical (and chronological) view of our feelings

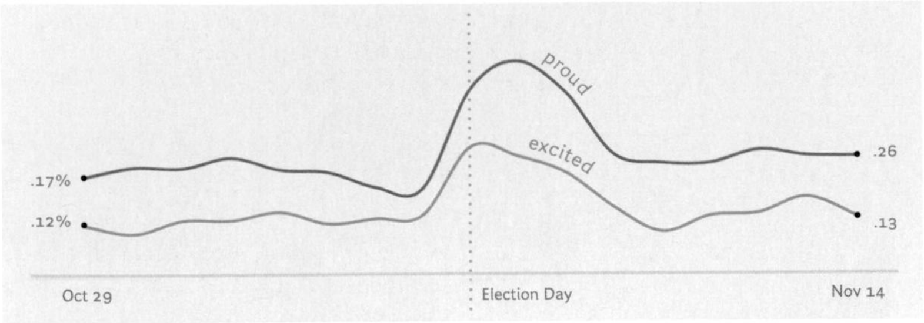

Obama's Election Day / Nov. 4, 2008
There was a dramatic spike in excitement and a swelling sense of pride, which lingered for several days after the election, during the palpable state of national euphoria.

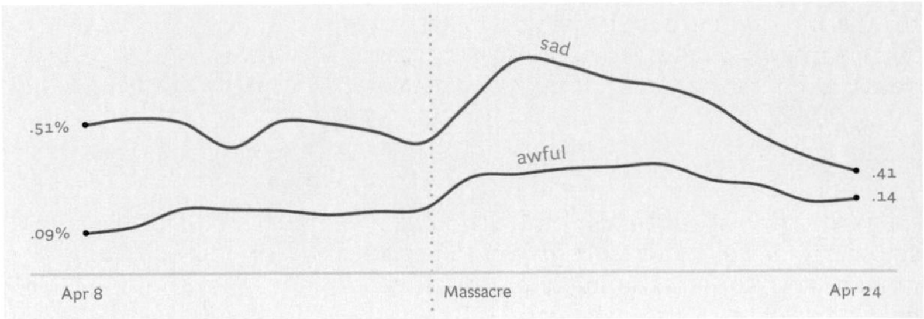

Virginia Tech Massacre / Apr. 16, 2007
There was a steady rise in sadness and feeling awful, both of which remained high for some time afterward, taking about a week to return to normal levels.

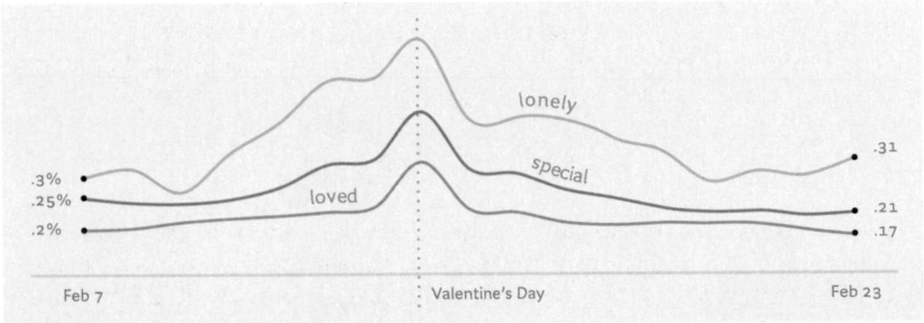

Valentine's Day / 2006–2008 average
Loneliness sees the biggest rise, starting a few days before Valentine's Day and remaining high for a few days afterwards. Feeling special and loved is also typical of the holiday.

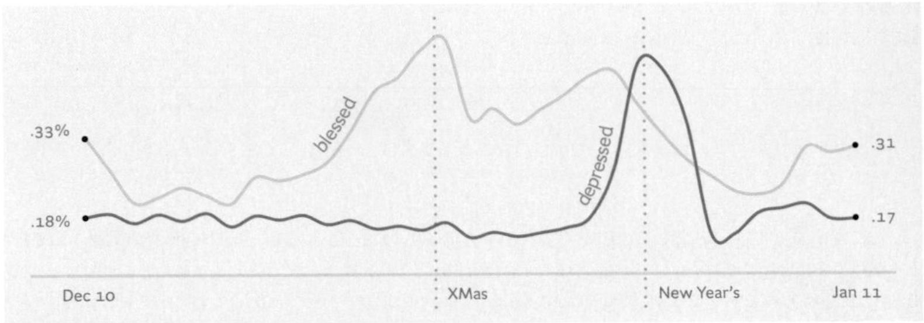

Christmas / New Year's / 2006–2008 average
Feeling blessed is common during the holidays, when people are home with the family. Depression rises sharply just before the new year. Back to business as usual in January.

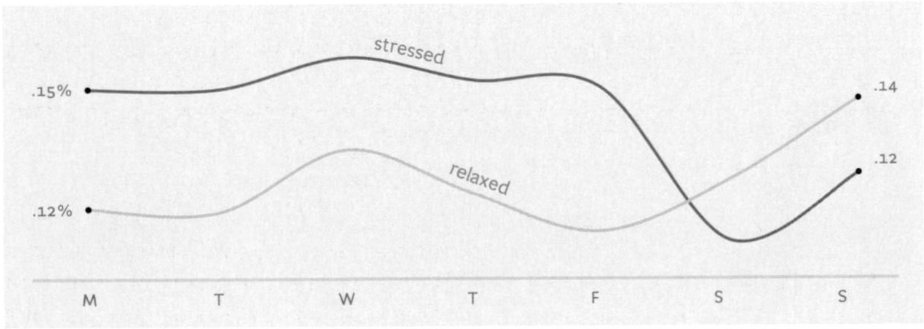

Stressful Weeks
Stress is high throughout the work week, but begins to decline on Friday, just as relaxation starts to rise, climbing to its Sunday high. Stress begins again on Sunday.

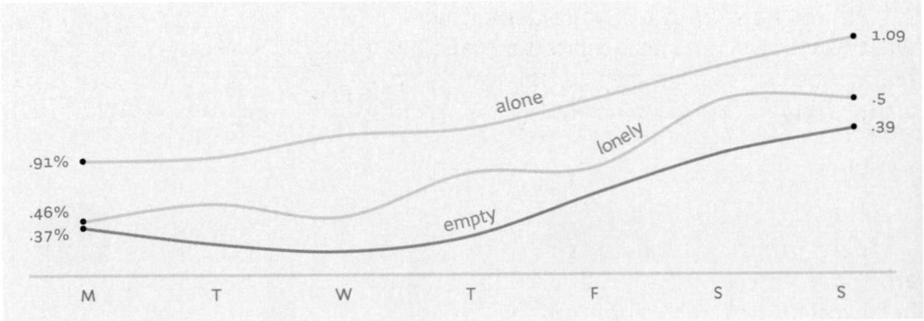

Lonely Weekends
Loneliness and emptiness rise steadily during the week, peaking on Sunday. Saturday night is the loneliest of all, which can make Monday (the least lonely day) a welcome relief.

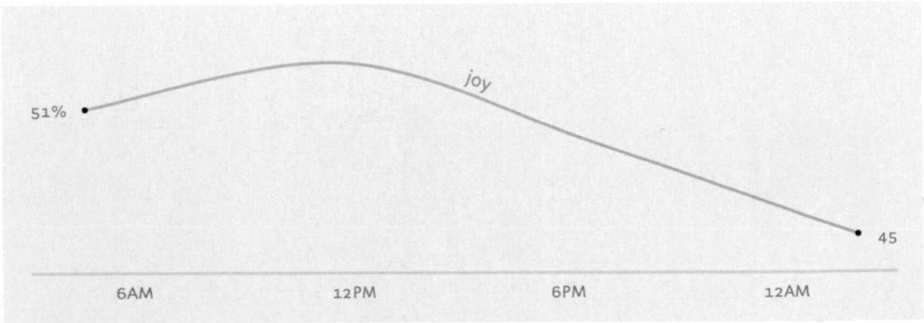

Joyful Mornings
Joy is high in the morning, and peaks just before lunchtime, before beginning its steady decline through the rest of the day as food coma and fatigue set in.

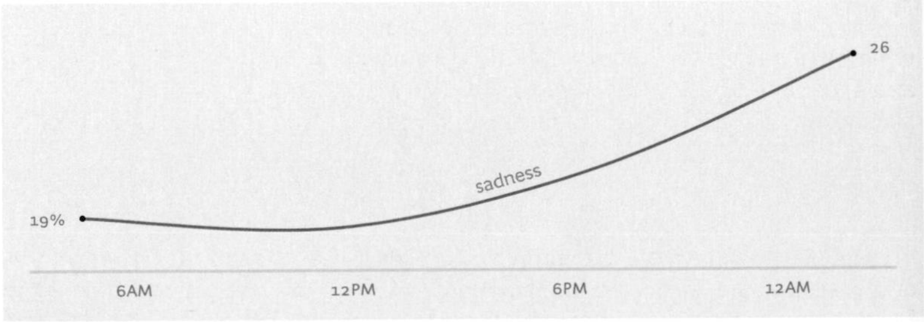

Sad Nights
Sadness is low in the morning, lowest around lunchtime, and begins to rise as the day presses on, peaking just before we go to sleep.

12:00 AM

• i don't feel like i have people i can trust people that i can call at **12am** because i can't stop crying and i want to hurt myself i used to have those people even if it was just one now i have none

1:00 AM

• i was home in bed by **1am** but woke feeling like the bottom of an ashtray in an irish bar • i don't feel like arguing about something i can't change when it's **1am**

2:00 AM

• i feel bad for leaving in the middle of the night during the best post-sex cuddling i've ever felt but i hadn't eaten all day and mcdonald's was calling my name at **2am**

3:00 AM

• i've just been drinking alot partying doing stupid shit dealing with feelings hooking up with random guys at parties going to parks at **3am** drunk dialing people and alot of bad stuff

4:00 AM

• i woke up at **4am** today feeling so lonely and frightened • i crawled into bed with hilton at **4am** and fell asleep in his arms feeling very pleased to have someone to come home to

5:00 AM

• i feel knackered after being woken up by a seagull at **5am** i wish i could've blasted it across the street with both barrels of a shotgun instead i had to make do with shouting like hell at it

6:00 AM

• i will admit that the **6am** shoulder kisses and light arm rubbing made me feel so at peace • i woke up around **6am** feeling weirded out about a dream i had

7:00 AM

• i wish they would just go away along with all the dreams and all the make it fucking stop feelings at **7am** in the morning • i could wake up at **7am** and feel so fresh and eager to get to work

8:00 AM

• i had 2 cups at **8am** and i am still shaking my heart is racing and i feel like i could jump off a building and fly • i feel as if there is a huge black pit in my stomach and it's only **8am**

9:00 AM

• i woke up at **9am** feeling like i'd just won the lottery even though i'm broke • i woke up at around **9am** feeling pretty good because i got a lot of sleep for once

10:00 AM

• i opened my eyes at **10am** and after having some toast and some coffee i began to feel human again • i routinely sleep through alarms and generally do not feel alive before **10am**

11:00 AM

• i don't know how a cough medicine taken at 11pm can make me still feel drunk at **11am** but by george i am loaded • i just pretend i'm drunk at **11am** and i feel like a bad ass rock star

12:00 PM

• i did feel bad about the yelling and the tv watching but also congratulated myself that in a hellacious week i managed to hold off drinking at **12pm** which i think is a mark of good parenting

1:00 PM

• i walked out of my house at 8am feeling motivated and i walked back in around **1pm** feeling absolutely drained and wrecked • i woke up at **1pm** today feeling like refried ass

2:00 PM

• i think i woke up around **2pm** feeling completely numb i bit my lip and actually drew blood but i didn't feel it • i've started to feel tired and a bit dizzy in the afternoons around **2pm**

3:00 PM

• i feel myself wanting to scratch my eyes out around **3pm** everyday • i didn't begin to feel betrayed by you until about **3pm** when the headache and queasy stomach started to kick in

4:00 PM

• i felt really good for a while then around **4pm** i started to feel like utter crap • i just want to bury my head in a pillow and sleep or cry until about **4pm** and then i start to feel a little better

5:00 PM

• i was feeling annoyed between **5pm** and 7pm worst fucking time frame ever invented • i can't believe it's almost **5pm** i've accomplished nothing and i feel like crap about life in general

6:00 PM

• i love being able to go out for a run at **6pm** whenever i want to and end up looking sweaty and gross and feeling amazing • i left the office a little after **6pm** feeling very stressed and moody

7:00 PM

• i sat down last night around **7pm** and began writing up my thoughts and feelings • i feel like people don't do anything after **7pm** around here if it doesn't involve intoxication

8:00 PM

• i had an odd feeling that she might show up and surprise me so around **8pm** i started cleaning • i belong in a city not some small town where everything but the internet cafe closes at **8pm**

9:00 PM

• i feel like i've been on the run the entire day and it's now **9pm** and i can finally breathe • i feel like my left hand will permanently smell of artichoke since i've been holding one since **9pm**

10:00 PM

• having someone who will cope with my emotional extremes at **10pm** is a very good feeling • i usually feel i can't sleep before **10pm** but i guess i've been more exhausted than usual

11:00 PM

• i went to bed at a reasonable hour **11pm** but i still feel like crud • i finally got home after a long and eventful day at **11pm** feeling rested and yes even at peace with my life

A Hard Day's Night

Feelings felt mainly in the morning and feelings felt mainly at night (by percentage)

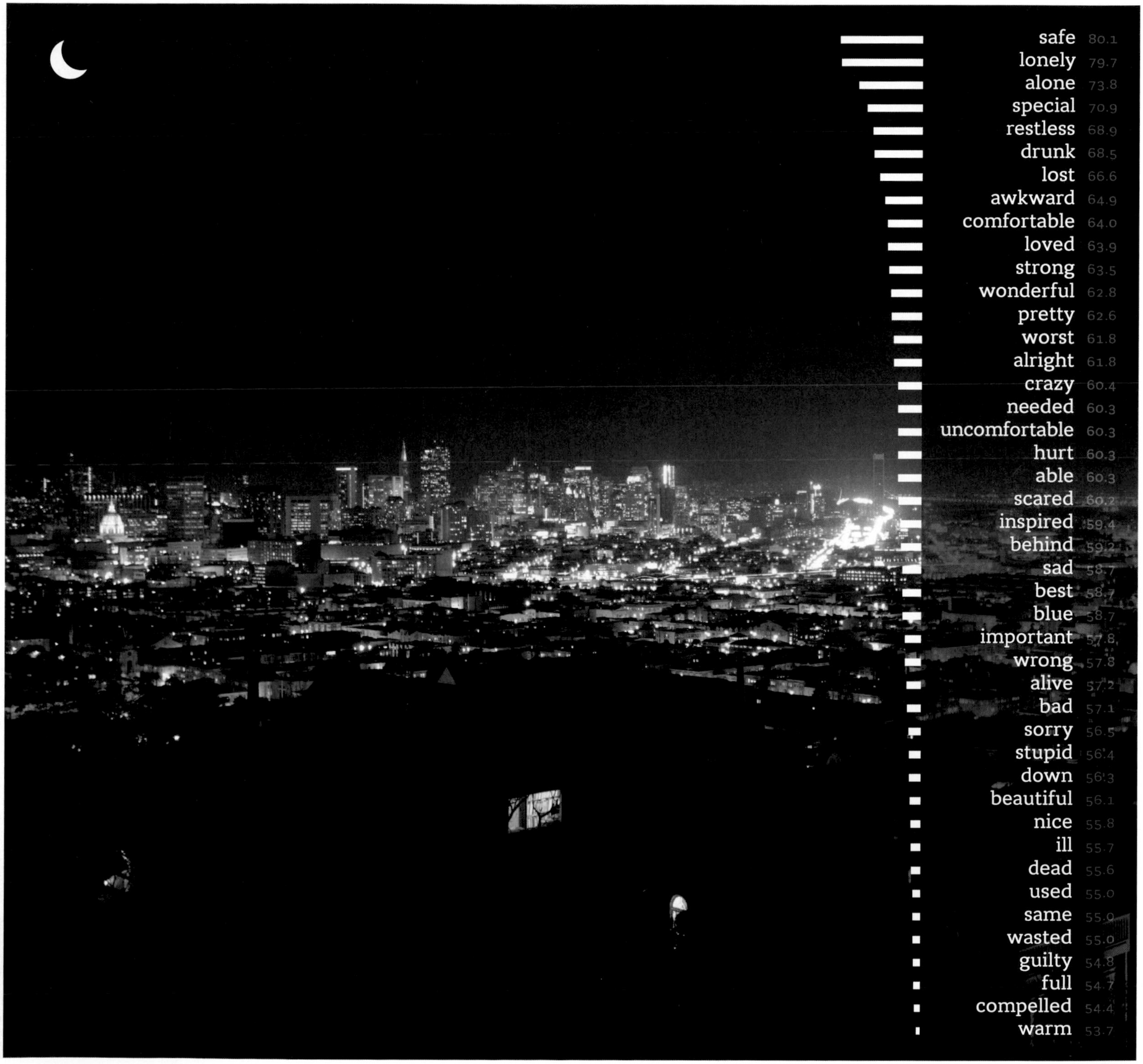
safe 80.1
lonely 79.7
alone 73.8
special 70.9
restless 68.9
drunk 68.5
lost 66.6
awkward 64.9
comfortable 64.0
loved 63.9
strong 63.5
wonderful 62.8
pretty 62.6
worst 61.8
alright 61.8
crazy 60.4
needed 60.3
uncomfortable 60.3
hurt 60.3
able 60.3
scared 60.2
inspired 59.4
behind 59.2
sad 58.7
best 58.7
blue 58.7
important 57.8
wrong 57.8
alive 57.2
bad 57.1
sorry 56.5
stupid 56.4
down 56.3
beautiful 56.1
nice 55.8
ill 55.7
dead 55.6
used 55.0
same 55.0
wasted 55.0
guilty 54.8
full 54.7
compelled 54.4
warm 53.7

The Geography of Emotion

Geographical insights into our feelings, focusing on the U.S., where the vast majority of *We Feel Fine*'s feelings originate

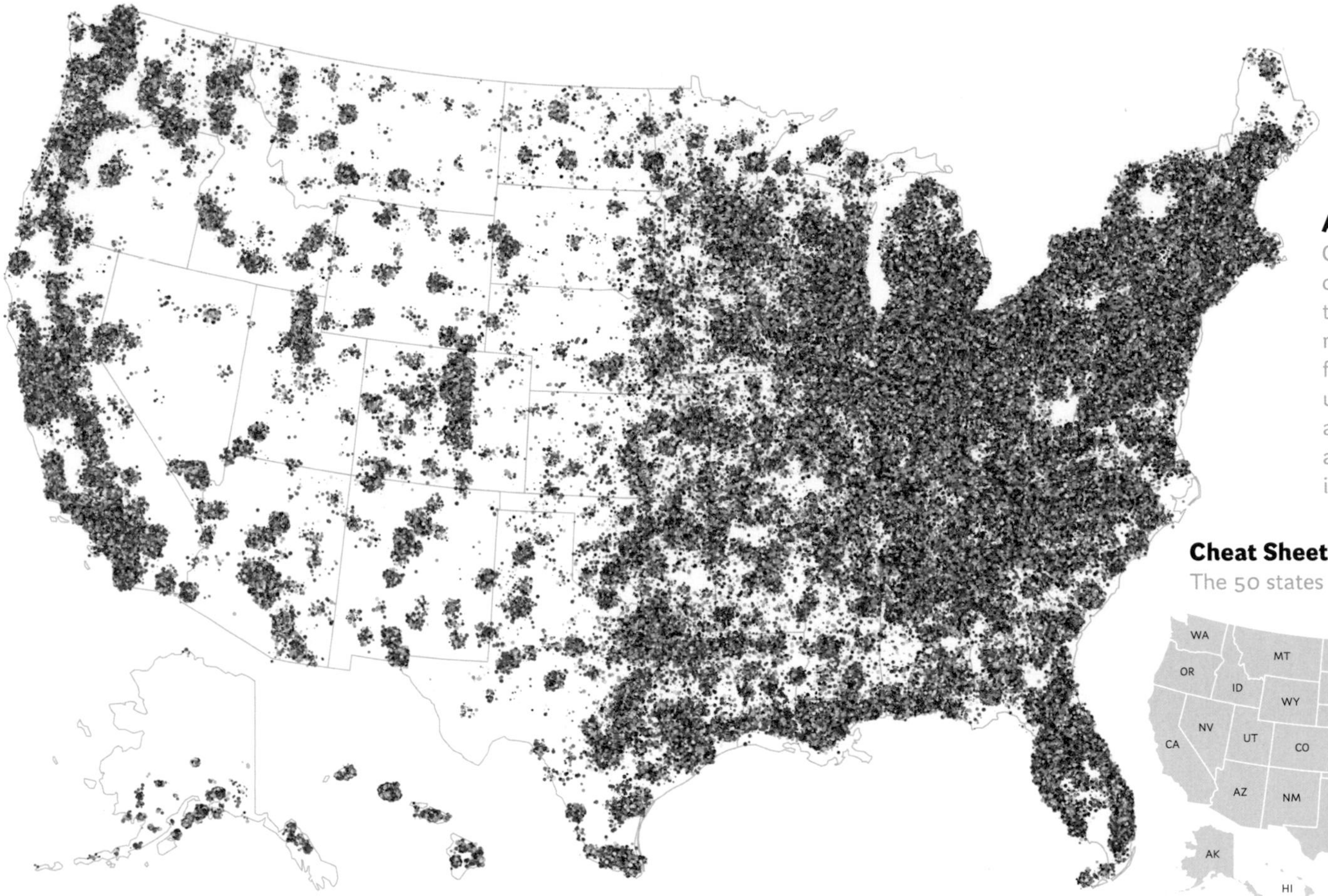

American Emotions

Geographic distribution of feelings throughout the United States. The majority of feelings come from people living in urban and suburban areas, a demographic reality affecting all the statistics in this book.

Cheat Sheet

The 50 states

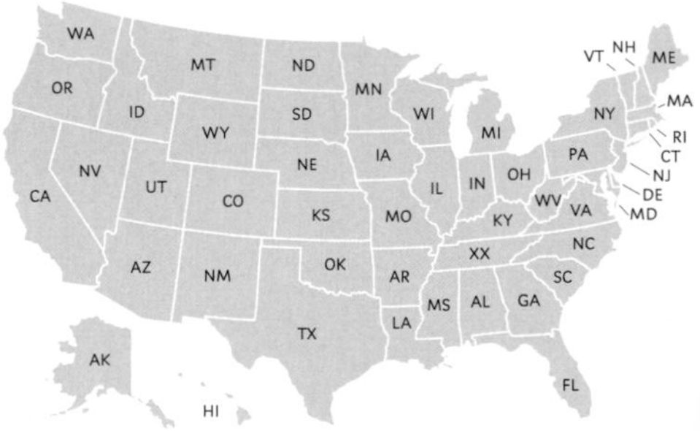

Most Religious Countries *

The U.S. leads the English speaking world in feelings about God.

United States	**.68%**
Australia	.58
Canada	.47
United Kingdom	.46

Most Sexual Countries *

The U.S. is slightly prudish about sexuality, while Canada is randy!

Canada	**.65%**
Australia	.63
United Kingdom	.62
United States	.52

Most Family-Oriented States

Rural farming states and Mormon Utah are big on family.

West Virginia	**.87%**
Arkansas	.82
Kansas	.81
Utah	.80
Oklahoma	.71
Kentucky	.70
Texas	.69
Tennessee	.68
North Carolina	.68
New Mexico	.67

States that are among the poorest 15 in the nation, in GDP per capita.

Most Career-Oriented States

States with high GDP and big cities are big on career.

New York	**.87%**
Illinois	.85
Massachusetts	.84
Minnesota	.84
Texas	.81
California	.78
Oregon	.78
Georgia	.77
Maryland	.75
New Jersey	.72

States that are among the richest 15 in the nation, in GDP per capita.

Most Drunken States

States with big college towns dominate the drunken list.

Wisconsin	**.22%**
Massachusetts	.21
Oregon	.20
Colorado	.19
Michigan	.18
Illinois	.18
Pennsylvania	.17
Arizona	.17
Indiana	.17
New York	.16

States with colleges on *The Princeton Review*'s Top Party Schools List.

* Only English-speaking countries

Rankings are by percentage of all feelings that contain the words "god," "sex," "family," "career," and "drunk," respectively.

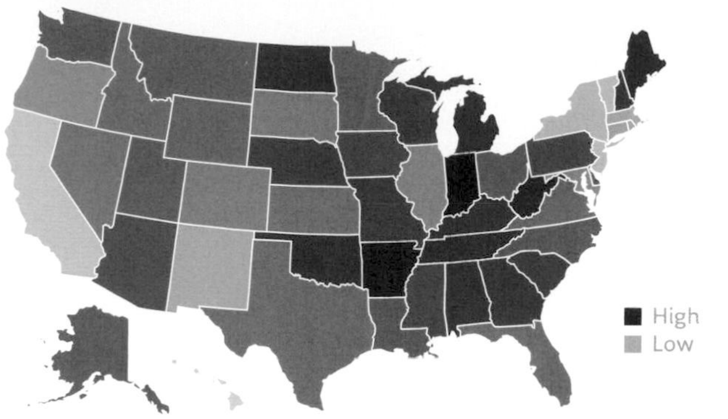

Feeling Happy

Some of the richest states (New York, California, Massachusetts, New Jersey, Illinois) are those that feel least happy, while many that focus on family (Arkansas, West Virgina, Tennessee, Oklahoma, Kentucky) feel happiest.

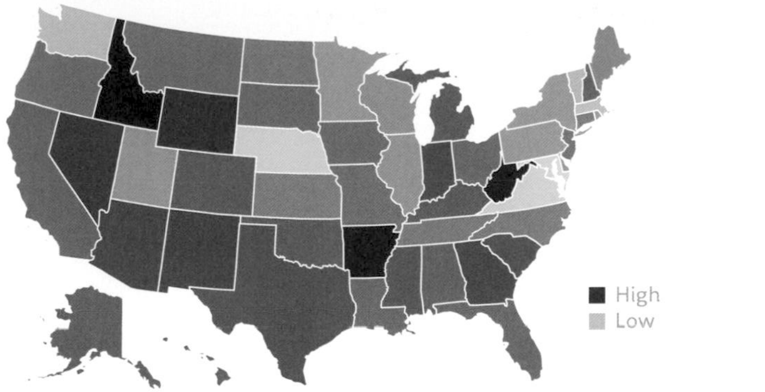

Feeling Lonely

Loneliness is highest in big states with small populations (Idaho, Wyoming, Nevada, New Mexico, Arizona), and in states with few or no big cities (West Virginia, Arkansas). Loneliness is lowest in Nebraska, Virginia, and Maryland.

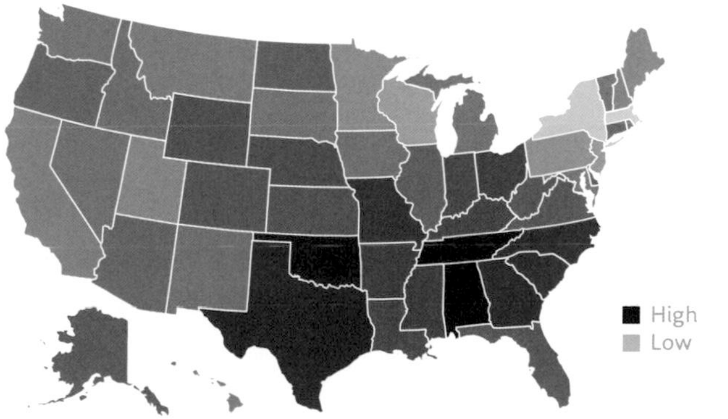

Feeling God

The so-called "Bible Belt" is also an emotional Bible Belt, as feelings about God are strongest in Oklahoma, Tennessee, Alabama, Texas, and Georgia. Feelings about God are lowest in New York, Massachusetts, and Wisconsin.

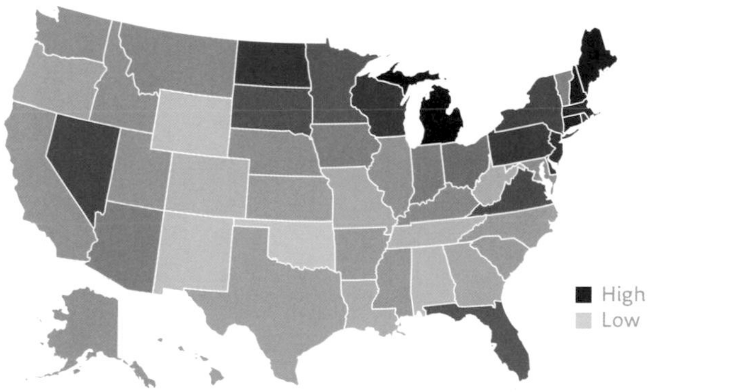

Feeling Sick

Cold weather seems to be the main cause of sickness, as chilly northeastern states (Maine, New Hampshire, Michigan, Pennsylvania, Wisconsin) feel most sick. States with older populations (Florida, Nevada), also feel quite sick.

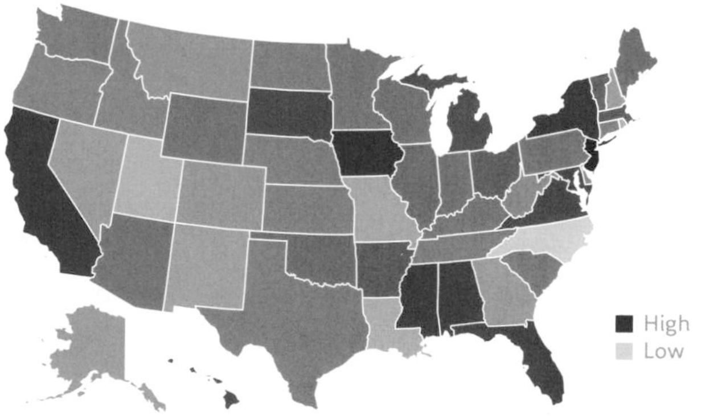

Feeling Fat

Some of the thinnest states (California, New York) are those that feel the fattest. Of the states with high obesity levels, some feel very fat (Mississippi, Alabama), while others don't feel too fat (Louisiana, Missouri), even though they should.

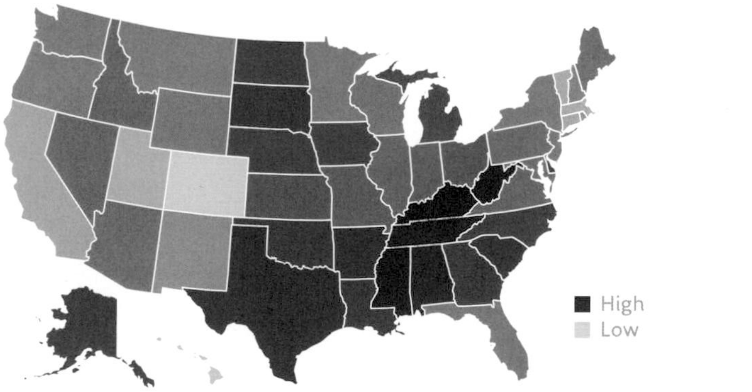

Being Fat

The 15 fattest states (in 2008, by obesity level) are Mississippi, West Virginia, Alabama, Louisiana, South Carolina, Tennessee, Kentucky, Oklahoma, Arkansas, Michigan, Indiana, Georgia, Missouri, Alaska, and Texas.

At a Glance: Feelings

Statistical summaries of the 50 feelings featured in this book

Feeling and its color	Rank in usage	Gender dominance	Age breakdown in 10-year blocks	Related feelings often felt by the same people	Main reasons for feeling this way	Prevalence over time % from 2006–2009	
afraid	142	**53%**	**40s**	**scared**, hurt, ashamed, mad	**love**, being hurt, loss, rejection	0.1	0.07
alive	43	**55%**	**50+**	**dead**, awake, strong, cool	**happiness**, pain, music, crying	0.27	0.25
alone	13	**53%**	**10s**	**unloved**, unwanted, isolated	**lovelessness**, friendlessness	0.96	0.56
ashamed	78	**55%**	**30s**	**disgusted**, embarrassed, afraid	**behavior**, actions, country, past	0.16	0.14
awesome	134	**52%**	**10s**	**cool**, excited, incredible	**love**, diet, friendship, good news	0.1	0.1
awful	46	**62%**	**20s**	**upset**, pissed, sick, disgusted	**fever**, flu, sleeplessness, overeating	0.29	0.26
bad	2	**54%**	**10s**	**bitchy**, rude, mad, nasty, mean	**the poor guy**, celebrities, money	4.65	3.52
beautiful	107	**64%**	**10s**	**sexy**, smart, ugly, touched	**good hair**, body image, confidence	0.11	0.11
better	1	**53%**	**10s**	**healthier**, stuffy, recovered	**feeling loved**, talking, sleeping	6.73	4.82
blessed	48	**65%**	**40s**	**thankful**, humbled, grateful	**love**, friendship, family, community	0.15	0.55
comfortable	10	**52%**	**50+**	**familiar**, relaxed, shy, nervous	**being at home**, job familiarity	0.81	1.15
cool	103	**54%**	**10s**	**refreshed**, calm, hip, naked	**air temperature**, breeze, popularity	0.13	0.13
crazy	76	**62%**	**20s**	**wild**, insane, helpless, mad	**fatigue**, losing control, opposite sex	0.15	0.1
depressed	40	**51%**	**10s**	**suicidal**, hopeless, angry	**no apparent reason**, clinical, winter	0.37	0.21
dirty	74	**63%**	**30s**	**gross**, disgusted, clean, cheap	**not showering**, voyeurism, sex	0.15	0.16
drunk	180	**54%**	**20s**	**sober**, giddy, insane, dizzy	**beer**, punch, wine, shots	0.12	0.03
empty	31	**51%**	**10s**	**hollow**, meaningless	**lovelessness**, loss, loneliness	0.4	0.3
excited	93	**51%**	**20s**	**nervous**, apprehensive, scared	**school**, friends, new job, vacation	0.11	0.15
fine	29	**60%**	**50+**	**okay**, awake, alright, regular	**waking up**, enough sleep, normality	0.38	0.6
good	3	**53%**	**40s**	**healthy**, fresh, happy, wonderful	**losing weight**, sleep, exercise	4.08	4.02
grateful	161	**62%**	**50+**	**humbled**, thankful, wonderful	**love**, friendship, family, opportunity	0.05	0.12
great	11	**56%**	**30s**	**sore**, amazing, wonderful	**exercise**, losing weight, sleep	0.94	1
guilty	4	**57%**	**40s**	**selfish**, mad, angry, ashamed	**money**, overeating, leaving, sex	1.58	1.72
happy	12	**53%**	**10s**	**content**, joyful, sad, satisfied	**love**, friendship, school, family	0.93	0.82
helpless	75	**57%**	**40s**	**hopeless**, suicidal, useless	**losing control**, pain, illness	0.17	0.12

Feeling and its color	Rank in usage	Gender dominance	Age breakdown in 10-year blocks	Related feelings often felt by the same people	Main reasons for feeling this way	Prevalence over time % from 2006–2009
horrible	26	61%	10s	**mad**, ugly, selfish, upset	**illness**, hurting others, money	0.5 – 0.32
human	112	56%	50+	**real**, awake, normal, capable	**sleep**, showering, bath, exercise	0.11 – 0.12
hurt	32	59%	10s	**angry**, abused, rejected	**pain**, love, betrayal, harsh words	0.37 – 0.28
jealous	174	55%	10s	**envious**, insecure, angry	**couples**, ex, romantic intrigue	0.07 – 0.07
lonely	22	52%	10s	**unloved**, isolated, homesick	**friendlessness**, lovelessness	0.65 – 0.41
lost	15	54%	10s	**confused**, clueless, unsure	**loss of friendship**, missing love	0.83 – 0.58
loved	35	60%	10s	**appreciated**, respected	**relationships**, friendship, family, god	0.4 – 0.41
lucky	34	55%	50+	**wonderful**, thankful, grateful	**significant other**, friends, family	0.29 – 0.54
miserable	98	52%	50+	**unhappy**, depressed, hopeless	**ilnness**, sleeplessness, school, job	0.17 – 0.14
naked	171	54%	50+	**bare**, exposed, pure, vulnerable	**no clothes**, missing accessory	0.06 – 0.07
normal	64	52%	50+	**human**, numb, average, healthy	**meds**, sleep, coffee, recovery	0.2 – 0.18
old	17	52%	40s	**aged**, worn, ancient, mature	**age**, pain, kids, fatigue	0.72 – 0.67
overwhelmed	67	63%	40s	**pressured**, stressed, frustrated	**love**, school, business, emotions	0.18 – 0.19
proud	56	52%	50+	**ashamed**, smart, brave	**myself**, country, achievements	0.19 – 0.27
sad	14	58%	50+	**angry**, depressed, disappointed	**love**, loneliness, depression	0.8 – 0.76
sexy	173	64%	30s	**gorgeous**, attractive, naughty	**being loved**, clothing, black lingerie	0.06 – 0.09
sick	7	55%	10s	**dizzy**, tired, nauseous, sore	**eating**, headache, common cold	1.49 – 0.88
small	73	52%	40s	**insignificant**, unimportant	**insignificance**, god, the universe	0.15 – 0.27
sorry	6	51%	40s	**poor**, pathetic, homeless	**myself**, someone else, family, kids	1.2 – 1.28
special	36	54%	10s	**unique**, appreciated, valued	**being loved**, caring, birthdays, gifts	0.37 – 0.34
stupid	19	58%	10s	**worthless**, mad, pissed, dumb	**unrequited love**, sharing feelings	0.7 – 0.35
terrible	33	54%	10s	**upset**, poor, fucked, mad	**lost love**, hurting friends, pain	0.38 – 0.31
ugly	149	63%	10s	**unwanted**, fat, unloved	**being fat**, bad hair, fatigue	0.1 – 0.05
weird	21	52%	10s	**awkward**, strange, confused	**self-expression**, new emotions	0.62 – 0.41
young	90	52%	50+	**immature**, dumb, shy	**aging**, kids, hairstyle, fun	0.11 – 0.1

At a Glance: Everything Else

Statistical summaries of the 2 genders, 5 ages, 13 cities, 4 weathers, 6 holidays, and 10 topics featured in this book

Who

Who	Feeling count* 2006–2009	Emotiveness index	Happiness index	Sadness index	Top feelings in this group	Prevalence over time % from 2006–2009
Men	683,970	**3.0** / 10	**6.6** / 10	**2.8** / 10	**better**, good, bad, sorry, alone, down, great, lost, guilty	11.04 – 1.61
Women	985,764	**7.0** / 10	**5.9** / 10	**3.5** / 10	**better**, bad, good, sorry, alone, guilty, down, lost, sick	8.5 – 3.4
10s	1,523,290	**4.0** / 10	**4.6** / 10	**4.0** / 10	**better**, bad, good, sick, guilty, alone, down, sorry, happy	18.43 – 6.01
20s	2,312,671	**4.5** / 10	**6.1** / 10	**2.8** / 10	**better**, bad, good, guilty, sorry, sick, down, well, alone	28.68 – 5.33
30s	393,100	**7.5** / 10	**7.8** / 10	**1.7** / 10	**better**, good, bad, guilty, sorry, well, down, great	3.81 – 1.03
40s	90,222	**8.5** / 10	**8.6** / 10	**1.5** / 10	**better**, good, bad, sorry, guilty, well, down, great, alone	0.72 – 0.25
50+	23,865	**9.0** / 10	**9.0** / 10	**1.0** / 10	**better**, good, bad, well, guilty, great, sad, comfortable	0.18 – 0.09

Where

Where	Feeling count* 2006–2009	Population 2007 est.	GDP per capita 2007 $USD	Top feelings in this city	Prevalence over time % from 2006–2009
Boston	21,993	616,535	47,000	**better**, bad, good, guilty, well, sick, great, down	0.25 – 0.1
Chicago	44,698	2,836,658	51,100	**better**, good, bad, guilty, down, well, sorry, comfortable	0.55 – 0.17
London	43,767	7,355,400	62,423	**better**, bad, good, guilty, sorry, sick, down, ill, well, happy	0.5 – 0.15
Los Angeles	37,807	3,849,378	53,000	**better**, bad, good, guilty, sorry, down, sick, comfortable	0.41 – 0.15
Moscow	3,721	12,382,754	16,800	**good**, better, bad, sorry, happy, sad, down, alone, guilty	0.03 – 0.01
Mumbai	1,146	13,662,885	7,000	**good**, better, bad, happy, guilty, sad, sorry, down, different	0.01 – 0.01
New York	33,335	8,274,527	61,000	**better**, bad, good, guilty, well, comfortable, sorry, down	0.35 – 0.11
Paris	3,009	2,167,994	46,000	**better**, good, bad, guilty, sorry, down, tired, well, happy	0.03 – 0.02
San Francisco	25,966	764,976	58,000	**better**, good, bad, guilty, sick, well, down, great, sorry	0.27 – 0.12
Seattle	48,268	594,210	56,000	**better**, good, bad, guilty, well, sorry, sick, comfortable	0.61 – 0.24
Sydney	32,604	4,284,379	39,000	**better**, bad, good, sick, guilty, sorry, down, happy, tired	0.43 – 0.08
Tokyo	4,284	12,790,000	34,000	**better**, bad, good, sorry, lonely, comfortable, sick, well	0.03 – 0.02
Toronto	41,149	2,503,281	40,900	**better**, bad, good, guilty, sick, sorry, well, down, great	0.57 – 0.14

* Note that feeling counts don't add up to the total number of feelings in the *We Feel Fine* database, as demographic information for feelings is sometimes unavailable.

When

When	Feeling count* 2006–2009	Date of this holiday	Distinctive themes for this weather / holiday	Distinctive feelings for this weather / holiday
Sunny	276,679	N/A	**sun**, shine, rays, clouds, moon, melting	**bright**, cheerful, warm, lovely, optimistic, special, happy
Cloudy	638,876	N/A	**sunny**, rainy, skies, storm, silver lining	**gloomy**, dreary, cold, cool, depressed, afraid, lonely
Rainy	110,843	N/A	**pouring**, drops, gloomy, storm	**gloomy**, cold, dreary, cheerful, melancholy, miserable, sleepy
Snowy	22,565	N/A	**christmas**, mountains, icy, roads	**freezing**, cold, wet, peaceful, excited, alive, glad
Christmas	9,803	Dec 25	**santa**, holiday, gifts, spirit, tree	**festive**, cozy, joyful, magical, cheerful, spoiled, generous, excited, giddy
Election Day	13,290	Nov 4, 2008	**vote**, returns, november, patriotic	**patriotic**, confident, proud, depressed, beautiful, excited
Halloween	13,739	Oct 31	**costume**, candy, parties, dressing up	**excited**, lame, awesome, shitty, silly, blah, sexy, creative
July 4th	14,576	guess	**patriotic**, parade, celebration, citizens	**patriotic**, american, political, proud, excited, free
New Year's	23,160	Jan 1	**eve**, resolution, christmas, celebration	**hopeful**, drunk, happy, optimistic, excited, ready
Valentine's Day	14,683	Feb 14	**roses**, candy, couples, gifts, cards	**romantic**, cheesy, lonely, special, cute, forced, depressed, evil, fake

* Average annual count, normalized for crawler decay

Why

Why	Feeling count 2006–2009	Gender dominance	Age breakdown in 10-year blocks	Distinctive feelings about this theme	Related themes mentioned with this one	Prevalence over time % from 2006–2009
Blogging	10,325	• 57%	50+	**interesting**, public, boring	**rambling**, readers, venting	0.04 – 0.16
Body Image	64,645	• 52%	20s	**fat**, beautiful, ugly, sexy	**mirror**, makeup, scale, ass	0.95 – 1.04
Death	26,185	• 56%	10s	**numb**, scared, frightened	**agony**, suicide, mourning	0.2 – 0.17
Friendship	167,961	• 51%	10s	**supported**, close, supportive	**family**, coworkers, enemies	1.57 – 1.15
Kids	34,676	• 55%	30s	**blessed**, grateful, protective	**adults**, marriage, raising	0.2 – 0.35
Money	50,828	• 56%	10s	**generous**, rich, ambitious	**earning**, spending, saving	0.36 – 0.51
Relationships	54,002	• 53%	20s	**committed**, romantic, intmate	**commitment**, intimacy	0.41 – 0.42
Religion	6,860	• 54%	50+	**religious**, holy, trusting	**worship**, prayer, bible, faith	0.05 – 0.07
Sex	57,692	• 54%	30s	**sexual**, sexy, horny, naughty	**partner**, toy, lover, marriage	0.35 – 0.38
Work	323,616	• 52%	30s	**hectic**, stressful, busy	**quitting**, salary, desk, boss	2.51 – 2.56

The Buddha talking to his son, Rahula:

"...practice loving kindness to overcome anger. Loving kindness has the capacity to bring happiness to others without demanding anything in return. Practice compassion to overcome cruelty. Compassion has the capacity to remove the suffering of others without expecting anything in return. Practice sympathetic joy to overcome hatred. Sympathetic joy arises when one rejoices over the happiness of others and wishes others well-being and success. Practice non-attachment to overcome prejudice. Non-attachment is the way of looking at all things openly and equally. This is because that is. That is because this is. Myself and others are not separate. Do not reject one thing only to chase after another... I call these the four immeasurables. Practice them and you will become a refreshing source of vitality and happiness for others." –from Old Path White Clouds*, by Thich Nhat Hanh*

The Three Poisons

The Three Poisons (*Kilesa*) are said by Buddhism to be the root of all suffering.

Greed creates an inner hunger so that we always seem to be striving toward an unattainable goal. We mistakenly believe our happiness is dependent upon that goal, but once we attain it, we get no lasting satisfaction. Influenced by greed, we are never content.

- jealousy ● 0.07% of feelings
- desire ● 0.07%
- greed ● 0.02%
- lust ● 0.01%

Hatred reinforces our perception of duality and separation, thrusting us into vicious cycles of finding conflict and enemies everywhere, making us neurotic, never calm, and endlessly occupied with strategies of self-protection or revenge.

- anger ● 0.19% of feelings
- hatred ● 0.16%
- frustration ● 0.05%
- resentment ● 0.02%
- cruelty ● 0.01%

Ignorance is our wrong understanding of reality, our misperception of the way the world works, our inability to understand the nature of things exactly as they are, free of perceptual distortions. Influenced by delusion, we are not in harmony with ourselves, others, or with life.

- confusion ● 0.17% of feelings
- apathy ● 0.02%
- bewilderment ● 0.01%

The Four Immeasurables

The Four Immeasurables, or Sublime Attitudes (*Bramavihara*) are virtues that are said by Buddhism to be the essential nature of the enlightened heart. The Four Immeasurables provide antidotes to the Three Poisons.

Love (● 0.68% of feelings), or "loving-kindness," is defined as the unconditional desire for others to be happy, and is distinguished from selfish love, which is a form of greed. The opposites of love are hatred, anger, and aggression.

Compassion (● 0.01% of feelings) is defined as wanting others to be free from suffering, and is distinguished from pity, which is more distant. The opposite of compassion is cruelty.

Joy (● 1.48% of feelings), or more specifically "sympathetic joy," is defined as the unselfish happiness for others' happiness. The opposites of joy are jealousy and resentment.

Equanimity (● 0.22% of feelings), or "non-attachment," describes an even-minded attitude toward all beings and a clear-minded tranquility. Equanimity should not be mistaken for indifference, or "not caring," which is a form of egotism. Equanimity is the basis for unconditional, altruistic love, compassion, and joy for other's happiness. The opposites of equanimity are apathy, attachment, lust, and desire.

8 Conclusion Wrapping up

Tags: presence, awareness, non-attachment, acceptance

On May 30th, 2004, Lucy May Thompson was born in West Yorkshire, England, not breathing. Her father, Neil, thought she was dead. "At the same time," he writes on his blog, "I am telling Dawn 'Everything is OK, the baby is fine,' knowing how ridiculous it sounds. I couldn't tell Dawn what I really thought, not after the hell she had been through… I watched them carry Lucy's lifeless body to the corner of the room where they placed a mask over her mouth and manually squeezed the bag to try to get air into her lungs. This was obviously having no effect. All the while, Dawn was asking what was going on because from where she lay she could see nothing. I kept telling her it was fine and everything was going to be OK. She said to me, 'She's dead, isn't she?'"

Lucy May did not die that day. The hospital staff brought her to the neonatal unit and were able to revive her. But because of oxygen starvation, she developed cerebral palsy, epilepsy, and visual impairment, and cannot coordinate her movements. "She is a beautiful little girl," writes Neil, "who has had more than her fair share of bad luck and I am immensely proud of all she has achieved."[1]

Around 534 BC, a 29-year-old Indian prince named Siddhartha Gautama saw suffering for the first time. Having lived a sheltered life in his multiple palaces, he had not known old age or poverty, and upon seeing them decided to leave his kingdom and enter a monastic life, hoping to better understand the nature of suffering.

After years of asceticism and meditation, Siddhartha, later known as Buddha, came up with the principles of what would be known as Buddhism. He came to the conclusion that suffering is a natural part of life, and that the root cause of suffering is attachment, whether it be attachment to people, ideas, or even life itself. He reasoned that change is an inevitable part of life and we are bound to lose the things to which we become attached, and consequently we are bound to suffer in their loss or the fear of their loss. Conversely, attachment can also cause acquisitiveness and greed, which in their insatiability also lead to suffering.

His antidote to suffering was through a present, nonjudgmental awareness of all that arises. He believed that with awareness of the true nature of things, unselfish love and equanimity reign, and suffering is diminished. He preached that when an emotion arises, one should not cling to it, but neither should one suppress it. He suggested instead that one should take a Middle Way, compassionately forming a precise picture of the emotion and then letting it go.[2]

A couple hundred years later and several thousand miles away, the Stoic philosophers in Athens and Rome were preaching a similar philosophy. Their fundamental tenet was that fate is fickle, and that people have little control over what happens to them. However, reasoned the Stoics, it is possible to gain inner freedom even in the face of external uncertainty, by focusing on and maintaining an internal harmony with one's present circumstance and a Stoic nonattachment to externalities.[3]

Contrary to common belief, the Stoics did not encourage the suppression of emotions. Rather, like Buddha and his followers, they believed that ridding oneself of excess attachments to things outside of one's control would lead to the cessation of destructive emotions such as greed, hatred, fear, and envy. Also, like the Buddhists, the Stoics did not confuse non-attachment with aloofness. To the Stoics, non-attachment meant not holding on too tightly to any storyline, knowing that the world is always changing.

From left: Neil Thompson holding his daughter, Lucy May Thompson; a healthier Lucy outside in the park; Neil and Lucy on a slide.

Neil and Dawn had originally planned to name their daughter Holly May. "I don't know why but we changed our minds at the last minute and called her Lucy May and not Holly May," writes Neil on his blog on December 11th, 2007. "Lucy is such a pretty name and it has always suited her... For a long time after and still now sometimes I think about Holly. Holly was the little girl that didn't come to us. She was the little girl that we lost. Lucy came to us and I love her to bits and now I wouldn't be without her but the baby I dreamt about and prepared for when Dawn was pregnant was Holly. I can't help feeling that I lost Holly when Lucy was born and I think it took me longer to accept Lucy because I was grieving for that other little girl. In a small way I probably always will. I loved her but I never got to know her. I pictured her taking her first steps and saying her first words. I imagined her wedding and I thought about meeting her children for the first time. I see her now in all the little three year olds that I meet or see running around the supermarket. I wonder what she would have been like now and I feel cheated that I never got to find out. I have even thought about having a funeral for Holly May, planting a tree, making a small memorial or just something to signify that she is lost to me so that I can move on."[4]

A couple thousand years after Buddha and Marcus Aurelius, a young Jewish psychiatrist named Viktor Frankl was brought to Auschwitz. During his time in the concentration camp, he observed his own psychological reactions to the brutal circumstances under which he lived. He came up with a set of remarkable conclusions: "Between stimulus and response," he said, "there is a space. In that

Lucy looking off into the sun

space lies our freedom and power to choose our response. In those choices lie our growth and happiness."[5]

Frankl, like Buddha and the Stoics, suggested making use of that space between stimulus and response to obtain a precise, compassionate, and unattached view of the emotion. He describes an experience at the concentration camp where he was in tears from pain, had terrible sores from wearing torn shoes while marching in the dead of winter, and was preoccupied with his cold and hunger. He writes: "I became disgusted with the state of affairs which compelled me, daily and hourly, to think of only such trivial things. I forced my thoughts to turn to another subject. Suddenly I saw myself standing on the platform of a well-lit, warm, and pleasant lecture room. In front of me sat an attentive audience on comfortable upholstered seats. I was giving a lecture on the psychology of the concentration camp! All that oppressed me at that moment became objective, seen and described from the remote viewpoint of science. By this method I succeeded somehow in rising above the situation, above the sufferings of the moment, and I observed them as if they were already of the past. Both I and my troubles became the object of an interesting psychoscientific study undertaken by myself. What does Spinoza say in his Ethics?—'Affectus, qui passio est, desinit esse passio siulatque eius claram et distinctam formamus ideam.' Emotion, which is suffering, ceases to be suffering as soon as we form a clear and precise picture of it."[6]

By putting their emotions into words on their blogs, the millions of bloggers in the *We Feel Fine* database are also taking a step back, observing their emotions, and forming a more clear and precise picture of what it is they are feeling. In doing so, they are able to rise above their emotions. Little did they know what a beautiful collective picture they were building in the process.

"I like to think of Lucy as our surprise gift," writes Neil at the conclusion of his December 11th, 2007 blog post. "It is true that I didn't expect to have a daughter like Lucy and if I had expected it I probably would have been filled with dread. What Lucy has given us is something completely new and wonderful. Lucy shines like the brightest star on all our lives and continues to teach us that everything is not quite as it seems. I look back on the last three and a half years and feel really proud of everything she has achieved and also of everything Lucy has given us. I have a wonderful daughter in Lucy and I wouldn't change her for anything. Holly May will always be a memory of a life I used to have and I won't forget her. I will probably always selfishly miss doing all the normal things I planned to do with her but I like my new life and I love that Lucy is part of it. Lucy May has brought us so much more than I ever expected and she has given us a new and wonderful life."[7] ♥

1. Lucy May Thumpson. http://littlelucymay.blogspot.com/2007/12/11dec07-holly-may.html
2. Hanh, Thich N. *The Heart of the Buddha's Teaching*. (New York: Broadway, 1999).
3. Irvine, William B. *A Guide to the Good Life: The Ancient Art of Stoic Joy*. (New York: Oxford University Press, 2009).
4. Lucy May Thompson. See 1.
5, 6. Frankl, V. *Man's Search for Meaning*. (Kansas City, MO: Beacon Press, 1959).
7. Lucy May Thompson. See 1.

The Data

Average number of feelings collected per day : **10,043**
Total number of feelings in database : **12,989,739**
Total number of people in database : **2,231,263**
Number of known women : **985,763**
Number of feelings from those women : **1,311,802**
Number of known men : **333,277**
Number of feelings from those men : **683,970**

Total number of images collected by *We Feel Fine* : **2,388,363**
Number selected by viewers for online gallery : **6,824**

Number of feelings from teenagers : **1,523,290**
Number from people in their 20s : **2,312,671**
Number from people in their 30s : **393,100**
Number from people in their 40s : **90,222**
Number from people in their 50s : **23,865**
Number from people in their 60s : **7,048**
Number from people in their 70s : **3,643**

Number of feelings from the United States : **4,260,050**
Number from Canada : **392,701**
Number from the United Kingdom : **329,858**
Number from Australia : **219,526**
Number from Singapore : **116,067**
Number from China : **16,435**
Number from France : **9,591**
Number from India : **8,489**
Number from South Africa : **5,064**
Number from Iraq : **1,214**
Number from North Korea : **16**

Number of feelings from people in Chicago : **44,698**
Number from people in New York : **33,335**
Number from people in San Francisco : **25,966**
Number from people in Paris : **3,009**
Number from people in Baghdad : **151**

Number of occurrences of the feeling "better" : **429,876**
Number of the feeling "happy" : **72,839**
Number of the feeling "sad" : **68,826**
Number of the feeling "alive" : **22,916**
Number of the feeling "dead" : **12,696**
Number of the feeling "beautiful" : **9,960**
Number of the feeling "ugly" : **7,353**
Number of the feeling "horny" : **1,376**

Number of sentences that contain the word "work" : **347,896**
Number that contain the word "play" : **106,895**
Number that contain the word "friends" : **167,961**
Number that contain the word "family" : **72,895**
Number that contain the word "god" : **84,817**
Number that contain the word "sex" : **61,612**

Number of people who felt loved on Valentine's Day : **242**
Number who felt lonely : **172**

The Code

Number of spoken languages tracked by *We Feel Fine* : **1**
Number of computer languages used by *We Feel Fine* : **7**
Total number of lines of code : **26,377**
Number of lines of backend code (Perl, MySQL) : **11,361**
Number of lines of frontend code (Processing, HTML, PHP, Javascript) : **9,104**
Number of lines of book statistics code (Java) : **3,132**
Number of lines of book graphics code (Processing) : **2,780**
Number of servers : **5**
Number of servers named optimusprime : **1**

The Book

Number of publishers we pitched : **12**
Number of offers * : **6**
Number of rejections ** : **6**

Number of hours worked on this book : **9,700**
Number of high-fives the authors exchanged while writing this book : **147**
Number of stern lectures the authors received from their agent : **3**
Number of swims Jonathan took while writing this book : **286**
Number of bags of shredded mild cheddar cheese Sep ate while writing this book *** : **56**
Average number of phone calls per day between the authors while writing this book : **3.1**
Number of e-mails exchanged between authors while writing this book : **3,867**
Number of cross-country flights taken by authors to meet with each other : **12**
Number of bloggers contacted to seek photo usage permissions for this book : **12,765**
Number who responded : **1,973**
Number who agreed : **1,629**
Number who thought our inquiries were spam : **a shitload**
Number of e-mails exchanged with bloggers : **14,956**
Number of bloggers with photos in this book : **1,143**
Number of montages in this book : **1,148**

The Bank

Number of dollars received for this book (advance) : **150,000**
Percentage of sales (once advance is repaid) the authors will receive in royalties : **10**
Number of dollars spent for our servers : **10,367**
Number of dollars spent for bandwidth and colocation (2005-2009) : **15,480**
Number of dollars in commission paid to the authors' agent : **22,500**
Number of dollars spent paying the authors' research staff : **134,238**
Number of dollars spent buying books for the bloggers who contributed : **25,381**
Number of dollars the authors netted from this book at publication time : **(−57,966)**

The Rest

Number of Google search results for "wefeelfine.org" : **42,800**
Number of pageviews for wefeelfine.org : **6,426,018**
Number of Sep's parents who think he's handsome : **1**
Number of Jonathan's parents who "don't understand the concept of pointing and clicking" as it relates to computers : **1**
Number of Jonathan's parents who think he should forget computers and go back to oil painting : **2**

* We had offers from Bloomsbury, Clarkson Potter, Gotham, HarperPerennial, Scribner, and Simon Spotlight Entertainment.
** The publishers who passed were Collins, HarperStudio, Hyperion, Little Brown and Co., Riverhead, and Viking Studio.
*** Sep loves shredded mild cheddar cheese.

Index

Blue text denotes a montage, indicating its page number and position on page.

Credits

Sep Kamvar
Author
San Francisco, CA

Jonathan Harris
Author + Designer
Brooklyn, NY

Hannah Johnson
Research Assistant
Sherman Oaks, CA

Raul Gomez Valverde
Design Assistant
Madrid, Spain

Matt Vidulich
Research Assistant
Oakland, CA

Kate Derrick
Project Assistant
Louisville, KY

Jesse Ashlock
Research Assistant
New York, NY

Dayna Crozier
Research Assistant
St. Louis, MO

Whitney Frick
Editor
New York, NY

Beth Wareham
Editor
New York, NY

Kate Bittman
Publicist
New York, NY

Erin Malone
Agent
New York, NY

Emily Ebbers
Handwriter
San Carlos, CA

Hannah Knafo
Handwriter
Brooklyn, NY

Jackie McGraw
Handwriter
Atherton CA

Mandy Mohindra
Handwriter
Milpitas, CA

Lynn Nguyen
Handwriter
Milpitas, CA

Jessica Tran
Handwriter
Milpitas, CA

Selected Photo Contributors

Listed by montage web code (includes all contributors who submitted portraits)

Photo Contributors Listed by montage web code (see p. 21 for details)

C1 Michelle Pickett Chicago, IL, **C2** Jessica Sanchez, **C3** Elise Watertown, NY, **C4** Sandy Martin Rockwall, TX, **C5** Brittany Jane Mrva Valrico, FL, **C6** Rachel Elaine Arnold Port Saint Lucie, FL, **C7** Rosie Hardy, **C8** Isabel Brown Raleigh, NC, **C9** Jessica Yong Kuala Lumpur, Malaysia, **C10** Jami Dwyer, **C11** Jennie Sommerkamp Germany, **C12** Courtney Tran Burnaby, BC, **C13** Chalica Pack, **C14** Jim Looper Greenwood, SC, **C16** Judith Fernando Phillippines, **C16** Kirsty, **C17** Shannon Ward Baltimore, MD, **C18** Rob Jonesboro, GA, **C19** Kate Stimac, **9A** Amanda Seebaugh Parkersburg, WV, **9B** Neusa Quaresma Hollywood, FL, **9C** Elsa De la Fuente Medellín, Colombia, **10A** Jamie Naughton Redlands, CA, **10B** Claire Cameron Toronto, **10C** Joodie, **10D** Jenny Hughes DuBois, PA, **10E** Shinobu Takagi Nascimento Yokosuka, Japan, **11A** Sara Luzia, **11B** Sonny Semansco Japan, **11C** Amy Belk New York, NY, **11D** Lauren Sweetland Sacramento, CA, **11E** Pamela Boutin Atlanta, GA, **11F** Genevieve Flynn Halifax, Nova Scotia, **11G** Kristie Gould, **11H** Katarzyna Slapak Krakow, Poland, **11I** Abby Rosenberg, **14A** Meghan Orr Wheaton, IL, **30A** Nathaniel Ndosi Williamstown, NJ, **30B** Tono Rondone Orlando, FL, **30C** Azami Abd Rahman Kuala Lumpur, Malaysia, **30D** Matt Gilluley Manchester, UK, **30E** Jeff Rogers New York, NY, **30F** Paul Dyson Calgary, AB, **30G** Michael Killingbeck Anderson, CA, **31A** Chris Calavas, **31B** Corey Middleville, MI, **31C** Scott R. Moulaison Jersey City, NJ, **31D** Franz Gabriel San Francisco, CA, **32A** Lyndal Tucciarone North Parramatta, Australia, **32B** Emma Neely Butler, PA, **32C** Diane Dennis UK, **33A** Natalie Johnson Leicestershire, UK, **33B** Jennifer Van Grove San Diego, CA, **33C** Paula Andrea Silva Fajardo La Serena, Chile, **33D** A.J. Kenneally Melbourne, Australia, **33E** Karen Coleman Minneapolis, MN, **33F** Erin Van Krimpen Brisbane, Australia, **33G** Nikki Hawkes Clayton, NJ, **34A** Reid Michael Garnett Lake Worth, FL, **35A** Brian Shafer Schenectady, NY, **35B** Kelsey Elyse Sullivan Cabot, AR, **35C** Elena Lin Singapore, **35D** Matthew Redente New Haven, CT, **35E** Tatianna Nasr Singapore, **36A** Michael J. Dowswell Dumfries, Scotland, **36B** Leonora Epstein New York, NY, **36C** Terri Van Benthuysen Point Pleasant, NJ, **36D** Cornelia Kofler Vienna, Austria, **36E** Alexey Aleshin Moscow, Russia, **37A** Jessica Van Beber, **37B** Sara Booth Burlington, ON, **37C** Eve Kemp Auckland, New Zealand, **37D** Jennifer Egurrola Auckland, New Zealand, **38A** Joe Plocki Greenville, SC, **38B** Julien R. Aleksandres Lexington, KY, **38C** Duane Romanell Belleville, NJ, **38D** Angela Ward-Brown Winchester, UK, **38E** Michael Verhoef Trentham, Australia, **39A** Stephanie Newton Simi Valley, CA, **39B** Ginger Davis Allman Springfield, MO, **39C** Jason Farrell Beaver Dams, NY, **39D** Karen Rubado Auckland, New Zealand, **39E** Jonathan Harris Brooklyn, NY, **40A** Tonya Blowe, **40B** Robin Vanyi-Anderson Hoquian, WA, **40C** Ginger Davis Allman Springfield, MO, **40D** Adrian Price Christchurch, New Zealand, **41A** Delia Nilson Yucca Valley, CA, **41B** K.R. Murali Krishna Bangalore, India, **41C** Michael Stephens Mishawaka, IN, **42A** Grace E. Davis Santa Cruz, CA, **42B** Tarn Peter, **42C** Katherine Stock Cascade Locks, OR, **42D** Steven Forrest Borrego Springs, CA, **42E** Stephen H. Foster, **43A** Thomas Peters Kalamazoo, MI, **43B** Susan M. Kennedy Sachse, TX, **43C** Judy Baxter Hahira, GA, **48A** Alexander Haga Kingsport, TN, **49A** Sarah Winfrey Whittier, CA, **49B** Fred Heurtin Baton Rouge, LA, **49C** Scott Craft Portsmouth, OH, **49D** Shannon Langdon Altus, OK, **50A** Sharon Walker Brisbane, Australia, **50B** Laura Kuah Rockville, MD, **50C** Ryan Tomorrow Brooklyn, NY, **50D** Veronica Lyons San Antonio, TX, **51A** Isha Gutierrez Miami, FL, **51B** Sascha Assbach Troisdorf, Germany, **51C** Catherine Henderson Springwood, Australia, **51D** Catherine Ehlers Somersworth, NH, **52A** Amy Deck Lancaster, PA, **52B** Stacy Wisegarver Champaign, IL, **52C** Janessa Douglas Lauderhill, FL, **53A** Jason Barbieri Middletown, CT, **53B** Trina Luciano Watertown, CT, **54A** Nadyne Kasta Montreal, QC, **54B** Brandon Lim Toronto, ON, **54C** Jennifer Florinki St. Lansing, MI, **55A** Claudia M. Trejo-Miller Brighton, CO, **55B** Roland Bouman Leiden, The Netherlands, **55C** Alex Guelff London, UK, **55D** Stephen Allinger Surrey, BC, **56A** Casha Arzola Valparaiso, IN, **56B** Josh Bisker New Rochelle, NY, **56C** Ryan Garwood West Lafayette, IN, **56D** Mitchell Campbell Windsor, ON, **56E** JP Norvell Chicago, IL, **57A** Ryan Curtis Elizabethtown, TN, **57B** Jennifer Wilmoth Orange, CA, **57C** Christopher Gutierrez Chicago, IL, **58A** Analiese Stinson Sutton, MA, **58B** Indira Birnie Chelsea, UK, **58C** Kamika Campbell Decatur, GA, **59A** Brad Knapp Dallas, TX, **59B** Leila-Anne Cavé Santa Rosa, CA, **60A** Nicole Sagert Ontario, **60B** Andrew Malone Somerville, MA, **60C** Kaylie Sim & Zackary Lee, **61A** Adrien Arnao Washburn, WI, **61B** Sneha Srivastava Uttarpradesh, India, **61C** Ward Pettibone Providence, RI, **61D** Kelly Price-Colston Fayetteville, AR, **61E** Sean Blood Mansfield, OH, **62A** Richele Philippot Winnipeg, MB, **62B** Kulpariya Wilaichit, **62C** Anonymous by request, **63A** Lori Butler Austin, TX, **63B** Vicki June Lake City, SC, **63C** Shannon Summersby Eversley, UK, **64A** Kristen Franklin Portland, OR, **64B** Leah Shannon British Columbia, **64C** Jenelle Rittenhouse Philadelphia, PA, **65A** Kimberly LaBombard Davidson, NC, **66A** Kristiana Silver Salt Lake City, UT, **66C** Mike Larson San Luis Obispo, CA, **66D** Marissa Kristal St. Paul, MN, **67A** Laurie Kelley Absarokee, MT, **67B** Sanwaree Sethi Moscow, Russia, **67B** Huiyan Singapore, **67C** Judy Kamilhor, **67D** Gillian Gauthier Orangeville, ON, **68A** Betty Williams Cape Girardeau, MO, **68B** Katie Hughes, **68C** Matthew McQuilkin Seattle, WA, **69A** Jane E. Brattland Oslo, Norway, **69B** Nathaniel Ndosi Williamstown, NJ, **70A** Trevor Bunch O'Fallon, MO, **70A** Samuel Lippke Long Beach, CA, **70B** Amanda Herzberger Shelburne, VT, **70C** Haley Richardson, **70D** Valeria Fuso Rome, Italy, **71B** Liann Chin Casey Miami, FL, **71C** Conguita Sacavé, Portugal, **71D** Andrew Mercer Walnut Creek, CA, **72A** Jessica Roy New York, NY, **72A** Josh Becker New York, NY, **72B** Kathleen Thomas Oklahoma City, OK, **72C** Maggie Carey Portland, ME, **72D** Robby Bailey Toccoa, GA, **73A** Pariya Kaligi, **73B** Rachel Valdez Schertz, TX, **74A** Sarah Waldorf South Pasadena, CA, **74B** Stephanie Yoo Ocean, NJ, **74C** Taryn Chieko Kagawa, **74D** Valerie Goh Singapore, **75A** Desiree Claridy Las Vegas, NV, **76A** Kimberly Domanico North Adams, MA, **76B** Andrea Olivier Austin, TX, **76C** Michelle Antonisse Silver Spring, MD, **77A** Natasha Krohn Imperial Beach, CA, **77B** Scott Bridges Brunswick, Australia, **78A** Lucy Brindley Isleworth, UK, **78B** Richard Piatt London, UK, **78C** Macy Rashelle Amin Chandler, AZ, **79A** Esther Simpson London, UK, **79B** Katrina Huller New Paltz, NY, **80A** Delaney Lindley Hurst, TX, **80B** Rachael Chan Selangor, Malaysia, **80C** Mary Bogdan Montreal, QB, **81A** Paige McCullough Burnaby, BC, **81B** Rodolfo Antonio Rivas Nunez, **81C** Anonymous by request, **82A** Faith Minnich Harrisburg, PA, **82B** Michi Chu Wayland, MA, **82C** Steph Calvert Long Beach, CA, **82D** Alyssa Polizzi Alameda, CA, **82E** Ehrrin Pittsburgh, PA, **83A** Megan Butcher Ottawa, ON, **83A** Manon Blouin, **83B** Laura Barnhouse Somerset, UK, **83C** Carolyn Scotchmer Bayfield, ON, **84A** Amanda Nelson Marietta, GA, **84B** Heidi Gumpert Waterloo, ON, **85A** Rebecca Roach, **85B** Jessica Zollman San Francisco, CA, **85C** Danny Robbins, **85D** Rachel Hynes Seattle, WA, **86A** Jocelyn Geboy Chicago, IL, **86C** Norma Clark, **87A** Michael Gnos Kuessnacht, Switzerland, **87B** Fabrice Ducouret Sartrouville, France, **87B** Kellianne Caulfield Cottage Grove, OR, **87C** Nicole Chiu Benowa, Australia, **88A** Jay Joslin Asheville, NC, **88B** Daniel Go Caloocan City, Philippines, **88C** J.J. Soh Singapore, **89A** Jennifer Westfall-Kee Pasadena, CA, **89B** Amy Belk New York, NY, **89C** Doug Spesert Van Nuys, CA, **90A** Sara Strickler Richmond, VA, **90B** Rachel Rogers Dover, NH, **90C** Tara Camilli Denver, CO, **90D** Kiona Van Rhee-Wilson Raleigh, NC, **91A** Chris Brennan San Francisco, CA, **91B** Michele-Pierre Raynaud-Bardon Beziers, France, **91C** Kate Pearson Lincolnshire, UK, **92A** Carolina Valenzuela, **92B** Rachel Green Dix Hills, NY, **93A** Charlotte Broad Wolverhampton, UK, **93B** Dave & Billie Tulk Perrysburgh, OH, **93C** Audra Knoxville, TN, **94A** Molly Kenefick Oakland, CA, **94B** Rachel Pine London, UK, **94C** Chris Whetstone, **94D** Laurel Black Beaverton, OR, **95A** Michael La-Cour Ditleusen, **95B** Blu Stephens, **96A** James Mathias Nashville, TN, **96B** Caitlin P. Abber Brooklyn, NY, **96C** Catherine Gottemaker Marietta, GA, **96D** Helen Lewis, **97A** Teresa Knezek Two Rivers, AR, **97B** Hannah Johnson Sherman Oaks, CA, **97C** Desiree Lyndsey, **98A** Christina Marie Brown Fredericksburg, VA, **98B** Lillyling Shanghai, China, **98C** Alice Pearland, TX, **99A** Mr. & Mrs. Barbeler Maryborough, Australia, & Albert, SK, **100A** Dusty Smith Moline, IL, **100B** Otto Wahl, **100C** Joel Rakes Nashville, TN, **101A** Polina Gribov Pawtucket, RI, **101B** Torley Wong Langley, WA, **103A** Christopher Gutierrez Chicago, IL, **103B** Amanda Bendis Bel Air, MD, **103C** Grace Anne Orpilla, **103D** Anthony Gratto Gainesville, FL, **104A** Kelsey Fry, **104A** Jo Parker, **104B** Meghan Stanbrough Sunnyvale, CA, **104B** Ali Bruzek Bloomington, MN, **105A** Rachael Oglesby West Columbia, SC, **105B** Amir Alfatakh Kuala Lumpur, **106A** Sarah Cruise Dublin, Ireland, **106B** Sarah Hill Cambridge, UK, **106C** Deepsha Surrey, BC, **107A** Marynka Egremy Navarro Cancun, Mexico, **107B** Mohammed Al-Rehaili Jeddah, Saudi Arabia, **107C** Anna Marie-Grace Serrone Sunnyvale, CA, **108A** Wayne Mackeson West Linn, OR, **108B** Terry Osterhout Orange, CA, **108C** Desiree Alegre Badalona, Spain, **108D** Elsa Alpehenaar Heiloo, The Netherlands, **109A** Marie Jane, **109B** Michael Dailey St. Petersburg, FL, **110A** Unaiza Nasim Dubai, United Arab Emirates, **110B** John Ashby Bristol, UK, **110C** Doug Spesert Van Nuys, CA, **110D** Kimberley Maurice West Vancouver, BC, **111A** Noelle Meridith Deigan Encino, CA, **111B** David Maybury Los Angeles, CA, **111C** Joanna Siew Eindhoven, The Netherlands, **111D** Brittany Hildebrandt Toronto, ON, **112A** Luke Healey Ames, IA, **112B** Bernard W. Barnes Rural Hall, NC, **112C** Paul Zollo North Hollywood, CA, **113A** Melissa Carey Philadelphia, PA, **113B** Michael Sangree, **113C** Jyn Meyer Portland, OR, **113D** Shawn Mueller Mountain House, CA, **114A** Teena Gerhardt Bloomington, IN, **114B** Vicky, **114C** Christine, **114D** Marilyn Kass Brookline, MA, **115A** Liz Sergison Livonia, MI, **115B** Mindy & Erik Helmer Portland, OR, **115C** Zen Law Singapore, **116A** Jon Ward Cambridgeshire, UK, **116B** Adriana Uribe Buenos Aires, Argentina, **116C** Alice Judge-Talbot London, UK, **116D** Julia Test San Francisco, CA, **117A** Cliff Ramos, **117B** Andrea King Mullens, WV, **117C** Heather DeVilbiss Henderson, NV, **118A** Brienne Griffin Baraboo, WI, **118B** Willemijn Lammers Amersfoort, Holland, **118C** Holli Gould Makati City, Philippines, **118D** Sunday Williams Olympia, WA, **119A** Stephanie Barkin, **119B** Alicia Carrier Portland, OR, **120A** Olivier Bloemendaal Rotterdam, The Netherlands, **120B** Trea Brown Decatur, GA, **120C** Teneisha Sprague Antrim, NH, **121A** John Yarbrough Thomaston, GA, **121B** Karran Sahadeo North Bergen, NJ, **121C** C. Oliver Godby Reading, UK, **121D** Salina Cole Brooklyn, NY, **122A** D. Tuazon California, **122B** Jess Machin Powys, UK, **122C** Maureen Flynn-Burhoe Calgary, AB, **122D** Mariyam Fazeela Abdul Samad Melbourne, Australia, **123A** Mimi Herrmann Charlotte, NC, **123B** Hannah Armstrong Portland, OR, **123C** Ana Carlos Marinha Grande, Portugal, **123D** Amanda Maxwell Port Moody, BC, **123E** Karen Cardoza Fremont, CA, **123F** Kristen Gregg Nashville, TN, **124A** Anna Klimek Squamish, BC, **124B** Feyza Celiktas Bursa, Turkey, **124C** David Summers Coolin, ID, **125A** Sara Solfanelli New York, NY, **125B** Pamela Siebert Overland Park, KS, **125C** Danell Norby, **125D** Sara Patalita Fort Wayne, IN, **126A** Alyssa, **126B** Brighton Metz Sandy, UT, **126C** Andrea King Mullens, WV, **126D** Cathy Chaput Ancaster, ON, **127A** Heather Hurd Lusby, MD, **127B** Natalie Johnson, **128A** Heather Curley, **128B** Jenna Sicuranza New Bedford, MA, **129A** Wendy O'Malley courtesy of Feastoffun.com Chicago, IL, **129B** Olivia Wright Brooklyn, NY, **129C** Alison Kinton, **129D** Victoria Palmer Cape Coral, FL, **129E** Annie Spencer USA, **129F** Mandy Williams Gateshead, UK, **130A** Jesper Nilsson Uddevalla, Sweden, **130B** Angela Klueber Louisville, KY, **130C** Paul Moody, **130D** Sara Taylor Cincinnati, OH, **131A** Stephen Gaddis Mexico Beach, FL, **131B** Christine Sanwald Shirley, NY, **131C** Angela Wagner Asheville, NC, **131D** Amir Hossein Keyhani, **131E** Justin Evans Ledyard, CT, **132A** Louise Barkuus Copenhagen, Denmark, **132B** Melanie Del Prete New York, NY, **132C** Anya Kopricica **133A** Meghan Colson Portland, OR, **133B** Heather Armstrong Victoria, BC, **133C** Paula LaValle Amherst, MA, **134A** W. Harold Cooley Cadillac, MI, **134B** Meshary Mohammed Al Obaid Kuwait, **134C** Mohammed Al Jumaah Al Nasiriyah, Iraq, **135A** Nancy Chen Zaandam, The Netherlands, **135B** Lisa Royland Gorham, ME, **135C** Emily Wilsoncroft Oakland, CA, **135D** Andrew West Stratford-upon-Avon, UK, **136A** Peter The Turk Boston, MA, **137A** Rebecca Martz-Burley Dickinson, ND, **137B** Joanne Kerr Glasgow, Scotland, **137C** Martin Memory Brighton, UK, **138A** Dan Sal, **138B** Meredith Farmer Portland, OR, **139A** Janelle Sumabat San Diego, CA, **139B** Richard Cody Oakland, CA, **140A** Dr. Lisa Eastman Kansas, **140B** Sadalit P. Van Buren Boston, MA, **140C** Marloes Nijssen, **141A** Melissa Miller New Paltz, NY, **141B** Erin Edwards Duvall, WA, **141C** Bill Baar St. Charles, IL, **142A** Clarice Yuen, **142B** Natalia Buia Brampton, ON, **142C** Charlie Honig Newton, MA, **142D** Kamryn Behee Carrollton, TX, **142E** Jan Guest Beeston, UK, **143A** Lina Novang Frolunda, Sweden, **143B** Danae Lawson, **143C** Rosetta Argento Melrose Park, IL, **143D** Vicky Chalmers Falmouth, UK, **144A** Emily Murrin La Grange Park, IL, **144B** Annalise Prodor Edmonton, AB, **144C** Jo, **144D** Carley Inman Denver, CO, **145A** Marek Papala, **145B** Dorothee Bond Washington, D.C., **145C** Bridget Lenderman Conway, AR, **146A** Jesse Malmed Santa Fe, NM, **146B** Rhonda Judeich-Yount Scottsdale, AZ, **146C** Monique Valderrama Singapore, **147A** Camille Ong, **147B** Lisa & Chris Krug Grovetown, GA, **152A** Seema Narayanan Vijinapura, India, **152B** Byrth, **152H** Grant MacDonald Toronto, ON, **153A** Mark Lucas Stannington, UK, **153B** Scott Rennie, **153C** Leonel Escota Jersey City, NJ, **154A** Mia Brigette Ting Manila, Philippines, **154B** Rachel Thompson Middletown, CA, **154B** Mariam Boone Tulsa, OK, **154H** Lori Cochran Durango, CO, **155A** Joey Ramone Sheffield, UK, **155B** Yosuke Fukushima Tokyo, Japan, **156A** Kate Pearson Lincolnshire, UK, **156B** Leley Noronha Arlington, TX, **156C** Sandra Go Taipei City, Taiwan, **156H** Kiki Brown Bear Philadelphia, PA, **157A** Teja Sauer, **157B** Illina Simeonova Astoria, NY, **157C** Laura Pinggera Vero Beach, FL, **158A** Mark Cunnington Alfreton, UK, **158B** Beth Hong Montreal, QC, **158H** Mary Gordon Thermopolis, WY, **159A** Suzanne Pettersson Hagersten, Sweden, **159B** Tim Stone, **159C** Jennifer Cloer Hillsboro, OR, **159D** Parrish Baker Kansas City, MO, **159E** Hiroshi Tazawa Sydney, Australia, **159F** Margarita Cherkasova St. Petersburg, Russia, **160A** Stephanie Heliker San Diego, CA, **160B** Montine Rummel Seattle, WA, **160H** Cheryl Guthrie Columbia, MO, **161A** Deborah Dilley Salt Lake City, UT, **161B** David Moore Lauderdale Lakes, FL, **161C** Michelle Vespe Buckeye, AZ, **161D** Becky Seipelt Murfreesboro, TN, **161E** Kimberly Vanilla Tong Jean-Lee Selangor, Malaysia, **162A** Kathie DiCesare Winter Park, FL, **162B** Shawn Graham Phoenix, NY, **162C** John David Nuno Jr., **162D** Brooke Medlin Kettering, OH, **162H** Nikki David Lake Forest, CA, **163A** Brian Leon Winston-Salem, NC, **163B** Garry Wilmore, **163C** Jennifer Clark Los Angeles, CA, **163D** Sarah Rummel, **164A** Mandee Edwards, **164B** Tim Ove Bsanesoy Bergen, Norway, **164C** Kristen Barreiro Las Vegas, NV, **164D** Guenevere Feldman Boston, MA, **164E** Angela Regas Iowa City, IA, **164H** Kevin Osborn Newton Heights, MA, **165A** Andrea Bruce Ottawa, ON, **165B** Kimberly, **165C** Kristen & Shawn Glazier Malone, NY, **165D** Danielle Blair Lethbridge, ON, **166A** Justin Eisinger San Diego, CA, **166B** Drew O'Bryan, **166C** Neil Gilham Edmonds, WA, **166D** Matthew McQuilkin Seattle, WA, **166H** Linda Martin Rockville, MD, **167A** Beverly Williams Granby, CT, **167B** Kevin Bond Raleigh, NC, **168A** Amanda Como Sydney, Australia, **168B** Eric Dwyer, **168C** Robyn Skwarczek La Grange, IL, **168D** José Nieves Utado, Puerto Rico, **168H** Nick Humphries Thousand Oaks, CA, **169A** Robin Owens Oklahoma City, OK, **169B** Sarah Kennard Mesa, AZ, **170A** Meghan Anderson, **170B** Terry Johnston, **170C** Randi Tan Singapore, **170D** Robert Miller Austin, TX, **170E** Jenny Rural South Carolina, **170H** Michael Ejercito Janesville, WI, **171A** Joseph Abken Kenmore, WA, **171B** Vicki Moore San Mateo, CA, **171C** Alex Guelff London, UK, **176H** G. Rowland Williams Lexington, MA, **178H** Kevin Lam Toronto, **180H** Daniele Dalledonne Trento, Italy, **182H** David A. Galvan Sherman Oaks, CA, **184H** Sergei Rogozhnikov St. Petersburg, Russia, **186H** Premshree Pillai, **188H** Mark Interrante Silicon Valley, USA, **190H** Belen & Miguel A. Sanz Madrid, Spain, **192H** Wyatt Hatfield Los Molinos, CA, **194H** Chethan Shankar Jersey City, NJ, **196H** Giuseppe Angele, **198H** Thomas Birke Berlin, Germany, **200H** Nathan Bergeron Chatham, ON, **206A** Kimberly Horne Ottawa, ON, **206B** Dennis Hurd New Westminster, BC, **206C** Vanessa Muscat Adelaide, Australia, **207A** Jeffrey Reisberg River Forest, IL, **207B** Lydia White San Francisco, CA, **207C** Triin Vihur London, UK, **207D** Krista Bruce Kingston, ON, **207E** Kari Noser Houston, TX, **208A** Brent Young Winnipeg, MB, **208B** Angela Auclair Long Sault, ON, **208C** Jon & Joy Madison Renton, WA, **208D** Carina Enright Taunton, MA, **208E** Clorie Van Tuyl Rogers, AR, **208H** Gareth Taylor Blackwood Gwent, UK, **209A** Andrea King Mullens, WV, **209B** Linda Malie Colorado Springs, CO, **210A** Matt Parsons Sidmouth, UK, **210B** Susan Schroeder Coraopolis, PA, **210C** J.M. Cornwell Colorado Springs, CO, **210H** Massimo Rizzo Agrigento, Italy, **211A** David Matte Toronto, ON, **212A** Erin Williams courtesy of socialcrisis.net Brooklyn, NY, **212B** Melinda Markey Vancouver, BC, **212C** Angela Johnson Masset, BC, **212D** Ans Deblauwe Tienen, Belgium, **212E** Shannon Tervo Madison, WI, **212H** Tor Sauder Vancouver, BC, **213A** Sean Higgins, **213B** Allison Fennel Warrenville, IL, **214A** Anna McLean Howell, NJ, **214B** Christine Morgan Rainbow City, AL, **214C** Timothy Johnson Urbandale, IA, **214D** Kristy Alley Memphis, TN, **214E** Andrew Dart Cambridge, UK, **214H** Marit Welker Boise, ID, **215A** Janice Matthews, NC, **215B** Joshua Paul Grantham Alpharetta, GA, **215C** Sara Deacon Woodbridge, VA, **215D** Yoon Ee Chuan, **216A** Genevieve Faust Green Lane, PA, **216B** Christine Nute Taylor, MI, **216C** Anna Palmer, **216C** Alyssa Synsteby, **216H** Tracy R. Olson Victoria, BC, **217A** Alice Braehler Innkreis, Austria, **217B** Kathleen Harris Reno, NV, **217C** Maureen Sill North Ridgeville, OH, **218A** Brittney Townson Toronto, ON, **218B** Ellie Smith Lebanon, MO, **218C** Valerie Korber Davidsville, PA, **218D** Katharine J. Moriarty Groton, CT, **218H** Finn Pröpper Düsseldorf, Germany, **219A** Sarah Davis Harrison, TN, **219B** Victoria Camp Belle Mead, NJ, **220A** Shelby Jones Rochester, MI, **220B** Alexandra Glyptis Athens, Greece, **220C** Jason Roberts, **220H** Juancho Reyes Dumaguete City, Philippines, **221A** Syeda Mushda Ali Dhaka, Bangladesh, **221B** Joseph Collette, **221C** Steven Meiers Los Angeles, CA, **221D** Darya Sipyeykina Tucker, GA, **222A** Coy Pink, **222H** Carlos E. Cáder, **223A** Catalina Loves, **223B** Monkeytwizzle Glasgow, Scotland, **223C** Wilhelmina Wang Hanover, NH, **224A** Michael Glover Brooklyn, NY, **224B** Ryan Ward, **224C** Lauren Rose, **224D** Haizam Shah Singapore, **224H** Templeton Elliott Norfolk, VA, **225A** Julia Lauren Aaker Teaneck, NJ, **225B** Nina Hiironniemi Tampere, Finland, **225C** Katie Fish, **282A** Sarah Hyatt, **282B** Peter Sabath, **282C** Lorna Keuning Brooklyn, NY, **282D** Amber Gregory San Francisco, CA, **282E** Jaclyn Pennoyer Silver Spring, MD, **282F** Margot Thorseth Edmonton, AB, **282G** Elijah James Majeski Washington Township, MI, **283A** Natalia Buia Brampton, ON, **283B** Lee Kurzweil, **283C** Meg Willis, **283D** Julia Westenberg Detroit, MI, **283E** Cari Ann Wayman, **283F** Somer Canon Philadelphia, PA, **283G** Nobara Hayakawa Bogotá, Colombia, **284A** Trithemius, **284B** Paul Moody, **284C** Sarah Brown Cambridge, UK, **284D** Charlotte O'Brien, **284E** Faith Minnich Harrisburg, PA, **284F** Jenna Marcum, **285A** Natalie Dirks Chicago, IL, **285B** Zélie Thornborough Amherst, MA, **285C** Graeme Seabrook Watertown, NY, **285D** Caroline Amico High Point, NC, **285E** Lynn Hall La Mesa, CA. Additional thanks to the thousands of other bloggers whose words are included in this book. Keep on doing what you do.

Montages

Every montage image featured in this book

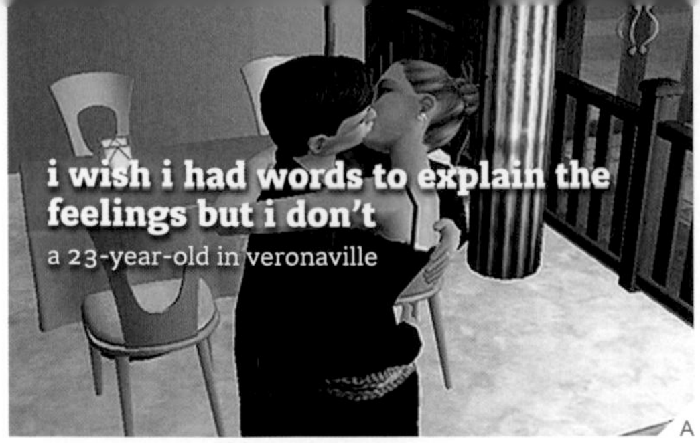
i wish i had words to explain the feelings but i don't
a 23-year-old in veronaville
A

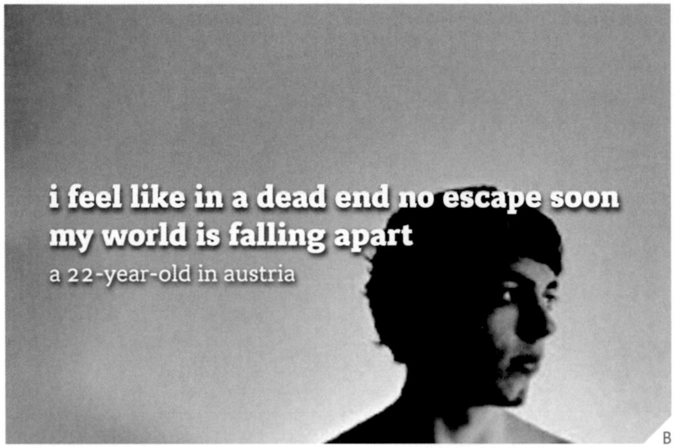
i feel like in a dead end no escape soon my world is falling apart
a 22-year-old in austria
B

i seem to have two to three days of feeling yucky on the chemo
a woman
C

i feel like accomplished or something
a woman
D

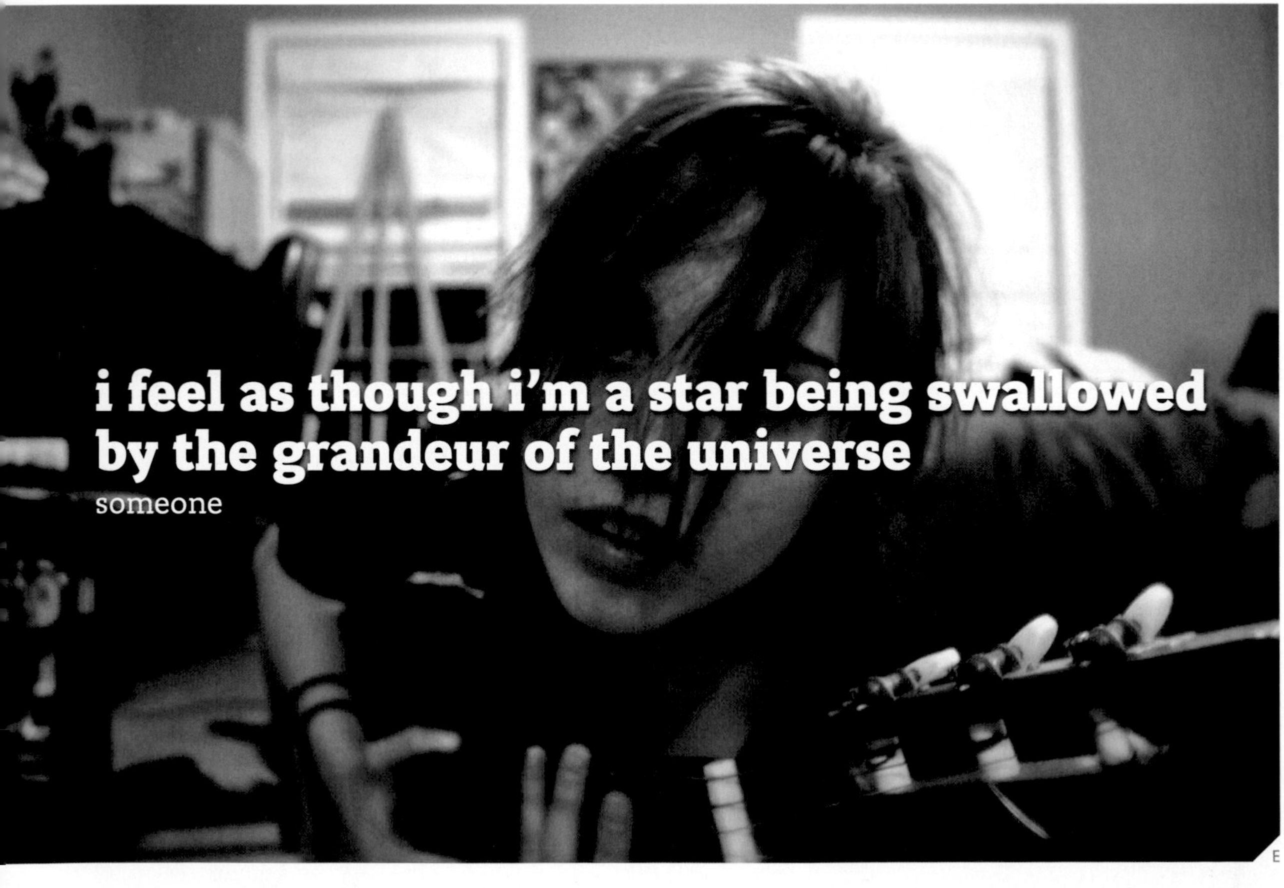
i feel as though i'm a star being swallowed by the grandeur of the universe
someone
E

i feel an emptiness
a woman
F

G
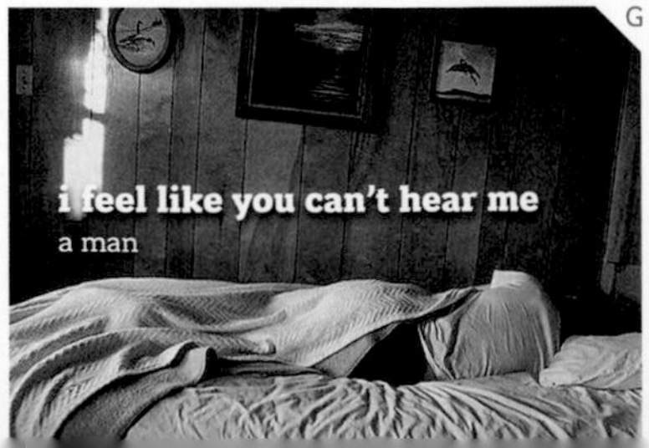
i feel like you can't hear me
a man

i don't feel anything
someone
A

i feel like a fragile clay
a woman
B

i feel less alone
someone
C

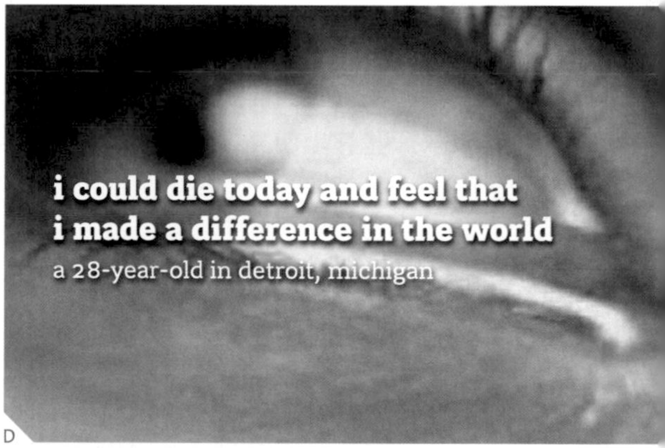
i could die today and feel that
i made a difference in the world
a 28-year-old in detroit, michigan
D

i have this incredibly strong longing feeling and
deeply miss experiences i have never had
someone
E

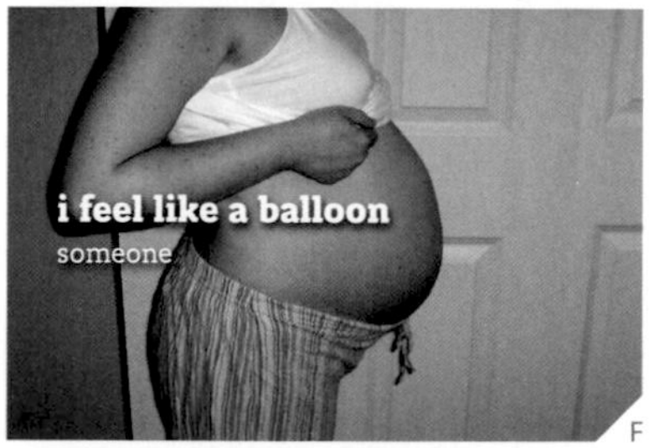
i feel like a balloon
someone
F

G
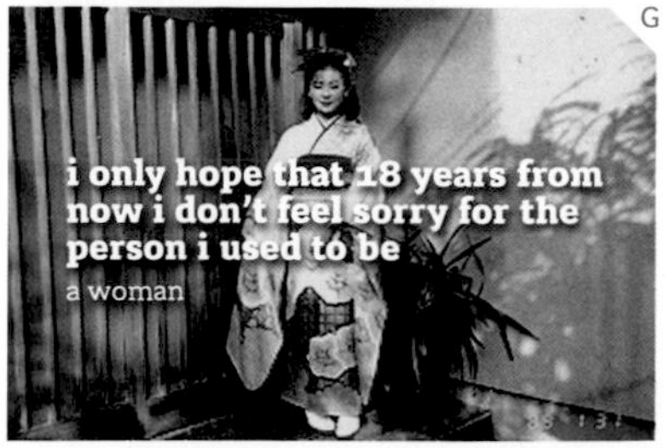
i only hope that 18 years from
now i don't feel sorry for the
person i used to be
a woman

i feel like i'm in the center of that light circle
a man
A

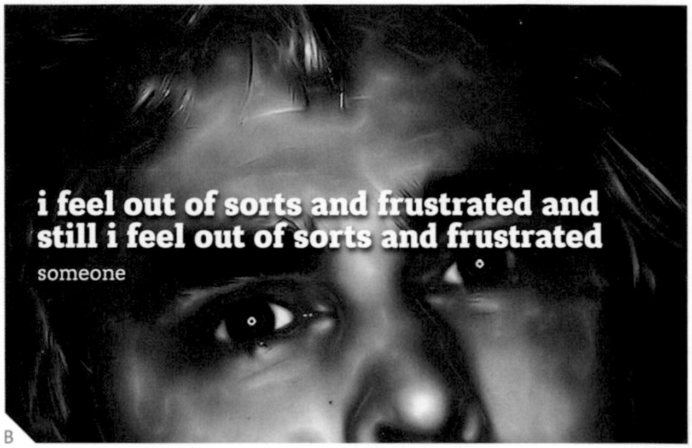
i feel out of sorts and frustrated and still i feel out of sorts and frustrated
someone
B

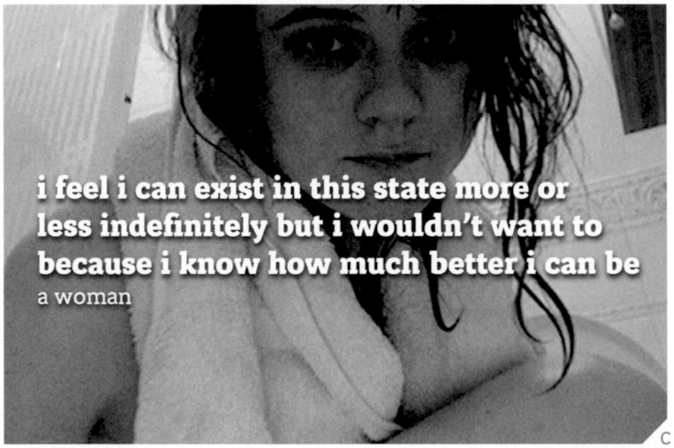
i feel i can exist in this state more or less indefinitely but i wouldn't want to because i know how much better i can be
a woman
C

i love how i feel today
someone in cape coral, florida
D

i feel like i meet god here more than anywhere else in the world
someone
E

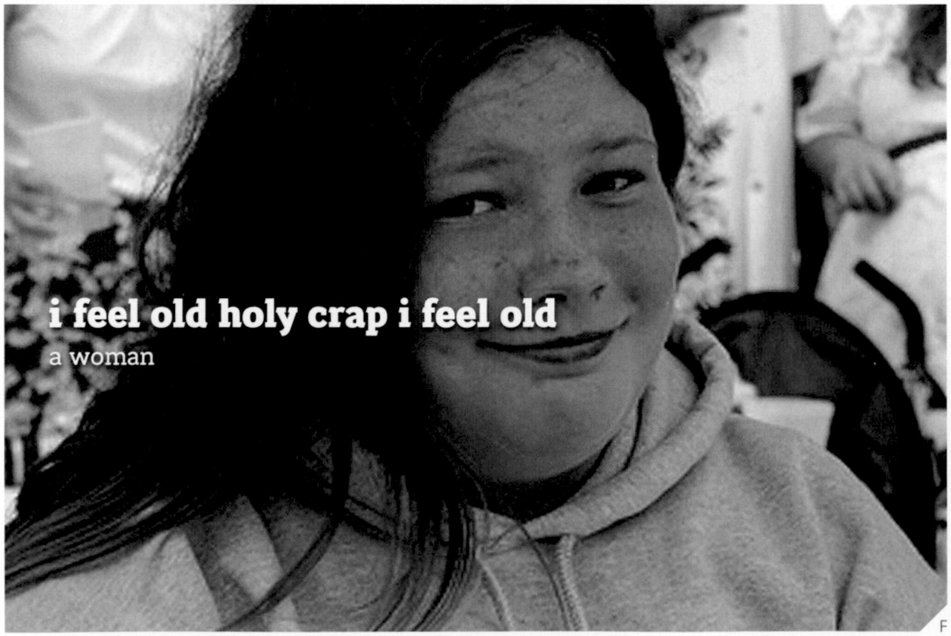
i feel old holy crap i feel old
a woman
F

i hope it's a feeling that lasts
a 30-year-old woman

A

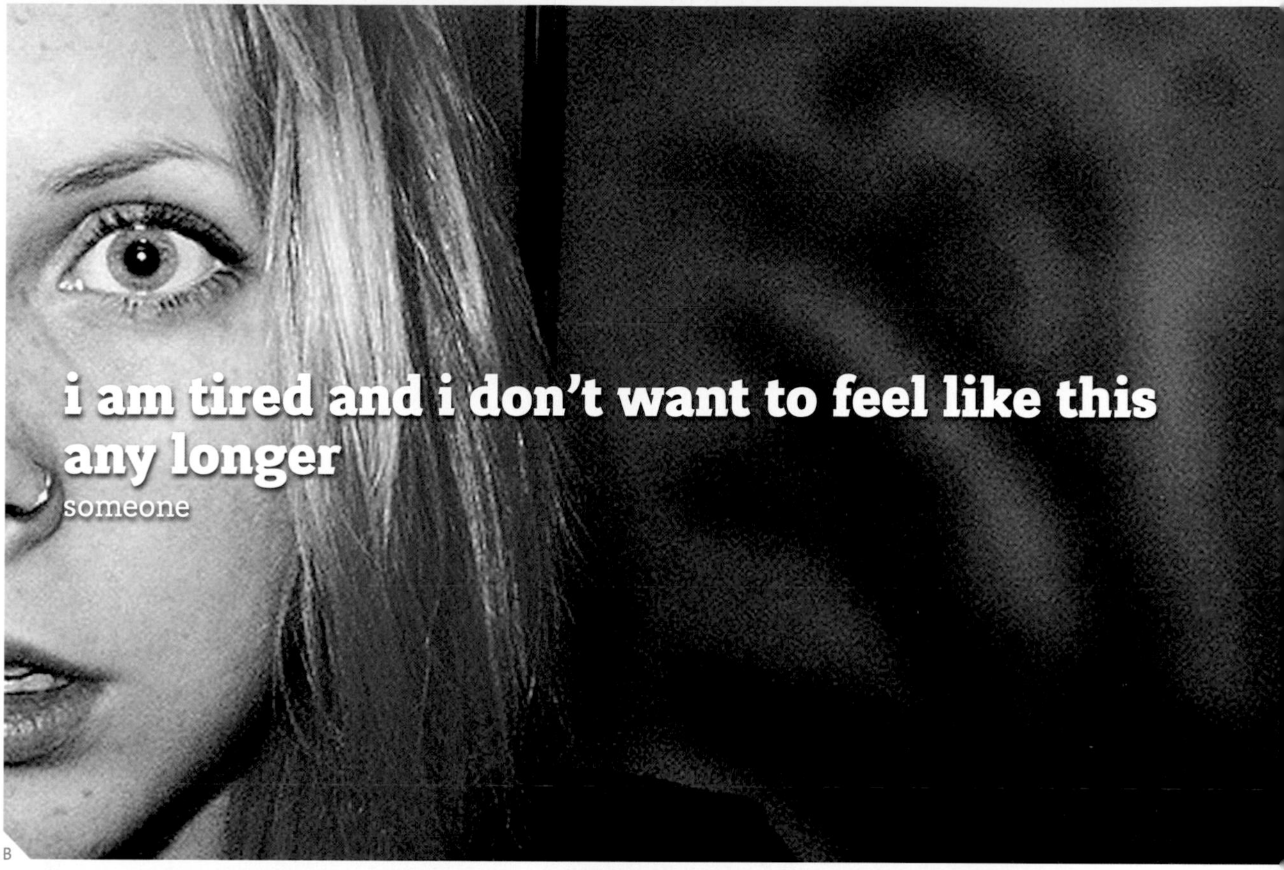
i am tired and i don't want to feel like this any longer
someone

B

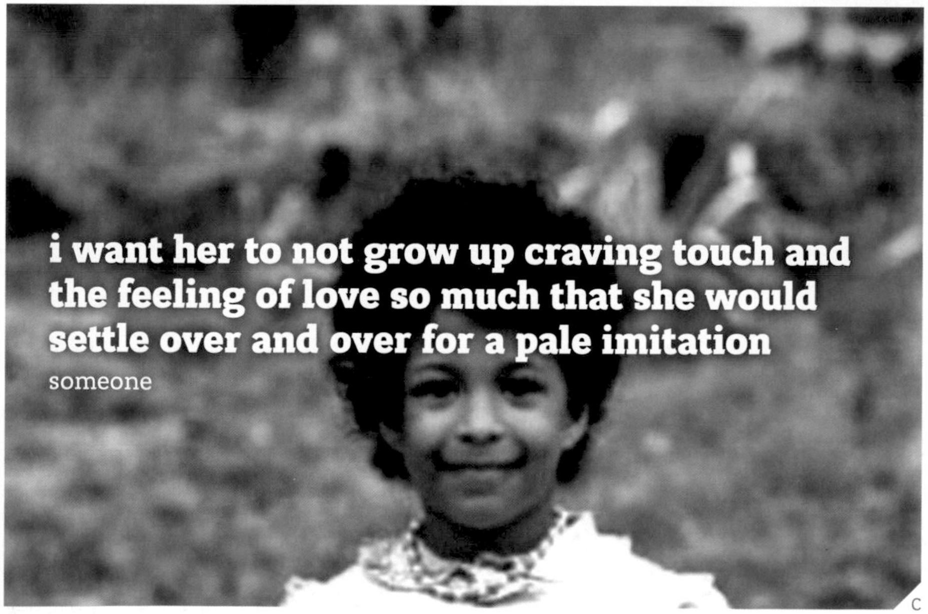
i want her to not grow up craving touch and the feeling of love so much that she would settle over and over for a pale imitation
someone

C

i hope you feel better soon
a woman

D

E

i feel calm
someone

• i don’t know what emotion to feel i need to pick one before i implode / a 28-year-old in s
the head of this group / a man • i feel like i’m halfway between a priest and a sci-fi action
crying at the drop of a hat / a 20-year-old • i always gave up after the rejection but i feel
losing my mind and all i want to do at the end of the day is curl up in my comfy warm bed /
shitty / a 25-year-old in the united states • i just had this feeling that it wasn’t a lie / a 20
no reason or overreact about something stupid or just walk around my apt at night shaking
like i have to lower my admittedly high expectations when it comes to relationship nd lov
the love that i felt / a 28-year-old in indianapolis, indiana • i feel alone most of the time / a
• i feel dead inside lonely and helpless when i should be enjoyin a lil space and hangin out in t
/ a 24-year-old in keene, new hampshire • i feel at home around the 4th graders / a man •
my brother serves our country with his life i’m proud of him for feeling that great sense of s
and the fact that there wasn’t a crowd there made me feel like i had the whole place for m
using a knife and fork and prefer the hands / a man • i constantly feel like people try not
i feel so blessed for it / a woman • i truly feel as if i have lived the american dream / a wo
• i feel so sorry for my poor husband / a woman • i feel vulnerable lonely confused / a w
• i feel like the weight on my shoulders is lighter / a woman • i dont understand my mor
much / a woman • i constantly feel my life is under a magnifying glass / a woman • i feel a
afraid to feel admiration for anyone / a 38-year-old in madison, wisconsin • i’m happy but i
• i feel exceedingly sorry for the new girl though obviously not enough to really do anythi
all / a 28-year-old in ithaca, new york • i can’t actually express how i feel or put words to
for females / a 28-year-old in chicago, illinois • i still care for him and i have this feeling i
• i feel like my brain’s turned to mush / a 27-year-old in sheffield, united kingdom • when
old me / a 27-year-old • i feel like i’m always hanging out with the exact same poeple ove
in new york • i feel i’ve neglected him with my work at the hospital / a 26-year-old • i feel
telling someone i’m gay / a 26-year-old in the united kingdom • i not only feel incredibly
/ a 26-year-old in las vegas, nevada • i feel like my time is so limited and it’s only been wo
being so nice and respectful towards peoples feelings is finally starting to loosen up from m
me / a 25-year-old in milwaukee, wisconsin • when i’m in chicago i feel alive / a 2 year-
this situation is a reminder that no matter how hard i try or how much better i th k i m g
know that he wanted me so much / a 21-year-old in the united states • i kind of feel like i
/ a 21-year-old in white plains, alabama • i feel pretty lonely and really homesick but i’m
shown or done in the way i need to feel fulfilled / a 21-year-old in japan • i wanna feel a k
a conflict in the past / an 18-year-old in singapore • i feel like i’m doing it all wron 1
old from maine • i used to be happy that’s how i know that the feeling the medication give
sick heart sinking feeling deep down inside my stomach / a 17-year-old • i feel like this co

a • i should make a section called beautiful artists because i feel like david bowie would be
a man • i feel like a knife just stabbed me in the heart / a man in new york city • i feel like
vant to persevere this time around / a 30-year-old in costa mesa, california • i feel like i'm
ear-old • i'm angry at myself because i have everything anyone could every want and i feel
ld in yokohama, japan • i get so uneasy and restless and anxious that i burst into tears for
se i feel so uncomfortable in my own skin / a 24-year-old in kentucky • i am sick of feeling
-year-old in indianapolis, indiana • i feel like someone squeezed out all of the beauty from
-old in the united states • i feel the need to be home now more than ever / a 22-year-old
amas / an 18-year-old • i've never dived into any one religion because i feel it's all or nothing
mber being their age and the challenger exploding and feeling like crying / a man • i know
/ a man • i feel like i've been turned upside down / a man • i thought the sky was beautiful
man • i love the feeling of dried up salt water on my skin / a man • i feel uncomfortable
me and just don't listen / a woman • i inherited this sense of humor from my father and
i feel ridiculous taking my own photo but i decided to finallly try the webcam / a woman
• i feel sorry for people who do not drink / a woman • i feel the end is near / a woman
lad and as much as i feel sorry for both of them sometimes i cant help but love them very
welcome as a curry fart in an airplane / a 38-year-old in darwin, northern territory • i am
e a jerk for possibly making someone else especially a friend of mine feel bad / a 38-year-old
ut it / a 28-year-old in the united kingdom • i still don't feel excited about the new year at
year-old in lafayette, louisiana • i do however feel unfulfilled by not exploring my desire
will since when i let someone in i don't forget them / a 28-year-old in berkeley, california
ay off an old credit card it feels like i'm untying a little ribbon that keeps me tethered to an
ver again it's nice to change things up / a 27-year-old • i feel like giving up / a 27-year-old
d about my relationship and my sexuality there isn't really much that phases me except for
alf the time i actually am / a 26-year-old in japan • i feel both self righteous and insecure
e i've had to work so much / a 26-year-old in smyrna, tennessee • i think the strain of me
t / a 25-year-old in alexandria, virginia • i feel naked constantly but i think it'll be good for
feel like a kitty right now / a 25-year-old in lancaster, new york • i can't help but feel like
will never be normal / a 25-year-old • i could feel his happiness and it made me happy to
act differently or that you won't like me because i'm not as happy and hyper as i used to be
cared as i was / a 21-year-old in naples, florida • i know both of them loved me it wasn't
crush me and break me down / an 18-year-old in brazil • i feel so guilty we had
old in virginia • i just feel annoyed that i wasted my life doing this / an 18-year-
n't real happiness / an 18-year-old in portland, oregon • i see him and i get that
ack from the dead thing has given me a second chance / a 48-year-old

i feel like nobody reads books to the end anymore
a 30-year-old man in brooklyn, new york